THE LAST TREK

THE LAST TREK

A Study of the Boer People
and the Afrikaner Nation

by

SHEILA PATTERSON

LONDON

ROUTLEDGE & KEGAN PAUL LTD.

First published in 1957
© *by Routledge & Kegan Paul Ltd.*
Broadway House
68–74 Carter Lane
London, E.C.4.
Printed in Great Britain by
W. & J. Mackay & Co. Ltd.
Chatham.

CONTENTS

SECRETS OF THE KINGDOM

British Radicals from the Popish Plot to the Revolution of 1688–1689

Richard L. Greaves

Stanford University Press • *Stanford, California* • *1992*

Stanford University Press
Stanford, California
© 1992 by the Board of Trustees of the
Leland Stanford Junior University
Printed in the United States of America
CIP data are at the end of the book

Published with the assistance of
The Florida State University

To
Ted and Judith Underwood,
and to
Christopher Hill,
Doyen of Stuart Historians

Preface

This volume completes a trilogy, the first two volumes of which were *Deliver Us from Evil: The Radical Underground in Britain, 1660–1663* (New York: Oxford University Press, 1986) and *Enemies Under His Feet: Radicals and Nonconformists in Britain, 1664–1677* (Stanford, Calif.: Stanford University Press, 1990). The trilogy covers dissident activities in England, Scotland, Ireland, and British exile communities on the Continent from the restoration of the monarchy in 1660 to the revolution of 1688–89. The first volume explores radical undertakings from the uprisings of John Lambert and John Venner to the northern rebellion in 1663; the second encompasses militant activity from the Second Dutch War to the period following Charles' proclamation of an indulgence in 1672; and the third extends from the Popish Plot to the "Glorious Revolution," with special attention to the Bothwell Bridge insurrection, the so-called Rye House conspiracies, the Argyll and Monmouth rebellions, and radical involvement in the revolution of 1688–89. The trilogy thus underscores both the continuity and the geographical range of radical activity in all three kingdoms from the restoration to the revolution—or perhaps more accurately, from revolution to revolution.

I use the anachronistic term "radical" to refer to the more extreme forms of dissent, both political and religious. Radicals endorsed active disobedience to laws they found offensive. This disobedience took such forms as physical resistance to authorities, the publication of illegal works, acts of rebellion, and even assassination. Some radicals were republicans, but as Gary De Krey has remarked, "the true measures of radicalism are not to be found in republican institutional blueprints but rather in advocacy of a wide and free electorate, accountable government, and individual rights secured through appropriate actions, including resistance."[1] Many radicals were nonconformists, although some were members of the established church while others had no significant religious interests. Not all nonconformists were radicals, however, nor is the term "radical" synonymous with particular dissenting groups, such as General Baptists or Congregationalists (Independents). On the contrary, radicals were to be found among all Protestant groups in late Stuart Britain.

I would add two further caveats. First, we must understand Stuart radicals in their own context, not that of modern radicalism. Although Stuart radicals did not espouse a common vision of the society to which they aspired, they were united in their dislike of arbitrary government, Roman Catholicism, prelacy, and the persecution of Protestants. This was their frame of reference, and we must understand them in these terms rather than employing anachronisms. Second, in analyzing the nature and significance of radical activity in late Stuart Britain I am neither suggesting that I approve of its tenets nor contending, as did Whig historians, that they were destined to triumph. On the contrary, while some have found favor with later ages, others have been repudiated or discarded as obsolete. Historiographically, this trilogy will, I hope, contribute to the emerging reevaluation of late Stuart Britain undertaken by such scholars as Lois Schwoerer, Richard Ashcraft, Gary De Krey, Jonathan Barry, William Speck, and Janelle Greenberg.

Much of this volume deals with the controversial conspiracies collectively (and misleadingly) known as the Rye House Plot. Whether these conspiracies actually existed has been disputed since the 1680s. More recently, such historians as Maurice Ashley and Tim Harris have essentially discounted the existence of the plotting because of the nature of the evidence; in Harris' judgment, "there is no evidence to suggest that such groups ever did contemplate such a rebellion," and Ashley calls the Rye House assassination plot "one of the great historical myths."[2] Other scholars, such as Ashcraft, De Krey, and Barry, believe the conspiracy was real. Indeed, the Argyll and Monmouth rebellions in 1685 can be seen as an outgrowth of the Rye House plotting, as Robin Clifton and Peter Earle suggest.

The fourth category consists solely of Robert Ferguson, a Scottish minister who had served as John Owen's assistant. Although Ferguson was never captured, he wrote a reasonably full account of the conspiracy.

The fifth group comprises the only two major figures who went to their executions denouncing all involvement—Sir Thomas Armstrong, a Monmouth associate, and Algernon Sidney, who repudiated the authorship of his own political treatise, "Discourses Concerning Government," in which he extolled republican polity. Their professions of innocence are not credible.

Thus most of the key figures admitted at least some degree of complicity in plotting against the crown. Confession did not automatically save them from the executioner's block; Russell, Walcott, and Holloway, for instance, perished despite their admissions. Moreover, two or more witnesses corroborate virtually every *major* point. Discrepancies exist with respect to detail, but this is hardly surprising given the fact that the elapsed time between the earliest events and their recording by some of the witnesses amounted to five or more years; that numerous meetings were involved; and that no records of the proceedings were kept. Such records as do survive—especially letters from Argyll and a document pertaining to the division of London into twenty recruiting districts—support the accounts. Precise agreement concerning details would render the testimony highly suspect by suggesting that witnesses simply repeated one another.

For biographical information on many of the figures referred to in this book, the reader may consult the *Biographical Dictionary of British Radicals in the Seventeenth Century*, edited by Richard L. Greaves and Robert Zaller (3 volumes; Brighton: Harvester, 1982–84), and A. G. Matthews, *Calamy Revised* (Oxford: Clarendon, 1934; reprinted 1988). At the suggestion of Stanford University Press's reader, I have appended a select bibliography of the principal primary sources used in the trilogy.

Dates are given in the old style (which was ten days behind the new style used on the Continent) except in those instances where the inclusion of both old- and new-style dates (thus, e.g.: 2/12 March) enhances clarity; the year, however, is taken to commence on 1 January rather than 25 March.

R.L.G.

The problem of evaluating the evidence is complicated by the origins of the conspiracy in the context of the Popish Plot, when both Whigs and Tories freely engaged in subornation, severely undermining the integrity of the judicial system. John Kenyon's landmark study *The Popish Plot* does not fully reveal the extent of the abuse of the court system by men motivated by political gain and self-preservation. The sorry specter of subornation, played out against a background of two decades of radical agitation and domestic espionage, must make any historian extremely wary in assessing the Rye House evidence.

The nature of this evidence is varied. Fifteen key figures who made substantive statements fall roughly into five categories. The first of these comprises four men, each of whom confessed freely in the early stages of discovery and testified for the prosecution against his former colleagues. Each is vulnerable to charges of self-serving as well as possible prevarication. This group includes Josiah Keeling, who turned informer and provided the government with its first substantial opportunity to crush the conspirators. A late recruit, Keeling knew little and had never been in contact with anyone of prominence. Much more valuable is the extensive testimony of Robert West, the staunchly Whig barrister of the Middle Temple. Although parts of his confession incorporate hearsay, the basic outline stands up very well when compared with the testimony of others; his contacts were limited to middle- and lower-level conspirators. More problematic is the evidence of Colonel John Rumsey, a Cromwellian veteran and customs collector at Bristol, whose recollection was sometimes garbled. The most enigmatic of this group was William Lord Howard of Escrick, who had a predilection for conspiracy: a member of the Leveller faction that had schemed to restore the monarchy in the 1650s, he was briefly imprisoned; after spying on the Netherlands in the Third Dutch War, he worked as an agent for William of Orange, twice going to the Tower for interrogation.[3] Although Howard embellished his story, its general framework withstands critical scrutiny.

The four men in the second category made relatively full confessions after they were captured. Two of them—Ford Lord Grey, an outspoken Whig, and Nathaniel Wade, a Bristol attorney—were apprehended in the Monmouth rebellion. Although Grey's statement is self-serving, occasionally vague, and based at times on hearsay, when the second-hand passages are discounted and allowance is made for incidental factual errors, his account is reasonably sound. Wade's testimony, refreshingly candid and largely devoid of self-serving comments, frequently corroborates the statements of others. Like Grey and Howard, he could testify about his personal involvement with such major figures as the earl of Shaftesbury, the duke of Monmouth, and William Lord Russell. The third figure, William Carstares, an intimate of the earl of Argyll and another of William of Orange's intelligence operatives, confessed only under torture. The last man in this category, James Holloway, a Bristol linen merchant, provided a detailed account of his involvement in the schemes of West and his associates.

The four men in the third category admitted a degree of complicity in the plotting but said little about their activities. Three of them were executed, two of them (Russell and Walcott) for their role in the Rye House plotting. Russell not only confessed having been present in a cabal that discussed an attack on the king's guards, but also admitted, "I have heard many things & say'd some things contrary to my duty." Notes of the confession of Captain Thomas Walcott, a Shaftesbury intimate, are meager, but he admitted involvement in the conspiracy: Shaftesbury, he said, had enlisted him in "an Vndertaking to Assert the peoples Just Libertyes, which were in hazard," and he identified the commanders of the proposed rebellion as Shaftesbury in London, Monmouth in Taunton and Bristol, Russell in Devon, and Lord Brandon in Chesire. His testimony substantially agrees with West's account.[4]

Monmouth, who is also in the third category and was executed, had a personal meeting with Charles and James in November 1683 in which he acknowledged "his guilt, & the share he had in the Conspiracy"; he also gave "an account of the whole conspiracy, naming all those concerned in it, which were more then those [who] had allready been mentioned by severall Witnesses." In December 1685, the fourth man, John Hampden, who had previously been found guilty of a misdemeanor—conspiracy to launch an insurrection—on the basis of Howard's testimony, pleaded guilty to charges of high treason when the state acquired, in Grey, a second witness.

Acknowledgments

As I bring this trilogy to completion I am keenly aware of my indebtedness to many people and institutions, including three fine historians who died while this work was in progress, Richard Schlatter, Roger Howell, and J. Leitch Wright. A fellowship from the American Council of Learned Societies under a program funded by the National Endowment for the Humanities made some of the research possible, as did financial assistance from Florida State University. Their generosity helped to offset some of the almost prohibitive expenses amassed in the course of recurring (but always pleasant) research trips to Great Britain. The staffs of the following libraries were both gracious and efficient: the Public Record Office (Chancery Lane), the British Library (especially the Department of Manuscripts), the Bodleian Library, the House of Lords Record Office, Dr. Williams's Library, the Huntington Library, the Library of the Religious Society of Friends (Friends' House, London), the National Library of Scotland, the Edinburgh University Library, the University of Nottingham Library, the University of London Library, the John Rylands Library, and the record offices in Somerset, East Sussex, Dorchester, Cheshire, Chester, and Cumbria (Carlisle and Kendal, where I was helped especially by James Grisenthwaite). Robert Zaller and Howard Nenner generously agreed to read the complete manuscript and offered much constructive criticism, as did the anonymous reader for Stanford University Press; any errors are, of course, my own responsibility. Portions of this work were presented in lectures at Yale University and the British Seminar at the Huntington Library, where I received helpful comments from David

Cressy, Lamar Hill, J. Sears McGee, and others. Four attorneys have shared their expertise with me: John Harrison Rains III and David Davis, both of whom are historians in their own right, and Sandra Duffy and Robert D. Greaves. Dr. Thomas Wood, medical examiner for Leon County, Florida, and Michael J. A. Thompson, a Yorkshire physician and a descendant of Robert Atkinson, who participated in the northern rebellion of 1663, discussed technical aspects of the earl of Essex's death with me. For scholarly advice and support I am also happy to thank Larry Abele, Richard Ashcraft (whose magisterial study of John Locke appeared as research for this book neared completion), J. Wayne Baker, Jonathan Barry, Bernard Capp, Gary De Krey, Janelle Greenberg, Paul Hardacre, David Mock, Michael Mullett, Geoffrey Nuttall, Lois Schwoerer, Paul Seaver, Leo Solt, Keith Sprunger, David Underdown, and Dewey Wallace. I owe a special debt to many scholars for their published work; they include Julia Buckroyd, Robin Clifton, Peter Earle, Kenneth Haley, Tim Harris, and J. P. Kenyon. Norris Pope has once again been a model editor, Nancy Atkinson a superb copy editor, and Stanford an exemplary press.

This book is dedicated to Ted and Judith Underwood, whose unwavering friendship and support extend back to our days in graduate school, and to Christopher Hill, whose unrivaled knowledge of Stuart England has been a constant inspiration. My family has been steadfast in its love and encouragement; I wish in particular to acknowledge a debt to my father, who died while this book was in press. I extend a very special and deeply personal expression of gratitude to Judith, to Sherry and Stephany, to Robert and Lili, and to Ted and Judith.

Contents

SECRETS OF THE KINGDOM

Prologue

Perhaps no issue aroused more concern in British politics in the period 1673–88 than James' Catholicism, particularly as it was a convenient symbol of court policies deemed by many to threaten traditional liberties and Protestant convictions. Although Catholics in England constituted only 2 percent of the population, anti-Catholicism was firmly embedded in the national consciousness as a result of the Marian burnings, the papacy's futile attempt to deprive Elizabeth I of her crown, the influx of seminary priests and Jesuits, the infamous Gunpowder Plot, and the "popish conspiracy" of the early 1640s. Caroline Hibbard observed of the latter period, "Of the two slogans of 'tyranny' and 'popery' that would be raised against the king's government, if not against the king himself, 'popery' was the most potent and the more universal."[1]

In the early sixteenth century the reformer John Bale had identified Antichrist with the papacy, a theme on which many subsequent English Protestant authors would expound as they painted a picture of the alleged spiritual tyranny of the Roman church. Coupled with this theme as its secular mirror image was the Stuarts' purported attempt to impose the tyranny of arbitrary government on the three kingdoms. Neatly linking these themes, in 1679 William Bedloe, one of the Popish Plot informers, proclaimed England to be the bulwark of liberty and Protestantism against the papacy's threat to inundate the world with tyranny and superstition.[2]

The sense of danger was heightened by the seemingly unstoppable march of Catholicism on the Continent. Although temporarily checked by Habsburg reverses in the Thirty Years' War and Crom-

well's defeat of Spain, Catholicism was again on the march commencing in the 1660s. This was particularly so in France, which increasingly threatened its Dutch and German neighbors. Moreover,
Louis XIV's government subjected the Huguenots to mounting ha-
rassment, including the demolition of churches built since the pro-
mulgation of the Edict of Nantes. French repression culminated, of
course, with the policy of billeting troops in Huguenot homes beginning in 1681 and the revocation of the edict itself four years later.
The English watched these events with mounting concern and periodically collected funds for the relief of persecuted Protestants on
the Continent.[3] The fate of the Huguenots under Louis XIV's regime complicated the efforts of those in Charles II's court who
looked to France as a model for strengthening royal authority and
reinforcing it with a large army and a centralized bureaucracy. Those
who favored such endeavors, including Charles and James, were inclined to pursue a pro-French foreign policy. However, this gave
critics of the court an opportunity to rally their supporters by de-
claiming the twin dangers of "popery and tyranny."

The stage was set in the early 1670s by the Treaty of Dover, the
1672 Declaration of Indulgence (which allowed Catholics to worship
in their homes as well as licensing Protestant nonconformists), and
the growing public awareness of James' conversion. The resulting
outcry, focused on the indulgence and the suspending power on
which it was based, prompted Charles to cancel the declaration and
accept a Test Bill in 1673 that excluded Catholics from positions of
power. James resigned his offices, as did his political ally Thomas
Clifford, also a convert to Catholicism. The eventual victor in this
struggle was Sir Thomas Osborne (earl of Danby from 1673), whose
policies were not only anti-French and anti-Catholic but hostile to
the nonconformists; increased royal authority continued to be a major goal, though to be achieved, according to Danby, by an alliance
with the Church of England and a core of parliamentary supporters
loyal to the court. Danby's ascendancy was virtually assured when
Anthony Ashley Cooper, earl of Shaftesbury, was dismissed as lord
chancellor in November 1673 because of his opposition to James'
marriage to Mary of Modena, a Catholic whose family had strong
ties to France. The possible implications of this marriage for the

succession became a matter of increased concern as hopes faded that Charles would procure an annulment of his own marriage to Catherine of Braganza and take a Protestant wife. The Dutch effectively used James' marriage to underscore their warnings that the Anglo-French alliance was part of a conspiracy to impose Catholicism and absolutism in England and Scotland.

England's withdrawal from the Third Dutch War in early 1674 only partly alleviated such concerns, not least because of valid suspicion that Charles remained sympathetic to France and Catholicism. Issues of foreign policy and religion were complicated by an unfolding political drama that pitted Danby and Sir Joseph Williamson, who succeeded the earl of Arlington as secretary of state in September 1674, against Shaftesbury, the duke of Buckingham, and their supporters. Danby proved unable to obtain parliamentary approval for a supplementary test that would have prohibited officeholders from attempting to alter the government of church or state, but the attempt of his critics to impeach him likewise failed. Increasingly, the domestic struggle focused on Shaftesbury's demand for more frequent parliaments and concomitant claims that the Cavalier Parliament had legally dissolved because of the unconstitutionally long prorogation from November 1675 to February 1677.[4] For protesting the continuation of this Parliament Shaftesbury, Buckingham, the earl of Salisbury, and Philip Lord Wharton were incarcerated in the Tower; Shaftesbury was not released until February 1678, seven months after the others. Aaron Smith, one of the earl's attorneys, fled when the House of Lords ordered his arrest for impugning the legitimacy of the new parliamentary session.

Danby's Protestant-oriented foreign policy and championship of the Church of England temporarily undermined the radicals' effectiveness in castigating the government as tyrannical and papist. For a time, in fact, some of the king's chief critics in the House of Commons received funds from the French government to encourage their obstruction of royal policies.[5] Danby's greatest achievement in foreign policy, the betrothal of Mary, James' daughter, to William of Orange in October 1677, seemingly underscored the Protestant commitments of England and Scotland, as did the subsequent creation of an Anglo-Dutch alliance against France and the dispatch of an army to Flanders in May 1678. Charles, however, was playing a duplicitous game, having secretly agreed with France in 1676 not to reenter the war as an ally of the Dutch. Danby and James, moreover, pondered using an army to impose greater royal authority.[6]

Unpersuaded by Charles' apparent embrace of an anti-French foreign policy, the king's critics zealously resumed their efforts to tar the court with the brush of tyranny and popery. As early as 24 June 1676, Francis Jenks, a Cornhill linen draper, had reiterated this theme in a speech at the Guildhall: he warned of a Catholic plot to replace Charles with James, which purportedly threatened lives, liberty, property, and Protestantism. Andrew Marvell took up the theme in *An Account of the Growth of Popery* (1677), charging that unnamed perpetrators were attempting "to introduce a *French Slavery*, and . . . *Roman Idolatry*," both of which were "crimes of the Highest Nature."[7] The notion of a popish plot thus became a convenient weapon with which to attack Danby and the court, undercutting the earl's efforts to champion a Protestant foreign policy. Arbitrary government, a charge to which Danby's efforts to manage Parliament rendered him suspect, was shrewdly linked to France and Catholicism. The radicals, whose hostility to the court had dropped sharply following the implementation of religious toleration in England (and to a lesser degree in Scotland and Ireland) only to mount again as persecution slowly intensified, were quick to seize on the notion of a popish plot to attack the government. Well before Titus Oates and Israel Tong made their sensational allegations in August 1678, dissidents had revived the notion of a Catholic conspiracy as a means of attracting popular support and berating the court. Among their concerns was the likelihood of James' succession. As Marvell observed in his "Dialogue Between the Two Horses": "If e'er he be King, I know Britain's doom. / We must all to the stake, or be converts to Rome." Undaunted by their previous failure to topple or at least impose limitations on the monarchy, the radicals were ready to renew their campaign against "*French Slavery*" and "*Roman Idolatry*." At stake was the future of three realms. The long decade that ensued was second in importance in British history only to the midcentury revolution.

"All That Oppose Popery"

═══ ONE ═══

The Popish Plot and the Radicals

As he prepared for his morning walk in St. James' Park on 13 August 1678, Charles II first learned of an alleged Catholic plot to assassinate him. The bearer of the news, Christopher Kirkby, a dabbler in chemical experiments, was a friend of Dr. Israel Tong, minister of St. Michael's, Wood Street, London. Tong, who was convinced that Catholics had been responsible for the great fire of London in 1666, was the source of Kirkby's allegations, but Tong had in turn received some of his information from Titus Oates, whose father Samuel had been a Baptist chaplain in the New Model Army. Titus had converted to Catholicism in March 1677, later claiming his intent had been to infiltrate the Jesuits in order to investigate Tong's belief in a Catholic plot. Shortly thereafter, Oates was expelled from Catholic colleges at Valladolid in Spain and St. Omers in France; he returned to England in late June 1678. Apparently driven by a desire for revenge, he informed Tong on approximately 1 August that he had evidence of a Catholic conspiracy to assassinate Charles and incite rebellions in the three kingdoms.[1]

Two years later, in August 1680, Tong's son, Simpson, testified before the Privy Council that his father and Oates had invented the conspiracy, forged some of the letters to substantiate it, and subsequently worked closely with the earls of Shaftesbury and Essex and with Philip Lord Wharton. Shortly thereafter, however, he repudiated this allegation. Nevertheless, no serious historian now questions the fact that the Popish Plot was manufactured by Oates and Tong. What is not fully understood is the extent to which the intrigue was linked to the English radicals.

Popery, Politics, and the Radicals

The Popish plot's premier historian, J. P. Kenyon, suspected connections between its inventors and earlier radicals, specifically suggesting that a Captain Oates executed at York in 1664 "for his share in a misty 'Presbyterian' Plot was almost certainly a relative of Titus Oates."[2] The captain was in fact Thomas Oates, of Morley, Yorkshire, who had an estate worth more than £300 per annum, and who died for his role in the northern rebellion of 1663. I know of no evidence to link Thomas and Titus. Kenyon was, however, on stronger ground in asserting that Israel Tong was a relative, possibly a brother, of Thomas Tong, executed in December 1662 for his role in a plot named after him.[3]

Two of Thomas Tong's associates in his 1662 scheme were Edward Radden, a former post office employee who lived near Exeter, and Captain Humphrey Spurway of Tiverton, Devon; both had escaped execution by fleeing to the Netherlands. Spurway was subsequently implicated in the planning that led to the northern rebellion of 1663, in which connection he probably met Thomas Oates and Lieutenant-Colonel Ralph Alexander. In 1666, the latter played a key role in a conspiracy to overthrow Charles and reestablish a commonwealth; Spurway too was allegedly part of that scheme, for which one of the leaders, Colonel John Rathbone, was executed. There was subsequently a report that Titus Oates himself—who was only sixteen or seventeen at the time—had been involved in the Rathbone conspiracy; if so, his participation must not have come to the attention of the authorities, for the following year he was admitted to Gonville and Caius College, Cambridge. Through the mediation of Thomas Blood, Alexander and Spurway eventually obtained pardons for their treasonable activities. Although Edward Radden had died, his brother William, a General Baptist and an attorney, was closely associated in the late 1670s with Spurway, Alexander, the General Baptist Thomas Parsons, and the radical bookseller and General Baptist Francis "Elephant" Smith.[4]

When Oates returned to London from St. Omers in late June 1678, he associated with Radden and Parsons. From Oates and Francis Smith, Radden and Parsons gathered and transmitted "news" to "the most dangerous Babtists [sic] in Devon and Dorsett" as well as to dissidents in Bristol and Somerset.⁵ The historical records offer no hint that Radden, Spurway, Parsons, Alexander, or Smith contributed to or initially knew of the manufacture of evidence concerning the purported Catholic conspiracy, but not insignificantly Oates and Tong contrived their allegations while they were associated with persons of distinctly radical convictions—men who undoubtedly shared the deep hostility to and suspicion of Catholics that were particularly marked among radicals.

In his appearance before the Privy Council on 28 September, Oates laid out the alleged Catholic plans for uprisings in Scotland, Ireland, and England. As the investigation continued in the ensuing days, the government began making arrests and seeking further information. One of the avenues of inquiry involved a Mr. Rumboll, who provided information to Secretary of State Henry Coventry that had been obtained from a Mr. Nevill, who lived in Ireland. Presumably his account related to purported Catholic activities on that island. The episode may be significant if Rumboll was in fact Captain Richard Rumbold (or Rumball), a former Cromwellian officer who would subsequently play a key role in the Rye House Plot. If so, this may have been the first attempt by radicals to manipulate the alleged scheme for their own ends. In any event, another dissident, the Scot William Carstares, who would later serve as William of Orange's agent in the radical community, testified in November during the treason trial of William Staley, son of a Catholic banker in London, who had publicly threatened to kill the king. Although Carstares' charge against Staley is plausible, especially if Staley was inebriated at the time, his motives in giving evidence were later questioned by Gilbert Burnet, perhaps with some justification.⁶

As Oates and the unscrupulous William Bedloe subsequently competed with each other in the invention of new fictions about the Popish Plot, an atmosphere of suspicion and fear grew, compounded by political maneuvering on the part of those who sought personal advantage. In December, officials in Dublin announced the discovery of a conspiracy to assassinate the duke of Ormond, the lord lieutenant, after finding suspicious letters in one of the streets. They arrested Michael Jephson, whose father, Colonel Alexander Jephson, had been executed for his role in the Dublin plot of 1663. The younger Jephson had supposedly acted for religious reasons as well as a desire to avenge his father's death. His confession implicated two secular priests, Plunket and Birne; authorities also found a letter addressed to Jephson from a Jesuit named Owens in Calais encouraging him to assassinate Ormond. The lord lieutenant took the Catholic threat seriously, perhaps with good reason, although there is apparently nothing to link the Jephson affair with the tales of Oates and Bedloe.[7]

As Oates expanded his accusations, his contacts with radicals increased. Colonel Henry Danvers, a veteran plotter who was intimate with Radden and Spurway, also drew close to Oates. An informant subsequently reported that in the spring of 1679 Oates met with a "private cabal" on a daily basis. This group centered around the earl of Shaftesbury and allegedly included such prominent Whigs as William Lord Howard of Escrick, Ford Lord Grey, Sir Thomas Player, and Sir George Treby. Also associated with these men was Major John Breman, a civil war veteran who had previously been imprisoned for his radical proclivities and who was apparently close to Danvers.[8] Unwittingly, Oates, with his tortuous, shifting account of Catholic subversion, provided a critical link between the Country opposition to Charles and the traditional radical underground represented by such men as Breman, Danvers, Spurway, Francis Smith, and Alexander. This nexus would subsequently provide the context for the conspiratorial activity traditionally known as the Rye House Plot.

Whatever influence Spurway and his radical colleagues had on Tong and Oates in 1678, by the following spring Oates had become a tool of Shaftesbury. As lord president of the Privy Council beginning 21 April 1679, he relentlessly investigated the alleged conspiracy. In the meantime, Charles had dissolved the Cavalier Parliament in January, summoned a new one to meet on 6 March 1679, and ordered the strict enforcement of laws against recusants. By this point local magistrates were already investigating Catholics, demanding recognizances of them, and confiscating their weapons.[9]

Because of the alleged Catholic threat the new Parliament met in an atmosphere of tension. On 27 April, during a debate in the House of Commons on the king's safety, Player announced that he had seen correspondence between James and the pope, the clear implication being that England and Rome would be reconciled when the duke succeeded to the throne. Speaking to this issue, Lord Russell ominously warned: "If we do not something relating to the Succession, we must resolve, when we have a Prince of the Popish Religion, to be Papists, or burn. And I will do neither." After further debate the Commons resolved: "the Duke of *Yorke's* being a Papist, and the Hopes of his coming such to the Crown, has given the greatest Countenance and Encouragement to the present Conspiracies and Designs of the Papists against the King, and the Protestant Religion." The House of Lords, however, never approved the resolution. Nevertheless, on 15 May an Exclusion Bill was introduced in the Commons; on the second reading it passed by a majority of 207 to 128. Adamantly opposed to the bill, Charles prorogued Parliament on the 27th, and eventually dissolved it on 12 July.[10]

By this time a belief was spreading in the country that the nation was endangered by the twin threat of popery and tyranny. As early as October 1678 some nonconformists, attuned to the embattled status of Protestantism on the Continent, particularly in France, had suspected the French of responsibility for the scheme, while others adjudged it more serious than the infamous Gunpowder Plot. The king himself soon fell under the shadow of suspicion, and by January there were fears that Parliament would be prorogued in order to smother the investigation. Such sentiments, observed William Clarke of Sandford, made people "mightily afrayd of Popery, and ill Times," adversely affecting even the economy: "Whether through a pannicke Fear, or just Apprehension I cannot say, but soe it is, the news which came from Westminster the Beginning of the last month hath soe much sunke the Souls of this Country men, that Wee must expect to feel the Effect of it in the Abatement of our Rents this next year" as the cloth trade declines and wool prices fall. Members of the Green Ribbon Club, which disseminated Whig propaganda, reportedly complained, "The Nation is sold to the French," and "Popery & arbitrary Government is intended" by an inner clique at Whitehall consisting of James, the duchess of Portsmouth, the lord treasurer, and the French ambassador. The declining fortunes of Protestants in France and central Europe made the Popish Plot a serious matter to many English people.[11]

Emotions were fanned by doggerel:

> How nere shall be a prince of Wales
> That wears a Roman Nose.
> What ere pretences can there be
> Sure something is contriving,
> And he is blind that cannot see
> The Plott is still a driving.

Passions were excited as well by the revival of public demonstrations against the pope, the reputed whore of Babylon. London apprentices were encouraged to march on Whitsun Monday and Tuesday, not only to protest against popery but to demand the punishment of the earl of Danby. The Green Ribbon Club organized a major demonstration in London on 17 November 1679, the anniversary of Elizabeth I's accession, which culminated in the burning of the pope in effigy, although no direct attack was made on the duke of York.[12]

Taking advantage of the king's illness, James and his supporters mounted an offensive of their own in September. The duke of Monmouth, the king's son by Lucy Walters, was relieved of his position as captain-general of the army on the 12th and ordered into exile. Shaftesbury was dismissed from the Council on 14 October, and the next day Parliament was prorogued before it could meet. James also gave his blessing to a harebrained scheme to frame Shaftesbury and other Whig leaders for treason. Forged papers were planted in the chamber of Colonel Roderick Mansell, a Whig and former servant of the earl of Essex, by Thomas Dangerfield (alias Willoughby), an associate of Elizabeth Cellier, a Catholic midwife with ties to the duchess of York. When Council members investigated the papers, conveniently "discovered" by Dangerfield, they were sufficiently suspicious of him to have Cellier's house searched. After incriminating documents were found in a meal tub, she was arrested and Dangerfield confessed.[13] His allegations led to the apprehension of other Catholics, including the earl of Castlemaine and the countess of Powis.

Among the Whigs whom the Cellier group had hoped to implicate were Monmouth, Lord Gerard of Brandon, Sir Thomas Armstrong, Sir William Waller, and, incongruously, Thomas Blood, the ex-plotter who had been a government agent since 1671. Ironically, the previous February some had suspected Blood of contriving the Popish Plot with Oates and Bedloe.[14] In fact, as part of the Tory offensive against the Whigs, Blood was engaged in a scheme to accuse the duke of Buckingham of treason and buggery. Among Blood's associates was Thomas Curtis, a participant in Cellier's effort to discredit the Whigs through a bogus Presbyterian plot, and Morrice Hickey (alias George Higgins), an Irishman who later tried to save himself by claiming he had information that the imprisoned Catholic peers in the Tower were scheming to establish popery by military means. In June 1680 Blood, Curtis, and two associates were found guilty of conspiring against Buckingham. Blood appealed to James for help, attributing his problems to the fact that he had kept "the Common Welth party in Awe and [had] broke[n] the Necke of Sir William Waller." He followed this with a protest to Secretary Jenkins, underlining the extent to which his counterespionage activities had made him disliked among his former radical colleagues: "I am asalted by the Duke of Bukinghym, and all the Commonwelth party, who though they know I never medled or made with any of the Concernment they Charged me with, yet have they not spared to spend 10000 pound upon me to get me out of their way knowing that I have beene a Check upon their disloyall Actions this nine Years, and remaine so still, being so interwoven in their interest." Caught in the act of trying to frame Buckingham for treason, Blood died in disgrace on 24 August 1680. So suspicious had some become of his actions that even his death was thought to be a ruse; that question was settled only after his grave was opened and a jury examined his corpse.[15]

Although the attempt to destroy Buckingham failed, royal supporters were more successful in dealing with Sir Robert Peyton, a wealthy Whig merchant and member of the Green Ribbon Club. He was briefly lured away from his Whig friends by the earl of Peterborough, Cellier, and the astrologer John Gadbury. When Dangerfield turned on Cellier, he also accused Peyton of complicity in

Catholic intrigue and support for James.[16] Then, in January 1680,
Cellier and Gadbury charged that when Peyton had joined them he
outlined Whig plans to establish a commonwealth by armed force if
Charles had died in the summer of 1679. Dangerfield subsequently
changed his story, claiming that Cellier was responsible for a Catholic intrigue to implicate Presbyterians in a fictional conspiracy. Bailed
in February, Peyton was discharged in May 1680, presumably chas-
tened by the imbroglio.[17]

The ease with which false charges could be lodged against the
Whigs did not dissuade Shaftesbury and his allies from prosecuting
alleged Popish plotters. In this endeavor the earl gained a new compatriot when the earl of Essex was dismissed as lord treasurer and
subsequently failed to obtain reappointment as lord lieutenant of
Ireland. It was undoubtedly at Essex's urging that Shaftesbury dispatched agents to Ireland in early 1680 to obtain incriminating material against the archbishops of Dublin and Armagh. By late March
he had enough information to tell the Council of purported plans
for a general massacre of Protestants in Ireland, to be accomplished
with foreign assistance. The Councillors, however, denied his request for an investigation by a select committee of lords, retaining
the matter for their own leisurely purview.[18]

Shaftesbury's efforts to compel Charles to convene a new Parliament fared no better. The king responded to petitions from London
and the provinces with two proclamations, dated 10 and 12 December 1679, charging that the petitioners promoted sedition and rebellion, and directing magistrates to prosecute the offenders. The
proclamations notwithstanding, the petitioners, many of them nonconformists, redoubled their efforts.[19] As if the link between the Popish Plot and the demands for Parliament to sit were not obvious
enough, Oates and Bedloe accompanied Sir Gilbert Gerard to Whitehall to deliver a petition from the people of Westminster and Southwark calling for new elections. When the goldsmith Thomas Dare
presented a similar petition from Taunton, Somerset, to the Council,
his provocative speech resulted in a fine of £500. Secretary Jenkins
must have been reminded of the influential petition drives of 1641
and their contribution to the outbreak of civil war.[20]

Public gatherings, by nature an obvious stage for the rehearsal of grievances, became a matter of special concern. Loyalists were terrified by a march of young, mostly nonconformist artisans in Bristol on 30 January 1680; known to be critical of the government, they may have been inspired by John Row and Joseph Tiley, two future Rye House conspirators, both of whom were arrested at this time on charges of seditious speech and taken to London. The episode underscored the deepening divisions in local Bristol politics between what Jonathan Barry has called "the military and clerical party" on the one hand and the nonconformists and their allies on the other. At Bath, nonconformist ministers reportedly stirred up feelings by telling people that the king would "let in" Catholicism as a result of James' influence; "under feare of Popery they endeavor[ed] to inflame the people into rebellion." On 7 April the Privy Council prohibited unauthorized bonfires and fireworks, even on festival days, because dissidents had been turning "those Meetings into Riots and Tumults." Exaggerated fears of popery, coupled with long-standing concerns among nonconformists about arbitrary government, provided Shaftesbury and his associates with a natural constituency in the country. Yet the real danger from the government's standpoint came not from the common people but from nonconformists of substance. As Secretary Jenkins told Sidney Godolphin on 23 September: "I have advice this day from among the small-Craft of Sectaries, that there is nothing to be feard from among them; the Danger is from the Wealthy dissenters that pretend the fear of Popery, but under that pretense drive at the change of Government into a Commonwealth."[21]

Probably at Shaftesbury's urging, Monmouth began a progress in July 1680 that was clearly designed to demonstrate popular support for the Whigs. Among those who made arrangements for the journey were Colonel John Rumsey, "a rigid Presbyterian" and sometime customs collector in Bristol, and Colonel John Scott, formerly an agent for the duke of Buckingham but more recently in Shaftesbury's employ.[22] Monmouth's journey took him from Reading, Bath, and Bristol to Exeter, where he received an enthusiastic welcome and enjoyed the hospitality of Sir William Courtenay. The reception at Oxford in September was tumultuous, with the crowd shouting, "A Monmouth, no York, no Bishop, no Clergy, no University." Not surprisingly, Henry Sidney informed William of Orange in October: "[The duke has] more credit in the countrey then one can imagine and, as long as he is kept out of the Court, it will encrease dayly." Indeed, Sidney believed the duke's popularity would soar if the king again dissolved Parliament, as he had done in July 1679, to save the succession for James. That assessment, of course, proved to be unduly pessimistic, but Monmouth continued to enjoy substantial favor, especially among the lower orders. After attending a banquet held in his honor by "the sea-faring men" of the London area in December, he basked in the plaudits of the crowds "from one end of the Citty to the other." [23]

The impact of the Popish Plot and the commencement of the exclusion controversy can be seen not only in the petitions and demonstrations sponsored by the Whigs but in the numerous allegations of seditious or improper language. It should, of course, be remembered that this barometer of dissident feeling was present throughout the 1660s and 1670s, although the tone and substance shifted somewhat as the Popish Plot unfolded. On the eve of the intrigue, one could hear the usual outbursts against the king's sexual promiscuity as well as language deemed subversive of the government or reminiscent of interregnum radicalism. Slingsby Bethel was said to have called Charles and James bastards, while a Dartford man, who claimed to have known the Leveller John Lilburne, boasted that he was "for noe King in England nor for any head of the Church but Jesus Christ." A Darlington gunsmith, perhaps demented, declared that he had "the power of a king & that the king would beare the name & he would beare the Rule." More importantly, even before the succession became a political issue, James was the object of "base & scandalous language." Those who shared such feelings would have welcomed efforts to exclude him from the throne. [24]

The plot and especially the exclusion debate had the effect of sharpening dissident expressions and focusing most of them on the duke of York. A Bath alderman, Walter Hickes, declaimed that "he did not care a [fart] for any popish mayor or Alderman . . . neither did he care a [fart] for the Duke of York, for he was a Rouge; A Raskall; A traytour; A Reble & A son of a whore." His sentiments were echoed by a Middlesex man, who denounced James as "A

Pimpe And a Sonne of A Whore"; ironically, it was Monmouth, not James, who was illegitimate. Numerous accusations were made of "dangerous and seditious words," a charge customarily employed against those who had labeled Charles or James papists or had denied the latter's right to the throne. The nonconformist Stephen Standen boasted in December 1680 that Parliament would exclude James and that the lord mayor would prevent the king from proroguing Parliament until it had done so. With equal spirit, his wife, Sarah, insisted that if the duke of York returned to London, she would throw stones and dirt in his face, "& tell him to his face, he was a Rogue and a Traytor to his nation."[25] It is impossible to ascertain how widespread such feelings were, but they must have been considerably more extensive than the extant evidence suggests, not least because most dissidents would have used discretion in speaking to strangers. Moreover, numerous potential witnesses must have opted not to bring charges so as to avoid legal entanglements.

The Catholic Scare and the Radical Press

The atmosphere of anti-Catholicism was nourished throughout the period of the Popish Plot by a somewhat vitriolic publication in newssheet format entitled *A Pacquet of Advice from Rome*, to which was appended *The Popish Courant*. Masquerading as history, the *Pacquet* was a polemical digest of the errors of Catholicism for readers unable or unwilling to peruse the scholarly tomes already in print. The *Courant*, on the other hand, focused on contemporary events and satirical treatments of Catholic practices. Stemming from the surge of interest in the Popish Plot, the first issue of the *Pacquet* appeared on 3 December 1678, published by Langley Curtis and written by the Whig pamphleteer Henry Care. In 1679 Curtis also published the first 31 numbers in a bound volume entitled *The Weekly Pacquet of Advice from Rome*, and the following year he put out the ensuing 47 issues in a second volume. After completing four more issues between 4 and 25 June 1680, Care was arrested and tried at the Guildhall on 2 July on a charge of libel, with intent to scandalize the government. Although the jury found him guilty,[26] he returned almost immediately to his desk and composed another number, which was probably published on 9 July (though it is undated). His legal difficulties prompted him to change the title to *The New Anti-Roman Pacquet*, and then to *The Anti-Roman Pacquet*, while the *Courant* was renamed *The Popes Harbinger*. On 3 December, Care boldly re-titled his publication *The Weekly Pacquet of Advice from Rome Re-stored*; sixteen issues later he dropped the last word from the title, a clear indication that censorship was in a state of severe if temporary decay. Two further volumes of collected issues were published, the last of which continued through the number that appeared on 18 August 1682.

Care kept his readers abreast of developments in the Popish Plot and repeatedly satirized attempts to manufacture belief in a Presby-terian plot. "Ever since 78," he made the Catholics say, "we have been beating a Bush to start a *Presbyterian Plot*, which to this very day [March 1681] is no where to be found, but in *L'Estrange's Pamphlets*." Sir Roger L'Estrange had, of course, long been an enemy of radical and nonconformist authors because of his campaign to regulate the press, and Care played on that hostility, satirizing him *inter alia* for a "pretended . . . Patent for *Fart-cracking*." L'Estrange and his fellow conservative Nathaniel Thompson were accused of publishing "the Grossest Scandals that were vented in a civil State, on purpose to divide *Protestants* and create Misunderstandings and Jealousies be-tween the King and His People." In response to continued allega-tions of Presbyterian or republican plots in the *Observator* and *Her-aclitus*, Care challenged L'Estrange, Thompson, and their associates to name the supposed perpetrators so they could be duly hanged. "If ever a *Popish Successor* mount the Throne, such shams" as the reputed Presbyterian plot will, Care asserted, "become excellent *Chaffer*, cur-rant *Church-Coyn*, and be *preach'd* up by the *Black-Robe* to be *Jure Divino*." The *Weekly Pacquet* was intended not only to drill into readers the insidious perils of Catholicism but also to enlist their support in the exclusion struggle on the side of the Whigs, namely "all that are soberly *loyal* and oppose *Popery*."[27]

When allegations of the Popish Plot were initially made, the gov-ernment directed its attention to publishers and printers of Catholic books, such as Nathaniel Thompson. But by December 1678 a re-ward had been offered for the apprehension of the printer of two of

Edward Coleman's letters to Father François La Chaise, Louis XIV's confessor, and a forged letter from James to the same priest. This was probably the handiwork of a radical printer such as Francis Smith, but in any case it was apparently the motivation for a more general search for unlicensed publications and works hostile to the state or the established church.[28] However, not until the fall of 1679, by which time the exclusion issue had come to the fore, did the underground press again become a serious problem for the government. As early as August, the lord mayor and aldermen of London, angered by the open sale of seditious books and scurrilous pamphlets, directed the marshal and constables to arrest offenders. The gesture was futile, for four months later Secretary Coventry complained that libels were sold every day at the very gates of Whitehall. A proclamation of 31 October offered a reward of £40 to anyone who disclosed the author or printer of a seditious publication in the forthcoming year.[29]

The publications of primary concern dealt, expectedly, with the Popish Plot and the succession. Andrew Marvell's *Account of the Growth of Popery* (1677), which accused Catholics of plotting not only to destroy Protestantism but also to introduce tyranny, had made Catholicism an explosive issue even before the revelations of Oates and Tong.[30] The Whig Charles Blount, building on Marvell's legacy, used his anonymous *Appeal from the Country to the City* (1679) to blame Catholics for both the great fire of London and the 1679 Covenanter rebellion in Scotland. Oates, of course, had warned that Catholics disguised as Protestant zealots were planning an uprising north of the Tweed, and Blount unabashedly attributed the rebellion to "disguis'd Priests and Emissaries." Had it truly been "a Fanatical Plot" as the government claimed, "the same Party would certainly have risen in *England*." Not surprisingly, Blount also argued against a Catholic successor, insisting such a ruler could not be fettered by laws because his power would be based on an army rather than Parliament.[31]

In February 1680 the state accused the bookseller Benjamin Harris, an associate of Shaftesbury's banker, Peter Percival, of responsibility for the printing and sale of the *Appeal*, although the author could not be identified. The book, opined Sir George Jeffreys, was "as base a piece as ever was contrived in hell, either by papists, or the blackest rebel that ever was." The work was doubly provocative because its appearance immediately preceded Monmouth's return from his exile in the Netherlands. By this time Harris was intimately associated with Shaftesbury, who, with Oates, had sponsored his newssheet, the *Domestick Intelligence*, commencing in July 1679; copies circulated in the Netherlands, sparking a protest from the English consul in 1681. For issuing the *Appeal*, Harris was fined £500 and pilloried. Unable to pay, he was incarcerated in Newgate until late December, during which time his paper was not published. The Privy Council ordered his reimprisonment in February 1681, and his paper was again suppressed the following April.[32]

Harris' trial was part of a government campaign against dissident booksellers, publishers, and coffeehouse keepers that had been launched in the late autumn of 1679. Among those taken into custody were John Claypoole, printer of the *Domestick Intelligence*, who had previously been arrested in July 1678, and the bookseller Matthew Turner, for allegedly printing the *Compendium or View of the Late Tryals*.[33] Another was Francis Smith, the associate of Spurway and his colleagues as well as Titus Oates. Smith too had earlier been in trouble with the authorities, not least for having helped to publish the notorious *Mirabilis Annus* (1662). Now he was propagating allegations of the Popish Plot, as in *Some Observations upon the Trial of Sir George Wakeman*, and assisting the Whigs, in part by printing some of their petitions. L'Estrange aptly called him "the principall Agent for the Presbyterians [i.e., the future Whigs] in their Trade of Libells; being entrusted with their Manuscripts." In June 1678 an informer glimpsed part of the title page of a Whig work Smith was handling that pertained to the calling of a new Parliament.[34] A year and a half later Smith was jailed for publishing allegedly seditious queries pertaining to the Association formulated in Elizabeth's reign in response to the threat posed by Catholic conspiracies; the parallel to the contemporary Popish Plot was obvious. Freed on a writ of habeas corpus, Smith was arrested again on 7 January 1680 for publishing *A New Years-Gift for the Lord Chief in Justice Sc[rog]gs*, only to be released the following day on another writ. An informer (whose report is undated) claimed not only that Smith acknowledged that he was printing *A New Years-Gift*, but also that Smith had been visited in prison by Lord Howard of Escrick (a future Rye House conspirator) and Claypoole, and that the latter had inquired if Smith had heard from Shaftesbury or seen Sir Robert Peyton. The testimony is probably reliable and underscores Smith's ties to Whig leaders. In February he was fined at the Guildhall for publishing *Some Observations upon the Trial of Sir George Wakeman*.[35] Jane Curtis, Langley's wife, was convicted the same day of publishing the allegedly seditious satire on Scroggs.[36]

While the government tried to bring the radical press to heel, in part by a proclamation of 12 May 1680 to suppress unlicensed newssheets, Whig efforts were under way to demonstrate Monmouth's legitimacy. As early as 1662, rumors had begun circulating that Monmouth's mother, Lucy Walters, had secretly married Charles.[37] In the spring of 1680 rumor spread that a black box, supposedly containing the marriage contract, had been given by Dr. John Cosin, bishop of Durham, to his son-in-law, Sir Gilbert Gerard. On 24 April, Gerard told the Privy Council he had no knowledge of such a box or a marriage contract, but his assertion did little or nothing to squelch rumors. John Wildman's cousin, William Disney, whose father had been a royalist colonel in the civil war, confessed to Essex and Jenkins that he had been investigating the matter on his own, but denied that he had been employed to do so by Colonel Mansell. Disney turned up assorted reports, all of a hearsay nature.[38] The king himself denied having married anyone but Queen Catherine, but like many rumors this one attracted believers simply through its frequent reiteration, thanks in part to the radical printers. The story was spread in *A Full Relation of the Contents of the Black Box* (1680) and *A Letter to a Person of Honour Concerning the Black Box* (1680), the latter by Robert Ferguson, a Scottish minister with "a great Roman nose," a shuffling gait, and close ties to Dr. John Owen, the Whig M.P. Thomas Papillon, and ultimately Shaftesbury; Ferguson had returned from the Netherlands the previous December under government suspicion that he was involved in conspiratorial undertakings. Large quantities of Ferguson's *Letter* were seized in the Royal Exchange in May, but other copies found their way throughout the country, aided in part by financial support from Monmouth and Shaftesbury.[39] Among those responsible for spreading the tale of the black box were Tong, Francis Smith, and Sir Thomas Armstrong, one of Monmouth's confidants.

Printers and booksellers furthered the duke's cause in other ways as well. One, who was arrested for his deed, had printed an equestrian portrait of Monmouth with the caption "his Royal Highness." When Monmouth undertook his triumphal tour through the west country in the summer of 1680, Benjamin Harris published an account of the duke's alleged cure of a young woman suffering from the king's evil (scrofula)—an obvious allusion to Monmouth's royal lineage.[40] Thus radical booksellers such as Harris and Smith provided a crucial link between the Whigs and members of the older radical underground, such as Danvers, Spurway, and Alexander; the Popish Plot and exclusion controversy provided the context in which that link was forged.

The Politics of Exclusion and Subornation

Against this tense backdrop, Parliament met on 21 October 1680, with the king willing to accept statutory limitations on the powers of a Catholic successor but firmly set against excluding his brother. The Lords' unwillingness to approve the Exclusion Bill sent up from the Commons left the Whigs embittered and frustrated.[41] In a speech to the Lords, which Francis Smith subsequently published,[42] Shaftesbury rehearsed the Whig case against James. The duke, he averred, changed his religion "to make himself a Party, and such a Party that his Brother must be sure *to dye* and be *made away*, to make room for Him." The Popish Plot was laid directly at James' feet, it being "his Interest and his Design." Shaftesbury complained about efforts to turn the plot into a Presbyterian conspiracy. There must, he insisted, be no funds for Charles until Parliament is assured that "*the King is ours.*" To Charles he said boldly, "*Change your Principles, change your Court, and be your self.*" Charles must surely have been convinced by now that the enactment of a statute excluding James would eventually lead to civil war, since the duke would undoubtedly have resorted to the sword to claim his heritable right. The king therefore dissolved Parliament in January 1681 and summoned another to convene at Oxford in March. For good measure, he also dismissed several supporters of exclusion from the Privy Council, including the earls of Essex and Sunderland.[43]

The exiles in the Netherlands followed these events with intense interest. According to William Carr, the English consul, they attempted to convince the Dutch that Charles intended to compel the Oxford Parliament to do his bidding and that James was raising troops in Scotland, but they also insisted that members of Parliament would travel to Oxford accompanied by armed retinues prepared to defend their interests. At the "Brownist" church in Amsterdam, Carr reported, a minister had preached that the time was near when all nations would be converted to the true faith, as described in the book of Daniel, and that "Antichrist must downe," but only after the godly—probably those in England first—had suffered persecution. Among the members of this congregation were John Phelps, a former member of the regicide court; Henry Cromwell's son, Oliver; Phelps' son as well as the sons of the regicides Thomas Harrison and Daniel Blagrave; Israel Hayes, who had provided hospitality to Colonel Mansell in 1680; and at least three Fifth Monarchists. As recently as September 1680, Sir William Waller had presented an address to this congregation, which Carr summarized thus: "[He] rendered our affaires in England in a bad Estate, & most malitious[ly] tould some of our Magistrates strange Lyes of our King." According to an unidentified informer, Waller was in Utrecht in January 1681, where he arranged for 4,000 pair of pistols and 2,000 firelocks to be shipped to England via Rotterdam.[44]

In England the deepening atmosphere of confrontation affected the Whigs in diverse ways. Those of a more moderate bent apparently wanted to draw back, for a number of former Whig members did not seek reelection and Whig strength in the new House of Commons declined slightly. Others, however, were increasingly embittered by the court's refusal to endorse exclusion. In response to the earl of Feversham's boast that he would march 20,000 armed men through London to show support for the court, Sir Thomas Player retorted that 20 good men would stop him in Cheapside. There would be no money, he warned, for the Whitehall whores or arbitrary government, even if Charles summoned Parliament all the way to York. Moreover, Player declaimed, the Commons had the right to dispose of the crown as it saw fit, the succession being "as Alterable as the Changing of Pipes."[45]

The previous Parliament had made it apparent to prominent Whigs that exclusion could never succeed without the king's support. Summoning Parliament to Oxford, a town mostly loyal to royal interests, signaled Charles' unshaken opposition to the Whig program. As a result, much of the hostility hitherto directed largely at James, unpopular royal ministers, and court "whores" henceforth encompassed Charles as well, though Shaftesbury and his supporters continued to believe that the king would ultimately embrace exclusion. If the withholding of supply was by itself insufficient to prevent dissolution of the Parliament, the Whigs were seemingly strengthened by a plan to impeach the Irish Catholic Edward Fitzharris, a government informer caught attempting to plant treasonable documents on Whig leaders. Not only would his impeachment incriminate men close to James, but Charles presumably could not dissolve Parliament until Fitzharris' case was resolved without creating the appearance of a coverup.[46] Fortunately for the king, the House of Lords refused to hear the impeachment charges because Fitzharris was a commoner. Believing himself financially secure with a promised subsidy from Louis XIV, Charles was undeterred by Whig pressures and dissolved Parliament on 28 March 1681 as the Commons debated a new Exclusion Bill. Whig efforts to achieve a parliamentary solution to the succession crisis—never realistic once statutory limitations were ruled out—had been effectively stalemated. Charles subsequently issued a declaration promising to convene Parliament frequently, but this was greeted with cynicism in some circles. "That is," opined a Chester silkweaver, "as if I, or another shold break your head & then speak you fair, or give you a plaister."[47]

The court struck next to eliminate Fitzharris, now not only an embarrassment but also a threat since he had changed his story and was prepared to testify that James, the queen, and Danby had been a party to Sir Edmund Godfrey's murder, and that an envoy of the duchess' father, the duke of Modena, had offered him £10,000 to assassinate Charles. With Shaftesbury and his associates in attendance, Fitzharris was tried in the King's Bench; as a show of fairness,

the government approved a list of counselors that included such
Whigs as Sir George Treby, Sir Francis Winnington, and Henry Pollexfen. Their contention that Fitzharris could not be tried in a lower
tribunal after having been impeached in the Commons was rejected,
and on 9 June he was charged with the authorship of *The True Englishman*, an indictment of Charles for arbitrary rule. The principal
witness for the crown was a sometime radical named Edmund Everard of Gray's Inn, who in 1673 had allegedly been involved in a
conspiracy to assassinate Monmouth, and in December 1678 had accused Scottish Catholic nobles of participation in the Popish Plot.[48]
According to Everard, Fitzharris had composed a seditious tract that
was to have been given to Father La Chaise with the understanding
that it had been written by a nonconformist and represented dissenting views. Oates claimed that Everard had told him the tract was
also to have been mailed to leading Whigs, after which the authorities would be tipped off that the Whigs had the work in their possession. The court itself, averred Oates, was involved in the scheme.
This allegation was fortified by the testimony of Sir William Waller,
Lord Howard of Escrick, and Henry Cornish, a Whig sheriff of
London. In his defense, Fitzharris asserted that he had in fact acted
with the court's approval, but only to ferret out conspiracies against
the crown. The author of *The True Englishman*, he insisted, was
Everard.[49]

While the Whigs endeavored to tarnish the court by pointing to
the Fitzharris case as a conspiracy to foist a bogus plot on them, the
Tories countered by depicting Fitzharris as a willing dupe of unscrupulous Whigs. After his wife, Anne, was arrested in June on suspicion of misprision of treason, she claimed that Essex and one of Sir
Edmund Godfrey's brothers, the latter acting as a representative of
the "Protestant" lords, advised her to persuade her husband to accuse Charles, Catherine, and James of the conspiracy. Essex allegedly
added Danby to the list for good measure. During the Oxford Parliament, she said, Waller and Sir Robert Clayton had made the same
proposal, while John Rouse, a future Rye House conspirator, had
wanted her husband to blame Charles and James for the fire of London. Although the charges and countercharges make this case somewhat murky, Anne Fitzharris' claims are not altogether implausible

and in fact are essentially compatible with what we know of Whig strategy at Oxford. Moreover, they were partially corroborated by her husband at his execution.[50]

The jury believed neither Edward Fitzharris' unlikely contention that he had been engaged in the king's secret service nor his attempt to blame Everard for writing *The True Englishman*. Found guilty, he was executed on 1 July, the same day that the last victim of the Popish Plot, Archbishop Oliver Plunket, went to the scaffold.[51] Although Kenyon has suggested that Fitzharris was "the first victim of the 'Tory Revenge,'" he was nothing more than an unscrupulous informer whose pliability and duplicity got him into trouble with both sides. He did not die a Whig martyr, but was instead reviled by the Whigs as a rogue who deserved to be hanged. Yet despite their ultimate condemnation of Fitzharris, dissidents continued to distribute copies of *The True Englishman*, which was reprinted in 1682 under the title *Treason in Graine*.[52] The seamy episode helped to keep allegations of the Popish Plot alive, and Langley Curtis capitalized on this by publishing *An Impartial Account of the Sham Plot or the Murder of Godfrey Discovered*.[53]

In the aftermath of the Oxford Parliament and in the context of the Fitzharris case, some Tories apparently attempted to suborn potential witnesses. One of the king's secretaries, who was not named, reportedly offered Captain Henry Wilkinson £500 per annum to testify against Shaftesbury, and Justice Edmund Warcup allegedly tried to suborn Thomas Sampson to do the same.[54] Before Everard became a government informer in June 1681, he had, he claimed, been pressed by the earl of Clarendon, Warcup, and his friend David Fitzgerald, a Popish Plot informer, to accuse Shaftesbury and Oates of treason. Fitzgerald supposedly showed Everard articles of treason that could be used against the earl, including charges that he had intended to establish a republic and had commissioned Ferguson to write a history depicting Charles II's government as treasonable. Robert Bolron, who, with Lawrence Mowbray, had been responsible for inventing stories about a Catholic conspiracy in Yorkshire, similarly contended that he had been solicited by Warcup to testify that the Whig peers had urged him to accuse James, Catherine, and others of treason. Mowbray asserted that the Irishman Bryan Haines had told him in April or May that the Popish Plot witnesses no longer enjoyed the support of the king or the citizens of London, and that to make a fortune it was henceforth necessary to accuse the Presbyterians of plotting. That declaration rings true. The Irishmen Haines, John and Dennis Macnamara, Edward Ivy, and Bernard Dennis as well as the Welshman Edward Turberville allegedly urged Mowbray to join them in falsely accusing Monmouth, Shaftesbury, Howard of Escrick, Lord Grey, Lord Lovelace, and others.[55] Such, at any rate, was Mowbray's story in late August.

Two months later the mercurial Mowbray told a different tale, blaming the Whigs for suborning him. Everard and William Lewis, the latter acting as an agent for two of Shaftesbury's associates, John Harrington and Thomas Shepherd, had, he explained, suborned him to testify against John "Narrative" Smith, John Macnamara, Haines, and other state witnesses. Thereafter he and Bolron were accused of framing a charge of subornation of perjury against crown witnesses, at which point Mowbray was bailed by Shaftesbury's agents, including John Atherton and Benjamin Wetton, and given a weekly allowance. Mowbray was then pressed to swear that Warcup had endeavored to suborn him to accuse Shaftesbury of treason. When he made these allegations in late October, Atherton and Wetton tried to bribe him to withdraw his charges and continue working with them, but he refused.[56]

In the meantime, on 11 June 1681, two days after Fitzharris had been accused of writing *The True Englishman*, a warrant was issued for the arrest of Lord Howard of Escrick on suspicion of high treason; the following day he was incarcerated in the Tower. Howard's radical roots and fascination with intrigue ran deep. A Baptist and a Leveller in the 1650s, he had been involved in a Leveller conspiracy to overthrow the Protectorate. Reconciled to Charles at the Restoration, he operated as a government spy in the Netherlands during the Third Dutch War before switching sides to serve William of Orange. More recently he had become a prominent Whig and a supporter of both Oates and exclusion. James, he reportedly snarled, was "a great Rogue & a Papist," while "the King was as great a Papist as the Duke if he durst to shew it & as great a Rogue." While Parliament sat in the autumn of 1680, he and Colonel Mansell had allegedly encouraged Fitzgerald to declare the truth, convinced it would implicate both James and Charles and lead to their execution. According to one informer, Howard denounced the king as the "head" of the Popish Plot and proclaimed that "the Queen did deserve the worst of Deaths."[57]

Now Howard found himself accused by Anne Fitzharris of composing *The True Englishman*, but he protested that he was innocent of "soe horrid, & detestable a Crime" ; she later retracted her charge. Although Howard sued for habeas corpus and proclaimed his innocence in King's Bench, he was remanded to the Tower. On 21 June, as prosecutors presented their evidence to the grand jury, they sensed that some of its members gave no credit to the testimony of Fitzharris and her maids, the crown's principal witnesses. Apart from their statements, the case rested on papers confiscated from Howard; at first they were thought to contain the principal points of *The True Englishman*, but instead they proved to be notes for a speech at the Oxford Parliament against a Catholic successor. Rather than risk a verdict of *ignoramus*, the prosecution withdrew the indictment.[58]

A fresh opportunity to try Howard presented itself the following month when William Carr, the English consul in the Netherlands, accused him of treasonable conduct during the Third Dutch War. The principal charges were these: Howard had received money from the enemy by selling passports obtained from William of Orange; Howard and Pierre du Moulin, a French refugee, had advised the States General to blockade the Thames; Howard had provided the Dutch with information about the English fleet in 1673 and given Carr treasonable papers to be printed; at Leyden, Howard had persuaded Dr. Edward Richardson, architect of the 1663 northern rebellion, to translate seditious documents for the insurgents; du Moulin had written *An Appeal to Parliament* in Howard's company in 1673, possibly with Howard's help. To prove these allegations in an English court required a second witness, but the king was sufficiently interested to authorize Carr's return in late October 1681 to discuss the charges. Despite the discovery of a second witness to some of the alleged acts, a royal servant named Henry Bulstrode, Howard was not prosecuted.[59]

The state was more successful in its efforts to convict Stephen College, a London joiner and an avid Whig. Legally he was charged with and convicted of high treason for having conspired to seize the king when the Parliament met in Oxford, but in practice the trial was a referendum on both the reliability of key Popish Plot witnesses and the Whigs' attempt to portray themselves as victims of a Catholic-inspired conspiracy to implicate them in a Presbyterian plot. The trial, in other words, was a facet of the political struggle between Whigs and Tories over the use and meaning of the Popish Plot. While the issue of exclusion per se did not figure in the trial, College's acquittal would have been a substantial propaganda boost for the Whigs, whose fundamental aim at this point was to block James' accession. College himself was a well-intentioned pawn in the political struggle. Initially he and his cause triumphed, for the Middlesex grand jury, whose members had been selected by the Whig sheriffs Slingsby Bethel and Henry Cornish, returned a verdict of *ignoramus* when he was charged with sedition at the Old Bailey on 8 July. Because most of his reputed crimes had occurred at Oxford, however, he was indicted to stand trial there on 17 August. This time Charles insisted on a jury "of Men rightly principled for the Church & for the King."[60]

College inclined to Presbyterianism because of its commitment to reform, but he attended both Presbyterian and Anglican services and favored the accommodation of Presbyterians in the state church. Above all, he was virulently anti-Catholic, professing that the Church of Rome was "pernicious and destructive to human societies, and all government."[61] By his own admission, he became a zealous investigator of the Popish Plot, an intimate of Oates and Tong (who lived and finally died in his house), and a witness in the trial of William Howard, Viscount Stafford. Such activities brought him to the attention of powerful Whigs. When Parliament convened at Westminster in October 1680, Monmouth and Grey summoned him to a tavern[62] where several other peers and more than a hundred members of the Commons had gathered, presumably to discuss political strategy and the state of the kingdom. They were also concerned about their safety, suspecting that the Catholics might try to

replicate the Gunpowder Plot. College was commissioned to conduct a thorough search of the buildings at Westminster, after which
he was affectionately known in Whig circles as "the Protestant
joiner."[63]

On the eve of the Oxford Parliament, College met Bryan Haines,
who claimed he was wanted on suspicion of treason.[64] College and a
friend, Captain (John?) Brown, a former Cromwellian officer who
would die before the trial, listened to Haines' story about a Catholic
conspiracy to destroy Parliament when it convened at Oxford. The
scheme purportedly entailed an army that would land or be recruited
in the north while a French force secured Ireland; the duke of York
would be the commander-in-chief. Fitzgerald was supposed to assassinate Shaftesbury, for which purpose he had allegedly asked Haines
to enlist the support of his cousin John Macnamara. Haines had obviously concocted the tale in the hope of saving his own life with
Shaftesbury's assistance. Like his friend Tong, College was prepared
to believe any antipapist allegations, and may well have made at
least some of the indiscreet statements of which he was accused
in his trial. The sentiments were certainly common enough in radical
circles: the king was a papist himself because he refused to prosecute
Catholics; he intended to introduce popery and arbitrary government; "he came of the race of buggerers, for his grandfather king
James buggered the old duke of Buckingham." The language reportedly degenerated to the level of character assassination: "Old Rowley
[Charles] was afraid, like his grandfather Jamy, and so ran away like
to beshit himself."[65]

College later admitted that he and others had been worried about
a Catholic assault on members of Parliament as they traveled to or
met in Oxford, and for that reason he had armed himself with a pair
of pistols and a sword, and had journeyed to Oxford as a bodyguard
for the earls of Huntingdon and Clare, Lord Howard of Escrick,
Lord Paget, and two of Howard's friends, Captain Brown and Don
Lewis, clerk of Derbyhouse.[66] Before leaving London, College distributed blue ribbons emblazoned "No Popery, No Slavery." In Oxford he was a guest in the homes of Sir Robert Clayton and Lord
Lovelace, in both of which he allegedly continued his seditious
speech. At Lovelace's, and previously in London, he reputedly sang

seditious ballads, notably *A Ra-ree Show*, printed copies and the original manuscript of which were subsequently seized in his London house; he denied he was the author or even responsible for their presence in his home.[67] Charles, the object of the ballad's satire, was made to state his parliamentary objectives thus:

> But if *they* would come out, with a hey, with a hey,
> Let them first make a Vote, with a ho,
>   To yield up all they have,
>   And *Tower Lords* to save,
> With a hey, Trany nony nony no.

The ballad also alluded to the extraordinary debate over exclusion between Shaftesbury and the marquis of Halifax in November 1680, and to the religious implications of the latter's victory:

> For if he should escape, with a hey, with a hey,
> With *Halifaxes Trap* with a ho,
>   He'd carry good *Dom. Com.*
>   Unto the Pope of *Rome*,
> With a hey, Trany nony nony no.[68]

When College and Haines met again following the dissolution of the Oxford Parliament, the latter claimed to possess information about the murder of Godfrey that incriminated Danby and corroborated Fitzharris' testimony. In return Haines wanted Shaftesbury to procure a pardon for him. College duly carried the message to Shaftesbury, who, though suspecting trickery, tried but failed to obtain a pardon for Haines. Fitzharris' wife subsequently came to College's home with Haines to reinforce the latter's assertion that Edward Fitzharris wanted him pardoned. Shaftesbury, however, would proceed no further without a signed confession from Haines, which the latter refused to provide.[69]

A warrant for College's arrest was issued on 28 June, and his trial at the Old Bailey followed ten days later, as we have seen. Faced with the subsequent trial at Oxford on 17 August, he obtained permission to seek legal counsel from two Whig lawyers, Aaron Smith, who had previously advised Oates, and Robert West, who lodged with John Locke during the trial.[70] Like College himself, three of the chief witnesses against College had testified against Viscount Stafford: Edward Turberville, Stephen Dugdale, and John "Narrative" Smith. Turberville, an ex-Dominican and ex-Benedictine, was currently a soldier of fortune. Although College was married and the father of two children, he had apparently engaged in a homosexual liaison with Turberville in Lord Lovelace's house at the time of the Oxford Parliament. (The fact that Oates too was a homosexual raises the possibility that pressure might have been brought on these men to testify falsely against others.) Dugdale, formerly Lord Aston's land steward, was a gambler, embezzler, and, like Turberville, an ex-Catholic. "Narrative" Smith had been ordained to the priesthood in the Catholic Church and still considered his ordination valid. The fourth principal witness was Bryan Haines.[71]

From the witnesses the prosecution pieced together an account of how College and his confederates had armed themselves before leaving London for Oxford, allegedly to seize and possibly to execute Charles. According to this account, Parliament would then meet in the Guildhall to address the nation's grievances. College, Haines testified, had boasted that his group had 1,500 barrels of gunpowder in London and could raise 100,000 men at an hour's notice. College's closest allies in this scheme were said to include Don Lewis, Captain Brown, and Captain Clinton, reputed heir of the earl of Lincoln. Supposedly this was a republican intrigue, for the conspirators had no intention of elevating Monmouth to the throne. College, claimed Haines, explained that they had made an idol of the duke to cloak their activities: "though we praise his actions, yet we cannot endure him." This seems to have been a calculated attempt to split the Whigs, and Haines may have been coached to make the remarks about Monmouth by someone in court circles with precisely that aim.[72]

College built his defense on the thesis that the accusations against him were the work of Catholics determined to destroy true Protestants by a bogus Presbyterian plot. "The papists' design is to make a protestant plot to turn off their own, and they begin with me." To buttress his argument he relied primarily on the testimony of other Popish Plot witnesses, notably Oates, Bolron, and Mowbray. The latter two, who had been in the service of a West Riding baronet before allegations of the Popish Plot surfaced, were now in the pay of Aaron Smith and Oates.[73] According to Oates, Turberville had originally told him he had nothing to say against College, but he changed his mind after concluding, "the protestant citizens [Whigs] have deserted us." If true, this would explain why several of the Popish Plot witnesses turned against College, and thus indirectly against the Whigs. For his part, Bolron asserted that "Narrative" Smith had promised him a substantial reward if he testified that Shaftesbury and College had been conspiring against the king. Mowbray similarly attested that Smith had pressed him to accuse the earl.[74]

This left the court in the position of having to make a choice between the conflicting accounts of two sets of Popish Plot witnesses, the credibility of all of whom was undermined by the conflicts to some degree. Accepting the testimony of Oates, Bolron, and Mowbray would have lent credence to the theory that the Whigs were the victims of a sham plot and thus implicitly strengthened their self-professed image as defenders of the nation against popery and tyranny. In his summing up, George Jeffreys, counsel for the crown, left no doubt as to the state's position: "If Dugdale, Smith, and Turberville be not to be believed, you trip up the heels of all the evidence and discovery of that [Popish] plot." It took the jury a scant thirty minutes to reach a guilty verdict, and on 31 August, College, admitting only that he had spoken rashly, was hanged, drawn, and quartered.[75] "I willingly submitt, and earnestly pray: mine may be the Last protestant Blood, that murdering Church of Rome may shed in Christendome: and that my Death may be a far Greater Blow to their Bloody Cause, than I Either have or Could have been By my Life."[76] The allusion to the Marian burnings was unmistakable, as College unequivocally cast himself in the role of a Whig martyr.

College's trial offered the Tories not only an opportunity to embarrass their rivals but also a chance to undermine the Whigs' ability to utilize the Popish Plot for their own ends. The state's effective use of three major Popish Plot witnesses to prosecute a symbol of Whig militancy left the Whigs in an awkward position, especially after the rough handling Oates had received during the trial. His credibility was now openly questioned, Tong was dead, and College had failed to persuade the judges and jury that the Whigs were victims of a Catholic endeavor to depict them as traitors. The trial was a clear-cut Tory victory. At root, the prosecution of College proved to be a trial run of the credibility of most of the key witnesses who could be used against Shaftesbury, the government's primary target, and in that respect the guilty verdict provided the incentive to proceed against the earl. Yet both sides paid a price, for the ensuing months were filled with unnerving allegations and rumors of plotting, most of them the product of imaginative minds inspired by the conspiratorial tales that surfaced in College's trial.

Shaftesbury Under Siege

On 1 July, three days after College's arrest, the government issued warrants for the apprehension of Shaftesbury and the confiscation of his papers; the following day he was confined in the Tower as a close prisoner. Shaftesbury's efforts to sue for habeas corpus or emigrate to Carolina in return for his release were unsuccessful, and the case was not heard at the Old Bailey until 24 November.[77] The earl's associate William Hetherington, also incarcerated, was accused of high treason by John and Dennis Macnamara, "Narrative" Smith, Ivy, Dennis, and Sampson. John Wilmore, the foreman of College's first jury, was sent to the Tower on 15 August on suspicion of high treason for allegedly having threatened to pull down the "idol" at Whitehall, namely Charles. Eight days later another Shaftesbury agent, John Harrington, was arrested and interrogated by the Privy Council.[78]

The legal jeopardy in which Shaftesbury found himself in 1681 was the result not only of his campaign for exclusion but also of his relationship with Popish Plot witnesses. After having zealously encouraged and supported them (sometimes financially), he found himself faced in early 1681 with the possibility that some of them would enter Tory employment. Hetherington was of the same mind, according to "Narrative" Smith. Behind this mounting concern was an awareness that the Tories were trying to suborn witnesses. Before he abandoned his Whig friends, Dennis swore that Fitzgerald had striven to persuade him "to forswear all he had sworn before." In August 1681 Oates, Aaron Smith, Bolron, Everard, Robert Blaney, Samuel Starkey, and a Catholic named Hee claimed that an Irishman known as Lamport "would have suborned lately to have sworne Treason against the Earl of Shaftesbury."[79] Shaftesbury's pending trial can only have intensified his awareness of the potential danger of Popish Plot witnesses who might turn against him.

In mid-1681, Shaftesbury and some of his supporters seem to have launched their own campaign to persuade witnesses to perjure themselves. Wilmore had reputedly tried to suborn William Lewis, a convicted forger, and Hubert Bourke to allow themselves to be called as prosecution witnesses in Shaftesbury's trial but once on the stand to testify that they had been bribed to accuse the earl; they were also to make allegations damaging to the credibility of the witnesses against Shaftesbury and College. A Yorkshire attorney named Brownrigg subsequently contended that the earl's secretary, Samuel Wilson, and his steward, Thomas Stringer, had asked him to testify in College's trial against "Narrative" Smith and John Macnamara by accusing them of having been suborned to blame College falsely. Brownrigg refused. Lewis claimed that he had persuaded Anne Fitzharris to retract her testimony (presumably against Howard of Escrick) at the behest of Harrington, a Shaftesbury agent, and that he had subsequently discussed this with Slingsby Bethel and Titus Oates, neither of whom trusted her.[80]

While he was associated with the Whigs, Everard had reportedly endeavored to entice Mowbray to accuse Hyde, Halifax, Jenkins, and other Tory notables of trying to suborn him to testify about an alleged Presbyterian plot. Mowbray was also asked to attest that this group, along with Jeffreys and Justice Warcup, had suborned "Narrative" Smith, Turberville, Macnamara, and others to charge Shaftesbury and his party with treason. According to Mowbray, John Ayloffe, a member of the Green Ribbon Club and an associate of Everard's, similarly pressed him to suborn crown witnesses as well as Justice Warcup. In early October, Wilson met with Lady Howard of Escrick to ponder ways to dissuade witnesses from testifying against her husband. About the same time, Bolron, who had by now defected from Whig benefactors, accused Peter Norrice, a Shaftesbury supporter, of soliciting his assistance in charging Warcup with attempted subornation.[81]

Rampant subornation, whether real or alleged, severely compromised the judicial process, not only rendering all charges of conspiracy unusually suspect but leaving political leaders, particularly those hostile to the court, vulnerable to their enemies' unscrupulous manipulation of the judicial system. While it would be rash to give much credence to any single allegation, the weight of the evidence suggests that both sides endeavored to influence witnesses improperly, often encouraging them with monetary support. So serious was the problem of subornation that the crown ordered the attorney general not to summon Bernard Dennis and John (or Dennis) Macnamara as witnesses against College because the latter was prepared to call Fitzgerald to testify that these men had previously been suborned to accuse the queen of treason.[82]

The problem of subornation was compounded by the fact that some magistrates who took depositions not only failed to submit them to the government and the appropriate sessions but in some cases dispersed copies among dissidents. Those accused of this practice included the Whigs Sir Patience Ward and Sir Robert Clayton as well as the Tory Sir George Jeffreys. Ward, for instance, putatively mishandled the depositions of Anne Fitzharris, Robert Bolron, and John Zeal, who had accused Edward Ivy of being the first to proclaim a Presbyterian plot. Warcup was notably suspicious of Justice Wolstenholme for providing Secretary Jenkins with copies rather than originals of depositions by Anne Fitzharris, Everard, Mowbray, and Bolron. Obtaining the originals was important not only to assess their accuracy but to ascertain if, as Warcup believed, Fitzharris' statement, written in a Scottish dialect, had been composed by Robert Murray, a radical Scot of Gray's Inn. Should this be provable, Warcup thought, Murray could be prosecuted for subornation as well as for scandalizing the king's ministers.[83]

In September and October 1681 the government explored several ways to discredit or eliminate potentially troublesome or unreliable witnesses. Warcup wanted to charge Oates with blasphemy or another crime because he was "supported in Creditt by the dissenters, to baffle the Kings witnesses before all Courts, and to bee a most Creditable witnes in any Parliament, against any Persons whome the Dissenters designe[d] for Ruine." Ayloffe, Harrington, Murray, and Edward Norton, another future Rye House plotter, were summoned before the Privy Council for allegedly having attempted to suborn Bolron, Mowbray, and others.[84] When Shaftesbury's group commissioned agents in Ireland to investigate the backgrounds of assorted Irish witnesses, an unidentified royalist acknowledged that the reputations of the latter were questionable in light of previous charges of perjury, burglary, horsetheft, and other crimes. Afraid that Shaftesbury's people would induce the Irish witnesses to accuse royal ministers of bribery or subornation,[85] he proposed that the Council return the Irishmen to their homeland and keep them in custody on the pretext of needing their testimony to prosecute Sir John Davys, Major John Butler, and others. Those targeted for return were the Macnamara brothers, Sampson, Ivy, Bernard and George Dennis, Bourke, Edmund Murphy, and Eustace Comins. Not until late February 1682, however, did the Council order the removal of Murphy and "three or four others."[86]

While Shaftesbury awaited trial, his friends apparently considered a plan to rescue him. Successful escapes had occurred before, including those of Danvers and Captain John Mason, but none had involved what it would take to liberate Shaftesbury. The key informer in this instance was Sir James Hay (or Hayes), who had initially met the earl in November or December 1680, when the two men discussed Shaftesbury's interest in Carolina. The earl reportedly made no attempt to conceal his contempt for Charles from Hay: "The King will never doe good[;] he is now a papist in his hearte and followes none, but his owen wilfull ways and Evill Counsellers, but I will fynd a way very shortly to make him and them know themselves, and make them doe such things, as will be for the good of the nation."[87] As late as August 1681, Hay was presumably still on good terms with Shaftesbury, whose secretary, Samuel Wilson, reportedly told one William Bird not only that thousands would perish in London if the state tried to execute Shaftesbury, but also that Hay would be "better provided for" if he stayed in England and was loyal to the Good Old Cause than if he migrated to Carolina. About the same time, Hay also seems to have boasted that College "would be secured for they would raise an Army of 25000 Men against the King." After Bird reported the conversation to magistrates, Hay apparently turned informer himself to avoid prosecution. The Whigs "would in a Short time . . . make all true Protestants flourish that were concerned in the Cause, And [as] for such Lordes as had been advisers against them their heads should be torne from their bodyes." Some 40 men of "Eminent Estates & Quality," Wilson had allegedly said, had recently come to London to procure money, secure Charles, and force him to accept "termes" that would save the three kingdoms from ruin.[88]

Obviously Hay would be of no use in the forthcoming Shaftesbury trial, but the discovery of a fresh plot was welcome because it would injure the Whigs' chances in the forthcoming London mayoral election; the Tory, Sir John Moore, was in fact chosen. Hay claimed to have learned from Wilson and Benjamin Clarke, a Fleet Street milliner, about a plan to liberate Shaftesbury, burn London (for which Catherine of Braganza, the Catholic queen, would be blamed), and overthrow "Papisticall and . . . Arbitrary Government." Clarke, he implausibly averred, had a list of all Protestants who would "entrust their Estates with those noble persons upon any designe to further Gods Cause," but Clarke later denied this, and no list was found. Wilson supposedly assured Hay that the conspirators had ample supplies of money to tap, and that financial management was in the hands of Bethel, Treby, Clayton, and others.[89] Their ultimate goal, Hay attested, was to replace Charles with Monmouth, but they were also said to be planning the execution of six Tory peers—Lauderdale, Clarendon, Feversham, Halifax, Hyde, and Arlington—and the lord chief justice, Francis North. According to Hay, Wilson outlined a plan by which Shaftesbury would confess to a fictitious plot by various Whigs to overthrow the government, thereby obtaining his own release while those he accused went to prison. He would then carry through the real plan to seize the king, after which the jailed Whigs would be released. Hay reportedly indicated that Shaftesbury had instructed him to communicate the scheme to Bedford, Clare, Grey, Essex, and Salisbury, and he implicated Captain Aldridge, whose father had served as a colonel under Robert Overton in Scotland; Hay charged that Captain Aldridge had traveled throughout Scotland and England to ascertain the strength of the garrisons. Although Wilson and Clarke were arrested and interrogated, the state had insufficient evidence to prosecute; Wilson was bailed on 28 November. Hay's rendition was probably for the most part fictitious, but it may have evolved from a kernel of truth, for Shaftesbury's secretary and other friends of the earl's had probably discussed ways to prevent his execution. Nathaniel Hartshorne, an aide to the Whig attorney Richard Goodenough, would testify in 1683 that his master, Francis Jenks, and Richard Nelthorpe discussed the assassination of the king on the eve of Shaftesbury's trial, although this and similar accusations were probably only the grumblings of a disgruntled former employee.[90]

Shortly before Shaftesbury's trial the government again tested the judicial waters by indicting John Rouse, who had been in Sir Thomas Player's employ, for high treason on 17 October. The king, Rouse had allegedly boasted, would gain nothing by proroguing and dismissing parliaments, for ultimately the Lords and Commons would compel him to accept James' exclusion. More importantly, Rouse had reportedly argued that the king had forfeited his crown by abusing his subjects. Rouse was also accused of having attempted to suborn Bryan Haines to swear that Charles had been involved in the great fire of London and the murder of Sir Edmund Godfrey. At the Old Bailey the jury distrusted the witnesses, including "Narrative" Smith, and the bill was returned *ignoramus*. The state considered retrying Rouse in Westminster, where the offending words had reputedly been uttered, but dropped the idea.[91]

When Shaftesbury was finally tried on 24 November, his jury was packed with Whig jurors by the Whig sheriffs, Thomas Pilkington and Benjamin Shute; the jurors included Sir Samuel Barnardiston as foreman, Thomas Papillon, former sheriff and prominent Whig M.P., and Michael Godfrey, the late Sir Edmund's brother. The prosecution had one piece of potentially incriminating documentary evidence, the plan for an Association that had been confiscated from Shaftesbury's house. Although the document was not mentioned in the indictment, it was nevertheless introduced in the trial by the prosecution. Asserting that James had countenanced and protected the Popish plotters, and that he had used his influence to employ mercenaries as well as to prorogue and dissolve parliaments unreasonably, the author (or authors) of the plan insisted that Charles was in danger of being murdered by those who wished to make way for his brother. Therefore defenders of Protestantism proposed to unite, under a sacred oath, to preserve their religion, laws, liberties, properties, and monarch. The heart of the oath embraced the principle of exclusion: "I will never consent that the said J. D. of Y. or any other, who is or hath been a papist or any ways adhered to the papists in their wicked designs, be admitted to the succession of the crown of England; but by all lawful means, and by force of arms if need so require, according to my abilities, will oppose him" as well as those who reject "the just and righteous ends of this Association." Forces would have to be raised, but those who took the oath pledged that these troops would obey the orders of the "present" (Oxford) Parliament while it sat, and thereafter the majority of the members of both houses who subscribed to the Association, and the officers they appointed. In short, the Association was to be based on both its Elizabethan predecessor and the experiences of 1642, and the draft resembled a proposal that had been broached in the House of Commons on 15 December 1680. As damaging as the draft was, the prosecution could not identify the handwriting in it or explain how the manuscript had gotten into Shaftesbury's closet.[92]

Apart from the draft Association, the prosecution had eight witnesses to support its contention that Shaftesbury had conspired to depose and execute Charles and to alter the government. Three of them had previously testified against College: "Narrative" Smith, Bryan Haines, and Edward Turberville, although the latter had little to say against Shaftesbury. Edward Ivy, Haines' associate, had provided evidence against College before the latter's trial but had not been called by the prosecution. The others were an equally motley lot: the Macnamara brothers, Bernard Dennis, a former Catholic priest recently converted to Protestantism by Gilbert Burnet and Robert Ferguson, and John Booth, who had likewise been ordained as a priest. Shaftesbury was already widely known to have endorsed the testimony of such men in prosecuting the Popish Plot, and his plight was therefore more serious than is sometimes thought. The thrust of their testimony was that the earl had not only castigated the king as a papist but planned to resist him with force if he dealt with Parliament violently, even to the point of beheading him. According to Haines, Shaftesbury intended to crown himself or the duke of Buckingham, or establish a commonwealth. John Macnamara recalled that the earl had insisted that Charles "ought to be deposed as well as king Richard the second, and that the duchess of Mazarine was one of his cabinet council, and that he did nothing but by her advice." [93]

Predisposed toward Shaftesbury, the principal jurors relentlessly questioned the credibility of the witnesses and tried to shake their stories by probing details and exposing inconsistencies. Although they failed in this endeavor, the jury nevertheless returned a verdict of *ignoramus*. [94] The trustworthiness of the witnesses was on the whole highly dubious, but some aspects of their testimony are plausible. First, it is likely that Shaftesbury and others were concerned for their safety when they went to Oxford, and that the earl made preparations for an armed guard. The key figure in the guard was Captain Henry Wilkinson, who had allegedly recruited Booth, but Wilkinson, in the King's Bench prison for debt, refused to testify. Secondly, Shaftesbury and his agents had probably attempted to suborn witnesses, as was testified. Dennis, for instance, claimed that the earl had praised his testimony concerning the Popish Plot but had asked him to speak "more home and positive" against the queen and the duke of York, taking care to corroborate what others were saying. Finally, it is difficult to see what Haines hoped to gain by lying when he confessed having visited Shaftesbury to propose forcing Charles' hand by instigating a rebellion in Ireland; the earl, he said, rejected the idea. Yet the evidence suggests that Shaftesbury was open to the idea of taking some kind of action in 1681 to prevent James' succession, though not an Irish uprising. [95]

The extent to which the Whig cause had achieved popular support was immediately apparent in the streets of London when the *ignoramus* verdict was announced. Bonfires and ringing churchbells marked Shaftesbury's triumph. In the words of a Tory bard:

> The *Rabble* to shew their *Loyalty*; . . .
> Did in full shouts with the *Jury* agree; . . .
> They Bonfires made, with great Applause,
> And all to maintain the *Good Old Cause*. [96]

The demonstrators, some bearing swords, cried, "No Popish Successorr, No York, A Monmouth, a Buckingham," and "God blesse the Earle of Shaftsbury." They came, they said, "to give the Irish Evidence a shoute & alsoe a faggott stick." The witnesses against the earl had to be escorted to the Savoy palace by a strong guard to protect them from the ebullient mobs. With the court's sanction, the mayor, Sir John Moore, issued a proclamation prohibiting unauthorized bonfires, and he also doubled the watch and appointed six militia companies to assist the constables in maintaining order. "Never any thing was so strange," grumbled the duke of York, "as the behavior and doings of the grand-jury, nor so insolent and seditious as what was done after it in the Citty by the rabble."[97]

But the court was not without supporters, who frowned on the verdict in Shaftesbury's trial. The Cheshire grand jury condemned not only his reputed Association but all those who presumed "to ruine the Monarchy, & enslave their Country." Further, they warned that such endeavors could plunge the nation into another civil war in the name of "Religion & the Common good."[98] The specter of the 1640s was very much in evidence four decades later.

A Seditious Press?

The depth of the popular support for Shaftesbury attested to the effectiveness of the radical press, which had popularized the cause of exclusion and kept readers informed of political and legal developments. Government efforts to curb the press were feeble and largely ineffective. While the Oxford Parliament met, Charles ordered the lord mayor of London to find and punish the authors and distributors of seditious papers, the intent of which was "to putt all into a Combustion, that they who [had] nothing of their own to loose [might] mend themselves in a publick Confusion by Rapine upon others." The London *Gazette*, which reflected the government's position, chimed in by condemning the allegedly false and malicious accounts in the pamphlets. The *Gazette* had no use for Francis Smith, whose newssheet, *Democritus Ridens*, fanned the fires of exclusion, in part by likening James to the persecuting Roman emperors, Decius and Titus. Smith pointedly asked his readers "whether the Church of *England* [would] not seem as Monstrous and Strange, to have a Papistical Head joyned to a Protestant Body, as it would be to see the Body of a Sheep have the Head of a

Woolf?"[99] The real danger, Smith cautioned, was the output of the *"Popish* Presses,"* by which he particularly meant the publications of his archrival, Nathaniel Thompson.[100] For publishing a newssheet entitled *Protestant Intelligence* beginning in February 1681, Smith was committed to Newgate prison on a charge of high treason on 15 April.[101]

In addition to radical newssheets, the government was also disturbed by the publication of purportedly seditious pamphlets and broadsides.[102] In April, officials committed Lawrence Morris to the Ely jail for dispersing such material, especially 1,400 copies of *Vox Populi, Vox Dei: or, Englands General Lamentation for the Dissolution of the Parliament*, printed by Thomas Braddyll.[103] Accepting the Popish Plot as real, the anonymous author depicted the people crying out "with one Voice, *No Popish Successor*, no *Idolater*, no Queen *Mary* in Breeches, no Tyrant over the Conscience, no new persecutor of *Protestants* in our Land." Dismayed by the dissolution of Parliament, he urged the people to petition the king and set forth their "Complaints and Lamentations." The tract contained no hint of disrespect for Charles, let alone any talk of revolution. Nevertheless, an anonymous Tory writer retorted that the tract was nothing but a compendium of the views of the Long Parliament—"the *Epitome* of *Bradshaw*, and *Cooke*"—as well as an affront to both king and Parliament. Although the anonymous Whig author had overstated his case, his encouragement of further petitioning helped sustain popular unrest. The principal theme of the Whig-oriented petitions to members of the Oxford Parliament, published collectively as *Vox Patriae* (1681), was "No Popish Successor, no *French* Slavery." In May an exasperated government prosecuted the printer and publisher of an address from Norwich on the grounds that it was a seditious libel.[104]

With its attention devoted primarily to the Oxford Parliament (21–28 March) and the Whig trials in 1681, the government was less concerned with substantive Whig tracts, such as Elkanah Settle's *The Character of a Popish Successor* (1681) and John Phillips' sequel, *The Character of a Popish Successor . . . Part the Second* (1681), than with newssheets and broadsides that reached a broader segment of the population and could therefore more readily influence public opinion.[105] The *Impartial Protestant Mercury* repeatedly attacked the credibility of Nathaniel Thompson, the purveyor of hard-core Tory propaganda, accusing him of popery and lying. The "whole work" of Thompson and L'Estrange was said to promote "the Interest of the Papists; [to] Divide, and Exasperate His Majesties Subjects, and to render the *Protestant Religion* contemptible."[106] In late September the government issued warrants for seven authors of newsletters, four of whom were employed by John Cotton; he had already been arrested in June. All four admitted to the Privy Council that the source of their information was John Claypoole, who was thereupon bound over. Three weeks later the Council examined three more men accused of publishing seditious newssheets and pamphlets: Richard Janeway, Richard Baldwin, and James Vade.[107]

The Council was particularly interested in Janeway, whom it suspected of publishing the anonymous *No Protestant-Plot*. As L'Estrange surmised, it was from the same hand as *A Just and Modest Vindication of the Proceedings of the Two Last Parliaments* (1681), which had also appeared anonymously. Both were by Ferguson. His *Vindication* not only challenged the king's right to dissolve Parliament before it had dealt with all pending petitions and bills, but blamed Charles' opposition to the exclusion bill on a "few ill men" who were "Creatures" of James or French pensioners. James himself was excoriated for "his vehemence in exalting the Prerogative . . . beyond its due bounds, and the principles of his Religion which carr[ied] him to all imaginable excesses of cruelty."[108]

By this time such themes were fairly common, but the Council was attracted to *No Protestant-Plot* because it argued Shaftesbury's innocence even before his trial got under way. Ferguson accused Warcup and the ubiquitous Fitzgerald of managing the plot against the earl, warning, "While we are hearkning after the noise and bug of a *Presbyterian* Plot, we be not overwhelmed and destroyed by a *Popish* one." Plausibly, Ferguson found no reason for Shaftesbury to have confided in such insignificant men as Fitzgerald, "Narrative" Smith, and Dennis. He also argued that the verdict in College's case was uncompelling because the judges denied College access to his papers and recourse to a solicitor during the trial. Fitzharris, Ferguson admitted, had written the libel for which he was executed, but only because Catholics had persuaded him to do so. Now, Ferguson insisted, the Catholics were ultimately responsible for the charges against Shaftesbury and were part of an international conspiracy: "We are the bolder to charge the *Roman Catholicks* for being the Contrivers and Forgers of this *Presbyterian* Plot, not only because it is of the same stamp and complexion that Mrs *Celliers* was, and designed to involve the same persons in the guilt of it, which hers did; but because we had the news of it from *Rome* and *Paris*, ere ever the tidings of it could fly thither from hence."[109]

Francis Smith likewise used the press to build support for Shaftesbury before his trial. After Smith's appointment as printer of the House of Commons (whose speaker, William Williams, was his counsel) on 30 October 1680, he published *The Speech of a Noble Peer*,[110] probably written by Shaftesbury though never delivered in the Lords. Because it questioned the king's trustworthiness, the Lords had it burned in January 1681. Undaunted, Smith reissued it on 19 September, an act for which he was convicted at the Guildhall on 12 November. What if any influence the radical press had on Shaftesbury's jurors is, of course, impossible to assess, although it would not be unreasonable to assume they were aware of the campaign in his behalf. Janeway's paper, the *Impartial Protestant Mercury*, was certainly incensed at the severity with which Shaftesbury was prosecuted as well as the efforts of "the *High-Flyers*" to spread the fiction of a Protestant plot.[111]

The abortive attempts to convict Howard of Escrick and Shaftesbury aggravated the political struggle, especially in the tense atmosphere, inimical to debate and compromise, that followed the precipitate dissolution of the Oxford Parliament. An early instance of this was the 110-page Postscript Thomas Hunt appended to the 1682 edition of his *Argument for the Bishops Right in Judging in Capital Causes in Parliament* (written prior to October 1679). Censured by L'Estrange as "one of the most Scandalous Libells against the Royall Family: the Succession, the Clergy, and the Kings Interest, and Party that has yet come out,"[112] the Postscript denounced the concept of *jure divino* government and averred that the succession was a purely civil matter to be determined by the people's will. Although normally hereditary, the succession, Hunt contended, could be altered "by the unlimited Power of the Legislative Authority" to save the nation. Purveyors of fictitious plots were castigated for irresponsibly raising the specter of 1641 and for making "Fanaticisme . . . more intolerable than Popery." Hunt blamed the bitter divisions that had plagued the country in the aftermath of the Popish Plot on the "new principles" of *jure divino* monarchy. He even accused Catholics of writing libels that they passed off as the work of Protestant "Fanaticks," thereby discrediting the latter. Most provocatively, he adjured that no one betray England and Protestantism "by pretending the example of the patience, and sufferance of the Primitive Christians for [English] rule." Here indeed was a clarion call to resist tyranny and popery.[113]

Other radical works quickly followed, although not all were freshly written. A revised edition of John Sadler's 1649 book, *Rights of the Kingdom*, appeared in 1682, arguing for an elective monarchy, explaining the conditions under which legal fealty could be dissolved, and maintaining that Parliament could not be dismissed until all petitions had been settled. The relevance to circumstances in 1681–82 was unmistakable, given the Whig campaign to substitute Monmouth for the duke of York as Charles' heir. L'Estrange understandably protested that Sadler's book was treasonable.[114] Other works from the revolutionary era found their way back into print, notably Nathaniel Bacon's *An Historical Discourse* (1647) and *The Continuation of an Historical Discourse* (1651), which refuted the contention that royal authority derived from the Norman conquest. Bacon's work was, Corinne Weston and Janelle Greenberg have noted, "a thinly disguised enunciation of the community-centered view of government that made Anglo-Saxon England the major source of Stuart political institutions." The bookseller John Starkey commissioned the printing of 750 copies of a combined edition in August 1681. The anonymous author of a government memorandum probably composed in June 1682 deemed the *Discourse*'s purpose antimonarchical and noted "that it was Dedicated to the Service of a Rebellion." Indeed, Bacon had candidly opined in his sequel: "As I found this Nation a Common-Wealth, so I leave it, and so may it be for ever; and so will it be, if we may attain the happinesse of our Fore-Fathers the ancient Saxons." In March 1683, on the eve of the disclosure of the Rye House Plot, copies of Henry Parker's *A Political Catechism* (1643) were found in a London tavern frequented by Oates. Parker had advocated that the king is subject to the law, that royal power originates in the people, and that Parliament is the supreme judge of all disputes between the sovereign and his subjects.[115]

Legal issues were also at the root of two controversial tracts by Edward Whitaker, whose *Ignoramus Justices* (1681) challenged the legality of an order by the Middlesex grand jury in January 1681 to suppress conventicles. Because the penal legislation dealing with recusancy, he argued, applied only to Catholics, he warned constables not to enforce either the acts or the arbitrary and illegal warrants issued by the grand jury. Although Whitaker was incarcerated in the Tower for high treason in July 1681, he refused to keep silent. In *The Second Part of the Ignoramus Justices* he turned to the exclusion issue, contending that kingship is an office and trust reposed in the monarch by the law of the land. The English government is *"Jure Divino, and the Ordinance of God, but the Modes and Forms were ever yet left to Man, which in all Countries whatsoever, have been chalked out by the People themselves."* He went on to reject the notion that James' hereditary right was more important than the welfare of the country. In October 1682 the court of King's Bench found Whitaker, whom the king deemed "a dangerous fellow," guilty of seditious speech at Bath for having denied that Charles I had been murdered and that the civil war had been a rebellion.[116]

Ferguson continued the Whig attack in *The Second Part of No Protestant Plot* (1682), charging the fabricators of the alleged Presbyterian conspiracy with ulterior motives, namely of seeking to supplement crown revenues with forfeited estates, justify arbitrary power, discredit the advocates of exclusion, and conceal the Popish Plot. Ferguson helped lay the philosophical foundation for active resistance as well: To debar the innocent from legal protection, he insisted, is

in effect, to cancel all bonds, by which Subjects are tyed to their Prince; & destroy all *Pleas* & Arguments, which may influence their Consciences to obedience and subjection. And whensoever Laws cease to be a security unto men, they will be sorely tempted to apprehend themselves cast into a state of War, and justified in having recourse to the best means they can for their shelter and defence.

Ferguson thus embraced the traditional radical conviction that arbitrary government should be forcibly overthrown. This position was a significant departure from pamphlets on exclusion that had argued the Whig case in terms of Parliament's sole right to settle the succession.[117]

Ferguson used *The Third Part of No Protestant Plot* (1682) to comment directly on the charges against the earls of Shaftesbury and Argyll. John Macnamara's testimony against the former, he alleged, had in fact been provided by none other than Secretary Jenkins. In broader terms, Ferguson complained that Catholics exercised so much influence over those who governed England that papist conspirators were not tried whereas Protestants were persecuted. He correctly contended that parliaments had been called, prorogued, and dissolved after Charles had consulted with Louis XIV.

The case for active resistance to James' succession was reinforced by Samuel Johnson, chaplain to William Lord Russell. In *Julian the Apostate*, published by Langley Curtis in 1682, Johnson defended the right to keep James from the throne. Passive obedience in this situation, he declared, contravened Magna Carta. In his judgment, the oaths of allegiance and supremacy had been designed to uphold Protestantism and would be violated if used to facilitate the introduction of popery. Resistance under these circumstances was therefore legal. Like Thomas Hunt, he rejected the example of the primitive church's suffering as proof that Christians in the 1680s should not take up arms to defend their faith; instead he implored them to act like the Christians in Julian's reign, who "were in full and quiet possession of their Religion" and entitled to protect it. The royal prerogative, which was "no . . . boundless Pit of Arbitrary Power and Self-will, but . . . limited, stated, and certain," did not convey the authority to reimpose popery.[118]

In addition to bringing out a new impression of *Julian the Apostate*, which had sold out within months of its publication, Jane Curtis (Langley's wife) published *The Perplex'd Prince* in September 1682. Dedicated to Lord Russell by the author, T.S., this semifictional but pointedly political account of Charles II commenced with the degeneration of his father's Solomonic rule into a period of war and poverty, followed by his deposition and the rule of a tyrant (Oliver Cromwell). While exiled in France, the book's hero, Prince Charles, privately married Lucilious (Lucy Walters), who bore him a son,

Heclacious (Monmouth). After Charles was restored to the throne, the Catholics, inspired by the Prince of Purdino (James), concocted the Popish Plot to eliminate him. Purdino was also the villain responsible for the attack on Shaftesbury. The Catholics were blamed as well for "the Calvenian [Presbyterian] Plot," which they had invented to divert attention from their own machinations. *The Perplex'd Prince* was not a revolutionary work; its account of the interregnum was largely negative, and it contained no hint of active resistance. On the contrary, T.S. contented himself with admonishing Charles to ponder the meaning of his tale.[119]

As seditious as the radical arguments were, harassed authorities continued to devote most of their attention to suppressing newssheets and broadsides, undoubtedly because of their popular appeal and brutal candor. Much of the latter was directed at L'Estrange, an "impudent Popish Writer," and Thompson, "the *Jesuites Conduit-Pipe*" and "a most *Malitious Lyer and Slaunderer*." In clever allusions to the *quo warranto* process for remodeling corporations, which the government was effectively using to diminish Whig influence in the parliamentary boroughs, several radicals questioned Charles' right to rule: "Each Quo Warranto doth to Question bring, / What WARRANT Cities had, that made him King?" Under the popular title *Vox Populi, Vox Dei*, another broadside asked: "We the People of England (finding our Parliaments dissolved) do, in the name of God, demand of Thee Charles Stewart, Quo Warranto art thou King of England?"[120] The same taunt appeared in *Macs Tryumph in Imitation of the King of Poland's Last Will & Testament*, reputedly by Elkanah Settle: "With Quo Warrantoes Romes new fireballs / More Malicious then the flames itt felt before." Mac—the duke of York—might "Survive to mount a Throne," but only because of "That all forgotten League with Rome and Hell / The Letters for which Martyr'd Coleman fell." Settle gave his verse to James Bowes of London, but with instructions to show it only to such Whigs as Essex, Anglesey, Macclesfield, Stamford, Grey, and Brandon.[121]

To stem the flow of such publications, the government stepped up its prosecutions in 1682, beginning with the Council's interrogation of Langley Curtis and Richard Janeway in April for having allegedly printed false and seditious news; Janeway had been indicted the pre-

vious February for printing unlicensed pamphlets.[122] Janeway confessed that the writers for his *Impartial Protestant Mercury* were
Henry Care and Thomas Vile, both of whom might have inserted
"some indecent Expressions & reflecting passages" after being provoked by Thompson. Janeway was tried and acquitted in May, as was
Samuel Harris, who had reportedly distributed *Treason in Graine*,
the tract—originally entitled *The True Englishman*—for which Fitzharris had been executed. Harris was again prosecuted in Michaelmas term, as were other radical authors, publishers, and booksellers,
including Care, Baldwin, Jane Curtis, and the astrologer John Partridge.[123] In December a grand jury in London indicted not only
Care and Curtis but also Francis Smith, his sister Eleanor and their
father, Vile, Starkey, and others, all for writing, printing, or publishing materials that libeled the king and government.[124] Included in
this group was Shaftesbury's steward, Thomas Stringer, who had
been apprehended as he submitted to a printer two manuscripts
defending the Association. The author, Stringer confessed, was the
elusive Ferguson.[125]

Ferguson was also accused of having written *The Second Part of the
Growth of Popery*, a copy of which was presented to Monmouth by
Francis Smith in November. It was printed for Smith by Braddyll's
wife. Copies were apparently available only to those with tickets,
some of which were given to Monmouth for distribution. L'Estrange had heard of the work, probably before its publication, as
early as January 1682. Justice Warcup denounced it as a treasonable
pamphlet, not least because it castigated Charles and his ministers as
conspirators. Ferguson denied writing both this work and *A Vindication of the Association*.[126]

The state's efforts to prosecute radical authors, printers, and publishers failed to deter them. In January 1683 Baldwin published
Hunt's *Defence of the Charter, and Municipal Rights of the City of London*, a slashing attack on remodeling at the expense of dissenters. "By
this new Form of Corporations, it will be in the Power of a *Popish*
Successor, to put the Government of all corporated Towns in *England* into the hands of *Papists*," and thus to extirpate the Reformed
religion. It was madness, Hunt insisted, for one party of Protestants to dominate another in such fashion that Catholics would be

brought into the corporations, and thus fill the next Parliament with "Papists, and Red-coats." Preachers should not be heeded, he admonished, if they exhorted obedience more extreme than the laws commanded—an indirect way of suggesting disobedience to tyrannical demands. Magistrates seized the book on 15 January.[127]

The mission of the radical press in the early 1680s was thus twofold. On the one hand it provided an opportunity for Whig theorists to make their case before a rather broad audience, including those who would sit in the next Parliament, whenever it might be called. On the other hand, the newssheets and broadsides helped maintain support for exclusion at the popular level by relentlessly attacking James, his supporters, and popery. Testimony to the importance of the radical press was given by Shaftesbury's secretary, Samuel Wilson, in September 1681 when he told Sir James Hay, "Care & Janeway by their Papers continue the Peoples hopes of a Reformation, which does more kindnesse then a 1000 Men in Armes."[128]

Popular Discontent

Ample evidence indicates that radical views were quite widely embraced. The long-standing tendency to castigate the king and his court for their lasciviousness continued, but interest in the way Charles governed and the perceived threat posed by a Catholic succession was increasingly evident. Suspicions abounded that Charles as well as James was Catholic, as did fears that the king intended to rule arbitrarily.[129] He "Governes as well by a Trust from us, as by Inheritance," protested one man, while a resident of Bath argued, "It is not fitt for the Prerogative . . . [that] so great power should bee in the Crown" at the people's expense. Thus the views of Whig political theorists seem to have made headway among common folk. Some accused Charles of emulating Louis XIV; however, Sir James Johnson of Yarmouth reportedly observed, "The King off france could whore well & governe well, our King could whore well, but not governe." In a similar vein, a newsletter circulating in Northamptonshire complained that the duchess of Portsmouth "with a Cabinet Caball of a few such others had the management and conduct of all the greatest affaires of the Nation."[130]

Animosity toward Charles and especially James was increasingly manifest. The duke of York was derided as a traitor, a pimp, the son of a whore, and a bastard, while the king was ridiculed as "the Greatest Mongrell in England," a rogue, a petty prince, and, like his brother, a prostitute's son.[131] Early in 1682 someone "offered . . . an Indignity" to the portrait of James in London Guildhall. Others drank curses to the royal brothers, an act for which three young Chichester men were charged with high treason in April 1683.[132] Monmouth was generally popular in these circles,[133] but sentiment was growing for another commonwealth. One of John Rouse's jurors was overheard saying that "Popery could not be rooted out under any other Government in this Nation, then a Common-Wealth." For Colonel Dering, not even a mixed monarchy was acceptable, for "a Monarchy which was limited, was like a Turd in a Chamber pot."[134]

Given such views, it is hardly surprising to find evidence of people willing to take up arms to prevent James' succession, precisely as some Whig theorists had advocated. A Lambeth woodmonger, disillusioned with Charles, allegedly advocated that the people organize to "cutt him and all the rogues at Whitehall off." The Cirencester attorney Miles Sandys used an Elizabethan statute (1 Elizabeth I, c. 1) to justify rebellion against James on the grounds of his Catholicism, while a Captain Baker reportedly threatened, "[I will] pistoll the Duke of Yorke if ever I meete him, I will send a brace of bulletts into the head of him, because he is a Villaine and a Traitor against his Brother."[135] In December 1682 an anonymous paper found in the church of St. Giles, Cripplegate, urged nonconformists, "[Use the] Swoord of Justice to Cut of[f] and Confound all shuch Enemies that beare rule," including Charles, who promotes "the Intrest of his father the pope and brother a[n] Enemie to god." On the eve of the disclosure of the Rye House Plot, talk of an uprising or assassination attempt spread, possibly encouraging the belief of some conspirators that a popular insurrection was feasible. "Scepters & Crownes," opined the mayor of Rye, "must tumble downe."[136]

Popular hostility manifested itself as well in public demonstrations, such as those that occurred in connection with hotly contested shrieval elections in London in 1680 and 1682 and in the mayoral election at Rye in 1682.[137] At Walsall, Staffordshire, bonfires blazed and church bells pealed in 1681 at the news that Parliament was considering an exclusion bill. Another demonstration took place in November 1682, when Londoners commemorated the Gunpowder Plot. Hundreds marched through the streets shouting, "Noe Yorke, noe Yorke, a Monmouth, a Monmouth," and "A Monmouth, a Monmouth, Stand to it, we'll make him king." Before the trained bands could restore order, the demonstrators broke windows in the homes of Tories, lit fires, and assaulted their enemies.[138] The following April a town-gown riot erupted in Oxford when royalist students challenged townsfolk as they drank Monmouth's health and offered "Confusion to York." After one student was clubbed, a crowd of some 200 stoned and chased a proctor who had taken a prisoner, and then tried to storm Oxford Castle.[139] The following month, more than a thousand people rioted at Taunton, a hotbed of discontent, as they celebrated their civil-war victory over royalist forces. Magistrates were stoned and denounced as "a packe of Rogues."[140] Although celebrations of major events, such as the Gunpowder Plot, had often led to violence in the past, the riots of 1682–83 were unusual because they occurred within a relatively brief span of time and reflected the titanic political struggle then under way.

Contemporaries—including the duke of York[141]—who saw parallels between the early 1680s and the early 1640s were not mistaken. Fear of popery was as pronounced in the later period as in the earlier, thanks to the unscrupulous encouragement of self-serving informers. Whereas the government's control of the press did not collapse as completely in the later period as in the early 1640s, radicals had relatively little difficulty getting their views into print. Competing newssheets sharpened the public's interest in the major issues, particularly the question of succession and the broader problems of arbitrary government and the security of Protestantism. This time, however, revenue was not an issue, nor in any direct way were economic considerations, other than the general threat of arbitrary rule to security of property. Much of this crisis was the product of fear: the broad concern that as king, James might reintroduce the kind of persecution that had made Mary's reign notorious, and worry too that the Stuarts would rule in imitation of Louis XIV, especially since Charles seemed quite able to govern without parliamentary grants. In a narrower sense another kind of fear was perhaps more significant, namely the growing awareness among Whig leaders that the court had begun to turn against them the very techniques and informers they had nurtured in fanning the Popish Plot. Subornation became a two-edged sword. With the crown itself as the prize, the struggle was played out with an intensity not seen since the 1640s. In this context militant Whigs and old-line radicals began exploring more daring options to prevent James' succession, and thus was born, in the English context, the skein of conspiracies traditionally known as the Rye House Plot.

"Fight the Lord's Battles"

TWO

The Turbulent Northern Kingdom

While English dissidents focused their attention on the exclusion crisis, the alleged Popish threat, and the ensuing web of treasonable charges and countercharges, militant Scottish Covenanters, undeterred by the failure of the Galloway rebellion in 1666, continued to wage a bitter struggle for their religious principles, including the right to worship in assemblies which were deemed illegal by the state. The inability of the Stuart regime to resolve the embittered religious disputes doomed the northern kingdom to further plotting and insurrection.

The Conventicle Struggle

Wedded to the principle of religious uniformity, mitigated only by the policy of limited indulgence of moderate Presbyterians who attended their local presbyteries and synods and restricted their services to parishioners, the government found itself repeatedly frustrated in its efforts to quash conventicles. That frustration was largely responsible for the disastrous decision in November 1677 to order a force of Highlanders into the western shires to crush the "growing disorders and insolencies." Additional forces were readied at Newcastle and Belfast, martial law was imposed, and in January and February the Highland Host did its repressive work, exacerbating the tensions by disorderly actions of its own.[1]

The authorities fined dissidents, quartered alien troops in their homes, and forced heritors to subscribe to bonds that made them responsible for the behavior of their tenants. Officials confiscated weapons, prohibited residents of the western shires from keeping any but the poorest horses, stationed garrisons in strategic locations, and destroyed illegal meetinghouses.[2] Because the nobility and gentry in the west were suspected of encouraging militant Covenanters, they were confined to their homes. Arrested conventiclers were increasingly forced to subscribe to bonds promising good behavior; for some, refusal meant banishment to Jamaica or Virginia. The intent was clearly to intimidate dissidents, and the impact of the violent tactics extended beyond the Scottish borders. The Highlanders "destroy all," marveled a Cumberland observer; their actions "hath putt a terror" into nonconformists in Ireland, Sir George Rawdon reported.[3]

Although repression undoubtedly cowed the timid and reinforced the split within the Presbyterian ranks that stemmed largely from the indulgence policy, it served only to inflame militants. Before the Highlanders thrust themselves into the western counties, John Welsh reportedly warned a huge throng of his followers that they faced the gallows and should therefore "fight the Lord's battles with their swords in their hands." Once the Host had done its work, he excommunicated the heritors who had subscribed the bond, and defied the government by continuing to preach to massive conventicles, including ones at Chirnside in the southeast, Colmonell in Ayrshire, and Dumfries in the west.[4] The evidence suggests that this latest campaign of repression had little or no effect on the frequency with which conventicles were held. Late in the spring the king himself admitted that the number of field conventicles had actually increased.[5]

The government's tougher stance prompted greater militancy on the part of the conventiclers, who were quick to rearm, probably with supplies from the Netherlands. According to Robert Smith, a Covenanter from Dunscore, Dumfries, much of the money collected at conventicles beginning in late 1677 was used to purchase weapons and ammunition. Additional funds may have come from England; after he was arrested in Ireland in late 1677, the preacher (John?) Douglas confessed that London friends of the Scottish Covenanters had already sent them £2,000 and had promised more.[6]

Evidence of rearmament is indisputable. Horsemen with weapons at a Fife assembly in May 1678 prevented the militia from disbanding it, and armed conventiclers who had gathered to hear John Blackader forced militiamen in the same county to flee. A party of soldiers dispatched by the governor of the Bass prison was disarmed by East Lothian conventiclers, who killed one of the troopers.[7] Between 7,000 and 10,000 people, some of them bearing weapons, gathered near Maybole, Ayrshire, in August to hear Welsh and at least eleven other ministers over a three-day period. According to one report, they "preached up the Solemn League and covenant [which in 1643 had pledged to maintain the Reformed faith in the three realms], and the Lawfullnes, conveniency and necessity of defensive armes, befor and after their sermons modeleing themselves, drilling, and exerciseing themselves in faits of armes." After the meeting Welsh brazenly marched into Ayre accompanied by such "considerable guards" that the magistrates feared to arrest him; one of them may have been an Englishman, Colonel (James?) Fox, who reportedly traveled with Welsh about this time. Another of the prominent militants, Donald Cargill, preached to large throngs in the west throughout the summer. The forces available to the Privy Council were so minimal that it opted not to employ them against conventiclers for fear the troops would receive "an affront." The government was unable to maintain its authority throughout much of Scotland without recourse to a good-sized army, although Charles was fortunate that most of the illegal worshipers were defiant only with respect to their right to worship, not royal authority per se.[8]

The pattern of illegal meetings and periodic violence extended throughout the fall and into the winter of 1678–79, when activity slowed because of harsh weather. When a government party of 16 attempted to disband a conventicle of 1,500 at Whitekirk, East Lothian, in September, another soldier was killed. Although the judges subsequently ruled that those who attended a conventicle in arms or incited people to violence could be tried for murder, the jury in this case refused to return a guilty verdict; nevertheless one of the accused, James Learmont, was eventually executed for attending a field conventicle. The same month, 14,000 Presbyterians met for three days on Skeoch Hill, near Irongray, Kirkcudbright, some of them having come mounted and armed from as far away as Lanarkshire and Nithsdale. Covenanting ministers preached openly in Dumfries, fueling fears of a rebellion by the "fanatics," and one observer noted that the militants had been especially successful recruiting young itinerant clergy.[9]

As concern mounted that "the strength of the Kingdom" favored the Presbyterians, the government again dispatched troops to restore order, but to little effect. Conventiclers, especially in Fife, were initially ignored, complained the archbishop of St. Andrews, and two conformist ministers who had provided information about them faced threats of death. The state proclaimed Welsh, Samuel Arnot, and Gabriel Semple traitors, but all three eluded capture. Not surprisingly, Covenanter sermons in this atmosphere were sometimes decidedly militant. "There is a sword coming," thundered Cargill. In the hills near Dumfries, an unnamed Covenanter lashed out "against the King and his Government," declaring, "All those thatt hath taken the Bond and payes the Supply Laid upon the Subjects . . . are Damned In Hell."[10]

The illegal assemblies were additionally troublesome because they served as distribution points for illegal literature, much of which was imported from the Netherlands and England. From Rotterdam, John Hay shipped copies of *Naphtali, or the Wrestlings of the Church of Scotland for the Kingdom of Christ* (1667), in which the two authors—lawyer James Stewart of Goodtrees (son of Sir James Stewart, former provost of Edinburgh) and the minister James Stirling of Paisley—not only justified the Galloway rebellion but provided the Covenanters with a record of their own martyrs; this work also circulated widely in Ulster.[11] Hay also supplied copies of sermons by conventicle preachers such as Welsh and John Walwood as well as the acts of the General Assembly.[12] Those who attended field conventicles could also obtain such works from England as *A Plea for Peace* and William Jenkins' *Celeusma, seu clamor* (1679).

Other books of interest to conventiclers were published in Scotland; among them were John Brown's *An Apologeticall Relation, of the Particular Sufferings of the Faithfull Ministers & Professours of the Church of Scotland, Since August, 1660* (1665), which upheld the legitimacy of resistance to persecutors; the same author's *The History of the Indulgence* (1678); and Robert MacWard's *The Poor Man's Cup of*

Cold Water, Ministered to the Saints and Sufferers for Christ (1678),
which especially commended victims of persecution in southwestern
Scotland. MacWard denounced Scottish rulers for rejecting the Covenant and persecuting the saints—actions tantamount to insurrection
against God. It is necessary, he thundered, "for *all who will live Godly
in Christ Jesus to suffer persecution*, and it were a madnesse to entertain
other thoughts, since our time is a time of Defection and shameful
Apostasy, which hath ever been a time of hot persecution." [13] Charles
himself was well aware of the threat posed by MacWard and Brown,
for in 1676 he had insisted, in accordance with the Treaty of Breda,
that the Dutch banish them along with the commander of the Galloway rebels, James Wallace. The States General finally acquiesced in
January 1677, but Brown was allowed to stay in the country because
of ill health and MacWard went into hiding. [14]

The Scottish conventicle problem spilled across the border into
Northumberland, forcing Charles to dispatch troops to restore order
in the spring of 1678. Frequent meetings there, Monmouth complained, tended "to the great disturbance of the publick peace."
When, in September 1678, authorities learned that Welsh intended to
address a large conventicle, they dispatched soldiers to search for the
dissidents. Fourteen or fifteen Scots ambushed the party, killing a
trooper. [15] The king deemed conditions on the border so serious that
he ordered Monmouth and his troops to assist the duke of Newcastle
in suppressing field services and arresting the preachers, while the
magistrates of Newcastle-on-Tyne received instructions to prosecute
seditious conventicles held in their town by English nonconformists.
The magistrates were less than zealous in performing that task, and
Newcastle grumbled that the militia was "of little or noe use." Nevertheless the presence of Monmouth's forces seems to have quieted
the border. In the process, the authorities captured William Veitch
(alias George Johnstone), "a notorious Ring-leader of the Seditious
Field-Conventiclers," who had been sentenced to death *in absentia*
for his alleged role in the Galloway rebellion of 1666. Although the
king initially ordered that Veitch be returned to Scotland, both
Monmouth and Shaftesbury interceded in his behalf, and he obtained his release in July 1679. [16]

Suppressing the conventicles was rendered more difficult both by the relative ease with which offenders could flee to northern Ireland and by the ability of dissidents to obtain fresh supplies of weapons. Although the duke of Ormond, lord lieutenant of Ireland, received instructions in September 1678 to guard the straits between Scotland and Ireland, a substantial number of Covenanters nevertheless succeeded in escaping to the Belfast area. Officials in Ireland were concerned about the impact of Scottish Covenanters on their island; "this countryes dance will be after their pype," Sir George Rawdon warned in January 1678. Neither Scottish nor Irish authorities were able to stop the illegal importing of weapons from the Netherlands. In Scotland itself blacksmiths in the west made poleaxes and other weapons for conventiclers. To compound the government's problems, Bo'ness shipmasters refused to transport Dutch arms intended for the king's forces because "their Conscience would not permitt them to cary home these Armes to disturbe the People of God from the Exercise of their Religion."[17] The conventiclers' determination to worship as they deemed appropriate and to defend themselves from government repression was a serious threat to civil peace in Scotland.

The Road to Bothwell Bridge

As conventiclers increasingly armed and organized themselves to repulse government units, violent incidents grew apace. In late 1677 some 60 to 80 followers of John Welsh not only refused to surrender a field preacher but shot at a royalist party commanded by Captain William Carstairs, killing one of its members and demanding that Carstairs "render himselfe prisoner in [the] name of God and the Covenant els he was to expect noe quarter."[18] Conventiclers in Edinburgh fired at the mayor with guns and assaulted him with swords in March 1679, threatening to kill him if he attempted to break up their services. Orthodox clergy were beaten at Torphichen and Bo'ness in 1677 and at Bara (near Haddington) in June 1679. A normally reliable informant reported in February 1679 that the "Phanatiks" were scheming to seize Edinburgh Castle, although nothing came of this.[19]

The confrontations escalated at Lesmahagow, Lanarkshire, in late March 1679, when a party of armed men attacked two or three troopers in their quarters. When the commander of a royalist force in Lanark learned that an illegal service would be held in Lesmahagow, a party of 20 dragoons arrested 6 or 7 persons en route to the meeting. The main body of conventiclers, however, was defended by approximately 300 foot soldiers and 60 men on horseback, the latter carrying pistols and some carbines. Approximately 120 of the foot had muskets, while the rest were equipped with halberds and pitchforks. When ordered to disperse, the worshipers retorted: "Farts in the King's teeth, and the Counsells, and all that has sent yow, For we appear here for the King of Heaven." Firing erupted on both sides and eight dragoons were temporarily captured. The Council responded by dispatching more troops, with orders to arrest the conventiclers, search for weapons, and seize the horses of persons unable to demonstrate their loyalty.[20]

As the violence spread, two soldiers were killed and others wounded on 20 April at Newmilns, Ayrshire, possibly by Covenanters. Following the arrest of Walter Scott, a conventicler and former magistrate, at Renfrew, a tumult erupted in which a laird serving as sheriff-depute was beaten. In their report to the Privy Council, the commissioners investigating these incidents as well as the Lesmahagow clash concluded, "[The field conventiclers have] framed a designe of keeping strong and armed conventicles in many distant places of designe to necessitat your Lordships to keep his Majesties forces togither in considerable numbers, that so they may in all uther places debauch the people." The militants also hoped to prevent the payment of the king's forces by hindering the levy of the assessment (cess), in part by kidnapping, killing, or beating troops collecting the money or those billeted in private houses.[21]

The state's policy of intensified repression, including billeting, transportation overseas, stiff fines (4,000 merks for a woman who attended one of Welsh's services), and bonding, provoked more hostility on the part of the Covenanters. In fact, the policy incited the growth of extremism. On 3 May a small group of zealots, ostensibly setting out to avenge themselves on William Carmichael of Easter Thurston, an ardent sheriff-depute notorious for his prosecution of Covenanters, happened upon a coach carrying James Sharp, archbishop of St. Andrews, at Magusmuir, a few miles from St. Andrews.

Calling him Judas and seeking revenge for the executions of the 1666 Pentland rebels as well as James Mitchell and James Learmont, the attackers shot the archbishop and then killed him with repeated sword-blows to the head. His daughter and servants were allowed to escape without harm.[22]

Two of the assassins—David Hackston of Rathillet, and his brother-in-law, John Balfour of Kinloch—were lairds; one, Andrew Guillan of Balmerino, was a weaver, and the others were sons of tenant farmers in Fife.[23] The Council issued a proclamation for the arrest of the assassins the following day, and ordered the heritors and masters of Fife and Kinross to bring their tenants and others living on their lands to St. Andrews, Cupar, Kirkcaldy, or Dunfermline for interrogation. Nevertheless, the assassins escaped by taking refuge with other militant Covenanters. Of the nine, Hackston (as discussed below) was caught and executed in July 1680, professing to the end that the killing of the archbishop was justified and no act of murder; Guillan met the same fate in July 1683.[24] Another assassin, James Russell of Kingskettle, twice escaped in Ireland, and may have done so again after his third arrest there, in October 1680. A fourth killer, Robert Dingwell of Cadham, died fighting with the Covenanters at Drumclog in June 1679, and George Balfour and George Fleeming served with Argyll in 1685. The fate of the remaining three is unknown.[25]

Although murdering Sharp had not initially been the objective of Hackston's band, the attack was a natural outgrowth of the Covenanters' increasing willingness to respond to repression with assaults on orthodox clergy, magistrates, and soldiers.[26] Sharp's assassination further escalated the violence by inciting the most militant wing of the Covenanters to launch the rebellion that the government had been expecting for some time.

The conventiclers to whom Hackston and his confederates fled for safety had been merged from smaller groups in the Lanark and Ayr regions. They had joined forces, said one Covenanter, "that thereby they might be in a better Capacity to assist & encouradge one another in keeping up a publike Testimony, by keeping up the Lords ordinances & worship & defending themselves." The leaders of the group included Robert Hamilton, younger son of Sir Thomas Hamilton of Preston and Fingalton, and the preachers Donald Cargill and John King, chaplain to Lord Cardross' wife. Throughout the early months of 1679 the conventiclers met in different places. On several occasions they were discovered by government troops, but the latter normally retreated in the face of the armed strength of the worshipers. When the soldiers finally tried to break up a conventicle, several were captured, disarmed, and forced to listen to two sermons before being released.[27]

After Hackston, Balfour of Kinloch, and James Russell had joined Hamilton's group, it convened at Avondale on 25 May and decided to revolt. Hamilton, Hackston, and others met with Cargill and John Spreul, the town clerk of Glasgow, to draft a declaration, which the conventiclers duly approved at Strathaven. They rose, the declaration averred, in defense of the National Covenant and the Solemn League and Covenant, and they protested various statutes, including those that had established royal supremacy, episcopacy, the indulgence, and 29 May as a day of thanksgiving. On Thursday the 29th a body of some 80 armed men rode into Rutherglen, affixed the declaration to the market cross, and set fire to copies of the offending acts, at least partly in retaliation for the earlier burning of their own Covenants. The rebels considered marching on Glasgow, but the unexpected arrival there of royalist forces under Captain John Graham of Claverhouse dissuaded them.[28]

By the time Claverhouse reached Rutherglen the Covenanters had left, but he arrested John King, Thomas Douglass, and two others near Strathaven. The rebels planned to hold a service, he learned, on 1 June near Loudoun Hill, east of Darvel, Ayrshire.[29] Claverhouse found his soldiers arrayed against approximately 1,400 or 1,500 men, and in the ensuing battle, fought on marshy land at nearby Drumclog, he lost 3 officers and 28 men before retreating to Glasgow. That night Hamilton, Balfour, Hackston, and other rebels were guests of the countess of Loudoun, and Hamilton apparently conferred privately with the earl himself. The following day the insurgents attacked the city twice, but, having no artillery, were repulsed with heavy losses by the forces of Lord Ross.[30] The Council subsequently ordered Ross to march his troops to the Edinburgh area as part of a general rendezvous, thus leaving Glasgow to the rebels. The latter occupied the city briefly, pillaging and burning houses belonging to Lauderdale and the bishops.[31]

In the days that followed, the rebels' numbers grew as other Covenanters seized an opportunity to act in defense of the Reformed religion and to extirpate popery and prelacy. Among the newcomers were Sir Hugh Campbell and Sir George Campbell, both of Cessnock, who provided 400 lances; John Welsh, who had been in Ulster and for whose arrest there was an outstanding reward of £500 sterling; and John Blackader. The previous month Blackader had told a Livingston conventicle, "When you come forth with swords in your hands, to defend the worship of God, it is well; but whatever you endeavour with your hostile weapons, I would have you trust little to them." The essential precondition, he had insisted, was adequate spiritual preparation: "I see a readiness to appear and defend the cause by instruments of war, which is, indeed, warrantable in its season; but oh! if this qualification be not added, all else will little avail."[32]

Whatever advantage the rebels gained by the new arrivals was more than offset by the resulting squabbles, which Blackader aptly described as "hot contentions, alienations, [and] mutual upbraiding." Two principal factions competed, the more extreme but smaller of which was led by Robert Hamilton, with the support of Hackston, Balfour of Kinloch, Andrew (or Alexander) Henderson, John Paton, William Cleland, and Walter Smith, clerk of the rebel council of war. The ministers in this faction were Cargill, Thomas Douglass, John Kid, and a Mr. Kemp. Richard Cameron and his brother Michael, both of whom shared the views of this group, were in the Netherlands seeking to purchase weapons. Direction of the second faction was in the hands of ministers, including Welsh, their leader; Samuel Arnot; George Barclay; and James Ure. In mid-June this group was bolstered by the arrival of Major Joseph Learmont, a veteran officer of the Galloway rebellion.[33]

Hamilton's faction was determined to repudiate the indulgence, the clergy who accepted it, and the king; the latter had, charged this group, "deprived us of the gospel and was seeking our destruction." Welsh's people, however, insisted that such issues be left to a parliament or general assembly, that the indulged ministers not be condemned without a hearing, and that Charles not be castigated inasmuch as the people had sworn to defend him. Although Welsh and his supporters opposed the indulgence, their unwillingness to condemn indulged clergy publicly without a proper forum made the Hamilton faction bitterly suspicious. Tension increased when the council of war, which Hamilton dominated, unsuccessfully tried to restrict the pulpit to those who would denounce the indulgence without qualification. In the judgment of Welsh's group, "it was the height of supremacy to give instructions to ministers [on] what to preach."[34] The latter dispute amounted to a role reversal, for ordinarily the Welsh faction rather than its opponents was willing to embrace a small amount of Erastianism.

These two feuding groups did not represent the full spectrum of Presbyterian opinion. Even among the rebels a few, including Blackader, urged a nonmilitant course of action. Others, such as Gabriel Semple, opted not to join the insurgents because of Hamilton's presence. Hamilton and his followers, Semple claimed, "would either Command all, or else they would Mutiny." Some, such as Patrick Gillespie and James Nesmith, had tried to unite all Presbyterians in a campaign to obtain a general indulgence, but on the understanding that no one would accept liberty to preach unless it were granted to all. Conservative Presbyterians, of course, had already embraced the limited indulgence offered by the government. Divisions among the Presbyterians were thus so pronounced in late 1679 that Semple aptly described them as "a Plague."[35]

In the weeks following the Drumclog triumph, rebel leaders would have been well advised to devote their energies to the acquisition of weapons and supplies, future strategy, and military training. Instead they were paralyzed by internecine feuding, most of which concerned the drafting of another declaration, particularly the points regarding indulged clergy and the king. The factions were "very hot on both sides," Ure reported. Hamilton's faction also insisted on observing a day of humiliation before publishing the declaration, but Welsh's group persuaded them to relinquish this demand in return for a statement in the declaration acknowledging "sins and engagement of duty." Before the declaration was in a form acceptable to Hamilton, Welsh slipped away to Glasgow to have it printed, further embittering Hamilton's supporters.[36]

Welsh's declaration, which was fastened to the market cross in

Hamilton, Lanark, set a markedly defensive tone by reciting charges of persecution, ranging from fines to execution and banishment, and efforts to prohibit conventicles and thus the preaching of the Gospel. The godly, it declared, had been patiently "groaninge under the overturninge of the worke of reformation, the Coruptions of doctrine, the slightinge of worshipe—despyseing of ordinances, the Changeing of Ancient church disciplinge & Governement," as well as the ouster of faithful clergy from their charges and the intrusion of inadequate, scandalous persons in their places. Threatened with violence by royalist forces, especially those commanded by Claverhouse, they had fought back only in self-defense and now were compelled "to take this last Remedie," the magistrates having "shutt the doore against any supplication." Thus justifying their recourse to arms, the Covenanters promulgated three aims: (1) to defend the Reformed faith, presbyterian polity, and the "kingly Authority" of Christ over his church; (2) to support Charles II "in the preservation & defense of the true religion & liberties of the kingdome" ; and (3) to obtain a free parliament and general assembly to redress their grievances, prevent the dangers of popery, and extirpate prelacy.[37]

By 18 June the rebels were on the verge of a complete split between the two factions. "We were fully resolved to separate" from Hamilton's party, Ure observed.

We were so hot on both sides, that we expected still to have gone by the ears. We intreated them to stand to the declaration, to let us go on against our enemy, and to let all debates alone till a free parliament and a general assembly. They told us, we were for an indulgence, and they would sheathe their swords as soon in them who owned it as they would do in many of the malignants.

The insurgents avoided a complete breach only when the Hamiltonians decided not to push their opposition to the declaration for the time being. Two days later the arrival of nearly 1,000 men from Galloway bolstered the rebel forces.[38]

While the Covenanters debated, the government readied a substantial army under Monmouth's command. Concerned about secret correspondence between the rebels and dissidents in Northumberland, the king also ordered an additional 500 militiamen into Berwick, and similar precautions were undertaken for Carlisle. The gov-

ernment directed Halifax to dispatch one or two frigates to prevent
the shipment of weapons to the rebels from Ireland.[39] Preliminary
skirmishes erupted between loyalist units and Covenanters, especially
those from Fife who were en route to join the main band encamped
variously at Glasgow, Hamilton, and Bothwell. Because of heavy
rains and delays in preparing the artillery and procuring ammunition, royalist troops were not ready to leave Edinburgh until 17 June;
Monmouth joined them two days later at Blackburn.[40]

At the peak of their strength the Covenanter forces encompassed
some 8,000 men, but as Monmouth's army approached, the number
dwindled to perhaps 6,000, apparently 1,600 of whom were cavalry.[41] In contrast, the duke had 10,000 soldiers as well as reserves
who could be summoned from Ireland[42] or northern England. By
the 20th Monmouth had advanced to within eight miles of Hamilton, where the insurgents had been joined by Robert Stewart,
brother of the laird of Galloway, and several other gentlemen.[43]

The following day Lord Melville, who accompanied Monmouth,
dispatched a messenger to Welsh and David Hume, informing them
of the imminent arrival of a mighty royalist army and urging them
to petition Monmouth for acceptable terms. Given the duke's friend-
ships with Presbyterian peers in England, he may have supported
this tactic. In any event, Melville, who favored the suspension of
prosecution against nonconformists, feared that a decisive royalist
victory would inflict irretrievable damage on the Presbyterian interest in Scotland. After some debate, the Covenanters agreed on a petition, which Hamilton duly signed. Like their recent declaration, it
commenced with a defensive tone: They had suffered violence and
oppression, and had no hope of redress. Their lives had been embittered by "evell bondage," so that "death seamed more eligible then
Lyfe." It was, they said, an act of providence that Monmouth had
come to Scotland and was averse to bloodshed. They sought only to
lay their grievances before him, and to that end they requested a safe
conduct for their representatives to attend the duke in the hope of
procuring speedy, effectual redress. Monmouth, however, refused to
discuss their grievances until the Covenanters had laid down their
weapons. Both armies thereupon positioned themselves to the north
of the town of Hamilton on opposite sides of Bothwell Bridge,

which the Covenanters barricaded with stones, cartwheels, and other objects.[44]

The battle, which commenced early on 22 June, went badly for the rebels, who were woefully short of artillery and gunpowder, and whose commanders were inept. At least one minister countermanded orders from the rebel council of war, thereby ruining such tactical advantage as the Covenanters had initially enjoyed. When the insurgents were repulsed, they made another crucial error by failing to destroy the bridge. The battle became a rout, with the craven Hamilton himself being among the first to flee. Royalist accounts report that between 200 and 900 rebels were killed and another 1,100 or 1,200 captured. "The Lord, in his holy providence, . . . [was] pleased to order it so for our humiliation and further trial," reflected George Brysson, who fought at Bothwell Bridge; "the time to deliver his church was not yet come."[45]

Scottish hard-liners, such as Linlithgow, wanted harsh punishment for the malefactors, but Monmouth, with his ties to English nonconformists, was not so inclined. In general, the king was persuaded to continue his policy of limited indulgence, allowing house but not field conventicles south of the Tay, except in Edinburgh, Glasgow, Stirling, and St. Andrews; indulged clergy had to provide surety for good behavior, but the offer was not open to the Bothwell rebels. Two of the renegade preachers—King and Kid—had been apprehended almost immediately, the latter apparently on Monmouth's assurance that his life would be spared. Both, however, were executed in August despite King's plea that he had attempted to persuade the insurgents "to loyaltie and Christianitie." The total number of executions remained nevertheless surprisingly small, at least until December 1682, when the exasperated government adopted a more stringent attitude toward recalcitrant rebels.[46]

Apart from the leaders of the insurrection and Sharp's killers, the state was willing to release most prisoners who subscribed bonds for their good behavior. When the deadline for the indemnity passed, the Scottish Council directed Lauderdale to give the Lords of the Justiciary discretion to extend it as circumstances warranted, and on 1 November, Charles authorized people to take the bond if they could satisfactorily explain why they had not previously done so.[47]

The Council did, however, want 300 to 400 rebels exiled to foreign plantations as an example. To this end, 258 were put on *The Crown of London* on 27 November, but the ship sank off the Orkney coast, and most of the prisoners drowned. In the meantime, 30 men were tried on 26 August on charges of treason and denying that Sharp's killing had been murder; 24 saved themselves by taking the bond, one was acquitted, and the remaining five were executed in December on the site of Sharp's assassination.[48] A year later James Skene, brother of the laird of Skene, received the death sentence; an obdurate rebel who told the Council that Sharp's killing had not been murder, he insisted that a state of war had existed between Covenanters and royalists, which made it legal to slay not only the king's soldiers and Councillors but Charles himself. Similarly unrepentant, James Robertson died in December 1682 after justifying his participation at Bothwell Bridge on the grounds of self-defense; the Covenanters had fought, he averred, not out "of treason and rebellion but dewtie," especially "to represse tyrannie & defend the opressed" from a monarch who had been "robing the churches liberties and usurping the royeall prerogatives of chryst Jesus."[49] More than a dozen others, including the attorney John Dick and the Galloway and Bothwell rebel John Paton, were executed between 1682 and 1684.[50]

Most of those who had fought at Bothwell Bridge escaped. Some fled to England, the Netherlands, Ireland, and even North America, although most probably stayed in Scotland.[51] A number of the latter would fight again, just as some, including Joseph Learmont, John Maclellan of Barscobe, and John Cuningham of Bedland, were veterans of the 1666 Galloway rebellion.[52] The Council was less lenient toward the lairds who had taken up arms, 35 of whom lost estates in Galloway and Dumfries.[53] The policy of selective punishment coupled with widespread leniency failed to break the militant wing of the Covenanters. John Whitelaw, one of those eventually executed, died defiant, affirming the Covenant and condemning not only popery, prelacy, and Erastianism but Charles Stuart "and all his procedings, becaues they [were] against God and His law and againest all bearing ofice under Him." His last letter, dated 28 November 1683, was a jeremiad that warned, "The Lord hath a great contrevarsy with thir cowinated [covenanted] lands for aposticy and baksliding from Him and for pergwry and unfaithfwll dealing in the maters off God." Yet God, he claimed, held out the promise of a remnant—a theme especially dear to the Covenanters. The final statement of Arthur Bruce, another convicted Bothwell rebel, was no less fiery. A follower of Kid, King, Cameron, and Cargill, he attributed the disaster at Bothwell to Judases within the Covenanting camp. He too decried the king: "[I leave my] testimony against Charles Stewart quhich is sitting upon the throne and is making it his work to persecut and destroy all the preciouse things of our Lord." [54] At most, the state's policy of leniency to those subscribing the bond weaned the less militant away from their fiery colleagues, reinforcing in the latter a strong sense of identity as the persecuted, godly remnant. This extreme faction, with its unshakable conviction of divine mission, its repudiation of Charles' government, and its willingness to take up arms and even assassinate officials, posed a more serious destabilizing threat to the Stuart regime in Scotland than modern historians have recognized.

The Scottish uprising heightened fears of related disturbances in northern Ireland, where reports of an imminent Presbyterian rebellion circulated in 1679. Militants attempted to disrupt the flow of mail to England in the hope of delaying orders from the king to call up additional troops, but their efforts failed. A force of 300 cavalry and 2,000 foot soldiers secured Dublin, while other troops reinforced the garrison at Carrickfergus and took up stations on the Antrim coast. [55] Ulster Presbyterians had in fact been meeting in very large conventicles, including ones that numbered 3,000 or more near Coleraine and at Ballykelly and Castlefinn, and 2,000 outside the walls of Londonderry. As in Scotland, many of the worshipers bore arms, and some boasted that they were "able to breake all Ireland"; their preachers proclaimed a gospel of civil disobedience, insisting that when the magistrates failed to punish sin, the godly had a "dutie to supply that desert." [56] Ireland, however, remained calm, suffering no more than a temporary economic slump caused by fear of an incipient rebellion. Various Presbyterian clerics professed their loyalty to the duke of Ormond, prompting Charles to reaffirm his willingness to tolerate peaceful nonconformists while suppressing militants. [57] The policy was generally effective, for in the ensuing years nonconformists in Ireland were peaceful, although some continued to hold outdoor meetings and thus went to prison.[58]

The Cameronians

In the immediate aftermath of the Bothwell defeat, field conventicles seem to have temporarily ceased in Scotland, although by the spring of 1680 their number was again on the rise. William Veitch, who had been arrested on suspicion of having been a Galloway rebel, obtained his release after insisting that he had not fought in the Pentland Hills in 1666. He returned immediately to Northumberland, where he continued to minister to conventicles.[59] Blackader, in contrast, stayed in Scotland, though he normally preached in house conventicles; at Southfield, Cramond, he exhorted some 4,000 worshipers in a field, and soldiers dispersed his meeting at Bo'ness. The more militant clergy were clearly chafing at the bit: "How furious their preachers are," noted one of Lauderdale's correspondents, "who would be faire at worke againe." Despite the fact that in March 1680 the Council had appointed a special committee to suppress conventicles, the following month the Councillors complained that illegal field meetings continued, with some Bothwell rebels who had subscribed the bond in attendance. "Severall turbulent persons," especially Walter Denoon and John Hepburn, were holding services in the fields of Moray, Nairn, and Inverness; Hepburn went so far as to sneer at "all house Sermons [as] Dunghill Conventicles." Illegal meetings were a problem too at Inverkeithing, Fife; at the Grange, Roxburgh, where James Ker preached; at Easter Crichton, East Lothian; and even outside Edinburgh, where a field conventicle gathered. Both Lieutenant-General Thomas Dalziel and the earl of Moray observed an increase in the number of such conventicles in April.[60]

The most militant of the conventicles in the post-Bothwell years was a band of zealots who looked for leadership to Richard Cameron, a protégé of the exiles John Brown and Robert MacWard. Ordained at their hands in Rotterdam, Cameron returned to Scotland in October 1679 and joined forces with several Bothwell fugitives, including Donald Cargill, David Hackston, and Robert Smith. Another major figure was Henry Hall, laird of Haughead, Teviotdale, who had a long history of dissident activity. He had moved to Northumberland about 1665 to avoid persecution for his nonconformist views, but returned to Scotland the following year and was arrested as he attempted to join the Galloway rebels in the Pentlands. After his release from prison with the aid of the earl of Roxburgh, he went back to Northumberland, where he was a member of the party that in September 1678 ambushed troopers dispatched to prevent John Welsh from holding a conventicle. Forced to flee England, Hall cast his lot with the Bothwell insurgents; their defeat prompted him to seek refuge in the Netherlands. Returning to his homeland early in 1680, he accompanied Cargill, especially in the area around the Firth of Forth.[61]

The core of the Cameronian message was prophetic and apocalyptic: dreadful judgments lay in store for Scotland, but hope was held out for a penitent remnant. "God is saying this day to his people in Scotland," proclaimed Cargill in May 1680; "I can doe nothing against the wicked, untill you be closer walkers with me, and then Judgment shall quickly fall upon them."[62]

In the fall of 1679 Cameron preached to a field conventicle numbering some 3,000 persons, who flouted the government by meeting near the home of Sir Robert Dalziel. Other conventicles followed, including one at Tinto Hill attended by more than 3,000 worshipers, many of whom bore arms. Shortly after the duke of York's arrival in Edinburgh on 4 December, Hackston proposed to a gathering of more than 20 Cameronians at the home of Lady Gilkerscleuch that they assassinate James. Robert Smith subsequently confessed that he and Michael Cameron had orders to determine whether men carrying concealed swords could gain access to the duke. En route, however, they were recognized and chased, and Smith subsequently fled to England.[63]

The government obtained substantive information about the Cameronians when, on 3 June 1680, a party of horse guards sought to detain and interrogate Cargill and Hall at Queensferry. Although Cargill escaped during the ensuing skirmish, Hall was killed. In a portmanteau belonging to one of the men the soldiers found a "new Covenant"[64] pledging to liberate the church from the thralldom and tyranny of prelacy and Erastianism, and to restore the "civill rights & liberties" of both the church and the people. The statement included a lengthy indictment of Scottish monarchs and most of their advisers for arbitrary government, imposing tyranny in lieu of government by the king and freely elected parliaments, rewarding evil and punishing good, burning the Solemn League and Covenant, and oppressing the civil rights and consciences of the people. The "new Covenant" urged believers to disobey the evil commands of their sovereigns: "[We declare them] to be no lawfull rulers, as they have declared us to be no lawfull subjects." The declaration even repudiated the principle of government by a single person as "being most lyable to inconveniencies . . . and aptest to degenerat into tyranny." Law, according to the Cameronians, must be grounded largely in the Old Testament, though excluding the Judaic provisions for slavery, divorce, and polygamy. Cognizant of the affinity of these views with those of the Fifth Monarchists, the Cameronians boldly endorsed this heritage: "If this be ther fyfthe monarchie wee both are and ought to be such and that according to his word." With the Fifth Monarchists they shared a fervent apocalypticism, a strong attraction to the legal principles of the Old Testament, and a willingness to employ violence in the cause of God. The declaration repudiated the Act of Supremacy as blasphemous, insisting that the church must be governed by God rather than an earthly monarch, and castigated ministers who accepted the indulgence. In essence, the declaration was a sweeping condemnation of virtually everyone in a position of authority.[65]

Government officials apparently realized that the Cameronians were a small group, but they were uncertain how many sympathizers might heed their revolutionary call. As early as 4 June, Dalziel alerted Lauderdale that the Cameronians would shortly take up arms "if thair num[b]ers disapoint not thair Expectations." Four days later the Scottish Council issued a proclamation offering a reward of £100 sterling for the apprehension of Cameron and others to be named. The new threat was undoubtedly a factor in the king's instructions for the maintenance of the peace in Scotland, issued on 12 June. Collectively the earls of Rothes, Argyll, Moray, and Queensberry, the bishop of Edinburgh, and Charles Maitland, Lord Hatton—or any three of them—were directed not only to suppress field conventicles and apprehend and punish Bothwell fugitives but to secure disaffected persons whenever they had probable grounds to expect a rebellion.[66]

While the Council was investigating the Queensferry declaration, the Cameronians struck. On the afternoon of 22 June a party of 21 mounted zealots, with swords and pistols drawn, rode into Sanquhar, Dumfries. After the band sang a psalm, the minister Thomas Douglass spoke, Cameron's brother Michael read a declaration and then affixed copies to the cross and the church, and Richard Cameron denounced the king and the state church at length.[67] The Sanquhar declaration, which identified the group as "the Trew Presbeterian Antiprelatick Anteristain Persecuted Partie in Scotland," vowed support for such "government & governors as the Word of God & the Covenant allow[ed]," but specifically disowned Charles Stuart as a tyrant, a perjurer, and a usurper. The declaration reaffirmed the Rutherglen proclamation of May 1679 while repudiating Welsh's statement of June 1679 because it was "taken in the kings intrest." The Sanquhar manifesto went on to denounce the duke of York as a professed Catholic and protested his right of succession to the throne—an issue that was, of course, already exercising Whigs in the English Parliament and would shortly link radical Covenanters with English conspirators in the Rye House plotting.[68]

After dispatching troops to engage the Cameronians, the government issued a proclamation on 30 June offering a reward of 5,000 merks for Richard Cameron, 3,000 each for his brother Michael, Cargill, and Douglass, and 1,000 apiece for their followers. The rebels, however, were undaunted. On 8 July, Cargill preached on Isaiah 49, which refers to a time when the world's sovereigns will bow before the godly and lick the dust from their feet. The Galloway rebels had failed in 1666, he told his followers, because they had taken the Covenant at Lanark "in the King's interest." Since the Restoration, he thundered, the actions of Charles and those on whom he had bestowed power demonstrated that "its impossible to manifest the royall prerogatives of Jesus Christ, & manifestly avow so much his civil rights: & since its so declared, we must ather quatt [quit] him as King, or Christ. Indeed . . . I am for no King but

Christ."[69] Relatively few heeded Cargill's call to overthrow the Stuart regime; the *Gazette* put the final rebel count at 140, but the real number may have been half that. Royalist troops defeated them at Aird's Moss, near Muirkirk, Ayrshire. More than two dozen militants died on the field, including the Cameron brothers. Although the elusive Cargill again escaped, the soldiers captured David Hackston, one of Archbishop Sharp's assassins. Hackston was hanged, drawn, and quartered in Edinburgh on the 30th, professing to the end the principles of the radical Covenanters. Of the king he said, "Where Authority disowns the Interest of God and States it self, in opposition to Jesus Christ, it is no more to be owned, and . . . the Authority of the King was such."[70]

The Cameronians should perhaps have been left alone, for they were probably less dangerous than their ideology suggests, although the duke of York deemed three of those who were executed in December 1680 "the boldest and stubernest rogu[e]s I ever heard of." Another captured rebel, Archibald Alison, who was executed in August 1680, testified that he had gone to conventicles in arms only to hear the Gospel "truly and faithfully" preached, not to attack the king's forces. The band was prepared to fight, he insisted, only in self-defense. Scottish officials were alarmed, however, by papers found in Richard Cameron's possession that contained this revealing statement: "The people are much influenced by rebells and fugitives who live in holland, to all their madd and rebellious practises, and . . . these rebells are as dangerous to the government as if they keeped their caballs here." The key supporters of the Cameronians were the more militant Scottish exiles in Rotterdam and Utrecht, such as MacWard and Brown, who were also suspect because of their ability to influence merchants doing business with the Dutch. A letter dated 7 January 1681 from one exile (W. S[hields]) contended that believers could not in good conscience regard the laws of those who had repudiated the Solemn League and Covenant as just or binding; such persons, including Charles II, had forfeited their right to rule.[71]

Cargill led his pursuers on a merry chase. On 12 September 1680 he preached to a large, armed field conventicle at Torwood, southeast of Stirling. There he wielded the weapon of excommunication, "the sword of the Lord," without respect of persons, he said, as it had been used by Ambrose, bishop of Milan, against the Emperor Theodosius. After rehearsing the nature of excommunication as a tool to purge the church of evil, he launched into a litany of charges against the high and mighty, commencing with the king himself: "I being a minister of Jesus Christ and having authority & power from him Doe in his name & by his Spirit Excommnicat, cast out of the true Church & delyver up to Satan Charles the 2d King, Defender, or rather Tyrant, and Destroyer." The crimes with which he was charged included renouncing the Covenant, supporting popery, employing the army to repress the godly, granting pardons to murderers, committing adultery, and inebriety. Cargill then excommunicated six others: the duke of York for idolatry; Monmouth for suppressing the Covenanters at Bothwell Bridge; Lauderdale for "dreadfull blasphemy," apostasy from the Covenant, persecuting the godly, adultery, and violating the Sabbath; Rothes for establishing popery at Charles' command, adultery, drunkenness, and (like Lauderdale) breaking a promise of indemnity to James Mitchell; Sir George Mackenzie, the lord advocate, for apostasy, prosecuting the godly in court, and pleading on behalf of capital offenders; and Dalziel for ordering the army to repress true believers, "Injurious deeds in the exercise of his power," and a lascivious life. Cargill's band posted copies of the excommunication in Torwood.[72]

Cargill spent the ensuing months preaching to conventiclers in Lanarkshire, Fife, and Ayrshire. In September, at Black Hill, north of Lanark, he proclaimed that the time would soon come when the elect would be avenged for their suffering and martyrdom.[73] He was in Edinburgh on 11 November to meet with James Skene and others to discuss the assassination of Charles, James, and assorted government officials. With Thomas Douglass and others, Cargill reportedly visited northern England in the winter on a recruiting mission. During the spring and early summer of 1681 his sermons focused on suffering and preparation for death as well as fidelity to the Covenant and the importance of not succumbing to the enemy. He found time as well to renew his condemnation of the indulged clergy, whom he called the voice of the devil, and to hold out hope of a remnant in the imminent day of judgment. The recurring themes of martyrdom and vengeance were all the more vivid as worshipers waved two cloths stained with the blood of the executed Covenanter Alexander Stewart and cried out for revenge.[74]

According to several reports the Cameronians permitted women to preach and excommunicate, but not administer baptism. Women, in fact, seem to have constituted the majority of Cargill's followers. Two women—Marian Harvey, a servant in Bo'ness, and Isabel Alison of Perth—had been captured at Aird's Moss and hanged, although three women arrested for attending the notorious Torwood conventicle were released with a warning that they would be beaten if they persisted in attending illegal services.[75]

The authorities finally arrested Cargill and two followers at Covington, southeast of Lanark, on 12 July 1681. With two other Bothwell rebels they went to the gallows in Edinburgh the same month. Unrepentant to the end, Cargill condemned the indulgence and ministers who embraced it as betrayers of God's interest. Persecutors of the godly, he admonished, faced divine judgment as "creualle and bloody murderers." Equally impenitent, the ministerial student Walter Smith, who repudiated the king's right to appoint judges or summon parliaments, proudly averred that he followed in the steps of James Guthry, the Stirling minister who had been executed in 1661. The state hanged five more Cameronians near Edinburgh in October, one of them after his hand had been cut off and nailed up with an inscription of his boast that he would slay all usurpers, including Charles II. Another five Cameronians found themselves banished. Most of the executed could have saved themselves by acknowledging the king's authority, but one, representative of all, said that "he could not purchase his Life at so dear a rate."[76]

Conventiclers Under Attack

Against the background of the Cameronian disturbances the government continued its futile effort to curb field conventicles. On 14 May 1680, Charles, citing his disappointment that the suspension of the provisions against house conventicles on 29 June 1679 had not ended illegal services in the fields, issued new, tougher regulations. He prohibited house conventicles and Presbyterian meeting houses within a distance of one mile of any parish served by a regular incumbent; banned presbyteries and synods as "grand nurseries of schisme and sedition"; extended from two miles to twelve the zone around Edinburgh within which dissenting clergy could not minister; forbade nonconformists from exercising ecclesiastical discipline or obtaining licenses "in any parish where the generality, the cheife and intelligent persons" were "regular and orderly"; and denied nonconformists who had been banished from any parish or corporation in England the right to preach in Scotland.[77]

The occasion for these restrictive measures was not primarily the Cameronian disturbances, which served as a convenient justification for the new policy, but shifting political circumstances. As Julia Buckroyd has demonstrated, the initiative for the tougher provisions came from the English bishops, whose primary objective was the reduction of Monmouth's influence. Much to James' consternation, Monmouth's popularity among moderate Scots had increased substantially because of his support for the indulgence policy following his victory at Bothwell Bridge. The stage was therefore set for an alliance between Monmouth's opponents in both realms. The Scottish bishops happily concurred with the suggestion to implement a tougher policy, and the result was largely the handiwork of James, Lauderdale, and William Sancroft, archbishop of Canterbury.[78]

The Scottish Council expeditiously implemented the new instructions, convinced that the recent indulgence "in its former latitud produced . . . insufferable disorders." The Councillors investigated prominent conventiclers for activities that had occurred as far back as 1679 and punished magistrates who had been remiss in prosecuting illegal religious meetings.[79] The crackdown undoubtedly inhibited some conventiclers and certainly prompted a number to seek refuge in northern England, but both field and house conventicles continued in the ensuing months. They ranged across the country from Fife and East Lothian to Galloway and Wigtown, and from Dumfries and Roxburgh to Perth. House conventicles even met in Edinburgh and Aberdeen. "Manie incendiarie schismatiques," complained the Scottish bishops in November 1680, "are in severall corners of this land yet keeping up house and field conventicles." Among those who preached at field meetings were Alexander Haisty, reportedly a Bothwell rebel; Thomas Forrester, who was sympathetic to the Cameronians; and John Blackader, whose preaching on Dalskairth Hill outside Dumfries attracted people from Galloway, Nithsdale, and Annandale.[80] Some conventicles enjoyed the support of socially prominent persons. Katherine Rigg, Lady Cavers, who associated with such preachers as Cargill, Douglass, and Semple, hosted an illegal service in her home in November 1680, at which some of the more than 300 in attendance could not squeeze into the house; the same month she supported an illegal fast led by Matthew Selkirk at Philiphaugh, near the town of Selkirk. Both the sheriff of Philiphaugh and his deputy were sympathetic to the conventiclers and to such rebels as John Welsh and Captain Alexander Hume (or Home). Lady Caldwell was imprisoned in Blackness Castle for attending illegal services. Margaret Hamilton, Lady Gilkerscleuch, who had been incarcerated in the Edinburgh Tolbooth for aiding rebels and going to conventicles, continued to do both after her release in August 1681.[81]

Although Dr. Francis Turner, the duke of York's chaplain, complained in June 1681, "Our John a Leyden party [the Covenanters] growes not more numerous to appearance, but more extravagantly wild in their notions, and divided into many hopefull schismes amoung themselves," by year's end the field conventicles had diminished because of the policy of holding landlords accountable for the actions of their tenants. The archbishop of St. Andrews, in fact, warned Archbishop Sancroft that implementation of an indulgence could undermine the successes of the repression.[82]

The ease with which dissidents could find haven south of the Tweed complicated the problem of curtailing conventicles. Among such militants were Welsh, who died in England in January 1681, Semple, and James Fraser of Brae. At Ford, southwest of Berwick, Semple preached in both the fields and the parish church to people who came on foot over distances as great as 30 miles; when he spoke in the church not even half of those who came could find space inside.[83] In late 1680 approximately 2,000 Scottish and English nonconformists met at Downham, Northumberland, to hear four unidentified preachers. Conventicles in border towns such as Berwick and Crookham undoubtedly included both Scots and English, thereby facilitating communications between nonconformists in the two kingdoms. The English Privy Council was understandably concerned in the spring of 1681 because "a great number of Persons disaffected to the Government [had] lately in a very unusual manner, kept unlawfull meetings" in Berwick.[84]

Evidence of relations between Scottish and English dissidents is sketchy. Communications from Scotland in early 1682 suggested that the Bothwell insurrectionists had received assistance from unnamed Englishmen, but this cannot be substantiated; as previously noted, however, an Englishman named Colonel Fox had been a companion of Welsh's before the uprising. After investigating the possibility of English aid for the rebels, Rothes and the bishop of Edinburgh concluded in 1680 that much of the unrest in Scotland began south of the border and was encouraged by Englishmen. Their inquiries, however, focused on the efforts of two Whigs, Sir James Rushout, M.P. for Evesham in the exclusion Parliaments, and Thomas Percival, a Cambridge attorney who had visited Scotland to seek support for an exclusion bill in the English Parliament. Charles deemed these activities suspicious and ordered ill-intentioned persons arrested.[85] No less dangerous for a government determined to impose religious conformity, however, was the ability of armed conventiclers to move almost at will across the border, blatantly defying both statutes and magistrates.

A substantial number of Scottish conventicle sermons have survived. Many of them, such as the 39 on Hosea 2: 19–20, seem harmless and free of sedition at first glance. The Hosea sermons concentrate on the importance of faithfulness to God, adherence to one's vows, and fulfillment of one's duties. But these obligations are set forth in the context of the Covenant, and worshipers would therefore have heard these sermons as reminders of the special sense of identity and mission that characterized the Covenanters. Believers must engage to be the people of God: "Keep true & faithfull unto him," even, by implication, at the cost of disobeying earthly rulers. Divine judgment is inevitable: "The justice of God stands ready to strike the Last & fatall stroke." Cargill made similar statements in his lectures on Genesis 19. What made such sermons dangerous was not so much their surface content but the associations with the Covenant theme, especially when enunciated in a manifestly illegal service, guarded in some instances by men wielding swords and guns. Other sermons, such as Cargill's on Isaiah 49, were blatantly seditious.[86]

An indication of the laity's sensitivity to the Covenanter message is apparent in the letters of James Simpson's widow and her son. A regular correspondent with John Brown and Robert MacWard in the Netherlands as well as the assassin David Hackston, Mrs. Simpson was accused by the bishop of Edinburgh in December 1680 of having supplied "intelligence to all the Rebells," including Cameron and Cargill. In a letter of 8 May to her son, she referred to "the pretious & persecuted Remnant" in Scotland and "the vertous old principls of the church of scotland," both favorite Covenanting themes. She also reiterated one of the Covenanters' strongest convictions: "The lord is about to purge his church of . . . [evil] Ministers & professors & will more & more discover them." Her son Richard's response reflected the pronounced nonconformist concern with the purported Catholic threat: "Truly the prevalency of the popish interest has been a grievous tryal to these nations, and is like to produce the most tragicall effects."[87] The same concerns and depth of commitment were manifest in the gallows speeches of Covenanter rebels. Those who attended the conventicles must have grasped the implications of such themes as judgment, remnant, obedience to God regardless of the cost, and covenant obligations.

Continued violence against conforming clergy—whatever the motivation[88]—lent credence to fears of further assaults by irate Covenanters. The minister of Livingston, West Lothian, was attacked in 1680, the same year that Cargill's partisans threatened to kill the minister of Carriden, West Lothian, after he reported Cargill's activities to the government. Covenanters were almost certainly responsible for severely beating the minister of Manor, Peebles, in September 1680; "if all the curats and oppressors of Christs cause had the like stroak," they told him, "it would be well for the Kirk of Scotland." The following year John Gray and four other "rebells" wounded the minister of Tarbolton, Ayrshire, and warned him to leave the parish within a month or face death. Early in 1682 "Hoome and Nisbett"— probably Captain Alexander Hume and John Nisbet, a Northumberland native and former student at the University of Edinburgh who would shortly become involved with English conspirators—were allegedly plotting to assassinate the bishop of Edinburgh.[89] About the same time, frightened conformist clergy in Northumberland rode in arms after a "Horrid attempt" had been made on one of their number. In Edinburgh itself a cleric was attacked as he prepared to preach, and a minister was assaulted while he conducted a service in the parish church at Prestonpans, East Lothian, in April 1682. Not surprisingly, as the duke of York prepared to leave Scotland he urged the Council to be vigilant in protecting the bishops and the conforming clergy. Nevertheless, several days later some 300 men and women physically assailed a conformist cleric at Dron, south of Perth.[90]

The occasion of the assaults at Prestonpans and Dron was the government's attempt to fill vacancies caused by the refusal of incumbents to subscribe to the Test, which affirmed royal supremacy in spiritual as well as temporal matters. Because of the recent Act of Succession (1681), taking the Test was tantamount to endorsing the probability of a Catholic succession to the throne and the supreme governorship of the church. This was too much for many moderates, approximately 50 of whom relinquished their parishes.[91] Although some ministers forthrightly criticized the Test, they were quietly allowed to continue preaching by some of the bishops because of their peaceful deportment.[92]

The controversy over the Test created serious dissension in the Scottish Council. Both the lord president, Sir James Dalrymple, and the clerk-register, Sir Thomas Murray, refused to subscribe; Dalrymple in fact opted to go into exile in the Netherlands. More significant for the future of the radical cause were the qualms of the earl of Argyll, who eventually subscribed after stipulating that he did so only as far as the Test was "consistant with itselfe and the Protestant religion." His political enemies seized on this qualification as an excuse to expel him from the Council and imprison him on charges of treason in November 1681. "I confesse," reflected the duke of York, "I was much scandalised at his proceding in that affaire; for, if he had either frankly taken it, or positively refused it, nothing would have been sayd to him." Because the paper setting forth Argyll's position was deemed to reflect adversely on the king's authority and the Test Act, he was tried and found guilty on 12 and 13 December. On the 20th he escaped in disguise from Edinburgh Castle; three days later the lords commissioners of the justiciary sentenced him to die as soon as he could be apprehended. A search of his chamber in the castle turned up documents that the Council determined to be seditious, but Argyll safely made his way to London. The attack on the earl, which stemmed primarily from political motives, was largely responsible for driving him into radical circles; by April 1682 he was reportedly with Robert Ferguson, who would shortly play a pivotal role in the Rye House conspiracy.[93]

The United Societies

While the government focused its attention on Argyll, the Cameronians, disorganized and without a minister after Cargill's arrest, regrouped. On 15 December 1681, delegates gathered at Lesmahagow in Lanarkshire to establish the United Societies. They made provisions for a circular letter that would be transmitted fortnightly or at least monthly, for regular meetings of the constituent societies in the shires, and for general sessions every three months. According to the Bothwell veteran Alexander Gordon of Earlston, whose initial contact with the group occurred shortly after its inception, the organization comprised approximately 80 local societies with a total membership of perhaps 6,000 or 7,000 persons. His figures probably err on the high side, but nevertheless the United Societies was apparently larger than historians have suspected. The local groups met, Earlston said, once or twice weekly in the hills and woods to sing, pray, and read Scripture. The general meetings included not only worship but also inquiries about spiritual growth, the collection of funds for the needy, and discussions of security.[94]

Thoroughly convinced of the justice of their cause, the Lesmahagow convention drafted a manifesto to be posted at Lanark on 12 January 1682. It not only endorsed the Rutherglen and Sanquhar declarations but incorporated a scathing six-point indictment of Charles. He had violated, it asserted, the "noble constitutione of church and state"; exalted himself, "exceeding al measure devine or human, tyranically obtruding his Will as a law" in civil and ecclesiastical affairs; irresponsibly dissolved parliaments; used his tyrannical prerogative to style himself supreme head; imposed exorbitant taxes, "grinding the face of the poor"; and endeavored to perpetuate tyranny beyond his own reign by imposing the Test, repugnant to all Protestants. The United Societies therefore claimed the sanction of divine, natural, and "ancient" civil and ecclesiastical law for their rebellion. Their professed goal was the extrication of the Scottish nation from tyranny and the restoration of church and state as they had existed in Scotland in 1648–49.[95]

At noon on 12 January, as scheduled, 40 horsemen and 20 people on foot posted their declaration in Lanark, distributed copies to the people, destroyed a cross, and publicly burned the Test and all the records and parliamentary statutes they could find in the bailiff's house. Although the militants were in Lanark for two hours, neither the magistrates nor the residents made any effort to stop or apprehend them, for which laxity they were subsequently punished.[96]

The Scottish Council responded vigorously, ordering troops to Lanark and publicly burning the Solemn League and Covenant, the Rutherglen and Sanquhar manifestos, the Queensferry statement, and the Lanark declaration. The king, observing that the problem of "wicked and rebellious practises" extended throughout much of the southwest, commissioned John Graham of Claverhouse as sheriff of Wigtown as well as sheriff-depute of Dumfries and the stewartries of Annandale and Kirkcudbright. Claverhouse received sweeping authority to apprehend and prosecute recusants, conventiclers, those who aided rebels or participated in illegal baptisms and marriages, and, except for heritors, all who had been involved in the Bothwell uprising and had not subscribed a bond to receive indemnity. Adam Urquhart, laird of Meldrum, and Major White subsequently received commissions as sheriffs-depute of Lanarkshire to punish not only those responsible for the Lanark manifesto but also conventiclers and recusants.[97]

When Claverhouse arrived in Galloway he found between 300 and 400 rebels who had not received the indemnity but had nevertheless enjoyed almost complete freedom since the revolt of 1679. He captured those he could locate and in the process quartered troops on rebel lands, rifled the Covenanters' homes, incarcerated their servants, and nearly starved their wives and children. Heritors had to sign bonds for the good behavior of their tenants but received exemptions from punishment for past offenses with the exception of assaults on clerics, aid to rebels, and attendance at field conventicles. When Claverhouse ordered roll taken at services in the parish churches and punished absentees, attendance dramatically increased. At the end of March, Claverhouse transferred his prisoners to Edinburgh, where most gained their freedom by taking the bond or subscribing to the Test. In October he claimed that he had "brok[en] a caball" in Galloway.[98]

Claverhouse's apparent success in Galloway prompted the government to issue comparable commissions in March for Haddington, Kinross, Perth, and West Lothian, where the crackdown subsequently produced satisfactory results. In other areas, including Ayrshire and Lanarkshire, resistance was considerably stronger and virtually irrepressible over the long term.[99] Proponents of harsh restraint were quick to claim success for their policy. There is, James boasted in May 1682, "no noise of feild conventicles any where, and the rebells in Gallow[ay] and other places [are] suing for parden and some of them deliver them selves up upon mercy and renounce all their covenants and damnable principels." Queensberry concurred but insisted that troops remain in the southwest, and Hamilton boasted in September that the region was even free of house conventicles; the archbishop of St. Andrews made a similar assertion in December. Yet the Council itself complained in the summer that assorted disorders, including conventicles and illegal baptisms and marriages, had actually increased in Ayrshire and the southeastern shires.[100] Magistrates received orders to prosecute offenders more vigorously, a policy whose implementation was reflected in reports carried in the *True Protestant Mercury* in the summer and fall of 1682. Exorbitant fines, the confiscation of property, and imprisonment were imposed, according to one account, with "Unparalleled Severity." The government ordered the transportation of some field conventiclers to New York and Carolina, while others escaped by fleeing into Northumberland.[101]

Among those caught in the dragnet were four Galloway insurgents: Joseph Learmont, one of the rebels' principal officers; John Maclellan of Barscobe, whose attack on Sir James Turner's soldiers had been the spark that ignited the uprising; Hugh Macklewraith (or McIlwraith) of Auchenflower; and Robert Fleming of Auchinfin.

Although all four were sentenced to death, each received a reprieve; Learmont was incarcerated in the Bass.[102]

Seven less-fortunate radicals went to the gallows in 1682, beginning with the Lanark weaver William Harvey, a Bothwell veteran and a member of the United Societies' band that had posted a declaration in his town in January. Robert Gray died in March after being convicted of treason for repudiating both the king's authority and the Test, and the Bothwell rebel Thomas Lauchlane followed him to the gallows in August. Three Cameronians were executed in December: the merchant James Robertson, who refused to denounce the Galloway and Bothwell uprisings and who was suspected of posting a statement against the Test on the church door at Stonehouse, Lanarkshire; John Finlay, who admitted he had been with the rebels at Drumclog in 1679, though without weapons; and William Cochran, who refused to answer an interrogatory pertaining to the right of subjects to take up arms against their monarch. The last person to face execution in 1682—Alexander Hume of Hume Castle—had attended field conventicles in arms but was accused of treason on highly dubious evidence for having participated in the rebellion of 1679. Neither the executions nor the continuation of repressive measures, including the punishment of uncooperative magistrates, could impose uniformity, especially in the southern shires.[103] The duke of York, habitually inept at assessing either political realities or the depth of Protestant concerns, failed to recognize the bankruptcy of this policy: "Truly tho I thinke it very hard to reconcile all people here to be very good freinds one with another," he wrote in December 1682, "yett I hope to be able to offer that to his Majesty which may make them all joyne in serving him, and secure this country entirly to him."[104]

Among those resolved not to be suppressed were the United Societies, which convened at Priest Hill in the parish of Muirkirk, Ayrshire, on 15 March 1682. There they appointed Alexander Gordon of Earlston as their representative to "foreign nations" with a view to conveying the story of Scottish persecution and the United Societies' opposition to popery, prelacy, and Erastianism. The following month Earlston and his assistant, John Nisbet, went to London, whence Earlston alone left for the Netherlands. Delegates to the March meeting also decided that each man in the United Societies should acquire arms for self-defense. The group met at Tweedsmuir, Peebles, on 15 June and in Edinburgh itself on 11 August, 11 October, and 10 January. In the Netherlands, Earlston and his brother-in-law Robert Hamilton, brother of the laird of Preston, sought financial assistance and a place to emigrate. They obtained the support of William Brackel, a Dutch minister at Leeuwarden in Friesland, who endorsed their views on strict discipline and separation from the state church. The way was then open to send four men to the Netherlands to study for the ministry. Of the six who volunteered, four were chosen by lot; three of them—James Renwick, John Flint, and William Boyd—thereupon left for the University of Groningen, where their presence troubled less-militant Covenanters in Rotterdam and Scotland. The latter feared that the radical tenets of the students from the United Societies would prove harmful to the Presbyterian cause when the young men returned to Scotland. The fourth, John Nisbet, a Northumberland native who had studied at the University of Edinburgh and had allegedly been involved in a plot to assassinate the bishop of Edinburgh, remained in the London area, where he was a tutor in the home of the Congregationalist minister Matthew Meade (alias Richardson) at Stepney. Contacts between the United Societies and Shaftesbury's circle apparently were initiated through Nisbet and Meade.[105] By December 1682, Nisbet had written to Earlston, using the latter's alias—Alexander Pringle—and "signifying what was done" at the behest of the United Societies. Nisbet thereupon reported to Renwick (alias Henry Emerson), with an additional message that may have pertained to projected radical activity, especially since these dissidents are known to have couched their scheming in commercial terms:

As for writting a Letter concerning the bill I sent[,] the gentleman most concerned thinks it needless[.] Only he with the rest would have you know that it is out of Love to the cause they understand that party is suffering for, & particularly in token of their respects to Mr. Caroll (to wit his fellowes). If you writ any thing direct it for me to be given to Mrs. [Elizabeth] Gaunt & [t]hat the discourse be generall to them all.[106]

At their meeting on 14 February, held in the parish of Eaglesham, south of Glasgow, the United Societies issued an invitation to five ministers to preach and administer the sacraments to them. Three of the five—Michael Bruce and the Galloway rebels Alexander Peden and Samuel Arnot—were in Ireland, but neither they nor the other two—Thomas Forrester and John Hepburn, both of whom had preached at field conventicles—accepted. The Societies' failure undoubtedly stemmed primarily from their position on tyrannicide, an issue they addressed in an undated "Apollogetick Call of the United Presbiters to the Ministers in the Church of Scotland": "Its objected by some of you, that wee cannot Depose a tyraunt untill wee sett up another magistrate: To which wee answer, Is it not known that Salus populi est suprema Lex." Because the people "have all power radically in themselves," they can "assume the fiduciall Trust" and bestow it on another person or retain it themselves until "the Lord choise such as he will establish." In most respects—with the obvious exception of the theocratic overtones in the last sentence—this was similar to the position John Locke would soon espouse.[107]

The same general meeting in Eaglesham parish also received a letter from Nisbet in London. Although it was "darkly written," the delegates ascertained that unnamed militants in England were prepared to join them and desired information about the Societies' plans. The representatives appointed Thomas Lining, George MacVey, and Robert Goodwin to draft a reply and also directed that "friends" in Edinburgh prepare a similar response, both of which would be considered at the next general meeting. Assuming that the English militants were Congregationalists or Baptists, the delegates concluded that formal union was impossible, although they were prepared to answer additional inquiries; none came.

The meeting on 14 February further resolved that the United Societies would defend themselves with force of arms in the event of an attempted popish massacre—another reminder of the potency of anti-Catholic feelings. To this end the representatives decided to commence military training in units comprising members from three or four contiguous societies. They even adopted a national password: "Reformation."[108]

Shortly after the Eaglesham meeting the Societies received unspecified letters from the Netherlands that prompted them to recall Earlston to discuss "several weighty affairs." They also received a letter from Robert Murray, one of Shaftesbury's agents, written in cant using the metaphor of a marriage about to be solemnized. The record of the general meeting on 8 May reveals that the mysterious subject of the letter from abroad was the proposed uprising being planned in London by Monmouth and his associates. Earlston had first learned of the plot from Nisbet and Murray at the time of the 1682 London shrieval election. According to them the principal conspirators were Monmouth, Shaftesbury, and Ford Lord Grey, while the key Scots were Sir John Cochrane, Robert Baillie of Jerviswood, and Sir Hugh Campbell of Cessnock and his son. Not until December 1682 or January 1683, when Earlston was in the Netherlands, did he learn that Argyll had reportedly agreed to enlist 7,000 to 10,000 Highlanders as well as to obtain weapons, for which unnamed Englishmen would provide him with £10,000.[109]

Earlston (under the alias Alexander Pringle) subsequently received a letter from Nisbet dated 20 March 1683, which seemingly dealt with business matters but in fact related to the conspiracy. Appendix A reproduces relevant portions of the letter with the hidden meaning, which Earlston revealed following his arrest, interspersed in parentheses; the letter is a prime example of the "canting" language used by the radicals to communicate their secrets.

Recalled to England, Earlston met with Nisbet and Murray in London. The conspirators, he learned, would soon rebel in England, with six or seven simultaneous rendezvous at such places as London and Coventry. They expected thousands to support them in Yorkshire. Murray invited Earlston to meet with William Lord Russell, Philip Lord Wharton (whose loyalty they deemed uncertain), Ford Lord Grey, Robert Ferguson, and several ex-Cromwellian officers. Although Earlston declined, he subsequently received a letter in canting language dated 2 May from Robert Johnston, one of Grey's men, offering to accompany him to Scotland to confer with members of the United Societies. Johnston, however, apparently did not make the trip with Earlston.[110]

When the general meeting convened in Edinburgh on 8 May, Earlston reported on his activities in the Netherlands and almost certainly his discussions with Nisbet and Murray. The principal item of debate was whether to instigate a rebellion against the government; the majority ultimately resolved not to rise in arms except in self-defense or for the deliverance of their fellow believers. In keeping with the advice they had received from the Netherlands, the delegates decided to wait until the Spirit brought both parties "further light therein," especially since rebelling at that time would have exposed them to "the fury of the enemy." Of particular importance is the fact that the representatives expected others to rebel, for they expressed concern that some of their members would split the United Societies by joining the insurrection without the prior authorization of the general meeting. By this point they had learned of the plotting in England, and it was the question of their involvement in this conspiracy that made the debate so urgent.[111]

The general meeting formulated a statement to send to "the Confederators" in London; the delegates called it "The Reason of the Sufferings and Actings of the True (Though Greatly Reproached, and Persecuted) Presbyterian, Anti-Prelatick, Anti-Erastian Party in Scotland." Although they endorsed the right to revolt against any magistrate who contravened the laws and insisted on their rights as freeborn subjects, they declined to cooperate with "a malignant party" of men of blood and profanity or with sectaries in an uprising; to do so, they argued, would be to join "with the public sins whereof they are guilty." While the United Societies did not insist on fighting in an army composed solely of saints, neither would they do battle alongside those manifestly hostile to God's principles—men "against whom the sword of justice should have free course."[112]

The meeting of 8 May also renewed the Societies' previous attempt to recruit ministers by drawing up "A Call by the Remnant of the True Presbyterians of the Church of Scotland." Although the Societies felt the absence of ministers keenly, reports from Brackel about the progress of their students at Groningen were heartening. With an air of expectation and apocalyptic fervency, the delegates responded to him: "This is a ground of encouragement for us to hope that our God is returning to covenanted Scotland, to ride prosperously on the white horse of the gospel, conquering and to conquer; and to be head and king over his church."[113]

After the meeting Earlston and his servant, George Aitken (or Atkin, alias Edward Leviston), left for Newcastle, where they boarded a ship bound for the Netherlands. Before the vessel had left English waters on 1 June, both men were arrested and a box of documents they had desperately thrown overboard was retrieved. In the cache were copies of "The Reasons of the Sufferings and Actings" and "A Call by the Remnant" as well as the Societies' reply to Brackel, new commissions for Earlston and Hamilton, Nisbet's letter of 20 March to Earlston, and addresses of dissidents in London, Scotland, and the Netherlands, including those for Abraham Holmes and Jeremiah Marsden (alias Zachary Ralfson).[114] The government now had substantive evidence about the planned insurrection that was but one aspect of the so-called Rye House conspiracy.

"Let Nimrod End His Reign"

The Tangled Web of Whig Conspiracy

The jury's verdict of *ignoramus* in Shaftesbury's trial and the government's decision to drop the prosecution on 13 February 1682 proved
to be only a temporary setback in the Tory program to curb the
Whigs. The ensuing sixteen months witnessed one of the most intense political struggles in British history, particularly as the more
radical Whigs and their Scottish allies adopted extreme measures.

The Tory Policy of Repression and the Whig Response

As early as April 1681 the London *Gazette* had begun to publish a
lengthy stream of Tory-inspired addresses supporting the king. The
address from Southampton, for example, denounced both the popish and the "Phanatical, Ambitious, and Antimonarchical Parties,"
the intent of which was to enslave the country to the "Tyranny of an
Armed Multitude." The theme was often reiterated, with the twin
dangers characterized in terms of the Spanish Inquisition and "the
rigid severity of Geneva Reformers." The addresses repudiated the
Association, affirmed support for the traditional succession, recalled
the specter of civil war, and urged the vigorous execution of the laws
against Catholics and dissenters, both of which were represented as
threats to civil order. The court was determined to turn the public
mood firmly against Whigs and nonconformists, a policy that bore
fruit. During the fall of 1682 in Bristol, long notorious as a center of
radical activity, young "addressers" wore scarlet ribbons in their hats
emblazoned with the words *Rex & Haredes* ("the King and the
Guilds") to demonstrate their loyalty, "in opposition to the late fac-

tious *Blew*, and former *Green* Marks of the *Kings head* and other Antimonarchical Clubs."[1]

The impact of the Tory campaign was especially noticeable in the treatment of conventicles. In the fall of 1680 the earl of Anglesey had been able to reflect favorably on the "undisturbed libertie" enjoyed by nonconformists in London because they had been "found to be otherwise peaceable people & loyall subjects." Noting the absence of prosecution in the London area, Sir Leoline Jenkins remarked about the same time that "the true Season to suppresse Sectaries hath been long since Lost; they have putt us now upon the Defensive." Hardcore conservatives were, of course, displeased at this policy and agitated for the suppression of conventicles. Failure to repress them, in the judgment of one conservative, would threaten the king's prerogative, turn the parish churches into stables, and transform traditional liberties "into a Plebean Tyrannie."[2]

Some magistrates responded to the court's shifting mood in 1681 by vigorously repressing illegal religious meetings. Such was the case in Salisbury (where dissenters were physically abused), Leicestershire, and parts of Essex and Norfolk. In the autumn, efforts to curb conventicles were under way in Middlesex, Southwark, Stepney, Bristol, and Canterbury (where the conventiclers were armed).[3] Other areas followed in early 1682, including Cornwall, Devon, Gloucestershire, Hertfordshire, Dorset, the Isle of Ely, Nottingham, and Newcastle.[4] In light of the government's recent laxity, other magistrates were understandably hesitant to prosecute and looked to Westminster for explicit directions. Even after they had resumed a policy of repression, Middlesex justices were of such a mind, as were their counterparts in Monmouthshire (where conventiclers reportedly had fresh supplies of weapons) and the mayors of Lyme and Plymouth.[5] Despite the mounting conservative tide, some magistrates either were reluctant to prosecute conventiclers, as at Dover and Sandwich, or openly supported them, as at Reading.[6] Such actions stemmed from various motives, ranging from compatible religious convictions to a sense that prosecution was futile. Sometimes, as at Windsor, officials were slow to act for economic considerations: "Our magistrates here, are such as live by their Trades, & will not loose a Customer to execute a Law."[7]

The renewed campaign against illegal religious services met with considerable resistance, and inflamed feelings on both sides. Many dissenters would have agreed with their unnamed compatriot who denounced the Conventicle Act as contrary to divine law, which "no where alows Majestrates to Robb men of their goods & putt them in prison & to Ruin them for circumstanciall errors in Judgment about Religion." Conventiclers increasingly relied on lookouts to warn of approaching magistrates, helped their preachers escape, changed their meeting places, or even barricaded their doors. Nathaniel Vincent's meetinghouse in Southwark was designed for hasty egress: "Almost every seat that adjoins to the Sides of the Conventicle has a door like the Sally Port of a Fireship to make their escape by. And in each door, a smal Peep-hole like to Taverns & Alehouses door, to Ken the person before they let them in." Although some dissenters in the west and south began arming themselves, shots were apparently never fired. An orthodox cleric in Wiltshire, however, had his life threatened, and informers in London were "severely treated."[8]

The fruit of the Tory policy of repression was not conformity but defiance. When magistrates ordered Nathaniel Vincent to desist from preaching, he refused, citing the King of Kings as his authority; when the justices commanded his audience to disperse, they were drowned out by psalm-singing while the preacher made his escape.[9] One nonconformist congregation purportedly responded to the persecution by singing a hymn with an unmistakable allusion to Charles II's rule:

> By Babel, Once Confusion came;
>   Lord send it Once again:
> And in Confusion rayse thy Name,
>   Let Nimrod End his Reign.[10]

Defiance was blatant in Bristol despite the resolve of the sheriff, Sir John Knight, to quash dissent. By March 1682, when 86 Quakers and 52 Presbyterians had been recently committed, the prisons were overflowing. Although the mayor, Sir Thomas Earle, boasted in June that the conventicles had been wholly suppressed, three months later the *True Protestant Mercury* carried a report that 1,200 dissenters would soon be indicted.[11] In London the sheriffs connived to help the nonconformists in early 1682 by giving them advance notice that writs were about to be served on them, and some of the aldermen refused to act against conventiclers. Dissenters as well as Whig political leaders thus had a stake in the forthcoming elections. Tumults erupted in the City in June 1682 when magistrates attempted to curb the conventicles.[12]

The Tory campaign to curtail illegal religious assemblies and the widespread spirit of confrontation it provoked were important considerations among Whigs and nonconformists as they weighed their options in 1682. An indication of what might lie in store for dissenting clergy had come in November 1681 when eleven of them were prosecuted for recusancy and violating the Five-Mile Act and fined a total of £4,840.[13] Among the eleven were two ministers subsequently implicated in the Rye House plotting, Robert Ferguson and Matthew Meade. A third, John Owen, was closely linked to them, since Ferguson had served as his assistant beginning in 1674. None of the three, however, was deterred by the government's attempt to silence them. Meade did become more cautious, and when magistrates stormed his conventicle at Stepney in January 1682 they found someone else in the pulpit. Owen seems to have been more brazen; informers observed him preaching to his well-known Leadenhall Street congregation the following month, on which occasion he pointedly omitted the king from his prayers.[14]

Meade as well as Owen was familiar with Ferguson, and Owen's house was the site of a meeting between Ferguson and Francis Charlton. Owen's concern was reflected in his preface to *An Humble Testimony unto the Goodness and Severity of God in His Dealing with Sinful Churches and Nations*, published by Nathaniel Ponder in 1681. At this point, serious consideration of an insurrection lay in the future, though the implications of the Association are consistent with discussions of some form of active resistance. Owen knew that some of those to whom he preached were considering means of deliverance from the expected *"publick Calamities"*—an obvious reference to a Catholic succession—and he warned of potential danger: "But whereas they fix themselves on various and opposite *Ways* and *Means* for this End, the Conflict of their *Counsels* and *Designs* encreaseth our Danger, and is like to prove our Ruine." Owen went on to advocate repentance and *"universal Reformation"* as the only way for the country to avoid destruction.[15]

Whether Owen was trying to curb militant Whigs or create the impression of innocent piety for the dissidents in his circle is arguable. Beyond dispute, however, is the fact that in the critical year 1682 he enunciated a doctrine of active resistance in circumstances where religious and civil rights were threatened. After the Reformation, he averred,

the Protection and Preservation of Religion was taken up by sundry Potentates, free Princes and Cities, who had a legal Right and Power to protect themselves and their subjects in the Profession of it. It hath been and is at this day incorporated into the Laws, Rights and Interests of sundry Nations, which ought to be defended. And no instance can be given of any people defending themselves in the Profession of the Protestant Religion by Arms, but where together with their Religion their Enemies did design and endeavour to destroy those Rights, Liberties and Priviledges.[16]

Ferguson too espoused the legitimacy of active resistance. While the assertion of such tenets does not prove that either they or anyone else actually plotted an insurrection, it does outline the intellectual framework in which the discussion of options took place. It is particularly striking that these views were espoused in public at the very time the Tories had taken the offensive.

At the heart of that offensive was a concerted attempt to wrest control of London and therefore of its juries from the Whigs. Under the influence of wealthy, conservative aldermen, the elections for the Common Council in December 1681 produced enough Tory gains to leave the body evenly divided. Although the Whigs had clearly sustained a setback, the shrieval election scheduled for June 1682 was more important because it would determine whether the Whigs would continue to benefit from sympathetic juries. In the meantime the Whigs sought to advance their cause on several fronts, the most important of which involved plans for the expected summoning of a new Parliament. The earl of Essex, William Lord Howard of Escrick, Sir Patience Ward, and others began compiling information on those who allegedly promoted belief in "the presbiterian sham plott" and were encouraging the Tory addresses with their inflammatory link-

age of "Popish & Fanatique Plotts." Essex and his colleagues reportedly were scheming to impeach a large number of royalists, including
the queen, the duke of York, Clarendon, the three chief justices, Sir
George Jeffreys, Sir Leoline Jenkins, the marquess of Worcester, and
the earls of Halifax, Peterborough, and Feversham. These activities
led to suspicions of a Whig plot; Roger Morrice's "Entr'ing Book"
contains such a notation for early February 1682: "A new Plott is,
and hath been carryed on for many weekes by the Whiggs against
the Government, but no sufficient proofe comes in of it yet." The
mounting tension on both sides was evident when Howard, in the
presence of Essex, accused Halifax, with the backing of Secretary
Jenkins and Sir Edward Seymour, of having hired men to assassinate him.[17]

For his part, Shaftesbury embarked on a legal campaign designed
both to vindicate his name and to put his enemies on the defensive.
The heart of this endeavor entailed the initiation of legal action
against Richard Graham, the Treasury solicitor, and others on the
grounds that they had conspired to suborn witnesses against him.
The earl's legal targets ranged from Justice Edmund Warcup to such
informers as John Booth and the Macnamara brothers. Apart from
causing the Tories to divert considerable legal talent and money to
defend the accused, Shaftesbury's efforts collapsed when the lord
chief justice agreed to defense motions for a change of venue. Unwilling to risk losing in one of the counties, where the Tory addresses had already inflamed public opinion against him, Shaftesbury dropped his suits in May 1682. The legal skirmish underscored
the importance to both sides of controlling the juries; Warcup, for
instance, had been in fear of losing his estate because of Shaftesbury's
action, and the earl was now increasingly aware of the threat to
his position should the Whigs suffer defeat in the London shrieval
election.[18]

Commencing on 17 March 1682, a series of dinner parties was
hosted by leading Whigs, presumably to demonstrate the vitality of
their cause and perhaps lay the groundwork for the forthcoming
election. Among the diners were Shaftesbury, Monmouth, Essex,
Grey, and Howard of Escrick.[19] The Tories staged a rival dinner of
their own on 20 April, at which the featured guest was the duke of

York, who had arrived in London twelve days earlier. Whig efforts to counter this fete with a feast honoring Monmouth were blocked when, at the court's insistence, the lord mayor and aldermen banned it as an unlawful assembly. The Whigs' decision not to defy the prohibition was a strategic error, especially since both sheriffs, Thomas Pilkington and Benjamin Shute, were partisan Whig supporters. Although Whig defiance might have strengthened the crown's case in the *quo warranto* proceedings to replace the City's charter, a Whig show of force might equally have persuaded the Tories not to risk using trickery against their opponents in the imminent shrieval election. This dinner-party defeat, coupled with the dropping of Shaftesbury's suits and the king's refusal to summon a new Parliament, kept the Whigs on the defensive. "I heare from London," James told Prince William, "that the factious and phanatike party are much cast downe, by his Ma[jesty] having forbid their feast." Militant Whigs were not, however, willing to surrender.[20]

As their candidates for sheriff, the Whigs settled on two merchants who had served on Shaftesbury's jury, John Dubois and Thomas Papillon. The Tories tried to preempt the election by reviving the old custom of allowing the lord mayor to select one of the sheriffs, in this case Dudley North. Inevitable disputes forced a delay of the poll until 5 July, when the results gave the Whig candidates a clear triumph over North and Ralph Box. The Privy Council, however, refused to accept the tallies and ordered new proceedings. On 14 July the lord mayor, relying on a show of hands by a mere minority of the liverymen, declared North elected. The following day two competing polls were conducted in the Common Hall; the lord mayor chose to ignore the one that Papillon and Dubois had won, declaring Box the second sheriff. Box's decision to pay a fine rather than serve in such a contentious atmosphere gave the Whigs a second opportunity, but they continued to insist that no new poll was needed because Papillon and Dubois had already been legally elected. In September the lord mayor, supported by a majority of the aldermen, had recourse to another specious show of hands to declare Peter Rich, a political ally of Secretary Jenkins, the second sheriff. The Tories completed their triumph in October by electing one of their own, Sir William Pritchard, as the new lord mayor, but only after disqualifying enough Whig votes to alter the outcome. The king had won, but only by making a mockery of the election process and revealing his determination to destroy the Whigs politically. Moreover, at key points during the dispute, including the poll on 5 July, Whig partisans brandished weapons, and in September the lord mayor had to be rescued by armed supporters. As Gary De Krey has observed, the lord mayor's growing reliance on the trained bands and the royal guards to maintain order "only stimulated further resistance to 'military power.'" The hotly disputed shrieval election, De Krey notes, "seemingly marked a transition from the occasional Whig resort to rhetorical violence and physical force to the rationalization and legitimization of such behaviour as instruments in Whig party warfare."[21]

In the fall of 1682, political and religious dissent faced the gravest challenge of Charles' reign. With control of the City and the juries gone, the conventicles under attack, and no likelihood of a new Parliament, the Whigs had few options. The earl of Huntingdon and George Booth, Lord Delamere, had earlier made their peace with the king, but the rest of the leading Whigs held firm. One of Shaftesbury's agents, Robert Murray, met with Huguenots in Paris in August, possibly in connection with the Carolina project or perhaps to seek financial support for a projected insurrection in England. On 29 September, Shaftesbury prudently went underground and took the alias Mr. Tucker.[22]

When Shaftesbury went into hiding the radicals had nothing like an effective national organization, although many committed militants were affiliated with political clubs that provided an opportunity to share ideas and consider courses of action, such as supporting public demonstrations and publishing propaganda. Both the Whigs and the Tories had such clubs, which met in taverns, coffeehouses, and private homes. The clubs were not new to the period of the exclusion crisis; John Wildman, for instance, had presided over a republican club at Nonsuch House from 1658 until the early 1660s. The Tory club that convened in Fuller's Rents between 1679 and 1684 consisted of Danby loyalists, such as Sir Peter Pett, whereas the club that met at the Warder within Ludgate beginning in the fall of 1681 comprised Tories chiefly interested in supporting the court against the exclusionists. Organized by the earl of Ailesbury and others, this club provided an opportunity for close interaction between the Privy Council and the City's preeminent citizens; in a matter of weeks this group had nearly 300 members and soon played a role, according to Ailesbury, in the Tory triumph in the London shrieval election of 1682.[23]

The Green Ribbon Club, which J. H. Plumb once aptly called a "political dining-club," was of course the most famous Whig organization and was in existence by 1674. De Krey has noted that at least a quarter of its adherents were freemen of the corporation of London or involved in City politics; most were apparently nonconformists as well. Situated at the King's Head tavern in Fleet Street near the Inns of Court, the club numbered among its members Francis Jenks, Slingsby Bethel, John Freke, Lord Grey, Lord Howard, Robert West, Richard Goodenough, John Ayloffe, Richard Nelthorpe, Lawrence Braddon, Colonel Roderick Mansell, Sir Robert Peyton, Sir John Trenchard, Henry Booth, and John Row of Bristol. Most of these men subsequently became embroiled in the Rye House plotting, by which time they had subsidized journalists and encouraged antipapal bonfires on 5 November and the burning of papal effigies on the 17th, the anniversary of Elizabeth I's accession. When West's chamber was searched after his surrender in June 1683, magistrates found a record of the club's membership and the resolutions it had passed through 29 June 1681. Following his capture in 1685, Nathaniel Wade provided more names of club members, including his former fellow-conspirators Francis Goodenough, John Rumsey, Aaron Smith, Edward Norton, Robert Blaney, Christopher Battiscombe, Zachary Bourne, and the clothier Joseph Tiley of Bristol.[24]

Among other radical associations of note—29 of which have been identified in the London area alone—was the Nag's Head Club in Cheapside, which was linked to Shaftesbury. Its leaders included Jenks, who reportedly wanted to incite a mob to march on Whitehall and demand justice after the Whig defeat in the 1682 shrieval election, and Bethel, who allegedly boasted of getting even with the court. Shaftesbury also had ties to clubs that met at the Swan in Fish Street, the Angel near the Old Exchange, and the Queen's Arms. At the Swan during the winter of 1679–80, Shaftesbury, Grey, Howard, the earl of Huntingdon, and other peers addressed the need for Parliament to sit. Another group, this one with ties to Buckingham, often met at the Salutation tavern in Lombard Street. Its predominantly republican and Baptist members included Colonel Henry Danvers, Major John Gladman, the printer Francis Smith, Lieutenant-Colonel Ralph Alexander, William Radden, and Thomas Parsons. When Samuel Oates informed on these groups in mid-1682, he claimed the Nag's Head Club was disenchanted with the Salutation dissidents because of the latter's relations with the French; Buckingham and Wildman, among others, had indeed visited Louis XIV's court in 1678. In July 1683, James Harris would inform Secretary Jenkins that the Nag's Head Club had numbered 300, the Salutation group 50, and a club at the Angel and Crown in Threadneedle Street 200.[25]

Members of the Green Ribbon Club, notably Rumsey, Row, and Tiley, were in contact with the Horseshoe (formerly the White Hart) Club of Bristol, which had been organized to support the election of Sir Robert Atkyns and Sir John Knight to the House of Commons. Its secretary was the linen-draper Joseph Whetham, Nathaniel Wade's brother-in-law. In addition to Wade and his brother William, a grocer, the members included Thomas Scrope, son of the regicide Adrian Scrope; James Holloway, who would join the Rye House plotters; Drs. John Griffith and Ichabod Chauncey, the latter an Independent minister; and Rumsey, Row, and Tiley, who were also members of London's Green Ribbon Club. The Horseshoe group numbered approximately 120, but its rolls were destroyed before the state could confiscate them. Other than those who belonged to the Green Ribbon Club, applicants for membership had to provide surety to keep the proceedings secret. Members of the Horseshoe Club raised substantial sums of money, though the member who revealed this, the soap-boiler Samuel Gale, claimed not to know the purpose for which the funds had been used. A second Bristol group, the Mermaid Club, included some of the same members as the Horseshoe Club, such as Chauncey and Griffith, but apparently the Mermaid group did not become involved in the Rye House plotting.[26]

Extreme Measures: Early Plans for an Uprising

By the time Shaftesbury went into hiding, he and his closest associates had begun to reconsider a scheme first broached in 1680 in the context of the exclusion crisis. The evidence for this plan is found in the confession signed by Lord Grey in October 1685 after his arrest for complicity in the Monmouth rebellion, and is summarized in his testimony at the trial of Charles Lord Gerard of Brandon the following month. Shaftesbury's biographer, K. H. D. Haley, doubts the reliability of the confession because it is self-serving, vague about dates, short on objective evidence, and replete with reports of conversations. Equally wary, Doreen Milne noted Grey's attempt to exonerate himself as much as possible by accusing others, and questioned his reliability because of his endeavor "to present as a rational and closely connected narrative the disjointed meetings and plans of various groups of people." The confession indisputably served Grey's interests and is imprecise about dates, but when used judiciously and in conjunction with other sources it is a useful document. According to Grey, Shaftesbury first advanced the idea of using force to compel Charles to bar James' succession shortly after the House of Lords rejected the Exclusion Bill in November 1680. The only way to obtain such an act, Shaftesbury reportedly argued, is by force of arms, "for the King would rather throw away a hundred Brothers than loose his Crowne." At that time, according to Grey, he, Monmouth, Russell, and Sir Thomas Armstrong did not encourage Shaftesbury. Some nine months earlier, however, Henry Sidney had noted in his diary that Monmouth himself had resolved "to take up arms in case the King dies, for he will conclude him murdered."[27]

By the time Grey told his story in the fall of 1685, Shaftesbury, Monmouth, and Armstrong were dead, but it is difficult to see what he could have gained by fabricating an alleged conspiracy about radicals who were already in the grave. The pardon he sought required a reasonably full confession, the details of which harmonized with the facts already known to the government. Before Grey's testimony the public had been told that the conspiracy had commenced in 1682; Grey therefore had no reason to discuss events in 1680 unless he suspected the government already knew what had happened in that period as a result of Monmouth's private meeting with the king in November 1683. Although the specific details of that session were never revealed, Monmouth had reportedly made a full confession (see below, Chapter 6), including information new to the government.[28] Knowing this in 1685, Grey was not likely to have invented a story whose falsity would have cast doubt on the rest of his confession and destroyed his chance for a pardon. His confession was indeed self-serving, but that alone does not provide ample grounds to reject it as evidence. On the contrary, unsure of what Monmouth had told the king, Grey could not afford to lie. That his confession was sometimes imprecise and sketchy suggests its basic veracity; fabricating detail is easier than recalling it for events extending over a period of five years. Grey's testimony cannot be discounted, although it must be rigorously tested against other evidence wherever possible.

Some confirmation for Grey's account of the 1680 conspiracy can be found in the confession of Sir Thomas Player's servant, John Rouse, prior to his execution for high treason in July 1683. Rouse, a Scot, was a minor but trusted figure among the Whigs. After the dissolution of the Oxford Parliament he channeled £1,500 from the Whigs to various Irish witnesses, including Mrs. Fitzharris, and, like Shaftesbury, he was subsequently accused of treason but escaped with an *ignoramus* verdict.[29] After his arrest for complicity in the Rye House Plot, he testified that prior to the Oxford Parliament he had seen Monmouth, Russell, Grey, Armstrong, Major John Manley, and others gather at Shaftesbury's house, apparently to discuss an insurrection; confirmation of this, Rouse claimed, came from the earl's servants. From his presence at Whig political clubs he knew the Whigs were split between republicans and those who wanted Monmouth on the throne, and he blamed this division for the delay in implementing the rebellion.[30]

Initially thwarted by Monmouth and his associates, Shaftesbury and Colonel John Rumsey planned to launch an uprising at Taunton following the conclusion of Trinity term in June 1681. On the earl's behalf Rumsey had solicited the support of Nathaniel Wade, a barrister of the Middle Temple, shortly after the dissolution of the Oxford Parliament, but a few days later Rumsey told Wade "it was put off." "From that time the matter slept," reported Wade, "till about May the year following."[31]

Consideration of an insurrection revived again when Argyll, accompanied by William Veitch, a Covenanting preacher and former Galloway rebel, and Captain John Lockyer, formerly an associate of

Thomas Blood's, came to London following the earl's escape from
Edinburgh Castle in 1681. Lockyer helped Argyll find a hiding place
at the home of Lieutenant-Colonel Abraham Holmes, a veteran of
the radical community. One of Shaftesbury's pensioners, Edmund
Everard of Gray's Inn, stayed with Argyll in the same house, "the
ordinary resort of people ill-affected to the Court." Veitch informed
Shaftesbury of the arrival of Argyll, who took the alias Mr. Hope.
Shortly thereafter the cause of the two earls was publicly linked by
Robert Ferguson, who appended seven pages on Argyll's case to *The
Third Part of No Protestant Plot*. In March 1682, while Shaftesbury
sought revenge against his accusers in the courts and planned for the
sheriffs' election, Argyll tried to procure weapons from the Netherlands; dissidents, in fact, had been shipping arms from that country
to the British Isles the previous spring and summer. Although Argyll's agent, the Glasgow merchant John Campbell, virtually com-
mandeered a ship for this purpose in March, the earl's plan was
dashed when the vessel disappeared, its fate unknown.[32]

Argyll was apparently hoping at this point to use the weapons to
launch rebellions in Scotland and Ireland. To this end, Argyll con-
tacted Arthur Forbes, Viscount Granard. Although the latter had
dutifully compiled information on radical activities in northern Ireland for the government,[33] he was sympathetic with moderate Presbyterians, and his growing concern for the future of Protestantism
in the British Isles may have driven him, like the earl of Essex, to
consider militant action to prevent a Catholic succession. Veitch and
the Lord of Lorne, Argyll's son, arranged for Granard to meet the
earl at the Dolphin tavern in Lombard Street, where for several
hours they discussed "what they thought proper for them to do to
prevent the evils that threatened both church and state." Subsequent
to this meeting Veitch, now using the alias Captain Forbes, served
as a courier between Granard and Argyll. At their second and final
meeting, again at the Dolphin, the two men, Veitch claimed, had
agreed to join forces with Monmouth to launch an insurrection.
Granard reportedly pledged to send 5,000 troops from Ireland to
support Argyll after the latter had begun the rebellion in western
Scotland. However, an anonymous account by someone who had
been present for at least one of the meetings insists that Granard

refused to participate in a rebellion and urged Argyll to trust Charles and James. Any thought Granard may have had of supporting Argyll was rendered void when the government, alerted to their consultations, summoned the viscount to return from Ireland, where he had gone after seeing Argyll.[34]

Granard was no radical but a man who combined his Protestant convictions with political pragmatism. Although purportedly sympathetic to Monmouth and Argyll in 1685, he failed to support them, and in the revolution of 1688–89 forsook James only in 1690. Granard, in other words, was reluctant in practice to commit himself to any revolutionary political venture and would hardly have contemplated anything more in 1682 than an uprising limited to the exclusion of James from the succession and the ruling circle around Charles. Granard was undoubtedly the "Considerable Courtier" whose contacts with Argyll excited suspicion in Monmouth's circle. Interestingly, Captain Thomas Walcott testified in 1683 that Ferguson had informed him that Granard would "head" the Scots in Ireland, that he had presented two addresses to the king on Argyll's behalf, and that when these were rejected he and Argyll had dined together and "adjusted the matter," presumably their political aims.[35]

The king's illness in May 1682 triggered fresh discussions about forcing him to exclude the duke of York. When Monmouth, Grey, and Armstrong learned of Charles' ailing health, they convened at Shaftesbury's home to plot a course of action in the event the king died. After some deliberation they adjourned to enable Shaftesbury to consult with unnamed men in the City, whose support for an uprising he obtained, according to Grey, contingent on assistance from the earl, Monmouth, and Russell. When the conspirators reconvened the same May evening, Russell and Manley were present; at Shaftesbury's request Manley had already been to Wapping, where he obtained promises of support. The May cabal agreed that if Charles died they would rebel, with a view to summoning a Parliament to determine the succession; in the meantime they would use their weapons to protect themselves and the Protestant faith. This plan was dropped, according to Grey, when the king recovered, but the discussions were clearly not forgotten.[36]

About the same time a smith named Fox, according to his own

confession (March 1683), accepted a commission from the earl of
Clare's steward, a man named Cawdron, to assassinate the king.
Clare himself, of course, was a prominent Whig peer with ties to
Shaftesbury. Algernon Sidney and Richard Stretton, a Presbyterian
minister who preached at Shoemakers' Hall and other places in
London, were putatively allied with Clare in this scheme. In October
1683, during the government's investigation of the Rye House plot-
ting, Fox offered more information about Clare, as did Samuel
Starkey, who had been employed by Aaron Smith and Nathaniel
Hartshorne, Richard Goodenough's assistant.³⁷ The evidence for the
involvement of Clare, Sidney, and Stretton in an assassination scheme
is, however, insubstantial.

Argyll met secretly with Shaftesbury in the summer of 1682. Grey
would later claim that in these talks Argyll demanded £30,000 to
fund an insurrection in Scotland, and Ferguson remarked that Argyll
had indeed insisted on financial support. As Ferguson recalled, nothing substantive came of the discussions because neither earl trusted
the other. The failed negotiations, he said, proved only "what little
preparation . . . had been made for relieving themselves by forceable
means, & what small probability there was of bringing the Grandees
of the party, into union of Councils & endeavours for vindicating
the Rights & Liberties of their Country's."³⁸ According to Gilbert
Burnet, Argyll conferred frequently with Monmouth, which would
generally accord with Veitch's account, although nothing of substance is known about these discussions. Argyll was still in London
in August 1682, but by year's end he had fled to the Netherlands.
Veitch and Holmes remained behind to serve as his agents.³⁹ Judging
from the role that Argyll played in the scheming that continued
apace in late 1682 and early 1683, his talks with Shaftesbury and Monmouth in London may have been more meaningful than Ferguson
suggests.

Magistrates intercepted two letters, one partly encoded and the
second almost entirely in cipher, pertaining to Argyll's departure and
continuing discussions of an insurrection. Even decoded, the epistles
are so obscure that the government probably had little understanding of their contents. The partially encoded letter was directed to

the printer Francis Smith in Rotterdam by Ann Smith, a friend of Abraham Holmes and the wife of a wealthy sugar-baker who had hidden Argyll in London; in mid to late 1683 she and her husband would offer hospitality to Argyll in Utrecht, and in 1685 she would provide funds for his ill-fated expedition. In her letter, written on or shortly after 8 December 1682, she notified Francis Smith that an unidentified agent was en route to Rotterdam and possibly Amsterdam, in part to see him and perhaps to consult as well with Shaftesbury, Ferguson, and their compatriots. Mrs. Smith also informed the printer that another messenger—a friend of Gordon of Earlston's identified only as "Langlangs" (probably Robert Langlands)— was conveying something previously requested by Smith, presumably money, a manuscript to be published, or a recently printed radical work. This the messenger was to give to Earlston, with whom he was intimate according to Veitch. She also enclosed "a line" to her friend, which Francis Smith was to use as he saw fit inasmuch as "Mr. P." and Ferguson were well acquainted.[40]

The second letter was directed to "Mr. Wood's friend"—Argyll— by "Mark White," an alias employed by one of the earl's supporters. The author thanked Argyll for his letter of 27 November before expressing chagrin that the earl had left without telling him after previously engaging the writer "past retreat in ane affaire of that nature." The "busines," he feared, might ruin him. "You have taken the nearest and surest way to your own distruction and myn to goe to the place wher you now are [the Netherlands], when you know that ther Shafts[bury] and such other of that sort [are], so that if an angel would swear you innocent of medling [i.e., plotting] it wil not be beleeved." The author referred to previous plans to coordinate uprisings in Scotland and England: Regarding "the match," he wrote, you know how the young lady (Monmouth) will look on me "that could say nothing all this time. And you may be sure what you have done in going away will make the easiest things difficult." After announcing his intention to go to Scotland at the end of January, Argyll's associate complained that he suffered

for mens faults, I mean what are so esteemed in my unkle, father, and you, and am like to be ruined for endeavouring to serve my father and you, any other great difficulty as thogh the match [i.e., the uprising], she would yet be entertained. I know not [to] what length you will goe or if you wil al stand to what [I] shall . . . offer.

Although he refused to excuse the fact that Argyll had left him in the lurch, the author pledged: "I will once more try the matter and make the proposition so that the yong lady's best and greatest friend [Argyll?] may see it take." He promised to keep Argyll posted and hoped the earl would follow his advice. Although the precise meaning of the letter is unclear, it certainly refers to the possibility of continuing efforts for coordinated uprisings in the two kingdoms. The use of both canting language and a cipher underscores the sensitivity of the message.[41]

Well before Argyll left for the Netherlands the Shaftesbury circle began planning a general insurrection as a result of the London shrieval election. The resumption of serious discussion would have begun sometime after the Privy Council repudiated the poll of 5 July 1682, in which Papillon and Dubois had defeated North and Box, and possibly just after the lord mayor declared the Tory candidates elected on the 14th and 15th. Grey subsequently admitted that he had met with Shaftesbury, Monmouth, Russell, and Armstrong at Thanet House, the earl's home in Aldersgate Street. Fearing their lives would be in danger as soon as the new sheriffs took up their offices, Shaftesbury, Monmouth, and Russell allegedly argued for an insurrection. "Many" meetings reportedly followed.[42]

When Russell was tried for treason in July 1683, the draft of the speech he prepared for his trial emphatically denied that he had supported plans for an uprising:

That likewise is a Thing so wicked, & withall so Impracticable, that it never enter'd into my thoughts. Had I been disposed to it, I never found (by all my Observation) that there was the least Disposition or Tendency to it in the People. And 'tis known Rebellion cannot be now made here, as in former Times, by a few Great men.

Nevertheless Russell admitted that at Shaftesbury's house he had discussed the seizure of the king's guards. He objected to such a course, he claimed, because it could have led to Charles' murder, and Monmouth agreed. Indisputably, then, at Thanet House Shaftesbury,

Monmouth, Russell, Grey, and probably Armstrong (whom Russell did not mention) discussed an attempt to seize the king; the only significant dispute involves the position espoused in those talks by Russell and Monmouth. Whatever Russell advocated, by his own admission he neither ceased to associate with this group nor reported its treasonable discussions to the authorities. Moreover, his initial denial of any knowledge of such consultations renders his other protestations of innocence somewhat suspect.[43]

Grey did not record the date of the meeting at which the Shaftesbury circle decided to proceed with its plans, but it was probably in July 1682,[44] for one of the early recruits, James Holloway, subsequently testified that he had been enlisted about that time by Joseph Tiley. Holloway, a Bristol linen manufacturer, had received modest assistance from the earl of Essex in 1680 concerning a proposal to employ some 80,000 poor people in the linen industry; efforts to obtain parliamentary approval for the plan in the Oxford Parliament came to naught with its precipitate dissolution. According to Grey, the Thanet House conspirators decided that Shaftesbury and Russell would sound out London leaders for support, contingent on the willingness of other key parts of the country to take up arms. Russell agreed to ascertain the attitude of dissidents in the west by consulting with the Whigs Sir William Courtenay, Sir Francis Rolle, Sir Walter Yonge, Sir Francis Drake, and John Freke, a Shaftesbury ally. Monmouth, the cabal decided, would undertake a progress through Cheshire, the pretense for which would be determined after consultations with the earl of Macclesfield and his son, Lord Brandon, and Lord Delamere and his son, Henry Booth. Grey himself was assigned to canvas Essex with the help of Colonel Henry Mildmay and John Rotherham (or Rotheram), but this he refused to do, claiming that he could trust fewer than five gentlemen in the county and that Mildmay was "a formal, timorous blockhead, who desired nothing in this world, but being knight of the shire." "I believed him not forward enough for any thing above a Riot, and that at no time but his Owne Election neither, so [I] let it alone." The aspersions on Mildmay's character clearly stemmed from spite, for the colonel had voted for the Exclusion Bill and in 1680 had been brazen enough to trade barbs with the king. Despite Grey's refusal to canvas Essex, he remained a member of the inner cabal. Rotherham subsequently admitted that at the request of Thomas Stringer, Shaftesbury's steward, he had collected the names of the gentry in Essex from the bailiffs in the hundreds.[45]

According to Grey, Russell won the support of Rolle and Yonge, after which he directed Yonge to meet with Courtenay and Drake.[46] Freke too received instructions to confer with Drake and other western gentry. The key recruit in the southwest was Sir John Trenchard, formerly M.P. for Taunton in the three exclusion parliaments and president of the Green Ribbon Club, recorder of an opposition club in Taunton, and possibly a nonconformist. Upon being approached by Monmouth or one of his emissaries, Trenchard reportedly agreed to enlist at least 1,500 men in the Taunton area, a traditional hotbed of radical activity. The uprising would occur, Grey averred, after Monmouth returned from Cheshire. Corroborating evidence for this part of Grey's account is virtually nonexistent.[47]

The only other substantive testimony about conspiratorial activity in July came from Holloway. After his arrest in 1684 he claimed he had initially learned of the proposed insurrection from Tiley "about" July 1682. The conspirators, Tiley reportedly explained, feared that the new Tory sheriffs would believe any purported evidence against Protestants. Shaftesbury and the Protestant gentry had allegedly resolved to employ force to rescue the king from his "evill Councell, and bring them to Justice." To this end the conspirators were planning an insurrection in all three kingdoms, with activity in England to be centered in London, Bristol, Taunton, Exeter, Chester, Newcastle, and other places in the north. The plotters, Tiley allegedly told Holloway, must determine "how to Manage the affayres in Bristoll, for if [the Tories] proceed at Michaelmas in chuseing [the] Lord Mayor as they did the sherrifs, and to swearing of North & Rich it must begin in october or november, otherwise there will be some sham plot or other Contrived to take of[f] most of the stiring men in the last Parliaments." Holloway would purportedly receive further details from Nathaniel Wade.[48]

Tiley himself provided a very different version of events. In June 1686, Tiley, who had by then participated in the Monmouth rebellion, wrote to the informer Edmund Everard in an attempt to make his peace with the Stuart regime; he claimed he had left London for "the country" in July 1682, by which time he had made no contact with Monmouth, Russell, Grey, Armstrong, Essex, Algernon Sidney, or John Hampden; he did not mention Shaftesbury. Nor, Tiley claimed, had he heard of Holloway and "many others" subsequently accused of complicity in the plotting. Clearly, either Tiley or Holloway lied. In this case the presumption of truth must be accorded to Holloway, whose complicity is beyond doubt, whose confession was full (if sometimes exaggerated), and whose forthrightness failed to save him from the executioner. In contrast, Tiley's story, recounted to a known informer, is sketchy and unconvincing; he had joined Monmouth, he claimed, only because he had been falsely accused of complicity in the Rye House plotting.[49]

In late August 1682 Wade arrived in Bristol, where he was well known in dissident circles. Two years earlier he had been accused of attending not only conventicles but meetings where nonconformists "exercised themselves in feats of armes."[50] Wade reportedly confirmed what Tiley had told Holloway, adding that agents had already lined up crucial support. Wade and Holloway concluded that the "first onset" in Bristol would require 350 men, of whom 150 could be obtained from the Taunton area, which had more potential recruits than could be armed. A force of 350, in their judgment, could secure Bristol without bloodshed by using small ordnance to "scour" the principal streets rather than to kill. Holloway himself reportedly had several pieces of small ordnance and shot in storage. The conspirators would begin enlisting supporters, they decided, only after the date for the insurrection had been determined, but no further information came until November. West later claimed that another key Bristol radical, John Row, had told him that by the fall he and his associates had 500 cavalrymen ready to move into Bristol from the adjacent counties—brave but probably baseless talk.[51]

"God Save the Duke of Monmouth" : The Western Tour

Preparations for Monmouth's trip to Cheshire in September were under way throughout the summer. Word about the proposed visit had gone out in July—another indication that Grey was probably

telling the truth about the revival of the conspiracy that month.[52] Dr.
Matthew Fowler, a loyalist, fretted in late July that the duke's journey might trigger a rebellion: "The Whiggs finding their Cause and
party dayly declining in London, will endeavour what they Can to
buoy it up againe, by raysing some Considerable tumults in the
Country." This, in fact, is precisely what Ferguson claimed that
Shaftesbury had intended if Monmouth's reception were favorable.
Although Monmouth reluctantly agreed to lead a rebellion if conditions were right, his real purpose in visiting Cheshire was not to
incite an uprising but to confer with Macclesfield, Delamere, and
others, and to gauge the level of support for the Whigs following
their recent setbacks in Parliament and the London elections. On this
point Grey was manifestly correct.[53]

Monmouth went first to Staffordshire before parading trium-
phantly through Cheshire in the company of between 120 and 200
men on horseback. Crowds numbering in the thousands were attracted not only by Monmouth and the dignitaries in his entourage
but by the horse races at Wallasey. In addition to Sir Thomas Armstrong, the duke's entourage included such prominent Whigs as
Macclesfield, Delamere, Brandon, Roger Whitley, Leveson Gower,
and Henry Booth. Present too were members of families with ties to
the parliamentary forces in the 1650s, such as Sir Henry Ingoldsby,
who had commanded a regiment in Ireland and was a friend of
Algernon Sidney's, and Sir Robert Duckenfield, whose father had
served on Oliver Cromwell's Council of State. Nonconformists were
prominent among the enthusiastic well-wishers, many of whom
cried "A Monmouth, A Monmouth," or "Let Munmouth reigne."
Others sang a "Seditious Song with it's Author mentioning the pulling downe Altars, and that Monmouth shall reigne next." One zealot
boasted that he "cared not a F[art] for the King or Parliament, God
save the Duke of Monmouth." The duke's enthusiasts voiced their
desire for an elective monarchy, opposed the right of a Catholic to
inherit the throne, and "drank Confusion to Poperie." The duke's
progress, grumbled Dr. Fowler, "wanted nothing but a Vive le Roy
to compleat a Rebellion."[54] Although Macclesfield had reportedly
amassed large quantities of arms and ammunition, it would have

been foolhardy for Monmouth to have instigated an insurrection at this point given the absence of an effective organization, adequate supplies and funding, and the primitive state of the preparations at Thanet House.[55] An ugly riot was feasible, but not a successful uprising to secure his place as the king's heir.

The government, anticipating the duke's tumultuous welcome, had placed troops in the area on alert and had made provisions for constant surveillance and frequent reports to London. According to Sir Leoline Jenkins, Charles considered the progress "to be of very ill consequence to the publick Peace" and ordered an investigation to determine who was responsible and what had been done "to draw the Rabble together."[56] Unwilling to risk a popular rebellion in the duke's behalf, the king had Monmouth arrested on 20 September on charges of inciting a riot at Chester. The duke ordered Armstrong to ride ahead to London to obtain a writ of habeas corpus and, according to Grey, to deliver a secret message to Shaftesbury, Russell, and Grey himself. The Cheshire gentry were prepared to take up arms, the duke reportedly said, but he wanted the advice of his Thanet House colleagues as to whether he should come to London or return to Cheshire and launch a rebellion. Shaftesbury and Russell thereupon consulted with colleagues in the City, most of whom, according to Grey, urged Monmouth to rebel in Cheshire and promised to rise themselves if Russell would lead them. Shaftesbury purportedly concurred, noting that he had several thousand supporters in Wapping ready to act. Russell, however, opposed this plan, partly because he had discerned a mixed response in London, but mostly because the cabal had still heard nothing about preparations in the west, nor had they drafted a declaration or made provision for weapons, ammunition, and money, especially in Cheshire. The absence of a declaration was especially important to Russell, Grey recalled, because he disagreed with those supporters of Shaftesbury who wanted to reestablish a commonwealth. Before he left to convey this information to Monmouth, Grey was stopped by Shaftesbury, who asked him in private to tell the duke they had agreed to rebel. Grey refused to lie, for which, he averred, the earl never forgave him. Informed by Grey of the divided counsels, Monmouth opted to go to London, where he refused to provide surety for his peaceful behavior and was arrested again. Freedom came only when he obtained another writ of habeas corpus and posted the required bond; the relative ease with which he evaded imprisonment made Shaftesbury suspicious. Monmouth had apparently disclosed nothing, however, for on 7 October Jenkins indicated that Charles was still suspicious of the duke's motives and suspected the existence of a "deep-rooted" association.[57]

The only substantial evidence for this part of the conspiracy was provided by Grey. Although Monmouth subsequently admitted his involvement in plans for a general insurrection, details of his confession to the king in 1683 were never recorded. Russell, of course, had been executed prior to the duke's confession; he went to his death insisting he was innocent of "all designes against . . . [Charles], or of altering the Government." Strictly speaking, an insurrection that intended only to remove James from the line of succession was neither a plot against the king's life nor a scheme to overthrow monarchy. Grey may indeed have told the truth, for Russell had to admit, "I have heard many things & say'd some things contrary to my duty."[58]

As Grey recalled, he, Shaftesbury, Monmouth, and Russell met again at Thanet House in late September. Once more the earl allegedly pressed the case for an immediate insurrection, in this instance limited to London alone. Russell demurred, noting that Courtenay had reported that the west would soon be ready to act. At this Shaftesbury exploded, insisting that "patience would be our destruction" and warning that the preparations he had made in London would be discovered unless the insurrection began within a week. When he threatened to lead the uprising by himself, Monmouth, wiser from his Cheshire experience, countered by asking where the earl's 10,000 men were quartered. Monmouth subsequently "viewed severall Passes into the City," but Grey learned from Trenchard that the men of Taunton were not ready to act. Grey, Rumsey, Ferguson, and Armstrong thereupon met with Monmouth at the London home of the wine merchant Thomas Shepherd, later described by Thomas Sprat as "a Violent Nonconformist, and Disciple of *Ferguson*'s" ; there they decided to postpone the rebellion. Shortly thereafter, following the installation of the Tory sheriffs on 28 September, Shaftesbury went into hiding, obviously afraid that he might have to face a hostile jury. "When he was gone," Grey recalled, "'twas impossible for us to go on."[59] How wrong he was.

"Pull Downe Babylon" : The Projected November Insurrection

The events of the ensuing eight months are extremely complex, and untangling them is complicated by an abundance of testimony, some of it contradictory, much of it self-serving, and all of it dependent on the fallible memories of those who tried to recount events and conversations that had occurred months or even years earlier. Some of the testimony may have been fabricated, especially since everyone concerned had at least some awareness of the subornation problem in the Popish Plot. The possible motives of those who gave evidence, the degree to which allegations can be substantiated, and plausibility form the best basis on which to attempt a reconstruction of what actually happened. In any case, it is probable that prior to the time Shaftesbury went underground no conspirator had proposed assassinating the king or the duke of York. The goal of the cabal, first propounded in 1680 and then revived in July 1682, was only to compel Charles to bar James from the line of succession. Nevertheless, Russell's suspicions of Shaftesbury's republican supporters underscored a fundamental problem the leaders had failed to resolve. Nearly as serious were the temperamental differences between the cautious Russell and Shaftesbury, whose fears for his personal safety led him to consider rash action.

The circle of conspirators broadened in October 1682 with the addition of Lord Howard of Escrick. His staunch loyalty to the Whig cause and his Dutch ties made him an obvious ally of Shaftesbury after Russell and Monmouth had disappointed the earl. Although Howard probably embellished the story he recounted after his arrest and his decision to turn state's evidence, its general framework holds up when compared with other testimony.

The man Shaftesbury selected to arrange a meeting with Howard was Captain Thomas Walcott, a Baptist who had served in Ireland under Edmund Ludlow in the 1650s, and had been imprisoned in Dublin Castle after the Restoration as the alleged executioner of

Charles I. Walcott had subsequently been involved with Thomas Blood and Colonel Robert Phaire in the Liverpool conspiracy of 1665–66. In 1672 he promoted a scheme to restore the Long Parliament and abolish popery and prelacy, but like the Liverpool plot it came to nothing. L'Estrange described him as "Highly Enthusiastique, Bold, and Malitious." Essex, however, was sufficiently impressed with him to suggest that he would be a useful spy; this idea too was stillborn. In the summer of 1682 the earl asked Walcott, to whom he had been previously introduced by Howard, to leave Ireland, where he had an estate worth £800 per annum, for London; he did, but ostensibly to go to Carolina. Walcott later confessed that he had first learned of the plot in August or September. Before his execution he admitted that Shaftesbury had enlisted him in "an Vndertaking to Assert the peoples Just Libertyes, which were in hazard."[60]

On 1 or 2 October, Walcott, following the earl's instructions, took Howard to the home of a Mr. Watson in Wood Street, where Shaftesbury was hiding. As Howard remembered the conversation, the earl told him that all honest people were unsafe because of the new "Pseudo-Sheriffs" and that he could soon "reduce things to a better posture" with the assistance of the 8,000 to 10,000 men who were ready to fight for him. One of them was John Cantrell, a Spitalfields glover, who had pledged to command 400 or 500 men the previous summer; "men enough would be found" to support Shaftesbury, he reportedly said, "if the Lords did not hang off." After securing the City the earl's forces planned to overpower the guards at Whitehall with the help of 1,000 or 1,200 cavalry led by officers such as Major John Breman. Shaftesbury complained, said Howard, of the recalcitrance of Monmouth and Russell, though Grey seemed more willing to support him. The earl asked Howard to lead an uprising in Essex while Henry Herbert, fourth lord of Cherbury, and Colonel John Rumsey assisted him in London. Howard refused to commit himself without first consulting other peers, and thus conferred with Monmouth the following day. According to Howard, the duke denied any knowledge of Shaftesbury's plans, expressed concern that such actions could destroy him and "all the Party," and asked to meet with the earl.[61]

Howard duly conveyed Monmouth's request to Shaftesbury on the 5th,[62] but the latter declined to meet, fearful that the duke had reached a secret understanding with Charles. According to Howard, Shaftesbury also argued that his people were tired of waiting, that secrecy could not be maintained because too many people knew about the scheme, and that he was no longer willing to accept monarchical government. The earl further claimed that one of his compatriots had brought nearly 100 horsemen into London before Michaelmas day (29 September) at their own expense, and that this contingent was ready to return home. The man who led this cavalry unit, Howard later learned, was the one-eyed, "round trussed" Captain Richard Rumbold, a maltster who had once served as a lieutenant in Oliver Cromwell's regiment and may have participated in the 1663 northern rebellion. Among Rumbold's known associates were majors Childs and Holmes and Sir John Hartopp, a friend of John Owen's. Rumbold had reportedly heard William Carstares, who also became involved in the plotting, preach on numerous occasions at Theobalds, Hertfordshire.[63] That Howard acted as an intermediary between Monmouth and Shaftesbury is probable enough, but the details of this conversation were almost certainly fabricated for effect. The likelihood that nearly 100 rebel recruits spent a week in London without once indiscreetly revealing their presence or being observed strains credulity.

When Monmouth persisted in his desire to see Shaftesbury, the latter finally consented to meet with Russell and the duke on Sunday evening, 8 October, when he could move through the streets with minimal chance of being recognized. Before the appointed time he decided not only to break his engagement with Monmouth but also to change his hideout. It was probably at this point that Shaftesbury began his week-long stay in Ferguson's house, after which he moved to Captain Tracy's home in Wapping.[64]

By this time Shaftesbury had begun to consider the possibility of assassinating Charles and James, an action that would render Monmouth's support unnecessary and require considerably less money and fewer weapons and men. Moreover, as Ferguson later reflected (seconding Howard), the earl had "grown weary" of monarchical government and had become apprehensive "that the preparations towards an insurrection would not only require an expense, which few would so far open their purses as come up unto, but would prove so tedious & so liable to detection that he & many other[s] might come to be destroy'd." The first major conspirator to propose assassination was probably John Wildman, a former Leveller leader and associate of the duke of Buckingham, but more recently an intimate of Shaftesbury and Algernon Sidney. Ferguson, who tried to distance himself from responsibility for the assassination scheme, later claimed that "it had been sometime on foot & fomented and entertained by many" before he learned of it; on that point he surely exaggerated. Ferguson asserted that he had first heard assassination mentioned by "several of the little impolitick people," perhaps only an extreme instance of the anti-Stuart speech that had been commonplace for decades. When he told unnamed "party" leaders of "a more easie, cheap, safe, & compendious way for relieving our selves, than that of an Insurrection," they decided, he recalled, to take him into their confidence. The first to do so was described as "a gentleman . . . who is esteemed a great statesman & excellently versed in the Laws of England, tho never accounted very friendly to Kingship." At the time Ferguson wrote his account of the conspiracy (c. 1686–87), this man, a longtime acquaintance of his, was (said Ferguson) living in Amsterdam among the exiles. The person in question was almost certainly Wildman. In his view, reported Ferguson, the only rational course was to employ "some brisk lad's to destroy the King & Duke, whome he expressed by the name of stagge that would not be impaled, but leapt over all the Fences."[65]

Ferguson decided to investigate whether the notion of an assassination extended beyond the circle of republicans. For this purpose he visited Shaftesbury, to whom he made the argument that only Monmouth could persuade sufficient numbers of people to take up arms in defense of their rights. In response, the earl reportedly questioned the reliability of Monmouth, Russell, and others before admitting that he was considering "a more compendious way of Redeeming the nation than that of an Insurrection." With North and Rich about to take up their positions as sheriff, Shaftesbury despaired of an insurrection as too time-consuming to prepare.[66]

During his stay in Ferguson's home Shaftesbury not only reiterated his thoughts on assassination, according to his host, but "accounted it needful to raise such a hatred in the people of . . . Monmouth as that he should never be able either to arrive at the Throne, nor to get possession of a power, whereby to be in a condition to punish what had been perpetrated upon his Father & Uncle." Unable to dissuade the earl from his suspicion of Monmouth, Ferguson convinced him to meet with Francis Charlton, Shaftesbury's cousin and a confidant of the duke's. Charlton too failed to sway Shaftesbury.[67]

By his own admission, Ferguson reported to Monmouth that unnamed persons were plotting to assassinate Charles and James. Finding this course abhorrent, the duke pressed Ferguson "to penetrate into, & superintend all the steps & advances that should be made in it; & secondly, not only to do all I could towards hindering the execution of it, but to assure him of finding out way's & means how to prevent & obstruct it." In short, Monmouth commissioned Ferguson to serve him as an agent provocateur, a role hitherto roundly castigated in radical circles because of its use against dissidents by the Stuart regime. Ferguson acquiesced, but on the condition that two others serve with him. Monmouth immediately named Armstrong but deferred the final appointment until after he had consulted with Sir Thomas. In his confession Ferguson refused to name the third agent provocateur on the grounds that this person would become the target of republican vengeance, but he was reputedly "a person of known worth & honor" and an adherent of the Church of England; although named in the Rye House confessions, he was still alive in 1686. He was almost certainly Charlton. In 1683, after the government began investigating the conspiracy, it concluded that Ferguson "was the Common Agitator Entrusted by all Parties in the several Conspiracies," but Armstrong, Charlton, and Wildman also played crucial if less-documented roles as intermediaries between the two cabals. So effective was Ferguson in his role as agent provocateur that he was allegedly credited by Walcott with "the management" of the scheme, raising the possibility that he may have been a double agent working for Shaftesbury as well as Monmouth.[68]

By the time Ferguson met with his two fellow agents, Charles had gone to Newmarket and the conspirators were preparing to assassinate him as he passed the Rye House in Hertfordshire on his return.

According to Ferguson, Richard Rumbold was to command the assassins. In 1685, at his execution, Rumbold would deny that he had
agreed to "such a villany" as the king's assassination; Ferguson himself attested to Rumbold's sincerity, noting the latter's doubts about
the prospect of success and the likelihood of unintended (and unspecified) consequences. Ferguson instructed Armstrong to see that
Monmouth was in London on the day the king was scheduled to
return and to be prepared "to mount," both to protect himself and
to proclaim the people's liberties. Obviously thinking that Rumbold
and his men might indeed kill Charles, Ferguson insisted on preparations to take advantage of the deed. Attended by Armstrong, Monmouth obliged, apparently having decided to take advantage of an
assassination should it occur. Howard subsequently and erroneously
charged that Armstrong was to have led the party of assassins.[69]

Confirmation of a plot to assassinate the king and his brother in
October 1682 is found in the confession of Robert West, a barrister
of the Middle Temple, an alleged atheist, and a staunch Whig whom
Stephen College had consulted in 1681. Concerned about the safety
of his family in the event of an insurrection, West sought the advice
of Shaftesbury's colleague, Captain Walcott, shortly after 8 October
1682. An intimate friend of West's, Walcott confided that an uprising
had indeed been "projected" by Shaftesbury, but that the earl was
currently planning to have Charles and James killed as they returned
from Newmarket. Walcott reportedly "scorn'd" to participate in such
a "base and ungenerous" scheme. He would go to his death in 1683
insisting that he had never approved of any plan to murder the king.[70]

Though temporarily excluded from substantive participation in
the cabals after speaking too freely, Howard nevertheless gleaned
some information and apparently filled in imaginative details when
he later confessed. He knew, for instance, that radical action was to
have been taken when Charles returned from Newmarket in October, and Walcott had allegedly told him that the uprising would "begin at the He[a]d." Aware that Monmouth was opposed to assassination, Howard was undoubtedly lying when he claimed the duke
had suggested assaulting Charles with a party of 40 or 50 riders at
Newmarket.[71]

Further information pertaining to an alleged assassination scheme to be carried out in October 1682 surfaced in December 1685 when John Row, the former Bristol swordbearer whom other conspirators were trying to silence, confided in Edmund Everard, by that time an informer. As Everard reported the conversation, Rumsey had enlisted Row in October 1682 in a party of assassins who would kill James as he called on the lord mayor, Sir John Moore. Row appeared at the stipulated rendezvous, only to find neither Rumsey nor other assassins; he concluded that the colonel had been testing his reliability. Row further claimed that James Holloway subsequently showed him a letter from West or Nathaniel Wade written in "Dark expressions" about "the Removeing of the two Tables," by which the writer meant the assassination of Charles and James as they went to dine with Sir William Pritchard, the lord mayor–elect. The scheme, to which Rumsey was allegedly privy, fell through when the royal brothers canceled their plans. Corroboration of Row's assertions is lacking, but it is difficult to imagine how he hoped to gain a pardon by manufacturing lies about Rumsey, who by 1685 was a well-established crown witness. If, then, the essence of Row's account is reliable, he had been considered a possible assassin as early as October 1682.[72]

The collapse of the October plot convinced Shaftesbury to reconsider working with the Monmouth group for a general insurrection, although he still refused a face-to-face meeting with the duke. According to Ferguson, the earl did send frequent messages to Monmouth and Russell in favor of a rebellion. Monmouth pretended to be amenable, if only to restrain Shaftesbury from extreme courses. The earl "would undo us all," Grey reported having been told by Monmouth; "[the duke] found . . . [Shaftesbury] did seriously resolve to rise, and would not be put off from it, and therefore we must come in to him." Monmouth persuaded the others to delay the uprising until 2 November in the expectation of enlisting more support in the shires. He also wanted to examine the entry into the City from the lower end of Fleet Ditch to Snow Hill; this he did with Armstrong and Grey, as the latter admitted.[73]

Near the end of October, Grey and Ferguson conferred with Sir John Trenchard, who, reported Grey, claimed growing support for an insurrection in the southwest, especially the Taunton area. Their discussion was the prelude to a meeting that subsequently proved to be critical in Russell's treason trial. That such a meeting occurred is indisputable: Russell, Rumsey, Grey, and Ferguson acknowledged their attendance, as did Thomas Shepherd, who hosted the gathering at his home in Abchurch Lane at the beginning of November. Rumsey later explained, Shepherd "was looked on as a man of the greatest interest in the Citty and for that reasone the apoint[ments] were at his house that he might give an account [of] what was to be expected from them" (i.e., London radicals). Nevertheless there is disagreement about what took place at the meeting. By his own testimony Rumsey was there as Shaftesbury's delegate, in part to convey the earl's message that "it was high time to come to some Resolution about the Rising." Rumsey also confessed that Grey and Ferguson told him of their meeting with Trenchard, who had boasted to them that he could raise 1,000 foot soldiers and 200 to 300 cavalry in four hours.[74]

According to Grey, Ferguson also claimed to speak for Shaftesbury, who reportedly wanted the group to be reminded that he, Monmouth, Russell, and Grey had agreed in their last meeting to launch uprisings in London, Cheshire, and the southwest; the earl had, he claimed, completed his preparations and needed to act before he was discovered. If the others would not join Shaftesbury, Ferguson purportedly asserted, the earl would act alone.[75]

The extent to which Russell and Monmouth participated in this discussion is in dispute. Russell admitted having gone to Shepherd's house frequently; on this occasion he went at the duke's behest after Monmouth had expressed concern that "Shaftsbury & some hot men would undoe us all, if great care is not taken." At the session he heard "things said by some, with much more Heat, then Judgment; which I did sufficiently disapprove." Included in the conversation was renewed discussion about the feasibility of seizing the king's guards, but Russell denied having heard Rumsey deliver Shaftesbury's message. On this point he undoubtedly told the truth, for Ferguson attested to Russell's late arrival. Russell also insisted that he could not recall having heard anything about Taunton, Trenchard, or an uprising in the west. Yet Russell either had a poor memory or feigned forgetfulness, for he claimed he could not remember whether Ferguson had been at the session.[76] Russell's professions concerning a general insurrection have minimal credibility; given the fact that he provided his testimony while he was on trial for his life, he probably pretended to forget much that would have been self-incriminating.

As Grey recounted the discussion at Shepherd's house, Russell and Monmouth had agreed to support Shaftesbury but wanted to know where his "ten thousand brisk boys" were and how they were armed. Ferguson allegedly responded that the earl had fifteen or sixteen trusted gentlemen in the London area, each of whom had undertaken to appear with a specified number of recruits at the time appointed for the insurrection. Altogether they accounted for 5,000 men, but Ferguson insisted that five times that many would join them in the early hours of the uprising. The conspirators reportedly had some weapons and knew where to obtain more, and Ferguson claimed that Shaftesbury had purchased several cannons and three field carriages, "which were all buried" ; the authorities, in fact, subsequently found a carriage concealed in Wildman's house. Apparently satisfied with Ferguson's explanation, Grey confessed that he, Monmouth, and Russell had resolved to support Shaftesbury "and that all the strength we could make should be with us in the city, except our western interest."[77]

The conspirators, said Grey, decided to launch their rebellion in London on the night of Sunday, 19 November. Sunday evening was selected because the shops were closed and the streets filled with people, making it easier for rebel forces to rendezvous and pick up their weapons. "We considered, that if we were repulsed at London, we might play an after-game in the West." To that end they decided to inform Courtenay of their plans and send Trenchard to Taunton to help prepare their supporters. According to Grey, Monmouth's residence in Hedge Lane, Northumberland House (where the duke would be present), and Bedford House (with Russell in attendance) would each serve as a rendezvous for 500 men, while thousands of others would gather at four or five nonconformist meetinghouses. Although Grey named none of the latter, Monmouth confessed to the king in November 1683 that John Owen, Matthew Meade, George Griffith, "& all the considerable Nonconformist Ministers knew of the Conspiracy," but the summary of his account does not stipulate when they were informed.[78]

Additional evidence confirms the fact that several nonconformist clerics knew about the proposed insurrection. The minister William Carstares subsequently admitted that he had talked about it with Owen, Griffith, and Meade, but this discussion probably occurred in April 1683 after his return from the Netherlands. According to Howard, moreover, Ferguson arranged for Armstrong to meet with Meade, an action that riled Monmouth and his colleagues because Armstrong "was not fitt to treat with the Godly"; it is unclear, however, whether this meeting occurred in the fall of 1682 or the early months of 1683, after Shaftesbury's death. Secretary Jenkins obtained information in late October 1682 that two members of Meade's congregation had averred that "they must shortly pull downe Babylon and all the greate ones," and that the insurrection was scheduled for 5 November. Another nonconformist pastor who knew of the planned uprising, at least by May 1683, was the Seventh-Day Baptist Francis Bampfield; he did not support it, however.[79]

Whether any dissenting clergymen apart from Ferguson and probably Meade were party to the alleged plans in the fall of 1682 is impossible to ascertain, but a strong probability exists that the conspirators at least considered using some of the nonconformist meetinghouses as rendezvous. Local residents were accustomed to seeing large numbers of people flock to these buildings and presumably would have been suspicious only if they had noticed the absence of women. The authorities, who had been hearing rumors of plotting, may have suspected the involvement of nonconformists, for they again cracked down on conventiclers in early November. Among their targets were Owen, Ferguson, and Henry Danvers, who were prosecuted for having violated the Elizabethan Conventicle Act and the Corporation Act, and Meade, whose goods they distrained.[80]

As Grey explained their tactics, the rebels planned to attack between 11 P.M. and midnight on 19 November, moving against the trained bands at the Exchange and taking Newgate, Ludgate, and Aldersgate as well as London Bridge to prevent rapid communication between Whitehall and the Tower. With 2,000 men, they expected to secure key positions in the City while 1,000 foot soldiers and some cavalry under Macclesfield's command attacked the king's forces from the rear. Another unit would march across London Bridge, pass through Southwark and Lambeth, and then cross the Thames by boat to attack Westminster if necessary. However, they expected Charles to seek refuge in Portsmouth, disheartening his forces and enabling the rebels to control London within hours. With their strategy in place, the conspirators agreed to reconvene on 15 or 16 November. They may have sent information about their plans to Argyll, for William Spence (alias Butler), one of the earl's operatives, had come to London in October and left for the Netherlands on 8 November.[81]

Following the session Monmouth summoned Trenchard to confer with Grey at the duke's home. When Grey apprised Trenchard of the plan, the latter, surprised and apparently frightened,[82] insisted he needed two or three weeks to prepare his men, though he promised Monmouth he would leave for Taunton immediately and report as soon as he knew when his forces could be ready. Rumsey, Grey recalled, was either present at this meeting or arrived shortly afterwards, and pledged to attack Bristol with 200 cavalry if Trenchard or another commander would assist him. Long before Grey recounted these discussions, Rumsey had confessed that Shaftesbury had assigned him responsibility for Bristol; his confession also mentioned Trenchard's insistence that he have additional time to prepare his men, reportedly because they had to make provision for their families.[83] At least the gist, then, of Grey's testimony about the discussion with Trenchard and Rumsey is substantiated by the latter's prior confession. West subsequently added that the Bristol rebels intended to seize Henry Somerset, marquess of Worcester (the future duke of Beaufort), Peter Mews, bishop of Bath and Wells, and other Tories as well as Pendennis Castle. A relative of the governor of Chepstow Castle supposedly agreed to betray it.[84]

Several days later Grey, Monmouth, and Armstrong, who later admitted he had frequently attended the consultations at Shepherd's house, decided to get a firsthand look at the state of the king's guards at night. They went, said Grey, to the mews gate, the horse guards, and the Savoy, each of which the duke checked while the others waited. According to Grey, Monmouth was encouraged by what he saw. Partial confirmation of Grey's story is again found in Rumsey's earlier testimony: In one of the meetings at Shepherd's house, Rumsey had heard Armstrong agree to examine the state of the guards at the Savoy and the mews. Shepherd too confessed shortly after the discovery of the plotting (in June 1683) that Monmouth, Grey, and Armstrong had indeed reconnoitered the guards.[85]

Grey's ability to continue in the conspiracy was nearly terminated by a legal dispute involving his alleged abduction and seduction of his sister-in-law, Lady Henrietta Berkeley, with whom he had been having an affair for four years. When her father, the earl of Berkeley, attempted to stop it by procuring a writ *de homine replegiando*, Grey was incarcerated in the King's Bench prison on 6 November. Prosecuted by Sir Robert Sawyer and Sir George Jeffreys, Grey was bailed but never sentenced, and Sawyer, as attorney general, soon ended the matter by entering a *nolle prosequi*.[86]

When the plotters gathered again at Shepherd's house, presumably on 15 or 16 November, Monmouth, Russell, Grey, Armstrong, Ferguson, and Shepherd were present; Rumsey arrived near the end of the meeting.[87] Having had no communication from the southwest, the conspirators postponed the rebellion. According to Grey, Russell himself had dispatched agents to the southwest, but after his arrest Russell would claim he could remember nothing about any discussion at Shepherd's house concerning an uprising in the west or at Taunton or any mention of Trenchard. Nor had there been a discussion at Shepherd's, he insisted, of a surprise assault on the royal guards to launch the insurrection or even any discourse concerning the reconnoitering of the guards by Monmouth, Grey, and Armstrong. The evidence suggests that Russell lied about the discussions concerning the guards, but we have no incontestable proof that he sent agents to the southwest; the state produced none to testify at his trial, nor were any named. In any event, Grey asserted that the conspirators had agreed to meet again in ten to fourteen days, by which time they expected to have Trenchard's report. Taking advantage of the delay, Monmouth allegedly instructed Ferguson to have four more field-carriages made.[88]

The general thrust of the conspiracy is corroborated in West's confession, although it too must be used with caution because parts of it embody hearsay. During November, Walcott again approached West with information about a proposed insurrection in London and other areas of the country. Shaftesbury had enlisted Walcott (which the captain admitted), and the latter allegedly told West he expected to be commissioned a colonel of horse. Walcott wanted West to accept a commission under him and recruit some gentlemen of the Temple, but West declined, both because he considered himself physically unfit for battle and because he had a "mean opinion" of the scheme. Nevertheless he promised to loan Walcott a suit of armor.[89] Part of what Walcott reportedly told West agrees with the account of the conspiracy outlined above, including the appointed date of 19 November, but other details suggest that Shaftesbury apparently had a somewhat different scheme in mind. Walcott's version, as related by West, had Shaftesbury and Howard of Escrick commanding in London, Monmouth and Russell in the west, and Grey in Essex. Shaftesbury, in other words, presumably continued to seek a more broad-based uprising, while Monmouth and his friends had confined their efforts to London and the southwest. According to the Walcott-West account, the Shaftesbury people gave some thought to seizing the Tower, which they deemed feasible because the earl had friends in the garrison; success, however, would depend on preventing the king's forces from reaching the arms and ammunition. But, Walcott reportedly said, "the actuall possession of the tower was not of any great importance at first, and must follow their successe if they had any."[90]

The notes of Walcott's 1683 confession are regrettably meager, but the captain acknowledged complicity in the conspiracy and referred to the commanders as Shaftesbury in London, Monmouth in Taunton and Bristol, Russell in Devon, and Brandon (who wanted his participation kept secret from his father) in Cheshire. Walcott also admitted that Shaftesbury had told him the City had been divided into twenty parts, each with a "chief" who would recruit fifteen deputies—a scheme that would resurface in the spring of 1683. Thus Walcott's testimony substantially agrees with West's account. Grey added that he, Monmouth, Armstrong, Brandon, and Sir Gilbert Gerard met at the George and Vulture tavern to discuss the uprising in Cheshire, especially an assault on Chester Castle.[91]

As West allegedly learned from Walcott, Shaftesbury was drafting a revolutionary manifesto. Convinced that more than one version should be prepared and that the best be adopted, Walcott invited West, a barrister, to write one. The captain showed him a draft that recounted attempts in the reigns of James I, Charles I, and Charles II to introduce popery and arbitrary government, cited the monarchs' personal vices, and concluded "that the Government was dissolv'd, and the people at Liberty to settle another." Taking this to be a model, West declined on the grounds that he had insufficient historical knowledge. Grey too referred to a declaration, which he claimed had been read by Ferguson to one of the gatherings at Shepherd's house. Although Grey did not know who had commissioned it, he recalled that it had commenced with a general discussion of the purpose of government, then turned to the nation's grievances and the steps taken by Charles II to establish absolute government. The draft manifesto next justified recourse to arms to rectify grievances and to liberate the king from his evil advisers, the oft-repeated formula of rebels. The declaration demanded that Parliament be summoned to resolve disputed issues but proposed neither harm to Charles nor "considerable alteration in the government."[92] This was almost certainly a different version from the one Walcott showed West, but its existence lends credence to Walcott's statement that he (and obviously others) wanted to compare several drafts.

Shaftesbury and Ferguson in Flight

Word of the conspirators' decision to postpone the uprising yet again, presumably made on 15 or 16 November, was conveyed to Shaftesbury by Rumsey. Already upset by the plans of the Monmouth group to reduce the scale of the insurrection and distrustful of their resolve, especially Trenchard's, the earl decided he could no longer risk another treason trial by remaining in England. According to Ferguson, Shaftesbury learned from a friend at Whitehall that plans were under consideration to file new charges against him. At this point he met secretly with the earls of Essex and Salisbury. Of that meeting we know only what Essex recounted to Gilbert Burnet, apparently in December 1682: "Fear, anger, and disappointment had wrought so much on him, that lord Essex told me he was much broke[n] in his thoughts: his notions were wild and impractible: and . . . [Essex] was glad . . . [Shaftesbury] was gone out of England: but that he had done them already a great deal of mischief, and would have done more if he had stayed." Burnet had no reason to invent this account, which can only have meant that Shaftesbury confided his scheming to Essex and Salisbury. Shaftesbury, in fact, subsequently apprised Walcott that he had consulted Essex with the intention of persuading him to join the conspirators, but Shaftesbury did not tell Walcott Essex's response, or so Walcott claimed.[93] Apparently Essex and Salisbury made no attempt to dissuade Shaftesbury from fleeing to the Netherlands.

Details of Shaftesbury's flight were a closely guarded secret, though he probably took advantage of a major fire in Wapping on 19 November to escape. The government subsequently learned that he had been conveyed to Brill by Robert Locke, master of the *Hare*, shortly before 26 November. Captain Tracy, the earl's host in Wapping, arranged the passage, which Shaftesbury made in the company of Walcott, Ferguson, and a number of his servants. Ferguson, the object of a fresh warrant charging him with seditious publications, barely escaped arrest but left behind his *Second Part of the Growth of Popery*, which a Mr. Culliford printed. Before fleeing, Ferguson consulted with Monmouth and provided Armstrong and his fellow agent with what he called "a full account in what posture I had left things," including the names of those who had revived the assassination plot, "the chief instigator's" of which were, he averred, Rumsey and West.[94]

The ease and secrecy with which Shaftesbury, Ferguson, and Walcott made their escape are testimony to the effectiveness of the cross-Channel links in the radical community. The earl and his party went from Brill to Rotterdam, where they briefly enjoyed the hospitality of James Washington, a longtime radical agent and champion of the Good Old Cause who was now involved in smuggling dissident literature into England. On 2 December, Shaftesbury arrived in Amsterdam, where he was greeted by Sir William Waller, of Popish Plot fame, and other radicals. A concerned English government instructed its ambassador, Thomas Chudleigh, to commission someone to "look narrowly into his words and actions" and prevent

William of Orange from granting Shaftesbury his "countenance or Protection"; William, in fact, was quick to assure Chudleigh that he would not see the earl.[95] Chudleigh pressed William to prevent Shaftesbury from enjoying a haven in Amsterdam, but Chudleigh's superiors were less interested in where the earl stayed than in his activities.[96] The fact that Shaftesbury had left his wife in England suggested the possibility that his move to the Netherlands was only temporary; indeed, Chudleigh reported on 12 December that a member of the earl's entourage had indicated Shaftesbury's intention to return to England as soon as another Parliament was called. The following month the earl deposited £30,000 in an Amsterdam bank— enough to finance an insurrection had he so desired—but he died on the 21st. "My lord Shaftesbury is gone to answer in an other world for all the villanys & Treasons he comitted in this," Chudleigh reported with relief.[97]

Shaftesbury's plotting, his meeting with Essex and Salisbury, his flight to the Netherlands, and his association with the radical community there are indisputable. So too were the surreptitious gatherings at Shepherd's house variously attended by Monmouth, Russell, Grey, Armstrong, Rumsey, and Ferguson; nor can there be any serious doubt that these men discussed the possibility of an uprising designed primarily to exclude James from the line of succession. They claimed they had intended no personal harm to Charles or to monarchical government per se, yet they knew Shaftesbury was contemplating assassination and they clearly envisioned the use of force to compel the king to summon Parliament and sign an exclusion bill. Moreover, Monmouth was prepared to seize power if extremists killed the king. Like Ferguson, the duke was primarily interested in blocking James' accession and securing Protestant interests in the three realms. Nevertheless, these men apparently saw themselves as operating—however extreme their means—within the traditional constitutional framework.

Whether Shaftesbury would have found a monarchical solution acceptable in late 1682 is arguable. By November he had come to distrust the Monmouth circle and was above all concerned for his own safety. Although the government's effort to convict him of treason had failed, it permanently scarred his character and inclined him to favor a commonwealth. In his circle rather than Monmouth's, the notion of instituting a republic by assassinating the royal brothers received increasing consideration. One of the most enigmatic but potentially revealing pieces of evidence in this regard is West's extensive testimony. Although this has been dismissed by some historians as sheer fabrication, parts of it are corroborated by other witnesses, some of whom died for their crimes. The portion of West's confession that deals with November 1682 includes dramatic testimony about a proposed assassination, although the chronological details suggest the possibility of embellishment.

According to West, a few days after he had refused Walcott's invitation to draft a manifesto, the captain informed him that "the design was frustrated, and wholly laid aside." This would have occurred after the meeting at Shepherd's house (probably on 15 or 16 November) at which Monmouth and his friends postponed the rebellion. We know from Grey's account that Shaftesbury interpreted this decision to mean that the uprising had been permanently canceled, and Walcott, a member of the earl's inner circle, reflected Shaftesbury's outlook when he visited West. Shortly after West's conference with Walcott, Rumsey, who was the godfather of West's son John, purportedly gave the barrister a fuller account of what had been developing and differentiated between Shaftesbury's circle and "another Caball" consisting of Monmouth, Russell, Grey, Armstrong, and Ferguson. The plans of the latter group, Rumsey allegedly said, had been frustrated when Trenchard failed to enlist sufficient men in Taunton. This account accords with the record of events as we know them.[98]

West claimed he met Ferguson about this time, apparently meaning around the 16th or 17th, but the conversation he relates refers to the lord mayor's day (11 November 1682) as being "just at hand." West also averred that he met with Ferguson several times subsequent to this conversation to discuss their conspiracy, which had to be postponed when Ferguson fled to the Netherlands. West's chronology was therefore somewhat shaky, since the initial discussion with Ferguson (assuming it actually took place) had to have occurred shortly prior to the 11th, approximately a week before Walcott told him the projected rebellion had been canceled. West undoubtedly exaggerated the number of his meetings with Ferguson, who had to have left England by the 25th. The account of his treasonable conversations with Ferguson may well be embroidered, probably to enhance its appeal to the government, yet the fact that West, as a barrister, specifically confessed that he had personally argued the case for assassination suggests that the core of his account is true. Presumably it would have been safer for him to blame Ferguson for advocating an assassination scheme, but this would have risked a denial from the minister should he be apprehended. In his own account, Ferguson, as we have seen, cited West and Rumsey as the chief instigators of a revived assassination plot, and claimed they had argued its viability prior to his flight to Holland with Shaftesbury.[99]

A trace of bitterness is evident in West's description of Ferguson as a man

who allways pretended a great zeal and sollicitude for the protestant Religion, the rights and Libertys of the Nation, and [who] now bewail'd the imminent danger both were in from the Government. Though he discours'd well and fluently upon all Subjects, yet at arraigning the government he had a particular Excellency, and outdid himself, and was so unhappily successeful in it, that like a whirlpit, he drew in all men that came near him.

In their meeting shortly before 11 November, Ferguson had painted such a vivid picture of conditions in Scotland under the duke of York's rule "that captivity in Algiers seem'd a blessed condition in comparison." James' work north of the Tweed, Ferguson reportedly charged, was intended to lay the foundation for the establishment of absolute rule in both kingdoms with Catholic support. He had no patience for those who preached a doctrine of passive obedience as a handmaiden of the doctrine of providence, for God expected people to "assist themselves, suitable to the Exigency they are under," by force of arms if necessary.[100] Such views, of course, were part of the militant nonconformist heritage in Scotland out of which Ferguson had come, and West's attribution of such tenets to him rings true.

Having outlined the repression in Scotland and the case for active resistance, Ferguson purportedly concluded by noting that only two options were available, a general insurrection or assassination. In a startling admission, West confided that he had argued against an uprising:

The case [is] very different now from what It was in 1641, for besides the want of that seeming Authority of a Parliament, which men acted under then, the Militia, Navy, Forts and Ammunition [are] all in the hands of the Government, and the people as it were naked, and that such an Attempt would at the best entail a long war upon the Nation, and must end in the destruction of the King and Duke, or else would be in vain.

If the conspirators decided to act, West contended, assassination was the "more rationall" course.[101] According to West, Ferguson responded first by reiterating his conversations with Walcott and Rumsey and then by exploring possibilities to kill Charles and James. Ferguson allegedly proposed attacking when the royal brothers went into the City for the lord mayor's day celebrations, though West claimed he opposed this plan as too hazardous.[102]

Other meetings reportedly followed with Ferguson, Rumsey, Row, and Richard Goodenough. In these sessions, West claimed, Ferguson outlined at least three assassination schemes, the first of which proposed ramming the royal barge with a hoy; if this proved ineffective, the assassins could board the barge and sink it by ripping up one or two planks on the bottom. Alternatively, the conspirators could slay Charles and James as they rode through St. James' Park in their chairs. A third scheme proposed shooting the king and his brother as they sat in the royal box at the theater. Each of these plans required prior knowledge of the movements of Charles and James, hence Rumsey reputedly suggested that the conspirators purchase an office at court for one of their confidants. West claimed he had argued against the Thames plan because it involved too many contingencies and against the park scheme because of the improbability of finding the royal brothers together there. He confessed, however, that he and Ferguson had endorsed the theater plot, deeming the venue apt for the end of Charles and James: "In a playhouse they will dy in their calling." In subsequent meetings West pressed Ferguson to tell the group if Monmouth had been informed of their plans and if the duke would promise not to hang them "for helping him to a crown." Ferguson reportedly offered to seek a written statement from Monmouth guaranteeing freedom from prosecution—an idea so preposterous that Ferguson surely had no intention of raising it with the duke. Nevertheless, this concern, according to West, "dampt the Design and always clog'd it." At this point Ferguson left for the Netherlands with Shaftesbury and Walcott.[103]

Rumsey's confession is at variance with West's account of the November meetings at which assassination schemes were allegedly discussed. The colonel claimed that he had hired West as his barrister in late November or early December 1682, after which West told him there had been a plan to kill Charles as he returned from Newmarket the previous October. Three or four days later, Rumsey recalled, he met with Goodenough and others in West's chamber to discuss such a scheme, but the idea was dropped and not revived until February 1683.[104] Rumsey, in other words, said nothing about his involvement in assassination talks prior to Shaftesbury's flight; up to that point he would admit only participation in plans for a general insurrection. Because both Ferguson and West testified to the contrary, Rumsey's attempt to pass over the November meetings in silence must be viewed with considerable suspicion. Unfortunately, Richard Goodenough's confession is too fragmentary to be of use in evaluating West's account of these discussions.

Rumsey confessed in 1685 that he had conferred with the earl of Stamford after the postponement of the insurrection in November 1682. The earl, he opined, was not "a person in the King's interest, but [one] who would run into any design against the King." When Rumsey recounted what had happened at Shepherd's house, Stamford, allegedly upset that he had not been consulted, pressed the colonel to keep him abreast of developments. Rumsey and Richard Goodenough honored his request in the months that followed.[105]

By the end of November 1682 the radicals were badly fragmented, unable to agree even on a method to bar James from the succession. It is possible to identify at least five conspiratorial groups in existence at this time, linked by no more than occasional and often unreliable communication, mostly through Robert Ferguson. Two of the cabals—those centered around Monmouth and Robert West respectively—remained in England; those of Shaftesbury and Argyll were now centered in the Netherlands; and the United Societies constituted a fifth in Scotland.

"The Lopping Point"

FOUR

The Winter Cabals and the Rye House

Shaftesbury's retreat to the Netherlands in late November 1682 temporarily unsettled some of the English radicals, especially in Monmouth's circle, where fear of disclosure mounted. According to Grey, consternation also mounted because the duke's men knew relatively little about the radical contacts in London that Shaftesbury and Robert Ferguson had cultivated.[1] Only after the earl died on 21 January 1683 did Monmouth and his associates resume plotting.

To Kill a King: The West Cabal

Apparently undeterred by these concerns, Robert West's group continued to meet in this period. West himself referred to several sessions in December 1682, one of which was in his own chamber at the Middle Temple, henceforth the site of many gatherings because of its convenient location. The core of the group consisted of West, Colonel John Rumsey, John Row, and Richard Goodenough. Also present at the December meeting in West's quarters were Edward Norton, a gentleman of Ashe, Wiltshire, and a known Shaftesbury supporter; the barrister Richard Nelthorpe, a friend of Goodenough's; Goodenough's brother, Francis; and Joseph Tiley, the Bristol clothier. West later confessed they had discussed both assassination, "the Lopping point," and insurrection, "the Generall point." They rejected Ferguson's schemes to attack the king in St. James' Park or to sink the royal barge on the Thames, but most of the group purportedly endorsed a plan favored by Rumsey to kill Charles and James "under Bedford Garden wall in Covent Garden" as they returned from an evening performance at the theater. The conspirators planned for one group to fire into the royal coach, a second to shoot at the guards, a third to block the street and prevent the coach from escaping, and a fourth, consisting of 30 to 40 riders dressed as "casuall travellers," to rush in from surrounding streets as reinforcements. Although Nelthorpe objected on the grounds that assassination was "base and dishonorable," the others preferred to avoid an insurrection as too hazardous. Should there be a rebellion, they concluded that Portsmouth had to be secured, which Rumsey thought could be accomplished by getting the garrison inebriated; conspirators dressed as country folk could then seize the guns and turn them on the gates. But, West concluded, nothing was decided in Ferguson's absence.[2]

Although seven men allegedly were present with West for this discussion, little direct evidence exists to corroborate his account. As noted earlier, Rumsey confessed that he and unnamed others pondered an assassination scheme in West's room in early December, then dropped the idea until February 1683. This gathering must have been the meeting described by West, but Rumsey provided no details. In a self-serving letter to a known informer in 1686, Tiley admitted he had returned to London from a visit in the country around 23 November 1682 but mentioned no gathering until he attended a supper party at Rumsey's house in Soho Square around 27 December. He was, he claimed, so drunk that he could not remember the names of the other guests. He went back to the countryside, he insisted, and returned to the City only on 20 May 1683.[3]

Tiley's admission that he was present at Rumsey's house shortly after Christmas accords with West's acknowledgment of such a gathering. In addition to himself, West averred, the Goodenough brothers, Row, Robert Blaney, and possibly Tiley were there. Blaney, a clerk in the Middle Temple, confessed he had attended Rumsey's party on 27 December but remembered a slightly different guest list, including West, Richard Goodenough, Tiley, and Christopher Battiscombe of the Middle Temple, who had been invited by Row and was a friend of John Locke's. Battiscombe too confessed having been present with Row, West, Tiley, Blaney, and others. The guests, West admitted, spoke in general terms of an assassination and an insurrection "under the Cant of Sealing the writings, and Executing the Conveyances," but Charles and James were not explicitly named according to Blaney, whose testimony agrees very closely with West's. For greater clarity in their discussion, West, by his own admission, proposed that assassination be referred to as "Executing a Bargain and Sale, which is a short kind of Conveyance; and the Insurrection being a more tedious way, Executing a lease and Release which is a longer Conveyance." Virtually the same phrases were attributed to West by Blaney. They drank, Blaney remembered, to executing a bargain and sale, or a lease and release. Blaney and West concurred that this was the only meeting the former had attended, although Blaney admitted he had frequently asked West, Blaney, and Goodenough if "the Great Men" would act. They allegedly responded negatively. Once again, West's account holds up to scrutiny reasonably well.[4]

Several dissidents may have examined possible assassination sites in this period. On 9 January, as the king traveled through St. James' Park in his sedan chair, two men in disguise were spotted; one of them was overhead to say, "Dam[n] him, we shall never have such an occasion againe." Shortly before this, John Gibbons, Monmouth's footman and a self-proclaimed confidant of Sir Thomas Armstrong, reportedly examined Covent Garden with Row. According to West, Gibbons told Row that this was "a Convenient place to doe the Trick," and that the duke's family knew of the plot and "would be glad to have it done, but did not care to be seen in it." As hearsay, this part of West's statement has no evidential value, although Rumsey testified that Row had told him essentially the same story about Gibbons.[5]

Rumsey later claimed—preposterously—that on 30 January twelve to sixteen of the conspirators had gathered in a Watling Street tavern to celebrate the anniversary of Charles I's execution. Around a table covered with (animal?) heads had allegedly gathered West, Sir John Trenchard, Sir Walter Yonge, John Freke, Nathaniel Wade, Row, Tiley, apparently one of the Goodenough brothers, and others. Led by West, the "chairman," Rumsey recounted, they "told me the meaning and magnified the Deed and the Glorious Men that did it and Dranke healths to theyr memoryes." They offered a second toast, according to Rumsey, to those who would execute Charles I's sons.

Reports of such celebrations had circulated before, and Rumsey himself claimed such occasions had occurred regularly since the Restoration, but men conspiring against the government are hardly likely to have called such attention to themselves.[6]

The "Council of Six"

After Shaftesbury died, Monmouth and five colleagues—William Lord Russell, the earl of Essex, William Lord Howard of Escrick, Algernon Sidney, and John Hampden, grandson of the civil-war parliamentarian—organized what Howard grandiloquently called a "council of six." They first convened, he said, at Hampden's house, where they "propounded some General Heads" for future discussion: Should the insurrection begin in London, in the country, or in both simultaneously? Which counties were most likely to revolt? What men in those shires were the most useful and likely to support them? What towns could most readily be seized and used for rendezvous? What types of weapons were best, and where and how could they be obtained? How much money was required (Monmouth estimated £25,000 to £30,000), and how could it be raised without drawing attention? How could an uprising in Scotland be coordinated with the English insurrection, and which Scots should be consulted about it?[7]

Hampden would later admit that Monmouth and probably Russell and Sidney had come to his house, but he professed not to remember if Howard had been present; the Privy Council minutes make no mention of Essex in this connection. According to Howard, it was probably after this initial meeting that Monmouth and Essex visited the earl of Salisbury at Hatfield to secure his support for their endeavors. Given the fact that Shaftesbury had conferred with Essex and Salisbury prior to his flight to the Netherlands, Howard was probably truthful in reporting the meeting. Moreover, Sir John Burlace asserted that Essex had told him Salisbury had pledged his backing.[8]

Approximately ten days after their first meeting the six conferred again, this time at Russell's house, where they decided to seek an alliance with the earl of Argyll and his Scottish supporters. According to Howard, the six wanted to invite Lord Melville (who had helped Monmouth repress the Bothwell Bridge rebels), Sir John Cochrane, and Sir Hugh Campbell of Cessnock to London to learn about Scottish plans for an insurrection. Responsibility for dispatching an agent to Scotland was assigned to Sidney, who later reportedly told Howard he had sent the Whig attorney Aaron Smith at Nelthorpe's suggestion. Samuel Starkey, Smith's clerk, subsequently depicted his employer as a man who was convinced that Charles and his Council were at root papists "resolved to destroy all Old English Liberty & totally extirpate the Gospel of Christ," and who therefore believed "it was high time to Arme themselves against such horrid designes & repair their Late Lost Rights & Privileges." Among Smith's intimates were Simon Mayne, son of the regicide, and Thomas Haselrig, a relative of Sir Arthur's. The letter Smith carried to Scotland was allegedly written in cant about Carolina-plantation affairs. Various witnesses later testified that they had served as Smith's guides or had seen him on his journey to Scotland. The "council," Howard testified, determined not to reconvene, barring an emergency, until the Scots had arrived or a message from Scotland had been received.[9]

Reliable testimony to support Howard's account is relatively meager, although the six men indisputably met, for in his trial Russell admitted as much. He insisted, however, that they had talked only of "things in general," not a "formed design." Grey, of course, was not one of the six, but he and the earl of Stamford attended Monmouth when the duke visited Chichester (in part, perhaps, because of its proximity to Portsmouth) in early February.[10] On that occasion, Grey claimed, the duke told him about the "council" and its plans for insurrections in several parts of England and hopefully in Scotland as well. Monmouth, however, expected the group to break up because Essex, Sidney, and Hampden favored a commonwealth, a course that would require "the destruction of the king." Howard, the duke allegedly complained, would support whatever form of government promised him the greatest personal benefit. Consequently, Grey averred, Monmouth and Russell would remain in the "council" only if he joined, but this he refused to do unless the next meeting offered a reasonable prospect that the two factions could work together.[11]

Grey heard nothing more until March, when he received a letter from Monmouth in cant asking him to come to London. Shortly after his arrival, the duke and Russell allegedly told him the "council" had met four or five times, during the course of which meetings they had resolved to launch uprisings in London, Cheshire, the west, and Scotland. They had also, Grey claimed, sent for Melville, Cochrane, and one of Argyll's relatives (Sir Hugh Campbell of Cessnock) to learn how the Scots were inclined and to ask if Argyll could defeat royalist forces in Scotland if he were given the £10,000 he sought. Grey further claimed that Russell and Monmouth had told him Sir William Courtenay and Sir John Trenchard were prepared to support them. Howard's confession agrees with this, adding that Lord Gerard of Brandon and Henry Booth had pledged to raise troops in Cheshire. An unnamed witness would afterward claim that around Christmas 1682 she had heard Trenchard boast that he, the Speke family, and others were engaged in a "great work," with Monmouth himself their general, a further indication that Grey was telling the truth. In any event, Monmouth and Russell again pressed Grey to join the "council" as a counterweight to the republicans. Monmouth and Russell, Grey recalled, professed to want only a reconciliation between Charles and Parliament, and the duke was silent on the issue of the succession. Grey's reference to Russell's position accords with the latter's insistence that he had never advocated an alteration of the government, although he had "heard many things & say'd some things contrary to my duty."[12]

About this time, Rumsey called on Monmouth while the duke was dining with Lord Brandon. According to Rumsey, Brandon suggested that a party of 200 men, of whom he offered to recruit 20, could seize the king at Newmarket, presumably to compel him to endorse James' exclusion. Although Monmouth casually dismissed the idea, Brandon opined that this was a better scheme than the general rebellion the duke "and his Greate men was upon." On another occasion Brandon reportedly suggested to Rumsey that if a new Parliament should meet, the duke's supporters could storm the meetingplace, brandishing swords and pocket-pistols, while they secured the duke of York.[13]

The Rye House Plot

While the Monmouth cabal engaged in its discussions, West's group continued to meet independently. Shortly after Shaftesbury's death, Rumsey, Captain Richard Rumbold, and Richard Goodenough assembled, according to West, in West's chamber in the Temple. Both insurrection and assassination were discussed, but Rumbold reportedly "had no great Stomach to an Insurrection" and refused to participate in an attempted assassination unless it occurred on the road between London and Newmarket. Rumsey's subsequent confession partially corroborated West's report of this meeting (which Rumsey placed in February), adding that West and Goodenough had agreed to recruit assassins. However, Rumsey insisted that he had first met Rumbold, the proposed leader of the assassination party, when the four men gathered at the Angel tavern.[14] The disagreement on details in this instance is of minimal significance when compared to the fact that West and Rumsey concurred on the existence of the meeting, the substance of the discussion, and the parties involved.

In the week following the conference in West's chamber, this cabal reconvened, according to West, at the Salutation tavern in Lombard Street. After they decided to ask Ferguson to return, Rumbold allegedly suggested that a similar invitation be issued to Edmund Ludlow, but that idea was subsequently dropped when they could not find a means to contact him. They also resolved to draft "a Modell of Government" and prepare blank commissions for civil and military offices, with the latter to "run in the names of the Confederate Lords and Commons of England." After the meeting, West and Rumsey sought out Thomas Shepherd, who agreed to send a letter from West inviting Ferguson to return, ostensibly for the sake of his health. They also decided not to draft commissions and a model of government after Rumsey informed them of the most recent work of the Monmouth cabal, which, he noted, expected to be ready to act in late March.[15]

Again Rumsey's version agrees in substance with West's more structured account but differs from it in some details. Even before West's arrest, Rumsey had admitted that he, West, and Richard Goodenough had gone to Bridge's coffeehouse (in January, he thought), where they met Shepherd. All four were supposed to join Rumbold at the Salutation tavern to discuss the proposed assassination, but Shepherd was unable to attend owing to business obligations. The others met Rumbold as scheduled, but, opined Rumsey, they accomplished little. In his confession Shepherd too acknowledged his own absence from the meeting at the Salutation tavern, and he admitted that West, Wade, and a third person (obviously Rumsey) had come to his house and discussed assassination. Neither West nor Rumsey mentioned Wade's presence.[16]

The confessions of West and Rumsey disagree to some extent with respect to a draft of political principles intended for the perusal of Monmouth's group. The idea, said West, was Rumsey's, and the document was prepared by both men along with Wade, who had returned to the City from Bristol after recovering from an illness. Rumsey, however, claimed that the manifesto was the handiwork of West and Wade alone.[17] To the best of West's memory, the document contained eight basic points: (1) Elections for Parliament would be held annually on a fixed date. (2) Parliament could not be adjourned or prorogued without its consent, or dismissed until a new one had been elected. (3) Parliament would continue to consist of Lords and Commons. (4) Only peers who supported "the design" would retain their hereditary titles; all others would become life peers, with replacements to be chosen from members of the House of Commons when they died. (5) Parliament would control the militia and nominate or elect judges, justices of the peace, sheriffs, and other major military and civil officers. (6) A bill that passed both houses of Parliament but did not receive the prince's consent would be a binding law for one year, and would become a "perpetuall Law" even without the prince's signature if the next Parliament passed it. (7) The prince's council would consist of peers elected by the House of Commons and commoners elected by the House of Lords.

(8) The religious activities of all Protestant nonconformists would be tolerated.[18]

Rumsey would later claim that he had never seen a copy of any declaration, though he confessed that he had been present when parts of it were discussed. He recalled only that it involved liberty of conscience, a freely elected Parliament, the return of lands seized at the Restoration, and law reform. After further examination Rumsey admitted he had given a copy of "a Project of Government" drafted by Wade and West to Ferguson, who had just arrived from the Netherlands on 21 February. On this point West concurred. Ferguson allegedly told Rumsey that Algernon Sidney had also prepared a draft. Ferguson then reportedly offered to edit them into a single document.[19]

Ferguson's account is in fundamental agreement with the confessions of West and Rumsey, although it provides a broader perspective because of his role as an agent provocateur. He admitted receiving letters from both Shepherd and West "written in disguised terms importuning [his] return." Neither Shepherd nor West, however, realized that the decision to encourage Ferguson's return had originated with Armstrong and his fellow agent (Francis Charlton?), both of whom were allegedly concerned that the assassination plans were too far advanced for them to block. Afraid that the trust Ferguson enjoyed in West's circle might be jeopardized if he returned without their knowledge or approval, Armstrong suggested to Rumsey that Ferguson should be in London when the Scottish party arrived. Rumsey thereupon mentioned this to his compatriots, and the request to Ferguson ensued.[20]

In the meantime, Ferguson was helping Israel Hayes and other exiles in the Netherlands to formulate a series of political queries that reflected militant Whig concerns. One query included the assertion that Charles was not governing in accordance with the law or the Declaration of Breda. Another was immediately relevant to the scheming under way in England and Scotland: "Wheather the time be not drawing neare for a Redemption from Tyrany & papal plotts & that some bold brittaine stands in the gap & struck the first sturdy strocke."[21]

Ferguson reached London on Ash Wednesday, shortly before the royal entourage departed for Newmarket. On Friday, 23 February, Armstrong apprised him of the recent discussions concerning both an insurrection and an assassination; soon thereafter Ferguson met with Shepherd and then with Rumsey and West. Rumsey and West doubted that a general rebellion would materialize, partly because of the conflicting principles and slow procedures of the Monmouth group, and partly because the Scots had not yet arrived and money had not been obtained to subsidize them. West and Rumsey concluded, said Ferguson, "that there remained nothing practicable, but the Lopping point, meaning thereby the cutting off the King & Duke." When Ferguson reported this discussion to Armstrong, the two decided to proceed no further until Ferguson could consult with Monmouth, as the duke himself desired. Ferguson reflected:

Tho I had already discovered too much of Rumsey's inclination & spirit, to judg it either possible to withdraw from pursuing the forementioned [assassination] design, or that it would be safe directly to endeavour it, yet I thought that the putting some testimony of confidence & respect upon him, might both keep an esteem in him for the D. of Monmouth, & render him the less jealous of my self.[22]

To this end Ferguson twice arranged to confer with Monmouth at the home of Rumsey, but without the latter's participation. According to Ferguson the duke apprised him of the current status of the planned uprising, including efforts for an alliance with the Scots, and again expressed his abhorrence of assassination, urging Ferguson to do his utmost to prevent any attempt on the life of Charles or James. Rumsey too testified that Monmouth had twice been to his house to see Ferguson; Rumsey had talked with them on one of the occasions, but not about the conspiracy. Rumsey also noted that Armstrong had met with Ferguson at his home several times, but not in his presence.[23]

Although the accounts of Ferguson and Rumsey substantially agree on these points, the more detailed testimony of West varies in some particulars. After Ferguson returned from the Netherlands, he met, according to West, at the Five Bells tavern in the Strand with Rumbold and Richard Goodenough as well as Rumsey and West; they endorsed assassination but not a particular plan. Ferguson's account, of course, had mentioned neither the presence of Rumbold and Goodenough, nor an alleged second meeting at a tavern in Fleet Street—possibly the Castle, West reminisced—where the cabal explored several assassination schemes before deciding upon the notorious Newmarket plan.[24] Either Ferguson's account is incomplete or West was fabricating detail, but in any case the two men concurred on the substantive points: they had met shortly after Ferguson's arrival in England, and the West cabal was still pursuing an assassination scheme.

The testimonies of Ferguson and West further agree that ensuing gatherings occurred in West's chamber in the Temple—three in one week according to Ferguson, whose participation was allegedly endorsed by Armstrong (the third agent provocateur, presumably Charlton, being away in the country). The tone of the two accounts, however, is strikingly different. Once Ferguson had satisfied himself that West and his associates were "far from being in a condition to execute" an assassination plan, his attitude toward them became dismissive and his subsequent efforts, he claimed, were primarily concerned with preventing West and Rumsey from directing their hostility against the Monmouth circle. The key factor, according to Ferguson, was the changing attitude of Rumbold. In October the latter had expressed his willingness to lead a party of 20 assassins, but now he demanded 50 as well as a guarantee of indemnity from "persons of quality."[25] Ferguson, Armstrong, and their fellow agent, who had returned from the country, decided that Ferguson should speak with Rumbold in private. On that occasion, according to Ferguson, Rumbold indicated that he was reluctant to lead an assassination party, not least because John Wildman, "who had been the first proposer & mover" of the scheme, now urged him not to participate.[26] Ferguson attributed Wildman's change of heart to Algernon Sidney's successful effort to persuade Monmouth, Russell, and Essex to take Wildman into their confidence. Although Wildman was "not chosen into the number of the publick managers of affairs towards an Insurrection," Ferguson recounted, "yet . . . he was privately consulted upon all occasions, applied unto as the chief Oracle, & intrusted to prepare & draw up a Remonstrance of the grievances and oppressions of the Kingdom, and how far the King had invaded & subverted the Laws, even to the changing of the Constitution."[27]

The remaining months of the plotting were passed over with minimal comment by Ferguson, who was content to assert that the most intelligent of those who engaged in discussions of assassination, including himself, did so only to make certain such schemes proved abortive. Their real interest, he insisted, was to encourage an insurrection, which they deemed lawful, not least because planning an uprising was a "means of allaying the heats" of would-be assassins.[28] Compared to the zeal with which Ferguson participated in the assassination discussions in the late winter and spring of 1683, as noted by his compatriots, his own dismissive treatment of this period suggests a conscious effort to downplay his actions and evade responsibility for his eager encouragement of extreme measures. Had those methods led to the establishment of a republic, he was in a position to claim a major share of the credit, but when they failed to achieve that end, he depicted himself as a savior of the monarchy.

In his role as an agent provocateur, Ferguson took the declaration drafted by West, Wade, and probably Rumsey not to the full "council of six," as he had promised, but only to a few of them, presumably Monmouth and Russell. They rejected it, decrying its provisions, averred West, "as Limitations that reduc'd the prince to a meer Duke of Venice, which indeed was our Intention."[29]

From late February through most of March 1683, West's chamber was the scene of frequent meetings at which the key topic, by West's own admission, continued to be assassination. In addition to West and Ferguson, the cabal included Rumsey, Richard Goodenough, and sometimes Rumbold and Captain Thomas Walcott (who had returned to England with Ferguson). Shepherd promised to attend but did not, although Ferguson or one of the others allegedly kept him informed. They decided, said West, to kill Charles and James as they returned from Newmarket. An attack on the royal party as it traveled to Newmarket was ruled out because some of the king's guards would not have left London, a circumstance making it more difficult to seize control of the City. Rumbold reportedly suggested that the assault be made at his house, the Rye, near Hoddesdon, Hertfordshire, "upon the road side where the road is narrow, near the end of a stage when the Coach-horses and the Guards would be hid, standing alone and surrounded with a moat and a High wall, wherein a hundred men might ly undiscover'd." This site, however, presented two major problems: first, it lay some eighteen miles from London, where the assassins would need to go to hide, and second, it was not a guaranteed stop on the king's itinerary; the royal party might use an alternative route, as had happened, Rumbold allegedly said, about ten years previously when he and some friends had lain in wait to kill Charles, James, and Monmouth.[30] The story about a previous plot might have been a vain boast by Rumbold, an invention of West's to add color to his narrative, or, if Ferguson's assessment of the reluctant Rumbold is correct, the maltster's attempt to give pause to his colleagues.[31] Since Richard Goodenough also heard Rumbold recount this story, the second possibility can be ruled out. Against the last possibility, moreover, is the fact that Rumbold himself suggested the Rye House and, according to both West and Ferguson, agreed to command a party of 40 or more assassins—"*Hannibal and his Boys*," as the conspirators called them, alluding to the fact that Rumbold had lost an eye.[32] In any event, the plotters agreed to attack the king's party as it passed the Rye House en route to London.

As the conspirators turned to the problem of recruiting 40 to 50 men, they debated the respective merits of seeking either gentlemen "zealous for the Laws and Libertyes of the Nation, and possess'd with a full Apprehension that both were in eminent danger from the Government," or "fierce bigotted men in Religion, who were under an invincible fear and hatred of popery." For the sake of homogeneity they opted to seek religious zealots of the kind they had recruited in October. The recruiting was entrusted to Ferguson, Goodenough, and Rumbold. At Rumbold's insistence, Walcott agreed to lead a party that would charge the royal guards, but Walcott reportedly said he would refuse to storm the king's coach. Although Walcott had grave misgivings about attacking unarmed men, Ferguson, playing his role with unseemly fervor, purportedly insisted that assassination was a "pious Action, which he hoped to see receive a Nationall reward, and statues erected by a parliament for the Actors in it with the Inscription of Liberatores Patriae."[33]

The conspirators briefly considered placing Charles and James on trial, thereby asserting the people's authority and demonstrating the accountability of princes. Ferguson allegedly disposed of this idea in short order by arguing that Charles' and James' friends would rush to their defense if the royals were seized, whereas "few would stirr when they were dead." Moreover, "it was never thought Injustice to shoot or set traps for wolves, and tygers."[34]

As recruiting progressed, Ferguson, Rumbold, and Goodenough compared lists during one of their meetings. According to West, Ferguson recruited mostly Scots who were in London, while Rumbold targeted ex-soldiers and Goodenough enlisted men in East Smithfield and Wapping. West, who professed never to have examined the lists himself, could recall only five names: the London salter Josiah Keeling, "a hot-headed fellow" who had been excommunicated by a Baptist church and would inform on the cabal in June; William Hone, a joiner recruited by Goodenough who eventually confessed "that he did agree with Goodenough to Kill the Kinge & the Duke"; and three obscure men identified only as [James] Burton, a brassier named Gale, and a man named Manning. Hone, a "melancholy Enthusiast," had been Stephen College's apprentice and had once worked for Sir Robert Peyton. The astrologer John Partridge declined Goodenough's invitation to join them, claiming inability to ride a horse, but reportedly prophesied that James would not live beyond March or April and that Charles was "under an ill Direction, and the people would be victorious." At the group's request West tried to recruit a naval captain of American birth named Bon, who, they thought, could enlist sailors, but West was unsuccessful. According to West, the Goodenough brothers themselves agreed to serve in the assassination party, but later backed out after enough recruits had been enlisted.[35]

Arming the recruits also had to be considered. Rumbold reportedly insisted that his men have swords, pistols, blunderbusses, and carbines. Ferguson allegedly claimed to possess £600 for this purpose, which had been raised by Shaftesbury for the plot of October 1682 and conveyed to Goodenough. However, Rumsey later told West that the money had come from Francis Charlton. The weapons could be transported to the Rye House in long chests carried by market carts from Smithfield or under a layer of oysters in boats that plied the river Ware. Alternatively the recruits themselves could hide them under their coats.[36]

The plan of attack was simple. The day before the assault, the assassins would travel in pairs from London to a house owned by Captain Rumbold near the Rye House. Early the next morning Rumbold would send his servants to the market and lock his wife and children on the upper floor of the Rye House, enabling the assassins to rendezvous inside his gate. As the royal party approached around midday, one group would shoot some of the horses pulling the king's coach while two men blocked the road with a cart. A second party would fire into the royal coach and then wield swords if necessary. A third party, led by Walcott, would set upon the guards. The deed done, the attackers would either flee across the meadows and Hackney marsh to London or barricade themselves behind the walls around the Rye House and escape under cover of darkness.[37]

The plans became more elaborate as the plotters schemed to capture the Tower of London. This too, according to West's confession, would require three groups of men, whose goal was to seize its arsenal and prevent the garrison from destroying the City. The first band, consisting of at least a dozen men, would enter the Tower with concealed weapons on the pretext of viewing the armory and the crown jewels; a second group would similarly enter to see the lions; and a third would arrive in a coach and ask to visit the imprisoned lords. As the coach entered the Tower gate, members of the first band would kill one of its horses or overturn the coach to prevent closure of the gate, while the second group attacked the guards. At this point, some 300 to 400 compatriots, lodged in empty houses near the Tower, would storm through the open portal. In the course of the strike, they planned to kill or capture the commander, Colonel George Legge, the future Lord Dartmouth. The assault was timed to coincide with the arrival of the news of the assassination in London. The Tower's importance to the success of any attempt to overthrow the government had long been recognized, but the expansion of the assassination plot to include the storming of the Tower necessitated a substantial increase in the quota of recruits; instead of 40 or 50, West and his associates determined they required between 370 and 480. The more the plan expanded, the more improbable it became, especially when the cabal decided that a sizable body of armed men in the City was needed to prevent royalists from proclaiming Princess Mary queen. Presumably reflecting concomitant planning

for a general uprising, Ferguson purportedly assured the conspirators that "a good body of men under an eminent Commander would
be ready in the City to appear," some of whom could kill the lord
mayor, the sheriffs, and other officials.[38]

Still needing a revolutionary manifesto to set forth their aims to
the people, West asked Ferguson about a draft that Walcott reportedly claimed had been prepared the previous October. Ferguson allegedly confirmed its existence but refused to let West see the document, presumably, the latter concluded, for fear that his group
would have demanded its revision. West's people wanted four basic
reforms: the abolition of all taxes apart from an assessment on land
and a moderate excise on superfluous goods, with all revenues earmarked for "particular uses"; religious toleration; the naturalization
of all aliens; and the designation of England as "a free port."[39]

On some proposed reforms the conspirators could not agree. Ferguson, for instance, purportedly advocated the abolition of bishops,
deans, and chapters, who "eat the fat of the land without makeing
any return for it," but the others wanted such notions kept silent
at this point for fear of alienating the present tenants of ecclesiastical lands. Debate occurred as well over a proposal to have certain
Oxford or Cambridge colleges focus on "Mechanicall Arts, and
Agriculture" rather than training "a supernumerary clergy." This
suggestion, which echoed radical demands of the 1650s, was never
endorsed.[40]

The extent of the deep hostility toward the regime in West's cabal
is manifested in the fate it projected for its opponents. Once Charles
and James were dead, the first target would be Francis North, the
lord keeper (since December 1682), "the ablest and subtilest man, and
the principall adviser of all the Quo warranto's against Corporations,
and of setting up the Lord Mayors prerogative in manageing elections"; he would be tried and hanged for his role in the "murder"
of Stephen College. Rumsey argued for the execution of the marquis
of Halifax, who was formerly "of our party," knew its weaknesses,
and had incited the court to embrace oppressive policies. For his
views on the succession the earl of Rochester was also singled out to
die. So too were some of the judges, including those who had condemned Edward Fitzharris. "To have their skins stufft and hanged

up in Westminster Hall," opined West, " . . . would prove a better Reformation of the Law then twenty Acts of Parliament, of which the Judges have the Interpretation, and be an effectual means of deterring others from swerving from the Law to serve a Turn." The same fate was reserved for Sir John Moore, whose stuffed skin would be displayed in the Guildhall because, as lord mayor, he had betrayed the rights and liberties of the City. The Parliament building, they thought, was a fitting place to mount the stuffed corpses of the pensioners in the Cavalier Parliament, but even West, by his own account, refused to endorse Rumsey's alleged proposal to punish those who had opposed the calling of a new Parliament.[41]

Princess Anne, the conspirators decided, must live and marry "some honest Country Gentleman, and raise a breed for keeping out all Forraign pretences to the Crown." The king's illegitimate sons, Ferguson and Rumbold reportedly argued, must also be spared but forced to take up employment as porters, watermen, and torchbearers.[42]

Until a new Parliament could be elected, funds to run the government would be obtained from the hearth tax (receipts for the preceding six months were due), the excise office and customs house, and loans. Ferguson reportedly told the cabal that the new lord mayor would be Sir Thomas Gold or Henry Cornish, and that Thomas Papillon and John Dubois would be the sheriffs. If these men refused they would be "knocked on the head." According to West, Ferguson asked him to draw up a list of lawyers who would be acceptable for appointment to the bench, but he never complied.[43]

While these planning sessions were in progress, West, concerned for his safety, again pressed Ferguson to obtain written assurances from Monmouth that the conspirators would not be prosecuted. The duke reportedly declined, though he was probably never asked. When West thereupon suggested that some of Monmouth's dependents or servants participate in the assassination, Ferguson and Rumbold putatively suggested that the duke and the peers supporting him be killed if they refused to guarantee indemnity; but this is improbable. Even West's assertion that Ferguson assured the conspirators immunity from prosecution rings false if Ferguson was truly concerned to thwart an assassination attempt. If, however, West was telling the truth on this point, Ferguson would in fact have been a double agent, the possibility of which has previously been suggested. This part of West's confession probably distorted the truth. As Ferguson would later do, West claimed that he was now trying to thwart the planned assassination. Such, he said, was the true intent of his attempt to obtain Monmouth's written guarantee of indemnity or the participation of his servants or dependents. His failure to obtain either, West insisted, left him no choice but to continue plotting.[44] This feeble effort to shift some of the responsibility from his own shoulders is thoroughly unconvincing.

At the request of his colleagues West wrote to the attorney John Ayloffe, a former member of William of Orange's intelligence network in England as well as the Green Ribbon Club, asking him to come to London. Ayloffe, a nephew of the first earl of Clarendon, had apparently been associated with Charlton no later than November 1681, when he came to the assistance of Charlton's son in a dispute with Nathaniel Thompson, a publisher of Catholic books. Another letter was sent to Nathaniel Wade in Bristol "to acquaint him with the proceeding of the Bargain, that the writings would be seal'd such a day, viz the day prefix'd for the Kings return, and to desire him to get as many of his friends as he could confide in, to be ready" in case the royalists took up arms after the assassination. In Wade's absence the letter was eventually delivered to James Holloway, the Bristol linen merchant, who subsequently confessed to receiving it approximately 17 March (as discussed below).[45]

No other confession pertaining to the activities of West's group in the period from 21 February (when Ferguson returned) to 22 March (the date of the Newmarket fire) is as detailed as West's, but significant parts are corroborated by other witnesses. The substantive points of agreement in the accounts of Ferguson and Rumsey pertaining to the earliest meetings in this period have already been discussed, as has William Hone's corroborative testimony. Rumsey further admitted that subsequent meetings were held in which the recruitment of 40 to 50 men was deliberated; Ferguson, Goodenough, Rumbold, and West were present. Rumsey's confession also substantiates West's on other points, including Ferguson's assertion that he had £600 for their use and his promise to seek Monmouth's guarantee of indemnity for the assassins.[46] Rumsey, however, would not admit to having supported an assassination plan. Although Goodenough had virtually nothing to say about this period in his confession (made in July 1685), he did acknowledge that he had asked Hone and Keeling "to get men about the Rye businesse."[47]

As he faced the gallows, Captain Walcott acknowledged having been present, at Rumsey's invitation, with Ferguson and West in three or four meetings at which "the plot" was discussed. We talked, admitted Walcott, about "Asserting our Liberties and Properties as *English* Men, which were lookt upon to be Violated and Invaded." However, he denied having agreed to lead a sortie against the king's guards, since, if it had been successful, Charles would have been left defenseless and his person violated. Walcott admitted missing some meetings because of gout, but West, he said, had visited him and had spoken of "Lopping the Two Sparks," meaning the assassination of Charles and James. Like Rumbold, Walcott adamantly insisted he had never approved of an assassination.[48]

Further if less-direct support for West's account is found in Rumsey's testimony against Armstrong and in Keeling's confession. Although Armstrong proclaimed his ignorance of any assassination plans, Rumsey asserted that Armstrong had advised him that Ferguson "would undertake to gett the Business of Rye ready enough before the king's return." Armstrong and Rumsey then reportedly met with Ferguson, who claimed "he had some Scotchmen who would undertake the Business."[49] West, of course, had noted Ferguson's efforts to recruit Scots in London.

Keeling testified that Richard Goodenough had first approached him two or three weeks before Charles left for Newmarket, and again while the king was there. On the latter occasion Goodenough allegedly argued that the only way to prevent bloodshed was "to take off the king and Duke privately," and for this purpose Keeling agreed to recruit assassins. By his own admission Keeling spoke to three Wapping men for this purpose: the cheesemonger James Burton, the carver William Thompson, and the instrument maker Andrew Barber, a Baptist of Wapping. Keeling subsequently met with Rumbold at the Mitre tavern, where he agreed to go to the Rye House and participate in the assassination. His version of the proposed ambush accords with West's account. Barber confessed to attending this meeting in the Mitre tavern along with Burton and Thompson, and his account of the plan is likewise congruent with West's. Barber, however, thought that only James was the target, but even so he declined to participate further.[50]

Once again the substantive points in West's confession are borne out by corroborating testimony from other parties. Virtually all of the accused attempt to mitigate their own responsibility, but there is ample concurrence that a series of conspiratorial meetings occurred in the period preceding the Newmarket fire, that the principal subject of these sessions was a plot to assassinate Charles and James, and that the primary conspirators were West, Rumsey, Rumbold, Ferguson, Richard Goodenough, and Walcott.

Another series of events that West describes as having occurred "during this time" cannot be substantiated by hard evidence, although the only other person involved, Lord Howard of Escrick, apparently never refuted West's account. West's report of his purported dealings with Howard is not crucial to the case for the reality of the conspiracy, but, if true, it raises interesting questions about Howard's role and character. As West tells the story, Howard, whom he had previously known, took him to a tavern and there catalogued the "advances and stops" made by the court since 1680 to introduce popery and "slavery," concluding that the people had to act boldly to preserve their religion and their liberties. "Whether his Lordship were wholly ignorant of our design, or dissembled his knowledge of it and intended to pump it out of me, or for what other reason I can't tell," West mused. Howard purportedly suggested his own assassination plan, according to which Monmouth would lead a troop of 500 cavalry against the king's guards at Newmarket and kill the royal brothers; he would, he averred, participate in this endeavor. West insisted that he argued against Howard's scheme because of the impracticability of getting that many armed men to Newmarket without being discovered, but he said nothing of his own group's plans, assuming Howard knew of them because of his closeness to Ferguson and Walcott.[51]

Several days later, Howard and Francis Shute (who died shortly thereafter) came to West's chamber, where Howard suggested that West, Goodenough, and 8 others to be named should form a council.

Each councillor would then select 10 officers, who in turn would enlist 20 men, creating an army of 2,000 soldiers and 10 officers. These men would be armed and lodged in empty houses near the City gates and other strategic locations. At the appointed time the soldiers would close the gates, confiscate the weapons of the residents, and assassinate Charles and James. Again West insisted that he had rejected the proposal, citing his lack of military experience and his modest social standing. Howard thereupon suggested a council comprising ten men with military experience, including Rumsey, Walcott, Rumbold, Colonel Henry Danvers, and Captain Henry or Timothy Clare, a veteran of John Lambert's 1660 uprising. Howard wanted West to persuade these men to form the council and then select an additional five members, but West agreed only reluctantly to "try what might be done." He spoke solely to Rumsey, who refused to participate, and then reported to Howard that he had found no encouragement for the plan. Visibly upset, Howard did not see West again until Russell's trial for high treason.[52]

The only supporting evidence for West's dealings with Howard comes from Rumsey, who got his information from West. Rumsey did confess that West approached him about the proposed council of ten and that they agreed not to organize it.[53]

Although West's story of his meetings with Howard may be fictitious, no motive for creating this account is apparent. If the story is true, then either the so-called "council of six" was not kept informed of what West's group was doing, or Howard was not privy to all that his fellow conspirators knew, or he was trying to assess the validity of what Ferguson had reported about the West cabal by using a far-fetched proposal to get West to volunteer details of his own scheme. There is conflicting evidence on how much Monmouth may have known of the assassination plot, but he surely was aware that such plans were underfoot. Howard may therefore have been acting as an agent for the "council" to verify Ferguson's reports, although no evidence exists to suggest that Monmouth distrusted Ferguson. Given Howard's penchant for conspiracy, he was probably acting on his own in an effort to speed up action against the government.

West and his confederates expected the king to return from Newmarket approximately 1 April, but a fire broke out in the town on

Thursday, 22 March, forcing the royal party to depart early.[54] When Ferguson heard the news, he summoned "all partys" to meet on Friday evening in West's chamber. Rumsey (who had recklessly endangered his own life by dueling with Lord Lumley over a woman on the 17th), Walcott, Rumbold, and Richard Goodenough were present along with West and Ferguson. "We star'd upon one another like baffled Fools," West admitted, and in the face of a report that Charles would travel to Westminster the following morning they resolved "wholly to desist." The next day word came that the king had gone to Cambridge and would not return until Monday. Ferguson thereupon convened another evening meeting, but again the conspirators decided not to act, this time for fear that purchasing large numbers of horses and weapons on a Sunday would arouse suspicion. Ferguson nevertheless borrowed 40 guineas from Rumsey to buy arms, but, said West, the assassins refused to leave the City unless they also had horses, funds for which were not immediately available. Rumsey's account, although terse and conflated at this point, acknowledges that Ferguson summoned a meeting. Rumsey confessed that he had tried to persuade Goodenough and Rumbold to find men willing to attempt the assassination, promising to provide six himself, but the cabal declined to act because weapons and horses were not readily available. Rumsey also confirmed that he had loaned 40 guineas to Ferguson, adding that he did so at Armstrong's request. Although Ferguson had previously claimed to have £600 at his disposal, the money was in the hands of Charlton, whose location at that point was unknown.[55]

The projected assassination at the Rye House and the impact of the Newmarket fire were also reflected in two letters from West to Wade concerning supporters in Bristol. As previously noted, the first of these dispatches had been passed in Wade's absence to Holloway. As early as July 1682, as we have seen, Holloway had learned of Shaftesbury's proposed insurrection from Joseph Tiley, and the following month he and Wade, who confirmed Tiley's report, had begun discussing strategy to seize Bristol. Word later came that the uprising had been postponed. When Holloway went to London on business on 3 March 1683, he learned from Wade that new "Managers" had been appointed for the rebellion: Essex, Howard, Grey, Russell, Sidney, Hampden, Wildman, and an eighth person whose name Holloway had forgotten when he confessed in 1684. Wade also reportedly told him that the managers had dispatched messengers to Scotland and Ireland "to know their minds," after which a date and strategy for the uprising would be determined.[56]

About 12 March, Wade passed through Bristol in the course of a business trip for the earl of Stamford. While there, he introduced Holloway to Rumsey. Wade told Holloway that the messengers had not yet returned but that West had promised to write, using the alias Ingleston, if anything was determined while Wade was away in the west. Approximately 17 March a letter from "Ingleston" to Wade was delivered to the latter's brother in Bristol, Wade himself having left for Taunton by this time. Unable to understand its canting language, he showed it to Holloway, who similarly professed ignorance. According to Holloway, the letter asked Wade to get his clients together "the next Saturday come fortnight [31 March] to seale the writings, for that was the day appoynted." Given the conspirators' original belief that the king would return from Newmarket around 1 April, the letter was manifestly intended to warn Bristol compatriots to prepare themselves. When a messenger delivered the letter to Wade at Taunton, the latter too allegedly claimed not to understand its meaning, but he asked that any further correspondence be delivered to him at Bristol on the 24th. About three days later, Holloway recalled, a second letter arrived from West instructing Wade not to call his clients together, "for the time of sealing was put off." Not only was the plot real, but Wade clearly expected at least modest support in the Bristol area. The fact that Wade was in Taunton, a traditional hotbed of radicalism, on the eve of the planned assassination may not have been accidental, and the fact that he was there as Stamford's agent may justify extra caution in evaluating the earl's profession of ignorance about the conspiracy.[57]

What Did the Government Know?

Some historians have questioned the reality of the plotting because of the government's apparent ignorance of it until Keeling's sensational confession in June 1683. In fact, the state possessed information about the conspiracy well before this date. Unfortunately for the authorities, the early reports were part of an incessant torrent of accusations, suspicions, innuendos, and outright fabrications that stretched back to 1660 and beyond. Some of the accusations were true enough but many had no substance. After more than two decades and especially in the aftermath of the spurious allegations and rampant subornation characteristic of the Popish Plot, officials were understandably reluctant to credit informers' reports without substantive proof.

Information and rumors about plots to prevent James' accession had been circulating for some time. As early as 1681 the informer Lawrence Mowbray recounted a tale of an alleged plot by Shaftesbury, Monmouth, Grey, Howard, the earl of Huntingdon, and others to alter the government at the time of the third Exclusion Parliament. Late that summer Charles Blood reported a plan by dissidents to use force of arms to prevent James' accession to the throne. Among those named in the allegations were Buckingham, Colonel Henry Owen (brother of John, the Congregationalist minister), Colonel John Scott, Colonel Roderick Mansell, Captain John Hume, the Fifth Monarchist John Patshall, and Lieutenant-Colonel Ralph Alexander, who manufactured weapons for dissidents. On 30 January 1682, John Fitzgerald first reported an alleged conversation between Israel Tong and the earl of Essex that had taken place as long before as February 1680, in which Essex asserted that "the King was goeing to New Markett, And he should be Cutt off before his returne from thence." Fitzgerald also claimed he had heard Shaftesbury, Sidney, Wildman, and others speak treasonably. These allegations, which rather strikingly reflect the scheming that was then in progress, were made some sixteen months before Keeling's revelations. Finally, around January 1682, Hone ostentatiously posted a copy of the Magna Carta on Temple Bar gate, supported Monmouth as Charles' successor, and allegedly offered to sell weapons for use against friends of the court.[58]

In September 1682, Secretary Jenkins received a document from James Harris containing a radical prophecy that read in part as follows:

In the yeare 83 its thought the Mole [Charles II] will be Layd in the Coffin; and the younger Mole [Monmouth] & the old Lyon [James] will Contend for A Crowne but after 2 Battels there will Come A Sorte of People out of the Wood [London]; And will pull a Dead Mann [Ludlow] out of his grave [exile in Vevey], which shall head the people which Comes out of the wood and they with the Dead Man shall End the strife between the Mole & Lyon. Then there will be Long peace in the Land of Aries [England] & neither the Mole or Lyon shall Ever obtayne the Crowne.

Harris' reports to Jenkins, which commenced in August 1682, include lengthy accounts of gatherings at the Salutation tavern in Lombard Street in which John Rouse, who would be executed as a conspirator the next year, figures prominently. Much of the rhetoric was the typical Whiggish bluster, although on one occasion Rouse allegedly boasted that the duke of York would soon be dispatched to purgatory. Rouse reportedly had weapons hidden in his house, and reference was made to Alexander's having manufactured numerous coats of mail. Among those accused of participating in these gatherings were Alexander, Danvers, the bookseller Francis Smith, the Fifth Monarchist Walter Thimbleton, and Captain Humphrey Spurway, a former Tong plotter. The list of suspects also included the Baptists William Radden, Thomas Parsons, and Francis Smith, each of whom had been linked to Titus Oates in 1678. Further discoveries were difficult because Alexander suspected Harris, but in the fall of 1682 the latter informed Jenkins that Rouse had told him an insurrection was planned for 5 November (later delayed to the 17th); that Alexander, Spurway, Danvers, Smith, Oates, and Robert Perrott (a former associate of Blood's) were involved; and that "they would begin under the Notion of Papists the betterr to Incite the Mobile who would be Incouraged thereby." Around Christmas 1682, Radden allegedly boasted: "Wee will fall upon the King & Queen & all his dutches & hoores, the duke of yorke & his dutches & hoares with all the Court-party that were against the bill of Exclusion . . . for nothing shorte of A Commonwealth According to the designe of my deceased brother [Edward] shall satisfy us." Although much in Harris' reports was conjectural, his remarks about Rouse indicate that he had in fact acquired some information about the actual plotting.[59]

More substantive allegations were made by Sir Robert Viner (or Vyner) in February 1683. Through the tobacconist John Harrison, an informant with close ties to the radicals, Viner learned that a number of men had come into the City and obtained arms, including

bills (weapons with curved blades and handles) for persons unskilled
in the use of firearms. His informant reported discussions of "speedy
action" against James. The list of alleged participants is of special
interest because it includes the names of several radicals who were
engaged in the plotting, namely Rumbold, Hone, and Colonel
Owen. Many of the others had long histories of involvement in radical activity. Among them were colonels John Scott and Francis or
Richard Buffett; Lieutenant-Colonel Ralph Alexander; majors John
Breman and Edmund Rolfe; Captains John Mason and Edward
Cary; and Richard Halliwell, notorious for having aided Thomas
Blood in his attempt to hang the duke of Ormond and steal the
crown jewels.[60] Viner's informer probably provided no more than a
list of known radicals, but he may have identified some of the
men—especially the officers—recruited for the projected insurrection or even, in a few cases, the assassination plan.

Several days later another of Viner's informers gave him a list of
men suspected of having bills in their possession. Jenkins was now
sufficiently alarmed to present their allegations to the king and several peers on the night of 24 February. Charles was concerned to
learn who was making bills and battle-axes and how many had been
manufactured, especially since the informer had referred to thousands of them.[61] Under questioning, Harrison repeated the accusations, identifying the principal manufacturer as a smith named Bird
of Brick Lane, near Spitalfields. Hone, the weaver Thomas Trow,
and a man named Powell (a carrier engaged in the arms trade), he
said, were encouraging men to arm themselves and promising that
such "considerable" people as Buffett and Breman would lead them.
From one of his informers he had heard of a plan to seize the Tower,
while a number of disaffected people were allegedly discussing the
necessity of killing the king because of his oppressive government.[62]
Again, there is a distinct possibility that the government, through
Viner and Harrison, had obtained some hint of what was actually
happening, although the reports probably contained more rumor
and suspicion than fact.

As the time for executing the plot approached, more allegations
surfaced. In late March the government received information (as
noted in the preceding chapter) that Algernon Sidney, Richard

Stretton, and the earl of Clare were plotting to assassinate Charles and restructure the government. After discussing the report in a night session, the Privy Council ordered Jenkins to investigate. The secretary did not forget John Harrison's allegations, for on 17 April he ordered fresh surveillance of the suspects. Among other things Jenkins learned that Rumbold, "a Brisk man & of Interest," had been in London frequently; Hone "thirst[ed] for Blud" ; Colonel Owen had not been seen for five or six weeks, possibly, as some suspected, because he had gone to Ireland; and Alexander, in partnership with Major John Gladman, was still making armor.[63] Nothing in this report provided officials with sufficient justification to act.

Two weeks before Keeling revealed the conspiracy to Jenkins, Sir Robert Townshend of Coventry received an anonymous letter suggesting that its author might have acquired information concerning the planned insurrection from a minor recruit. The generalizations and extreme exaggerations in the letter rule out a principal conspirator as the source, and more likely indicate that the author was merely repeating the rumors of plotting that had periodically surfaced since the outset of the Restoration. Richard Ashcraft, who accepts this letter as genuine, believes it might have been composed by Walcott in connection with the latter's efforts to obtain a pardon, but Walcott was not arrested until 8 July, nearly six weeks after the anonymous letter had been written. The Association, as the letter's author called the alleged conspiracy, "is caried on with vigor," having agents in every county and corporation. It has "twelve principals in england unto whom all inteligences comes who sitt most dayes and gives orders." The Association reputedly intended to seize Charles and James and then compel the king to summon a Parliament and allow it to sit until the nation's grievances had been resolved. The conspirators had supposedly drafted a declaration similar in form to the Grand Remonstrance, citing the abuses of the reigns of James I and Charles I, justifying the civil war and regicide, and finally denouncing the debauchery, duplicity, and tyranny of Charles II. The absurdity of the accusations was amply manifested in the author's claim to have seen a list of more than 120,000 rebels with commissions. Assertions such as this undoubtedly made the government chary of crediting rumors of intrigue.[64]

As close as the government was to uncovering the plotting, it had learned nothing substantive about the conspiracy. Although at least a few of those involved, particularly Hone, had been careless in their speech, the authorities understandably found it virtually impossible to distinguish between fact and rumor. Jenkins, however, was clearly suspicious. In the meantime the web of conspiracy grew increasingly complex as the circle of intrigue widened.

"So Black a Design"

FIVE

Spring Conspiracies and Discovery

The failure of the plot to assassinate Charles and James as they returned from Newmarket did not dissuade the radicals from further scheming. In the ensuing months Monmouth's group focused its attention on the possibility of mounting coordinated rebellions in England and Scotland, whereas Robert West's cabal continued to explore ways to kill the royal brothers. Ultimately, however, West and his compatriots began implementing plans for a major insurrection in London to topple the Stuart regime.

Argyll and the Scottish Schemers

Robert Ferguson's pivotal involvement in the English cabals increased the possibility of an alliance with disaffected Scots, a particularly attractive option to Monmouth and his compatriots since it offered the potential for simultaneous uprisings in both kingdoms. Despite the theoretical advantages, however, the prospect of creating an effective alliance was sharply reduced by a variety of factors, not the least of which were lingering memories among militant Scots of Monmouth's suppression of the Bothwell Bridge rebellion. The duke's best hope involved a compact with the earl of Argyll, but the latter was now in exile, short of funds, and distrusted by the more extreme Covenanters. Radical prospects were further complicated by the personal ambitions of Monmouth and Argyll as well as the disparate aims of the dissidents, which ranged from the essentially secular interests of English republicans such as Algernon Sidney to the rigidly narrow theocratic program of the United Societies. Whether a shared hatred of popery and the duke of York as well as a firm commitment to fundamental Protestant tenets provided a sufficient foundation for cooperation remained to be seen, but Ferguson and others were manifestly interested in exploring the possibilities.

In the summer of 1682, Argyll and Shaftesbury had, of course, discussed the possibility of a revolt in Scotland, for which Argyll demanded English financial backing. Although the earls failed to reach an agreement, the possibility of cooperation remained alive. Shortly before Ferguson fled to the Netherlands in the fall, he obliquely hinted to a fellow Scot, William Carstares, that "for the saving of Innocent Blood, it would be necessary to cut off a few, insinuating the King and Duke." Carstares later recalled that this conversation had occurred in October or November 1682, by which time, as we have seen, the possibility of assassination had been broached in Shaftesbury's circle and Ferguson had accepted Monmouth's commission to serve as an agent provocateur. Whether Ferguson was trying to enlist Scottish assassins or merely learn through Carstares if the Scots had plans to kill Charles and James is unclear, but Carstares in any event repudiated the idea of assassination. "That's Work for our wild People in *Scotland,*" he retorted, alluding to the Cameronians; "my Conscience does not serve me for such things." [1]

Although Carstares disavowed assassination he displayed no qualms about supporting an insurrection designed to block James' accession and secure toleration for the Covenanters, and to this end he served as an important intermediary between some of the Scottish and English dissidents. As Carstares later confessed, James Stewart, brother of the laird of Coltness and author of *Jus Populi Vindicatum* (1669), wrote to him from the Netherlands in November or December 1682, indicating that substantial action could be undertaken in Scotland if financial backing could be obtained in England. With Stewart's approval, Carstares passed the letter to Thomas Shepherd, who promised to transmit its contents to unnamed persons in England. According to Carstares, Shepherd subsequently informed him that the message had been conveyed to Algernon Sidney in the presence of Colonel Henry Danvers, but that Sidney was reluctant to support Argyll because the earl was "too much affected to the Royal Family, and inclined to the present Church Government." [2]

Carstares subsequently went to the Netherlands, probably early in 1683, but not, he later insisted, with a formal commission to negotiate with Argyll. He apprised the earl of his discussions with Shepherd and of Stewart's request that the English provide £30,000 and enlist 1,000 cavalrymen and dragoons for Argyll. The earl allegedly agreed that if the thousand men could be recruited in England, he would lead them into Scotland and secure Edinburgh Castle. At Argyll's request, Carstares then talked with Lord Stair "but found him shy" and probably said nothing to him about their plans. Argyll also arranged for Carstares to confer with Lieutenant-Colonel Abraham Holmes. To facilitate future communications, Stewart provided Holmes and Carstares with a cipher and list of aliases, and additionally urged Carstares to persuade "the Party in *England*" to raise £30,000. Before Carstares returned to England, he received a letter from Shepherd indicating that the money could not be obtained.[3]

By the time Carstares reached London in early April 1683, a delegation had arrived from Scotland, ostensibly to discuss the Carolina project. The colony's proprietors, including Shaftesbury, had launched a new program to lure English and Scottish immigrants in the spring of 1682. The scheme appealed to a group of dissident Scots, including Henry Erskine, third Lord Cardross; Lord Melville; Sir George Campbell of Cessnock; Alexander Monro of Bearcrofts (an enemy of Lauderdale's); and Sir John Cochrane of Ochiltree, who had been discussing plans for a settlement in New York. The first shipload of immigrants had sailed in September 1682, and a number of Scots had settled in Carolina the following winter. Some were apparently motivated by the fate of William Lowrie of Blackwood, former chamberlain to the marquis of Douglas; Lowrie had been arrested in November 1682 and sentenced to death the following February for aiding fugitive ministers and Bothwell rebels. The Carolina scheme was of special interest to Scottish dissidents, not least because of the colony's potential usefulness as a refuge from persecution. "I find," observed Sir George Mackenzie, the lord advocate, "the Carolina project encourages much our fanaticks, thinking they ar now secur of a retreat." The duke of Hamilton, in fact, explicitly sanctioned the Carolina project because it reduced the number of dissidents in Scotland, and Charles himself endorsed the colonizing plans of Cochrane and Campbell.[4]

Cochrane, Campbell, and their compatriots were probably associated with Argyll's abortive effort to smuggle weapons from the Netherlands to Scotland in March 1682. Consideration of an insurrection continued alongside plans for a settlement in America. A letter dated 2 October 1682 to Cochrane and Campbell from Sir Patrick Hume of Polwarth, a longtime correspondent of Shaftesbury's, referred to the Carolina settlement or to plans for a rebellion:

I have made offer of foure of the sex undertakeinges you wer pleased to trust mee with, in these three shires of Barwicke, Roxbrugh, and Selkirk, to such persones whose concurrence others more judicious and I conceived might be of most use in the generall project, and did discover a pretty good relish of the busines [the settlement or the uprising], but the whole affaire being new and unknowen to most in these pairtes, there is more time required to consider of a busines of this nature before positive resolutions can be fixt upon.

James Murray, laird of Philiphaugh, would later confess that the conspirators corresponded in canting language about the Carolina project and furniture. Whatever the meaning of Hume's letter, by late January or early February 1683 the Monmouth cabal had learned that Cochrane, Campbell, and others were contemplating an insurrection and, as we have seen, had dispatched Aaron Smith (using the alias Clarke) to Scotland to invite key dissidents to London for the purpose of coordinating their uprisings.[5]

The first Scottish delegates had arrived in London by early April 1683, and others followed in early May. Among them were Sir Hugh Campbell and his son Sir George, Sir John Cochrane and his son, Robert Baillie of Jerviswood, Alexander Monro, Lord Melville, David Montgomery of Langshaw, the Covenanting minister William Veitch, Sir William Muir (or Moore) of Rowallen and his son William, John Crawford (or Crawfurd), and William Fairly of Bruntsfield. Some of them mixed with Scots already in London, particularly those who met weekly at the house of John Brown, the former servant of Alexander Johnston, son of Sir Archibald Johnston of Wariston. This group comprised Baillie (Wariston's son-in-law and nephew), Carstares, Veitch, the minister Robert Trail, William Gilchrist, Alexander Haisty (alias Person), Major Hume (Captain Alexander Hume?), and Robert Marten, former clerk of the Justiciary Court.[6]

In the meantime, the day after Carstares returned to London from the Netherlands, by his own admission he informed Cochrane, whose chaplain he had once been, of Argyll's request for £30,000 and his proposed use of a thousand troops. Taken to see William Lord Russell by Cochrane, Carstares recounted the message, but Russell, who had not previously known Carstares, was noncommittal. Carstares would later confess that shortly thereafter he had a chance encounter with Russell at Shepherd's house, where Russell told him his group could not raise such a large sum. "But if they had 10000 Pound to begin," Russell purportedly continued, "that would show People in" and lead to further donations. Since Russell had been convicted and executed long before Carstares recounted this conversation, he was probably telling the truth; he could have expected no favors from the government in return for such testimony. Russell, of course, had never mentioned any meeting with Carstares, although he admitted having heard "general discourses of many distressed people, Ministers and others of the Scottish Nation that were fled and that it were great Charity to relieve them."[7]

Carstares also conveyed Argyll's message to Ferguson, "who was much concerned in the Affair, and zealous for the promoting of it," and who claimed to be doing what he could "to get it effectuate." Zachary Bourne, a brewer with whom Ferguson sometimes lodged, subsequently confirmed that Carstares had called on Ferguson. According to Carstares, Ferguson also said he had spoken with John Wildman, an allegation reported by no other source. Ferguson was also reputedly dissatisfied with Algernon Sidney for "driving Designs of his own."[8]

As he later confessed, Carstares subsequently met two or three times with the leading Scottish dissidents in London, namely Cochrane, Baillie, Monro, Melville, the Campbells, Montgomery of Langshaw, and Veitch. According to Carstares they were principally concerned with raising money for Argyll. Melville, Monro, and the Campbells argued against a compact with the English on the grounds that the latter would never do more than talk, though Melville hoped Monmouth would lead them into battle in Scotland. Baillie, Veitch, and Carstares, however, preferred to seek English funds, and Carstares tried unsuccessfully to solicit money from John Freke. It was probably about this time that Carstares purportedly discussed plans for the rebellion with John Owen, George Griffith, and Matthew Meade.[9]

Concerned that militant Covenanters might take up arms prematurely, the London delegation dispatched Marten to Scotland to urge them to await the outcome of negotiations with the English.[10] As instructed, in May Marten conveyed the message, which included a letter to Hume and George Pringle, laird of Torwoodlee, from Baillie explaining that the English conspirators had agreed to raise £10,000—not the £30,000 Argyll had requested—to enable the earl to purchase Dutch arms. The earl of Tarras and two "zealous Sticklers for the Field-Conventicle-Meetings," James Murray, laird of Philiphaugh, and Hugh Scott, laird of Galashiels, were soon apprised of the news. In guarded conversations they discussed their options, finally deciding not to act until the English had rebelled. They noted the importance of securing the chancellor and treasurer and seizing the castles at Stirling and Berwick. In addition, they agreed to make an inventory of available weapons and line up potential supporters, and they adopted a password ("harmony") and a sign (loosening and redoing one or two buttons on the chest). The possibility of Argyll's invading the west was also noted, and Murray and Pringle accepted Marten's offer to order them suits of armor "of a new fashion, very light," in London. Tarras was instructed by Baillie to direct Veitch, now in Northumberland, to remain close to the Scottish border. Murray later admitted, "if the king were once free from the influence of the duke's counsels, they [the dissidents] were confident he might be moved to reform their abuses, and secure their religions and liberties." Tarras, Murray, Scott, and Monro subsequently confessed these undertakings.[11] At root their aims were compatible with those of Monmouth.

In the meantime, aided by William Spence, one of his key operatives, Argyll maintained contact with dissidents in England through encoded correspondence with Holmes. Carstares, who had a copy of the cipher and decoded one of the earl's letters, subsequently revealed that in it Argyll had intimated a willingness to join forces with Monmouth and follow his lead. Wishing to communicate this message to the duke, Veitch obtained copies of the letter and the cipher from Carstares and conveyed them to Ferguson for transmission to the duke. Although the government subsequently intercepted some of Argyll's correspondence and obtained the cipher, this letter apparently has not survived. Nor does Ferguson's account, which is strategically silent on the work of the Scottish delegates and the activities of Monmouth and Argyll at this point, provide either corroboration or further details. According to West, Argyll also corresponded with Wildman, addressing letters to him at a Southwark coffeehouse under the alias "West," but without the real West's knowledge.[12]

Thomas Shepherd, who became one of Monmouth's principal English contacts with the Scottish delegates, eventually confessed that he had learned of their arrival in London and of plans for uprisings in Scotland and England from Ferguson. The latter, according to Shepherd, had also apprised him of the scheme to assassinate Charles and James as they returned from Newmarket. Because of his prior acquaintance with Baillie's brother, a merchant in Bordeaux, Shepherd was kept informed of the delegates' activities by Baillie, whom Ferguson regarded as "the chief man for the *Scots*." Shepherd was also in contact with Monro and Carstares, and knew that Cochrane and the Campbells were involved. From Baillie, Shepherd learned both of Argyll's demand for £30,000 and of the inability of Russell and his friends to obtain the money. According to Shepherd, Baillie claimed that he had advised Argyll to be satisfied with £10,000 and that Charlton had undertaken to raise the money. Baillie further asserted, said Shepherd, that he had been in direct contact not only with Russell but with Monmouth, Wildman, and (he thought) Sidney. Baillie explained to Shepherd that they had agreed to raise £5,000 among themselves and a like amount in the City, and Shepherd subsequently confessed he had agreed to convey this money to the Netherlands to purchase weapons for Argyll's use. At one point Baillie also advised Shepherd (as the latter afterward testified) that Charlton had promised to raise the entire £10,000, but Charlton denied this, admitting only that he had subsidized Titus Oates. Shepherd averred that efforts to find even limited funds in London had failed and that no money had been deposited with him, though he would later testify that Sidney had collected some funds.[13]

Further information about relations between Monmouth's and Argyll's agents was subsequently provided in the confession of Col-

onel John Rumsey. When he told Lord Gerard of Brandon that no
monies had been raised, the latter "wondred at that, & what was
become of so many Rich men of the City of London engaged in this
matter," but he promised £500 for the "Scotch businesse" if twenty
other men made identical pledges. According to his own testimony,
Rumsey also disclosed to the earl of Stamford that the "council" had
invited the Scots to visit London for consultations, in response to
which the earl professed that he "was not inferior to any but my
Lord Russel," and engaged to recruit between 1,500 and 3,000 men
for an uprising.[14]

The arrival in April of the first Scottish delegates in London had
sparked new life in the Monmouth circle. Unfortunately the only
real account of what its members discussed is that of Ford Lord
Grey. Although some points in his story can be corroborated, most
of it is incapable of verification and may include inaccuracies. What
follows, therefore, is a provisional reconstruction.

Grey first learned of the Scots' arrival from Monmouth and Russell, who were heartened by Cochrane's report. In his discussions
with the English, Cochrane reportedly heard the duke and Russell
exhort Grey to emphasize pro-monarchical sentiment in Scotland to
undercut the republican proclivities of the earl of Essex and Algernon Sidney. When Grey and Russell met Cochrane a day or two
later, Cochrane unsuccessfully pressed Grey to provide the Scots
with horses from Northumberland. Before the full cabal convened,
Monmouth, Russell, and Grey met to formulate a strategy for the
imminent debate on a declaration and the question of whether management of the insurrection should rest with a general or a council.
Grey also claims that he registered his objections to William Lord
Howard of Escrick, whom he distrusted, and threatened not to attend a meeting of the conspirators if Howard were present.[15] To
strengthen their case, Monmouth and Grey went that night to Rumsey's house, where Ferguson rehearsed arguments to use against Essex and Sidney. Armstrong was also present at this meeting. Rumsey,
it should be noted, independently confessed that Sir Thomas Armstrong, who had frequently been in his home, was there on at least
one occasion with Monmouth and Ferguson, although Rumsey in-

sisted they did no more than complain about their general political condition. Rumsey made no mention of Grey's presence.[16]

Near the end of April, five of the six members of Monmouth's cabal gathered at Southampton House, Russell's London residence. Essex arrived in London too late to attend. As Grey recalled, Sidney spoke at length on the current state of affairs, stressed the importance of Scotland, and endorsed the solicitation of funds for Argyll. When Grey insisted that agreement first be reached on a declaration, Sidney retorted that because Charles had violated both the laws and his oath, the settlement of the country should be left to Parliament. Sidney capitulated, however, when Monmouth, Russell, John Hampden, and Grey endorsed monarchical government and blamed the realm's woes on the king's advisers. Disagreement also surfaced over management of the rebellion, with Grey arguing for a military commander and Sidney favoring a council (the present six and perhaps one or two others). The only possible commander, Sidney argued, was Monmouth, who should lead the forces in Scotland. Russell, Hampden, and Grey objected, insisting that western England would not rebel without his leadership. They did agree, however, to discuss at their next meeting a general declaration as well as means to raise money.[17]

Before they disbanded, according to Grey, the five decided that £10,000 should be speedily loaned to Argyll to enable the Scots to rebel by the end of June. (Carstares subsequently told Holmes the conspirators had agreed to raise £10,000 for Argyll.) Once the Scots were in arms, the cabal wanted them to dispatch a messenger to London, from where the news would be conveyed to Monmouth at Grey's house in Sussex. The duke would hide there to prevent the government from securing him when the fighting erupted. On receipt of the news, Monmouth would ride to Taunton to command Sir John Trenchard's men. Either Lord Russell or Sir Francis Rolle would join them, and another messenger would inform the earl of Macclesfield in Cheshire.[18]

Grey was absent when the cabal convened a week or so later, but Russell, Grey claimed, told him what had been decided. Essex and Sidney had reportedly agreed to draft a declaration that, as Grey put it, "would be to our minds," and the conspirators decided to raise as much money as possible among themselves to avoid discovery, although Hampden and Russell expected donations from friends in London. Grey himself pledged between £2,000 and £3,000, not £10,000 as was later stipulated.[19]

Shortly after this meeting, an upholsterer reported seeing a large quantity of arms in Grey's London house in Charterhouse Yard, and on 11 May the government issued warrants for Grey's arrest and the seizure of the weapons. Between 80 and 90 firelock muskets along with some armor were found concealed in "Bed matts in severall parcells and layd up in a little Darke Garret." The Council met until nearly midnight to consider the implications of Grey's arrest. When Grey was interrogated on the 16th he insisted the weapons had been purchased on his behalf by the late Henry Ireton's son about the time of the Oxford Parliament to "furnish" his three houses in Essex, Sussex, and Northumberland. Grey was released after he and two sureties provided recognizances totaling £20,000.[20]

A few days earlier the Whig cause had sustained another blow when Grey and thirteen others, including Richard Goodenough, Thomas Pilkington, Samuel Shute, Henry Cornish, Slingsby Bethel, Sir Thomas Player, and Francis Jenks were found guilty of instigating a riot in the previous shrieval election. On 26 June, Pilkington was fined £500; Grey, Cornish, Bethel, and Shute 1,000 marks; and the others amounts ranging from 100 to 500 marks.[21]

To avoid forfeiting his recognizance Grey retired to his Sussex home to await the insurrection. Unable to raise the promised £3,000 before his departure, he persuaded Russell to contribute the funds on his behalf, with repayment assured. The night before Grey left for the country, Monmouth expressed hope that there would be little bloodshed and that king and Parliament could reach an accommodation. The duke also allegedly reported that Macclesfield had made "a barbarous proposal" to assassinate James as a way to frighten Charles into reaching an agreement. Grey was still in Sussex when the conspiracy was discovered in June. He knew nothing about the intervening weeks, he said, apart from what Armstrong later told him when the two met as exiles in Cleves.[22]

The essential features of Grey's narrative of the events of April and May can be corroborated: the presence in London of the Scottish delegates; the problem of raising £10,000 for Argyll; the conflicting views of Monmouth, Russell, and Sidney on monarchical government; the discovery of a large quantity of weapons in Grey's London residence; Rumsey's admission that Monmouth, Ferguson, and Armstrong met in his home (though Grey was not mentioned by Rumsey). With the exception of the allegation against Macclesfield, nothing in this part of Grey's account is out of keeping with what we know of the various personalities, and we may therefore tentatively accept it as a reasonable record of what happened. If so, the most striking fact is the extent to which both Monmouth's cabal and the Hume group in Scotland expected to act only *after* someone else initiated a rebellion. As in 1685 and 1688, nothing would have been undertaken without the impetus of an invading force from the Netherlands.

Assassination or Insurrection? A Spring of Uncertainty

However unsavory to the minds of some conspirators, an assassination attempt required only a fraction of the money and manpower needed for a general insurrection. Nor was an invasion force necessary. In fact, the group of extremists that centered around Robert West continued to plot Charles' demise even after the king's premature return from Newmarket had disrupted their plans. West's account records frequent meetings in no less than six taverns (the Dolphin, the George and Vulture, the Castle, the Green Dragon, the Salutation, and the Young Devil) over a period extending from 31 March to the discovery of the plot. Although no other account is nearly as detailed, the testimonies of Colonel Rumsey and Josiah Keeling corroborate it at key points. West may have embellished his story, but the foundation is reasonably solid. More problematic are the reports of the Monmouth group that West attributes to Ferguson, and that do not accord with the views we know were held by the duke and his advisers. West could have fabricated the alleged comments by Ferguson, but this would have been an unlikely risk for a barrister to assume, especially since Ferguson could have forcefully rebutted West. More importantly, when Ferguson eventually told his version of the conspiracy, he passed over these months in silence, making no attempt to refute West. Apparently, therefore, the statements attributed to Ferguson by West were reasonably accurate. Ferguson, in his role as an agent provocateur, had deliberately misrepresented the position of Monmouth's cabal. If this interpretation is correct, West's account bears up rather well.

West and Keeling both acknowledge a meeting with Captain Richard Rumbold and Richard Goodenough at the Dolphin tavern in Bartholomew Lane. It occurred on 31 March, though Keeling mistakenly placed it a week earlier. The discussion turned in part on the weapons in Rumbold's possession, which, at West's insistence, were described in cant. Keeling gives the number as 6 swan quills (blunderbusses), 20 goose quills (muskets), 20 or 30 pair of crow quills (cases of pistols), and an appropriate amount of ink and sand (gunpowder and bullets), but he had a tendency to garble his facts. Since the subject of obtaining weapons arose at the next meeting, Rumbold was probably only indicating the weapons he thought a party of assassins would need. Rumbold also reported that the king had been accompanied by only a handful of guards on his return to London—six according to West, five according to Keeling, and four according to Rumsey (recalling a later discussion).[23]

Shortly thereafter a meeting was held at the George and Vulture tavern on Ludgate Hill, attended by West, Ferguson, Richard Goodenough, Captain Thomas Walcott, Rumsey, Rumbold, and (West thought) John Ayloffe and Edward Norton, who had arrived in the City a day or two earlier. Citing their lack of weapons and horses as the reason for not having attacked the royal party on its recent return from Newmarket, the conspirators resolved to purchase 10 blunderbusses, 30 carbines, and 30 cases of pistols. Ferguson reportedly offered to raise the money, and West agreed to purchase the weapons because, as he later confessed, he "had not been serviceable to the design any other way, and could make the best excuse for buying 'm, having a plantation in America whither I could pretend to send 'm as an Adventure." When the others asked Ferguson to purchase and arrange for the stabling of horses in addition to raising funds for arms, he balked, both because of the cost of their upkeep and because of the likelihood of detection. He allegedly claimed, however, that he had assigned an agent to locate an uninhabited house on the road to Hampton Court or Windsor that could serve as a base for a new assassination attempt. The conspirators also discussed the possibility of attacking Charles and James as they left the theater but discarded this idea since the court was expected to spend the summer at Windsor and Winchester.[24]

Rumsey admitted attending a meeting at which a decision to purchase arms was made, adding that West agreed to buy enough pistols, carbines, blunderbusses, and muskets for 50 men. Rumsey also mentioned the possibility of an assassination attempt at a theater, on the road to Hampton Court or Windsor, or during the king's Newmarket trip in the fall. This sounds very much like the session West described, although Rumsey placed it around the time of Charles' return to London. He apparently confused the meeting at the George and Vulture tavern with that of 24 March. About the same time Captain Walcott, Richard Nelthorpe, and one of the Goodenoughs asked the vintner of the Green Dragon tavern (as he later testified) if buff coats could be purchased in his neighborhood, supposedly for use if the Catholics rebelled.[25]

As promised, West, accompanied by Ayloffe, ordered weapons from a gunsmith named Daff (or Daft) near Temple Bar. As Daff afterward confessed, the order was for 15 blunderbusses and 30 or 40 cases of pistols. As part of the pretense that they were intended for shipment to America, West directed that they be "sanguin'd" to prevent rust and packed in sea chests stuffed with dried bran. But then he began to lose his nerve, thinking, like Walcott and Rumsey, that the Newmarket fire had been providentially sent to prevent the assassination. As he testified, he also had second thoughts after reading the chapter on conspiracy (XIX) in Machiavelli's *The Prince*, which underscored the likelihood that plots will fail, often as a result of disclosure by co-conspirators. Daff, however, protested when West tried to void the contract. Having paid nearly £100 for the weapons, West finally threatened to ship them to America unless his confederates came up with the money. Ferguson persuaded him that Francis Charlton, who served as the rebels' paymaster general, would give him the funds when he returned to London, but such was not the case. At Ferguson's instructions West then sent Rumbold to get the money from Wildman. When Rumbold could not find him, he allegedly reported that "the Major [Wildman] grew a very unintelligible man; for he had first encouraged him [Rumbold] to undertake the Assassination of the King and Duke and afterward seem'd to disswade him." West finally got his money from Ferguson just after Charlton was seen leaving the latter's house, having delivered the funds; this was subsequently affirmed, after the conspiracy was uncovered.[26]

While the weapons were being manufactured, West and most of the members of his cabal met two or three times at the Castle tavern in Fleet Street. Nothing was resolved, but Ferguson, playing his role of agent provocateur to the hilt, announced that consideration had been given (by the Monmouth group?) to a surprise attack on Windsor Castle with 500 horsemen, but the plan had been ruled out as too difficult. By this time (April) Ferguson had informed the West cabal that Sir John Cochrane and other Scottish agents were in London, and Ferguson's focus had shifted from assassination to insurrections in the two kingdoms.[27] It was probably about this time too that Ferguson consulted with Charlton, Richard Goodenough, and John Wildman at the latter's house.[28]

Further conferences followed, according to West himself, at the Castle tavern, the Green Dragon tavern in Snow Hill, and Ferguson's lodgings. West, Rumsey, Ferguson, the Goodenough brothers, Nathaniel Wade, Edward Norton, James Holloway, and sometimes Walcott reportedly attended. Rumsey, however, later insisted he did not meet with the conspirators for a period of five or six weeks, during which time West allegedly averred to him "that it was not fit to give it [the plot] over." West may in fact have been referring to a series of small gatherings, perhaps normally involving only three or four of the conspirators. This, at any rate, is suggested in Holloway's confession (discussed below). The vintner of the Green Dragon tavern subsequently confirmed that Ferguson, West, (Richard?) Goodenough, and Rumbold had met there privately on two occasions in April.[29]

During this period West and some of his associates heard Ferguson's account of discussions in the Monmouth circle following the arrival of the Scots. As West recounted Ferguson's reports, the Scots had demanded £30,000 to launch a rebellion on their own, or £10,000 if the English agreed to revolt as well. Monmouth's group had accepted the latter alternative, and Ferguson expected to take "the Bills" for the appropriate amount to the Netherlands. The earl of Argyll, he reportedly said, would return to Scotland to lead the insurrection, which would commence in late June or early July when the Scottish Council and its deputies were preoccupied with tendering a Test to recusants and punishing those who refused to conform—a calculated attempt to identify and prosecute hard-core Covenanters and their sympathizers. A messenger would notify Monmouth's group a day or two before the rebellion was launched, and confirmation would follow once the uprising had begun. This version accords reasonably well with Grey's account. Moreover, Scottish sources indicate that the Campbells began meeting frequently in Argyllshire in early May, when some of their leaders, including the laird of Auchenbrack, expressed their belief that the revolution would occur on Lammas (1 August).[30]

According to West, Ferguson outlined the projected uprising in England; West's report of this is considerably more detailed than the account of the uprising provided by Grey and somewhat at variance with it. Monmouth's group reportedly planned simultaneous uprisings in London, Taunton, Bristol, Exeter, Chester, and York, with "some person of Quality" leading the rebels in each place. Whereas Grey expected Monmouth and Russell to go to the west, Ferguson thought they would take charge in the City. The strategy for the London area is evocative of plans bandied about in real and presumed plots extending as far back as the early 1660s. Rebel parties would attack the Tower, the city gates, and the guards at the Exchange, the mews, the Savoy, and Whitehall. One party would invade the rear of Whitehall palace and seize Charles and James, while other bands would be stationed at Staines Bridge and on the Portsmouth road in case the royal party should attempt to flee to Windsor or the south coast. The lord mayor and sheriffs would be executed, and additional weapons would be seized at the artillery grounds in Moorfields. To prepare the people a remonstrance would be distrib-

uted several days before the rebellion. Rumbold told the group that
Wildman had shown him a draft that enunciated their grievances
"yet kept within the Law." [31]

All of these ideas could plausibly have been discussed at some
point by Monmouth and his colleagues. Nothing in the plan was
innovative, although the scheme was both brazen and unrealistic,
especially for a group short of money and lacking an organization
capable of turning out hundreds of men without the government's
prior knowledge. As Ferguson purportedly outlined the plan, London alone was to have had no fewer than seven places for recruits to
rendezvous: St. James' Square, Covent Garden, Lincoln's Inn Fields,
St. George's Fields, Spitalfields, Goodman's Fields, and Moorfields. [32]
Arming all of these men would have been a daunting task. Monmouth might indeed have dreamed of such an insurrection, but it
was beyond his means, and Ferguson undoubtedly engaged in flights
of fancy as he baited West's group with his story.

West and his associates were not wholly gullible. They wanted to
know, for instance, the source of the £10,000 with which Argyll was
to be provided. Grey, replied Ferguson, had agreed to raise the
money by mortgaging his lands if his colleagues promised to pay
their share, "but neither could that be adjusted." In the end the Scots
purportedly reduced their demand to £5,000; if so, this happened
after Grey had retreated to his estate in Sussex. When the Monmouth group could not provide even this sum, the Scots reportedly
resolved to proceed, "though they had nothing but their claws to
fight with." Ferguson and others, including the Scottish delegates,
thought Monmouth would lead the rebellion in Scotland if the
English refused to act. Ferguson also noted that the plans for joint
rebellions had failed because of a second problem, namely an unsuccessful effort by Sidney and Wildman to persuade the Scots to endorse a commonwealth and "the extirpation" of the Stuarts. [33]

According to West, Ferguson, determined that the insurrection
should materialize, promised to find money for the Scots and
claimed he had already received a pledge of £3,000, a point also
noted by Rumsey. They were probably telling the truth, for Holmes
afterward confessed that around the beginning of June 1683, Carstares, acting for Monmouth and Russell, had directed him to write

to Argyll about the money that would be remitted to him. Monmouth, Ferguson allegedly said, wanted to confer with West and Richard Goodenough to determine what could be done in the City. The duke was supposedly prepared to assume command if a contingent of 3,000 men could be recruited. Now clearly fabricating, Ferguson claimed Armstrong had agreed to assassinate James on the eve of the rebellion while visiting him on the pretense of revealing a plot. Apparently suspicious, West refused to confer with Monmouth or Armstrong; but Ferguson, said West, "continually insinuated into my friends, that It was unsafe to sit still, and we could not be more dipp'd [in treason] then we were allready."[34] Thus by mid or late May the Monmouth and West cabals were on the verge of expiring of their own accord, and Argyll had no reasonable expectation of substantive material assistance from the English. Ferguson, probably worried about the state of affairs in Scotland and undoubtedly enamored of his role as an agent provocateur, had fallen back on increasingly fictitious schemes and threats of imminent discovery.

This interpretation is largely borne out as well by Holloway's confession, the essential points of which harmonize with West's account. Holloway had been in London on 5 April, at which time he met West and inquired about the correspondence intended for Wade but that Holloway himself had received in Bristol, as we have seen. West thereupon swore him to secrecy and explained how the plot to assassinate Charles and James as they returned from Newmarket had been foiled. Holloway afterward claimed he had denounced the plan to West as cowardly and dishonorable, insisting that the king only needed to be freed from his evil Councillors. The following day Holloway met Ferguson at Zachary Bourne's house, where he learned that the Scottish delegates had arrived in London and were "treating with the Managers." At Rumsey's house later the same day the colonel allegedly told Holloway that "the Generall designe would come to nothing," although assassination "would put an end to all in little time." Again, Holloway claims he objected. He left for Bristol on the 7th and, with the exception of a letter from West that mentioned further delays, received no more news of the plotting until he returned to London with Wade and other Bristol men on business in May.[35]

Wade was the first to renew contact with the London conspirators, after which he remarked to Holloway that "all would prove a sham, for he [Wade] thought there was nothing intended." Both men then went to West, who again explained the failure of the March plan. This time, however, he also showed them "a parcell of armes" at his gunsmith's. They spoke next with Rumsey, who purportedly renewed his case for assassination, to which they objected. A session with Ferguson followed, at which he argued against assassination but held out hope for the imminent and successful conclusion of the talks between the Scottish representatives and the Monmouth group. More delays ensued because of difficulties in raising money for Argyll and in deciding when and how the English should rebel.[36] Like West's account, Holloway's reveals the almost total inability of the conspirators to solicit funds or formulate a workable strategy. By late spring 1683, the radicals appeared stymied.

London and Bristol: Preparations for Rebellion

As West later confessed, a chance meeting of seven of the conspirators at Richard's coffeehouse near Temple Bar in mid or late May breathed new life into the plotting. West, Holloway, and Rumsey agree on the substantive points. All three were present along with Wade, Walcott, Norton, and Richard Goodenough. Francis Goodenough was there as well, according to Holloway. The group quickly moved to the nearby Young Devil tavern, although Rumsey, no master of details, thought they had met in West's chamber. Rumsey purportedly told the others that if they could recruit 3,000 men in London, a "person of honour," whom they assumed was Monmouth, would command them. Rumsey indeed subsequently acknowledged that he had intended to invite the duke to assume command when the recruiting was finished; but in fact the conspirators would never complete that task. To enlist troops Holloway suggested they use the same method previously proposed both for London (by Shaftesbury) and for Bristol, namely the division of the London area into districts, each of which would be managed by an "eminent" person. As a number of plotters later confessed, they settled on twenty districts, with each head responsible for selecting ten associates and each of them in turn recruiting fifteen men. If each region produced the anticipated 161 men, the rebels would have an army of 3,220 "for the first push." Once the uprising was under way, they expected an additional 20,000 to 40,000 people to join them. The names of the chief managers (the revolutionary council) would not be revealed, they decided, until all the men had been recruited. Holloway was troubled, however, by the continued preference of Rumsey and West for "the Lopping business"—assassination.[37]

The following day "Morgan's large Map" of London was purchased and taken to West's quarters, where Wade, Holloway, Francis Goodenough, and West began dividing the London area into districts. Because of his earlier experience as undersheriff of London, Richard Goodenough assumed responsibility for finding a leader for each district. The more "forward" of these were apparently to be told the truth about their work, but the others would be informed that recruits were needed to defend against a French invasion or a popish massacre.[38]

About this time, as Richard Goodenough later confessed, he met with the earl of Stamford, Walcott, Rumsey, and a Mr. Rope at the Young Devil tavern, where they discussed seizing the Tower and "beating the guards out of the Town." After Walcott and Rope had departed, Stamford allegedly observed that the plan might work "iff the Cittizens were unanimous," and, according to Goodenough, the earl "agreed to further it all he could." Upon interrogation in 1685, Stamford denied complicity in the conspiracy, admitting only that he had provided Rumsey with an annuity and that he had known the Goodenough brothers. For his part, Rumsey acknowledged his agreement with Stamford for an annuity but denied having discussed the plot with the earl at the Young Devil tavern. Confronted with Goodenough's testimony, Rumsey finally confessed he had apprised Stamford of plans for an insurrection as early as the summer of 1681.[39]

Another round of meetings ensued at the Salutation tavern in Lombard Street and the Green Dragon tavern in Snow Hill, site of some earlier gatherings. Francis Goodenough and Bourne, who had been privy to "all the former parts of the Conspiracy," were now present, according to West. Bourne in fact later confessed he had attended meetings at the Green Dragon on 8 and 14 June and at the

Salutation on 11 June. Other sessions were held as well, including a gathering at the Salutation tavern on 7 June, West himself being absent on one occasion. The vintner at the Green Dragon recalled the meeting of 14 June as well as one some two weeks earlier. Those present, he said, included West, Rumsey, Wade, Walcott, and one of the Goodenough brothers.[40]

The conspirators were understandably eager to hear Richard Goodenough's reports of his recruiting campaign. He claimed, according to West, that the people were ready "to engage," although they would take up arms only "on terms of ease and advantage in matters of Religion, their Libertys and propertys, and security for their being perform'd." At the request of West's group, Goodenough asked Ferguson and Armstrong to convey this message to Monmouth. The duke's reply, West assumed, must have been positive, for at the next meeting Goodenough allegedly reported that one (unnamed) person had promised to enlist 1,000 men and, if necessary, "shew'm at a football match or other pastime upon Blackheath." William Hone too afterward admitted he had been told of a plan "to appoint a match of Hurlinge a Silver Ball" on Blackheath; those drawn to the match would be enlisted to attack the Tower. Other witnesses attested to talk of such a plan. Goodenough subsequently told his confederates that two hamlets had promised to supply 1,300 men and Southwark even more. During West's absence Goodenough reportedly claimed that seven of the districts had promised 3,700 recruits, and Bourne subsequently admitted the conspirators eventually reckoned they could call up 8,000 to 9,000 men.[41] By any standards these were grossly exaggerated numbers, which at most reflected the overly enthusiastic hopes of local leaders.

Bourne would later confess he had been asked (by Wade) to enlist approximately 160 men in the area of Bloomsbury, St. Giles', St. James', and Soho. Wade suggested that he ask persons he knew to recruit between 10 and 20 men apiece "to defend our selves." On 8 June, Wade took Bourne to the Green Dragon tavern, where they met with Rumsey, West, Walcott, Norton, and the Goodenough brothers. Bourne was pressed to accept the recruiting assignment, but West in particular urged him to say nothing to the ministers, who were "a parcel of Rogues and had ruined the People ever since

Constantine." The cabal was at first unsympathetic to Bourne's argument that the Congregationalists Matthew Meade and Stephen Lobb could be trusted, but at the Salutation tavern the following day they agreed to let Bourne approach Lobb in a very general way. This was, the conspirators decided, "the most probable way to raise a force."[42] The conspirators would have known, of course, that Lobb and Meade along with other nonconformists had been targets of the government in the preceding months, which might have made them receptive to proposals to act against the regime.[43]

The September 1683 confession of Edward Massey, an Essex man who had moved to London in November 1681 and whose contacts included Major John Gladman, Valentine Desborough (son of the late major-general), and friends of Trenchard, casts some light on Lobb's circle. Massey was introduced to Lobb in late December 1682 by Norwich Salisbury, a harness maker of Longacre, at the Bloomsbury house of a Mr. Read. Lobb, a known supporter of Monmouth, encouraged those who were present to stand firm for the cause in the expectation that God would soon deliver Charles into their hands. After Lobb left, members of his congregation reportedly stayed behind to "conclude the work" and urge Massey and the others to remain silent. Massey claimed to have had subsequent discussions about the plotting with men identified only as (John?) Anderson, Ogilby, Reson, Richard Heathaway, and Anthony Sandford, formerly a corporal in Oliver Cromwell's cavalry and now a Covent Garden shopkeeper. Anderson, Ogilby, and probably the others were associated with Lobb.[44] If Massey's confession, delivered under oath, is valid, Lobb and his people were prepared to support Monmouth well before Bourne approached them.

Major Gladman himself was at the center of a group of dissidents who met both at his house in St. Botolph's, Bishopsgate, and at the nearby home of (William?) Brand. Those present included Rumbold, Gladman's kinsman and a former member of his troop; Rumbold's brother William; Lieutenant-Colonel Abraham Holmes; Samuel Packer, who had been a deputy to Richard Goodenough when the latter was undersheriff and who now lived with and was employed by Goodenough; Captain Anthony Spinage, Packer's father-in-law and a veteran of the Lambert rebellion of 1660; Captain

Robert Scrope, a Cromwellian veteran; and Daniel Dyke, a General Baptist minister and a colleague of William Kiffin. Testifying under oath, one witness asserted that these "Consults" were held to determine "whether they should shutt them up or oppose them that troubled them." Suspicion was further increased by the fact that on the eve of the Oxford Parliament, Gladman had ordered several coats of mail covered with Indian silk. The dyer Thomas Lee, a Baptist who knew Packer, would subsequently testify that John Rouse had told him that Packer was cognizant of the plotting. Indeed, Lee admitted discussing the conspiracy with Packer himself at the King's Head tavern. Packer had his own handwritten copy of William Prynne's *The Soveraigne Power of Parliaments* (1643), originally composed to defend the parliamentary position in the early stages of the civil war; he was now trying to have it reprinted.[45]

According to his own testimony Bourne told Lobb on 12 June that the dissidents could help themselves only by taking up arms, and asked him "where he could find a good parcel amongst his people that he thought should stir" if the rebels acted. Lobb, who was related to Carstares' wife, reportedly answered that the people's spirits were low, though many "would make use of an opportunity if it was put into their Hands." But Lobb, Bourne continued, "would see no hopes of such an opportunity as yet, [for] we were too great Cowards." In his account West added that Lobb had promised Bourne to employ two zealous but poor men in his congregation to enlist others, and Bourne claimed Lobb had told him that two of his people (presumably the same pair) were in prison but would aid the conspirators after Lobb had obtained their release. It was apparently at this time that Walcott's suggestion to consult the Particular Baptist minister William Collins was rejected, presumably because they did not consider him trustworthy.[46]

Keeling was to have been another of the district leaders, with responsibility for the area around Wapping, East Smithfield, and Whitechapel. Richard Goodenough gave him a list of streets in the fourth district. This paper, which Keeling thought was in Goodenough's handwriting, was later turned over to the government. Goodenough and Keeling persuaded Hone to join them, and, according to West, Goodenough also enlisted Crispe Grange, a Westminster brewer who had spread the rumor about Charles' purported marriage to Lucy Walters (Monmouth's mother), and a Fleet Street hatter named Barnes. Goodenough admitted in 1685 that Grange had agreed to participate, but Barnes, he claimed, was untrustworthy.[47]

Another recruit was the dyer Thomas Lee, who confessed that Goodenough had enlisted him at the Salutation tavern after explaining how a group of gentlemen intended to restore the rights and privileges of the people. Goodenough wanted Lee to enroll others by playing up the threat of a foreign invasion, although Lee insisted he had not been selected as one of the twenty managers. Lee in turn recommended Charles Bateman, a surgeon with previous ties to Shaftesbury. Lee and Richard Goodenough would later testify that Bateman enthusiastically agreed to help enlist men and assumed responsibility for one of the districts. Bateman, however, denied all knowledge of the affair. Lee was indisputably involved in the recruitment of others, including the brewer and Fifth Monarchist John Patshall and several shadowy characters: Francis Eades, an "ancient Gentleman" named Francis Franks, the brewing partners Mr. Porter and Edmund Cole, and possibly the draper John Noyes (or Noice, who claimed to have denied Lee's invitation). Lee was also in contact with other alleged enlisters, such as the distiller Joseph How, the glazier John Atherton (a former agent of Shaftesbury's), the weaver James Wood, John Harris, John Armiger, and a Southwark apothecary named Read. Lee truthfully acknowledged he had discussed the conspiracy with Hone and John Rouse, both of whom confessed as much, and with Francis Goodenough, but he apparently exaggerated some parts of his story in a misguided attempt to please his interrogators or perhaps impress those he was attempting to enlist. He boasted, for instance, that 10,000 men could rebel at an hour's warning, that the conspirators had £20,000 "in Bank" to fund the enterprise, and that they would commence the uprising by sending a party of 300 men to Windsor to seize the "black bird & the gold finch," by which they meant Charles and James. Lee had apparently picked up the rudiments of ideas previously broached before creating his own version of what might happen.[48]

While West and his friends waited for Richard Goodenough to complete the recruiting, they tinkered with their insurrection scheme. As before, they would kill the lord mayor and sheriffs, seize the principal ministers of state, use the stipulated places of rendez-vous, and announce their aims to the people. Ferguson reportedly wanted to apprehend Sir Roger L'Estrange as well. To secure the streets and keep the royalists in check, the cabal decided to employ a party of 500 men on horseback, brought in from the home counties, to confiscate the horses of the Life Guard, and, if necessary, to use the Hackney coach horses. Ship guns mounted on drays would be utilized to clear the streets.[49]

An object of concern, the Tower received special attention. One proposal called for several conspirators to instigate legal actions in St. Catherine's court, which convened in the Tower. On the appointed day a substantial number of men would enter the Tower in the guise of plaintiffs, defendants, witnesses, and visitors, and then surprise the guards with the aid of reinforcements hiding in empty houses in the area. An alternative scheme called for one group of rebels, bearing hidden arms, to visit the Tower armory; a second to enter the Tower to see the royal menagerie; and a third to call on the imprisoned peers. Once in the Tower, members of the first party would overturn a coach in the gateway to prevent its closure, enabling 200 to 300 compatriots hiding in nearby houses to storm the Tower. Walcott, however, purportedly favored a night assault using a great quantity of faggots to burn down the gate. A variant of this plan called for a party of seamen to attack by water using hand grenades. Goodenough announced that through Keeling he had met an engineer (who proved to be Keeling's brother John) in possession of seven mortar pieces "made for the Tower which he would keep out for this service." With them, he said, the rebels could breach the walls in fifteen minutes, but West and his associates were dubious.[50]

The contents of the proposed declaration had yet to be settled. According to Bourne, the cabal accepted Goodenough's suggestion to draft a set of principles that could be given to Monmouth for his signature the night before the insurrection. In reconsidering the earlier draft prepared by Wade, West, and Rumsey, the conspirators reportedly agreed on five points: (1) control of the militia would rest in the hands of Parliament; (2) each county would choose its sheriff;

(3) parliaments would be elected annually and sit as long as they had business to transact; (4) liberty of conscience would be assured, apparently only for Protestants; (5) all English nobles who had acted "contrary to the Interest of the People should be Degraded." Some thought was also given to terminating or reducing the hearth tax. According to Bourne, Wade was assigned the task of preparing the new draft, which Rumsey would take to Monmouth. Not until 16 June, when the conspirators gathered at the George and Vulture tavern, did they receive Monmouth's reply: "That all of . . . [the five points] were things of moment, and that they could not be done without a Parliament but must be left to them, [and] that he would do what lay in his power towards the obtaining them."[51]

While Goodenough was still trying to find twenty district managers, Holloway returned to Bristol. In his last meeting with the London cabal, which occurred at the Green Dragon, he had objected as Rumsey again urged assassination, planned this time for Windsor Park. Holloway agreed, however, to support an uprising in Bristol, to which end the other conspirators allegedly promised to provide weapons and dispatch "some great person" to command the Bristol rebels. Holloway and others, presumably including Wade, subsequently planned a surprise attack on Bristol using approximately 200 local men and another 150 from Taunton. The Bristol conspirators, according to Holloway, included the apothecary Samuel Jacob, the mercer Thomas Tyler, and the sugar-baker Benjamin Adlam. The assault was scheduled for 4 A.M., after the watch had dispersed so as to avoid bloodshed. The Taunton recruits would arrive the previous day and receive weapons from their Bristol compatriots. Approximately 90 men would be assigned to overwhelm the mayor's guards, and the rest would be divided into units of 20 men apiece to secure 13 strategic posts in the city. Once the rebellion was under way, Holloway later confessed, they expected several thousand people in Bristol and the counties of Gloucester, Somerset, and Wiltshire to join them.[52] After the plot was disclosed, the mayor of Taunton heard testimony that many "ordinary men" in his town "had Strong beer given them a great while every day to be redy att an [h]ours warning to fight for monmoth & Transhard." This crude attempt to keep recruits near at hand commenced in mid-June, apparently just before Keeling made his revelations. Several inns were involved, the most important being the Red Lion, whose keeper, William Savage, was one of Trenchard's men.[53]

Disclosure

As the web of conspiracy widened, the chances of discovery increased significantly. Goodenough had hardly begun to enlist managers when the conspirators were "alarm'd with an intimation that all [their] designs were discover'd." A schoolmaster named Shanks, who lived near the Tower, reportedly told Keeling that he suspected him of involvement in a plot and offered to give him substantial cash and a position in the customs house worth £160 per annum if he disclosed it. Rumbold proposed to lure Shanks into the countryside "and knock him o'th head." Although West acquiesced, Shanks was apparently left alone, but Goodenough closely interrogated Keeling until he was convinced the latter had told the truth.[54]

On 29 May or 1 June, as Shanks and others later testified, an agitated Keeling had told them at the Fleet tavern in Cornhill that he had been "very much Sollicited by some greate person . . . to doe some businesse for him," the reward for which was a post worth £160 per annum, but that "he knew not of any thinge he could sware against any person whatsoever." Another witness recounted that Keeling professed that he had been "sent to by some that belonged to the Lords in the Tower," a reference to the earl of Danby and three Catholic peers. They reportedly told Keeling that he had been "Disobliged by his Freinds & that therfore this was a fitt time for him to be Rivenged of them."[55] The possibility that some of the peers imprisoned during the Popish Plot crisis engineered the disclosure of the Rye conspiracy is intriguing but not very plausible.

An alternative and more compelling explanation of the disclosure was put forth by Thomas Peckham, whose acquaintance with Keeling extended back to 1679, when both men were associated with a coal operation in Warwickshire. Chary about Keeling's association with factious persons, Peckham warned him as late as April 1683 to desist. On 9 June, Keeling asked Peckham if the latter could secure a pardon for him from the earl of Dartmouth in return for disclosing information about an assassination plot against Charles and James. Keeling admitted that he had already approached someone else, but that this person had warned the conspirators. On the 11th, Peckham persuaded Keeling to speak with John Graham, Dartmouth's servant, who in turn arranged a meeting with his master the following day. By noon Keeling had been taken to Secretary Jenkins, who interrogated him for five hours and subsequently procured a warrant for his pardon. In December 1683 he received his reward—a clerkship in the Bakehouse.[56]

Because two witnesses were required to convict someone of treason, Keeling's testimony by itself was insufficient. At Jenkins' request Keeling and his brother John, a turner and a Baptist, met at the Dolphin tavern on the 13th with Richard Goodenough, who spoke candidly about the assassination plot. As the Keelings reported the conversation, Goodenough claimed £20,000 had been promised on demand for distribution to the twenty principal recruiters, the money coming from Monmouth and his associates. Rumsey had agreed to advance from £800 to £1,000 for weapons, and Goodenough himself purportedly would donate £110 to £120 in gold and plate. Altogether they expected to field a strike force of 4,000. The insurrection would begin with the assassination of Charles and James at the "bull feast" in Lion Fields. Either Goodenough was deliberately misleading the Keelings or they considerably exaggerated their tale.[57]

After the Keeling brothers reported to Jenkins, he asked them to record what they knew of the conspiracy. John, however, was sufficiently troubled by his act of betrayal to dispatch a friend— apparently Thomas Lee—to warn Goodenough. West's group had become suspicious of Keeling on the 15th, when they learned he had been at Whitehall, although they were somewhat pacified by his insistence that he had only gone there on business. The following day Goodenough received the tip about Josiah Keeling from John's friend and the message was passed to West, who in turn informed Rumsey, Norton, and Wade the following morning. On the 18th, West, Rumsey, Norton, Wade, Richard Goodenough, Nelthorpe, and Ferguson gathered in Walcott's lodgings in Goodman's Fields.

Ferguson decided to stay in London for three or four days to receive the money destined for the Scots, and West opted to remain until he could put his legal obligations and personal affairs in order. With the exception of Walcott, who had had no dealings with Keeling, the others decided to seek passage to the Netherlands as soon as they could find a ship.[58]

As the conspirators pondered their options, West thought it was possible that Keeling would be "blown out of credit" and that they could rely on their solid reputations to rebut his accusations. Rumsey, however, proposed killing both Keeling and Sir Nicholas Butler, whom he suspected of having persuaded Keeling to defect. Instead they sent spies into the City to ascertain the latest developments. Some of those Keeling had accused confronted him, but he denied having betrayed them. They in turn urged him to escape to the Netherlands or face the gallows. In the meantime West and his compatriots made arrangements for Daff to send the weapons he had ordered to Gravesend for shipment to the West Indies. Before the ship could weigh anchor, however, government agents seized the arms.[59]

The crackdown commenced on the 19th, when the Council issued eleven warrants and ordered a search of the chambers of West, Goodenough, and Nelthorpe. Suspecting that the conspirators might try to flee abroad, government agents watched the ports. When Norton brought word of this to his fellow conspirators, they relinquished the ship they had hired and each man "resolv'd to shift for himself." Despite their dejection, several of them still gave some thought to calling up 1,000 supporters in London or the west, with Monmouth at the head, "and by venturing a push for't rather dy like men then be hang'd like dogs." Dispirited and bitter, Rumsey retorted that this was "a vain Imagination, for the people's hearts were down and our Great men were good for nothing." As West recalled, the pious Walcott "comforted himself with a prophetick faith, saying he was perswaded that God would yet deliver the Nation but did not approve of the Instruments who had at present undertaken it." The parting words attributed by West to Ferguson fit the latter's character and may well be accurate: "Gentlemen you are strangers to this kind of exercise, I have been usd to fly, I will never be out of a plot so long as I live, and yet hope to meet some of you at Dunbar before Michaelmas."[60]

Once the government began the crackdown, security measures were rapidly implemented. On 20 June, Jenkins directed the lord mayor and other officials to take special precautions for the security of the City, the Tower, Southwark, and Middlesex. A list of persons in the London area to be disarmed followed two days later. Comprising well-known Whigs and other radicals, virtually none of whom was implicated in the conspiracy, the list was a clear attempt by the government to strike at its critics. It included such Whigs as Sir Thomas Player, Thomas Papillon, Sir John Mallet, and John Dubois, and radicals such as the printer Dorman Newman and Edward Harrison, a Particular Baptist minister; another name, "Capt. Palmer," may have referred to the Fifth Monarchist Thomas Palmer, once an associate of Thomas Blood's. The list also cited all nonconformist meetinghouses and other places where conventicles had been held.[61]

On the 23rd, Jenkins directed all lords lieutenant to ensure that the officers of the militia were prepared, to keep dissidents under surveillance, and to disarm suspicious persons. In the weeks that followed, the lords lieutenant and their deputies as well as the mayors launched intensive searches both for the alleged conspirators (more than 80 warrants had been issued by the 23rd) and for weapons. Some of the magistrates acted with unseemly zeal: the earl of Anglesey's house, for instance, was "rudely" searched at midnight; most of his doors were broken down and his papers and books scattered. A proclamation dated 23 June offered a reward of £100 apiece for the apprehension of Rumsey, Walcott, Richard Goodenough, Nelthorpe, Rumbold, Wade, William Hone, James Burton, and William Thompson.[62] The seriousness with which the government viewed the threat was further underscored by careful searches of the houses of Parliament and the surrounding buildings as well as the Temple, by heightened security along the Scottish border and the coasts, by the doubling of the guards at Portsmouth, and by the king's decision on 14 July to reinforce the garrison in the Tower.[63]

Security measures were implemented in Scotland and Ireland as well. On 27 June, Charles ordered the Scottish Privy Council to have the borders searched and to arrest Monmouth, Grey, Ferguson, or "any Englishmen whatsoever" who had entered Scotland. Security in the northern kingdom was complicated by the continuing efforts

to seek out and punish the Bothwell Bridge rebels and the field conventiclers, some of whom went into hiding in northern England and
Ireland. Charles again focused on this problem on 15 September 1684
by commanding the masters of all ships entering or leaving Scottish
ports to identify their passengers to customs officials.[64] In Ireland,
Ormond dispatched troops to the north, kept the garrisons in readiness, and issued orders to examine passengers arriving in Ireland,
disarm conventiclers, and remove disaffected persons from the commission of the peace. The earl of Longford, master of ordnance in
Ireland, made an inventory of weapons manufactured by Dublin
gunsmiths and prohibited further sales without written authorization from the government. As late as August 1684 the earl of Sunderland instructed Ormond to arrest fugitives and return them to
Scotland, but the concern in this instance was primarily with Bothwell Bridge rebels. As in England, renewed efforts were made in
Ireland and Scotland to repress conventicles because of their alleged
role in fostering rebellious principles.[65]

Although the government implemented tighter security in Ireland, dissidents on the island figured only marginally in the scheming. Reports of seditious activity in Ireland in 1681 and 1682 by Captain John Nichols and a Mr. Hawkins were never substantiated.[66]
Apart from Walcott, the figure of most interest to authorities was
Colonel Henry Owen, brother of the Independent divine John
Owen. The colonel, who owned an estate near Carbury in county
Kildare, was in London in the spring of 1683, and often saw Ferguson at John Owen's house. Around the end of May or the beginning
of June the colonel called at the home of the earl of Anglesey concerning, he later claimed, business he was conducting for the earl in
Ireland. Monmouth, a rather frequent guest in Anglesey's home, was
present with (unnamed) other peers, but Owen insisted he did not
speak with the duke. The day before he left London on a trip to
Somerset, Owen was supposed to meet with Monmouth, but the
duke was reportedly not home. Owen arrived in Taunton on 12 June,
the same day Keeling initially confessed to Secretary Jenkins; Owen's
departure from London was thus not a result of the disclosure of the
plot, as Richard Ashcraft has suggested. Owen may have departed
on business connected with the proposed insurrection, for on the

21st he reportedly asked Robert Quary of Dublin, who had recently been a lieutenant with the army in Ireland, about the condition of those forces. He also allegedly told Quary there were between 80,000 and 100,000 "fighting" dissenters in London. Five days later a customs officer in Minehead arrested the colonel as he sought passage to Ireland. Released on bail, he was subsequently rearrested in Ireland, though he insisted he knew nothing about any conspiracy. Rumsey accused him of having provided money to support Aaron Smith's journey to Scotland, but Owen denied this, acknowledging only a discussion with Smith concerning a suit by John Owen's widow in Chancery concerning her portion. He admitted he had been with Nelthorpe, but only at a pub along with more than twenty other persons. Although the evidence against Colonel Owen was at best tenuous, he was rearrested and imprisoned in the fall of 1685.[67]

On 4 July magistrates captured another suspect—Thomas Slape (alias John Sealy) of Taunton—at Appledore, near Bideford, Devon, as he was en route to Ireland carrying fragments of a treasonable Scottish declaration. A few days later Walcott would confess that Ferguson had claimed the cabal expected between 20,000 and 30,000 Scots in Ulster to rebel. This was surely a gross exaggeration, although Slape may have been carrying a copy of a declaration intended for use in Ulster. Before his arrival in Bideford, Slape had been in Minehead at the time Owen was arrested there, though Slape denied seeing the colonel. An Exeter customs officer who investigated Slape's past accused him of being one of the militants who had robbed the exchequer at Taunton to raise money for the northern rebellion of 1663, after which he had allegedly fled to Ireland and subsequently fought in the Dutch navy against the English. Slape denied all this, insisting he had served in Ormond's troop and subsequently worked as Lord Arran's keeper in Ireland. He used an alias, he claimed, because of bad debts. In Taunton he had lodged with William Savage, keeper of the Red Lion tavern, where Trenchard's club had convened. Slape was imprisoned at Exeter.[68]

The government, then, failed to uncover any firm evidence, apart perhaps from the manifesto seized from Slape, that the conspiracy had involved Ireland. As in the case of the spurious Popish Plot, unscrupulous men took advantage of the allegations to invent stories of scheming. Owen O'Callaghan of county Limerick and Murgagh Downey claimed to have knowledge that Captain Seymour, son of Sir Edward Seymour, had dispatched letters from Waterford to Sir William Courtenay and other squires concerning a plot to put Monmouth on the throne. Charles, insisting that he abhorred "false swearing to the uttermost," denounced them for having "sworne such incredible & ridiculous things" and ordered them punished as vagrants and returned to Ireland. The incident is a further example of the parallels between the Popish and Rye House plots to which Jonathan Scott has called attention, although it does not disprove the substantive evidence about the scheming of Monmouth, Russell, West, and others.[69]

West confessed on 22 June, after persuading Sir George Jeffreys to intercede for him. In the days that followed he poured forth a detailed—and unmistakably self-serving—account of the plotting based on his own involvement and hearsay:

From the time I bought the arms, I was more passive, then active, was rather dragg'd, then went along in the Conspiracy, and never brought any one man into it, nor did any other Act then come to the Meetings. . . . I could not retreat with safety, and to break it was not in my single power, but I endeav'd to divert it in such a way as might render me least suspected; and to that end I us'd this method. When an Insurrection was principally intended, I laid open the hazards of it; and because the King and Duke were design'd for immediate destruction in that, as well as in an Assassination, I urg'd an Assassination as much the safer and more rationall villany; and when an Assassination was intended, I insisted on security from the Duke of Monmouth against prosecution for it, which I knew was not to be got.[70]

After escaping to the Netherlands, Rumbold wrote to West on 2 August: "When I consider what misery has fallen on our party by your evidence, I cannot thinke of you but with amusement and horror, as if you were borne for the Subversion of your Country and ruine of the protestant religion." But, Rumbold continued, when he reflected on the subtlety with which the royalists had deluded West into accusing the men he had recruited, Rumbold could not help feeling compassionate. This was especially so when he thought about the way West had given his interrogators hearsay information, "hallowing them upon Hone, Rouse and Walcot," concealing some, and naming others only after they had escaped "the gripes of popish cruelty." He admired West, he said, because he had saved himself and so many other worthy men at the cost of only three lives, two of them—Walcott's and Hone's—"inconsiderable"; moreover the loss of these two was blameable largely on Shepherd and Peter Percival. The blood of Russell (who had also been executed by the time Rumbold wrote) cried out for vengeance against Shepherd, Howard, and "that villaine Rumsey": "I am convinced [Rumsey] hath been the Duke of Yorks spie and trepan managed by the Duke of Beaufort ever since he was the little Lords privado." Rumbold closed by telling West that he could persuade the "party" to be charitable to him and thanking him for the zeal and sincerity with which he had led them "whilst there was any hopes of succeeding." West, he concluded, perhaps sarcastically, had saved his life: "For had not your wisdom directed me[,] Keelings villany had destroyed me."[71]

On the 24th, Rumsey surrendered to the duke of Albemarle and was interrogated by the Privy Council. Rumsey, who confirmed much of what West had confessed, was, recalled Sir Francis North, "thought a man of that Circumspection that he would Not venture in such a designe without very Considerable persons & great probability of success."[72] After receiving letters from Jenkins concerning the examination of West and Rumsey, the king decided on the 25th to return to London from Windsor the following day and interrogate the conspirators himself. On the 26th, Charles, though initially skeptical about the allegations, reportedly "declared he [was] sattisfied of the truth of this Conspiracy & further that all the eminent Fanatiques in England [were] concerned therein." Unlike his brother, James accepted the conspiracy as real from the moment of its discovery. By 31 July, Jenkins was convinced that the plot was "very generall & layd very deep."[73]

The most important of the "eminent Fanatiques" to whom the king referred were, of course, the members of Monmouth's revolutionary cabal. On the 25th the Privy Council had issued a warrant for the seizure of Sidney's books and papers and had posted a messenger outside Russell's home to monitor his movements. By this time Russell knew that Keeling had turned informant. After Keeling's brother had tipped off the conspirators, Nelthorpe and Norton had reported this to Russell, "desiring they would immediately take their swords in their hands, but his answer was that it was better some private men should suffer, than the Public be precipitated."[74] Russell then sought the advice of unnamed friends through his wife, Lady Rachel. Although escape was possible through the unguarded rear of Southampton House, Russell, responding to the argument that flight would be taken as an admission of guilt, determined to stay. Lois Schwoerer is undoubtedly correct in surmising that Russell thereupon destroyed his political papers.[75] Arrested on the 26th, he "appeared in very great Confusion" when he stood before the Privy Council, according to Sir Francis North. Sidney, Grey, Baillie, and the Campbells were also arrested on the 26th. Wildman and Trenchard, who had brazenly boasted that "a Trenchard had as much right to the Crown, as any Stewart," were apprehended two days later. By month's end, Hone, who had been arrested in Cambridge after stealing a horse, was in custody, as were Holmes and Breman. Magistrates also caught Sir William Muir; his son; William Fairly; and John Crawford. Shepherd, Burlace, and John Owen (who would die of natural causes in August) were interrogated but allowed to return to their homes, whereas Aaron Smith went to the Tower for having spoken dangerous words at College's trial, an offense of which he had been found guilty in the summer of 1682. Salisbury probably would have been questioned had he not died in May, and Macclesfield and several other nonconformist peers kissed the king's hand and professed their abhorrence of the conspiracy. Ingoldsby, though interrogated and released on bail, was never prosecuted, and Courtenay was left alone after sending the Council a written disavowal of any knowledge of the plotting. Messengers were dispatched in July to apprehend Drake, Yonge, Colonel John Birch, and Colonel Silas Titus.[76]

A number of key conspirators eluded arrest. Chief among them was Monmouth, who had fled by the time a messenger arrived at his London home with a summons on the 26th. The following day the king ordered the chancellor and Privy Council in Scotland to search for Monmouth, Ferguson, and Grey, who had escaped when the messenger escorting him to London fell asleep. On the 28th the government offered a reward of £500 apiece for the apprehension of these three and Sir Thomas Armstrong. Jenkins received a report that Monmouth and Armstrong had escaped by ship via Gravesend to Scotland, carrying with them weapons for 200 or 300 men; from Scotland the duke reputedly intended to invade England around late September. This information was spurious, for Monmouth had gone into hiding in Cheshire and soon found refuge at Lady Henrietta Wentworth's home in Toddington, Bedfordshire.[77]

Grey fled to Chichester, where he and Ezekiel Everest, a customs officer in that city, the steward-designate of Grey's estate at Midsummer, and an outspoken Monmouth supporter, found passage to the Netherlands in a ship commanded by Robert Locke, who had previously taken Shaftesbury abroad. Grey and Ferguson were spotted with James Washington in Cleves, where Armstrong joined them in August.[78] Wade and Nelthorpe made it to Yorkshire, whence they escaped to the Continent; both men joined Ludlow in Vevey for a time. Tiley traveled to Rouen, Paris, and, in late 1684, the Netherlands. Cochrane, Melville, the Goodenough brothers, Row, and Ayloffe also reached the Continent.[79] Others, however, were captured as they tried to flee. Among them were Bourne, Meade, and Nisbet, the agent of the United Societies who had lived with Meade.[80]

As the government's investigation continued, based largely on the testimony of West, Rumsey, and Shepherd, further arrests followed, including those of Walcott, Hampden, and Brandon on 8 July. The same day a warrant was issued for the apprehension of Lord Howard, who had ostentatiously and repeatedly insisted that there had been no plot, although he had eagerly offered to protect Sidney's papers (and valuables) following Sidney's arrest. The magistrates found Howard hiding in a cupboard behind his chimney. Taken before the king, "he fell A crying biterly, & desired pen & paper that he might recollect & discover what he knew." Although James happily told Prince William that Howard's confession "agrees exactly with what we know from others of the conspirators," the king himself remarked that Howard "was soe ill a man that he would not hang the worst dog he had on his Evidence." That would not stop the prosecution from using Howard's sometimes inconsistent testimony in trying his compatriots.[81]

Essex and Jenks were arrested on the 9th, followed several days later by Henry Booth, like Brandon a Cheshire radical, and Alexander Monro, one of the Scottish delegates.[82] Carstares (then using the aliases William Swan and Moor) was not apprehended until a search for weapons at Tenterden, Kent, accidentally led to his discovery at the end of July. Charlton and Lobb were caught in early August. Charlton, who was captured in Oxfordshire in the company of the solicitor Walter Vaughan, soon confessed his assigned role as paymaster general, including the contribution of a considerable amount of his own money, and acknowledged having conferred with Ferguson in the homes of John Owen, Zachary Bourne, and a cutler whose name he could not recall. Magistrates also arrested Christopher Battiscombe and John Friend.[83] The back of the conspiracies had been broken; securing the kingdom was now the government's paramount concern.

In Search of Weapons and Secret Documents

In addition to mounting the widespread manhunt for alleged plotters, the government was intent on confiscating arms from dissidents. Substantial numbers of weapons had been purchased in the context of the Popish Plot, many of which presumably remained in private hands and could have been used to arm insurrectionists. In 1681, for instance, the grand juries of Wiltshire and Dorset had expressed concern about the extent to which dissenters and Catholics wore arms in public and stored weapons in their homes. Numerous reports cited large quantities of arms in the possession of known dissidents, especially beginning around the time of the Oxford Parliament.[84] Understandably, therefore, the government took precautionary measures as West, Rumsey, and Shepherd began revealing information about the projected insurrection. At first the sense of urgency was so great that officers and magistrates had blanket orders to disarm the dissidents, but by 7 July the king had issued instructions "that this search be made with as little appearance as may be of a Military force" and in accord with law. Three days later he added that the search should be conducted with decency and discretion, and that small swords and fowling guns should not be seized.[85]

The government confiscated numerous weapons. Approximately 80 muskets had, of course, already been impounded from Lord Grey, and at the time he fled England he owed a saddler approximately £80 for saddles. Daff confessed on 21 June that he had delivered 15 blunderbusses and 30 or 40 cases of pistols to West earlier in the month, and that they had been shipped in a cart headed for Wapping. An initial search turned up nothing, but the weapons confiscated from a ship at Dover on the 23rd may have been those commissioned by West. Two chests of his weapons were subsequently discovered.[86] Two cannons and their carriages were found hidden under straw and wood in Wildman's cellar; the "threepounders," reflected the duke of York, were "very fit guns for a street." Two boxes of weapons were discovered in Rumsey's house. Although Norton was known to have recently purchased a new suit of armor, magistrates could not locate it, but they seized 7 pistols, 4 swords, a musket, a dagger, and a small parcel of powder. A suit of steel armor that Charlton had hidden in his house was impounded. Holloway's brother-in-law, a Birmingham shopkeeper, had concealed 9 muskets, and magistrates found weapons in Stamford's home. In Cheshire, where special attention was given to disarming all those who had attended Monmouth on his visit, Colonel Roger Whitley and his son Thomas each had 50 muskets in their possession. Weapons were also impounded from Henry Booth (though only three cases of pistols), the earl of Macclesfield, and others in the county.[87]

In neighboring Shropshire, officials unearthed a sizable cache of arms in the possession of Francis Forrester, his son William, and William Leeke. Between them they had 50 muskets as well as pistols and bandoliers. After the discovery of the plot these men tried to conceal the weapons, burying a large quantity of gunpowder and burning 50 pikes, whose iron heads were afterward found in the ashes by magistrates. Several men testified that Leeke, an avowed supporter of Monmouth, had tried to recruit them for an uprising, promising them horses and weapons if they agreed to fight. Rebels in this area were supposed to seize Shrewsbury Castle, which had weapons for 300 men, cannons, and 38 barrels of gunpowder.[88]

"A great many" weapons were seized in Somerset, including a chest of arms at Bridgwater. Confiscated records revealed that a disaffected Taunton shopkeeper named Baker had accepted delivery of four barrels of gunpowder the previous December. A search of Trenchard's house turned up only a pair of rusty pistols, a gun to kill deer, and another small firearm, but Trenchard admitted he had received advance notice of the search. His gunsmith confessed he had recently provided Trenchard with a case of pistols and two guns, one of which pleased him very much: "Such Guns as those will serve to take off the fellowes in Scarlet," a reference to the king's guards. From Trenchard's brother-in-law, John Speke, the authorities seized three carbines, two blunderbusses, eleven cases of pistols, and armor. Twenty cases of pistols and other weapons were found at Chard. John Friend of Taunton, a friend of Trenchard's with links to the Green Ribbon Club, had distributed a dozen muskets to his neighbors and reportedly had enough weapons to supply another 60 to 80 men.[89]

At scattered locations around the country other search parties discovered caches of weapons. At Audley End in Essex, for instance, they found eighteen muskets, fourteen pair of pistols, two carbines, and a wide range of armor. More than a cartload of arms was hauled away from the homes of two Nottinghamshire gentlemen; included were fourteen cases of pistols, four blunderbusses, four carbines, ten smaller guns, and seven suits of armor. Weapons were also confiscated from Northamptonshire gentry suspected of involvement in the projected uprising. Officials worried about the 300 to 400 armed men, including Sir Robert Clayton, at the Epsom spa.[90]

Although arms were impounded from dissidents in virtually every part of the country,[91] most officials were surprised by the relatively small number they found. Unlike Cheshire and Somerset, this was the experience of officials in such counties as Lancashire, Hampshire, Dorset, Buckinghamshire, Hertfordshire, and Sussex.[92] Nothing of consequence turned up in the East Riding, and although many were disarmed in the West Riding, the earl of Burlington observed, "The proporcion of Armes which will bee found in this Riding will not bee great, and this makes mee willing to hope, that the Infection of this Horrid Designe has not to any great degree reacht our Parts."[93] He was correct.

The inability of many magistrates to find substantial quantities of weapons in the hands of dissidents raised widespread suspicion that sufficient advance notice had been given to enable malcontents to move or hide the arms. The bishop of Bristol, the duke of Newcastle, and the earls of Bristol, Winchelsea, Rutland, Pembroke, and Lindsey all voiced this concern, and the king himself was convinced that dissidents had hidden most of their weapons.[94] Magistrates at Coventry were especially surprised not to have unearthed "the quantitys . . . expected" : "[We] have great reason to suspect they had notice of a search, and so predisposed of them."[95] Whether or not dissidents were alerted to an impending search, they certainly could have surmised the likelihood of one once the news of the plot's discovery began to circulate. Wildman was not the only radical who tried to conceal weapons, for others spirited them away in sacks of meal, under floor boards, and in the ground. Some entrusted their weapons to friends to conceal. West's clerk, for instance, asked an acquaintance to hide two blunderbusses and a musket in his cellar. The mayor and aldermen at Nottingham knew that many blunderbusses and pistols had recently been manufactured and sold in the town but could not locate them because the dissidents kept moving them around.[96]

Suspicion that many weapons were hidden was heightened by the reports of neighbors and informers, at least some of which proved to be accurate. Sir John Bowyer, "a very Factius man and a great favourer of the Desenters," had reportedly purchased about 100 muskets and possibly that many additional weapons for men on horseback. Captain John Lockyer, who had a long history of radical activity, had allegedly ordered approximately 60 blunderbusses in 1680–81.[97] Sometimes the authorities attempted to verify such reports by interrogating gunsmiths, two of whom confessed they had made 20 muskets and carbines in the past three years for Charlton and Leveson Gower, and that others were on order. When the Smithfield armorer Ralph Alexander, a former associate of Thomas Blood's, was arrested on 5 July, magistrates seized six or seven coats of a new kind of armor supposedly capable of repelling a musket bullet or a sword thrust.[98] Ultimately, then, dissidents had more arms than historians have suspected, though probably not enough to have launched an effective insurrection. More may have been en route from the Netherlands, but authorities learned too late about a vessel that had arrived between 16 and 19 June reportedly loaded with weapons.[99] By May 1684 the government had confiscated so many weapons that the lords lieutenant were given instructions for their storage in secure depositories.[100] It would, therefore, be a mistake to underestimate the number of arms to which the disaffected had access.

In addition to apprehending suspected plotters and impounding weapons, the government hoped to find incriminating papers. Success in this area was minimal since the conspirators had ample time to burn documents, as Russell almost certainly did. So too, apparently, did Wade, none of whose papers from the period after 1679 could be found. Direct proof that papers were burned is, of course, virtually nonexistent, although the sensitivity of dissidents to the importance of documents as evidence is reflected in the care taken by one man to examine printed papers in his brother-in-law's possession. He instructed the latter's apprentice to burn copies of printed addresses to Sir Patience Ward while he was lord mayor and another concerning the shrieval election. A militia captain found the ashes as he searched for weapons. One of Sir Samuel Barnardiston's servants admitted having burned one of his master's documents before Sir Samuel's arrest, and Hume allegedly ordered his son to destroy letters and papers he was conveying from London to Scotland.[101]

The government did get its hands on a variety of documents, including the papers seized when Alexander Gordon of Earlston was arrested (see Chapter 2 above), three sacks filled with copies of *The Second Part of the Growth of Popery*, encoded letters, and lesser materials. Another paper of Gordon's was found when Newcastle magistrates raided the house of John Mann in search of two Scottish ministers. They discovered "many Seditious books" (which unfortunately were not named in their reports) as well as some letters and papers, one of which they deemed sufficiently important to send to Secretary Jenkins. An eight-page discourse on the plight of the Scottish church, it castigated the early Stuarts as well as Charles II. Gordon, who signed the manuscript, condemned the Resolutioners as a corrupt party content to endorse episcopalian polity or Erastian supremacy and thereby to displace the ambassadors of King Jesus, the true kirk's only head. There are few Calebs or Joshuas, he lamented, who follow the Lord with their whole heart, and few who stand "on the bottome of ane covenanted interest." The government of apostate Scotland is therefore crumbling: "The lord hath justlie broken down the hedge and the walls of Governement and the lord may charge yea is charging Scotland as he did israell." [102] The reference was to Isaiah 5, which talks of bloodshed, the downfall of the nobility and multitude of Jerusalem, the humbling of the haughty, and the desolation of the land. This was, of course, the heart of the militant Covenanters' message, and its implications for the Stuart regime were obvious.

Of the papers that fell into the government's hands, the most important as evidence of the conspiracy were coded letters from Argyll addressed to "Master West" (Major Holmes) or his wife. When a packet of letters from the Netherlands directed to this "West" arrived in the post office on 25 June, the authorities, assuming the addressee was Robert West, confiscated them. The packet was to have been left with Leonard or Susanna Staples at the Southwark coffeehouse in Bartholomew Lane. Mrs. Staples acknowledged that similar packets had been delivered for the past year or so, and Holmes was arrested on the 26th. A week later government agents intercepted another coded letter from Argyll. [103]

The packet confiscated on the 25th contained a letter dated 19 June responding to Holmes' of the 15th, which apparently has not survived. Argyll indicated he could say little until he had met with Mr. Red (or Read), a code name for Carstares, but assured Holmes he would not desert "your service" (the proposed insurrection). "I doubt not," he continued, "after I have spoke with him, to convince you of what I shall then give you as my opinion and leave the issue to God," probably a reference to the amount of money he sought for weapons. Argyll was reluctant to say anything substantive about the planning until William Spence reached England with a sophisticated cipher: "When I once know Mr. B[utler, i.e. Spence] is with you, I can write at greater length of all your affairs." Then followed a cryptic comment that probably referred either to Argyll's latest proposal in the ongoing negotiations for financial support or to a secret shipment of weapons from the Netherlands to Scotland: "I will now long to hear how the last parcel of goods I sent you pleases the merchants. They were long of coming, but I hope are not yet out of time and whatever the fault is may be helped in the next parcel." [104]

Included with this document was an encoded letter to Argyll's wife employing a straightforward cipher based on the substitution of numbers for letters (40 = a, 41 = b, etc.). Deciphered, it reads as follows:

> If D[uke] M[onmouth] be made prisoner he is lost to al int[ent]s and purposes[;] thrice M[r.] Reds [Carstares'] proposition of every thing might secure Brand [= Scotland] without a box [= battle, a reference to Carstares' plan to seize Edinburgh Castle] and then to deale with Birch [= England][;] but it is not talking wil doe it and what is hapened needs not hinder but should further em. [105]

Word of Keeling's suspected betrayal had obviously been sent to Argyll by Holmes on the 15th. In response, the earl was clearly willing to consider striking in Scotland first, then in England, and to do this even if Monmouth were imprisoned. Moreover, Argyll erroneously concluded that the possibility of the disclosure of the plot would spur the conspirators to act.

The letter intercepted on 2 July was composed in a much more sophisticated cipher that combined numbers and words but used the latter in a seemingly senseless order. It began thus, for example: "West much may daily at F with *Bothwell* then or *Commission*." Unable to crack the code, Jenkins sent the letter to Dr. John Wallis, the eminent Oxford mathematician, at the king's request, but Wallis was unable to decipher the document. Its contents remained a mystery to the government until Spence confessed after being tortured in Edinburgh in August 1684. Holmes had previously admitted that this document was to have been conveyed to Ferguson by Carstares. [106]

Dated 21 June (n.s.), the letter contained Argyll's defense of his request for £30,000—"the least sum I thought could do our business effectually"—although he promised to keep an open mind until he learned what assistance the English intended to provide. In any case he did not "expect all from Browne" (Monmouth's group) but hoped "some considerable part of the horse" could be provided by the Scots. Given the fact that Scotland was defended by more than 1,200 horse and dragoons and at least 2,000 foot soldiers, Argyll thought he would need nearly 1,000 cavalry "for the first brush." There would be no time, he argued, to raise additional monies to purchase weapons once the insurrection had begun. "Is it not a small sum, and a small force," he asked, "to raise so many men with, and by God's blessing, to repress the whole power of Brand [Scotland], . . . besides the horse to be sent, need possibly stay but a little while to do a job, if future events do not bring the seat of the war to Brand?" Thus Argyll anticipated that there would be no need for long-term English assistance unless Charles decided to make his stand in Scotland, an eventuality that would be "yet more to the advantage of Birch [England]." [107]

The government also obtained a list of ciphers for Baillie, Carstares, Cochrane, Monro, and the two Campbells in James Stewart's hand.[108] Yet another document—this one seized when Charlton was arrested—accounted for expenses incurred primarily for the publication of radical literature after 15 May 1680. A total of £56 10s. had been expended for the printing of four titles, including two impressions totaling 3,000 copies of a tract dealing with the Black Box, and 1,000 copies of a work setting forth the case to indict the duke of York. Other funds were earmarked for the unnamed printer and a press. Ferguson himself had contributed eight guineas.[109]

The authorities also confiscated a list from Charlton containing the names of 55 men who had donated small sums of money (£5 apiece in the case of 10 men, 50s. each by the rest) for an unspecified purpose prior to February 1682. Among them were such conspirators as Essex, Russell, Grey, Hampden, and Charlton himself as well as several peers on the fringes of the conspiracy, namely Salisbury, Clare, and Wharton. Named too were a number of men the plotters referred to in connection with projected uprisings in the shires: Sir Walter Yonge, Sir William Courtenay, Sir Francis Rolle, Colonel Henry Mildmay, and John Freke. Others were well-known Whigs such as John Honeywood, M.P. for Essex, and Edmund Prideaux, M.P. for Taunton, both of whom had sat in the last two Exclusion Parliaments; Sir Samuel Barnardiston, the foreman of Shaftesbury's jury; Thomas Papillon, M.P. for Dover; and Henry Henley, M.P. for Lyme Regis, all three of whom had sat in all three Exclusion Parliaments; Sir James Rushout, M.P. for Evesham, who had enlisted sup-

port for the Whigs in Scotland; and Sir Robert Clayton. Honeywood apparently knew something about the conspiracy, for he was
seen weeping after Charles and James interrogated him. The list also
included Sir Peter Colleton, a cosponsor with Shaftesbury of the
Carolina project, and Sir John Sydenham and Ralph Montagu, both
of whom—like Charlton and Russell—had posted bail for the earl.
A few moderates and conservatives, including Sir Josiah Child of the
East India Company and Sir James Langham, the former high sheriff
of Northamptonshire and a member of Richard Baxter's congregation, were on the register.[110]

Several of these names—Mildmay, Honeywood, and Prideaux—
also appear on another mysterious list, this one written by an unknown person on a fragment of a letter dated 26 June 1683, two
weeks after Keeling's disclosure of the plotting. The second list also
contains the names of such known conspirators as Armstrong, Sidney, (Richard?) Goodenough, Nelthorpe, Rumbold, and Trenchard
as well as such prominent dissidents as Major John Breman, Major
John Gladman, Captain (Henry or Timothy) Clare, Ralph Alexander, John Harrington, and Sir William Waller.[111] The second list may
have been nothing more than a compilation by a government agent
of the names of potential suspects, but the overlap with the roster
confiscated from Charlton may point to a rather broad network of
persons willing to donate funds to support an insurrection or, in
some cases, to participate in one.

In Newton Stewart, Wigtown, Viscount Mountjoy's agents confiscated documents written in cipher from the house of Robert Trail's
shadowy brother. Robert, of course, had been part of the Scottish
group in London that included Carstares, Baillie, and Veitch. The
Trail brothers had corresponded, and they also had a sister who was
married to the prominent exile James Stewart, co-author of *Naphtali*.
When Trail's papers were seized, he fled to county Antrim (purportedly on business), took an alias, and boarded a ship bound for
America. Of all the Covenanters, he was deemed by Mountjoy "the
most dangerous, for parts, principles, and correspondence."[112]

Although the weapons confiscated by the government were fewer
than anticipated and the number of incriminating documents relatively modest, the conspiracies were real enough and probably

touched more dissidents than most historians have suspected. The plans of the various groups, however, had shifted perceptibly in April and May. Most members of West's cabal became increasingly chary of continuing with an assassination plan and focused more on a general insurrection. In the meantime Monmouth and his colleagues, who had once championed major uprisings, had pretty much determined to act only after Argyll had rebelled in Scotland. Argyll, however, could not revolt without substantial financial assistance from Monmouth and his allies, who were either unable to raise the necessary money or unwilling to entrust it to Argyll. Lack of trust may well have been the primary reason, for the earl felt compelled to tell Monmouth's council in his letter of 21 June: "I made the [financial] reckoning as low as if I had been to pay it out of my own purse; and whether I meddle [in the rebellion] or meddle not, I resolve never to touch the money, but to order the payment of necessaries, as they shall be received." [113] Had the money been forthcoming, Argyll would have invaded in 1683 instead of 1685. Whether Monmouth and his associates could have mounted a more effective uprising in 1683 from their principal bases in London, Somerset, and Cheshire is a moot question. The fact that the 1685 invasions were mounted by essentially the same people espousing fundamentally the same aims as the earlier Monmouth and Argyll cabals underscores the reality of the plotting in 1682 and 1683.

"That Net of Treason"

SIX

The Treason Trials and the Death of Essex

The controversy over the reality of the Rye House plotting originated while the investigations were still under way. With the memory of the Popish Plot still vivid, the king himself was initially dubious, and many people may have suspected from the earliest reports that "the news of a fanatick plott . . . will prove a sham." As early as 26 June some people were arguing that West and Rumsey had been "decoys from the beginning to draw others in." Still other observers, noted Sir Francis North, "suspected [the plotting] to be some artifice In order to disturb the Citty & promote some turbulent Elections for sherriffs." An indignant duke of York complained to Prince William that some were "so very malitious and so ill subjects as to say it is but a made plot of the court."[1]

The Particular Baptist William Kiffin referred in his autobiography to "the pretended plot" of Monmouth and Russell, and the Presbyterian Richard Stretton, who dismissed the conspiracy as no more significant than the northern uprising of 1663, nevertheless expected the Tories to make the most of it. The staunchly Tory *Observator* did precisely that in the summer of 1683, calling the conspiracy a natural outgrowth of Shaftesbury's Association, drawing a parallel between the new plotting and the events of 1641, and concluding that there was apparently "a *Conjunction* of *Commonwealths-men*, and *Separatists*, to *Overthrow* both *Church*, and *State*." Others, including John Bunyan's nemesis, Dr. Edward Fowler, attributed the origins of the plotting to the Catholics, ostensibly, said one accuser, to divert attention from themselves. Given the history of the Popish Plot, news of the confessions did not always assuage concern: "Innocent men

begin to fear least the really guilty should attone for treason by perjury; & revive the old trade of evidences, laying their plot at their
neighbours dores," the bishop of Oxford observed in July.[2]

From around the country came declarations expressing gratitude
for the failure of the conspirators—"Blood-thirsty Rebels and Assas-
sines," as they were called in Great Yarmouth, or "the most desperate
Atheistical and Turbulent Spirits," as an address from Wells, Somerset, described them. Declarations arrived from the council and
general assembly of Jamaica, officials on the West Indian island of
Nevis, the governor and council of New Plymouth, the governor and
general assembly of Connecticut, and the house of burgesses as well
as the governor general of Virginia. As in 1681, the volume of addresses was so great that the London *Gazette* sometimes doubled the
size of its issues (to two pages printed on both sides).[3]

At the assizes in Kent the nobility and gentry offered to organize
a troop at their own expense to defend the king. They explained:

The Number of . . . actuall Conspirators wee apprehend to be very dangerous & besides [we] have reason to believe that multitudes of Discontented
persons, some by their unwarrantable actions, Others by their virulent discourses against the Government have given fair hopes of falling into their
Assistance when the generall insurrection They designed in all parts of the
Kingdom should be set on Foot.

In Northamptonshire the grand jury, recalling purportedly seditious
support for Whig candidates in the last election and subsequent suspicious meetings, listed 51 disaffected persons who it thought should
provide security for good behavior. Among them were Ralph Montagu, who had helped post bail for Shaftesbury; Charles Fleetwood,
the former parliamentary general; and William Harbord, an outspoken advocate of exclusion and a strident critic of Halifax. Whigs,
nonconformists, and malcontents of all sorts were readily tarred
with the brush of sedition in the frenzy of accusations. The residents of Hereford town averred, "From those Hives of Faction the
Conventicles, did swarm these Hellish Monsters of Rebellion and
Treason, and will still do so, since in them Divisions are made and
Fomented, and a Disaffection to your [Charles'] Person and Government taught." The fervency of the Tory address from Wigan, Lan-

cashire, helped incite a riot directed against nonconformists, fore-shadowing, as it were, the Sacheverell violence of 1710.[4]

Such was the background against which the state launched the first wave of trials against five of the accused. Nevertheless there was not, it should be stressed, anything like a universal presumption of their guilt.

The Trials Begin: Walcott and Hone

To convict someone of treason in 1683 required two witnesses to the same treason, though not to the same act. The state was permitted to use the testimony of accomplices, even without corroboration, on the grounds that such persons were most knowledgeable about the alleged offense. The accused had no right to legal counsel before the trial, although the government sometimes allowed it. Once the trial was under way, a defendant had to admit the facts before counsel could advise him on a point of law; he had no right to counsel with respect to determining the veracity of disputed facts. Hearsay was not admissible, although witnesses sometimes blurted it out before the judge ruled it valueless. Not until 1689 did jurors have to be freeholders, but the accused could exercise 35 challenges to prevent the impaneling of unacceptable jurors. The accused had no right to a written indictment, although he could surmise the charges against him by the questions posed in pretrial interrogation. He did have the right to call character witnesses, a potentially valuable option because jurors in treason trials were often forced to discriminate between the conflicting testimony of witnesses and the accused.

In the space of a mere two days—12 and 13 July—the state tried five men: Thomas Walcott, William Hone, Lord Russell, John Rouse, and William Blague. Walcott was first, probably for two reasons: he had had links with Shaftesbury and the plan for a general insurrection as well as with West's cabal and the proposed Rye House assassination; and he had written to Secretary Jenkins, hoping for a pardon in return for a confession that promised to be more revealing than Keeling's. In its first trial the state needed an opportunity both to lay out the conspiracy and to procure a virtually certain conviction. With one or two guilty verdicts in hand the government could then strike quickly at Russell, an outspoken critic of Charles in the past and a member of Monmouth's revolutionary council.

At the Old Bailey on the morning of the 12th, Walcott, Hone, Rouse, and Blague were arraigned. All pleaded not guilty. With the lord chief justice, Sir Francis Pemberton, presiding, Walcott was tried the same afternoon. The state called four witnesses: Rumsey, Keeling, Bourne, and West. Much of their testimony was directed to the conspiracy in general rather than to Walcott's involvement, but what three of them had to say about the defendant was nevertheless incriminating. Keeling could only place Walcott in a meeting at the Salutation tavern during which West had allegedly remarked that he hoped to see Keeling lead an army in Wapping. Keeling's testimony was useful only in helping the state lay out the broad lines of the conspiracy. West accused Walcott of having told him about Shaftesbury's proposed insurrection, including Walcott's attempt to recruit West himself, and about various plans to attack the royal brothers. West also claimed that Walcott had mentioned Shaftesbury's interest in a declaration and showed him a paper reciting attempts to introduce arbitrary government and popery in the reign of the early Stuarts and Charles II. West and Rumsey noted Walcott's opposition to assassination as a cowardly act, but Rumsey also testified that the captain had expressed a willingness to command the party that would attack the king's guards near the Rye House. Both men placed Walcott in the meeting after the Newmarket fire, at which meeting they made plans to have West purchase weapons for them. According to Rumsey, West, and Bourne, Walcott was present when the cabal formulated the scheme to divide London into twenty districts. Rumsey and Bourne also placed Walcott at a later meeting in the Salutation tavern during which Goodenough gave his report on raising troops, and at a session held at Captain Tracy's (where Walcott lodged) after the discovery of the plot, at which session the conspirators decided to flee.[5]

Walcott had the opportunity to question each of the four government witnesses as well as to summon his own. He called only one—and that solely to support his claim that he had suffered from gout in the spring of 1683 and would therefore not have been a likely participant in a proposed assassination party. Apart from that argument he based his defense on two points, the first of which was that the state's witnesses had lied to save themselves. Pemberton would have none of this: "There is nothing more reasonable, nothing more just in the world, than to make use of some traitors to discover and convict the others, else would treason be hatched securely." Walcott also argued that he had only been guilty of misprision (concealment) of treason, having gone only to some of the meetings, and that by accident and solely to "hear news." He admitted having heard some discussion about assassinating the king but insisted he had always condemned such proposals. The solicitor general, however, scoffed that he had gone to the sessions only to learn of the latest reports: "No man that comes there would have been admitted merely for curiosity"—a telling point. More importantly, Pemberton rejected Walcott's attempt to limit his offense to misprision: "For a man to hear of treason accidentally, or occasionally, and conceal it, is but misprision; but if a man will be at a consult where treason is hatched, and will then conceal it, he is guilty of treason therein."[6]

Not only did Walcott admit to having attended meetings of the conspirators and participated in discussions of assassination but he had previously written a letter to Jenkins that was introduced in the trial. Composed after he saw his name in the royal proclamation, the letter acknowledges his guilt. He offered to inform Charles of everything he knew about radical activities in England, Scotland, and Ireland, "which I suppose may be something more than the original discoverer [Keeling] was able to acquaint his majesty with, especially as to Ireland." He had learned many things, he claimed, through his intimacy with "a Scotch minister [Ferguson], through whose hands much of the business went." Walcott also offered to go to the Netherlands and spy on the exiles.[7]

The jury took almost no time to find Walcott guilty, and he was executed on the 20th before a crowd estimated at 30,000, a testimony to popular interest in the plotting. On the gallows he blamed his imminent death on persons guiltier than he, "who Combin'd together to Swear me out of my Life, thereby to Save their own." Although he admitted having attended some of the conspirators' meetings, they were only concerned with asserting their "Liberties and Properties as *English* Men." Despite what he had hinted at in his letter to Jenkins, he insisted now that he knew of no Englishman or Protestant in Ireland who had been engaged in the plotting. His head and quarters, along with those of four colleagues, remained on public display until May 1689.[8]

Hone was tried on the morning of the 13th by the same jury that had found Walcott guilty. The previous day he had pleaded not guilty, but only after Pemberton refused to let him plead guilty to the Rye House conspiracy but not to the companion charge in the indictment, that of providing weapons. Keeling and West testified that Hone had been present at the Dolphin tavern on the day the conspirators discussed the number of weapons needed to kill Charles and James, but, West admitted, he arrived *after* these deliberations were concluded. Keeling, however, claimed that on one occasion Hone acknowledged he had been one of the party that had planned to assassinate the king and duke of York at the Rye House. West could say only that he had seen Hone in the company of one Mannius, another of the alleged assassins, and that Richard Goodenough had spoken to Hone "about a little job for the duke." The weakness of this testimony was offset by the fact that Hone had already conceded that Goodenough had recruited him to kill Charles and James. The state also produced two witnesses—Sir Nicholas Butler and Captain William Richardson, keeper of Newgate prison—who testified that Hone had previously told them of a plot to assassinate the royal brothers, using crossbows to fire from the steeple of Bow Church during the lord mayor's show. Hone acknowledged this conversation, but claimed he was only passing on something he had learned from a butcher associated with Thomas Blood. That plot had allegedly occurred some seven years earlier. Hone called no witnesses in his defense, Pemberton urged the jury to find him guilty, and the jurors did so without leaving the room.[9]

As in the case of Walcott, Hone's guilt is not in doubt. He admitted his complicity, though insisting to the end that he had been drawn in by Goodenough, who was professedly determined "to secure the Liberty & priviledges of the people." Hone was a bit player whose trial served primarily to underscore the reality of the assassination conspiracy. On the day of his execution, in a conversation with Dr. Thomas Cartwright, Hone plaintively remarked: "I never was at any of their meetings, none of their Cabals, but in a publick *Coffee-house* or *Tavern*, where they discoursed the matter of Fact: and I was to meet the *K.* and the *D.* of *York*, but I did not know at that time when, or where, nor what was my business."[10]

Russell: Misprision or Treason?

Hone's trial was but a warmup for Russell's, which convened around 9 A.M. the same morning, 13 July. Although Russell was entitled to 35 challenges in jury selection and invoked that right 31 times, he accepted one juror (Thomas Short) who had already sat in the trials of Walcott and Hone,[11] and who was therefore predisposed to accept the validity of the conspiracy.

At the king's insistence Russell was for the most part treated fairly, at least by the standards that prevailed in 1683.[12] Before the trial he was allowed to discuss his case with 4 barristers and a solicitor selected by his wife;[13] he was provided with a list of 60 to 80 prospective jurors before the proceedings commenced; he was allowed to call 11 character witnesses; and he was interrogated well in advance of the trial by members of the Privy Council, whose questions gave him a reasonable idea of the charges to be brought against him, and therefore more than two weeks in which to prepare his defense.

Russell's notes reveal diligent preparation. They also manifest that in defending himself he intended to attack the government's case on points of law and the credibility of its witnesses rather than call witnesses of his own to rebut the charges. From his lawyers he apparently learned that the state would base its charge on 25 Edward III, stat. 5, c. 2, or 13 Charles II, c. 1, for he scrutinized those statutes as well as pertinent commentary in Sir Edward Coke's *Institutes*. He planned to argue, for instance, that under the Edwardian statute, encompassing the king's death had to be demonstrated by an overt act, such as consultations about it, assembling to undertake it, providing weapons, or sending others to commit the assassination. Conspiring to levy war (which he knew he was guilty of) was not the same, he believed, as plotting the king's death. To levy war entails assembly for that purpose or actual fighting, but "conspiracy to Levy

War," he thought, "is no Treason." He also hoped to argue that the state needed two witnesses to prove the same kind of treason: "If one Proves the *Design, & Meeting*; Another the *Meeting*, but nothing of the *Intent*, this is but One Witnesse: For the last Proves nothing Ill." Russell, it seems, was cognizant that the state could establish his presence at suspicious gatherings, but since inference alone was not adequate proof (as Coke had argued), his defense would depend at least in part on the government's inability (he hoped) to produce two witnesses to testify that those meetings were treasonable.[14]

Russell intended not only to be alert for contradictions in the testimony of the witnesses but also to question their character. Because accomplices in a wicked action were not reputable, the substance of their allegations, he thought, was improbable, especially when made against someone of unblemished reputation. Moreover, he reasoned, "I may Examine the Witnesses, as to their Intimacy with mee. For it is not to be beleeved that a Person of Ordinary Discretion should venture his Life upon little, or no Acquaintance." Russell intended to attack Rumsey on the grounds that he had received "great Benefits" from Charles and James yet had, according to his own confession, plotted to kill both of them. "Who can think that this Ungrateful Man, who had Conspired to take away the Life of his Prince, who had bin so great a Benefactor to him, will stick at an Oath to take away my Life, when he hath hopes thereby to save his own?" Rumsey's pardon, Russell believed, did not make him a credible witness, for it removed the legal guilt but not "the Blackness & Basenesse of his Soul." The pardon forfeited the king's right to punish Rumsey but not "the Subject's Right to cover himself from the Testimony of one so Convict[ed]." By the time Russell reached the courtroom, however, this argument had already been rejected in Walcott's trial.[15]

Testimony about a planned rebellion in the west could be countered, Russell surmised, by disputing the likelihood of its success. It might also be asked why no witnesses had surfaced in the west so long after the discovery of the conspiracy, for had the plot been real, some presumably would have testified out of conscience or fear.

Russell came very close to confessing what he would later admit, namely that he had been guilty of misprision of treason. "The Words themselves," he said in an apparent reference to the alleged discussions of the conspirators, amounted to no more than concealment. "So that is the *Misprision* of a *Misprision*—For they import only an Expectation, & knowledge of that Rising, but no share that these then mett, had of it." [16] Russell may have considered the possibility of acknowledging that he had been guilty of misprision, but his counsel advised him against it, presumably because of the fuzzy distinction between this offense and treason per se. Moreover, Walcott's trial on the 12th demonstrated the ineffectiveness of such a defense.

Russell's decision not to confess misprision is debatable, but by his own subsequent admission he was guilty of at least this much. The draft of his concluding speech to the jury therefore rings untrue. After roundly denouncing assassination, consistently with his principles, as an "abominably Wicked, Rash, & Inconsiderate" action, he condemned insurrection with equal fervor but certainly less honesty: "[It] is a Thing so wicked, & withall so Impracticable, that it never enter'd into my thoughts." Another of his observations on insurrection may in fact go a long way toward explaining why Monmouth's council increasingly shied away from a popular uprising in England, and why so little progress was made in Bristol and Taunton toward the recruitment of volunteers: "Had I been disposed to it, I never found (by all my Observation) that there was the least Disposition or Tendency to it in the People." [17]

In the trial itself the state called four witnesses: Rumsey, Shepherd, Howard, and West, though Chief Justice Pemberton quickly dismissed West's evidence as hearsay because he could testify only to what Ferguson and Rumsey had told him about Russell. Rumsey placed Russell at Shepherd's house in late October or early November 1682 with Ferguson, Monmouth, Armstrong, and Grey. The discussion, he recalled, had concerned Trenchard's failure to recruit men at Taunton for Shaftesbury's proposed rebellion, and plans to ascertain the state of the royal guards at the Savoy and the mews. Shepherd corroborated Russell's attendance at this meeting and possibly a second, but could not recall if he had been present when Ferguson read a draft of a revolutionary manifesto. Most of Howard's testimony provided background information about Shaftesbury's planned insurrection; none of this information bore directly on Russell, and it was therefore discounted by Pemberton, but only after the jury had heard a detailed account. Howard did, however, identify Russell as a member of Monmouth's revolutionary council formed in January 1683 at Hampden's house; on that occasion, Howard asserted, they had discussed where the insurrection should begin. A second meeting of the cabal, also attended by Russell according to Howard, dispatched a messenger to Argyll "to settle an understanding with him," and others to Scotland to invite dissident leaders to London. This, then, was the crux of the state's case against Russell.[18]

Russell questioned each witness, but his effort was anemic. He conceded he had been at Shepherd's, but only to taste wine. No discourse about raising an army or surprising the guards had taken place. Although he had admitted in pretrial interrogation that he had been to Shepherd's a number of times, in the trial itself he claimed to have been there only once. Russell also acknowledged his presence at the meetings with Monmouth, Essex, Sidney, Hampden, and Howard, but they had gathered, he argued, "only to talk of news, and talk of things in general," and to listen to Howard, whom he described as "a man that hath a voluble tongue, talks very well, and is full of discourse." There had been "no formed design." Russell also put forth the arguments he had prepared in advance, and tried to undercut Rumsey's testimony by contending that the discussion to which the colonel referred had occurred before he (Russell) arrived at Shepherd's. Rumsey strongly disputed this.[19]

The most intangible aspect of Russell's trial was the impact of the news of Essex's death on the jury—an intrusion that in modern American law would result in a mistrial. The jury had hardly been seated when the attorney general, Sir Robert Sawyer, remarked that Essex "hath, this morning, prevented the hand of justice upon himself." The news of Essex's fate, Howard claimed during his testimony, "hath sunk my voice." In his closing argument Sir George Jeffreys used the earl's death as dramatic testimony to the reality of the conspiracy: "Who should think that my lord of Essex, who had been advanced so much in his estate and honour, should be guilty of such desperate things! which had he not been conscious of, he would scarcely have brought himself to that timely end, to avoid the methods of public justice." Lady Rachel Russell and Ferguson were probably correct in concluding that the references to Essex's demise swayed the jury, although how much is impossible to ascertain. In any event the jurors found Russell guilty on the afternoon of the 13th.[20]

Several days after the trial Russell petitioned the king for mercy, insisting that he had "never had any Intention or thought of doing hurt to your Majestys sacred Person," a claim that left open the question of an insurrection to bar James' succession. On the 19th, however, he referred to the real issue. After repeating his protestation of innocence with respect to any plot against the king's person or against the present form of government, he continued: "I know of noe designe now on foot against either yet I doe not deny but I have heard many things & say'd some things contrary to my duty." By this point Gilbert Burnet was ministering to him almost constantly. Burnet, in fact, would shortly be accused of writing Russell's gallows speech, the contents of which he accurately mentioned to Sir Edward Harley on the 19th.[21]

In that speech, delivered two days later, Russell justified his actions as efforts to defend Protestantism from popery. He had not been involved in a plot to change the government, he insisted, nor had anyone spoken to him about assassinating the king. He admitted, however, that he had been at Shepherd's house (at Monmouth's request) when those present discussed the feasibility of surprising the royal guards, and he confessed to having heard this idea mentioned on other occasions. He and Monmouth opposed such an undertaking, he claimed, when it was discussed at Shepherd's house. He heard people speak "with much more Heat, then Judgment," but he went to his death proclaiming that he was guilty only of misprision for having not reported the meeting at Shepherd's house.[22]

Russell clearly knew more than he revealed, and his resolve not to make a fuller confession was probably reinforced by his wife and Burnet. There is evidence that Burnet, acting at Lady Russell's direction, had the gallows speech printed the day before the execution. Allegations that Burnet had written the speech prompted the Privy Council to interrogate him several times in the ensuing week.[23] A strong probability exists that Burnet helped Russell draft his speech, probably with a view to protecting Monmouth and his associates; at the very least he discussed its contents with Russell.[24]

Sensitive to the potential propaganda value of Russell's statement, the Tories rushed retorts into print. Among them were *Animadversions on the Last Speech and Confession of the Late William Lord Russel* (1683), *Some Succinct Remarks on the Speech of the Late Lord Russel* (1683), and *An Antidote Against Poison* (1683), the latter published by the king's own stationer. Russell's authorship of his gallows speech was denied in *Animadversions upon a Paper, Entitled, the Speech of the Late Lord Russel* (1683). *A Vindication of the Lord Russel's Speech and Paper* (1683) was in fact a satirical attack on Russell. Such works underscore the trial's political importance, one manifestation of which has been a debate over Russell's guilt that has continued to the present day.[25] The evidence of Russell's guilt, however, is sufficiently strong to discredit traditional Whig protestations of his innocence.

Rouse and Blague at the Bar

The government managed to cram two more trials into the same day on which Hone and Russell were tried and found guilty. John Rouse and Captain William Blague both pleaded innocent; although their trials were separate, they had identical juries, six members of which had served as jurors for Walcott and Hone. (Rouse exercised several challenges, Blague none.)[26] The state produced three witnesses against Rouse, but one could testify only to an alleged offense for which Rouse had been acquitted in 1681. The principal witness, Thomas Lee, who had been enlisted for the uprising in London by Richard Goodenough, testified that he had subsequently reported to Rouse and Goodenough about his own recruiting efforts. Lee also testified that Rouse had informed him of the importance of seizing the king to prevent the insurrection from turning into a civil war, and of a plan to recruit sailors for an assault on the Tower by staging a competition for a golden ball on Blackheath. Moreover, Lee asserted that he had gone with Rouse and Mate Lee to study the best place to attack the Tower. After Keeling turned informer, Thomas Lee had tried to help Rouse hide by cutting his hair and giving him a wig. The second witness, Mate Lee, claimed that Rouse had enlisted him and had urged the importance of securing the king, the Tower, and Whitehall.

Rouse's defense centered around his claim that Thomas Lee had persuaded him to join the conspirators and that he had made notes of his conversations with Lee for the purpose of informing the authorities. Fearing that Rouse might try such a gambit, however, Lee had struck preemptively in his testimony by swearing against him. Rouse, who had no witnesses to testify in his behalf, was ultimately driven to self-deprecation: "I appeal to your lordship, and this honourable court, whether it is likely for me, who am such a silly person, to engage in such a devilish design." Unpersuaded, the jurors found him guilty.

The printed version of Rouse's gallows speech reiterated his contention that he had listened to Thomas Lee's discussion of the proposed insurrection with a view to reporting the conspiracy to the government. He confessed, however, that the plan to lure potential recruits to Blackheath was his, though advanced only to elicit more information. Although he insisted that he had attended no conspiratorial gatherings, he conceded: "I have been a hearer, and have understood too much of some kind of meetings" without reporting them. Rouse added that the conspirators had intended to march to Whitehall, swords in their hands, to demand their "Priviledges and Liberties." They did not intend to kill Charles, he insisted, "but only let the D. of *Y.* look to it: for he [Lee] was resolved upon it that he [James] should not succeed the King." At the conclusion of his remarks, Rouse acknowledged the justice of his own execution. He died on 20 July.[27]

In the ensuing trial of Blague, with whom Rouse had sailed to Virginia more than two decades earlier, the state again relied on Thomas Lee and Mate Lee as its witnesses. The former maintained that Blague had spoken with him on several occasions about the best way to attack the Tower, the captain favoring the use of ship-mounted guns from the Southwark side. Moreover, Thomas Lee placed Blague at a meeting in the King's Head tavern in Chancery Lane attended also by the Goodenough brothers, at which the alleged subject of discussion was the provision of £40,000 for the seamen. Mate Lee's testimony, however, was very weak since it involved no more than a theoretical discussion of the best way to seize the Tower and an oblique reference of Blague's to "tossing up a ball," probably an allusion to the Blackheath recruitment scheme. In his instructions to the jury Pemberton candidly referred to Mate Lee's account as "a dark kind of an evidence" and raised the possibility that the discussion about attacking the Tower may have been no more than "sportive, or a trial of skill." In the absence of firm testimony from two witnesses, the jury returned a verdict of not guilty.[28]

No further trials followed until November, when Sidney and Hampden were called to account. In both instances the government must have known it would be difficult to substantiate its case. Concern may have been intensified by Blague's acquittal and Pemberton's evenhandedness. The king, moreover, had become engrossed in the continuing interrogations, which suggests that the government itself was finding it increasingly difficult to evaluate the growing mountain of purported evidence, much of it irrelevant, hearsay, or innuendo. Nonconformists and Scots in particular were widely regarded as suspects in the plotting. Three days after Russell's conviction the *Observator* remarked: "I reckon Every man to be *Constructively* in it [the conspiracy], that went along with the *Dissenters* till *This Discovery*, and does not *now*, *Openly Renounce*, and *Abominate* the *Accused Interest*, and *Practices* of the *Whole* Party." Such inflammatory comments can only have encouraged the submission of more dubious accusations, the net effect of which was to slow the wheels of justice. As the investigation mushroomed, the government issued 140 more warrants in late July.[29] By that point Charles and his advisers were further distracted by the burgeoning controversy over Essex's death,[30] to which we now turn.

Essex's Death: Suicide or Homicide?

Essex had been arrested at his home in Hertfordshire on 9 July, apparently unconcerned about the crackdown on his fellow plotters, for he was picking peaches in his garden when the magistrates arrived. He was subsequently incarcerated in the same room in the Tower from which his father had been led to his execution in 1649. One servant, Paul Bomeny, attended him, and his security was the responsibility of Major Thomas Hawley, the gentleman porter in whose house in the Tower he was confined, and two warders, Thomas Russell and Nathaniel Monday (or Munday). On the 10th,

Essex told the Privy Council he knew of no "design" against the government or any proposed uprising in Scotland, and admitted only that he might have visited Lord Russell when Monmouth and Sidney were present, that he had seen Hampden, and that he and Bedford had gone to Hatfield to speak with Salisbury. When interrogated by Clarendon on the 12th, Essex claimed he knew nothing of a plot to assassinate the king but made no attempt "to vindicate him self from being in other designes upon the government." According to Sir Francis North, when Essex was before the Council he "appeared dejected, & said litle, but . . . he did Not Imagin any body would swear fals against him, and Made No Manner of professions of Duty, as he Might have Done If he would have appeared clear." [31]

Looking ahead to his own trial, Essex directed his steward to take shorthand notes the following day when Lord Russell was tried. It is clear that Essex was concerned about his health and safety in the Tower, for he ordered his servants to bring silver vessels in which his own cook could prepare his food as well as a considerable quantity of fine wine. The earl also requested a penknife to trim his nails, though one was not immediately available. A member of the coroner's jury would later testify that according to Bomeny the earl was in good spirits on the night of the 12th and ate well. The day of his death, according to a courtier, Essex consumed a hearty breakfast and "was not perceived to be in any disturbance of mind." He also inquired twice if the king had arrived, possibly hoping to appeal personally for Charles' clemency. [32] As late as the morning of his death, therefore, nothing suggests that he was contemplating suicide. Bomeny later testified that he had been melancholy, but no more than usual. John Evelyn (who knew Essex and was in no sense a radical), the earl of Arran, Ferguson, and Danvers all remarked that the earl's principles and temperament precluded suicide. He had, however, previously commended an earl of Northumberland for taking his own life and thereby preventing the loss of his estate to his family by act of attainder, and he had reflected that an alderman in Ireland who had slit his throat had experienced "an easy Kind of Death." [33]

On the morning of the 13th, Charles and James came to the Tower around 6 A.M. to view some new fortifications. Approximately two hours later they stood on a balcony of the lieutenant's house and watched as Russell was led away to the Old Bailey. Around 8:45, according to a witness named Peter Essington, James left the king, conferred with two men, and dispatched them in the direction of Hawley's house. Approximately fifteen minutes later the two men returned, smiled, and told the duke "the Business was done." James seemed pleased with the news.[34] Essington's account is indirectly substantiated by the testimony of two women who purportedly spoke to Thomas Ruddle, a soldier, at approximately 11:00 A.M. on the day of Essex's death. Ruddle, they said, claimed to have overheard James tell Charles that Essex "ought to be taken off." The king allegedly retorted that he wanted to spare the earl "for what his Father had suffered." Shortly before Essex's death, according to Ruddle, James left Charles and then dispatched two men to Hawley's house; they returned after the earl had died.[35] Ferguson would later conclude that James ordered the two men, whose names he would not reveal in the hope that one might confess, to kill Essex.[36]

On the morning in question Hawley left his house between 4:00 and 5:00 A.M. to open the Tower gates. A sentinel, John Lloyd, stood guard at Hawley's door, while upstairs Thomas Russell kept watch in a room directly opposite Essex's. Following his breakfast Essex again asked for a penknife from Bomeny, but the footman had not yet arrived with it and the daily order of provisions. Essex thereupon requested and received Bomeny's razor, after which Bomeny left to speak with Russell and then return to his own chamber. When the footman arrived, Bomeny took the penknife to Essex's room, only to discover that the earl had apparently gone into the watercloset and shut the door behind him. Bomeny left the room for approximately fifteen minutes, but when he returned the watercloset door was still closed. "I went against the door, and knocked three times, and said, My lord, my lord, and nobody answered: then I looked through the chink of the door, between the door and the wall, and I could see blood, and a little part of the razor. Then I called to the warden, and the people of the house, and they came up and found him there."[37] Such, in any event, was Bomeny's version of what had occurred.

Thomas Russell corroborated this account, adding that he rushed into Essex's chamber as soon as he heard Bomeny call out that the earl was sick. Finding the key to the watercloset door on the outside, he opened the door, but with some difficulty because Essex lay on his side with his legs (a foot, according to Bomeny) against it. The razor, according to Russell and Bomeny, lay beside the earl's body. This was substantiated by Nathaniel Monday, who claimed that he had been sitting outside Hawley's door smoking a pipe when he heard what he called "the first Noise of my Lords death." He ran upstairs, saw Bomeny and Russell trying to open the watercloset door, and assisted them by putting his shoulder to it. The razor, he recalled, was nine to twelve inches from the left side of the earl's neck. Bomeny, Russell, and Monday insisted that only Bomeny had been in the room with Essex that morning, and Lloyd initially averred that he had admitted no one to Hawley's house.[38]

According to Lawrence Braddon, the Whig attorney who subsequently conducted his own investigation of the death, Charles received word of Essex's demise while he was still in the Tower. He thereupon ordered William Lord Alington (Russell's brother-in-law), Thomas Howard, and "Sir C——" (Sir Hugh Cholmley?) to go to Hawley's house, detain those who had attended Essex, and ensure that everything remain untouched until examined by a coroner's jury. As "Sir C——" began taking testimony at Hawley's house, a messenger directed him to go at once to the Old Bailey to inform the attorney general of Essex's death. Although "Sir C——" initially protested, he followed orders, which Braddon suspected had not come from the king. Whether Alington (whose mind was surely on Lord Russell's trial) and Howard remained at Hawley's house is not mentioned, but there is no indication that they interrogated witnesses as the king had initially ordered.[39]

The deputy coroner convened an inquest the following day, by which time the corpse had been removed from the watercloset, stripped, and washed at Hawley's direction by a charwoman, Mary Johnson, and Major Webster. Hawley also had Johnson clean the watercloset and the main chamber. The jury therefore saw the corpse only after it had been washed and dressed in fresh linen. A request to inspect the clothes Essex had been wearing at the time of his death was brushed aside by the coroner as unnecessary.[40] On the basis of the testimony of two "chirurgeons," the jury concluded that Essex had slit his own throat, "giving unto himself one mortal wound, cut from one jugular to the other, and by the aspera arteria, and the windpipe, to the vertebres of the neck, both the jugulars being thoroughly divided." In addition to severing completely both jugular veins, the esophagus, and the trachea, the instrument, allegedly a razor, penetrated to the vertebrae at the back of the neck. There is some evidence, however, that the jury was coerced into rendering a judgment of suicide: in January 1685 one juror went to the King's Bench prison for reportedly complaining that he believed the jury had been "presepitated into that Verdict, and would never have past such a verdict if they had not been infatuated for he [the juror] did not believe that he [Essex] cut his own throat."[41]

The instrument with which Essex killed himself, according to Bomeny, was a French razor with a blade between 4.25 and 4.5 inches long and "no Spill or Tongue at the end." In other words, the user had to grasp the blade itself with his fingers. To cut anything of substance with such a blade one had to grip it between the thumb and the index and middle fingers, leaving approximately 2.75 inches exposed. Greater force could be exerted by grasping the razor with the thumb and three fingers, leaving about 2.25 inches of the blade uncovered. The depth of the cut (reportedly between 3 and 4 inches) in the earl's neck renders the official account of Essex's death improbable.[42]

One surgeon reported a 2-inch cut in the palm of Essex's right hand, and witnesses also observed two cuts on the right index finger (both on the inside, with one near the base and the other near the tip), another on the fourth finger, and a final one on the little finger.[43] Grasping a razor with sufficient force to cut one's neck could produce cuts, but the pattern of those on the earl's hand suggests a grip that left little of the blade exposed. Perhaps, therefore, the cuts resulted from Essex's struggle to defend himself from assassins.[44]

The disposition of the razor following the discovery of the body was contested. William Edwards, a thirteen-year-old boy, had opted not to go to the Merchant Taylor's School on the morning of the 13th when he heard that the king was visiting the Tower. The boy returned home about 10 A.M. and subsequently told Lawrence Braddon, who claimed to represent Essex's widow and Sir Henry Capel, that Essex had killed himself, that he had seen a hand throw a razor from a window, and that a woman wearing a white hood had emerged from the house to retrieve it. However, young Edwards subsequently retracted his story. Nevertheless virtually the same account was related by Jane Loadman, a thirteen-year-old girl who had also been in the Tower that morning. A sentry named Robert Meake also reportedly saw the razor being thrown from the window and a maid subsequently retrieving it, but he died under suspicious circumstances (as will be seen) before he could formally testify. The couple to whom he had told his story later recounted it in a deposition.[45] During the trial in February 1684 of Lawrence Braddon (who had endeavored to prove Essex had been murdered) and Hugh Speke, the sentinel John Lloyd testified that he had not seen a razor thrown from a window or a maid leave the house. In January 1689, however, he apparently confessed precisely the opposite: someone had indeed cast the razor from the window, the instrument narrowly missing Lloyd's head, and a maid had retrieved it. Nicks in the razor lent credence to the assertion that it had fallen from a second-story window.[46]

If the razor was in fact tossed from Essex's window—and the evidence for this is tenuous at best—this does not necessarily prove that the earl was murdered. Samuel Storey (who fought with Monmouth in 1685) would later depose that when Major Webster was arrested on 21 January 1689, he admitted throwing the razor out the window in a state of consternation. If the account of Webster's confession is valid, he probably threw the razor away before someone realized its potential usefulness in implicating Essex in suicide and its danger (if found in the Tower yard) in implicating him or his colleagues in murder. Webster reportedly acknowledged that he "knew not what he did."[47]

More fundamental is the question of access to Essex's chamber. As we have seen, Bomeny, Thomas Russell, and Monday were adamant that no one but Bomeny had been with the earl on the morning of his death, and Lloyd initially insisted that he had allowed no one to enter Hawley's house. In his confession of 21 January 1689, however,

Lloyd reportedly admitted that on the instructions of Hawley or one of his warders (Nathaniel Monday) he had indeed permitted Webster and one or two other men to go into the house. On the 22nd he told a justice of the peace that he had allowed two men unknown to him to enter around 8:30 A.M. with the warder's permission. He testified to this effect before a House of Lords committee in January 1689, noting that the two men who had entered were "well cloathed" but carried no swords. About an hour after their entry Lloyd heard a "trampling" in Essex's room, followed by a thump, and afterwards the thrice-repeated cry, "My Lord is dead!"[48]

Although Hawley averred that he had been away from his house from 4:00 or 5:00 A.M. until he received the news of Essex's death, another Tower warder, Richard Nicholson, testified that he saw Hawley at his home as he (Nicholson) was escorting Lord Russell to the Old Bailey around 8:00 A.M. Hawley would therefore have been in position to give Monday or Lloyd instructions to admit the assassins. The sentry Robert Meake reportedly saw the men enter Hawley's house. The following day an officer allegedly ordered Meake and other soldiers to say nothing about what they had seen or heard, but one Samuel Bampstone and his wife subsequently deposed that Meake related his story to them. Meake, they said, feared for his life; several days later his body was found in the Tower ditch. Ferguson claims he was murdered.[49]

If Lloyd was telling the truth when he testified to the Lords committee in 1689, Webster was a likely assassin. Another witness swore that Webster had boisterously displayed Essex's bloody handkerchief after his death. Webster, however, claimed that he had been summoned to Essex's room by Hawley following the earl's demise, and that he had removed Essex's cravat and searched his pockets for papers at Hawley's direction, after which he wiped his bloody fingers on the earl's handkerchief and "unknowingly" put it in his pocket. John Holland, an erstwhile servant of the earl of Sunderland's, was probably Webster's companion. Shortly after Essex's death, Holland, a convicted burglar and extortionist, received a blanket pardon through Sunderland's efforts, and Sunderland subsequently paid at least some of Holland's debts and gave him a pension of 3 to 5 guineas per week. In 1685 a London schoolmaster heard that Holland's acquaintances were whispering that he had killed Essex with a large knife for Sunderland.[50]

If Sunderland was a sponsor of Essex's murder, his motivation is not hard to ascertain. As secretary of state during the exclusion crisis, he, along with Essex and several other Privy Councillors, had supported the interests of Mary and William of Orange. In that context he voted for the Exclusion Bill in November 1680, subsequent to which the king dismissed him in January 1681. Through the efforts of the duchess of Portsmouth, Sunderland was reconciled to Charles and James in 1682 and restored to the Privy Council in July. By the following year he espoused pro-French, pro-Catholic views and received a pension from Barillon, the French ambassador. His determined effort to win James' favor paid off in 1685 when the new king, to the surprise of many, appointed Sunderland lord president of the Council and principal secretary of state. Could these honors have been at least in part a reward for Sunderland's arrangement of the murder of Essex?

James himself, of course, had sent two men to Hawley's house shortly before the earl's death, at least according to one witness (Essington) and the alleged report of a soldier who died shortly thereafter. The questionable testimony of Dorothy Smith, a servant of Mr. Homes', a Catholic who lived in Baldwins Gardens near Gray's Inn, also dealt with James. Smith insisted she had overheard Homes and his Catholic friends discussing Essex on 4 July. One claimed to have been with James, who purportedly wanted the earl poisoned. This plan, however, was rejected because it would look overly suspicious. After stabbing too was ruled out, the duke allegedly ordered Essex's throat cut. Approximately three days later, Smith testified, the group met again to plan the assassination and to disguise it as suicide. On the afternoon of the earl's death, they met once more at Homes' house, where one of the men slapped her master on the back and said, "the Feat was done." Homes reportedly asked if the earl's throat had been cut, and received a positive reply. The respondent allegedly continued, "He could not but laugh to think how like a foole the Earl of Essex look'd when they came to cut his throat." The only visitor Smith could identify was a Mr.

Lovet. Her account makes no mention of Webster or Holland and is probably a fabrication.[51]

A variety of circumstantial evidence suggests both that Essex was murdered and that his killers acted on behalf of one or more very powerful persons. The financial assistance Sunderland provided to Holland has already been noted. The morning after Essex's death Webster had 49 guineas in his possession, and for a time thereafter he "lived at a rate much above his Quality" despite losing several hundred pounds gambling. In 1684, Bomeny, who had been dismissed by the countess of Essex shortly after her husband's demise, received £50 in secret-service money, probably as a reward for his testimony in Braddon's trial. Since the other government witnesses were not paid, someone seems to have thought highly of his testimony. He also obtained a position in the horse guards, apparently from the duke of York. Three others met a very different end. The brutally maimed body of a warder named Hawley (not to be confused with the major), who had been in the Tower at the time of Essex's death and deemed it "a piece of Villany," was fished out of a river near Rochester in the spring of 1684; he had apparently been murdered. Robert Meake's body was found in the Tower ditch, and Thomas Ruddle, after being assigned to the East Indies, was shot to death at Fort St. George. It is of course possible that the deaths of these men, all of whom were potential key witnesses, were coincidental, but it seems unlikely.[52]

The violent deaths of Hawley, Ruddle, and possibly Meake were severe impediments to a thorough investigation of Essex's death after the revolution of 1688–89. A number of thoughtful contemporaries, including Essex's friend John Evelyn, seriously doubted the suicide story. So too did John Locke, who pondered legal action to vacate the verdict of the coroner's inquest and initiate a new inquiry.[53] So troubled was James' administration by Braddon's meticulous investigation that it put him and Hugh Speke, Sir John Trenchard's father-in-law, on trial in the King's Bench in February 1684 on a charge of attempted subornation. Both were found guilty; Braddon was fined £2,000 and imprisoned, and Speke was convicted of encouraging sedition (but not subornation), fined £1,000, and jailed.[54] The severity of the government's reaction may indicate a coverup,

although it is also possible that the court was afraid that an attack
on the suicide verdict would lead to widespread disbelief in the Rye
House conspiracy. As Roger L'Estrange told Jenkins, "the Murder
of the Earl of Essex is the mayn poynt they [the Whigs] Trust toe
and the next step in Consequence, will be to make a sham-plot
of this horrid Conspiracy. The whole design moves upon these
2 Hinges." [55]

The evidence concerning Essex's death, although not conclusive,
is sufficiently strong to suggest homicide. A plausible scenario can at
least be constructed. Sunderland, in a calculated effort to win James'
favor, may have initially proposed the assassination of Essex. When
the duke agreed, they settled on Webster and Holland as their
agents. On the morning of 13 July, James took his leave of the king,
who knew nothing of the plot, and sent Webster and Holland to
Mayor Hawley's house. On the basis of prior instructions from
James, Hawley ordered Lloyd to permit the two men to enter. When
they reached Essex's chamber a struggle ensued, Holland slit the
earl's throat with a knife (nearly decapitating him in the process),
and Webster panicked and threw the earl's bloody razor out the window. Someone quickly decided to retrieve the razor and leave it
rather than the knife as the pretended suicide instrument. Another
of Hawley's maids, Alice Evans (or Carter), then fetched the razor.
Russell and Bomeny probably had no direct involvement in the murder, although they may have had advance knowledge and would certainly have participated in the coverup. Approximately six weeks
after the earl's death, a letter initialed P.B. and, according to Braddon, in Bomeny's handwriting, was addressed to the dowager countess of Essex and left with one William Cadman. The author, promising to confess if the countess could obtain a pardon for him, told
her "that the DUKE of YORK and ——— were authorizing the
Murther." [56]

If Holland and Webster killed Essex at the behest of James and
Sunderland, what was the primary motive? Sunderland, of course,
must have hoped to ingratiate himself with the duke, a daunting task
for one who had so visibly supported exclusion in 1680. But what
could James have hoped to gain? Ferguson argued that "some about
St. James's and *Whitehall* were the contrivers and authorisers of that

barbarous assassination" because they feared what Essex knew about the Popish Plot and Catholic activity in general as a result of his work in Ireland and his service on the Privy Council. Moreover, Ferguson charged, the king's justices and ministers hoped to demonstrate the reality of the Rye House conspiracy—which Ferguson brazenly described as nothing but a "Court and Popish Sham"—by claiming that Essex had killed himself because of "the shame and horror of being concerned in so treasonabl' a design." Danvers offered similar arguments. Reflecting the court's position, North contended that Whig claims that Essex had been assassinated were part of their campaign "to perswade the world, that this Conspiracy was No generall designe of the party; but some weak Men drawne in by some spys & decoys of the court."[57]

Although the efforts of Ferguson and Danvers to link Essex's death to an attempt to cover up Catholic activity were groundless, both men correctly sensed the impact of the news of Essex's purported suicide on Lord Russell's jury. If James and Sunderland ordered Essex's assassination, they must have anticipated this impact and its probable effect in persuading many Englishmen that the Rye House conspiracy was genuine. Moreover, if killing Essex made Russell's conviction more likely, the cumulative effect was potentially even more important for the expected trials of other alleged conspirators. Without Essex's apparent suicide, Russell's jury might not have believed Howard and Rumsey. Had Russell been found not guilty, a similar verdict would almost certainly have followed in Essex's trial. When Tory attempts to convict Shaftesbury of treason collapsed, conspiracy ensued. Failure to convict Russell and Essex, the Tories must have reasoned, could lead to renewed and potentially successful efforts to exclude the duke of York or alter the government. That thesis would have provided ample motivation for James and Sunderland to commission the assassination of Essex.

Contrasting Fates: Monmouth, Sidney, and Hampden

On 12 July, the day before Essex's death, the government indicted a number of conspirators who had already fled, chief among them Monmouth, Grey, Armstrong, Ferguson, and the Goodenough brothers. Included as well were Rumbold, Nelthorpe, Norton, and the key figures associated with Bristol, namely Wade, Holloway, Tiley, and John Row.[58]

The hiatus in the treason trials, which gave, opined the bishop of Oxford, "courage to the party to dispute against the reality of the design," stemmed directly from the government's inability to find the necessary second witness to corroborate Howard's accusations against Sidney and Hampden. With Russell and Essex dead and Grey in exile, Monmouth was a possibility. After admitting nothing of consequence following his arrest in June, Wildman had been discharged on the 28th of that month. Ferguson was in the Netherlands, but Aaron Smith, whom Monmouth's council had dispatched to Scotland with Sidney's financial support, had been arrested on 4 July. Although, as one courtier remarked, Smith made "a large confession" in August, he admitted nothing that could be used against Sidney. As he told his interrogator in the Tower, "I could not say any thing that could touch an haire of Col Sydneys head." Cited at last before the King's Bench in late October, Smith was fined £500 and pilloried as punishment for his misconduct in Stephen Colege's trial, in which he had provided libelous advice and used seditious speech.[59]

Faced with Smith's unwillingness to accuse Sidney and compelled in any case to find a second witness against Hampden, the king, perhaps at the suggestion of the marquis of Halifax, decided to approach Monmouth in mid-October. The duke, as Charles knew, had been hiding at the home of his mistress, Lady Henrietta Wentworth, at Toddington, Bedfordshire. On the 13th, Halifax secretly traveled there with a message for Monmouth, which the duke noted in his diary: Charles "could never be brought to believe I knew any thing of that part of the Plot that concern'd *Rye-House*; but as things went, he must behave himself as if he did believe it, for some reasons that might be for my Advantage." Charles, in other words, wanted an acknowledgment from the duke that the conspiracy had been real. At Halifax's suggestion, Monmouth wrote to his father, but in guarded terms: "I am clear of this most horrid, and base accusation," he insisted, referring to the assassination plot, though he apologized for having done "many things" that angered the court. He had acted, he argued, in the belief that the duke of York had "intended to destroy me," but "I doe here declare to your Majesty that I will never ask to see your face more if ever I doe any thing against him [James], which is the greatest Curse I can lay upon myself." Monmouth was trying not only to win his father's forgiveness but also to placate James, who was ignorant of Halifax's mission and thought the duke had fled to the Continent.[60]

Monmouth had said nothing to further the prosecution of Sidney or Hampden nor even to pacify James. Charles, whose fondness for Monmouth was still apparent, advised him to remain at Toddington, although the two met clandestinely at Whitehall on 25 October and at Stepney on 4 November as a result of Halifax's efforts. By this point the state had decided to try Sidney by using his own writings as a second witness, a risky strategy. Monmouth may have told Charles enough at Whitehall or Stepney to lead the king to believe that the duke's own admission of guilt could be used against Sidney, but the latter's attorneys forced the government's hand by obtaining a writ of habeas corpus on 6 November. The following day the state hurriedly convened a grand jury, obtained a bill of indictment, and indicted Sidney on charges of high treason. Although Russell had been tried the day following his own indictment and had been unsuccessful in requesting a postponement, the attorney general himself asked that Sidney's trial be held on the 14th and willingly acceded to the defendant's request for an additional week's delay.[61] Such action on the prosecution's part may have been motivated by the expectation of a possible statement of guilt from Monmouth.

Written on 15 November, Monmouth's second letter, which Halifax drafted, was designed to pave the way for a *modus vivendi* with James, but it offered no new information about the conspiracy. "I never had a Criminall thought towards your Majesty," he averred, but he alluded darkly to inappropriate activity: "Whilst I was under the apprehensions of great anger and violence against me it might easely Corrupt my judgement." Pleading that incarceration in the Tower would be an "unnecessary mortification," he begged Charles to intercede on his behalf with the duke of York.[62] This is where matters stood when Sidney's trial began on the 21st. Clearly Charles had decided to proceed regardless of Monmouth's conduct.

By this time Sidney's barrister, William Williams, had plotted the strategy for the trial with meticulous care, but as in Russell's case, most of the attention focused on technical matters, including jury qualifications and challenges, the two-witness rule, the inadmissibility of hearsay, the untrustworthiness of testimony from confessed traitors, and a warning not to let the prosecution cite misdemeanors as evidence of treason.[63] Correctly surmising that the manuscripts seized when Sidney was arrested would be used against the defendant, Sidney's counsel advised him not to admit authorship. Sidney, however, was at first inclined to disregard this advice, as he explained in a letter to Hampden:

I doe nott yet know how my councell will suffer me to proceed in this businesse, but confesse . . . I am much inclined to admit [authorship of the papers], and telling the utmost nature, meaning, and intention of them, to put it upon a speciall Plea, that if such papers, soe written are treason, I am Guilty, if not not. In this I shall have god to be the defender of my innocence.[64]

In the end he followed the advice of his counsel, including Williams' detailed instructions on how to argue against the manuscripts if the chief justice admitted them as evidence. The heart of this strategy was to insist that the entirety of the manuscripts be read, not simply extracts, and to argue that the prosecution's interpretation of the writings was erroneous.[65]

Sidney's own thinking was revealed in a series of letters to Hampden as the two men explored legal issues pertaining to treason and exchanged the views of authorities and records of previous treason trials, especially those of Sir Henry Vane and Lord Russell. From the strictly legal standpoint Sidney was convinced that the state could not make its case: "On looking over the papers that you have seene, I growe to be very confident, that such rules being observed in proceeding against us as the Lawe requires, it is not possible to bring us into danger." But a favorable outcome would depend on having honest, understanding judges, and Sidney fully expected "all possible care" would be taken to prevent this. Indeed, he cautioned, "wee are to expect that manner of tricks will be used, if wee are brought to triall, and if such, wee cannot forsee doe start of, wee must answeare as well as we can." He pondered the possibility of arguing that merely imagining war against the crown was not treason, and that to make war is not the same as to imagine the king's death. Nor, he mused, can anyone be convicted of imagining the king's death in purely verbal terms unless killing the monarch is explicitly mentioned. Sidney, in short, wanted to turn his trial into a debate on constitutional law. In any event, his manuscript, he insisted, was far from completed, and thus hardly represented his final position. "If I had written a book ready to be published (as is pretended) to stirre up a rebellion in prosecution of what they say wee designed," he sarcastically observed, "you must needs have seene it."[66]

The crown's case rested on two basic contentions: first, that Sidney had conspired with others to kill the king and levy war, and to this end had sent Aaron Smith to Scotland to invite dissidents there to consult with the English plotters; and second, that he had written a seditious work designed to persuade the people of England that it was lawful to rebel. To provide the necessary background for the jurors, the prosecution called West, Rumsey, and Keeling, none of whom could cite more than hearsay about Sidney's alleged involvement. Despite Sidney's objections, Jeffreys allowed them to protract their testimony, conceding only that "all this evidence does not affect you, and I tell the jury so." Sidney's retort, "But it prepossesses the jury," was ignored.[67]

Lord Howard, the government's star witness, testified at length about Sidney's role in Monmouth's cabal. In mid-January, he recalled, he, the duke, and Sidney had decided to revive the insurrection plan, to which end Monmouth agreed to recruit Russell and the earl of Salisbury while Sidney approached Essex and Hampden. Howard then placed Sidney in meetings of the council of six at the homes of Hampden and Russell. The first of these sessions involved a general discussion of when and where to rebel, the funds that would be required (£25,000 or £30,000, according to Monmouth), and the need to coordinate with the Scots. At the second meeting, Howard testified, the conspirators resolved to send Aaron Smith, whom Sidney suggested, to Scotland to confer with Sir John Cochrane, Lord Melville, and Sir Hugh Campbell and his son Sir George. Sidney subsequently told Howard that he intended to give Smith

funds for the journey, and Howard estimated that Sidney had perhaps 60 guineas for this purpose. Although Jeffreys offered Sidney
the opportunity to question Howard, he declined, preferring instead
to attack Howard's credibility later in the trial.[68]

When the attorney general turned to Sidney's manuscript, he
made a point of citing it as "another overt act of the treason," a
carefully chosen phrase that not only pronounced the work an *overt*
act but linked it to the Monmouth cabal as an act of the *same* treason.
After three witnesses had expressed their opinion that the handwriting was Sidney's, the attorney general ordered the reading of substantive extracts (approximately 1,800 words). The key points were
these: as a man the king is subject to the law of God, and as a monarch he is subject to the people; like the Hebrews who threw off the
bondage of the pharaoh the people of England can shake off a harmful yoke; in the past when English monarchs "failed of their duties,"
the nobility and gentry called Parliament into session; the people are
"judges in their own case . . . because it is their own, and only concerns themselves" ; and "the general revolt of a nation from its own
magistrates, can never be called rebellion." As a final touch the
attorney general had the record of Russell's conviction read for the
jury, an act manifestly intended to remind the jurors that a comparable body had already found the evidence for the conspiracy
incontrovertible.[69]

In his defense Sidney attacked Howard's credibility, proving beyond doubt that Howard had denied the existence of a conspiracy
after Keeling's confession, and that Howard had subsequently remarked that he could not obtain a pardon "until he had done some
other jobs, 'till he was past this drudgery of swearing" by testifying
against others. Among those who attested to Howard's initial protestations of ignorance about a plot were the earl of Anglesey, the
earl of Clare, and Gilbert Burnet. Sidney heaped scorn on Howard,
referring specifically to his conduct during the crucial spring of 1683:
"[He] goes into Essex upon great important business, greater than
the war of England and Scotland, to what purpose? To look after a
little pimping manor, and what then? Why then it must be laid aside,
and he must be idle five weeks at the Bath, and there is no enquiring
after [the conspiracy]." Sidney refused to acknowledge the offending

manuscript as his, implying that it might not have been taken from his house and repeatedly arguing that it was, judging from the ink, probably twenty years old, not in his handwriting, and apparently an attack on Robert Filmer's *Patriarcha*. Following his counsel's advice, he argued, though unsuccessfully, that the state had to introduce the document in its entirety. Moreover, the writings, he argued, had "no manner of coherence, no dependence upon such design" as the prosecution charged. He knew nothing, he said, of Smith's trip to Scotland, nor had he heard the names of the Scottish emissaries until after his incarceration in the Tower.[70]

In his instructions to the jury Jeffreys professed that he would rather see many guilty men escape than one innocent person suffer, but he made his own views evident, in part by likening the principles in the manuscript attributed to Sidney to those that had led to the execution of Charles I in 1649. If, then, the jurors believed that Sidney was the author, this would be "a sufficient evidence, that he is guilty of compassing and imagining the death of the king." To undercut any doubts about using the manuscript as a second witness, Jeffreys declared: "it is not upon two, but it is upon greater evidence than 22, if you believe this book was writ by him." The evidence that convicted Russell, he added, was less than that marshalled against Sidney. As for Howard, he was a credible witness, the judge intoned, so that in reality the only question he left for the jurors to decide was whether or not Sidney had written the manuscript. It took the jury less than 30 minutes to return a guilty verdict.[71]

While the trial was in progress nothing was done about Monmouth. The following day, however, Charles told James about the negotiations with the duke, to which James at first objected vigorously but then reluctantly acquiesced. After a warrant for Monmouth's arrest was issued on 24 November, he surrendered to Secretary Jenkins the same day and requested a meeting with Charles and James. Throwing himself at the king's feet he acknowledged "his guilt, & the share he had in the Conspiracy," giving "an account of the whole conspiracy, naming all those concerned in it, which were more then those [who] had allready been mentioned by severall Witnesses." Again he reiterated his ignorance of the assassination plot, though he averred that John Owen, Matthew Meade, George Griffith, "& all the considerable Nonconformist Ministers knew of the Conspiracy." From Halifax, Sir John Reresby learned that Monmouth "had confessed the thruth of the late plott to the King and Duke, but would not give any publique evidence against the conspiratours." Monmouth sought the forgiveness of Charles and James, and on the 26th a formal pardon was issued. The king also gave him £4,000.[72]

Monmouth received his pardon on the day Sidney was sentenced to be hanged, drawn, and quartered. Seemingly baffled that the duke had not made an appearance before the trial, Sidney reflected on Monmouth's confession: "If this be his temper it can hardly be good." When he appeared before Jeffreys for sentencing, Sidney seized on the news about Monmouth to press his case for a new trial: "If there had been any thing in consultation, by this means to bring any thing about, he must have known of it, for it must be taken to be in prosecution of those designs of his: and if he will say there ever was any such thing, or knew any thing of it, I will acknowledge whatever you please."[73] Sidney was clearly gambling that Monmouth would not acknowledge the conspiracy in court, regardless of what he might have said to Charles and James. The state, after all, had not produced Monmouth as a witness against him. Jeffreys, however, brushed aside the request, forcing Sidney to fall back, unsuccessfully, on other, technical grounds in arguing for a new trial.[74]

Rumors of the lenient treatment of Monmouth fed popular suspicion in some quarters that Whig assertions of a sham plot might be valid. Apparently in an effort to silence such doubt, Charles, pressured by James, ordered the *Gazette* to publish the minutes of his statement to the Privy Council noting that Monmouth had made a full confession of his role in the plot.[75] An irate Monmouth protested that the announcement was injurious to him, and he must also have been troubled that it was used to justify Sidney's condemnation and might be employed against Hampden. Halifax tried to calm Monmouth by explaining that the impending end of term would mean the bailing of the principal alleged conspirators (Hampden, Lord Brandon, Henry Booth, Wildman, Trenchard, and Charlton), all of whom had filed writs of habeas corpus. The duke, Halifax insisted, could not be accused of treachery by his supporters, for these men would have remained in prison had he become the critical second witness against them.[76] Monmouth's friends, however, spread the word that he repudiated the *Gazette* story and castigated Howard as a liar.

Unchecked, such statements not only impugned the verdict in Sidney's trial but also threatened the state's case against Hampden. The king thereupon ordered Monmouth to acknowledge his confession in writing, but the resulting "finely worded" version was rejected as insufficiently explicit.[77] One of Charles' advisers prepared a draft for the duke to sign, which he did only after considerable persuasion from Halifax and after rewriting the document in his own hand:

I have heard of some Reports of me, as if I should have lessen'd the late Plot, & gone about to discredit the Evidence given against those who have dyed by Justice. Your Majestie & the Duke [of York] know how Ingeniously I have owned the late Conspiracy, & tho' I was not conscious of any design against your Majesties Life yet I lament the having had soe great a share in the other part of the said Conspiracy.

A second paragraph indicated that the letter was intended for the duke's "own vindication" and incorporated a promise never again to act against the king.[78]

The signed document was given to Charles, apparently on 5 December, but that evening Monmouth showed the original draft to Hampden's father, Trenchard, and Sir James Forbes. Forbes told the duke that "the Paper would make him Infamous and it would destroy many lives," whereupon Monmouth had him show the confession to Anglesey, who sent a written response to Monmouth advising against its submission. Forbes also took the document to Hampden along with the duke's apology and his insistence that Halifax had "persuaded and overborne him to doe it." Hampden protested to Monmouth that his statement "would hang me." In reality, the document, which Hampden later described as "a confession of the Plot," said nothing about him, but the impact on a jury of its affirmation of a conspiracy to mount an insurrection was impossible to gauge. Monmouth consequently instructed Halifax to retrieve the confession on the 6th. Visibly upset, Charles reluctantly complied with his son's request but ordered him not to return to court. After Forbes had reported the duke's decision to Hampden, Charlton, and

Wildman, he conferred again with Monmouth, urging him to save Sidney, presumably by testifying in his behalf. Although the duke "feard he could not," he agreed to discuss the possibility of helping Sidney with Hampden. Reports from London, Coventry, Chichester, the southwest, and the Netherlands indicated that dissidents were heartened by Monmouth's refusal to submit a signed confession. James, in contrast, was livid.[79]

Determined to implicate Monmouth further in the plotting, Howard pressed the Privy Council to interrogate Anglesey in January 1684. Although the earl refused to answer to anyone but the king, he professed ignorance of any criminal actions on Monmouth's part. Charles, presumably satisfied that the duke had revealed enough, opted not to question Anglesey.[80]

While political circles were engrossed with the changing fortunes of Monmouth, Sidney used his last days to draft a rambling but substantive apology, replete with legal arguments and historical references.[81] Conceding nothing, he roundly condemned the indictment as error-ridden, the chief justice as fraudulent and violent, the bench in general as irrational and ignorant of the law, the jury as packed and sordid, and Howard as a liar whose "fruitful fancy [was] spurred on by fear and restrained neither by conscience nor shame." The solicitor general was castigated for having "misrepeated the evidence on both sides to mislead the jury." Sidney again brazenly insisted that he knew nothing of the contents of the treatise attributed to him apart from the passages read in court, but he also reiterated his claim that this was an old work written to refute Filmer. The outcome of the trial, he averred, had been decided in advance, possibly as long ago as April 1683. The entire episode, he concluded, manifested the extent to which the regime was intent to establish "tyranny over consciences" to reimpose popery.[82] On 23 November he again wrote to Hampden, exonerating his defense counsel but castigating "the impudent violence of the Chief Justice [who] overthrew all." Since the conviction, he added, several "propositions have bin made unto me for saving my life, but I do not think them seasonable or decent. Thus might I have sent a petition to represent the irregularities of the proceedings against me, and as an oppressed person, desiring reliefe."[83]

Sidney had one more message for the world. Taken to the scaffold at Tower Hill on 7 December, the day after Monmouth was banished from the court, he refused to make a final speech but presented a written statement to the sheriff. He had prudently left a second copy with his secretary, Joseph Ducasse, who managed to have it printed shortly after the execution. Mostly Sidney remarked on the disputed treatise, the authorship of which he at last came very close to acknowledging. If Filmer could offer his views, Sidney reflected, "I know not why I might not have published my opinion to the contrary." His outlook was nevertheless defiant to the end. His judges were "blemishes to the bar," and his age was one "that maketh truth pass for treason." His enemies, he opined, had determined he must die to validate their belief that the conspiracy had been real. He saw his own death as a testimony to "that Old Cause in which I was from my youth engaged."[84]

The government had successfully prosecuted Sidney by using his writings as a second witness, but they had no comparable evidence with which to incriminate Hampden. Accordingly he had been indicted on 28 November (prior to his release on bail) for a misdemeanor, having allegedly conspired to launch an insurrection and to send an agent to Scotland to invite "evil-disposed subjects" of that country to visit England for consultations with the plotters. Prior to the trial which was set for 6 February, the government apparently made an effort to force Monmouth to testify against Hampden, leaving subpoenas on 25 January with servants at the duke's homes at Moorpark and the Cockpit and at the house of another servant in Westminster. Since no effort was made to find Monmouth at Toddington, the prosecution may have been posturing with a view to enhancing the appearance of Monmouth's—and Hampden's—guilt. This, in any event, was Ormond's judgment. Although this course would have been agreeable to Charles, putting the duke on the witness stand for questioning by both prosecutors and the defendant might not have been palatable to the king. For his part Monmouth slipped away to the Continent, and in April was seen in Brussels.[85]

Howard, once again the government's star witness, essentially reiterated the testimony he had given in Sidney's trial. Circumstantial corroboration was provided by four men who testified about Aaron

Smith's trip to Scotland and the subsequent arrival in England of
Baillie, the Campbells, and others. As Hampden's counsel, Williams
successfully blocked the attorney general's attempt to introduce the
record of Sidney's trial by arguing that his client had been "neither
party nor privy" to Sidney's offense nor had he been indicted for
the same crime. Williams based Hampden's defense on the same tactics that had failed to acquit Sidney, namely a lengthy attack on
Howard's credibility using such witnesses as the earl of Clare, Lord
Paget, Gilbert Burnet, and Sidney's secretary, Joseph Ducasse. Jeffreys refused to allow Williams to introduce the testimony of the earl
of Anglesey, who could not be in court because of illness, through a
third party: "Come, will you consent that what the duke of Monmouth has said, shall be given in evidence, and then I presume the
king's counsel will consent to your request?" Hampden himself said
virtually nothing during the trial.[86]

After presenting his defense Williams opted not to make a closing
argument, a tactic designed to deprive the prosecution of a final
statement. The chief justice's summation, Williams realized, would
be damaging enough. Jeffreys had already signaled the jurors that
the prosecution was correct with respect to Howard's credibility, the
very issue on which Hampden's defense rested. "Lord Howard is to
be believed, to all intents and purposes," the lord chief justice had
proclaimed, "for here is a record of the conviction of my Lord Russell, and of colonel Sidney." To drive this point home, he remarked:
"Essex had such an opinion of my Lord Howard's evidence, that he
thought fit to cut his own throat, rather than abide the trial."[87] Williams can only have expected more of the same in the judge's summing up, and Jeffreys in fact reiterated his opinion of Russell and
Sidney and the purported suicide of Essex. Noting that Monmouth
had allegedly denied the existence of a conspiracy, Jeffreys observed
that the prosecution's attempt to summon him was an effort "to
shew we are not afraid to have the truth come out." The lord chief
justice also underscored his belief that "if there were another witness
as positive against the defendant as . . . lord Howard," Hampden
could have been found guilty of high treason. Obviously aware of the
verdict Jeffreys desired, the jury found Hampden guilty. On 12 February the court fined him the staggering sum of £40,000 and or-

dered that he be imprisoned until it was paid, a sentence tantamount to life imprisonment.[88]

After Grey was captured in the Monmouth rebellion and therefore became available to serve as a second witness, the state prosecuted Hampden for high treason, in December 1685. Rather than contest the allegations, which were substantially the same as those in his first trial, Hampden pleaded guilty, following the advice of friends who argued that this course "could hurt noe man liveing, but my Lord Howard." Although he was sentenced to death, the king gave him a reprieve the following month, and in June 1686 his conviction was reversed on a writ of error in the court of King's Bench.[89]

Thus of the six members of the revolutionary "council," Russell and Sidney were executed, Howard and Monmouth were pardoned, Essex died under suspicious circumstances in the Tower, and Hampden was convicted of a misdemeanor and subsequently pleaded guilty to treason. With the other principal conspirators beyond reach on the Continent, the authorities lacked sufficient evidence for successful prosecutions and thus discharged Brandon (who had contemplated an escape attempt during Russell's trial), Henry Booth, Wildman, Charlton, Trenchard, and others on 12 February 1684, the same day Hampden was fined £40,000. Perhaps not coincidentally, Danby and the three surviving Catholic peers in the Tower (who had been arrested in connection with the Popish Plot) were released on bail the same day.[90]

The Scottish Trials and the Recourse to Torture

Evidentiary problems impeded prosecution of the alleged Scottish conspirators, although magistrates put out a wide dragnet to arrest suspicious Scots in England and Ireland following the arrest of Gordon of Earlston and the disclosures made by Keeling and Rumsey. Concern about Scottish aliens was exacerbated by Rumsey's assertion that Ferguson had claimed that 1,200 Scots—more than 300 of whom were in London and the remainder scattered throughout England—were prepared to support an insurrection. Many were supposedly former Bothwell Bridge rebels. West too sparked disquietude by his claim that Row had been advised by his Scottish friends that between 2,000 and 3,000 Scots, many of them Bothwell veterans, were in England and subject to the command of the Scottish delegation in London. Scores of Scots were interrogated and sometimes arrested; although some were well armed, many were harmless traders.[91] A number were Covenanters and in some instances fugitives from Scottish justice,[92] but few had any demonstrable links to the plotting.[93] Although most of the key Scottish agents, including Baillie, Monro, the Campbells, and Carstares, were in custody by the end of July 1683, only Gordon of Earlston at first confessed. The authorities, moreover, could not decipher Argyll's coded letters, which were discovered when Holmes was arrested in June.[94]

In late October the government decided to ship twelve Scottish prisoners from London to Edinburgh. Included in the group were Carstares, Baillie, Monro, the Campbells, Sir William Muir of Rowallan and his son William, Robert Murray, and Argyll's secretary, William Spence.[95] Transferring the prisoners to Scotland gave the authorities the option of using torture, which was legal north of the Tweed, and trying some of the men for their reputed associations with the Covenanter rebels. As an English citizen, Nisbet remained in England, although the state failed to locate the necessary second witness (in addition to Gordon of Earlston) to try him for treason.

In the meantime the government was working on a plan to persuade Sir John Cochrane, who had fled to the Continent, to submit to the king in return for clemency. Presumably this was predicated on a full confession and perhaps his testimony against his imprisoned associates. The authorities were clearly having trouble making a case against the Scots, and they were undoubtedly interested as well in the activities of the exile community. They had learned little by interrogating two of Cochrane's servants, who insisted that their master had come to London only in connection with the Carolina project. They admitted, however, that while there he had conversed with the Campbells, Lord Wharton, Gilbert Burnet's brother, and, on one occasion, Monmouth himself. The English envoy to the Netherlands, Thomas Chudleigh, had an agent contact Cochrane in the fall, but the latter professed his innocence of the plotting and expressed an unwillingness to return to Scotland because it had no right of habeas corpus. On 2/12 November, Chudleigh reported to Sunderland that Cochrane was filled with malice toward Charles: "[He] is hardened beyond all hopes of reclayming him, if it be not that he hopes by the means of his freinds to make his peace without acknowledging his guilt." Five days later Cochrane himself wrote to the earl of Middleton from Cleves professing his innocence.[96]

The government tried Sir Hugh Campbell in March 1684 on charges that he had "intercommuned" with and encouraged the Bothwell rebels in 1679, and that he had employed James Brown, a conventicle preacher, as his household chaplain. He was found guilty on these charges and not cited at all for his alleged involvement in the Monmouth conspiracy, but in June 1685 he and his son pleaded guilty to treason after Monro and Carstares had confessed. Although they forfeited their estates, their lives were spared and they were freed in August. Following Cochrane's capture and confession, they were again imprisoned, from October 1685 to January 1686.[97]

Legal proceedings against Cochrane and his son as well as Lord Melville and the earl of Loudoun had been initiated in Scotland in April 1684, though all were in exile. Most of the charges pertained to the Bothwell Bridge rebellion, in which the younger Cochrane, commonly known as Cochrane of Waterside, had participated. Ironically, Melville had fought against the Covenanters but was cited for having given them information about the strength and position of the king's forces while urging them to surrender. All four men were also accused of responding positively to Aaron Smith's invitation to visit London to consult about an insurrection. The younger Cochrane, though still not in custody, was found guilty of treason in April 1684 because of his Bothwell Bridge activities, and his estate was forfeited. On the basis of the testimony of Monro and Shepherd, the elder Cochrane was found guilty of treason (also *in absentia*) in May 1685 for his involvement in the Monmouth conspiracy. Both men were captured during the Monmouth rebellion. Although required to pay a substantial fine, Melville received a pardon in October 1686.[98]

The state made further headway in prosecuting the reputed Scottish conspirators in the late summer and fall of 1684 by using torture. Determined to force Spence to confess and to read the coded correspondence, the Privy Council subjected him to the boot (striking the wedge against his shin with the mallet eighteen times instead of the typical six or seven), prevented him from sleeping for at least five days and nights by dressing him in a hair shirt and pricking him until "the balls of his eyes [were] swolen as big as Tennis balls," and then crushed his thumbs with thumbscrews "till the broken bone was appearing thro' the skin." Faced again with the boot, he finally broke down, corroborating Holmes' confession and acknowledging the existence of three codes—one each for himself, Holmes, and Carstares. On the basis of Spence's testimony, Gordon of Earlston and Carstares were tortured. The latter named many who had allegedly known of the conspiracy, opening the way to a spate of new arrests. Among the detainees were Walter Scott, earl of Tarras and brother-in-law of the duchess of Monmouth; James Murray of Philiphaugh; Hugh Scott of Galashiels; and Sir James Dalrymple. Some, including Monro and Sir Colin Campbell of Ardkinglas, Argyll's cousin, confessed rather than undergo torture.[99] Among those who escaped were George Pringle of Torwoodlee and Sir Patrick Hume of Polwarth.[100] In return for their confessions, Carstares, Murray of Philiphaugh, and Scott of Galashiels received pardons, whereas the government opted to try Baillie and Tarras.[101]

In his trial on 23 December, Baillie was accused of traitorously attempting to bar James' succession, conspiring with the West cabal to assassinate Charles, scheming with Cochrane and Monro to send money to Argyll, and dispatching Robert Marten to Scotland to confer with Hume and other dissidents about an insurrection, including plans to secure the officers of state and the castles. Baillie, who had competent counsel, pleaded not guilty. The prosecution led off with the earl of Tarras despite the objections of Baillie's attorney that he was an alleged accomplice and himself under an indictment for treason. Tarras explained how Baillie had indicated his determination to go to London with Monro to urge the English to rebel, and how Marten had later delivered a letter in Baillie's hand to Pringle of Torwoodlee reporting on efforts to raise funds for Argyll, who had planned to land in western Scotland. Monro, who had originally professed ignorance of the planned insurrection, recounted the activities of the Scottish agents in London, and Murray and

Scott provided more details about Marten's mission to Scotland. Although the state had exempted Carstares from testifying in return for his confession, the prosecution introduced his written deposition; the defense objected unsuccessfully. This document's damaging account of Baillie's role in the deliberations about raising money for Argyll was corroborated by a written account of Shepherd's examination before Secretary Jenkins the previous December. To complete its case the prosecution produced Zachary Bourne's deposition to Jenkins, which depicted Baillie as "the chief man for the Scots, next to the lord Argyle," and accused him of helping Ferguson draft a revolutionary manifesto. Although a very sick man, Baillie vehemently denied involvement in any plot to assassinate the king or draft a manifesto.[102]

In his summation the king's advocate described Baillie as "the ringleader of all those who in this kingdom concurred with the English conspirators." Sensitive to the widespread allegations that the government had manufactured the plot to destroy its enemies, he went on to explain: "It was indeed fit and just to begin with the most guilty; so that if he be not convicted, there should no man be punished for this conspiracy; all the noise we have heard of it, is but a cheat, the king's judges have been murderers, all the witnesses have been knaves, and such as died for it, have been martyrs." Baillie's trial was a carefully orchestrated object lesson designed as much to shore up the government's tattered credibility as to convict a conspirator. "I have insisted so much upon this probation," the advocate concluded, "rather to convince the world of the conspiracy, than you that this conspirator is guilty." Convicted, Baillie was hanged and quartered on the 24th. He died professing his innocence of any plot to overthrow the government or kill the king and his brother. Like Holloway, he attributed his death to his zeal to preserve Protestantism from the popish threat.[103]

The way for Tarras to testify against Baillie had been prepared by the former's petition to the king in October 1684 acknowledging his guilt. The state nevertheless proceeded with his trial, in part at least to reinforce its contention that the conspiracy had been real.[104] In addition to the earl's confession, the prosecution introduced the earlier depositions of Murray and Scott. Adjudged guilty, Tarras was sentenced to death on 6 January, but Charles granted him a pardon and in June 1686 his estates were returned to him.[105]

Death for Outlaws: Holloway and Armstrong

The government captured and executed two more English plotters, James Holloway and Sir Thomas Armstrong, both of them outlaws, in early 1684. Following the disclosure of the Rye House plot, Holloway had traveled through Gloucester, Oxfordshire, and Somerset in the guise of a wood merchant before fleeing to France in late August 1683. On 4 October he sailed from La Rochelle with a cargo of brandy and other merchandise bound for Barbados, and thereafter, using the alias John Milward, he moved throughout the Caribbean until his arrest in January 1684. On the long journey back to England he reaffirmed his conviction that England was endangered by popery and arbitrary government, but he also promised to make a full confession, intimating that much had not been told. Thousands in England, Scotland, and Ireland, he asserted, had known of the projected insurrection, though few if any had been cognizant of the assassination scheme. Having said this, however, he also insisted that he would be loyal to his friends and an enemy to Rome, promising in doggerel to declare such truths that would scare the Tories. "I will no friend betray / But rather chuse to gang up Holbourn way."[106]

At first Holloway refused to make "any considerable confession, but on the contrary would trifle with his Majesty as some others have done." He quickly changed his mind, however, and confessed freely. Of the significant plotters with whom he had come into contact, Walcott was dead, West and Rumsey had turned state's evidence, and the remaining six (Ferguson, Wade, the Goodenough brothers, Norton, and Tiley) had fled to the Continent.[107] Having no apparent need for his testimony, the government tried him in the King's Bench for illegal flight after his indictment for high treason. Although the court was empowered to sentence him to death because of his attainder as an outlaw, the king offered to waive that judgment and permit Holloway to defend himself against charges of high treason. Since he had already confessed, Holloway threw himself on the mercy of the court. The outlawry, which carried an automatic sentence of death, therefore stood and no additional sentence was required. When a petition for mercy to the king proved fruitless, Holloway showed traces of bitterness: "I have cause to repent that Ever the King was Mercifull, not that I concerned my selfe depending upon Mercy if taken, but had he not been Mercifull to popish Plotters I had never been a Plotter. I never had a designe against the Kings life, but twas His and the Nations Intrest that Ingaged me in it."[108]

In his gallows comments on 30 April, Holloway insisted he had been party only to a plan to rescue Charles from his evil advisers and to punish those who were involved in the Popish Plot. "Had the Law been executed against Popish Offenders, I had never been concerned in any Plot." He had some parting counsel for the king: to prevent future conspiracies he urged Charles to summon Parliament, pass an act of oblivion for all plotters, and ban "news-mongers." Holloway's assorted statements are particularly striking as a revelation of the extent to which at least some of the conspirators conceived their activity as a response to the imagined perils of the Popish Plot. The dark shadow of Titus Oates was longer than is often recognized.[109]

The elusive Armstrong (alias Henry Lawrence) had gone to Cleves with Monmouth, Grey, and others, but by May 1684 he and Ferguson had traveled to Rotterdam.[110] While en route to Amsterdam to confer with other dissidents, he was seized at Leiden by one of Chudleigh's agents (see below, Chapter 7). With the approval of the provincial court of Holland he was returned to England under heavy guard, though many of the Dutch were incensed, viewing the extradition as a violation of their traditional practice of sanctuary.[111] Letters from Monmouth to Armstrong, seized when the latter was captured, indicated, according to the duke of York, that Monmouth had "neither minded nor would remember the caracter [i.e., the cipher] he had given that worthy assassinating knight"; the correspondence has apparently not survived.[112] On 14 June, three days after he had arrived in England, Armstrong was sentenced to death in the King's Bench on a charge of outlawry for high treason. Jeffreys denied his request for a trial. To the Privy Council he admitted only that he had often attended conferences at Shepherd's house and that he had seen Ferguson several times. Armstrong's final statement, contained in a paper given to the sheriff on the scaffold, professed innocence of any scheme to assassinate the king or alter the government. Had he been allowed a trial, he claimed, he could have disproved Lord Howard's accusations against him through the testimony of at least ten gentlemen as well as servants. Armstrong pointedly noted that Holloway had been offered a trial whereas he had not, even after claiming the right to one under the provisions of 5 & 6 Edward VI, c. 11.[113]

In Burnet's opinion, Armstrong probably would have been found innocent in a trial. The crown's case would have rested on the testimony of Rumsey and Shepherd, placing Armstrong in two meetings at Shepherd's house to discuss the deployment of the royal guards. Armstrong apparently had witnesses to prove his presence elsewhere on at least one of the occasions, and Burnet argued that Armstrong, a former captain of the guards, would have found it unnecessary to examine their disposition.[114] Nevertheless, it would have been prudent for him to do so, and the judges and jury might have allowed the witnesses a degree of latitude in estimating the dates of the meetings. The prosecution, moreover, would probably have introduced the record of Russell's trial, which noted the existence of those meetings. With Jeffreys to summarize the evidence, Armstrong, I believe, would almost certainly have been found guilty.

Royal Vengeance: Cornish and Bateman on Trial

Although attention shifted in the first year of James' reign to the fate of the Monmouth and Argyll rebels, the new king chose to have more alleged Rye House conspirators prosecuted. In at least three cases his motive was political vengeance: those of Henry Cornish, the outspoken Whig activist and leading financial supporter of Monmouth's cause in the City; Charles Lord Gerard of Brandon, a prominent Monmouth supporter and a member of the grand jury that had presented James as a recusant in 1680; and Charles Bateman, Shaftesbury's former surgeon and the obvious remaining target for a final attack on the earl. (Brandon's trial will be discussed in Chapter 8 in connection with those of Delamere and Stamford.)

Tried on 19 October 1685, Cornish pleaded not guilty to charges that he had conspired to kill the king and alter the government. He was unsuccessful in obtaining a postponement on the grounds that a material witness who could prove his innocence was in Lancashire. Rumsey, the first of the state's two witnesses, claimed that Cornish had arrived late for the meeting at Shepherd's house attended by Monmouth, Russell, Armstrong, Grey, Ferguson, and Rumsey himself. Ferguson, according to Rumsey, read a draft of the manifesto to Cornish, who approved its contents. Cornish heatedly denied having been present, although he acknowledged that he had visited Shepherd's house on a number of occasions despite a dislike of his "morals." The prosecution's second witness, Richard Goodenough, had been Cornish's undersheriff. The gist of his testimony concerned a conversation that had allegedly occurred around Easter 1683 at Cornish's home. As Goodenough recalled, he had commented on the plight of the Whigs: "Now the law will not defend us, though we be never so innocent; but some other way is to be thought on." To this Cornish purportedly replied, "I wonder the city is so unready [for rebellion], and the country so ready." Nothing in the conversation to this point was treasonable, but Goodenough, he claimed, then made a case for seizing the Tower, after which Cornish allegedly promised, "I will do what I can." In his confession of 20 July 1685, Goodenough indicated the two men had discussed the proposed uprising, and he also admitted they had conferred together about the insurrection on several other occasions at the Exchange in the City.[115]

In his defense Cornish argued that he had accepted Goodenough, whom he disliked, as his undersheriff only at Slingsby Bethel's insistence, and he called various witnesses to corroborate this fact as well as attest to his loyalty. Even more telling was the testimony of Shepherd, who insisted that the manifesto had not been read in the presence of Cornish, because he was "not looked upon to be of the company." Neither the prosecution nor the defendant made any attempt to call Lord Grey, the former because it knew Grey had not mentioned Cornish in his account, and the latter because he must have feared that Grey, like Rumsey, would lie. Shepherd's testimony cast serious doubt on Rumsey's story, and Goodenough's tale of his conversation with Cornish is dubious both because of the mutual dislike of the two men and because of the improbability that Goodenough would have revealed plans to seize the Tower to a man not known to be a conspirator. Nevertheless the jurors, one of whom (Thomas Oneby) had served in Russell's trial, found Cornish guilty. His scaffold speech, delivered on 23 October, contained a ringing declaration of his innocence: "The crimes laid to my charge were falsely and maliciously sworn against me by the witnesses." He spoke truthfully, for his death was in fact an act of judicial vengeance by James II.[116]

Charged with plotting to seize the king as well as the City, the Tower, and Whitehall palace, Charles Bateman was tried at the Old Bailey on 9 December 1685. Once again the prosecution used Josiah Keeling to sketch the outlines of the conspiracy, although he had no direct evidence of Bateman's involvement. Of the two obligatory witnesses, the first, Thomas Lee, explained how he had recruited Bateman at Richard Goodenough's request, noting, however, that Bateman seemed to have prior knowledge of the plot. Lee accompanied Bateman to Monmouth's house, and the surgeon subsequently related his plans to capture the Tower to Lee. Goodenough, who had received a pardon for his outlawry for high treason, testified that he and Bateman had discussed the proposed insurrection at the King's Head tavern in St. Swithin's Alley, and that the surgeon had promised to help recruit men. Bateman compelled Goodenough to admit that he might have been wrong about the place, but the latter insisted he had accurately recalled the conversation. After Bateman's efforts to undermine Lee's credibility by the testimony of other witnesses had failed, the jury found him guilty and he was executed on the 18th.[117]

The Trials in Retrospect

From the judicial perspective the Rye House trials as a whole were marred. Viewed even in the laxer context of seventeenth-century jurisprudence, standards of justice were violated in three key areas, the first of which involved the highly prejudicial use of Essex's alleged suicide to sway the juries in the trials of Russell and Sidney. The introduction of such information was especially heinous if Essex was murdered by Holland and Webster at the behest of James and Sunderland. In a modern court extant evidence would almost certainly be sufficient at least to indict Holland and Webster for murder and to cite James and Sunderland as conspirators. Standards of justice were also violated by the highly partisan role played by Judge Jeffreys, especially when in Hampden's trial he openly endorsed the credibility of Howard's testimony and backed his opinion with a reference to Essex's "suicide." Equally questionable was the role of torture, whether actual or threatened, in extracting confessions in Scotland in 1684. Although legal, its use was rightly protested by the duke of Hamilton, not least because of the dubious reliability of the resulting confessions. Judicially, therefore, the trials are a blot on the reigns of Charles and James.[118]

Doubts about whether justice had been served undermined the government's efforts to use the trials to prove that the conspiracies were real. The defensive comments of the prosecution in Baillie's trial are eloquent testimony to widespread disbelief. Convictions and executions failed to produce the desired goal of credibility, especially when condemned men such as Walcott, Holloway, and Baillie went to their graves steadfastly professing their innocence of many of the key charges. Nor did the state's heavy reliance on witnesses of dubious character, such as Howard and Keeling, lend much credence to the government's campaign. Sensing this, the Whigs were not reluctant to charge the Tories with manufacturing a sham plot for political purposes. As early as July 1683 an anonymous Whig "libel" depicted the Rye House arrests as part of a campaign to impose Catholicism on the country:

There is a rod in piss preparing to take of[f] some of the emminent Prottestants of England because Popery will not come else in easely. . . . We do expect there will be hundreds of Rumsies and Rumbolts &c: sett at worke to sweare & intrap men to take away there lives. . . . We suppose . . . [the sheriffs] are as the tide is and the Judges are accordingly corrupted.

The punishment of Sir Samuel Barnardiston, the most prominent critic of the conspiracy allegations, failed to stem such accusations.[119]

Unfortunately for the government, its poor handling of the trials undermined the general care with which it had undertaken the investigation of the conspiracies. The king's counsel, Sir Francis

North, who had played an integral part in the investigation and prosecution, subsequently reflected that the interrogators had asked no "leading question . . . by Naming any person that was suspicious beforhand, but onely such as arise Naturally from the Matter confessed"—an observation essentially borne out by the extant evidence. Ormond, who also participated in the investigation, made the same point: "We have never named any person to them [those being interrogated] that it may not be in theirs or anybody's power to say they have been terrified or bribed to accuse any particular person." As Richard Ashcraft has observed, "the government was generally careful in preventing witnesses in its custody from communicating with one another or allowing them to see the depositions of other witnesses."[120]

The plotting was real enough and the investigation—the use of torture in Scotland aside—reasonably fair, but the botched handling of the trials raised sufficient doubts to prompt people to question the reality of the conspiracies from the seventeenth century to the present. The government's ineptitude arose partly from its haste to prosecute, but this in turn was determined by its own uncertainty as to the extent of the plotting and its fear that other conspirators might yet be at work. The awkwardness of dealing with Monmouth was another constraint. If to later generations there would thus appear to be less to the Rye House plotting than met the eye, to the anxious government of Charles II it seemed that there might well be a great deal more.

"Insuperable Difficulties"

SEVEN

The Bungled Invasion Schemes

Although the ineptitude of the conspiracies to block James' accession had seriously weakened the radical cause, the goals of the plotters remained alive, especially in the exile community. The government's failure to recognize the potential scope of radical activity after the disclosures made by Alexander Gordon of Earlston and Josiah Keeling meant that a serious effort to arrest suspects got under way only on 21 June 1683. Many key conspirators were therefore able to make their way to the Continent, where they could avail themselves of the hospitality, financial support, and communications network of the exiles. As Chudleigh aptly remarked, the Netherlands is "a Country [in] which all that Party have but too many freinds which will be ayding to conceale them."[1] From this base, the exiles regrouped, and then, under the leadership of Argyll and Monmouth, invaded James' domains in the spring of 1685.

The Exiles Regroup

The exiles took extreme measures to protect themselves. Nathaniel Wade, Robert Ferguson, and Richard Nelthorpe paid John Row to stay in Switzerland, "fearing . . . he might turne a Discoverer of their Designs." Trenchard, at whose insistence Row had been forced into exile, was similarly concerned. On three occasions, prominent radicals threatened to kill Row to keep him quiet. The first time was in London. The second time, Sir Thomas Armstrong would have murdered Row at Cleves had Ford Lord Grey not intervened. The third time, Captain John Matthews, whom Row called Trenchard's "Bully

& Pensioner," threatened to stab him. Edmund Ludlow, at whose Vevey home Row stayed, urged the latter not to confess. Moreover, Grey and Armstrong allegedly discussed the possibility of commissioning someone to assassinate Thomas Shepherd and Colonel John Rumsey, whose potential testimony prevented Grey and Armstrong from returning to England.[2]

The government's efforts to monitor exile activities were crippled by recurrent tensions with Dutch authorities and difficulties in employing effective spies. Relations with the Dutch, for instance, had been sufficiently tense in November 1682 to prompt the States General to promulgate a resolution denying that they wanted war or that they were corresponding with "the King's factious Subjects." On 7 November, Thomas Chudleigh, the English envoy, was directed to remind the States General that any measures that threatened to rupture relations with England would be welcomed by dissidents, "who have now no other ressource than the malitious, and vaine hopes of a confusion which might be occasioned by the accidents of a Warr." The Dutch should know, Chudleigh was told, that they could expect no advantage by domestic upheaval in England, since London was "under a magistracy that will take no measures against the King."[3] Whitehall continued to operate on the assumption that the Dutch viewed English and Scottish dissidents as natural allies, especially in the event of a war between the two countries. Mutual suspicion coupled with the Dutch tradition of sanctuary virtually precluded coordinated efforts to arrest and extradite radical fugitives or even to keep an eye on exile activities.

Approximately five months before the plot was revealed, attempts had been under way to persuade Don Lewis, Samuel Pepys' secretary and a former friend of Stephen College's, to come to England and obtain a pardon in return for a substantive confession. William Carr, who had once been part of Pierre du Moulin's espionage network[4] and was now an agent for Secretary Jenkins, reported in April 1683 that one of his contacts, Mr. M[ounson?], alias B (Thomas Blunt, a radical who had turned informer), had employed Lewis as a spy to discover the intrigues of a cabal against royal interests. Among those involved were David Hackston, the Scottish assassin, and Thomas Dare of Taunton, whose house in Amsterdam was a center of radical activity. Although Charles was concerned that Lewis intended "to cheate him," he permitted his return to England following the initial revelations of the Rye House Plot. It quickly became apparent, however, that Lewis either could not or would not reveal anything substantive, and the king, who had, in Jenkins' words, "an extreme gracious tenderness of the lives of His Subjects," refused to allow him to testify against alleged conspirators. James dismissed the entire episode as a "silly contrivance of a new plot" by Lewis and the Whigs. Banned from England by Charles, Lewis returned to the Netherlands, where the dissidents suspected he was a spy and refused to trust him.[5]

Although Chudleigh had a number of agents in his employ, they were rarely able to do more than monitor some of the radicals' movements and report rumors about their plans. In September 1683, Sunderland instructed Chudleigh to dispatch to Cleves an agent not known to Armstrong and Ferguson, but who could recognize them. As a result of that mission, contact was established with Sir John Cochrane, who, as noted above in Chapter 6, had refused to return to Scotland. Some operatives in the Netherlands, notably James Hodgson and Ezekiel Everest (alias John Elton), reported directly (at least on occasion) to such English officials as Sunderland and Godolphin, raising a question as to how much Chudleigh knew of such reports. In May 1685, Thomas Vile, who had once written for Richard Janeway's *Impartial Protestant Mercury* and later acquired a reputation as "one of the Cheif Confidents of all those Traiterous Fugitives," sought employment from the Stuart court as a spy, as did a man named Ballard. The espionage network was inevitably complicated by the activities of double agents, such as Ensign James Denham, who pretended to spy on the Scottish dissidents in 1685 but sailed with the Argyll expedition.[6]

On 27 July 1683, Sunderland directed Chudleigh to seek Dutch assistance in the apprehension of Armstrong, Ferguson, and other fugitive plotters; to make inquiries as to Cochrane's whereabouts; and to insist that the Dutch expel Monmouth and Grey from the Netherlands. The States of Holland and Utrecht duly ordered the arrest of the conspirators, but their action was apparently only pro forma. Perhaps more representative of popular Dutch feeling was the

Utrecht bailiff who left his town rather than arrest Ferguson. A Rotterdam bailiff agreed to apprehend Armstrong and Ferguson, but only if Chudleigh located them for him.[7]

Chudleigh's agents first began to pick up the trail of the conspirators at Amsterdam in early August after questioning the sentinel responsible for Grey's escape. Although the sentinel indicated that Grey and Monmouth had gone to Germany, this, Chudleigh surmised, was "but a feint." In fact the two peers reached Cleves in mid-August. With them were five other men, probably including Armstrong and Ferguson, and Lady Henrietta Berkeley, who was approximately four months pregnant. Chudleigh's agents learned that the elector had promised to leave them alone and to warn them if Charles demanded their arrest. Argyll and Cochrane were in Cleves for a time in the fall, perhaps to discuss their options. Some of the fugitives may have returned to the Netherlands surreptitiously for brief visits, for Grey, Armstrong, Ferguson, and the Goodenough brothers were reportedly in Amsterdam in early October, and Grey and Lady Henrietta were apparently sighted at the Utrecht home of James Stewart less than a month later. Cochrane and several other Scots visited Wesel for approximately a week in mid-December, presumably to ascertain its suitability as a place to settle. By January 1684, as surveillance became more effective, Sunderland and Chudleigh could place Grey (alias Thomas Holt), Armstrong (alias Henry Lawrence), and Lady Henrietta in Cleves; Cochrane (alias Thomas Parsons) at Nijmegen; Ferguson (alias William Clark) in Amsterdam; and Richard Goodenough (alias George Smart), Francis Goodenough (alias Thomas Bryan), John Ayloffe (alias Richard St. John), Edward Norton, the London tobacconist Nicholas Locke, Mr. Smith, the wealthy sugar-baker, and his wife, Ann Smith, who had hidden Argyll in London in 1682, in Utrecht. Sir Patience Ward was also in Utrecht, although he did not associate with the fugitives. Wade (alias John Land), Nelthorpe, and Row were with Ludlow in Vevey, and Argyll was believed to be in Friesland.[8]

Intelligence reports suggested that the spirits of the exiles were surprisingly buoyant. By late August 1683 they were speaking "as if the King were weary of the Prosecution of the Plott & would be glad to lett it fall," though such hopes proved to be misplaced. About the same time expectations were high that New Englanders would defend their charter, presumably by force, against *quo warranto* proceedings, and there was talk as well that Charles and James could not expect to live long.[9] Rumors, such as one that Scotland was in arms, helped to raise their spirits, and so too perhaps did the prayers of English and Dutch ministers in behalf of persecuted Protestants in England as well as France and the German states.[10] The exiles were also undoubtedly aware that the Rye House prosecutions had only momentarily dampened radical sentiments at home. Some dissidents were, if anything, more convinced than ever that Charles II should receive the fate meted out to his father. As Broom Whorwood of Oxford had put it on the eve of the Rye House disclosures: "The Martyrdom [of Charles I] says he; the farterdom; if this King [Charles II] had been Served as his Father was, it had been the better for us all." The executions of Russell, Walcott, and their compatriots intensified resentment among some, as is reflected, for instance, in anonymous doggerel found at St. Olave's, Southwark:

> You Hippocrites leave off your Pranks
> To murther men and then give thanks
> Forbear your Tricks pursue no farther
> For God accepts no thanks for murther.

Optimism was also generated by the conviction that the dissidents enjoyed the protection of William of Orange because they placed his right to the English throne (presumably as Mary's husband) ahead of Anne's.[11]

Planning for joint insurrections in England and Scotland resumed in the spring of 1684. The initiative came from the Argyll circle when a London merchant named Rawlins indicated that he could raise £20,000 from his friends in the City if a suitable messenger could be found. Ayloffe agreed to go, but first he wrote to Wade in Vevey asking him to return to the Netherlands and help with the planning. At Ayloffe's request and undoubtedly with Argyll's approval, Wade extended a similar invitation to Ludlow, who was promised command of a rebel force in western England. The old warrior declined, pleading, Wade reported, that he had already "done his work . . . in the World and was resolved to Leave it to others."[12]

Despite Ludlow's refusal, preparations went forward. Chudleigh's agents noted that the conspirators began secretly purchasing considerable quantities of weapons "fit onely for common Soldiers"; Chudleigh surmised that they might have been intended for shipment to Scotland. Funding probably came from Ann Smith, Argyll's hostess. Ferguson was also the beneficiary of her support. Planning sessions were held in Rotterdam, a city popular with the Scottish exiles and the residence of such English dissidents as Dr. Edward Richardson, a key architect of the 1663 northern rebellion; James Washington, a veteran radical involved in the shipment of "factious" books to England (as was Argyll himself); and the Quaker merchant Benjamin Furly, whose previous radical associates had included Algernon Sidney and John Phelps. "A very zealus man for the good old Cause," according to Ezekiel Everest, Furly acted as an intermediary between radicals in England and exiles in the Netherlands. Among those present in Rotterdam in early May were Ferguson, Norton, Cochrane, and Wade. The government was sufficiently cognizant of these activities to issue a proclamation on 5 May to begin arming loyal Scots, having previously ordered the confiscation of weapons from Argyll's supporters.[13]

Variously using the aliases St. John and Hammon, Ayloffe went secretly to London; Chudleigh's informers thought he had gone to a German spa. The mission, however, was a failure, for the unnamed nonconformist ministers who were his principal target refused to see him because of his reputation as an atheist. After Ayloffe's return to the Netherlands, Sir William Ellis sent word that he would pledge £2,000. Nicholas Locke, the brother-in-law of the now deceased Mr. Smith and himself a man worth some £30,000, also returned to London, ostensibly to visit his two sons but probably to seek financial backing for the insurrection. Learning of his trip, Chudleigh suggested to the king that Locke could reveal much about the radicals if he were arrested and interrogated in England.[14]

Shortly before the Rotterdam "consults" Ferguson had traveled to Cleves to inform Lord Grey about the proposed insurrection, adding that he, Argyll, and others feared a repeat of the Bothwell Bridge fiasco if the Scots acted on their own. Ferguson was unsuccessful in pressing Grey to arrange for a meeting between Monmouth and Argyll, but Grey did agree to speak with the earl on his own. Subsequently, in May, Grey journeyed to Rotterdam, where he presumably met with the earl or his supporters, and certainly with Armstrong, on matters relating to Monmouth.[15]

The duke had gone to Brussels, where the marquis of Grana, governor of the Spanish Netherlands, granted him an annuity of £6,000 and appointed him colonel of a Spanish regiment. Armstrong, hoping to persuade him to serve the elector of Brandenburg instead, followed him to Brussels, as did Henry Booth after his release from the Tower. Reluctant to exacerbate relations with his father, Monmouth adamantly refused to visit Berlin, which Charles had placed off-limits. Armstrong then traveled to Rotterdam, where he and Captain John Matthews, his son-in-law, unsuccessfully pleaded for Grey to go to Brussels to intercede with the duke.[16]

In the meantime, at The Hague Lord Brandon arranged through Bentinck to meet with William. "No Englishman was ever known to be so highly caressd before by Monsieur Benting," grumbled Chudleigh. The prince, determined to preserve close relations with the Whigs, subsequently received both Brandon and Monmouth with great favor, prompting Charles II to have Chudleigh convey his displeasure to William, who was "a little embarrassed."[17] The English court was additionally irritated by reports—apparently false—that Henry Ireton, son of the major-general and grandson of Oliver Cromwell, had also enjoyed the prince's hospitality. Although Ireton had accompanied Brandon to the Netherlands, the two seem to have parted company almost immediately.[18]

The radicals plotting an insurrection had scheduled a meeting at Amsterdam in early June 1684. As they passed through Leiden en route to the gathering, Armstrong was captured by Chudleigh's agents, though Grey escaped and fled to Cleves.[19] Apparently at the Amsterdam session the other plotters realized they had insufficient funds to support uprisings tentatively scheduled for Michaelmas 1684. Rawlins' pledge of £1,000 did not materialize because of his death, and Christopher Vane, who lived in Utrecht and had promised £1,000, backed out after his wife objected. "The Expedition" was therefore postponed "and resolutions taken to endeavour what might be, to be ready" the following spring.[20]

The dissidents received more bad news on 4/14 July when George Barclay returned to Rotterdam from a mission to discern the state of affairs in Scotland. While there he had preached to a large conventicle attended by numerous armed men, but he also detected some discouragement because "so much of theire purposes are known."[21] The government had instigated sweeping security measures, including provisions for armed troops who could be called up by lieutenants on six days' notice. Lieutenants in sensitive areas had orders to interrogate former Bothwell Bridge rebels, their supporters, and any who "calumniate[d] the laws and government." The Privy Council was empowered, among other things, to require security from suspicious persons, disarm dissidents in Argyllshire, and punish ministers who had violated the terms of the indulgence. Additional security measures were implemented throughout the summer and fall as the government revealed its determination to prevent another uprising north of the Tweed. Three Argyll supporters—Colonel Menzies and the lairds of McFarland and Weems—were arrested in July, at which time a substantial number of weapons were confiscated from McFarland.[22]

An unidentified agent whose sources appear to be fairly reliable reported that at the time of the Barclay mission other emissaries had been dispatched to seek assistance. Cochrane, he said, had gone to consult the elector of Brandenburg and another agent sought the aid of Sweden's Charles XI, but because of the expense, the distance, and other commitments both rulers declined to help unless they received "great pleadges and security." Armstrong, the agent thought, would have returned to England in disguise had he not been captured; reports from others indicated that "England is like to play the Jade." The conspirators placed their chief hope in Scotland, where they saw evidence of "some resolution and courage." The setbacks to the rebels notwithstanding, this agent warned his superiors not to underestimate the radicals: "They are a partie in a desperat condition, and of desperat principles and practices, and seem now to be extending to theire extreamest reach."[23]

Once the decision to postpone the rebellion had been made, Argyll and several English exiles, including Richard Goodenough, went to Cleves. There Goodenough, presumably at Argyll's request, asked Grey if he would engage in an English uprising, particularly if Courtenay and other gentlemen of quality were involved. Grey's answer was noncommittal, and several days later Argyll and some of his followers left Cleves. So too did the English fugitives because of a request from the English government to the elector of Brandenburg. Grey, however, was allowed to remain.[24]

The capture of Armstrong, the ouster of the English fugitives from Cleves, and the continuing efforts of Charles' agents to apprehend them made security a paramount concern. During the summer of 1684 Cochrane and his son, a university student at Utrecht, visited several German courts "soliciting for a retreat to themselves & their poor afflicted Countreymen." By September they had returned to the Netherlands with positive news from Hamburg and Lüneburg. The government of the latter commissioned Sir William Waller to command a regiment, at the same time bestowing a captaincy upon Cochrane and a lieutenancy upon James Stewart, who was living in Rotterdam.[25]

Reports of heightened security in Scotland and the London area about the time the conspirators had originally intended to launch their insurrections persuaded them to become more secretive. In early October the constables of London and Westminster received orders to arrest III "disaffected and dangerous" persons, including Matthew Meade (indicted the previous December under the Elizabethan Conventicle Act), Henry Danvers, Stephen Lobb, George Griffith, Robert Perrott, Nathaniel Vincent, Francis Bampfield, and William Kiffin (whose weapons had been confiscated in the Rye House crackdown). The plotters attributed the increased security in England and Scotland to the fact that information about the projected insurrections had been given to too many of "our own friends." Planning for the spring 1685 uprisings, said Wade, would therefore be "kept very private," even from members of "our own Party." The inner circle saw an additional benefit from Waller's arrangements in Lüneburg: "Some of our talking People were encouraged to go, & others on purpose went to other places that the thing might be carryed on with less observation."[26]

While the conspirators tried to draw the veil of secrecy more closely around them, Chudleigh's attention was diverted—perhaps deliberately—by a spate of radical publications. In December 1683 he had been provoked by a work from the pen of the Huguenot refugee Pierre Jurieu; entitled *L'Esprit de Mons' Arnauld*, it criticized Charles and James. Deeming it "the boldest & the horridest Libell," Chudleigh persuaded William to have the States General prohibit its sale. Nevertheless a shipment of approximately 100 copies was sent to François Bureau, a London bookseller.[27]

In November 1684, Chudleigh's ire was roused even more by two anonymous pamphlets, both from Ferguson's pen,[28] published in the Netherlands: *An Enquirie into, and Detection of, the Barbarous Murther of the Late Earl of Essex* and *An Impartial Enquiry into the Administration of Affair's in England*. Both, Chudleigh thought, were the work of John Locke, who had ostensibly come to the Netherlands "for the benefitt of the Aire" but who, reported Chudleigh, "lives amongst the worst of our Traytors here." That number included Nelthorpe; Thomas Dare, with whom Locke stayed in Amsterdam; John Wilmore, the foreman of the London jury that had returned an *ignoramus* verdict in Stephen College's trial; Daniel Le Blon, who, with Wilmore, was apparently involved in purchasing weapons for Argyll; and Jacob Vandervelde, an Amsterdam bookseller whose shop was a meeting place for the radicals.[29]

Although Chudleigh had known Locke when both were at Christ Church, Oxford, he was mistaken in his attribution of these pamphlets. Ferguson wrote the tract on Essex using material supplied to him by Robert Cragg (alias John Smith), one of Monmouth's couriers, though Locke too, as Chudleigh may have known, found the government's suicide story unconvincing. Richard Ashcraft has made a compelling argument that *An Impartial Enquiry into the Administration of Affair's in England* also came from Ferguson's pen. In it Ferguson justified the right of rebellion against a ruler who failed to promote the common good by citing natural law and British history:

Any ruler who commands what God prohibits, or forbids what God enjoins, doth *ipso facto* depose himself, and instead of being owned any longer for a King, ought to be treated as a Rebel and Traitor against the Supream and Universal Soveraign. And to resist such is not to oppose Authority, but

Usurpation; nor is the dethroning those who have invaded the Right and Authority of their Maker, a deposing of Governours, but a delivering our selves from conspirators against their as wel as our King.

The real conspirators were Charles and James, who had challenged the rights and privileges of the people, in part by the frequent proroguing and dissolving of parliaments. Ferguson castigated Charles for his blatant immorality, his attack on the charters, and his appointment of Catholics to high offices as well as for ordering the fire of London and the assassination of Sir Edmund Godfrey. Ferguson further denounced the Stuart regime for its alleged sham conspiracies, including the Meal Tub Plot and the purported schemes to seize the king during the Oxford Parliament and launch a rebellion in Cheshire. For good measure he also blamed the court for the improper convictions of Argyll and Russell and the murder of Essex. Not surprisingly, Chudleigh castigated the tract as an "impudent and horrid Libell." [30]

The earl of Middleton ordered Chudleigh to identify the publishers of the two pamphlets and insist that the States General punish them, but Chudleigh doubted whether the States would act, owing to their half-hearted attempts to suppress Jurieu's book. In that instance, he explained to Middleton, the fine of 500 guilders only piqued people's curiosity and increased sales. When Middleton learned that both books had been translated into French, he renewed his instructions to Chudleigh. The latter thereupon prepared a memorial to the States General, but withdrew it when Gaspar Fagel, the grand pensionary, warned that it would only publicize the tracts; moreover, an existing law already prohibited the publication of libelous material. By early January 1685, Chudleigh could identify five booksellers in Amsterdam, a like number at The Hague, and four in Rotterdam who sold the tract dealing with Essex's death. [31]

In early January the Amsterdam magistrates mounted a search for the presses that had printed the offending books and issued a proclamation banning the vilification of Charles II in coffeehouses. One of those accused of the latter offense was the merchant Abraham Kicke, a steadfast friend of the radicals. [32] The magistrates also ordered the seizure of all copies of the tract about Essex, launched an investigation to determine who had printed *The Life of the King*, and commanded all printers not to issue anything "to the disservice of any forreigne Potentate." The sweep turned up another offensive work, *The Triumph of Adultery*, which Chudleigh deemed "as bad as any of the others." But the Amsterdam magistrates refused to punish the booksellers; in contrast a Leiden bookseller who sold a pamphlet critical of Fagel was fined 1,800 guilders. Finally, in response to a memorial from Chudleigh the States General resolved to punish the publishers of libelous material in the future with fines of 1,000 guilders and the closure of their shops for one year, though no action was taken against the booksellers. The rather lenient attitude of the Dutch was consistent with their historic tendency to enforce their press-control laws only rarely, and was compatible as well with the hospitality offered to British radicals, especially by Dutch republicans. Indeed, the ability of British radicals to survive owed a great deal to the Dutch.[33]

Dissent in Scotland and Ireland

Relatively subdued in the aftermath of the Rye House plotting, dissident activity in Scotland and Ireland soon began to increase. In September 1684, Captain Andrew Birch, who had been arresting large numbers of Scottish fugitives along the Scottish border, reported a conspiracy to seize Berwick and the castles in the region for Argyll. The key figures included Sir Patrick Hume and George Pringle of Torwoodlee, both of whom escaped.[34]

As early as January 1684 dissidents at Lesmahagow and Carstairs in Lanarkshire had liberated imprisoned rebels, confiscated property previously expropriated from Covenanters, and stabbed horses belonging to the dragoons. In June, 40 to 50 rebels were in arms at Glencorse, south of Edinburgh, and on 29 July a band of some 30 men attacked a royalist force conveying prisoners from Dumfries to Edinburgh at Enterkin, north of Thornhill.[35]

Much of this militancy was undoubtedly the work of the Cameronians, who remained defiant in the face of persecution and continued to hold general meetings. Copies of the documents seized when Earlston was arrested as well as a new commission were conveyed to Robert Hamilton at Leeuwarden by William Nairn in August 1683.

At this point the United Societies anticipated the receipt of printed copies of the sermons of Cargill and Cameron from the Netherlands, even as they prepared to send the sermons of John Welwood for publication. On 3 October 1683 the Societies wrote to "those who desire to Joine with the Cause of God in Dubline," insisting that the government's indulgence policy was Satan's work, "whereby Christs Crown was established upon a mans head, which some men, Loveing worldlie ease, more then Truth, embracing, they betrayed the Cause of God." The Societies were also in contact with a nonconformist group in Newcastle. In mid-November 1684 the Cameronians affixed copies of another of their declarations—"The Apologetical Declaration and Admonitory Vindication of the True Presbyterians of the Church of Scotland"—to church doors and market crosses, declaring war against Charles Stuart and vowing to slay his supporters. Such killing, they professed, was not murder because it was "for the sake of Religion." On the night of the 19th a rebel party comprising more than 30 men assassinated two royal guardsmen as they slept in an abbey near Edinburgh. Government troops cornered 11 of the alleged perpetrators in February 1685, killing 6 and hanging 3, but losing 2 of their own men in the fighting.[36]

Apart from the ubiquitous conventicles, Ireland remained calm until the fall of 1684. Continuing government efforts to procure the return of Scottish fugitives resulted in the arrest of John "Clubfoot" Campbell and David Montgomery of Langshaw.[37] In November magistrates in Ireland learned of a radical Covenanter document enjoining Presbyterians from supporting either clerics of the state church or moderate dissenters who prayed for the king. Subscribers of this document were exhorted to assist Scottish fugitives. The paper was ostensibly to have been sent to Glasgow, but was burned when James Caldwell, a Belfast bookbinder, and others could not obtain enough signatures. Caldwell believed militant Covenanters were "in the right and upon occacon he wold Joyne with them against all others." The propagation of such tenets prompted Sir Robert Colvill, a royalist, to advise Ormond's secretary that "these disorders will hardly be prevented unless the roote be plucked up[,] for tender dealing will never gaine upon people of such perverse principles." Caldwell may have been involved in plans for a Covenanter uprising in northern Ireland in December 1684, the alleged leader of which was to have been Gawin Hamilton of Liswine (Lisowen?), county Down. Authorities learned of the scheme from a Downpatrick carpenter whom Robert Camlin of Loughinisland, county Down, a radical recruiter, attempted to enlist. The alleged conspiracy was probably nothing more than the musings of irate malcontents, but Presbyterians in the north were increasingly observed at fairs and markets wearing arms.[38]

Monmouth Thwarted: Charles' Untimely Death

The Argyll and Monmouth circles went their separate ways in the fall of 1684. Argyll was determined to invade Scotland in the spring of 1685, though most of the English exiles, according to John Erskine, were "no ways forward to concur for the advancing of that design at present, as it was at present managed, and other affairs were situated." Monmouth had been well treated by William, who bestowed military honors on the duke and entertained him at Dieren, thereby signaling his continued support for the Whigs, especially their monarchical wing. Emboldened by this welcome, perhaps encouraged by the prince, and undoubtedly concerned by the capture of Armstrong and the attempt to seize Grey, Monmouth began hatching new plans of his own to undermine James. His servants had copies of Ferguson's tract expounding the case for Essex's murder, and one of them insisted that the duke of York would "suddainly be calld to account for it, & that wee shall see a strange change in England very quickly." Monmouth also conferred with Grey—their first meeting since they had fled to the Continent—to persuade him not to move to Switzerland. Explaining that he was about to undertake a secret mission to see Charles, the duke offered to intervene with the king on Grey's behalf. At this point Monmouth clearly entertained hopes that his father would accord him a place of prominence at the English court, at the least restoring his offices and according favor to a faction hostile to James.[39]

Monmouth left Dieren on 10 November 1684, ostensibly bound for Brussels, though he made surreptitious visits en route, presumably to consult with key exiles. "It appears," opined the Comte d'Avaux, the French ambassador, "as if there was somewhat in agitation." Once in London, Monmouth arranged to see the king with the help of an old friend, William Lord Alington, governor of the Tower. As William Veitch, the Covenanting minister, later recounted, Monmouth told Charles "anent the Duke of York and his jesuitical cabal's plotting how to take the king off the stage." Monmouth may also have spoken to Charles about Grey, but in any event the duke received jewels valued at £10,000. After Monmouth's departure Alington reportedly advised Charles to restore the duke to his former offices while James was in Scotland for the next session of its Parliament, and to ban from the English court all persons who supported James. This episode was at the heart of an intrigue in which the key participants were Halifax, William (concerned, as always, to keep England out of the French orbit), and Monmouth, all of whom were apparently attempting to isolate James at Holyrood. Further plans to this end were laid at the end of December, when Halifax secretly wrote to Monmouth with the king's approval, indicating that he could return to Westminster in February. James, who had orders to leave for Edinburgh the same month, may not have known of the intrigue. All came to naught, however, when Charles became seriously ill on 2 February 1685 and died four days later.[40]

Two days before Charles' death, Alington was poisoned, and suspicions soon surfaced that the king had likewise been murdered. Two physicians, Needham and Lower, who were present at the autopsy, told Burnet they saw two or three blue spots on the outside of the king's stomach, but the surgeons refused Needham's request to examine its contents and quickly disposed of it. Le Fevre, a French physician, "saw a blackness in the shoulder," made an incision, and discovered that "it was all mortified." A Catholic physician named Short suspected "foul dealing," although he may have been referring to the nature of Charles' treatment by the attending doctors rather than a suspicious cause of death. Short soon died after drinking a large draft of wine; before the end he said he was convinced that he himself had been poisoned. Among the others who believed that Charles had been poisoned were the duchess of Portsmouth, the earl of Mulgrave, Burnet, Delamere, and Veitch.[41] An investigation of these allegations lies beyond the purview of this book, but the case that Charles was poisoned appears to be extremely flimsy. Rumors of his alleged murder soon spread. At Barking, near London, an anonymous paper repudiated James' right to ascend the throne without the consent of the nation assembled in Parliament and cited among his alleged public atrocities the great fire of London, the murder of Sir Edmund Godfrey, the murder of the earl of Essex, and the poisoning of his brother. The charges would shortly be reiterated in Monmouth's declaration.[42]

After his visit with Charles on 30 November, Monmouth returned to the Netherlands, where he was frequently with William. The duke, Chudleigh reported, continued to be "highly caressd att this Court where he appear[ed] as one of the family." He continued to display an interest in the Anglo-Scottish regiment of Sir Henry Bellasis, which was on loan to the prince. Most of its officers were Monmouth supporters, and the duke was now interested in commissioning Captain Matthews as its major. As early as November 1684, Chudleigh had surmised that the purpose of such activity was to block James' accession. Chudleigh might have correctly guessed the duke's intent, but Monmouth himself kept his plans highly secret, even from Grey. The latter apparently had no idea that anything unusual was afoot, for while the duke was in England, Grey tried (unsuccessfully) to borrow £500 to purchase the command of a regiment in the service of the elector of Brandenburg. Not until late January did Monmouth ask Matthews to arrange a meeting with Grey, on which occasion the duke told Grey he had not seen Charles but provided details of an alleged plot at The Hague to kill Monmouth himself.[43]

In late January, Halifax wrote again to Monmouth to indicate that their plans were moving ahead. The duke made this entry in his diary: "A Letter from *L.* [Halifax] that my business was almost as well as done; but must be so sudden as not to leave room for 39's [James'] Party to counterplot. That it is probable he would chuse *Scotland* rather than *Flanders* or this Country; which was all one to 29 [Charles]." With restoration to royal favor seemingly within his grasp, Monmouth received the report of Charles' death with bitterness: "The sad News of his Death by *L. O cruel Fate!*"[44]

Invasion Plans

When William learned of Charles' death, which made Princess Mary the heir presumptive to the English throne, he advised Monmouth to leave his court, suggesting he accept a command in the imperial forces fighting the Turks. The duke instead remained in Brussels, where he hoped to receive a message—perhaps an invitation to return—"from the great men his friends in England." His stay was cut short when the marquis of Grana, governor of the Spanish Netherlands, tipped him off that Charles II of Spain had ordered his arrest. Surreptitiously returning to the Netherlands, Monmouth found refuge in Gouda with the help of James Washington.[45] His hopes for being restored to favor at court dashed, Monmouth again considered rebellion as a means not only to acquire personal power but to protect Protestant and parliamentary interests from James and his supporters. This required that he renew contacts with the radical exiles, whom he had virtually ignored in the first year of his exile in the hope of demonstrating to his father that he deserved to be welcomed back to court. Such dreams, however, had perished with his father.

While Monmouth pursued his intrigue with Halifax in the final months before Charles' death, Argyll's coterie plotted a spring insurrection. Among the planners were Phelps and Wade, but none of Monmouth's people, according to Wade, was involved. Government agents had virtually no success tracking this group throughout the fall and winter. Not since September, when unnamed radicals convened at Rotterdam and Utrecht, had Chudleigh learned much about dissident activities. Ferguson and (Richard?) Goodenough had reportedly left in November 1684 for Lüneburg to be with Waller, possibly because they were among those who talked too freely. Nelthorpe (alias Gardner) was planning to go to the same city with his wife and Waller's spouse. John Locke, who had been with Nelthorpe, was pondering a move to Utrecht, "the greatest nest att present of the King's ill Subjects," according to Chudleigh. Despite the scanty data, Chudleigh correctly surmised in mid-January 1685 that in Amsterdam "the Faction is still endeavouring by all ways to disturbe the Peace of His Majesty's Government & if possible to raise up Sedition & Rebellion among His Subjects."[46]

Both the Argyll and the Monmouth groups maintained contacts with supporters in the British Isles, using personal messengers and coded correspondence. Knowing this, the government employed agents to watch the ports, monitor traffic to and from the Continent, and confiscate suspicious documents. Thanks to the extra security measures ordered by James at his accession, magistrates apprehended two couriers in early February, William Spence, who posed as an art buyer but was a messenger for Argyll, at Harwich, and John Gibbons, Monmouth's servant, at Dover. Both couriers were carrying letters, most of which had been composed before the king's death.[47]

Richard Ashcraft has argued that the correspondence was written in cant and has ingeniously suggested possible hidden meanings.[48] In some cases such encoding was used, but substantial caution is necessary in determining which letters were in cipher and how they are to be explained. It would be tempting, for instance, to interpret the references to money in the correspondence carried by Gibbons as information about the transmission of or need for funds with which to purchase weapons. But on the eve of the king's death Monmouth was no longer thinking of an insurrection or an invasion but of a court intrigue that would accomplish his ends without bloodshed. If the letters in Gibbons' possession had any surreptitious meaning, they must have done no more than hint at the possibility of the duke's return to England. "I may see you this sumer," wrote Sarah Hubbard to Ann Mobury at Exton, Rutland. Another Hubbard letter offered to send lace or money and inquired about Mrs. (Mary) Percival, formerly a member of Shaftesbury's household and an acquaintance of John Locke's.[49] There is also the distinct possibility that the letters were perfectly innocuous and intended as a partial cover to explain the courier's trip. Certainly Monmouth was sensitive to Gibbons' need for an excuse, for he was instructed to say that the duke had dismissed all his servants. The real purpose of Gibbons' trip was therefore probably not the conveyance of coded letters but the transmission of one or more oral messages, in this case either to someone close to Halifax or to the duke's supporters. No hard evi-

dence can be adduced to support Ashcraft's suggestion that such encoded correspondence indicates Monmouth was aware of Argyll's
plans for an insurrection aided by English radicals.[50]

The letters in Spence's possession were probably devoid of political
substance. Mrs. Rawlins, undoubtedly the wife of the London merchant who had previously considered providing financial support for
a rebel invasion, wrote to the bookseller Samuel Harris in Utrecht,
asking him to send her a box and a trunk via James Washington. Both
men were part of the radical community, and indeed Mrs. Rawlins
sent greetings to a number of the exiles. Another letter, ostensibly
from Thomas Papillon to his wife, took advantage of the fact that
the bearer left for England "imediately" on news of Charles' death.
Argyll, who commissioned Spence, wished to communicate to allies
in London, hence Spence's rapid departure. But the important messages were undoubtedly transmitted orally, not in cant. Indeed, one
of the confiscated letters, from a London hosier named Whiting to
the preacher John Spademan in Rotterdam, indicated that Spence
would verbally report "how things were Carried here at present."
Spademan had ties to the Princess Mary.[51]

Word of the king's death inspired a flurry of radical activity. The
news, reflected Erskine, "did move [militant exiles] . . . as if fire had
been set to powder."[52] When Monmouth left for Brussels, Grey went
to Amsterdam, where Ferguson soon called on him to underscore
the importance of unity if the three kingdoms were to be maintained
and Protestantism preserved throughout Europe. Proposing a meeting between Monmouth and Argyll, Ferguson warned that if the
duke did not act speedily, others would proceed without him. Unable to convince Grey, Ferguson called on him later the same day.
This time Ferguson was more candid, explaining that for some time
Argyll had been in contact with prominent dissidents in Scotland to
plan a rebellion, and that a large quantity of arms and ammunition
had been purchased and Scottish officers now in Dutch or German
service recruited. Reluctant to return to the shadowy underground
of conspiracy, Grey suggested that Ferguson himself approach Monmouth in Brussels, but Ferguson declined.[53]

About the same time Sir Patrick Hume (alias Peter Pereson), who
had been released from a Scottish prison in December, left Utrecht

to meet with fellow Scots in Rotterdam. Ferguson may have refused to go to Brussels in order to attend this meeting, the discussions at which certainly reflected his views. Convinced that Charles' demise was part of a Catholic plot, the Scots invited Monmouth to Rotterdam.[54] There, according to Hume, he agreed that "if something were not timously done, the Duke of York would strenthen himself in armes, debauch or violent [i.e. violate] parliaments, so as in short time he should be able to oppress all good christians, and free spirits in the nationes, and setle Antichristianisme and tyranny at his pleasure."[55]

By the time Argyll, Cochrane, and his son joined their Scottish allies in Rotterdam, Monmouth had left for Friesland. Argyll declared that he was prepared to invade Scotland at once, having already received English money, with which weapons and a frigate had been purchased. Calmer heads must have urged caution, for Hume and others consulted with Monmouth a second time, apparently troubled in part by the duke's personal ambition. To assuage their doubts, Monmouth, who would have settled for a prominent role in a Protestant republic (akin perhaps to that of William in the Netherlands), promised he would not claim the crown without first taking advice, and that the common cause would take precedence. The caution of Hume and his colleagues was apparent in their refusal to act unless the English rebelled and "a ballance [was] fixed in Ireland, as that no danger might come upon Scotland or England from thence." They also wanted to make arrangements with Protestant states on the Continent to prevent Catholic intervention on James' behalf. For his part, Monmouth pledged to fight alongside the Scots if the English proved unwilling to take up arms. When the Hume delegation conveyed this information to Argyll in Rotterdam, the earl opposed Monmouth's direct involvement in Scotland because the latter knew so little of the countryside and had no experience leading "a few men in partyes."[56]

Meanwhile Grey's efforts to raise money to purchase a command in Brandenburg continued to prove fruitless, and his condition worsened when James procured his ouster from Cleves. Penniless, he returned to Amsterdam, where Matthews apprised him of the Scottish preparations and persuaded him to participate in the discussions.

Around 23 February / 5 March 1685 Monmouth came to Amsterdam to confer with Hume, Melville, two other Scots, and Grey. They discussed the proposed Scottish rebellion only in general terms, for Argyll was expected the following day. By this point the earl was so anxious to get under way that he was willing to serve under Monmouth in Scotland if the duke provided weapons and ammunition.[57]

Monmouth and Argyll met for several hours at the home of Thomas Dare in Amsterdam approximately 25 February / 7 March. Second-hand accounts of what occurred were provided by Hume, whose information came from Argyll, and by Grey, who relied on Monmouth. According to Hume, the duke accepted responsibility for England, most of Ireland, and relations with foreign states, while Argyll promised to be answerable for Scotland and northern Ireland. The earl purportedly asserted that 5,000 or 6,000 Highlanders, using their own weapons, would support him, and that altogether he could raise a force of 15,000. Even with 3,000, he boasted, he could tie up royalist forces in Scotland for a year. Monmouth informed Grey that the earl had nearly 10,000 weapons (a slight exaggeration), some field artillery, 500 barrels of powder, and ammunition. Argyll also claimed that he was purchasing three ships and would be prepared to sail in two weeks, though he agreed to a postponement if the English promised to mount a simultaneous uprising in their country.[58]

About the time Monmouth was telling Grey of his meeting with Argyll (25 February / 7 March or the next day), Cragg arrived from England on a mission for William Disney, John Wildman's cousin. Disney and his compatriots wanted to know whether the duke was involved in Argyll's invasion plans, word of which was obviously circulating in radical circles in London. Grey and Monmouth learned of Cragg's arrival from Wade and Tiley. Having never met Cragg, Monmouth had Ferguson interview him that evening. Grey claims that he and the duke conferred with Cragg the following morning, on which occasion Cragg reported that Wildman and his confederates wanted the duke to reach an agreement with Argyll and provide them with details of Scottish preparations. Cragg allegedly identified Wildman's associates as the earl of Devonshire, Richard Hampden (John's father), John Freke, and certain men in the City whose names Grey later forgot. Grey was dubious about Devonshire's commitment, but Cragg retorted that he and the earl had actively sought to prove that Essex had been murdered. Had Charles lived longer, Cragg claimed, Devonshire would have raised the matter in the Privy Council, but now he planned to discuss it in the House of Lords when Parliament met. Devonshire's friends, Cragg purportedly insisted, feared that he would be assassinated because of what he knew about Essex's death.[59]

Cragg offers a sharply different version of his first mission, claiming he saw only Dare and Ferguson. The latter reputedly informed Cragg that a "good understanding" existed between Monmouth and Argyll, that the earl hoped to sail for Scotland in a month, and that the duke would invade England two weeks later. Cragg insisted he was asked to return to London and raise money for Monmouth's weapons and ammunition.[60]

Such, in any event, was Cragg's version of the meeting. Ferguson, however, gave a different account to Wade and presumably to the duke as well, as Wade testified. Cragg, according to Wade, claimed he had come from Wildman (which may have been true, since Disney could have been acting as Wildman's agent). The errand was one of rapprochement: "[Wildman wishes] in the name of all the other Gentlemen of the Duke's Party in England to invite us to an agreement with the Duke of Monmouth, assuring us, that there was never a greater Spirit amongst the Common People in England for our purpose, and that if we would procure a good correspondence between my Lord Argyle and the Duke of Monmouth, [so] that they might act with united Councels[,] we should not want any reasonable sum of mony for the carrying on our design." According to Wade, Monmouth's promise to Argyll to invade England shortly after the earl landed in Scotland was based on Cragg's alleged pledge that the duke's English supporters would provide thousands of pounds in aid. Cragg or (more likely) Ferguson apparently lied.[61]

Following Cragg's first mission, Monmouth and Grey decided to map out their strategy in consultation with Wade and Tiley. Richard Goodenough would have been included but he was in Lüneburg. They decided to land in the southwest (at Lyme, Dorset, according to Grey, but the precise location was apparently not determined until later), after which their supporters in Cheshire would rebel. Once the royalist troops had left London for the southwest, dissidents in the City would rise. These events would be closely coordinated with Argyll's invasion to prevent the government from securing English radicals. Monmouth and his colleagues decided to seek £6,000 from their supporters in England, while the duke would pawn his plate and jewels to raise additional funds.[62]

Monmouth and his advisers selected Matthews and Christopher Battiscombe (who had an estate near Lyme) as emissaries to key radicals in England. The duke instructed Matthews to have Wildman arrange for him to confer with Macclesfield, Delamere, and Brandon about preparations in Cheshire. Devonshire was to have the options of rising in Derbyshire and joining forces with Macclesfield in Cheshire, as Monmouth preferred, or coming alone to the southwest. Charlton and his son were assigned to lead the rebels in Shropshire unless they were needed in London. Matthews also had orders to have Wildman convene a meeting of the four dissident lords to seek their advice for Monmouth. Speed, the duke impressed on Matthews, was essential so the insurrection could commence one or two days before the opening of Parliament on 19 May, at which time most of the lords lieutenant, their deputies, other militia officers, and Tory peers would be in London. The rebels would therefore have an excellent opportunity to seize militia weapons and horses and win the support of sympathetic militiamen.[63]

As soon as Matthews had set sail for England, accompanied by the son of the Congregationalist minister George Griffith, Monmouth gave Battiscombe his orders, directing him to go first to London, where Matthews could introduce him to the four peers, thereby enabling Battiscombe to confirm Matthews' instructions. With Freke's assistance Battiscombe was to enlist the support of key southwestern dissidents in preparing for Monmouth's invasion. Among them were Trenchard, Sir Francis Rolle, Sir Walter Yonge, Sir Francis Drake, William Strode, and Captain John Hucker of Taunton.[64]

Shortly after Battiscombe's departure,[65] Henry Ireton, Grey's cousin, arrived from England. Immediately sent back with instructions similar to Matthews', he was arrested when the packet boat docked at Harwich. Not only did the magistrates find no papers on him but he escaped in May.[66]

In the meantime Cragg reported to Disney in London, stressing

Monmouth's need for money. Two days later, after Disney had consulted with unnamed gentlemen, he reportedly told Cragg of their dismay at not having previously been consulted and their suggestion that the duke fight with Argyll in Scotland. The people of England were not inclined to help Monmouth, and, Cragg reported having been told by Disney, there was "a great backwardness in the gentlemen he had discoursed with." On such short notice, moreover, the likelihood of raising funds was slight. This was the message that Cragg, by his own testimony, carried to Monmouth; it was confirmed by Grey and Wade.[67] The latter, an Argyll confidant, also noted that Cragg had informed the duke that Wildman and his associates had been "exceedingly rejoyced to hear that [the exiles in Argyll's circle] were all agreed, and approved mightily of the Scotch Design, and that it was the Maj[o]rs Opinion that the Duke should attend the Success of that, and should come over incognito & lye hid in London."[68]

According to Cragg, Monmouth became irate when he learned of the "backwardness and coldness" of his friends in England, especially Wildman, whom he accused of wanting to dominate everybody. "He thinks by keeping his own purse-strings fast and persuading others to do the same to hinder me in this thing," complained the duke, "but he and they shall be mistaken." Monmouth's ire may have been sparked by Grey, who, said Wade, "upbraide[d]" the duke because Wildman "had governed him of late but would doe nothing for him nor advance one penny of money to help him." Cragg, Wade, and Grey agree that Monmouth instructed Cragg to return to London. Cragg and Wade note that the duke was willing to accept a smaller amount than the original goal of £6,000, perhaps as little as £3,000 (Cragg) or even £1,000 (Wade).[69] Cragg later testified that he was to seek the funds from Wildman, Hampden, and Sir Samuel Barnardiston (not Charlton, as Grey recalled). Both Cragg and Grey had some difficulty remembering the names of those designated by Monmouth to serve as his London managers, but both cited Wildman and Danvers. Grey mentioned the earl of Devonshire, Disney, Captain Thimbleton, and Major John Breman (who Cragg said would help get the country ready). Cragg also listed the Congregationalist minister Matthew Meade, recommended by Ferguson because "he had a good interest with the people about London."[70]

Concerned about the reaction of key continental states to the proposed invasion, Monmouth endorsed Ferguson's suggestion to have Dare confer with Jacob Boreel, the Dutch ambassador to the court of Louis XIV. Ferguson himself made inquiries of three other Dutchmen. Sympathetic, the Dutch promised to inform Monmouth's people of any demands made by James' envoy and of pertinent resolutions in the States General, and they promised safe haven in Amsterdam. According to Grey, the duke and his advisers also hoped to obtain support from several German princes and Charles XI of Sweden, but he provided no details.[71]

In early April, some three weeks after Matthews left for England, Monmouth received a report of his conference with Wildman. According to Wade, the letter indicated that Wildman had spoken to Matthews "only in Hieroglyphices and was Something Shie of the matter, but he believ'd he [Monmouth] should find the Cheshire Gent[lemen] in another humour."[72] Grey's rather different version of the report stipulated that Wildman had depicted a nation in ferment and had noted especially "a general inclination" in the country to rebel. Although some of the gentry were unreliable, Argyll's invasion of Scotland, Wildman supposedly claimed, would spur the "backward" in England to act.[73]

Once again, Cragg offers a different account of events in London and especially of Wildman's position. Returning to the City after his second mission to the Netherlands, Cragg reported to Disney as Monmouth had directed. The following evening Disney met Cragg at the Young Devil tavern to explain that Wildman was perturbed by the duke's willingness to "conclude the scheme of the government of the nation, without the knowledge of any of the people in England." Why, Wildman purportedly wondered, did Monmouth not send someone to England who could fully explain his intentions? When Hampden refused to see Cragg, a stranger, the latter asked Disney to convey to Hampden Monmouth's request that he seek funds from Barnardiston. Nothing came of this, nor could Disney obtain money from Wildman, who even refused to convene a meeting of managers for an uprising. Danvers was similarly reluctant, claiming he could not find suitable persons to join him. Disney was unable to locate anyone willing to approach Devonshire because of the latter's reputed dislike of Monmouth, and Disney's discussions with Delamere and others from Cheshire revealed considerable concern about, as Devonshire put it, "what model the Duke intends, or what it is they must declare for."[74]

The Argyll Expedition

By the time Cragg returned to the Netherlands around 20/30 April 1685, Argyll and his men were ready to sail for Scotland. Circumstances had made further delay impossible. His recruits, some of whom were from Lüneburg and others from William's army, had to be paid; they were also so prone "to tattle, that the matter began to be talked of as freely in Amsterdam & Roterdam amongst the Dutchmen as any other news." This was especially true after Argyll summoned his officers, who had been dispersed throughout Holland and Friesland, to Amsterdam. Urgency was also dictated by Boreel's warning that Bevil Skelton, the new English envoy, would demand that the States General seize the earl's ships.[75]

By the second week in April, Argyll was engaged in daily consultations with key supporters in Rotterdam. Monmouth himself was present, presumably to discuss their joint preparations and the contents of the manifestos that each group would draft. Although Monmouth was troubled by the earl's plan to spend some time in the western isles before invading the mainland, he pledged to set sail six days after Argyll's departure for Scotland, a promise that would prove impossible to keep because of difficulties in raising money and the late date at which his preparations commenced. The duke had departed for Delft by the time Argyll, Cochrane, Hume, Cleland, Pringle of Torwoodlee, and seven other Scots met in Amsterdam on 17 April to compare drafts of the declarations. Alterations were made so that they "adjusted . . . to one and the same purpose in the declarative pairt," although the accompanying narratives reflected the specific conditions in each country.[76]

Argyll's two declarations set forth radical aims. The first—"The Declaration and Apology of the Protestant People . . . of Scotland, with the Concurrence of the True and Faithful Pastors, and of Several Gentlemen of the English Nation Joyned with Them in the Same Cause"—denounced Charles' actions as tyrannical and apostate, condemned the deprivation of the godly clergy and the toleration of

Catholics, opposed a standing army and the Dutch wars, deplored the torture of William Spence and William Carstares in the Rye House investigations as well as the prosecution of Bothwell Bridge rebels, and repudiated James as lawful sovereign and the sitting House of Commons (because of allegedly fraudulent returns in 1685). The declaration promised to uphold Protestantism, suppress popery and prelacy, establish a new government (of unspecified form), restore those who had suffered under the Stuarts, and support the allies of Argyll and the Covenanters in England and Ireland. The second manifesto, entitled "The Declaration of Archibald Earl of Argyle," issued a call to arms, demanded the restoration of property confiscated from the earl and his father, and vigorously denounced James: "The Duke of *York* having taken off his Mask, and having abandoned and invaded our Religion and Liberties, Resolving to enter into the Government and Exercise it contrary to Law, I think it not only Just, but my Duty to God and my Country, to use my outmost endeavors to oppose and repress his Usurpations and Tyranny." [77]

The manifesto that Ferguson drafted for Monmouth and that his key advisers (especially Grey, Wade, and John Patshall) endorsed is a ringing summation of the radical movement's major tenets in the early 1680s and parallels Argyll's first declaration in many respects. "All the boundaries of the Government have of late been broken, & nothing left unattempted, for turning our *limited Monarchy* into an absolute *Tyranny*." Protestantism, proclaimed the declaration, had been undermined by popish counsels. Indeed the life of the usurper James was a lengthy conspiracy against the Reformed religion and the rights of the nation. Responsibility for the fire of London, the Third Dutch War, the Popish Plot, the murder of Sir Edmund Godfrey, the subornation of witnesses, and the assassination of Essex and Charles II were laid at James' feet. The litany of abuses included the violation of property rights, the corruption of the judicial system, packing the House of Commons through fraudulent returns, and the imposition of illegal charters. The only means of relief, the manifesto asserted, was a recourse to arms. "Now therefore Wee do hereby solemnly *declare* & *proclaime Warr*, against *James Duke of York*, as a *Murderer*, and an Assassin of innocent men; a *Popish Usurper* of the Crown; *Traytor* to the *Nation*, and *Tyrant* over the *People*." The rebels demanded the repeal of penal laws against Protestant nonconformists, annual elections for Parliament, the restoration of the ancient charters, the repeal of the Corporation Act and the Militia Act, life tenure for judges subject to good behavior, the repeal of the treason convictions of the Rye House plotters, and a prohibition against standing armies not authorized by Parliament. The manifesto acknowledged the legitimacy of Monmouth's title to the throne but left the disposition of the government to a freely elected Parliament.[78] Although the royalist victory at Sedgemoor would soon dash Monmouth's hopes, much of the program embodied in his manifesto was subsequently incorporated in the 1689 settlement.

Argyll's group sought and obtained the approval of exile ministers in Rotterdam, some of whom were invited to sail with the earl's forces. Argyll subsequently dispatched Pringle of Torwoodlee to Moray, Veitch to the borders and Northumberland, and Cleland to central Scotland to notify supporters that Argyll would arrive shortly. Veitch also had a commission to raise money for the purchase of weapons, horses, flags, and drums, and to recruit men, "especially old Oliverian officers."[79]

Although Veitch subsequently claimed he had provided pistols, swords, and money to many dissidents, Colonel Strother quickly learned of his activities and alerted the Scottish Council, forcing Veitch into hiding. We get a glimpse of Cleland's work on Argyll's behalf in an updated, partially encoded letter he sent to Cochrane:

I have this order to write in their names, that if Mr. Ker [possibly Robert Ker of Kersland, who had forfeited his estates because of complicity in the Galloway rebellion, or the Covenanting minister James Ker] be for the work of Reformation carryed on from the 38 to the 48, they are for him [Argyll]. . . . Keep you strong where you are, and keep the enemie in all great vexation as you can, till you see a beacon on Lowdoun hill. I hope in eight days, or thereby, all shall be in a flame. Send us intelligence to Moffet well [Moffat, Dumfries], if possible, where I shall have a man or a woman. . . . The enemie did prevent us as to horses, but we are minded to retake them. If you would frequentlie alarme the enemie, it would exceedinglie weaken them. In short things are brought to a probable posture.

The context suggests that Cleland wrote this in May 1685, by which time Argyll had landed in Scotland and was seeking support in Kintyre and Argyllshire.[80]

According to Grey and Wade, Argyll had between £9,000 and £10,000 with which to equip his expedition. Of this, said Grey, approximately £7,000 came from Ann Smith (whose son sailed with the earl and whom Argyll called "Mother"), £1,000 from Battiscombe, £1,000 from an unidentified merchant who had recently died in Holland, and nearly £1,000 from (Nicholas?) Locke. Some funds may have come from Scotland, for one of Skelton's correspondents in Bremen reported that the Scots had transmitted a substantial amount of money to "these partes" in the preceding three months. Wade, however, doubted that the Scots contributed anything; although Melville "was very busy with his advice yet as to his purse or Person he intended not to be concerned."[81]

With the aid of James Delap, a Scottish factor in Rotterdam, Argyll purchased three ships, leaving sufficient funds for at least 8,000 weapons, some or all of which were purchased in Friesland, and perhaps 500 barrels of gunpowder. Other weapons had been shipped to Scotland during the previous twelve months.[82] By 13/23 April the ships were being loaded. Argyll kept them in the Zuider Zee for four or five days, and then, having called at Amsterdam on 21 April / 1 May, he set sail for Scotland the following evening with fewer than 300 men on board.[83] William had made no effort to prevent Argyll from purchasing weapons and ammunition, nor did the Dutch fleet make more than a halfhearted effort to block Argyll's ships. Apparently not until the beginning of July did the prince decide to throw his support to James, though he at least feigned to be "exceedingly troubled" about Argyll's expedition and supported the States General's earlier resolution banishing James' rebellious subjects from the Netherlands.[84] While Argyll sailed and Monmouth continued his preparations, Skelton and William debated who would be exiled, a delaying exercise that enabled the prince to ponder his own moves. Among those who Skelton insisted must leave were John Locke and Sir James Dalrymple. In the meantime the prince, offering a curiously lame excuse for inaction, promised to banish Monmouth if he could be found.[85]

In the minds of many dissidents, Argyll's expedition was tantamount to a "Holy Warre." On the eve of its departure "above 20 Guifted brethren" were preaching on Argyll's behalf in Rotter-

dam, apparently with great success, for many of the women urged
their husbands to enlist. Both the English and the Scottish clergy
in Amsterdam proclaimed "that those who are not for them are
against them." Argyll's expedition, explained Erskine, was designed
to prevent "our native land from being again drowned in popish
idolatry and slavery." But the undertaking was also depicted by
Erskine as having a distinctly international importance: "The standing or falling of the Protestant interest in Europe depended in a
great measure upon the event of this undertaking in Britain"—
an observation more appropriate, in retrospect, to 1688.[86]

Argyll's expedition had unmistakable radical support. Among
those who sailed with the earl were John Balfour, one of Archbishop Sharp's assassins; the Covenanting ministers Robert Langlands, Thomas and John Forrester, and George Barclay, a Bothwell
Bridge rebel; Spence and Cochrane, who had participated in discussions for the proposed 1683 insurrections; William Denholm, laird of
Westshiels; the Rye House conspirators John Ayloffe and Richard
Rumbold; and Dr. William Blackader, eldest son of John Blackader,
another Bothwell Bridge veteran. Flags emblazoned with such mot-
toes as "For God, Freedom and Religion" and "From Popery[,]
herecy and seizure good lord deliver us" encapsulated the radical
program.[87]

Virtually from the outset, the expeditionary force encountered serious difficulties. After Spence and Blackader, Argyll's secretary and
physician, were captured in the Orkney Isles, the earl sailed to
Argyllshire, where he garrisoned Dunstaffnage Castle, one of his former possessions. Efforts to enlist men in Islay, Kintyre, and Argyllshire were relatively ineffective. By 30 May, three weeks of recruiting
had netted him approximately 2,500 men. Delayed only by a few
minor skirmishes, Argyll led his forces from Loch Fyne past Gare-
lochhead to the region between Dumbarton and Loch Lomond. As
royalist troops closed in, his army found itself surrounded on three
sides by royalist troops and short of provisions, at which point many
rebels deserted. After crossing the river Clyde into Renfrewshire, the
remaining troops lost their way in a bog and dispersed into small
groups. Argyll, who had demonstrated a woeful inability to command an army in the field, was captured at Inchinnan on the Clyde

on 18 June, and Ayloffe (who tried to commit suicide), Rumbold (who was wounded in the fighting), and Cochrane and his son were soon apprehended.[88]

The hard-riding religious zealots who constituted the United Societies had at first contemplated fighting for Argyll despite the fact that he was no Covenanter. In a general meeting on 28 May, however, they resolved neither to join with the "malignants, or sectarians in arms," nor to endorse Argyll's declarations "as the state of their quarrel, because it was not concerted according to the ancient plea of the Scotch Covenanters [especially the National Covenant and the Solemn League and Covenant], *&c*; and because it opened a door for a sinful confederacy." Nevertheless the Cameronians agreed to do what they could against "the common enemy," including issuing a proclamation repudiating James as the lawful king as well as the legality of the new Parliament and the "apparent inlet of Popery." The manifesto called on the godly to be faithful to their Covenant obligations and reminded them of previous persecution at the hands of "bloodie papists, the subjects of Antichrist." The same day a band of some 220 armed men affixed a copy of this protestation to the market cross at Sanquhar, Dumfries. Expecting Argyll to march south, the delegates scheduled another meeting for 4 June, at which time they could determine a course of action. By that date, however, royalist forces, including parties of Highlanders, were sufficiently numerous in the Dumfries region to prevent the meeting. The United Societies could do no more than facilitate the escape of two of Argyll's ministers, Barclay and Langlands. Rescuing them provided an opportunity for informal negotiations at the general meeting on 24 July to restore relations between the United Societies and mainline Covenanters, but not even the Argyll debacle and the triumph of a Catholic sovereign could persuade these feuding religious factions to heal their breach.[89]

Had the Covenanters united in support of Argyll, and had the earl landed straightaway in Ayrshire or Kirkcudbright, the Scottish rebellion might have tied up more royalist troops and provided Monmouth with a greater opportunity for success. Certainly discontent with the regime was deep and widespread on the eve of the rebellion, and the government did not take Argyll's threat lightly. The earl of

Perth reported to Archbishop Sancroft on 1 July, "Many enthusiastique fanaticall men wanted only a head to get together to: no man
was lyke to be more acceptable to them than Argyle." The rebels too
had assessed their potential strength as substantial, especially, as
Erskine reflected on 11 July, since they had enjoyed those assets in
1685 that had been so obviously lacking at Bothwell Bridge, namely
leaders of birth, an adequately organized army, and sufficient weapons and ammunition. Erskine could explain the calamitous defeat
only in religious terms: "The Lord was pleased to crush the undertaking, and make his people bare of all those, wherein I fear they too
much trusted, not looking to the Lord only." In fact, Argyll failed
for several reasons: his decision to land in the Highlands, which gave
James time to get his troops in the field; internecine rivalry among
the Covenanters; and delays in Monmouth's invasion. James' hand
was further strengthened by the decision of the States General, taken
on 30 May / 9 June, to send three Scottish regiments from the Netherlands to Britain.[90]

Monmouth: The Last Gamble

While Argyll was preparing to sail, Cragg reported to Monmouth
that no money had been raised in England, a point on which the
accounts of Grey, Wade, and Cragg concur. Grey and Wade also note
that Wildman had argued that funds were unnecessary because the
duke's supporters in England were well armed. Grey's account includes a good deal of additional information purportedly imparted
to Monmouth by Cragg, including the probably unfounded assertion that Danvers and other Monmouth allies had prevented an uprising when James was crowned—a rebellion "designed by some
hot headed men in London" who had brought 500 of their supporters from Hertfordshire and Essex. Supposedly only news of
Monmouth's impending invasion had kept them from implementing
their plans. According to Grey, Cragg told the duke that Wildman
had spoken with Devonshire, Delamere, either Macclesfield or Brandon, and others, as he had been directed, and concluded that the
people were generally ready to rebel. More than 500 armed and
mounted men were prepared to rise in London, said Cragg, and

similar bands waited in Bedfordshire and Buckinghamshire. The London group planned to leave the City before the duke's arrival on the pretense of visiting the spa at Epsom, and at the appropriate time attack the royalist forces at Kingston, Staines, and Egham. Others in London would meet at a prearranged rendezvous and march to unite with the duke. Sir Francis Rolle, moreover, had supposedly agreed to lead an uprising in Hampshire. According to Grey, Wildman also sent word that Monmouth should assume the title of king, procure "a broad seal," and in his manifesto threaten severe punishment to those who opposed him.[91] If such a message was in fact delivered to Monmouth by Cragg, and if the duke believed even half of it, he was badly served by his supposed allies in England.

Even before Cragg's final visit to the Netherlands Monmouth had pawned his jewels, plate, and other possessions in Rotterdam, raising some £3,000. He subsequently pawned goods belonging to Lady Henrietta Wentworth, and her mother. Sir Patience Ward pledged £500 in collateral to help the duke obtain a loan through the agency of Daniel Le Blon, and additional monies were forthcoming from Ann Smith (£1,000), Nicholas or John Locke (£400), Barnardiston, and William Rumbold (Richard's brother, £100). Altogether Monmouth had approximately £5,500 with which to equip his expedition. Assisted primarily by Wade, Le Blon, and Robert Archer (who had sent printers with Argyll), the duke was able to purchase two small ships, nearly 1,500 pieces of body armor, 100 muskets and bandoleers, 500 pikes, 500 swords, 200 to 250 barrels of gunpowder, four small cannons, and a small number of pistols and carbines. In addition he hired and equipped a 32-gun frigate, the *Helderenburgh*, to serve as an escort. "All the Armories in the Countrey," reported Skelton, were manufacturing weapons for the rebels.[92]

Monmouth's state of mind about this time can be ascertained from a letter he wrote to someone in the southwest, possibly Trenchard or Battiscombe (though Wade knew of no response from the latter). The document was composed in May, as its references to the makeup and outlook of the new Parliament show. "They [the M.P.s] will be ready to make their Peace as soon as they can, rather than hazard themselves upon an uncertain Bottom." He promised to follow whatever advice had been proffered to him by his correspondent, but he was worried: "Whatever way I turn my thoughts, I find insuperable difficulties." Their circumstances, he reflected, were desperate, a probable reference to his inability to obtain funding in England and the pressure to act quickly since Argyll had already left. Realistically, Monmouth knew his chances for success were slim: "Judge then what we are to expect, in case we should venture upon any such Attempt at this time." Promising to meet his friend at the appointed time and place (Lyme Regis), the duke urged him to ponder in the interval "the Improbabilities that lye naturally in our way."[93] Judging from the prints they produced, some of Monmouth's supporters in the Netherlands were more confident, or at least sought to convey that impression. One depicted the duke in "a warlyke Posture," while another showed a decapitated James, his severed head between his legs "with the stump part of the neck upwards & his Crowne reverse & over his neck these words *Non Plus Ultra.*"[94]

While the ships and goods were being readied, another envoy, the cabinetmaker John Jones, arrived from London in late April with a message from Disney. According to Grey, the duke was urged to hasten before "some hot-headed action" was instigated by London radicals. Jones later testified, however, that he had informed Monmouth that Disney did not want him to come to England but urged him to stay in the Netherlands or go to Scotland. The delay, in any event, was not of the duke's making but was occasioned by the presence of English warships in the channel and the resulting need to hire and equip the *Helderenburgh*. By Grey's reckoning this took an additional two weeks.[95]

When Monmouth was nearly ready to sail he dispatched Cragg to inform Wildman and the peers who supported the duke of his imminent arrival and to instruct them to be prepared to take up arms. Upon his arrival Cragg reported to Disney and also to Ralph Alexander, who was asked to provide the duke with a suit of armor and to recruit six officers in the City to join him in the southwest. Monmouth also wanted Wildman to send him five or six good horses for his personal use. In the City itself the duke wanted his managers— notably Wildman, Danvers, and Meade—to meet daily and to launch an uprising as soon as royalist troops left for the southwest. In addition he asked that a press be ready to print relevant materials and that a reliable messenger service be established.[96]

Because Cragg's departure was delayed for several days by inclement weather, Monmouth dispatched Jones with similar instructions as well as a sealed document to be opened at sea containing details of the landing site at Lyme Regis, Dorset. Upon his arrival in England on 27 May, Jones was to see Wildman, to dispatch William Brand to inform Sir Robert Peyton of their plans, and to have Matthews contact Macclesfield, Brandon, and Delamere. Matthews was also "to send one Post to that place [Lyme Regis] that was named in the Note to receive Intelligence of his landing, and that [note] should be brought to his Friends [in London] immediately." Monmouth wanted the Cheshire lords to march their troops to Taunton. Because Matthews and Wildman were out of town when Jones arrived, Jones asked Disney to convey these instructions to Macclesfield, Brandon, and Delamere. He later insisted he had not known if Disney had done so, though Samuel Storey, who subsequently fought with Monmouth, claimed Disney did deliver the instructions. Moreover, Delamere admitted leaving London on the 27th, using the alias Brown, supposedly to visit a sick child. On the day of his departure, he left the following letter for Wildman:

I have received yours & am of your opinion that we are near our Verticle point, & I fear the decree is gone out against us, if some continue long where they are, & some thought so very necessary & others so litle. I wish I had Cause for clearer thoughts. Yet I will omit nothing that on my part ought to be done: I have fixed the Militia of this County [Cheshire] & am taking horse for Chester to setle the Militia of that City where I expect a good reception, if it be worth the trouble of a letter you shall have it; I hope we have in these parts twenty thousand [who] will stand by uss to the last which is some comfort. My service to Mrs. Wildman. I have a project which if it succeed will please you.

Delamere returned to London the night of 3 June, discouraged, perhaps, because his fellow peers had not joined him; whether they could have mounted an effective insurrection is arguable, but there was considerable popular disaffection in Cheshire. In any event, Jones himself eventually joined Monmouth at Lyme Regis.[97]

Cragg's account of the reaction of Monmouth's supposed allies to news of his imminent arrival is an appalling record of distrust, jealousy, ineptitude, and cowardice. Wildman refused to meet with Danvers, and neither Wildman, Macclesfield,[98] nor Brandon would make firm plans until the duke had landed. No money was forthcoming for weapons and ammunition. Although Danvers made several attempts to persuade Meade to return to the City, the latter's friends urged him to stay in Essex; he came only when it was too late to help. Some of the reluctance to act stemmed from the fact that Monmouth had not landed approximately a week after Cragg's arrival,[99] as had been anticipated, but even when Jones brought word that the expedition had sailed the internal bickering undermined any realistic possibility for an uprising in the City. With the exception of Delamere, the Cheshire lords, who had insisted on attending the opening of Parliament to avoid suspicion, found it impossible to leave London. As Monmouth had instructed, Disney and his friends did send two messengers, Brand and Thomas Chadwick, to the Red Lion tavern in Taunton to await new orders from the duke, with the message, Grey claimed, that "several thousands" under Danvers' command were prepared to rise as soon as Monmouth gave his approval and the Cheshire insurrection was under way. Disney also met with Wildman and Charlton, but Wildman was "in a cold temper," presumably because Delamere had declined to act until Parliament recessed.[100]

The duke took with him a contingent of only 83 men, including a cohort of former Rye House conspirators: Grey, Wade, Nelthorpe, Ferguson, Tiley, and the Goodenough brothers. Ayloffe and Rumbold had, of course, sailed with Argyll. A small group of experienced officers was recruited from a variety of sources: Major (or Colonel) Thomas Venner, son of the Cromwellian Fifth Monarchist; Captain Foulkes, who had once threatened to kill Chudleigh's secretary and had been cashiered from the English regiments in Dutch service; Captain Robert Bruce, a Scot, formerly a mercenary in the Brandenburg army; Captain John Tillier and Captain Thompson, both also former mercenaries; and Ensign Thomas Parsons had served with a brigade in Amsterdam. Others, such as Major Abraham Holmes (personally recruited by Monmouth), Major Manley, Captain Matthews, and Colonel (or Captain) Richard Buffett (or Bovett), were veterans of the radical movement. None apparently was experienced with cannons, for the duke commissioned Captain Anton Buys, on leave from the Brandenburg military, to handle his field artillery. One of the more infamous radicals (recruited by Brand) was the Fifth Monarchist Robert Perrott, a former accomplice of Thomas Blood in an attempted theft of the crown jewels. Dare served as Monmouth's paymaster.[101]

After Disney learned that Monmouth had landed in Dorset, he conferred with Danvers, Cragg, and an unidentified friend of the colonel at the Steel Yard in London. In Disney's judgment Monmouth enjoyed considerable popular support in the City, making its seizure possible after the royalist troops had departed to confront the invasion force. But the London conspirators could not agree, according to Disney, on the appointment of a commander, an impasse underscoring the critical communications problem between London and Monmouth's troops. Although Peyton was deemed the most capable leader, he was unpopular with the people and disgusted with the "party." When Disney suggested that Danvers assume command, the latter reacted angrily, saying that he "could not nor would meddle with nothing that was thus confused," especially when Wildman, Meade, and other key figures refused to formulate a plan. Danvers did agree to meet with Meade, who had finally come to London. About that time Disney was arrested, whereupon Danvers and Meade went into hiding. Following the arrival of Major John Manley with a message from the duke to act speedily, a final conference was held at the Bull Head tavern in Bishopsgate Street on 5/15 July. Danvers and Peyton, Cragg thought, were among those present, although Cragg himself did not attend because his wife and one of his children were fatally ill.[102]

According to a separate account (provided by Everard on the basis of information from the radical printer John Bringhurst), Peyton, after previously consenting to command an uprising in the City, reneged; he claimed he had "better intelligence then they, which made him Judge that it was then too late to undertake anything, & he cursed them as cowardly & prateing fools." By that point it mattered not, for on that Sunday, 5 July 1685, Monmouth's forces were crushed at Sedgemoor, near Bridgwater in Somerset, having failed in their attempt to overrun royalist troops in a daring night attack.[103]

"The Nation Delivered"

EIGHT

The Radicals and the Revolution of 1688–1689

For a quarter of a century before the Argyll and Monmouth rebellions British dissidents had talked of and periodically laid plans for a general insurrection as well as less ambitious plots directed at the Stuart regime. All of these efforts were dismal failures. Not even the great Whig leaders of the early 1680s—Shaftesbury, Essex, Russell, Sidney, and Hampden—could mount an uprising with the limited aim of excluding the duke of York from the line of succession. Ironically, Charles' affection for Monmouth, coupled with Halifax's skilfull intrigues, may have come closer to achieving that objective than all of the Whig efforts after the dissolution of the Oxford Parliament. But whether Charles intended simply to restore Monmouth to a position of favor at court (as is likely) or, more ambitiously, to alter the succession is a secret the king carried to his grave.

The Argyll and Monmouth rebellions and the various conspiracies collectively known as the Rye House Plot had a profoundly negative impact on the radical cause. In suppressing these activities the government destroyed or neutralized every English and Scottish radical leader of the first rank and many of the middling order. The regime's only conspicuous failure was its inability to curtail the activities of two of the three men most responsible for articulating the ideology of the movement, John Locke and Robert Ferguson; of the leading radical thinkers and propagandists, only Sidney perished. Although the radical leaders were systematically cut down or, in the case of Grey and Wade, persuaded to turn state's evidence, the ideas of the movement lived on and many were incorporated into the 1689 revolutionary settlement.

Rebels on Trial

The crackdown following the disclosure of the Rye House plotting deprived the dissidents of men whose leadership was sorely needed by Monmouth and Argyll. But probably nothing could have saved the earl from his own staggering incompetence, most vividly revealed in his stubborn determination to base his revolt in the Highlands rather than the factious southwest, as James Stewart had urged. Had Argyll listened to his advisers, had he landed in the southwest, had the Cameronians and moderate Covenanters flocked to his banner, and had Monmouth not suffered serious delays, the outcome of the Scottish insurrection might not have been so predictable. Apprehended on 18 June 1685, Argyll was executed in Edinburgh twelve days later under a sentence of death pronounced against him in 1681. He died praying for God to "restrain the spirite of profanitie, atheisme, superstition, poprey and persicution," and to "provide for the securety of his church that Antichrist nor the gates of hell may never prevaill against it."[1]

Among those captured when Argyll's expedition collapsed, as we have seen, were two Rye House conspirators, Richard Rumbold and John Ayloffe. Tried at Edinburgh in June, Rumbold freely confessed his involvement with Argyll. He remained unrepentant to the end, however, insisting that he had never participated in any plot to assassinate the king. Tried on 26 June, he was hanged, drawn, and quartered the same day. Ayloffe, after recovering from his attempted suicide, was taken to London, where he adamantly refused to provide information against his former associates. The state executed him on 30 October.[2]

Monmouth's chances were ruined by external factors as well as misjudgments. Organizing late and with fewer resources than Argyll, he was hurt both by delays and by the earl's failure to strike in southwestern Scotland. Once Parliament had convened, its staunchly Tory membership—the fruit of Charles' restructuring of the corporations—loyally supported the new king. Virtually trapped in London, the Cheshire lords (with the exception of Delamere) were effectively neutralized; hence any possibility of raising the northwest for

Monmouth was destroyed. Danvers lacked both the stature and the mandate to command, and Wildman, the bluster of his rhetoric notwithstanding, shirked his responsibilities in London. As Wade aptly remarked, Wildman was "a man of cunning, very able to draw others into snares and keep out himself." Trenchard, so often viewed as a stalwart of the radicals in the southwest, fled into exile even before the duke's arrival, apparently aware that the gentry would not rise on Monmouth's behalf. To justify his betrayal of Monmouth, he subsequently averred that William would be a better sovereign than the duke because the prince was "lesse burdensome to the People by his frugall & carefull management."³ The insurrection, as Peter Earle has argued, could have been won, especially if the duke had launched an assault on Bristol, where a sizable dissident community could have disrupted royalist defenders; according to Richard Goodenough, however, the rebel leaders had no contacts in this strategic city. Even Sedgemoor might have been a rebel victory had the duke's men surprised the sleeping royalist troops.⁴

Although the duke's commitment to radical principles has often been questioned, with some justification because of his undeniable personal ambition, in the end he chose to make his stand when numerous others were content to offer excuses for their inactivity. As a prisoner, he groveled in the hope of saving his life, undoubtedly embittered by the failure of Wildman, Danvers, Delamere, Macclesfield, and others to take up arms. The title of king, he said, had been forced on him. "The People so basely left me," he complained in his final statement, thereby precluding him from "the restoring of their Rights & Priviledges." Selecting his words with care, he concluded by quoting his grandfather: "I die a Martyr for the People." The ultimate responsibility for his failure rested not with the people, however, but with those he trusted to lead them. Monmouth was beheaded on 15 July, one week after he was discovered, dressed in peasant clothing and hiding in a ditch. The executioner struck five blows. After the first the duke "turned his head a little and looked up, and after the second or third blow [he] did speak a word or two, when Catch [the executioner] seemed to intermitt or lay down the Axe."⁵ Ten days later an unidentified dissident copied a manuscript version of George Wither's *Vox & Lacrimae Anglorum* (1668), with its call to keep the Good Old Cause alive: "Renowned Patriots, open your eyes, & lend an eare to the justice of our cryes. As you are Englishmen (our blood & bones) know 'tis your duty to regard our groans. On you next God, our confidence relyes. You are the Bullwarks of our liberty."[6]

Altogether the state tried nearly 1,300 Monmouth partisans, of whom approximately 250 were executed and some 850 were sentenced to be transported to the West Indies; many of the latter escaped in England or died during the voyage to the Americas. Another 200 or so perished in prison or received pardons. The heinousness with which some of the executions were carried out redounded negatively on James, as reflected, for instance, in the observations of the Quaker John Whiting: "There were eight Executed, Quarter'd, and their Bowels burnt on the Market-place [at Ivelchester, Somerset]. . . . Forcing poor Men to hale about Mens Quarters, like Horse-Flesh or Carrion, to boil and hang them up as Monuments of their Cruelty and Inhumanity, for the Terror of others . . . lost King *James* the Hearts of many." The legal executions were not the only ones; the royalist soldiers had summarily killed approximately 100 rebels after the battle of Sedgemoor.[7] Few radicals of even modest prominence were among those captured and executed; the most significant were the Rye House plotter Richard Nelthorpe, Monmouth's emissary Christopher Battiscombe, the printer William Disney, and Abraham Holmes, a friend of Argyll's with a long radical career; the crown-stealer Robert Perrott died of his injuries in captivity. The state also executed the Particular Baptist minister Sampson Larke, who had ridden with the rebels, and Alicia Lisle, widow of the regicide John Lisle, because she had harbored a fugitive. For freely confessing, Grey won a pardon despite having joined with Ferguson and others in proclaiming Monmouth king; Wade too obtained a pardon.[8] Altogether, more prominent dissidents received pardons than sentences of execution. Among the pardoned were Richard Goodenough, Wade, West, Cochrane, James Burton, Henry Ireton, and Nicholas and Joshua Locke. Pardons followed in 1687 for Lord Brandon, Stephen Lobb, Sir Francis Drake, and (as will be seen) many exiles, and the following year for Rumbold's brother William.[9]

The government's reluctance to prosecute these men stemmed not from mercy or political calculations but primarily from the difficulty of convicting conspirators as distinct from rebels. Grey, Wade, and Goodenough escaped because the state needed their testimony; Grey was also aided by the earl of Rochester, who had a life interest in Grey's estate. Financial considerations were a factor in the pardon of Edmund Prideaux, who bribed George Jeffreys, "that bloody Nero" in the words of one rebel, with £14,500 to spare his life. As we have seen in Chapter 6, the state successfully prosecuted Cornish and Bateman in the aftermath of the rebellion, but for offenses associated with the Rye House conspiracy. With Grey the state had a second witness to convict Hampden of treason, but the latter, having a misdemeanor conviction already on record, prudently admitted guilt and had his death sentence commuted in 1686 (though he was fined £6,000).[10]

The government had considerably less success when it prosecuted the Cheshire lords, an obvious target given their collective prominence in the factious west. Delamere, Brandon, and Stamford went to the Tower in July, but Macclesfield, following a proclamation for his apprehension in September, fled to the Continent. Tried in November 1685, Brandon was accused of complicity in the Rye House plotting, including conspiracy with Monmouth and Macclesfield to compass Charles' death, to raise money for an insurrection, and to seize Chester Castle. The state once again called on Keeling to outline the plot, though Brandon cut this short by admitting its existence. Rumsey, the first of the government's key witnesses, described a meeting in Soho Square in which he informed Brandon of the progress of negotiations with the Scots and noted the shortage of funds; Brandon allegedly promised to donate £500. Rumsey also recalled an after-supper conversation in Monmouth's presence during which Brandon observed that it would be easy to seize Charles at Newmarket or Windsor with 300 men, of whom he could recruit 20. Grey, the crucial second witness, placed Brandon in a meeting at the George and Vulture tavern attended by Monmouth, Armstrong, Sir Gilbert Gerard, and Grey himself; in part they discussed Brandon's responsibility for Cheshire, including Chester Castle, in a general insurrection. A third witness, the tobacconist and Monmouth rebel Thomas Saxon, claimed that Brandon had informed him of plans for an uprising to put Monmouth on the throne, and that he had seen a letter from Brandon to the duke inviting the latter to be king. Although Brandon insisted on his innocence, it took the jury less than an hour to find him guilty. Intercession by the queen and Lady Brandon brought a reprieve on 1 December, and he was eventually released, in January 1687.[11]

The crown's case against Delamere, who was tried in January 1686, was based on his alleged involvement in preparations for the Monmouth rebellion. Lacking the usual two witnesses, the government attempted to prove the charges by documenting "substantial Circumstances joyned to one Positive Testimony," the latter being Saxon's assertion that Delamere, Sir Robert Cotton, and John Crew Ostley had asked him to carry a message from Delamere's Cheshire home to Monmouth; the purported communication pressed the duke to postpone the insurrection until midsummer because they could not raise £40,000 and enlist 10,000 men until that time. Delamere, however, demonstrated that neither he nor Cotton nor Ostley was at his home at the time alleged by Saxon. The rest of the state's case essentially rested on testimony by Grey, Wade, Richard Goodenough, and Jones pertaining to the role Monmouth had expected Delamere to play in Cheshire and the messages intended for him. No one, however, had been in direct contact with Delamere. Not only did the jury return a verdict of not guilty, but Saxon was subsequently convicted of perjury for his testimony in this case.[12]

The government fared no better against the earl of Stamford, likewise accused of high treason. Taken before the court of King's Bench on a writ of habeas corpus in February 1686, he was bailed and ordered to appear at the bar of the House of the Lords on the first day of its next sitting. Two months later, however, he received a pardon.[13]

The Exiles: Keeping the Flame Burning

A surprising number of Monmouth's partisans—several score according to Robin Clifton—made their way to the Continent. Among them were such central figures as Ferguson (who got through Feversham's army by forging the earl's name on a pass), Wildman, Danvers (who had avoided arrest by hiding in his own house), and Charlton, as well as Norton, Manley, and Tiley. Two of the duke's officers, Matthews and Foulkes, would later obtain commissions in William's army. Sir John Thompson, the earl of Anglesey's son-in-law, arrived around the beginning of August 1685; Thompson was reportedly carrying jewels worth thousands of pounds, possibly to fund new radical activity.[14] Trenchard appeared in Amsterdam about the same time, and Macclesfield fled to the Netherlands the following month. Sir Patrick Hume hid in Scotland until mid-August, at which time he escaped to Ireland and thence to Bordeaux and Geneva. Other dissidents, including Carstares, John Locke, Slingsby Bethel (alias Watson), Sir Patience Ward, James Washington, and Sir Robert Peyton, had remained in the Netherlands during the expeditions of 1685.[15]

Despite the losses sustained in the Argyll and Monmouth ventures, the exile community remained surprisingly vigorous. This was partly owing to the militancy of its ministers, one of the most outspoken of whom was John Hogg at Utrecht, a man ambassador Skelton deemed as dangerous as Ferguson. Although disappointed when Monmouth declared himself king, Hogg remained loyal to the rebel cause and even tried to uphold morale during the black days of July by discounting stories of royalist victories. The "Brownist" church in Amsterdam prayed for the deliverance of the rebels, some of whom had once worshiped in their midst, and offered thanks "in Covert Expressions" for Ferguson's safe return.[16] When Matthew Meade ministered to that congregation in November, Everard observed, he prayed "with a foaming mouth . . . that Babylon might be destroyed in England & her brats dasht against the walls"—a reference, mused Everard, to "moderate Christians whether Roman Catholiks or church of England & may be some great persons." John Wilmore (who had been foreman of the jury in Stephen College's trial in London), the bookseller Samuel Harris, Meade's son, and Walter Cross, Sir John Thompson's chaplain, spoke derogatorily of James II, helping fan the flames of discord. Harris, a republican and a Baptist who admitted dispersing "many of the late dangerous papers," declared that he hoped "to be in England *to see his Majesty have the same end as Monmouth had*," and Sir Robert Peyton "mightily inveighed" against monarchy.[17]

Perhaps inevitably, the exile community experienced substantial internal division and mutual recrimination during the year following the invasions. Some bitterly castigated Danvers and Meade for supposedly persuading the people of London and Wapping not to rebel on the grounds that God would "cause Deliverance & ruine Babylon in his own way." Anger was understandably directed against Trenchard because he had fled to France before the invasion, and at Thomas Parsons because he had deserted the duke after the first skirmish. Ferguson was reportedly angry with Wildman for having given Monmouth "desperate & wicked Councells." Suspicion was heightened by fears that more of their number would turn state's evidence, as Wade and Grey had done. Bitterness against Grey brought accusations that he had fathered an illegitimate child at Cleves and lied about the mother's status in order to have the baby baptized.[18] Cragg, the fugitives worried, had information that could bring many to the gallows, including Sir Samuel Barnardiston, Titus Oates, and Braddon. Before Cragg confessed, the rebels had offered him an annuity worth £50 per annum if he came to the Netherlands, and Manley was irate because a late-arriving fugitive had not stabbed Cragg before leaving England.[19] Threats were also made against Peter Perry (Parry), son of a Taunton clothier, who had served Monmouth as a cornet of horse but sought a pardon in early 1686 in return for information about his associates.[20]

Further dissension in the exile community stemmed from religious differences. Everard described two basic groups, on the one hand "*the Brownists* and Enthusiasts," or self-proclaimed "Godly Party," and on the other hand "the ungodly Party" headed by Matthews. The latter group purportedly "employ[ed] all their time and mony . . . in drinking & nightly Revells & Disorders to the great Scandall of the Dutch & the godly English inhabitants." Although this was obviously an exaggeration, it is nevertheless a salutary reminder that not all radicals developed their ideology in connection with religious beliefs. The godly party, according to Everard, consisted of three groups. The first comprised Meade and his associates, who were supposedly pleased that Monmouth had failed; Everard apparently misunderstood their cautious demeanor in the aftermath of the rebellion. A second godly faction, whose members included Manley, Venner, and Mercy Browning, expected the overthrow of Babylon and the inauguration of Christ's visible kingdom on earth within three years. "These doe of their absolute power down into the pitt of hell all those that possesse five hundred pounds a year; they are of the rich that cant be saved." Everard identified a third godly component consisting of former Popish Plot witnesses, including Robert Jenison, Miles Prance, William Hetherington, and Hubert Bourke.[21]

Although Westminster renewed its efforts to persuade the Dutch to banish English and Scottish fugitives from the Netherlands, magistrates were slow to act despite assurances to the contrary. Fagel promised to seize Ferguson or any other rebel found in Holland, but arrest warrants passed through so many hands, Skelton complained, that the targets received advance notice to flee. This happened at Rotterdam in December 1685 when Skelton persuaded local officials to arrest James Stewart, "the great adviser of the [Scottish] Party." Although on the list of persons to be banned, Samuel Harris lived openly with his family in Utrecht and met regularly with other dissidents.[22] Bethel, Ward, Matthews, Norton, and other radicals appeared openly in Amsterdam, and by mid-November Skelton could write to Middleton of "the Swarms of Fugitive Rebells" in that city and Utrecht.[23] Matthews was even made a burgher of Amsterdam (though under a pseudonym) some three months after being released on bail because no one would testify against him. At Middleton's urging, William promised in early December 1685 to ask the Amsterdam magistrates to apprehend Matthews, Danvers, and Manley; when the officials refused, Skelton suggested that a more "private way" had to be found. A search for fugitives in that city in late December proved fruitless. The depth of sympathy for the dissidents among some Amsterdamers was manifest in their reaction to news of Monmouth's death: "The wrong head had bin Cutt off."[24]

The duke of Cleves, who expressed a desire to keep fugitives from settling in his territory, was more cooperative. No rebels had returned to Cleves as of mid-September, but Wildman reportedly arrived late the following month. John Locke was living there in November, while Lord Wharton and his chaplain, John Howe, neither of them fugitives, were in Emmerich, where Locke and Cross visited them, as did Ward and the Quaker merchant Benjamin Furly the following February.[25] Wildman was also in Emmerich in the fall of 1685. By year's end Thompson, Foulkes, and Venner—the latter threatening to avenge his father's death—were all in Cleves. The magistrates there agreed only to arrest Ferguson, who was reportedly in the region, because his apprehension had been ordered by the elector of Brandenburg. Other fugitives, including Captain John Tillier and Ensign Thomas Parsons, found refuge in the lands of the bishop of Münster.[26]

The radicals generally moved around frequently, making it difficult for Skelton and his spies to monitor their activity. Ferguson, "the grand Criminall & head of all the mischief," as Everard called him, was not terribly secretive when he first arrived in the Netherlands with Barnardiston. Skelton's agents knew Ferguson visited Ann Smith, probably to recount details of Monmouth's failure, and he met with other dissidents, known as "the Clubb," at the Amsterdam house of James Stiles (who had previously been indicted as a Rye House conspirator) and at the home of Daniel Le Blon. Among other members of "the Clubb" with whom Ferguson consulted were Thomas Hunt (alias Briggs), the Whig pamphleteer, and John Starkey, a former associate of Shaftesbury's and Stephen College's; Starkey was recently alleged to have called Jeffreys a "damned rogue" and to have hoped to see James hanged. Accompanied at this time by Norton (alias Willoughby) and Barnardiston, Ferguson soon began to keep his whereabouts secret, even from most exiles, an indication of the distrust that was increasingly common among the dissidents. Between August and early November, he was reported at Middelburg, Amsterdam, Danzig, Leiden, Rotterdam, and Lüneburg before disappearing.[27] He was apparently spotted again near Emmerich in early January 1686, and a month later he surreptitiously returned to Amsterdam disguised in "a very ragged patcht & dark suite." Government agents then lost track of him for four months until he was seen in Amsterdam and possibly in Danzig in the company of Ensign James Denham, a former double agent who had cast his lot with the rebels about the time he sailed with Argyll.[28]

In June, Ferguson was also reported en route to see Ludlow in Switzerland or to visit a wealthy widow in Cleves, but Skelton suspected he was still in Amsterdam; his alleged movements were of sufficient interest to be chronicled in an Amsterdam newspaper.[29]

Occasionally government spies gleaned information about what the radicals were discussing. At a gathering in Amsterdam in October attended by Israel Hayes and others, Starkey, referring to the revocation of the Edict of Nantes, expressed concern about an Anglo-French alliance to destroy Protestantism and predicted a return to persecution akin to that in the days of Mary Tudor. About the same time, several informers, including Everard and Thomas Vile, shared the sentiment reported by a visitor to Amsterdam: "There was never soe much Impudence & Implacable hatred express'd as there's now shew'd by those Sons of Belial the Fugitives now in Amsterdam," who expected an imminent upheaval in England. They were allegedly toasting the damnation of both James and his government, and Trenchard was purportedly boasting that he would lead the dissidents himself rather than see their efforts fail again. He was meeting in "a Caballing Room" at the Croom Elbow coffeehouse in Amsterdam with Matthews, Manley and his son, Tiley, Starkey, Hayes, Wilmore, and others.[30]

In Utrecht, Sir John Thompson, whose house was described as "a private receptacle to the devote Brethern," was the focal point of another group of radicals, including Walter Cross. Thompson had been instrumental in bringing Meade to the Netherlands in October. The same month he entertained Starkey, who presumably apprised him of the views of dissidents in Amsterdam. Sir John also had a private meeting with Captain James Thompson (alias Henderson), a Scot who had served on the Argyll expedition; with him came Charnock, a former retainer of Lord Grey's. Another visitor in Sir John's home was John Scrope, grandson of the regicide and a former companion to Monmouth and Grey.[31] Early in October, Sir John and Sir Patience Ward (alias Delawne) went to Cleves to see Wharton, while Cross traveled to Emmerich to invite Wildman to join them.[32] Sir John reportedly sailed to England in early November, but Cross, who had been linked to both the Rye House plotting and the Argyll invasion (to which he had contributed £20), remained behind. Cross and approximately 40 other Scottish exiles met in Sir John's house, and Erskine heard John Howe preach there in January 1686.[33]

Other dissidents, both Scots and English, met at the Utrecht home of Lady Kersdale, whose husband had been killed at Bothwell Bridge and whose son John had been captured in the Argyll rebellion. Meetings were also held at the houses of Samuel Harris, an associate of Sir John Thompson's, and Thomas Papillon, whose chaplain was John Alsop (alias Browne); Papillon was in close contact with Thompson and Cross. Altogether, said one intelligence report (and others agreed), "the Congregation of English at Utrecht are aboute 200 people continually goeing between Amsterdam and utrecht likewise from utrecht to Amsterdam severall times in the Weeke to consult their partyes." In the spring and summer of 1686 alone, those who called at Utrecht included Stewart, Starkey, Danvers, Matthews, Parsons, Captain William Savage (former keeper of the Red Lion tavern in Taunton and a Monmouth rebel), George Speke, and the earl of Sutherland, who would support William in 1688.[34]

Utrecht was also home to Slingsby Bethel after he moved from the Amsterdam residence of Abraham Kicke. "Many of The Fraternity" went to Utrecht to consult with Bethel, Skelton noted. Bethel had ties to Howe, and his nephew, Captain Goodwin, was a confidant of Colonel Sir Henry Bellasis, whose Anglo-Dutch regiment had gone to England during the Monmouth threat. Bethel sent Goodwin to England with instructions to keep him apprised of Parliament's actions.[35]

From their base in the Netherlands the radicals maintained contact with associates in England with the cooperation of "Phanaticall Skippers" such as Edward Holbridge of Boston, Lincolnshire, and couriers such as William Fowler, who carried coded letters in a basket with a false bottom. Among those who used Fowler's service was Danvers, who corresponded with a Mrs. Carr in Leadenhall Street, London, probably the widow of the notorious Colonel Gilby Carr. Prominent women couriers, such as Elizabeth Gaunt and Jane Hall, were no longer available by the fall of 1685 because the authorities had learned of their work; Gaunt, in fact, was arrested in September on charges of high treason.[36]

Nevertheless James' government failed to destroy the radicals' communications network. For their part, the radicals had to determine how best to carry on their opposition to the detested Stuart regime.

Radical Weapons: The Press and the Factory Schemes

Although Disney had been executed in June 1685 for his role in publishing Monmouth's declaration, the community of radical printers in the Netherlands survived. Awnsham Churchill and his brother, on whose press the manifesto had been printed, were in Amsterdam in the summer and fall of 1685, engaging in "secret Conferences" with such rebels as Trenchard and Manley. John Bringhurst, the Quaker who had helped print the declaration, arrived there in November, as did the London bookseller Thomas Malthus and the printer Thomas Chadwick.[37] "The Presse has been formerly, and is of late made the Chiefe Toole of Sedition both in Church & State," complained Everard as he surveyed their activity.[38] He regarded the widow Mercy Browning as "the Retailer & Printresse of all [these] factious Pamphlets." In March 1686 she was preparing to print a "virulent" pamphlet on Essex's death; copies of Ferguson's tract on that subject had been shipped to the Netherlands the previous October.[39]

Although the radical printers were generally able to publish almost at will, at Skelton's urging William persuaded the States of Amsterdam to prohibit the sale of Monmouth's final statement.[40] Similar attempts to prevent the printing of an almanac by John Partridge ultimately failed after he switched title pages and disclaimed responsibility for the printing (but not the authorship). Publication of the almanac was primarily encouraged by Sir Robert Peyton, but Partridge's circle also included Trenchard, Malthus, Kicke, and the Amsterdam bookseller Jacob Vandervelde, "a notorious bookseller for the Rebeles interest" who had once harbored Argyll. Partridge's almanac predicted a Catholic massacre in Ireland in March 1686 as well as James' death. The almanac as well as *Mrs. Elizabeth Gaunt's Last Speech* were printed in Dutch as well as English. An untitled broadside, also from one of the dissident printers in Holland, used parallel columns in English and Dutch to satirize James' desire for a standing army. Hidden among unbound books, such works were smuggled into England. Fear of a hostile reaction on the part of merchants persuaded the radical printers not to publish the purported vision of a west-country man depicting "bloodshed & action in England this year [1686], & of the Restitution of the right heir to his own." The allusion was to Monmouth, sightings of whom had been widely reported in the aftermath of his defeat and execution. Thus publications from the radical press helped keep the radical cause alive and elicited support from Dutch sympathizers.[41]

The publication in Dutch of books hostile to James was undertaken with Dutch assistance. Some support came from William Brackel, the militant cleric with ties to the Covenanter extremists in Scotland, who was now the pastor of a Rotterdam church. William's opponents, alert to the fact that the prince's wife was heiress presumptive to the thrones of England and Scotland, probably helped fund works critical of the Stuart dynasty. British radicals, of course, found Amsterdam, Delft, and Leiden—all strongholds of opposition to William—congenial places of residence.[42]

A potentially more potent weapon than the radical publications was the establishment of a linen and woolen factory at Leeuwarden in Friesland and a woolen factory at Lüneburg, southeast of Hamburg, both of which could manufacture cloth less expensively than it could be imported from England. The factories would provide employment for dissident exiles, whose profits could be used to fund assorted radical activities ranging from anti-Stuart publications to insurrection, a point grasped by Everard when he called them "seminaries of rebellion."

Waller had initially attempted to found a woolen manufactory at Bremen in late 1683. Negotiations to establish one in nearby Lüneburg eventually succeeded, and in early 1685 he went to England to recruit workers. With the financial backing of Nicholas Locke, a Baptist or Quaker who had once engaged in the tobacco trade with the English colonies, the Lüneburg enterprise was sufficiently prosperous to worry English cloth merchants in Hamburg. By May 1686 the manufactory had a capital stock of 36,000 guilders, loans worth an equal amount, and a work force of approximately 400, some of whom were cloth workers who had fled the southwest when Monmouth was defeated. They obtained much of their wool from Pomerania and marketed the finished cloth in Amsterdam and elsewhere. Waller was unsuccessful in his attempts to persuade the linen workers in Leeuwarden to relocate in Lüneburg, but the latter city was already the home of a factory founded by Vincent du Bois that made linen and fine thread.[43]

Friesland, which had long been home to many Scottish exiles (including Argyll, who had a small estate there), was a natural site for another factory. "All sorts of Phanaticks," complained Skelton, were encouraged to settle in Friesland. The Cameronians, as we have seen, had sent Alexander Gordon of Earlston and Robert Hamilton to Leeuwarden to obtain William Brackel's endorsement of their narrow religious tenets. Brackel, renowned as "a zealous encourager of all the Rebells," persuaded his Reformed colleagues to ordain Scottish ministerial students, two of whom he sent back to Scotland "to preach Sedition & Rebellion." He also supported the translation into Dutch and publication of works by Scottish dissidents, thereby helping create a favorable climate for the exiles. By February 1684 he had accepted a pastorate in Rotterdam, but he maintained contacts with friends in Leeuwarden. Some of the exiles there apparently sailed with Argyll or Monmouth, and shortly before the duke's defeat Ann Smith and Starkey made a special trip to Leeuwarden, possibly to seek additional funds or weapons.[44]

Joseph Tiley (alias George Neale), who had proclaimed Monmouth king at Taunton, negotiated favorable terms with the Dutch for a cloth factory at Leeuwarden: workhouses with 60 looms and fulling mills constructed at state expense; an interest-free ten-year loan of 25,000 guilders; a twenty-year exemption from taxes for employers and workers; rent-free housing; 380 child laborers at no cost the first year; a contract to produce uniforms for the Friesland militia; payment of the salaries of a minister and his assistant for an exile church; and a pledge to employ more English professors at the University of Leeuwarden. Under the terms of this agreement Tiley calculated that the manufactory could produce cloth for 15 percent less than could its competitors in England, and without the cost of transportation.[45] Working capital was provided by Tiley; his principal assistant, Joseph Hilliard, a west-country clothier who had once traveled to the southwest to find a suitable landing place for Monmouth's troops; Christopher Cooke, whose woolen factory at Wilton had employed more than 600 workers before the Monmouth rebellion; Hugh Crosse, formerly a merchant at Bishop's Hull; prominent radicals such as Trenchard, Danvers, and Bethel; and various Dutch merchants, including Henry Uylenbrock, who had helped Le Blon and Thomas Archer equip the *Helderenburgh* for Monmouth, and who had provided hospitality for Grey, Armstrong, and Ferguson after the Rye House conspiracy failed. Another Dutch supporter was William Brackel, whose involvement in the publication of radical literature has previously been noted.[46]

By the spring of 1686 the Dutch had constructed workhouses (one of which was 90 feet long, 30 feet wide, and 6 stories high), a fulling mill, and furnaces and had installed 60 or more looms. Twenty English workers had arrived and Tiley was receiving numerous inquiries from interested persons in northern and western England, though 500 families had been expected by this point. Difficulty locating a carpenter who knew how to build English-style looms and mills caused some delay, and there were doubts if the quality of the water was adequate for fulling. Progress was slow, and Tiley even objected to two proposed ministers, Meade and Alsop.[47]

Consideration was also given to founding a third cloth factory in the neighboring province of Groningen, where dissidents had also settled. In January 1685 a group of them—probably Scottish Covenanters—had "erected a Tribunall amongst themselves [and] Inquired into his Majesties Rights, and afterwards very formally deposed him [James II] declaring all persons Traytors that should adhere to him." Manley spearheaded the effort to establish a factory at Groningen, but the project was apparently stillborn despite the fact that some exiles preferred the site to Lüneburg, which was deemed more vulnerable to pressures from James for their arrest.[48]

Royal Efforts to Diffuse the Radical Threat

James was sufficiently worried by the factory projects to seek the advice of his attorney general as to how he could prohibit trade with the rebels, and he renewed his complaints to William about their refuge in the Netherlands.[49] The king's most effective weapon was a royal pardon, a course favored by Nicholas Locke and Everard, although the latter soon suspected that the Leeuwarden scheme had been contrived simply to frighten James into granting a pardon. Exceptions to the general pardon, issued in March 1686, excluded various key figures in the cloth factories, such as Tiley, Hilliard, and Danvers. Such men therefore attempted to persuade their workers that the pardon was untrustworthy, that their neighbors and enemies at home would castigate them as traitors, that liberty of conscience would be denied them in England, and that James' reign would not last long. Edmund Everard tried to counter these efforts by employing Hunt and Trenchard to convince workers that the pardon did indeed encompass them, but Trenchard, despairing of a pardon for himself, tried for a time to dissuade Tiley from seeking one.[50]

On 10/20 May 1686, Skelton's efforts to persuade the States General to banish all dissidents excluded from the general pardon apparently succeeded, which turn of events gave him hope that the "Rebellious Marchants whoe were the Promoters and Assisters of Monmouths designe & private Abetters of that Party" could be driven out. However, political realities rendered the decision largely ineffectual. The States of Holland were reluctant to act unless Friesland did the same. When Friesland rejected the proclamation of the States General, Kicke and his allies denied the validity of the document, which in any case was of questionable effectiveness against those who had been made burghers. Once again the Dutch, motivated by economic considerations as well as their tradition of refuge and probably a degree of hostility to James, effectively ignored English pressure.[51]

By this point, frustration over Dutch reluctance to expel militant exile leaders had prompted James and his advisers to launch an alternative policy, namely the offer of pardons to hitherto-excluded dissidents who were willing to accept the regime and in some cases provide intelligence about radical activities. On 27 March / 6 April 1686, Joshua Locke, whose father Nicholas was a major financial backer of the factories at Leeuwarden and Lüneburg, notified Skelton that he wanted a pardon. Aware that he had been excluded from the general pardon, he offered to help block the "designed Staple" at

Leeuwarden and the factory at Lüneburg, "his Stock (as he sayes) being theire maine support, which once drawne out the whole Trade must vanish." The earl of Middleton insisted that Joshua must first prove his loyalty to James by "Breaking the Manufactary in Lunenbourg & Leewarden."[52] Skelton's agent, Captain Slater, confirmed the Lockes' willingness to withdraw their financial backing from the factories and worked out a similar arrangement for Cooke and Crosse; all four men subsequently received pardons.[53]

By early June, Tiley, who had decided to make his peace with James' regime, told Everard that he was seeking to terminate the Leeuwarden project, in part by putting off investors who had shown themselves willing to put up £10,000 to become partners. Mindful of his own investment, he wanted James to recompense him for the inevitable losses that would be sustained if he abrogated his contract with Friesland. While Tiley was in the process of disbanding the Leeuwarden factory, others tried to raise fresh funds to keep it operating. After receiving a pardon on 27 March, Hilliard returned to England to sell estates belonging to himself, Cooke (who was in no hurry to fulfill the conditions of his pardon), and others.[54] By the beginning of July, Everard informed Middleton that both the Leeuwarden and the Lüneburg factories had been "ruined by bringing over Tily." Although the latter was left with debts of 6,000 guilders, Cooke, Peyton, Norton, the minister John Shower, and Joseph Flight all pledged funds for his relief as a means of speeding their own pardons. A final effort to save the Leeuwarden factory was made by Israel Hayes in August, possibly at the instigation of Macclesfield, his tenant in Amsterdam. Having no funds of his own, Hayes was rebuffed by the Dutch, who presumably deemed the project too risky. Waller fared no better in Lüneburg after he lost his financial backing, leaving him vulnerable to English pressure that he be banned by the elector of Brandenburg.[55]

A number of other exiles sought and received royal pardons. Among them were Samuel Barnardiston, whose friends cited his youth and the influence of his governor, John Shower, but the latter also was pardoned after insisting he had tried to dissuade his charge from supporting Monmouth. Slater, who had served as an intermediary for Nicholas and Joshua Locke, also assisted Norton, Trenchard, and Meade. Although Norton confessed he had been involved in "Shaftsbury's Plott" (but to a lesser degree than West and Rumsey alleged), he sought not only a pardon but the return of his estate. Because his father had helped Charles II escape after the battle of Worcester and his mother had given the king 500 pieces of gold, Norton obtained his pardon, though for a time he delayed accepting it because of the £500 or £600 demanded of him; he was back in England in December 1686.[56] In the meantime Trenchard,[57] having despaired of a pardon, was trying to persuade Peyton, Bethel, and John Speke, his brother-in-law (who had offered Skelton £800 for a pardon), not to accept theirs should they be tendered. Trenchard— and Bethel (who denied complicity in the Rye House plotting and the 1685 rebellions)—finally received pardons in December 1687. Speke, his brother Hugh, and his parents, George and Mary, obtained pardons in February of the same year. Peyton's, however, was denied.[58]

Approached by Slater in April 1686, Meade maintained he had taken up residence in the Netherlands only for reasons of conscience, and that he was a zealous proponent of the royal prerogative and the loyalty and obedience of subjects. Sensitive to royal concerns about the exiles' cloth factories, he also claimed to have been instrumental in persuading the "Trading Men" to terminate their plans. Before he moved from Amsterdam to Utrecht in June 1686, Meade preached against the use of violence to oppose princes or reform the church, and he also tried to dissuade Manley and other extremists from attempting to kill Everard. Two months later Meade, seeking Skelton's assistance in obtaining a pardon, avowed: "[My only offense was] Nonconformitie; for which I have been under the severitie of the Law for eight years together."[59] He made no mention of his alleged involvement in either the Rye House plotting or the Monmouth invasion. About this time he was praying "so hartily" for James II "that all the whiggish auditory were amazed att it," and he was still trying to persuade wealthy members of his former congregation to return to England. Although Meade sometimes touched on millenarian themes in the pulpit, Skelton was impressed with the loyal tenor of his sermons and thought he would be "very usefull in keeping the Seamen & other Rabble among whome he lived in theire dewty." A pardon was forthcoming in March 1687.[60]

Pardons sometimes had major conditions attached, as did those of Joshua Locke and Hugh Crosse, noted above. Another case is that of Lieutenant Thompson, who had fought in the Monmouth expedition; Skelton agreed to obtain a pardon for him if he located Ferguson or helped apprehend Matthews, Manley, and John Balfour of Kinloch, the Scottish assassin. In June 1686, Thompson reneged on his agreement and openly boasted that he, Matthews, and others would be employed by the Friesland government. Like Peyton, Danvers sought a pardon in vain, while others, such as Matthews, Manley, Ferguson, and Wildman, apparently had no interest in making their peace with the Stuart regime.[61]

While the pardoning process was under way, English authorities continued their campaign to persuade the Dutch to banish the rebels, with James himself complaining to William about the lack of action. In June 1686 the States General finally agreed to implement the provision in the Treaty of Breda requiring the rebels to leave the country within fifteen days or risk the loss of their goods and face execution. But magistrates in such places as Friesland and Amsterdam were habitually reluctant to act against the dissidents, not least because they were still hoping for financial advantage from the cloth factories. The radicals, however, could not be sure of continuing sympathy from these officials. Trenchard, Tiley, and Nathaniel Hooke, formerly Monmouth's chaplain, had gone to Leeuwarden the previous month, believing it was safer than Amsterdam. By late summer others, including Macclesfield, Hunt, and Bethel, had left for the German states, though Skelton complained to Middleton that "many of the Rebells are yet bare faced at Amsterdam."[62]

The new menace to their sanctuary inflamed some radicals. Manley threatened to murder Everard, as has already been noted, and in June 1686 the latter was assaulted by Rotherham, a merchant and one of Manley's confederates. When Slater and others tried to capture Ferguson the following month, a hostile crowd that included Kicke and his son threatened them, and in early September, Samuel Harris and dissidents in Utrecht, having discovered the identity of one of Skelton's spies, severely injured him.[63] Skelton subsequently sent Everard to France to protect him from the rebels. But violence was not a radical monopoly: John Lisle had been killed by an Irish assassin in 1664. Ludlow's life had been threatened, and by early July 1686 an Irishman named Sidnam and a Welshman named Davis had arrived in Utrecht to make Ward, Bethel, and other dissidents "taste of the Ditche water of this Towne."[64] They failed.

Skelton seems to have had a short list of radicals he wanted to apprehend and return to England for trial. Gaspar Fagel, the grand pensionary, promised to help him take Matthews and Bethel, but Skelton was properly dubious. In October 1686, Slater seized Peyton near the Rotterdam docks, where James' yacht was moored, but before the captain could get his prisoner aboard, Peyton's screams attracted a crowd of Dutch sympathizers. Slater had no choice but to turn Peyton over to the Dutch authorities, who soon released him since his name did not appear on the recent list of rebels to be banned. Both Amsterdam, where Peyton was a burgher, and Rotterdam complained about Slater's action in the States of Holland, which in turn dispatched a delegate from each city to file a protest with William. The Dutch arrested Slater and ten other English officers. James disclaimed responsibility for Slater's action and the Privy Council registered its disapproval, but proceedings for Peyton's return were not canceled until March 1687, apparently in connection with James' efforts to procure the release of Slater and his men. William finally arranged their release, though they lost their commissions.[65]

The elusive Ferguson, "the Scotch firebrand . . . who can not live out of a conspiracy," as Bishop Fell aptly remarked, was the man Skelton most wanted. As we have seen, Ferguson was variously reported in Amsterdam, Danzig, Cleves, and en route to Switzerland in June 1686. By early July he had gone to Utrecht, where he preached to a private gathering at the home of John Howe and visited Ann Smith. About the same time he sent a note to Tiley, apparently unaware that Tiley had become an informer, agreeing to meet in Amsterdam.[66] For two days after their meeting Tiley said nothing until Slater questioned him. Hoping to learn Ferguson's whereabouts, Slater had asked Nicholas Locke to inquire if Ferguson was interested in a pardon. Ferguson, who was staying with Matthews, agreed to see Locke only if the meeting were arranged by Sir Cornelius Vermuyden. Slater then approached Tiley, who admitted he had seen Ferguson—now very wary and devoting his time to writing—two days earlier. From Tiley, Slater learned that Ferguson was staying in a house in which all the windows facing the street had been plastered up. By the time Slater persuaded the magistrates to act, Ferguson had fled across the roof tops of neighboring houses, leaving Slater and his men to face a hostile crowd.[67] An embittered Everard complained to Skelton that his work in the Netherlands had been ruined, for the dissidents had "raised a mutiny of the People" against Slater and himself by claiming that the privileges of Amsterdam had been "invaded."[68]

Ferguson, who was now short of money, fled from Amsterdam disguised as a soldier. He went first to Lüneburg, where he apparently saw Erskine's brother, and then traveled to Utrecht and conferred with Erskine. Little is known about Ferguson's movements in 1687 and most of 1688, either because Skelton's successor as English envoy, Ignatius White, marquis d'Albeville, was inept or (less likely) because, as an occasional spy for Louis XIV, White had no interest in helping James track down a radical so potentially disruptive to the Stuart regime.[69] A baseless report circulated in England in March 1687 that Ferguson had been captured, and the following month d'Albeville told Middleton that Ferguson was at Geneva. Nine months later he asked Middleton not to issue a pardon for some of the rebels still living in Amsterdam (especially Tiley and Row) because he hoped to obtain their assistance in apprehending Ferguson. He also expected help from Nicolaas Witsen, an Amsterdam burgomaster, but he, like Ferguson, would shortly be aiding William in the revolution of 1688–89.[70]

Although dissidents in the Netherlands had boasted as early as July 1685 that they would soon get their revenge "with a farr greater Power" should Monmouth escape, his defeat dampened further plotting until the radicals' ability to remain in the Netherlands was threatened and the offer of pardons isolated the more extreme dissidents. James' efforts to reduce the militant threat to his regime by granting pardons ultimately proved counterproductive.[71] At first the exiles did little more than hope for an economic downturn of sufficient magnitude in England to "bestirr" the people to act. Manley and other extremists likewise thought irate people might help them "have another tugg for it" after the government began questioning titles to certain former church lands.[72]

Heightened security measures imposed during and immediately

after the Argyll and Monmouth insurrections kept Ireland and Scotland reasonably under control throughout James' reign. Conventicles remained a major irritant in Scotland, although the king was primarily concerned only with those that met in the fields, such as one numbering around 3,000 Covenanters that gathered on the border. As before, many conventiclers bore arms. Orthodox ministers in Scotland continued to be targets of periodic violence; James Lawson of Irongray, Kirkcudbright, was physically attacked and denounced as a "papist dog" in 1685 because he prayed for James, and in July 1686 an armed band of approximately 40 militants assaulted the minister at Kirk of Shotts, Lanark. Moreover, dissidents rescued imprisoned zealots from royal authorities on three occasions, including one assault on the tollbooth at Ayr. Although baseless, rumors of Catholic plotting in Ireland were discomfiting to Protestants. The level of discontent with James remained sufficiently high, especially in Scotland, to encourage the exiles that a successful uprising might in fact be mounted against him.[73]

Plotting Redivivus: James Under Attack

The first apparent indication of a new conspiracy came in late April 1686, when Captain Segar, a German who had formerly served in the Danish navy, traveled from Amsterdam to consult with Skelton at The Hague. Kicke, he asserted, had engaged him to command one of six ships to transport rebels and weapons from Amsterdam and Utrecht for a "second disturbance." The principal conspirators had allegedly inspected 6,000 firearms in Utrecht, placed an order for an additional 12,000, and recently shipped large quantities of pistols and other weapons to Scotland. Some of those who were involved, Segar claimed, were pardoned rebels who had gone to England to raise money for the cause by selling their estates. Segar had almost certainly invented his story, apparently in the hope of extracting funds from Skelton.[74] Equally dubious was a contemporaneous letter to Skelton from an anonymous Amsterdam trader purportedly describing a new conspiracy involving rebels excepted from the royal pardon. They could raise an army of 10,000 at short notice, the author claimed, and would eventually triple their number, arming the recruits with weapons smuggled from the Netherlands. The conspirators allegedly planned to use a look-alike to persuade the commoners that Monmouth had not been executed. Interestingly, about a month and a half earlier a young man from Earl Shilton, Leicestershire, who had arrived in the southwest too late to fight for Monmouth, was in the Netherlands posing as the duke's son. The charade, which reminded Everest of the Perkin Warbeck episode, had been conceived by a Somerset minister and had Waller's support but was repudiated by Matthews and Trenchard because the young man bore no likeness to the duke's son.[75]

More substantive information about a new plot surfaced in the summer of 1686 when Sir Duncan Campbell, Argyll's son-in-law, told Tiley of a scheme by Donald Cargill's band to kill James as he traveled through the border country en route to Edinburgh for his coronation. When that scheme failed to materialize, radical Scots, including Captain William Cleland (alias Cunningham), plotted with Manley, Wildman, and others, and as part of their conspiracy sent an agent named Hedrington back to England, apparently with answers to queries from radicals in London. Matthews, who was probably involved in the new plan, shortly thereafter denounced James as "that great Catterpillar who destroyed the Nation" and promised that by April 1687 "they would make the Pope to Shake." When Captain Tillier boasted that preparations for a new rebellion were under way, Skelton had him arrested at Mechelen (north of Brussels) in September. The following month Fagel too remarked that he had learned of a "new designe" from a Scot in Rotterdam.[76]

According to Fagel, his informant had described the new conspirators as Fifth Monarchists, but Skelton, who was by now beginning to pick up accounts of plotting, told Middleton that an insurrection by Fifth Monarchists was improbable because they were "Insignificant & [in] number inconsiderable."[77]

Whether Fagel knew it or not, on the same day Skelton wrote to Middleton a group of Scots secretly banded together. Erskine, who was part of the group, recorded in his journal: "We entered into a society and order [by] which we designed close amity. All the members were to mentain four principalls, viz., Liberty, religion, loyalty and honour, all which were explained and cleared at the first erection." The other charter members were Baillie of Jerviswood the younger, Walter Seaton, John Lamotte, James Wishart, and a Mr. Sinclair, his wife, son, and daughter. They agreed to use "severall signs whereby to know one another, every member having the seal and badge of the order." One week after this meeting Erskine conferred with Carstares, on whom William relied for knowledge of the radicals' activity, and Robert Chiesley (or Cheislie), another former Argyll supporter. Erskine recorded the subject of neither this discussion nor that which occurred six days later with James Johnston, Burnet's nephew and a member of the prince's intelligence service.[78]

Judging from the cryptic entries in his journal, Erskine seems to have played a key but unspecified role in the exile community. In December 1685 he and five other Scots—Cleland, John Guthry, Walter Lockart of Kirkton, George Pourie, and James Bruce—had decided to remain in or near the Netherlands in the event, Erskine explains, "the Lord gave us an opportunity of going home to serve our country." Erskine was subsequently in frequent contact with other dissidents, including Lord Stair, Lord Colvil, Patrick Hume (eldest son of Hume of Polwarth), the Cameronian John Nisbet, and the ministers Robert Blair, Thomas Hogg, and George Barclay. He met too with such English radicals as Hunt, Lieutenant Thompson, and Ann Smith, and with the Dutch bookseller Vandervelde. Erskine's frequent presence at the sermons of Meade, Howe, and Cross, several of which were delivered in the homes of Papillon, Sir John Thompson, and Lady Kersland (Robert Ker's widow), would have kept him in contact with other radicals; he attended at least one service, for instance, with Danvers and Ward.[79] Presumably Erskine used these meetings to explore ways to advance his "four principalls," especially "Liberty" and Protestantism.

After d'Albeville replaced Skelton, the government's ability to monitor radical activities sharply declined, unfortunately for James just as pressures on William to intervene in English affairs were increasing. In September 1686, Lord Mordaunt had unsuccessfully urged the prince to invade, and William was not persuaded to change his mind after Everard van Weede, Heer van Dijkvelt, reported the results of his meeting with Mordaunt, Halifax, Devonshire, and six others at the earl of Shrewsbury's home the following

January. Since the prince probably made his decision to invade only after he had learned of Queen Mary's pregnancy, the radicals in the Netherlands must have continued to ponder action of their own throughout 1687. William presumably knew of such efforts through the work of Carstares, his principal link with the militants.[80]

In early 1687 unidentified dissidents attempted to inflame feeling against James by publishing hostile libels in the newspapers of Amsterdam, Rotterdam, Leiden, Utrecht, and Dort, but d'Albeville blocked them by paying the gazeteers not to publish the stories. Many of the exiles as well as moderates in the British Isles were calmed when James issued a declaration of indulgence for England in April and a comparable proclamation for Scotland in June. The latter won Stewart's approval, though Carstares' refusal to return to his homeland reflected the deep suspicion of other dissidents. Reports that hard-core militants expected imminent unrest in England, Scotland, and Ireland prompted d'Albeville to dispatch spies to "penetrate these Encouragements," but their efforts led only to a short and incomplete catalogue of eighteen radicals in four Dutch communities. One of the eighteen, the Monmouth rebel John Parsons, who had been in Amsterdam with Peyton, Wildman, Matthews, Francis Goodenough, and others, was audacious enough to appear at The Hague, but d'Albeville refused to have his men arrest him for fear they would be "massacred." As usual, the Dutch protected the fugitives.[81]

The government obtained a possible glimpse of radical activity in August 1687 when Henry Bodham, an Amsterdam broker, informed the royal agent William Carr that he had been asked by dissidents to purchase three or four ships to be used for another invasion of England. The group purportedly had a fund of 300,000 guilders with which to buy weapons and boasted that 10,000 men would take up arms in London when they landed. According to Carr's account, several unidentified men had arrived from London to discuss "their designe." The information may be credible, since Bodham, a member of the "Brownist" church in Amsterdam, had numerous ties to the radical community: Argyll had once lodged in his father's house, the same building where Monmouth once met with associates; Argyll's son now lived with Bodham's mother; Bodham's sister was close to Matthews and Wilmore; and Bodham himself was often with Peyton. Carr also reported a secret meeting involving several dissidents at a village between Leiden and Haarlem in mid-August, and additionally noted that William Lord Paget, currently in Amsterdam, received numerous English visitors. Paget, who was Richard Hampden's father-in-law and a man with ties to noncon-formists, may have been on a mission related to the simultaneous trip of Frederick van Nassau, Heer van Zuylestein, the prince's agent, to England following James' dismissal of his prorogued Parliament the previous month. Zuylestein's mission was not only to assess James' likely plans but also to establish contacts with the king's critics and secure a communications network with them. Paget probably had instructions to create similar ties with the exiles.[82]

In the meantime James had determined to procure the return of Burnet, who had arrived in the Netherlands in May 1686 and had taken up duties as one of William's advisers, thanks to Halifax's influence. In Burnet the prince had not only a man familiar with British affairs but a foremost Protestant propagandist. Honoring the con-ditions of his appointment, Burnet initially eschewed any contact with the English radicals in Amsterdam or their Scottish counter-parts in Rotterdam, castigating both groups as "the dark men of the last age." He even preached a sermon at The Hague in May 1687 denying the right of subjects to take up arms against their sovereign. Yet by this point Burnet was associating with radicals, and the pre-vious month he had acquired a house in Utrecht, a city that was home to approximately 150 English and Scottish families, including (at that point) Danvers and Alsop. Although some of the Dutch clergy despised him as "a man full of cheat & fraud," he moved freely in government circles. In May 1687, Burnet was ordered to surrender to authorities in Edinburgh on charges of high treason. Instead he became a naturalized Dutch citizen and obtained the services of a bodyguard from William.[83]

Burnet's name figured prominently in the burgeoning press cam-paign against James' regime. The publication of Burnet's letters to Middleton in the summer of 1687 brought a protest from Westmin-ster to The Hague. Libels were appearing on a daily basis, d'Albeville complained in August (with exaggeration); among them was *Reflec-*

tions on His Majesties Proclamation for Liberty of Conscience, a work attributed to Burnet. At least some of these publications were being smuggled into England; in August the government received a tip that two parcels containing scandalous libels intended for William Spence or his assigns were on a ship that had just arrived from Holland. Dissident publications, some of which were published in England, were then shipped throughout the country. Richard Lambert, a bookseller in York, admitted receiving 50 copies each of Burnet's reply to his citation to return to Scotland on charges of high treason (which included his letters to Middleton), *An Answer to a Paper Printed with Allowance, Entitled, A New Test of the Church of Englands Loyalty* (London, 1687), and *A Letter, Containing Some Reflections on His Majesties Declaration of Liberty for Conscience* (1687).[84]

The Declaration of Indulgence James issued in England on 4 April 1687 was a calculated attempt to provide relief from the penal statutes for his fellow Catholics and to negate one of the most appealing elements of the radical program, namely religious liberty for Protestants. The Scottish experience had already demonstrated that even a limited indulgence could sow dissension among critics of the established church. Reaction among English Protestants was varied. Some, such as William Penn and Stephen Lobb, were ready to endorse the policy of toleration; most, however, were chary, both because Catholics were among the beneficiaries and because the declaration was based on the use of the prerogative to suspend statutes. Among the exiles, Ferguson and Wildman, who, with Burnet, were the chief propagandists, made their opposition known, hoping to keep the exiles firmly opposed to James and to counter the efforts of Penn and Lobb to build support for James' policy at home. Ferguson attacked Penn in *An Answer to Mr. Penn's Advice to the Church of England*; Wildman, in a broadside entitled *Ten Seasonable Queries Proposed by an English Gentleman in Amsterdam to His Friends in England*, warned Protestants not to trust James but to remember Catholicism's history of persecution, most recently on the Continent.[85]

Probably the most important publications shipped to England in this period focused on a letter from Fagel to James Stewart, whom the king had appointed to the Scottish Privy Council to administer the indulgence in the northern realm. The letter, which Carstares conveyed to Stewart in November 1687, clearly applied to England as well as Scotland. Fagel explained that William supported the repeal of the penal laws against nonconformists while leaving the Test Act in place, a calculated appeal to both nonconformists and Tories. When James refused to endorse the prince's proposal, copies of Fagel's letter—perhaps as many as 50,000—were printed in Amsterdam and shipped to England under the title *Their Highness the Prince and Princess of Orange's Opinion About a General Liberty of Conscience*. This document as well as edited versions of Stewart's letters to Carstares (with the latter's name removed) were also published in Dutch, French, and Latin to ensure that William's European allies understood that he wanted toleration for nonconformists and Catholics without challenging the traditional monopoly of office by members of the established church—the conditions, in other words, that prevailed in the Netherlands. Johnston, the chief figure responsible for distributing this literature, kept the Dutch court apprised of events in England by means of encoded messages written in invisible ink on letters concerning business affairs.[86]

As this propaganda campaign unfolded, James redoubled his efforts to apprehend Burnet or procure his banishment from the Netherlands. The latter course was complicated by Burnet's Dutch citizenship. When d'Albeville protested that Burnet's primary allegiance to the king was not transferable and that the Dutch were obligated to surrender him under the terms of the Treaty of Breda, Fagel agreed to exile him only if James "would give an Act that others should not be us'd in the same manner." Effectively checked, James offered a reward for Burnet's capture and dispatched a royal yacht to the Netherlands to bring him home. Not only was the scheme foiled when someone tipped off Burnet, but it failed to dissuade him from further attacks on the regime.[87]

The pamphlet campaign against James intensified in the Netherlands during the spring and summer of 1688 as anonymous writers accused him of murdering Essex, burning London, poisoning Charles II, and plotting with a midwife to substitute a baby boy should the queen give birth to a female (a charge made as early as April).[88] In *A Discourse to the King*, which was sold in the Netherlands by 25 May / 4 June, a radical poet firmly linked the notion of a baby-switching scheme to the country's deep-seated anti-Catholicism:

> We've seen the Land where Romes Imps scarce might dare
> To breath, become like their own native air.
> We've seen *Romes Locusts*, Hell's most damned brood,
> Oreflow these Islands, like a *Stygian* flood.
>
> . . .
>
> And now Thou'rt prompted by that cursed Faction,
> To cheat us with a Brat of base extraction,
> T'exclude thine Heir, our greatest consolation,
> That Thou to Rome may'st Sacrifice the Nation,
> To make thy free-born people stand in aw
> By a Tyrannick, Military Law.

In the author's mind, this was but the latest in a series of popish plots that included those of 1641 and 1678:

> Had we our Slavery under Rome forgot?
> All its destroying arts? Its *Hellish Plot*
> In *seventy eight*? Was our remembrance gone
> Of its Infernal rage in *forty one*? [89]

Allegations that the Prince of Wales, born on 10 June 1688, was not really James' son were common among the Dutch and provided fodder for more pamphlets. [90]

Prince William and the Radicals

An alliance between William and the British radicals did not come easily. The prince knew that in the past radicals such as the duke of Buckingham, Algernon Sidney, and John Hampden had had contacts with the French court, and he was concerned as well by nonconformist clerics whose view of James had been favorably swayed by his toleration policy. Some radicals in turn must inevitably have worried about William's reputed authoritarian tendencies, a favorite criticism of Dutch republicans. But the prince had been careful to maintain ties with the radicals since the early 1670s, and by now his key agents included Carstares and Johnston. Important too was

Richard Hampden's endorsement of William, which Johnston solicited. For a decade and a half the prince had kept the channels of communication with the radicals open; in the crucial months of 1688 it would have made no sense to cut those links.

So effective was William's communications network that little more than its outlines can be reconstructed. Zuylestein, as we have seen, was the primary architect, establishing the key links after his arrival in England in August 1687. Paget's secret meetings with exiles the same month may have been part of the plan. The principal figures in England, not all of whom were radicals, included Sir Henry Sidney (who had earned William's trust while commanding British regiments in Dutch service between 1681 and 1685), Johnston, William Forrester, the earls of Devonshire and Carlisle, Sir James Herbert, James Rivers, and Henry Powle. They sent intelligence about such matters as James' plans, the court's preparations for parliamentary elections, the attitude of military officers, and the impact of the propaganda campaign against James to Zuylestein, Dijkvelt, and William Bentinck. Working with Carstares, Bentinck also maintained ties with Scotland.

Tension between William and James increased in January 1688 when the latter asked the States General to repatriate the six British regiments in the Netherlands. With roots going back to the origins of the Dutch Republic, these regiments comprised English, Scottish, and Irish troops recruited in the Netherlands. Although the republic funded them, they were primarily loyal to the house of Orange and were of substantial value to William. Increasingly concerned that these regiments had become the home of political and religious partisans critical of his regime, James determined to recall them once Louis XIV had promised to underwrite the cost of maintaining them in England. On 9/19 February the Dutch refused James' request, agreeing only to honor the right of officers to resign their commissions and return to England as private persons. Between 40 and 60 officers, approximately a quarter of the total, returned, leaving an officer corps loyal to William. Those who stayed, complained d'Albeville, "presume to give out that the Protestant Religion is att the Stake; and men of no Religion pretend now to have tender Consciences." "I am informed from the several garrisons where the Brigade is," he wrote in late April, "that the Crumwellians were never more animated against the King, then they appear to be." For the most part the regimental vacancies were filled by men who came to the Netherlands to serve William. Although some were simply mercenaries, others were committed radicals, such as John Cutts, a Monmouth rebel, and the Covenanter Henry Erskine, Lord Cardross.[91]

James Kennedy, Middleton's agent at Rotterdam, learned from an English fugitive of "a project in England, and elsewhere, to bring over recruites" disguised as workmen or travelers. He also discovered that several Irish officers in William's employ were negotiating with the captains of two Dublin ships to transport recruits to the Netherlands in secret. In the spring both Kennedy and d'Albeville reported the arrival of officers and men from England, Scotland, and Ireland. Sir William Waller came from Hesse in May, but for the most part fugitives moved so openly and frequently in Amsterdam that d'Albeville no longer thought their presence worth noting. Four men-of-war, according to Kennedy, were manned almost entirely by veterans of the Argyll and Monmouth rebellions. At the end of September d'Albeville estimated that an additional 300 to 400 Englishmen and Scots had arrived to join William.[92]

Well before that time William had resolved to intervene in Britain. The decision came in May 1688, when Admiral Edward Russell warned him that the English would rebel on their own if William declined to lead them. If he chose to stay on the sidelines, the prince risked either a total victory by James or the establishment of another republic devoted to colonial and mercantile expansion. Acquiescing to these arguments, he insisted that Russell and Herbert obtain pledges of support, which were forthcoming on 30 June in the "invitation" from Sidney, Russell, Devonshire, Danby, Shrewsbury, Lord Lumley, and Henry Compton, bishop of London. The previous day the archbishop of Canterbury and six other bishops had been acquitted on charges of seditious libel for having denied the legality of the dispensing power; their action had been provoked by the king's order that the clergy read his second Declaration of Indulgence in their pulpits. The crowds, hitherto alarmed by the prospect of unchecked Catholicism, greeted the news with unbridled enthusiasm.

The mood of the radicals brightened perceptibly as they followed the rapidly unfolding events. As early as the beginning of June the fugitives in the Netherlands rejoiced at the prospect of a general pardon that would include even Ferguson and Peyton, but when James finally issued his declaration on 27 September, they "scorn[ed] to take their pardons," convinced "they must have them in spite of their enemies." As the radicals watched and engaged in preparations for the invasion, Ferguson, expressing what they must all have believed, exulted, "Monmouth went altogether upon hopes, but now there is all assurances that can be desired."[93]

The radicals were not, however, as successful in shaping William's declaration as they would have liked. According to Burnet an early draft, including Danby's notes, was presented to William in August 1688 by Sidney, Johnston, Shrewsbury, and Russell. The executioner had already claimed relatives of three of these men: Russell's cousin, William Lord Russell; Sidney's older brother, Algernon; and Johnston's father, Sir Archibald. Sidney and Johnston had been largely responsible for persuading William to use the press in his campaign against James, Johnston in particular having encouraged the prince to spread doubts about the legitimacy of the Prince of Wales.

William submitted the draft of the proposed declaration to his English and Dutch advisers, prompting debate between moderates who wanted to focus exclusively on James and radicals who sought to condemn the abuses of Charles' reign as well; the latter course would have alienated Tories and effectively limited William's appeal to Whigs and nonconformists. The radical case was enunciated primarily by Wildman, who prepared an alternate draft (now lost), Macclesfield, and Mordaunt. Burnet's account castigates Wildman as a spiteful meddler and attributes to him a barely credible threat not to aid William unless the original draft were modified. The pragmatism of Sidney, Russell, and Shrewsbury convinced William, but Wildman subsequently publicized his points in *The Memorial of English Protestants* (November 1688), which accused Charles of having been a pensioner of Louis XIV and an enemy of free parliaments and Protestantism. Charles' reign, Wildman contended, had laid the foundation for James', which was part of a pervasive conspiracy against Protestantism. In the meantime, William himself, despite reservations about the declaration's promise to call a free Parliament and abide by its decisions, accepted the principles outlined in the draft, had Fagel revise it, and commissioned Burnet to translate and slightly abbreviate it. Lois Schwoerer has persuasively argued that William, who overestimated the strength of the radicals, probably accepted the English proposal in part to head off the more extreme demands of Wildman and his associates.[94]

Soon published in four languages—English, Dutch, French, and German—*The Declaration of His Highness William Henry, Prince of Orange, of the Reasons Inducing Him to Appear in Armes in the Kingdom of England* deplored the dispensing power as a device to implement arbitrary government, condemned James' pro-Catholic policies, and called for a free Parliament and the enactment of measures to preserve Protestantism. The declaration also demanded a parliamentary investigation into the supposed legitimacy of the Prince of Wales.[95] Ferguson and his Scottish allies drafted a declaration for their kingdom, an edited version of which William accepted. It too was published in four languages.

When William finally got under way on 1/11 November, a number of veteran radicals sailed with him. Among them were Ferguson, the inveterate plotter, and his brother, who had recently been promoted to a captaincy, as well as Wildman and Waller. Matthews, Manley, and Parsons, who had fought with Monmouth, would again lead some of their former compatriots. Sir Robert Peyton and the earl of Leven each commanded one of the two regiments comprising exiles, and Sir Duncan Campbell, angry because his estate had not been restored when he was pardoned for high treason, was in charge of a company. "Every Englishman and Scot, of whatever political complexion, from practical or theoretical republicans such as Wildman or Fletcher of Saltoun to alienated tories such as the Earl of Macclesfield, were offered carte blanche and a free passage to swell the numbers." The Scots who accompanied William included Argyll's son, William Carstares (who conducted a service of thanksgiving for the prince after his troops had landed in England), Sir Patrick Hume, and several men wanted in connection with the archbishop of St. Andrews' assassination in 1679. William Cleland and Dr. William Blackader had already gone to Scotland as agents in August; the latter, carrying encoded correspondence, was arrested and imprisoned in Edinburgh.[96] "All our English Rebells are vanish't and believ'd on board these Ships," Petit had observed as early as 29 August / 8 September. On the eve of William's departure d'Albeville similarly remarked, "All the Traytors of England and Scotland and Irland goe along," a statement that appropriately (though hyperbolically) underscored the radicals' collaboration with the prince.[97]

In England, William received the assistance of other veteran radicals, the most important of whom was probably Delamere, whose uprising in Cheshire effectively prevented James from bringing Irish troops through Chester. On 16 November, Delamere issued a rousing call to his tenants, exhorting them to take up arms or financially support others who could do so:

Can you ever hope for a better occasion to root out POPERY and SLAVERY, than by joyning with the *P*. of *O*. whose Proposals contain and speak the desires of every man that loves his Religion and Liberty? . . . I am to choose whether I will be a *Slave* and a *Papist*, or a *Protestant* and a *Freeman*. . . . Our Deliverance must be by force. . . . If the K. prevails, farewel Liberty of Conscience. . . . I am willing to lose my Life in the Cause.[98]

Delamere and his men, garbed in blue, received an enthusiastic welcome in Manchester as well as among his own tenants, and in Newcastle-under-Lyme his speech "was much Hosana'd by throwing up hatts &c." At Nottingham he and Devonshire publicly resolved to investigate the deaths of Essex, Russell, Sidney, Cornish, Godfrey, and others. The earls of Stamford and Manchester organized armed support for William in Nottinghamshire, and Trenchard arranged for financial support. Such noted dissidents as Lord Lovelace, Colonel John Birch, and Sir Francis Drake also rallied to William's cause.[99]

One of the more unsavory contributions to William's cause was made by Hugh Speke, who had been imprisoned for his inquiry into Essex's death and whose brother Charles had been executed as a Monmouth rebel. In 1709 he claimed that James had commissioned him to ascertain the strength of William's forces after they landed, but instead he assumed the role of a double agent and, at the prince's behest, sent inflated accounts of the invading force to James. With an unidentified gentleman, according to Speke's own testimony, he drafted William's so-called "Third Declaration." Left with a friend in London to be printed when Speke notified him by letter, it was designed to fan the flames of anti-Catholicism. To prevent the burning of London and Westminster by Catholics or the French, the manifesto, first distributed in London on 8 December, called on magistrates to disarm Catholics. Obviously intended as well to intimidate James' supporters, the "Third Declaration" not only asserted that the prince enjoyed enormous popular support but ominously proclaimed that those who had betrayed the Protestant faith or subverted the laws of England had forfeited their lives. Speke also insisted he had sent letters throughout the country disclosing "an universal Conspiracy of the *Irish* and their Popish Adherents, to make some desperate Attempt." At least three of James' key supporters—Jeffreys, Father Edward Petre, and Robert Brent, a Catholic attorney—were apparently sufficiently alarmed by the outburst of anti-Catholicism to make plans to flee.[100]

Speke's attempt to claim a substantial share of the credit for disarming Catholics in England and Ireland raises the question of radical responsibility for the widespread violence against Catholics during the revolution. Apart from the possible influence of Speke's manifesto, there is no evidence that dissident leaders instigated these disturbances. Rather they appear to have been the outgrowth of mounting animosity toward Catholics at the popular level on the part of Tories as well as Whigs. Hostility toward Catholics was, of course, endemic in English public life. The memory of the Popish Plot had hardly subsided when James' accession intensified fears of popery. In 1686 anti-Catholic riots had erupted in London and Coventry, and early in the same year Scottish malcontents demolished the chapel of the earl of Perth, whom they threatened to kill, and rioted and demonstrated against papists in Edinburgh. Against a background of rising tension as England awaited William's invasion, a London mob wrecked the Carmelite chapel in Bucklersbury and burned its vestments and altar furnishings on 29 October.[101] On the morning of 5 November at Reading, a town "as factious as any place in England," a crowd stoned a Catholic chapel while mass was being said, and that evening troops had to be called out to prevent more than 200 persons armed with long poles from destroying the building and burning an effigy of the pope. Six days later irate Londoners, agitated by rumors of gridirons, spits, and cauldrons intended for the destruction of Protestants, attacked the monastery of St. John's, Clerkenwell. Not surprisingly, the mob, more than a thousand strong, turned on Henry Hills, the king's printer, on 12 November, breaking his windows and threatening to assault him. Elsewhere angry crowds demolished a Catholic chapel in York, sacked another in Newcastle, and endangered a third in Norwich.[102]

A crescendo of anti-Catholic activity was clearly building before Speke began circulating the "Third Declaration," which William had supposedly issued on 28 November. Speke's manifesto may have aggravated the agitation,[103] as reflected in antipapal outbursts in Bristol, where "the rabble" demolished a Catholic chapel and burned its contents, and in Oxford, Shropshire, and Suffolk. Despite Delamere's efforts to dissuade crowds in Worcester "from any such Arbitrary and tumultuous doeings," they defaced or destroyed Catholic chapels. Violence also struck Cambridge, where demonstrators attacked priests and destroyed vestments and other accoutrements of Catholic worship at Sidney Sussex College. After James fled Westminster, thousands of people took to the streets on the night of 11 December, destroying the Franciscans' house and chapel in Lincoln's Inn Fields and ransacking the residences of the Spanish ambassador and the diplomatic representatives of Florence and possibly Venice, in the process burning the Catholic ornaments. The house of the French ambassador was left alone, purportedly because he had paid artisans on time. Attacks were also renewed against the chapels at Bucklersbury, Lime Street, and St. John's, Clerkenwell. Although the trained bands had been called out, the following night "the mobile were up again in a numerous body, and proceeded to pull down several popish houses: they carried away and burnt, in books, pictures, goods, money, and plate . . . to the value of near 100,000*l*." Attacks were also mounted on buildings in Soho and the Haymarket where Catholics were believed to have stored gunpowder, and again on Henry Hills, who lost at least two cartloads of books as well as presses and stamps to the flames. "A universall terrible Alarme was taken all over London and Westminster," observed Roger Morrice, "with a fear and confident persuasion that they should have their throats cut by the French and by the Papists." People locked themselves in their homes and burned candles in the windows throughout the night. This was, opined Morrice, "the great terror."[104]

Also in December, mobs attacked the earl of Dover's house at Clevely Park, near Cambridge, and paraded him on a saddleless horse through neighboring towns and villages; the earl of Peterborough's home near Northampton; Lord Aston's residence at Standen, Hertfordshire; and "many other Papists houses," in some of which large quantities of weapons and gunpowder were reportedly found. Had it not been for the militia, a similar fate would have befallen Hatfield House, the splendid mansion of the earl of Salisbury. A story in the London *Gazette* dated 16 December frankly admitted that the arson, plundering, and demolition of Catholic residences and chapels had spread throughout England. Hysterical reports that Catholics were massacring Protestants in Ireland were numerous. Throughout much of England—especially in Buckinghamshire, Northamptonshire, Leicestershire, and Staffordshire—fears were widespread, particularly after mid-December, that Catholics and disbanded Irish soldiers intended to slit the throats of Protestants. "In very many townes throughout the Nation," noted Morrice, "they staid up all night upon the Watch, and the Countrey came crouding in, and sent all the Horsemen and Armed foot men they could raise &c in to them." Magistrates—Delamere and Whitley among them—confiscated weapons from the Catholics. At Carlisle the citizens stayed up one night fearing that the garrison itself would massacre them. Not surprisingly, many terrified Catholics fled from their homes.[105]

Catholics and orthodox clergy alike were victims of mob violence in Scotland: assaults on the clergy in the southwest were probably the work of Covenanters, but the mob that invaded Holyrood, desecrating royal tombs, ransacking the chapel, and ousting the Jesuits from their nearby seminary, was undoubtedly as diverse in its makeup as its English counterparts. This was notably so after the royalist troops defending Holyrood had killed approximately a dozen demonstrators and wounded three times that many. "Hitherto the Students and Apprentices had made up the Bulk of the Rioters; but now the Inhabitants in general ran to their Arms, and the malcontent Leaders came out into the Streets, publicly espous'd the

Quarrel, and offer'd their Service, which was gladly accepted." By the time the mob had triumphed, several soldiers had been killed, the Jesuits' residence had been destroyed, and the homes of several Catholics had been plundered.[106]

Apart from Speke's claim, there is no evidence that prominent dissidents were responsible for inciting this orgy of anti-Catholic destruction. Unlike the popular agitation in London in 1668, which was largely the work of apprentices,[107] the mobs of 1688 were apparently more diverse. To the extent, however, that militant nonconformists and radical printers and publishers had long maintained a drumbeat of antipapal criticism, they were at least partly responsible for the violence. No direct blame can attach to William, whose anti-French policy depended on alliances with Catholic states such as Spain, and who was exonerated by Speke of complicity in the "Third Declaration" in 1709. Yet the prince probably benefited by the agitation, since the need to halt the spreading disorder presumably encouraged Whigs and Tories to reach early accommodation on a revolutionary settlement.[108] Indeed, the positive reception accorded James on 16 December by Londoners following his capture by Kentish fishermen probably stemmed from a desire to quell the disorders.

James' cause was undermined by widespread hostility toward him at home, the initially cautious reaction to William in England and Scotland notwithstanding. Some of the hostility was rooted in long-standing radical criticism of the Stuart regime. Those on whom the king relied were frankly worried about the simmering discontent among the masses. In October, for instance, the duke of Norfolk kept part of the militia in a state of readiness to prevent "ill-affected" people from joining the enemy, and on 2 November he cautioned Middleton not to fire the beacons in the event of William's invasion until the lords lieutenant and the gentry were "in a posture to gouvern the rabble"; the latter, the duke observed, "are so unsteady, & in some parts so ill affected that it might as well guide them where wee would not have them go, as shew them where they should."[109] Another royalist warned that the king could not rely on Devon or most of Cornwall, and after William had landed the earl of Bath, writing from Plymouth, informed Middleton that the militia was unreliable. The duke of Beaufort feared for the safety of Bristol "considering the universall disaffection of the next County," and Sir John Reresby complained that royalists were in "a bad Condition" in Yorkshire. Indeed, observed John Evelyn in early October, "the universall discontent, brought people to so desperate a passe as with uttmost expressions even passionately seeme to long for & desire the landing of that Prince, whom they looked on as their deliverer from popish Tyrannie." [110]

Their warnings proved to be correct, although many reacted cautiously to the prince. William received a warm welcome in Exeter, where many commoners flocked to his banner and others supplied him with information about royalist activity. At Reading more people apparently prayed for the success of the "Rebels" than for James, and most of the residents of Nottingham and York rejoiced when the earls of Devonshire and Danby respectively took control of their towns for William. Although it would be foolhardy to deny the centrality of William and, in Evelyn's exaggerated words, "all the eminent mobility & persons of quality throout England" in accomplishing the revolution, their task was considerably eased both by the popular hostility toward James and by the endemic anti-Catholicism, both of which had been nurtured in part by the radicals. That William was aware of this is revealed in his reliance not only on Burnet, the moderate Whig, but also on Ferguson, a notorious radical, as his primary clerical spokesmen in the weeks following the invasion. Sword in hand, Ferguson had helped set the tone by preaching to a Presbyterian congregation in Exeter on the theme, "Who will rise up for me against evildoers?" Moderates such as the earls of Clarendon and Aberdeen were understandably troubled by the fact that radicals such as Ferguson and Wildman were "in the Prince's Train." Carstares, the prince's chaplain, was there too, providing advice and spiritual sustenance. [111] If the revolution cannot be depicted as an uprising of the masses against their social betters, neither can it be properly understood without according due importance to the role of radicals, whose principles and deep-seated hostility to James sustained the exile movement and fanned popular hostility at home. Radicals such as Ferguson and Wildman participated in the invading force and contributed to the propaganda effort that aided William's success.

For the moment at least, William's triumph was a source of joy for the radicals. As far away as Jamaica, exiled Monmouth rebels exulted at the news: "[We rejoiced] when we that were in captivity heard of this glorious Revolution, that the captive Leader [James] was gone into captivity, and King William settled in the throne of the king-dom." No one more effectively expressed radical sentiments in the first blush of success than Matthew Meade, who, on 31 January, preached on the theme of providence in the Merchants' Lecture (Broad Street, London) and to his former congregation at Stepney. His reference to the story of Abimelech in Judges 9 had unmistak-able parallels to the reign of James II, including the duke's alleged murder of his brother: "He had not reigned above three *years*, but the same hands that Crowned him, sought to Depose him. It should seem he was a cruel man, and had a hand in his Brethrens Blood, to make his own way to the Throne; and therefore the righteous God would not suffer him to inioy it long." Indeed, England's plight had been desperate, its rights, property, and religion endangered, "all things being fitted to let in Popery upon [its people] like a Flood." So bigoted was James, thundered Meade, that he had hazarded three kingdoms in his quest to impose Catholicism, the "poisonous Prin-ciples" of which were disseminated by priests and Jesuits with the aid of corrupt judges and Catholic justices of the peace. To this vin-tage anti-Catholicism Meade added an indictment of James for main-taining a standing army replete with popish officers and for remod-eling the charters. Like Isaac, Britain had been "laid upon the Altar, and bound with the Knife at the Throat," only to be delivered at the crucial moment by providence. Meade undoubtedly voiced the feel-ings of the radical community in January 1689 when he epitomized the revolution as a triune blessing: "the Throne emptyed of Popery; the Nation delivered from Slavery; the People of God in possession of their Liberty."[112]

Epilogue

"For Our People, & for the Cities of Our God"

Neither the radical threat to the Stuart regime nor the radical impact on the revolution of 1688–89 should be underestimated. In the space of 28 years radical elements participated in seven insurrections, the first six of which they indeed mounted: the 1661 Venner uprising, the 1663 northern revolt, the 1666 Galloway insurrection, the 1679 Bothwell Bridge uprising, the Argyll and Monmouth rebellions in 1685, and the revolution of 1688–89. An eighth revolt, which the government only narrowly averted, was planned by radicals for Dublin and Ulster in early 1663, and other uprisings were seriously considered. The most militant radicals also posed an ongoing threat to the government by their endorsement of assassination as a legitimate political tool. Although only one prominent official, the archbishop of St. Andrews, was in fact assassinated, at least two other significant attempts were made, an earlier one on the archbishop and another on the duke of Ormond. By his own admission, Thomas Blood nearly murdered Charles at Battersea in 1670, and the Rye House plotters, however inept they seem in retrospect, laid plans to kill both Charles and James. Covenanters periodically attacked royalist troops in Scotland, killing several and wounding many, and the Cameron-Cargill faction in Scotland loudly denounced the legitimacy of the Stuart government and demanded its overthrow. The radical movement in general, particularly its more extreme elements, clearly posed a continuing threat to the regime that could not be ignored.

The radical challenge drew strength in part from the fact that dissidents could be found in all three kingdoms as well as in exile centers in the Netherlands, Switzerland, and (in the 1680s) several

German states. Never, though, did the radicals mount the much-discussed simultaneous insurrection in all three realms. English dissidents did nothing of consequence to support the major Covenanter rebellions in 1666 and 1679, and not until 1685 was military activity undertaken in Scotland and England at approximately the same time. Ireland never became the scene of a radical uprising, though the north in particular was a convenient refuge for Scottish fugitives; security considerations, which involved Protestant militants as well as Catholics, tied up both money and troops in Ireland throughout the period. In addition to supporting the cause of the Netherlands in the Second Dutch War and Prince William's expedition in 1688, the exile community provided weapons, ammunition, printing presses for radical books, and sanctuary for the dissidents. Moreover, the hospitality provided for the radicals in the Netherlands was a constant irritant in Anglo-Dutch diplomatic relations and eventually contributed to James II's suspicion of William's motives.

The only significant break in radical militancy throughout the period occurred in the aftermath of attempts to assassinate Charles and Ormond in 1670 and of Blood's theft of the crown jewels the following year—schemes that suggest radical disillusionment with the more ambitious general insurrections. Between 1672 and 1678 the radicals were generally quiet, thanks to the implementation of religious toleration in England. Radical activity during the Third Dutch War was confined to espionage intended to force England to withdraw from the fighting. These endeavors involved relatively few dissidents. Militancy revived in the late 1670s in Scotland and England primarily from religious considerations, notably mounting fear of Catholicism and heightened resentment, especially in Scotland, toward the policy of religious repression.

Religious issues were fundamental to the radical cause. Toleration for Protestant nonconformists was the most crucial single issue; a policy that permanently granted such freedom would have substantially reduced the radical threat to the government. Fears of religious repression were intensified by a growing paranoia toward Catholicism, especially from the late 1670s onward. As Jonathan Scott has argued, the Popish Plot cannot simply be dismissed as an outbreak of mass hysteria or a tale of credulity and folly. On the contrary, it was, as he notes, characterized by a systematic and "pitiless determination and a cold-blooded cruelty." Colored by the memory of the Marian persecutions and played out against a background of aggressive Catholicism on the Continent, including the growing repression of Huguenots in France, the Popish Plot culminated a hatred and fear of Catholics that extended from the Smithfield burnings through the papal bull *Regnans in excelsis*, the Gunpowder Plot, the purported plotting in 1640 and 1641, and the tales of Titus Oates and Israel Tong.[1]

As in the early 1640s, many feared that the court or its supporters were determined to quash the prosecution of Catholic conspirators: "Some are very much concerned to bury the Plott," observed Roger Morrice, "that so there might be no outcry against Popery." Shaftesbury and his associates in turn were quick to exploit fears of popish conspirators for their own ends; in the judgment of Edmund Everard, a radical who turned informer, the "popish plott was made a Shasberian Engine to prepare for a more reall one, & to keep the nation in agitation, in pannik & Jelousies." Although the ensuing Whig plotting was real enough, the aim was not simply to agitate the nation but to prevent the accession of James, a man later adjudged by radicals to be, in the words of Nathaniel Hooke, Monmouth's chaplain, "a bloudy Romanist, Ignis & ferrum, a deceiver, usurper, an Invader." Blatant attempts to manipulate anti-Catholic concerns do not detract from the fact that antipapist sentiment was both widespread and a matter of deep conviction. Perhaps no more eloquent testimony of this exists than the confession of the Monmouth rebel John Coad, a carpenter from Stoford, Somerset: "After the death of King Charles II and the advance of the Duke of Yorke to the Crowne, Popery and arbitrary government did more visibly appear in continuall and unwearyed plotting and contriving to weaken the Protestant party, which gave great cause of feare of the subversion of our Religion and Liberties, from which we had great hopes of deliverance by the Duke of Monmouth's appearance." William Speck has underscored the importance of "paranoia about popery" in alienating James' subjects and contributing to his overthrow. The bitter anti-Catholic demonstrations that occurred in 1688 gave special urgency to the widespread rumors of Catholic activity, including stories of Catholic arson in Doncaster, Huddersfield, and Penistone. "Religion," concluded Speck, "was thus at the heart of the Revolution," as indeed it was at the core of the radical movement.[2]

The Stuart regime recognized the importance of religious issues for the radicals, as reflected in their oft-repeated and not always unwarranted accusation that conventicles were nurseries of sedition. Most illegal services were undoubtedly harmless, apart from inculcating the notion that under certain conditions disobedience to state laws was not only permissible but obligatory for true believers. The significance of encouraging citizens to evaluate government edicts with a view to disobeying those not in accord with scriptural principles must be recognized. Without such a mind-set on the part of dissenters, efforts to obtain widespread acquiescence for James' ouster and acceptance of William and Mary as lawful sovereigns would have been more difficult. But conventicles were also associated with militant activity, one of the more obvious examples being Thomas Venner's use of a Fifth Monarchist congregation to launch his revolt. Conventicles played a major role in the origins of the two Covenanter rebellions, and the wider specter of meetings in the hills and fields attended by huge congregations of armed and sometimes violent worshipers was unsettling in Scotland and Northumberland, and to a lesser degree in Somerset and Wiltshire. Conventicles were probably a key recruiting ground for the abortive Dublin rebellion and the 1663 northern insurrection, and we know that those who planned a general uprising in 1682 and 1683 hoped to enlist men from dissenting congregations. Nonconformist churches in the Netherlands provided a convenient setting in which exiles could keep abreast of schemes directed against the Stuart regime and raise money for the purchase of arms and ammunition to be shipped to militants in the British Isles. Victorian efforts to depict nonconformists as peaceful men and women interested exclusively in the pursuit of godly worship and pure lives must be substantially altered as we recognize how deeply some dissenters opposed the Stuart regime, even to the point of endorsing violence. Restoration nonconformity was much more complex than we have recognized, encompassing a range of political views as diverse as (though not coextensive with) the religious tenets dissenters espoused.

The compass of religious views represented in the radical community was broad, including not only all major varieties of nonconformity but also the Church of England and possibly atheism (allegedly Robert West was an atheist). Most of the leading radical ministers in England—John Owen, Matthew Meade, Stephen Lobb, George Griffith, Jeremiah Marsden, Edward Richardson— were Congregationalists, whereas their Scottish and Irish counterparts, such as Andrew McCormack, John Crookshanks, William Veitch, Donald Cargill, and Richard Cameron, were Presbyterians. Paul Hobson and Henry Danvers were Baptist lay preachers. Common concerns were often more important than differences of polity; for example, after the Presbyterian Robert Ferguson came to England, he became Owen's assistant. Among the laity Lord Russell and James Holloway were Anglicans; Thomas Blood, Gilby Carr, Stephen College, Margaret Hamilton, Isabel Alison, and Edward Warren Presbyterians; Nathaniel Wade, John Breman, Slingsby Bethel, and Richard Salway Congregationalists; and Thomas Walcott, Richard Rumbold, Ann Smith, and Francis Smith Baptists. Other radicals had less precise religious preferences. Edmund Cole attended both Presbyterian and Anglican services, as did William Hone, who also worshiped with the Congregationalists. Thomas Lee "incline[d] to be an Independent & was allwayes unsetled in [his] Religion," whereas Josiah Keeling tasted "of all sects, at Last [becoming] an Anabaptist." Christopher Battiscombe, who died professing to be "a true Protestant," manifested a dislike of denominational labels, an aversion shared by such moderate nonconformists as Richard Baxter and John Bunyan.[3] Other nonconformists considered themselves religious but apparently knew little about controversial tenets; the men John Manley rallied at Lyme Regis in November 1688 to support William were described as "Stout sturdy Fellows, Pretending to Fight for Religion, and not one to Twentye Knowes what it is."[4]

The Friends, whose sense of identity as a spiritual group was intense, were radical with respect to their religious and social views, but very few were willing to fight against the government. As late as 1685 a handful of Quakers followed Monmouth's banner, though few of them actually bore arms. Chief among the militant Friends was Thomas Plaice, whom the duke commissioned to recruit the independent-minded Clubmen of Somerset by citing the twin dangers of popery and foreign (French and Irish) invasion; Plaice himself did not fight, but Quakers such as Francis Scott and John Hellier did.[5] Fear of the Quakers had contributed in a very modest way to the restoration of traditional government in 1660, but in the ensuing decades their activities, though hardly predominantly quiescent, had at best only a minimal impact on the revolution of 1688–89.

For many in the radical community, religious issues were paramount, but a host of secular concerns were espoused as well. Chief among these was the demand by some radicals for the restoration of republican government. On no issue were dissidents more divided than the question of what kind of government they wanted, but two overriding considerations prevented this division from destroying the radical movement: common hostility to arbitrary rule, a charge frequently lodged against the Stuart regime and a rallying cry often linked to antipapist sentiments; and a shared concern to achieve religious toleration for all Protestants. Prior to 1688 the radicals' best opportunity for success, the Monmouth rebellion, would probably have preserved monarchical rule, but on a firm Protestant foundation, with a greater role for Parliament and freedom of religion for Protestants. The 1666 and 1679 rebellions had expressed more limited aims, focusing primarily on the Covenanters' religious program— liberty of conscience for Protestants, the establishment of a presbyterian polity in the state church (to be governed by the General Assembly), the restoration of deprived ministers, and the termination of episcopacy and fines for recusancy. The Covenanters also articulated secular concerns, particularly hostility to taxes and billeting. English dissidents were likewise angry about taxes, including the excise, customs, and poll and hearth levies, but they manifested concern as well about the negative impact of religious repression on trade. The Vennerites had demanded reform of the debt laws, the abolition of primogeniture and of capital punishment for theft, and the introduction of democratic government in towns and guilds. By the late 1670s the most important constitutional issue involved the lengthy, ostensibly illegal prorogation of the Cavalier Parliament and resulting demands for new elections, though this was soon overshadowed by the exclusion crisis and the ensuing controversy over the charters. Throughout the period discontent with the moral standards of the court in particular and the nation in general remained high. Radicals were angered as well by the regime's normally amicable relations with France. Many of these issues, of course, had religious overtones that stoked the radicals' hostility.

Local concerns also were important for the radicals, as the recent studies of Gary De Krey and Jonathan Barry have demonstrated for London and Bristol respectively. The radical tradition in London, which considerably antedated the Whig movement, was rooted not only in religious concerns and national political issues but in a quest to establish corporation government according to democratic principles. Moreover, the Francophile policies of Charles II deeply troubled many Londoners, not least the people alarmed by the Popish Plot and the merchants and artisans worried about French competition. Against this background the Whigs tried unsuccessfully to maintain control over the corporation, only to be frustrated in 1682 by a Tory lord mayor and a Tory-dominated aldermanic bench that engineered the election of Tory sheriffs, thus depriving the Whigs of control over the juries. Whigs were soon purged from key positions in the City, and magistrates stepped up the prosecution of nonconformists. The resentment and fear these actions engendered were key factors in motivating such City radicals as Richard Goodenough, Henry Cornish, Slingsby Bethel, Sir Patience Ward, Francis Jenks, and a host of lesser dissidents. The politics of finance was also involved, particularly with respect to the East India Company, whose receipt of a new charter from the king in 1683 enabled Sir Josiah Child and his Tory allies to prevent Thomas Papillon and his associates from broadening the base of investors. The threat to Whigs and nonconformists in London drove many of them to embrace radical principles. Yet by 1688 many of the City Tories had themselves been victimized by James' ill-conceived attempt to win Whig and nonconformist support by restoring the City's original charter. These developments help to explain why London accepted William in 1688.[6]

In Bristol too the Popish Plot aggravated existing tensions. Prior to 1678 the prosecution of dissent had been sporadic, with most members of the corporation unwilling to sanction serious repression, particularly in light of the substantial number of nonconformists, some of whom were politically and financially prominent. This began to change as Whig-Tory divisions emerged and Tories launched a campaign to exclude Whigs from the corporation. The Tories' hostility to nonconformity led to increased persecution, directed now against all dissenters rather than primarily the more radical Baptists and Quakers. The twin threat to civic participation and the right to worship in nonconformist congregations prompted Bristol dissidents such as Nathaniel Wade and John Rumsey to engage in the Rye House plotting. As in London, James' attempts to return Catholics to public life alienated many Tories, though he won the support of Wade and some of his Whig allies. However, many Whigs and Tories, like their counterparts in London, found common cause in supporting William.[7]

The case for the importance of the radicals throughout the period from the restoration to the revolution rests in part on the precautions and countermeasures that they forced the government to employ. Until recently, modern historians have tended to ignore the radical threat during the Restoration era, but this was a luxury the governments of Charles and James could not afford.[8] The task of monitoring the radicals was daunting, particularly for the secretaries of state who ultimately had to evaluate the unstanchable stream of reports from agents, magistrates, and well-wishers in the three kingdoms and abroad. Included in their information were hard evidence of dissident activity, hearsay accounts of suspicious doings, lists of conventicle preachers and sometimes those who heard them, intercepted correspondence, allegations of treasonable speech, registers of known dissidents in the capital and elsewhere, reports of the arrival and departure of suspicious persons at the ports, and word of the movements of known or suspected radicals on the Continent. At virtually any moment the government had the names of hundreds of persons before it in current and recent reports; the register of the Scottish Privy Council alone contains the names of scores of Covenanters known to have attended unlawful assemblies or performed such illegal acts as physically assaulting orthodox clergy. Some of the information came from paid agents and informers, both at home and abroad, whose livelihood depended on their ability to provide data. While this created obvious temptations to fabricate allegations, future employment must have been contingent on the general reliability of their information. For the most part, the government behaved circumspectly in evaluating the reports; wholesale arrests were generally limited to periods of genuine danger, such as that following the disclosure of the Rye House plotting, but even then most dissidents were not detained for long periods unless the state had evidence of illegal activity against them.

The radical threat forced a government habitually short of funds to expend money for intelligence services. Between midsummer 1660 and October 1662, Joseph Williamson theoretically disbursed £1,480 to Sir Edward Nicholas' agents, but £500 of this was in fact a personal loan to the secretary. Clearly in its early years Charles' government had little appreciation of the need for systematic intelligence services, but the incessant plotting finally changed that attitude. In the latter part of the reign the senior secretary of state received £3,000 per annum for intelligence, the junior secretary £2,000.[9]

The seriousness with which the government came to regard the radical threat is also apparent with respect to the forces employed to quash the insurrections. To suppress the Vennerites the authorities called out the trained bands, elements of the Life Guards, more than a troop of horse, and 200 men from the duke of York's regiment of foot; another 700 cavalry arrived after the rebels had been crushed.[10] Lieutenant-General Thomas Dalziel, who had principal responsibility for repressing the Galloway rebels, commanded 7 troops of horse (c. 560 men) and up to 3,000 foot soldiers, and hundreds of others were raised by Scottish nobles.[11] Monmouth suppressed the Bothwell Bridge insurgents with an army of 10,000 and had reserves that could be called up from northern England and Ireland.[12] Although authorities in England and Scotland were always able to muster enough men to quash the uprisings, the cumulative effect was eventually felt at the time of the Argyll and Monmouth invasions, neither of which was as insignificant as many historians have assumed. The earl of Feversham and John Churchill were justifiably disappointed with the fighting capabilities of the militia and therefore preferred to rely on the army. Viscount Cholmondeley was frankly embarrassed when only 8 men mustered for his troop. By the time Monmouth had been defeated, James had 15,700 men in arms, a number to which he would add another 4,000 by year's end in recognition, at least in part, of the fact that the militia alone was incapable of ensuring the kingdom's security.[13] The radical threat therefore played a role in the decision to increase the size of the regular army—a determination that eventually contributed to the political difficulties that helped topple James.

The Stuart regime crushed every insurrection apart from that of 1688, but it failed in its efforts to stamp out radical ideas, whether by censorship or by imprisoning or even executing dissidents. Indeed, far from repressing radical ideology, the government's policy of executing dissident leaders and plotters in 1683–85 had the effect of expanding the pantheon of martyrs that included the executed regicides. The revolution of 1688–89 enshrined Russell, Essex, and Sidney as the preeminent trinity in this pantheon, the heroes of a Whig martyrology that would be revered for two centuries.

Radicals contributed to the revolution of 1688–89 at all levels. John Locke, Robert Ferguson, and John Owen helped shape the intellectual framework; Mordaunt first urged William to mount an invasion; Ferguson and other Scottish exiles drafted the original version of William's Scottish declaration; radicals participated in William's expedition and others rallied to his banner after he reached England; Carstares was at William's side, offering advice and spiritual counsel; and Ferguson tried to inspire nonconformists. As Lois Schwoerer has demonstrated, radical Whigs did much to shape the revolutionary settlement, and nonconformist ministers such as Matthew Meade helped win popular support for the new regime. The revolution of 1688–89 essentially achieved the program of the Monmouth rebellion—a limited monarchy, toleration for Protestants, an enhanced role for Parliament in the political process, and a Protestant succession. The radicals, of course, had no single set of goals and thus could not have unambiguously triumphed under any circumstances, but these elements were surely at the heart of any radical agenda. The revolution of 1688–89 thus fulfilled many of the radicals' hopes, and in that sense Monmouth, Argyll, and their associates prepared the way for William even as the core of their program became that of the political nation.

William himself recognized the contribution of the radicals to his success, as many of his appointments indicate. Memberships in the English Privy Council went to Delamere, Grey, Macclesfield, Mordaunt, Sidney, Trenchard, Stamford, and Richard Hampden; Hume and Melville became Privy Councillors in Scotland. Sidney and Trenchard would serve as secretaries of state in England, as would Melville and Johnston in Scotland. Hume received the lord chancellorship in Scotland and Aaron Smith the position of treasury solicitor in England. Three radicals—Capel, Hume, and Sidney— were soon elevated to the peerage, while others, including Delamere, Grey, Melville, and Mordaunt, were promoted within the peerage. The king knighted Pilkington, Trenchard, and Wildman. Among the treasury commissioners were Delamere, Grey, Mordaunt, Sidney, and Richard Hampden. Brandon, Delamere, Macclesfield, Mordaunt, Sidney, and Stamford received lord lieutenancies, and at least a dozen radicals (including Brandon) served as deputy lieutenants. Radicals won seats in both the Convention and the Parliament of 1690, and at the local level a number of radicals were elected mayors (including Pilkington in London) or aldermen. Numerous others served as justices of the peace. Three Rye House plotters—Zachary Bourne, John Gibbons, and Thomas Lee—obtained appointments as messengers of the Chamber, while their colleague John Row became king's waiter at the port of Bristol. To Wildman went the postmastership-general, in which capacity he dispensed patronage; several radicals—Macclesfield, Brandon, Papillon, Ferguson, Cragg, John Speke, and Argyll's son (the tenth earl)—sought his assistance, mostly to find positions for friends, as did Sir Henry Capel on behalf of one of his brother's former retainers. William had apparently tired of Ferguson, who received only an appointment as housekeeper at the Excise Office. (See below, Appendixes B and C.)[14]

Perhaps the most eloquent testimony to the lasting influence of the radicals is the enshrinement of many of their principles, in whole or in part, in the 1689 Declaration of Rights and the Act of Toleration. The radicals were not, of course, the sole proponents of these principles, virtually all of which were deeply rooted in the past, but the radicals' level of commitment and activism were surely crucial in the adoption of these principles in the revolutionary settlement. The northern rebels of 1663 and the Galloway insurgents of 1666 had protested against all taxes, but Monmouth's declaration (written by Ferguson) manifested more sophistication in complaining about the illegal collection of the customs and part of the excise: "Nor hath he [James] been more tender in trampling upon the *Lauws* which Concerne our *Properties*, seeing by two Proclamations, whereof the one requires the collecting of the *Customes*, & the other the continuing that part of the *Excise* which was to expiere with the late Kings death, he hath violently & against all the Lauws of the Land broken in upon our *Estates*." The fourth article in the Declaration of Rights addressed this by prohibiting financial levies without parliamentary approval. The eloquent protests in the Argyll and Monmouth manifestos against the inhumane treatment of dissidents found expression in the tenth article, which prohibited cruel and unusual punishment—a principle reiterated in the American Bill of Rights. Both of the 1685 declarations also condemned fraudulent electoral returns, a point dealt with in the eighth article, which insisted on free parliamentary elections. Moreover, the sixth article of the Declaration of Rights prohibited a standing army without Parliament's authorization, echoing the Argyll and Monmouth manifestos. Although the duke's demand that parliaments be chosen annually was too extreme for the Convention, the latter nevertheless, in the thirteenth article, endorsed the principle that parliaments should meet often (a provision clearly implying frequent elections). The twelfth article's condemnation of fines and forfeitures imposed prior to conviction probably reflects the concern in Monmouth's declaration about the imposition of "Exorbitant fines for *no Crimes*." [15]

Thus in varying degrees six of the thirteen articles in the Declaration of Rights embrace principles previously enunciated in radical manifestos. No less indebted to a radical precursor is the Declaration's opening statement: "Whereas the late King James the second, by the Assistance of divers Evil Counsellors, Judges, and Ministers, imployed by him did endeavour to Subvert and extirpate the Protestant Religion, and the Lawes and Liberties of this Kingdome." These lines echo the words of Ferguson in Monmouth's manifesto, which condemned James for wanting "to see the *reformed Protestant Religion*, and such as profess it *extirpated*; popish *superstition* and

Idolatry established; . . . the *Liberties* & rights of the *English people* subverted." The Act of Toleration, which bestowed religious freedom on all Trinitarian Protestants, crowned the radicals' achievement. Monmouth and Ferguson's call for judicial tenure based on good behavior was endorsed by William, though absolute security of tenure was assured only in 1701 by the Act of Settlement. Although the revolutionary settlement of 1689 did not legally embody freedom of the press, the ability of radical authors and printers to withstand censorship for three decades had established that principle in practice. Henceforth censorship was imposed only in the private realm—by authors on themselves or by publishers with an eye to sales.[16]

Far from being insignificant, the radicals had a major impact on the Restoration era, the revolutionary settlement of 1689, and subsequent generations.[17] If in some respects the events leading up to and including the Restoration can be called an "experience of defeat," the revolution of 1688–89 was an important, albeit partial, victory for the radicals. This was, of course, more so for the constitutional monarchists than for the republicans. Had Algernon Sidney lived, he would have been disappointed to see not only the triumph of William, whom he detested, but the defeat of English and Dutch republicanism. Nor did the revolution, despite its unmistakable roots in the revolutionary upheavals of the 1640s and 1650s, mark the triumph of the people as envisioned by such midcentury radicals as John Lilburne, William Walwyn, and Gerrard Winstanley. Indisputably a compromise, the 1689 settlement incorporated tenets dear to the radicals—the rule of law in conjunction with the ascendancy of statute over monarch, parliamentary control of taxation, free elections, restrictions on a standing army, judicial restraints, toleration for Trinitarian Protestants—into the political fabric of England and Scotland. Above all, the events of 1688–89 manifested the fundamental radical conviction that a government which has exceeded the limits imposed on it—and is therefore deemed to be tyrannical—can legitimately be resisted. In practice, the revolutionaries embraced the theory of resistance championed by John Calvin and John Owen, which required the leadership of nobility or magistrates, rather than the more radical view of John Knox, John Locke, and Robert Ferguson, who proclaimed the people's right and duty to rebel. Many of those who helped to topple James were, of course, reluctant to admit that they were resisting at all, but their actions clearly indicated otherwise. Nor were all revolutionaries reluctant. The declaration of 25 December 1688 from the nobility, gentry, and commoners of Nottingham contained a ringing endorsement of the right to resist: "We count it rebellion to resist a King that governs by law, but he was always counted a tyrant that made his will the law; to resist such a one we justly esteem it no rebellion, but a necessary defence." [18]

The framers of the Declaration of Rights praised William for "delivering this Kingdom from Popery and Arbitrary Power," deliverance demanded by the radicals for nearly three decades. His triumph, to which they contributed and for which they were rewarded, was far more than a palace coup d'état. By affirming the supremacy of statute, circumscribing government with law, and providing modest religious toleration, the revolution made possible the economic growth that set the stage for Britain to become the home of the Industrial Revolution and the greatest imperial power in history.

REFERENCE MATTER

Appendix A

John Nisbet's Letter of 20 March 1683 to Alexander Gordon of Earlston

Sir; On Saturday last I had the occasion of seeing a letter from you . . . at the reading of which I was not a little troubled, considering my full resolutions [to come to the Netherlands[1]] signified to you in my last; for effectuating of which I had spoke for passage . . . : and that very week I was set upon by that gentleman with whom I stay [Matthew Meade], and Jo. Johnstoun [Murray] with some others to stay but a month, and if that did not accomplish somewhat in hand to help trading ("the design of rising in arms"), then I should be no longer detained. After I was prevailed to retract so far, I ordered Jo. [Murray] . . . to give you an ample account of matters ("a letter under the metaphor of marriage, and that by the marriage, he understood a rising designed there"); and withal, Jo. was desired by our friends from Scotland [Cochrane, Baillie of Jerviswood, and the Campbells of Cessnock] to stand here in my place, the like engagements of secrecy, &c. being taken ("an ingagement of secrecy and some queries to try if they agreed in principles"), and thereupon I ordered him to shew you the grounds of my staying [in England], and to desire if you inclined to cross the water to come this way. . . .

In my last, or it precedent to it, I shewed you that trading was very low here, and many breaking, which has made the merchants . . . to think that desperate diseases must have desperate cures ("their people, viz. the dissenters were breaking in their stocks by excommunications and other courses, and therefore they were resolving upon desperate courses which was rising in arms"); and while they must have some stock, it will be better to venture out,

than to keep shop and sit still till all be gone, and then they shall not
be able to act, but let all go: which resolution I thought a thing not
to confide in, seeing the most of them are fire-side merchants, and
love not to venture where storms are any thing apparent ("some that
lived at their ease and quiet would not venture to rise, when they
saw much danger"). But about my departing they shewed the model
of affairs in such order ("they had shewn to Jo[hn] N[isbet] a model
how they would go about their affairs in order to their rising"), that
I see venture they must, and venture they will; whereupon [Nisbet]
first demanded how our trade would be carried on. Answer, they
knew well what goods had proven most prejudicial to the trade, and
therefore they thought to insist upon negatives ("they resolved to
agree in what they would put down, which he thinks was the whole
government, civil and ecclesiastic, but that they would not determine
positively what they would set up"), in which whatever I proposed
is assented to, as I find ("he [Nisbet] had stated the grounds of the
quarrel relative to the present government, and . . . they had assented
to it"); and thus they thought best to still some criticks in the trade
("the Scotch fanaticks"): and by this means first to endeavour the
dispatching the old rotten stuff ("the dispatching of the sectaries or
the present government, but rather thinks it was the last") before
they order what to bring home next. This looked somewhat strange
to me, but when I consider all circumstances, I think they for themselves do best in it: for our merchants I made account only to have
had some stock for to set the broken ones up again ("the Scotch
fanaticks to be helped by contributions"), and so bid them here farewell, and they to try their way, and we ours ("the English was for
rising in arms, but the Scotch fanaticks were for delaying some
time"); since they think fit that some of these whom we have
found . . . treacherous dealers ("both the sectaries and the present
government who had formerly broke their government") in our
trade, consulted, and accordingly have done: whereupon I fear, or
rather hope that our merchants [dissenters], though broke, will
rather desire to live a while longer as they are [i.e., under persecu-
tion], than join with such, &c. to advance the trade; unless surer
grounds of their fidelity be gotten, than is, or can be expected. . . .
They think it is almost at a point to set forward ("their being ready

for rendezvous"), if they had their factors home, who are gone to try how the country will like such goods, as they are for, or against the making sale of ("emissaries ... sent out both in Scotland and England from London to try the people's inclinations to a rising and to incite them to it"). Friends, I mean merchants ("the meetings of the fanaticks in Scotland" [i.e., the United Societies]), wrote to me, that after I had spoken to you [Earlston], possibly you might come this way [return to Scotland], the better thereby to advise them what to do in this case, for I have signified somewhat of it to them, but not so far as this; because I thought to have seen you long ere this time. But I hope you will not misconstruct of my staying, seeing in it I designed nothing but advancement of our trade ("the carrying on of the rising"); but once this week these factors sent for will be here, and then matters will in instanti, either off or on, break, or go through ("when these factors [agents] came in they expected money for buying of arms and then they would instantly have risen"). Wherefore in reference to friends, I desire you will advise me what to do, if you cannot, or think it not convenient to come here; if you do, let a letter precede, and if any strange thing ("the insurrection") fall out this week or the next, I will again post it towards you. . . . The Whiggs are very low as well in city as in the suburbs, all meetings [conventicles] being every Sunday beset with constables to keep them out, and what they get is stolen, either at evening or morning. . . . My endeared respects to yourself and B[rackel] with the young men [Renwick, Flint, and Boyd] arrived [at Groningen]. . . . Matters ("the present intended rebellion") are full as high as I tell you. Farewell. . . .[2]

Appendix B

Select List of Offices and Honors Received by Radicals in the Aftermath of the Revolution of 1688–1689

Dates in parentheses indicate the time at which incumbency commenced. The list does not include all offices and honors.

Archer, Robert: waiter at the quays for oranges and coarse goods (1689).

Atherton, John: landwaiter at the customs house, London (1689).

Barnardiston, Sir Samuel: commissioner for assessment, Suffolk (1689); deputy lieutenant, Suffolk (1689?); commissioner for public accounts (1690).

Bethel, Slingsby: member, committee to draft the regulations for the Bank of England.

Birch, Colonel John: commissioner for assessment, Herefordshire and Lancashire (1689); high steward, Herefordshire (1689); deputy lieutenant, Herefordshire and London (1689); auditor of the excise (1689); commissioner for disbandment of the New Raised Forces (1689); commissioner for assessment, London (1690).

Blackader, William: royal physician (c. 1689).

Blaney, Robert: commissioner for the office of clerk of the pipe (1689); commissioner for traitors' estates (by 1692).

Bourne, Zachary: messenger of the Chamber (by 1690).

Breman, John: major, volunteer regiment of horse, London (1689); deputy governor, Isle of Wight (1692).

Campbell, Sir George, of Cesnock: justice clerk (1690); commissioner of excise, Ayr (1690); member, Court of Justiciary (1690); commissioner of the Exchequer (1690); sheriff of Ayr and bailie (alderman) of Kyle Stewart (1690).

Capel, Sir Henry: Treasury commissioner (1689); Lord Capel of Tewkesbury (1692); lord justice of Ireland (1693); lord deputy of Ireland (1695).

Carstares, William: moderator, General Assembly, Church of Scotland (1689); principal, Edinburgh University (1703).

Clayton, Sir Robert: commissioner for assessment, Buckinghamshire, London, and Surrey (1689); justice of the peace, Surrey (1689); deputy lieutenant, London (1689); commissioner of customs (1689); colonel, Orange Regiment (1689); farmer of the post fines (by 1690); commissioner for assessment, Norfolk (1690); president, Honorable Artillery Company (1690).

Colleton, Sir Peter: commissioner for public accounts (by 1691).

Courtenay, Sir William: commissioner for militia, Devon (1688); commissioner for assessment, Devon (1689); deputy lieutenant, Devon (1689).

Delamere, Henry Booth, Lord: Privy Councillor (1689); Treasury commissioner (1689); chancellor of the Exchequer (1689); lord lieutenant, Cheshire (1689); *custos rotulorum*, Cheshire (1689); earl of Warrington (1690); mayor, Chester (1691).

Denholm, William, of Westshiels: officer of the Mint (1689); commissioner of excise, Lanark (1690); master of the Mint (1690).

Drake, Sir Francis: justice of the peace, Devon (1689); commissioner for assessment, Devon (1689).

Ferguson, Robert: housekeeper of the Excise Office (1689).

Forrester, William: commissioner for assessment, Salop (1689); justice of the peace, Salop (1689?); clerk of the Green Cloth (1689); knighted (1689); commissioner for assessment, Gloucestershire (1690); justice of the peace, Westminster (1691).

Gerard of Brandon, Charles Lord: commissioner for assessment, Cheshire, Lancashire, and Middlesex (1689); deputy lieutenant, Wales (1689); lord lieutenant, Lancashire (1689); *custos rotulorum*, Cheshire (1690); major-general, regiment of horse (1694); lord lieutenant, North Wales (1696).

Gibbons, John: messenger of the Chamber (by 1690).

Grey, Ford Lord: Privy Councillor (1695); earl of Tankerville (1695); commissioner of trade (1696); first commissioner of the Treasury (1699); lord justice (1700); lord privy seal (1700).

Hampden, John: declined ambassadorship to Spain.

Hampden, Richard: Privy Councillor (1689); lord of the Treasury (1689); chancellor of the Exchequer (1690).

Hume, Sir Patrick, of Polwarth: Privy Councillor (1689); Lord Polwarth (1689); sheriff-principal, Berwickshire (1692); lord of the Court of Session (1693); lord chancellor (1696); earl of Marchmont (1697).

Ingoldsby, Sir Henry: adjutant general.

Johnston, James: envoy to Brandenburg (1689); joint secretary of state, Scotland (1692).

Lee, Thomas: messenger of the Chamber (by 1690).

Lovelace, John Baron: captain of the gentlemen pensioners (1689); chief justice, royal parks and forests (1690).

Macclesfield, Charles Gerard, earl of: lord president of the Council of the Marches of Wales (1689); Privy Councillor (1689); lord lieutenant of Gloucester, Hereford, Monmouth, and North and South Wales (1689).

Melville, George Lord: secretary of state (1689); high commissioner (1690); earl of Melville (1690); lord privy seal (1691); president, Privy Council (1696).

Mildmay, Henry: commissioner for assessment, Essex (1689).

Monro, Alexander, of Bearcrofts: clerk to the Court Martial (Council of War) (1689); commissary of Stirling (1690); commissioner to Parliament (1690).

Montgomery, David, of Langshaw: lord of the Session (1690).

Mordaunt, Charles, Viscount: Privy Councillor (1689); gentleman of the bedchamber (1689); lord lieutenant of Northamptonshire (1689); first lord of the Treasury (1689); earl of Monmouth (1689); water-bailiff of the Severn (1689).

Murray, James, of Philiphaugh: sheriff of Selkirk (1689); lord of the Session (1689); Lord Philiphaugh (1689).

Norton, Edward: captain in Viscount Mordaunt's regiment of foot (November 1688); major of marines (1691).

Papillon, Thomas: alderman, London (1689); commissioner for assessment, London and Dover (1689); justice of the peace, Kent (1689); deputy lieutenant, London and Kent (1689); commissioner for lodemanage court, Cinque Ports (1689); commissioner of victualling for the navy (1689).

Pilkington, Sir Thomas: commissioner for assessment, London and Northamptonshire (1689); alderman, London (1689); deputy lieutenant, London (1689); lord mayor, London (1689); colonel, White Regiment (1689); justice of the peace, Kent (1689); commissioner for preventing the export of wool (1689); knighted (1689).

Prideaux, Edmund: commissioner for assessment, Devon and Middlesex (1689); justice of the peace, Devon and Middlesex (1689).

Row, John: king's waiter, port of Bristol (1689).

Sidney, Sir Henry: Treasury commissioner (1689); Baron Milton and Viscount Sidney of Sheppey (1689); Privy Councillor (1689); gentleman of the bedchamber (1689); colonel, king's regiment of footguards (1689); lord lieutenant of Kent (1689); lord justice, Ireland (1690); secretary of state (1690); lord lieutenant of Ireland (1692); master-general of the Ordnance (1693); earl of Romney (1694); lord justice, England (1697).

Smith, Aaron: treasury solicitor (1689).

Speke, George: deputy lieutenant, Somerset (1689).

Speke, John: commissioner for assessment, Somerset (1689); deputy lieutenant, Somerset (1691).

Stamford, Thomas Grey, earl of: high steward, Leicester (1689); Privy Councillor (1694); commissioner of Greenwich Hospital (1695); commissioner of trade and foreign plantations (1695); lord lieutenant of Devon (1696); *custos rotulorum*, Leicestershire (1696); chancellor, Duchy of Lancaster (1697).

Stewart, James: lord advocate, Scotland.

Tarras, Walter Scott, earl of: commissioner of supply, Roxburgh (1691); captain of militia horse (1691).

Trenchard, John: receiver-general, Somerset, Dorset, and Bristol (November 1688); comptroller of customs, Bristol (November 1688); chief justice, Chester and Flint (1689); king's serjeant-at-law (1689); chief justice, Denbigh and Montgomery (1689); chief justice of the Council in the Marches of Wales (1689); knighted (1689); recorder, Taunton (1690); secretary of state (1692); Privy Councillor (1693).

Waller, Sir William: prizer and butler of wines (1689); gentleman of the privy chamber (1689).

Ward, Sir Patience: deputy lieutenant, London (1689); commissioner for assessment, London and the West Riding (1689); commissioner for preventing the export of wool (1689); commissioner of customs (1689); colonel, Blue Regiment (1689).

Whitley, Colonel Roger: gentleman of the privy chamber (1689); justice of the peace, Flint (1689); commissioner for assessment, Cheshire, Chester, and Flint (1689); *custos rotulorum*, Flint (1689); commissioner for the disbandment of the New Raised Forces (1689); mayor, Chester (1692).

Wildman, John: commissioner for assessment, Westminster, Berkshire, and Wiltshire (1689); postmaster-general (1689); alderman, London (1690); justice of the peace and deputy lieutenant, Middlesex (1692); knighted (1692).

Yonge, Sir Walter: deputy lieutenant, Devon (June 1688); commissioner for assessment, Devon (1689); commissioner of customs (1694).

Appendix C

Select List of Radicals Elected to the Convention and the Parliament of 1690

Barnardiston, Sir Samuel: 1690 (Suffolk)
Birch, Colonel John: 1689, 1690 (Weobley, Herefordshire)
Clayton, Sir Robert: 1689 (London); 1690 (Bletchingley, Surrey)
Drake, Sir Francis: 1689, 1690 (Tavistock, Devon)
Forrester, William: 1689, 1690 (Much Wenlock, Salop)
Gerard of Brandon, Charles Lord: 1689, 1690 (Lancashire)
Hampden, John: 1689 (Wendover, Buckinghamshire)
Hampden, Richard: 1689 (Wendover, Buckinghamshire); 1690 (Buckinghamshire)
Manley, Major John: 1689 (Bridport, Dorset)
Mildmay, Colonel Henry: 1689, 1690 (Essex)
Papillon, Thomas: 1689, 1690 (Dover)
Pilkington, Sir Thomas: 1689 (London)
Speke, John: 1690 (Taunton, Somerset)
Thompson, William: 1689, 1690 (Scarborough, Yorkshire)
Trenchard, Sir John: 1689 (Thetford, Norfolk); 1690 (Poole, Dorset)
Ward, Sir Patience: 1689 (London)
Whitley, Colonel Roger: 1689 (Chester)
Wildman, John: 1689 (Great Bedwin, Wiltshire)
Yonge, Sir Walter: 1689 (Ashburton, Devon); 1690 (Honiton, Devon)

Notes

See the bibliography for full information on primary sources cited below only by title or author and title.

Abbreviations

Add. MSS	Additional Manuscripts, British Library
Ashcraft	Richard Ashcraft, *Revolutionary Politics & Locke's "Two Treatises of Government"* (Princeton, N.J.: Princeton University Press, 1986)
Baxter	Stephen B. Baxter, *William III and the Defense of European Liberty 1650–1702* (New York: Harcourt, Brace & World, 1966)
BDBR	*Biographical Dictionary of British Radicals in the Seventeenth Century*, ed. Richard L. Greaves and Robert Zaller, 3 vols. (Brighton: Harvester, 1982–84)
BL	British Library
Blackader Mem.	Andrew Crichton, *Memoirs of Rev. John Blackader*
Bodl.	Bodleian Library, Oxford
Burnet	*Burnet's History of My Own Time*
CCRO	Chester City Record Office
ChRO	Cheshire Record Office
CJ	*Journals of the House of Commons 1547–1714*
Clifton, *LPR*	Robin Clifton, *The Last Popular Rebellion: The Western Rising of 1685* (London: Temple Smith; New York: St. Martin's, 1984)
Cokayne	G. E. C[okayne], *Complete Peerage of England, Scotland, Ireland, Great Britain and the United Kingdom*, rev. V. Gibbs, et al., 14 vols. (1910ff.)
Copies	*Copies of the Informations and Original Papers Relating to the Proof of the Horrid Conspiracy Against the Late King, His Present Majesty, and the Government*

Cowan	Ian B. Cowan, *The Scottish Covenanters 1660–1688* (London: Victor Gollancz, 1976)
Crookshank	William Crookshank, *The History of the State and Sufferings of the Church of Scotland, from the Restoration to the Revolution*, 2nd ed., 2 vols. (Edinburgh: Andrew Stevenson, 1751)
CSPD	*Calendar of State Papers, Domestic Series, 1603–1714*
CumRO (C)	Cumbria Record Office, Carlisle
CumRO (K)	Cumbria Record Office, Kendal
D'Avaux	Jean Mesmes, Count D'Avaux, *The Negotiations of Count D'Avaux, Ambassador from the Most Christian King, Lewis XIV, to the States General of the United Provinces*, vol. 3
DWL	Dr. Williams's Library, London
Earle, *MR*	Peter Earle, *Monmouth's Rebels: The Road to Sedgemoor 1685* (New York: St. Martin's, 1977)
Erskine	*Journal of the Hon. John Erskine of Carnock. 1683–1687*
ESRO	East Sussex Record Office
EUL	Edinburgh University Library
Evelyn	*The Diary of John Evelyn*
Ferguson, "Rye House"	Robert Ferguson, "Concerning the Rye House Business"
Foxcroft	H. C. Foxcroft, *The Life and Letters of Sir George Savile, Bart., First Marquis of Halifax*, 2 vols. (London: Longmans, Green, 1898)
Greaves, *DUFE*	Richard L. Greaves, *Deliver Us from Evil: The Radical Underground in Britain, 1660–1663* (New York: Oxford University Press, 1986)
Greaves, *EUHF*	Richard L. Greaves, *Enemies Under His Feet: Radicals and Nonconformists in Britain, 1664–1677* (Stanford, Calif.: Stanford University Press, 1990)
Grey, *Debates*	*Debates of the House of Commons from the Year 1667 to the Year 1694*, ed. Anchitel Grey
Grey, *SH*	Ford Lord Grey, *The Secret History of the Rye-House Plot: and of Monmouth's Rebellion*
Haley	K. H. D. Haley, *The First Earl of Shaftesbury* (Oxford: Clarendon, 1968)
HLRO	House of Lords Record Office
HMC	*Historical Manuscripts Commission, Reports*
Holloway	*The Free and Voluntary Confession and Narrative of James Holloway*
Hume	Sir Patrick Hume, "A Narrative of the Events Which Occurred in the Enterprize of the Earl of Argyle in 1685"

JRL	John Rylands Library, Manchester
Lacey	Douglas R. Lacey, *Dissent and Parliamentary Politics in England, 1661–1689* (New Brunswick, N.J.: Rutgers University Press, 1969)
Last Speech	*The Last Speech & Behaviour of William Late Lord Russel. . . . Also the Last Speeches, Behaviour, and Prayers of Capt. Thomas Walcot, John Rouse Gent. & William Hone Joyner*
Letters to Aberdeen	*Letters, Illustrative of Public Affairs in Scotland, Addressed by Contemporary Statesmen to George, Earl of Aberdeen, Lord High Chancellor of Scotland. MDCLXXXI–MDCLXXXIV*
Luttrell	Narcissus Luttrell, *A Brief Historical Relation of State Affairs from September 1678 to April 1714*
Mackenzie	[George Mackenzie], *A True and Plain Account of the Discoveries Made in Scotland, of the Late Conspiracies Against His Majesty and the Government*
Milne	D. J. Milne, "The Rye House Plot with Special Reference to Its Place in the Exclusion Contest and Its Consequences till 1685" (Ph.D. thesis, University of London, 1949)
Morrice	Roger Morrice, "Entr'ing Book, Being an Historical Register of Occurrences from April, Anno 1677 to April 1691," DWL
MVB	*Memoirs of Mr. William Veitch, and George Brysson, Written by Themselves*
NLS	National Library of Scotland, Edinburgh
NUL	Nottingham University Library
Plomer, *DBP*	Henry R. Plomer, *A Dictionary of the Booksellers and Printers Who Were at Work in England, Scotland and Ireland from 1641 to 1667* (London: Blades, East and Blades for the Bibliographical Society, 1907)
Plomer, *DPB*	Henry R. Plomer, *A Dictionary of the Printers and Booksellers Who Were at Work in England, Scotland and Ireland from 1668 to 1725* (Oxford: Oxford University Press for the Bibliographical Society, 1922)
Prideaux	*Letters of Humphrey Prideaux Sometime Dean of Norwich to John Ellis Sometime Under-Secretary of State 1674–1722*
Prinsterer	G. Groen Van Prinsterer, ed., *Archives ou Correspondance Inédite de la Maison D'Orange-Nassau*, 2nd ser., bk. 5, 1650–88
PRO SP	Public Record Office (London), State Papers
Reresby	*Memoirs of Sir John Reresby*

RPCS   *The Register of the Privy Council of Scotland*
Shields   Michael Shields, *Faithful Contendings Displayed* (Glasgow: John Bryce, 1780)
Sprat   Thomas Sprat, *A True Account and Declaration of the Horrid Conspiracy*
SRO   Somerset Record Office
ST   W. Cobbett and T. B. Howell, eds., *Cobbett's Complete Collection of State Trials and Proceedings*
Ure   James Ure, "Narrative of the Rising Suppressed at Bothwell Bridge," in *MVB*
Welwood   James Welwood, *Memoirs of the Most Material Transactions in England*

Preface

1. Gary S. De Krey, "The London Whigs and the Exclusion Crisis Reconsidered," in *The First Modern Society*, ed. Lee Beier, David Cannadine, and James Rosenheim (Cambridge, Eng.: Cambridge University Press, 1989), p. 480.

2. Tim Harris, *London Crowds in the Reign of Charles II: Propaganda and Politics from the Restoration Until the Exclusion Crisis* (Cambridge, Eng.: Cambridge University Press, 1987), p. 208; Maurice Ashley, *John Wildman: Plotter and Postmaster* (New Haven, Connecticut: Yale University Press, 1947), p. 239.

3. *BDBR*, s.v. "Howard, William."

4. *Copies*, p. 129; PRO SP 29/428/4.

Prologue

1. Caroline M. Hibbard, *Charles I and the Popish Plot* (Chapel Hill: University of North Carolina Press, 1983), p. 238.

2. Bedloe, *A Narrative and Impartial Discovery of the Horrid Popish Plot*, p. 2.

3. See, e.g., JRL Legh of Lyme MSS (newsletters to Richard Legh, 9 and 14 Jan. 1686; 6 Nov. 1686; 10 Feb. 1687); CumRO (C) MSS DRC/5/4, fols. 254r, 261r–v; HMC 29, *Portland*, 3: 392, 396, 405.

4. Cf. [Holles], *Some Considerations upon the Question, Whether the Parliament Is Dissolved*.

5. Lacey, pp. 86–92.

6. John Miller, *Popery and Politics in England 1660–1688* (Cambridge, Eng.: At the University Press, 1973), pp. 147–53.

7. Jenks, *Speech Spoken in a Common Hall*; Marvell, *Account of the Growth of Popery*, p. 8.

Chapter 1

1. John Kenyon, *The Popish Plot* (Harmondsworth: Penguin, 1974), chap. 3.

2. *CSPD 1679–80*, p. 597; PRO SP 29/414/80; Kenyon, *Popish Plot*, p. 62.

3. Greaves, *DUFE*, pp. 116–24, 180–96; Kenyon, *Popish Plot*, p. 62.

4. Greaves, *DUFE*, pp. 176, 178, 186, 194–95; Greaves, *EUHF*, pp. 34, 222; PRO SP 29/420/36, 137; 29/421/7, 30; 29/437/85.1. Smith acquired his sobriquet, which served to distinguish him from other printers with the same surname, from his public sign, the Elephant and Castle.

5. PRO SP 29/420/122; 29/421/7, 30.

6. PRO SP 29/406/182; 44/334, p. 573; Kenyon, *Popish Plot*, pp. 76–80; *CSPD 1678*, pp. 425–28, 431–34, 444; BL Add. MSS 25,124, fol. 158r; Burnet, 2: 156–61; *ST*, 6: 1501–12.

7. London *Gazette*, 1368 (26–30 Dec. 1678); BL Add. MSS 21,484, fols. 42r–43r.

8. PRO SP 29/415/19; 29/420/36; Greaves, *DUFE*, pp. 67, 69, 96, 203.

9. CumRO (C) MSS D/LONS/L 13/1/20; CCRO MSS ML 4/495, 498, 508. There had been earlier crackdowns on Catholics, as in February 1675. CCRO MSS ML 4/491.

10. *CJ*, 9: 605; Grey, *Debates*, 7: 140–41, 147; *CSPD 1679–80*, p. 195.

11. SRO MSS DD/SF 3109; PRO SP 29/406/243; 29/411/16, 22; Jonathan Scott, "England's Troubles: Exhuming the Popish Plot," in *The Politics of Religion in Restoration England*, ed. Tim Harris, Paul Seaward, and Mark Goldie (Oxford: Basil Blackwell, 1990), pp. 112–14. As in previous decades, spurious reports of mysterious troop movements heightened tension. PRO SP 29/408/4; 44/29, p. 303; 44/52, p. 120.

12. BL Add. MSS 61,903, p. 121; PRO SP 29/411/155; Kenyon, *Popish Plot*, pp. 214–15.

13. A Mr. Swithwick subsequently testified that Dangerfield had told Mr. Hill he had been "planted" in prison by Shaftesbury, Buckingham, and Oates "to insinuat himselfe into & to bee acquainted with the Catholiques, to Collour or to strengthen his Evidence." According to Swithwick, Hill claimed Shaftesbury and his colleagues aimed not only at the Catholic lords in the Tower but also at Charles and James. BL Add. MSS 62,453, fol. 2r. This testimony, dated 2 April 1680, is probably fictitious, but it reflects at least the growing perception of how closely Shaftesbury worked with Oates. Mansell had been cashiered from his post in Ireland in February 1678 after speaking disparagingly of Viscount Granard. PRO SP 63/338/142.

14. PRO SP 29/411/72; 29/412/57; London *Gazette*, 1456b (30 Oct.–3 Nov. 1679); 1457 (3–6 Nov. 1679); 1458 (6–10 Nov. 1679); *Domestick Intelligence*, 37 (11 Nov. 1679); Kenyon, *Popish Plot*, pp. 216–17.

15. *Protestant (Domestick) Intelligence*, 58 (23 Jan. 1680); 59 (27 Jan. 1680); 60 (30 Jan. 1680); 62 (6 Feb. 1680); 63 (10 Feb. 1680); 64 (13 Feb. 1680); 66 (20 Feb. 1680); 68 (27 Feb. 1680); 70 (5 Mar. 1680); 72 (12 Mar. 1680); 77 (30 Mar. 1680); PRO SP 29/414/23, 26; *CSPD 1679–80*, pp. 561, 568; BL Add. MSS 4107, fol. 32r.

16. Cambridge University, Pepys Library, Misc. MSS 7, p. 490. See Grey, *Debates*, 7: 358–59, for Peyton's position.

17. *HMC* 36, *Ormonde*, 4: 571; Luttrell, 1: 29; London *Gazette*, 1476 (8–12 Jan. 1680); 1515 (24–27 May 1680); *CSPD 1679–80*, p. 370.

18. PRO SP 29/414/80; *CSPD 1679–80*, p. 426.

19. London *Gazette*, 1467 (8–11 Dec. 1669); 1468 (11–15 Dec. 1679); *CSPD 1679–80*, pp. 309, 364; CumRO (C) MSS D/LONS/L13/1/18.

20. Kenyon, *Popish Plot*, p. 211; London *Gazette*, 1488 (19–23 Feb. 1680); 1501 (5–8 Apr. 1680); *CSPD 1679–80*, pp. 566–67.

21. London *Gazette*, 1482 (29 Jan.–2 Feb. 1680); 1486 (12–16 Feb. 1680); 1498 (25–29 Mar. 1680); 1502 (8–12 Apr. 1680); PRO SP 44/62, p. 87; Jonathan Barry, "The Politics of Religion in Restoration Bristol," in *Politics of Religion in Restoration England*, ed. Harris, Seaward, and Goldie, pp. 172–73.

22. BL Add. MSS 25,124, fol. 71r; PRO SP 29/417/116. Rumsey's father had reputedly been "a most notorious Incendiary in the late Troubles" as well as a surveyor of royalist estates. Scott, a double agent during the Third Dutch War and then an agent for the French, was also linked to Francis Jenks, a radical City linen draper, and John Wildman. Sources cited above; Bodl. Rawlinson MSS A175, fols. 164r, 193r–v; Ashcraft, pp. 130–32, 248.

23. Prinsterer, pp. 418, 421, 424, 459; Haley, pp. 586–87.

24. PRO SP 29/401/108, 227, 228, 229; 29/404/89, 89.1, 237; 29/405/97, 126; 29/406/102; 44/28, fol. 210r; 44/334, pp. 420, 538–39; *CSPD 1678*, p. 377. One of the more outspoken attacks on prelates was directed against the bishop of Norwich: "a viper not fitt to live, You Limbe of Satan, . . . you biteing Satan." PRO SP 29/405/123.1; cf. 123.2.

25. PRO SP 29/413/31; 29/414/159; 29/415/42; 44/54, p. 65; 44/334, pp. 569, 577, 586; *CSPD 1679–80*, p. 411; BL Add. MSS 25,124, fol. 199r; London *Gazette*, 1488 (19–23 Feb. 1680); 1498 (25–29 Mar. 1680); 1511 (10–13 May 1680). Cf. BL Egerton MSS 2985, fol. 216r–v.

26. *ST*, 7: 1111–30; *CSPD 1679–80*, p. 536.

27. *Weekly Pacquet of Advice from Rome*, 3: 312, 319, 376, 391–92; 4: 232.

28. PRO SP 29/407/79; 44/54, p. 12; 44/334, pp. 554–55, 596; London *Gazette*, 1368 (26–30 Dec. 1678).

29. London *Gazette*, 1432 (7–11 Aug. 1679); BL Add. MSS 25,125, fol. 81r; *CSPD 1679–80*, p. 269.

30. PRO SP 29/401/237; 29/402/143; 29/403/27, 27.1; 29/405/77, 122; 29/406/37; 44/334, pp. 457, 514, 522, 525.

31. [Blount], *Appeal from the Country to the City*, pp. 5–6, 9, 24–25.

32. PRO SP 29/417/12; *ST*, 7: 925–32; *CSPD 1679–80*, p. 397; *Protestant (Domestick) Intelligence*, 65 (17 Feb. 1680); BL Add. MSS 37,981, fol. 6r; *BDBR*, s.v. "Harris, Benjamin." No issues of the *Domestick Intelligence* were published between 16 April and 28 December 1680.

33. *Domestick Intelligence*, 43 (2 Dec. 1679); London *Gazette*, 1469 (15–18 Dec. 1679); PRO SP 44/28, fol. 216r; London *Gazette*, 1467 (8–11 Dec. 1679); 1486 (12–16 Feb. 1680). Turner was fined 100 marks in the King's Bench. London *Gazette*, 1522 (17–21 June 1680).

34. Greaves, *DUFE*, p. 213; *ST*, 7: 257; PRO SP 29/401/225; 29/404/236 (cf. 29/442/49).

35. London *Gazette*, 1469 (15–18 Dec. 1679); *Domestick Intelligence*, 48 (19 Dec. 1679); 49 (23 Dec. 1679); 54 (9 Jan. 1680); *ST*, 7: 931–37, 956–57; PRO SP 29/417/209 (which probably should be dated 1680, not 1681).

36. *ST*, 7: 959–60; London *Gazette*, 1484 (5–9 Feb. 1680); *Protestant (Domestick) Intelligence*, 63 (10 Feb. 1680).

37. *CSPD 1679–80*, p. 472; London *Gazette*, 1509 (3–6 May 1680); Pepys, *Diary*, 3: 238.

38. BL Add. MSS 32,095, fol. 198r–v, 200r; Add. MSS 28,094, fols. 71r–72r; Morrice, 1: 470.

39. PRO SP 29/433/8, p. 6; 44/56, p. 22; London *Gazette*, 1848 (2–6 Aug. 1683).

40. PRO SP 29/413/85, 118, 119; 29/414/55.1; 44/62, pp. 25–26; *CSPD 1679–80*, pp. 466–67, 594; BL Add. MSS 62,453, fol. 99r. In September 1680, Smith and Curtis were indicted for printing an act of the London Common Council with animadversions, but the jury returned a verdict of *ignoramus*. Morrice, 1: 265–66.

41. The bill was rejected in the Lords by a vote of 63 to 30. For a list of the 30, see BL Add. MSS 51,319, fol. 55r.

42. When Smith was charged in January 1681 with publishing Shaftesbury's speech, the jury returned a verdict of *ignoramus*. *True Protestant Mercury*, 8 (18–22 Jan. 1681).

43. [Cooper, earl of Shaftesbury], *Speech Lately Made by a Noble Peer*.

44. BL Add. MSS 37,981, fols. 2r–3r, 4r; PRO SP 29/415/8.

45. PRO SP 29/417/50.

46. BL Add. MSS 47,021, fol. 273v; *CJ*, 9: 709–10.

47. J. R. Jones, *The First Whigs: The Politics of the Exclusion Crisis 1678–1683* (London: Oxford University Press, 1961), pp. 156–81.

48. *HMC* 32, *Thirteenth Report*, Appendix 6, pp. 141–45; Kenyon, *Popish Plot*, p. 61; Haley, pp. 630, 647.

49. *ST*, 8: 330–96; *Tryal and Condemnation of Fitz-Harris*. Cf. *True Protestant Mercury*, 19 (26 Feb.–2 Mar. 1681).

50. PRO SP 29/416/37; *CSPD 1680–81*, p. 313; Fitzharris, *Confession*, esp. p. 5; Grey, *Debates*, 9: 180–83.

51. *True Protestant Mercury*, 51 (29 June–2 May 1681); *CSPD 1680–81*, pp. 340–41.

52. Kenyon, *Popish Plot*, p. 234; PRO SP 29/416/7, 51; 29/417/30; *CSPD 1680–81*, p. 655; *True Protestant Mercury*, 142 (13–17 May 1682).

53. *CSPD 1680–81*, p. 310. Concern was also aroused by the unauthorized publication of *Arraignment and Plea of Fitz-Harris*, an account of Edward Fitzharris' case. *Impartial London Intelligence*, 4 (11–14 Apr. 1681). The fear of popery remained strong even among many loyalists. In July 1681, Westmorland magistrates, for instance, petitioned Charles: "Secure us against Popery and all other our Just Fears." CumRO (C) MSS D/LONS/L13/1/21.

54. PRO SP 29/417/46; *CSPD 1680–81*, pp. 606–7.

55. PRO SP 29/416/81, 115, 116.

56. PRO SP 29/417/62.

57. PRO SP 29/415/149; 29/417/89, 194; 44/54, pp. 74, 75; *BDBR*, s.v. "Howard, William." Because of his accusations, the informer Charles Rea was assaulted by Howard on 6 April. Rea claimed that in 1679 Player and Clayton had offered him £11,000 to assassinate James and more than £1,000 to kill the duchess of Portsmouth. PRO SP 29/415/118, 119, 150.

58. *CSPD 1680–81*, pp. 317, 321–22, 331, 656; PRO SP 29/416/13, 18, 19, 21; Luttrell, 1: 100–101, 102.

59. BL Add. MSS 35,104, fols. 19v–21v, 28r; 37,981, fols. 57r–v, 59r–60r, 63r, 65r–66r, 67r–v, 69r–70r, 71r, 73r, 86r–v.

60. *ST*, 8: 562–67; PRO SP 44/62, pp. 198–99, 222, 224, 225; Morrice, 1: 309, 310.

61. *ST*, 8: 720, 722.

62. At one point College claimed he had been summoned by Monmouth to the Sun tavern, and at another by Grey to the Crown tavern. *ST*, 8: 624, 719.

63. *ST*, 8: 624, 719.

64. This was Haines' claim; there is a warrant dated 20 June 1681. PRO SP 44/54, p. 76.

65. *ST*, 8: 592, 597, 605, 606, 608, 609, 612–13, 624, 678, 707. Cf. PRO SP 29/416/172; 29/427/10 (against James), 81.

66. *ST*, 8: 613–14, 624, 625, 649, 664, 692, 720. College was also accused of having a carbine, a coat of mail, and a helmet. The total value of the armor, alleged the attorney general, was double the worth of his estate. *ST*, 8: 589. Cf. PRO SP 29/416/70. William Smith, Thomas Blood's confederate in the rescue of Mason and the attempted assassination of Ormond, also went to Oxford conspicuously armed. PRO SP 29/416/70; cf. 29/416/132.

67. *ST*, 8: 595–96, 599–600, 602, 603, 611, 613, 614, 617, 625, 664; PRO SP 29/416/112.

68. In *Raree Show: or the True Protestant Procession* (1681), a Tory author retorted by castigating the Whigs as "the Club of a Pack of ingenious friends / that made *Charles* a Scotch Pedlar in the *Rare show*."

69. *ST*, 8: 679–80.

70. PRO SP 44/54, p. 77; Prideaux, pp. 139–40; Kenyon, *Popish Plot*, p. 125; *ST*, 8: 551–52; Morrice, 1: 311–12. A second warrant for College's arrest was issued on 4 July. PRO SP 44/54, p. 80. In July 1682 Smith was convicted of providing College with seditious material to help him in his trial; he fled to avoid punishment. *True Protestant Mercury*, 156 (1–5 July 1682); London *Gazette*, 1735 (3–6 July 1682).

71. *ST*, 8: 600, 607, 615.

72. *ST*, 8: 593, 609; *CSPD 1680–81*, p. 378.

73. *ST*, 8: 659; PRO SP 29/416/132; Morrice, 1: 312. Bolron subsequently deposed that in return for this support he was to swear to whatever Edmund Everard dictated. He also asserted that Smith, Everard, John Ayloffe, and the Scotsman Robert Murray (who passed information to Shaftesbury) told him they had acted at the earl's behest. Everard dictated the mostly false charges Bolron made against Justice Edmund Warcup and John "Narrative" Smith. PRO SP 29/416/132.

74. *ST*, 8: 638, 652–53, 655–56.

75. *ST*, 8: 710, 716–24; PRO SP 29/416/133; 44/54, p. 94; BL Add. MSS 61,903, p. 173; BL Sloan MSS 1008, fol. 317r; Morrice, 1: 313.

76. PRO SP 29/416/112. This is a different version of College's statement from the one recorded in the *State Trials*. See also PRO SP 44/62, pp. 268–70. A royalist satirized College's death in *Whiggs Lamentation, for the Death of Colledge*. In contrast, dissidents in Chichester angrily proclaimed that "his blood would certainly Cry for Vengence." PRO SP 29/416/164; cf. 29/418/16.

77. PRO SP 29/416/39; 44/54, pp. 77, 81, 82; 63/341, p. 97; *CSPD 1680–81*, pp. 340–41, 534; Morrice, 1: 309.

78. PRO SP 29/416/23, 39, 50, 98; 44/54, pp. 89–90; *CSPD 1680–81*, p. 406; London *Gazette*, 1645 (22–25 Aug. 1681). Cf. PRO SP 44/54, p. 95.

79. *ST*, 8: 794–95; Morrice, 1: 312.

80. PRO SP 29/416/7, 125, 179; 29/417/24; 29/424/5. Cf. PRO SP 29/418/169; 44/62, p. 261; *CSPD 1682*, pp. 140–41.

81. PRO SP 29/415/207; 29/417/24, 104, 115. Cf. PRO SP 29/417/62. In October, Francisco de Faria of London deposed that the previous July Everard had tried to persuade him to accuse Warcup of suborning him. Everard, however, had switched sides in June, and if the substance of de Faria's charge

is true, Everard's attempt had to have been made no later than the beginning of that month. PRO SP 29/417/33. As late as October 1682 de Faria and Mowbray accused Lewis of claiming that the king was trying to discredit the Whigs, in part by planting the Association in Shaftesbury's closet. With his friends John Zeal and Bolron, Lewis allegedly charged Jenkins and the Council with soliciting them to accuse Shaftesbury and the Presbyterians of plotting. De Faria and Mowbray also asserted that Lewis had asked them to accuse "Narrative" Smith and Macnamara of trying to suborn them to testify about a Presbyterian plot. PRO SP 29/421/15. Less than two months before the disclosure of the Rye House Plot, Lewis informed on Henry Manfield (a younger son of Lady Ancrum's) who had allegedly hoped to manufacture a new popish plot by planting incriminating papers on Walter Jones, a supposed priest. PRO SP 29/424/3, 3.1, 5.

82. PRO SP 44/62, p. 259.

83. PRO SP 29/416/177; 29/418/128; *ST*, 8: 635–36; BL Add. MSS 41,819, fol. 58v; 41,820, fol. 86r.

84. PRO SP 29/416/179, 180.

85. On 4 October, Wilson reportedly conferred with Lady Howard of Escrick about suborning witnesses against her husband. PRO SP 29/417/15.

86. *CSPD 1680–81*, p. 502; PRO SP 29/418/127.

87. PRO SP 29/417/129.

88. BL Stowe MSS 186, fols. 48r–49v.

89. PRO SP 29/416/155; 29/417/19; BL Stowe MSS 186, fols. 48r, 49r–50r.

90. PRO SP 29/416/150, 162; 29/417/2, 19, 32, 35, 36; 29/427/22; 44/54, p. 104; BL Stowe MSS 186, fols. 43v, 48r, 49r; *CSPD 1680–81*, pp. 509–10; *True Protestant Mercury*, 94 (26–30 Nov. 1681); London *Gazette*, 1660 (13–17 Oct. 1681); Charles Firth and Godfrey Davies, *The Regimental History of Cromwell's Army*, 2 vols. (Oxford: Clarendon, 1940), 2: 548. Cf. PRO SP 29/421/172. According to Roger L'Estrange, Hartshorne was a forger. PRO SP 29/428/85; cf. 29/430/79.

91. PRO SP 29/417/44, 46; 44/54, p. 77; London *Gazette*, 1661 (17–20 Oct. 1681); *True Protestant Mercury*, 82 (15–19 Oct. 1681); *CSPD 1680–81*, pp. 521, 525, 622.

92. BL Add. MSS 29,577, fol. 401r; *ST*, 8: 781–87, 803; Haley, pp. 677–78. The plan of Association is printed in [L'Estrange], *Brief History of the Times*, pp. 100–106.

93. *ST*, 8: 636–37, 793, 795–96, 798–801, 813–14, 816, 819. Cf. PRO SP 29/417/193, 193.1.

94. *ST*, 8: 821. Among those who provided bail for Shaftesbury was William Lord Russell; Monmouth offered to help. Ford Lord Grey helped to bail Howard of Escrick. Morrice, 1: 318. After the trial John Dubois, one of the jurors, reportedly observed: "[It is] a great greefe to many good people

that it should be Treason to call the King a papist. Why may not a man call a spade a spade?" This suggests that the jurors did not repudiate the views of Charles allegedly held by Shaftesbury. PRO SP 29/417/135.

95. *ST*, 8: 788–91, 800, 815, 826.

96. *True Protestant Mercury*, 93 (23–26 Nov. 1681); *CSPD 1680–81*, p. 611; *Ignoramus-Justice*.

97. PRO SP 29/417/115, 119, 120; *CSPD 1680–81*, p. 591; Prinsterer, p. 537.

98. CCRO MSS QSF/82, fol. 278r.

99. PRO SP 44/62, pp. 141–42; London *Gazette*, 1607 (11–14 Apr. 1681); *Democritus Ridens*, 5 (11 Apr. 1681); 6 (18 Apr. 1681).

100. *Democritus Ridens*, 12 (6 June 1681); cf. 5 (11 Apr. 1681). In February 1681 a London grand jury indicted Thompson and the bookseller Joseph Hindmarsh for publishing *Presbyterian Pater Noster, Creed, and Ten Commandments*, a conservative but sacriligious satire. Note this line: "I believe in *John Calvin, Baxter* and *Jenkins &c.* his dear Sons our Lords, who were Conceived by the *Spirit of Fanaticism*, born of *Schism* and *Faction*, suffer'd under the *Act of Uniformity*, were Silenced, Dead and Buried." PRO SP 44/54, p. 58; *True Protestant Mercury*, 17 (19–23 Feb. 1681); 18 (23–26 Feb. 1681); 19 (26 Feb.–2 Mar. 1681).

101. London *Gazette*, 1608 (14–18 Apr. 1681).

102. Seditious pamphlets circulated in the Netherlands as well. In May 1681, Carr discovered two of them, *Answer to His Majesties Declaration* and *Project for a Successor to the Crown*. He immediately commissioned refutations, which he had printed in Dutch. BL Add. MSS 37,981, fol. 36r.

103. PRO SP 29/415/122. A copy of *Vox Populi, Vox Dei* is bound in BL Egerton MSS 2134, fol. 5r–v. For Bradyll see PRO SP 29/417/152; Plomer, *DBP*, pp. 45–46.

104. *Vox Populi, Fax Populi*, p. 13; *Impartial Protestant Mercury*, 8 (16–19 May 1681); *CSPD 1680–81*, pp. 370–71. In July, John Smith, publisher of *The Current Intelligence*, was indicted for issuing a justification of the Norwich address. *Impartial Protestant Mercury*, 23 (8–12 July 1681).

105. Cf. PRO SP 29/415/165. A broadside printed for Benjamin Harris and also sold by Langley Curtis warned that destruction was imminent unless a political settlement on the succession issue was reached. BL Add. MSS 38,849, fol. 109r–v.

106. *Impartial Protestant Mercury*, 33 (12–16 Aug. 1681); 34 (16–19 Aug. 1681); 44 (20–23 Sept. 1681).

107. *CSPD 1680–81*, pp. 318, 477; PRO SP 44/54, pp. 100, 102; London *Gazette*, 1660 (13–17 Oct. 1681). Cf. PRO SP 29/416/163, 178. Cotton's four writers were Henry Paris, Christopher Fleet, Henry Goodyear, and Thomas Collyns. PRO SP 44/54, p. 103. The other three men who were arrested were Claypoole, Wood, and a Mr. Gravely.

108. *Impartial Protestant Mercury*, 51 (14–18 Oct. 1681); PRO SP 29/417/56 (cf. 28); [Ferguson], *Just and Modest Vindication*, pp. 1, 28, 30. John Locke was erroneously suspected of having written *No Protestant-Plot*. Prideaux, p. 115. Ferguson subsequently admitted having written the work. Bodl. MSS Smith 31, fol. 30r.

109. [Ferguson], *No Protestant-Plot*, pp. 9, 12, 13, 18–19, 21–22, 28–29.

110. The speech was printed by James Astwood, who was also responsible for printing College's *Ra-ree Show* and various issues of *Weekly Pacquet of Advice from Rome*. PRO SP 29/424/147, 151; *CSPD 1683*, 1: 178, 301.

111. PRO SP 29/417/83; London *Gazette*, 1668 (10–14 Nov. 1681); Morrice, 1: 295, 317; *CSPD 1680–81*, pp. 137, 564; *Impartial Protestant Mercury*, 63 (25–29 Nov. 1681); cf. 64 (29 Nov.–2 Dec. 1681).

112. PRO SP 29/417/153.

113. Hunt, Postscript to *Argument for the Bishops Right*, pp. 10–12, 37–38, 42–43, 46, 51–52.

114. [Sadler], *Rights of the Kingdom*, pp. 11ff., 24, 318; PRO SP 29/418/33, 112. L'Estrange suspected that Baldwin was the publisher. *Impartial Protestant Mercury*, 82 (31 Jan.–3 Feb. 1682).

115. PRO SP 29/419/85, 171; 29/423/10, 10.1; Bacon, *Continuation of an Historical Discourse*, p. 307; Corinne Comstock Weston and Janelle Renfrow Greenberg, *Subjects and Sovereigns: The Grand Controversy over Legal Sovereignty in Stuart England* (Cambridge: Cambridge University Press, 1981), p. 66. Cf. Janelle Greenberg, "The Confessor's Laws and the Radical Face of the Ancient Constitution," *English Historical Review*, 104 (July 1989): 622–23.

116. [Whitaker], *Ignoramus Justices*, pp. 11–18; PRO SP 29/418/112; 44/54, pp. 83–84; [Whitaker], *Second Part of the Ignoramus Justices*, pp. 28–30, 33; PRO SP 29/420/157; London *Gazette*, 1669 (30 Oct.–2 Nov. 1682); Morrice, 1: 342.

117. [Ferguson], *Second Part of No Protestant Plot*, pp. 1–2, 4–7, 19.

118. [Johnson], *Julian the Apostate*, pp. v–ix, xxii–xxv, 68–69, 71, 73–75, 77, 82, 92–93. *Julian* sparked interest in the Rotterdam exile community. NLS MSS 500, fol. 27r.

119. NLS MSS 500, fol. 27r; PRO SP 29/422/59; T.S., *Perplex'd Prince*, passim.

120. *Impartial Protestant Mercury*, 81 (27–31 Jan. 1682); 91 (3–7 Mar. 1682); 115 (26–30 May 1682); PRO SP 29/418/88 (*Vox Populi, Vox Dei*); 29/421/221; cf. 29/418/98.

121. PRO SP 29/421/75, 75.2.

122. *CSPD 1682*, pp. 68, 146–47; *True Protestant Mercury*, 129 (29 Mar.–1 Apr. 1682); London *Gazette*, 1709 (3–6 Apr. 1682); Morrice, 1: 327. In

March, Jenkins ordered the customs commissioners to search for subversive books being smuggled into the kingdom. PRO SP 44/66, p. 68.

123. PRO SP 29/419/8, 9; 29/421/118; *True Protestant Mercury*, 142 (13–17 May 1682); Morrice, 1: 341; *CSPD 1682*, p. 211. Baldwin published Ferguson's *Third Part of No Protestant Plot*, and the *Impartial Protestant Mercury*, 75 (6–10 Jan. 1682), assigned him responsibility for the first two parts as well.

124. PRO SP 29/421/118; cf. *CSPD 1682*, p. 533. Eleanor and Francis Smith were fined in April 1683 for continuing to publish radical works. PRO SP 29/423/87. In the spring of 1683 Starkey was in the company of Aaron Smith, Thomas Braddyll, Samuel Harris, and Alexander Dare. PRO SP 29/424/86, 114.

125. PRO SP 29/421/118; 44/68, p. 168; NUL MSS PwV 95, p. 63.

126. NUL MSS PwV 95, p. 63; PRO SP 29/418/34; 29/421/76, 115, 137, 169, 170; 29/424/86, 102, 104. Neither work appears on a list of books Ferguson later admitted writing. Bodl. MSS Smith 31, fol. 30r. Shortly before the disclosure of the Rye House conspiracy in June 1683 a warrant was issued for Ferguson's arrest because of his reputed authorship of unnamed treasonable and scandalous works. PRO SP 44/54, p. 163.

127. PRO SP 29/422/25; Hunt, *Defence of the Charter*, pp. 5–6, 10, 32–34, 45; *CSPD 1683*, 1: 17. For the setting of Hunt's tract in the context of London politics see Gary S. De Krey, "The London Whigs and the Exclusion Crisis Reconsidered," in *The First Modern Society*, ed. Lee Beier, David Cannadine, and James Rosenheim (Cambridge, Eng.: Cambridge University Press, 1989), pp. 472–74.

128. BL Stowe MSS 186, fol. 48r.

129. PRO SP 29/415/189; 29/417/47, 54.1; 29/419/43; 29/425/54; *True Protestant Mercury*, 98 (10–14 Dec. 1681). Cf. PRO SP 29/413/95 concerning an allegation that George Speke, whose brother Hugh would subsequently fan anti-Catholic hostility in the revolution of 1688–89, denounced Charles and James as papists and defended Monmouth as the rightful heir.

130. PRO SP 29/416/38; 29/417/59; 29/421/54.1, 146; 29/429/19.

131. PRO SP 29/416/127; 29/418/16, 19; 29/420/4, 100; 29/422/26, 41, 68, 99, 100, 122; 29/424/148; 29/429/173; 44/68, p. 190; *CSPD 1680–81*, p. 507; *CSPD 1682*, p. 43; *Impartial Protestant Mercury*, 50 (11–14 Oct. 1681); *True Protestant Mercury*, 79 (5–8 Oct. 1681).

132. London *Gazette*, 1690 (26–30 Jan. 1682); PRO SP 29/415/178; 29/422/4, 5, 98; 29/423/91.

133. PRO SP 29/417/54.1; 29/422/5, 98; 29/424/154; 29/425/137, 247; 29/429/173.

134. PRO SP 29/416/92, 102, 123; 29/417/51; 29/419/46; 29/422/99; 29/424/154.

135. PRO SP 29/420/6; 29/421/29, 96; 29/422/180; 29/428/69; BL Stowe MSS 186, fol. 45r. Cf. PRO SP 29/420/15; 29/421/215; 29/429/101, 165, 166, 167.

136. PRO SP 29/416/79; 29/421/112; 29/423/38 (cf. 39); 29/425/70; 29/428/35, 68; *True Protestant Mercury*, 166 (5–9 Aug. 1682); BL Stowe MSS 186, fol. 45v.

137. PRO SP 29/414/22; 29/417/87; London *Gazette*, 1733 (26–29 June 1682); *ST*, 8: 187–298. The victorious candidates in London in 1680 were Henry Cornish and Slingsby Bethel; the latter appointed Richard Goodenough, a Whig attorney formerly tied to William of Orange's agents, as his undersheriff. PRO SP 44/62, p. 66. Secretary Jenkins complained bitterly the following year that of the 49 jurors Goodenough had returned for Middlesex, only two attended the established church; the rest were "desperate Sectaries, most of them Fifth-Monarchy men." PRO SP 44/62, p. 334.

138. PRO SP 29/421/67; *CSPD 1682*, p. 528; London *Gazette*, 1772 (9–13 Nov. 1682).

139. PRO SP 29/423/90, 99; 29/424/9, 34, 34.1, 34.19, 34.20, 34.23, 34.31; 29/437/4; 29/438/9.

140. PRO SP 29/424/62, 103, 133, 145, 145.1, 145.4.

141. Prinsterer, p. 437. Cf. "Theophilus Rationalis," in *Multum in parvo, aut vox veritatis*; Scott, "England's Troubles," pp. 123–25.

Chapter 2

1. *RPCS*, 5: 272–73, 291, 300–301, 516; PRO SP 29/338/141; 29/400/77; 29/407/77; 63/338/158; Greaves, *EUHF*, pp. 90–91.

2. PRO SP 29/401/148, 183, 189; 29/402/73.1; *HMC* 29, *Portland*, 2: 47; *RPCS*, 5: 296–98, 319–27, 345–46, 349–55, 365–67, 369–70, 375–76, 379–81, 389–90, 395–97, 404–11, 413–17, 457, 459, 512, 514–16, 520, 522–23, 533–45, 547–50, 553, 556–57, 559–65, 567, 572, 588–89. Cf. BL Add. MSS 32,095, fols. 176r–177r.

3. PRO SP 29/401/189; 29/402/138; 29/405/211; 29/408/6; 63/338/143; *HMC* 29, *Portland*, 2: 47; *RPCS*, 5: 464–65, 472, 474, 488; 6: 59; BL Add. MSS 23,243, fol. 7r. Cf. Add. MSS 23,242, fol. 1r.

4. *HMC* 29, *Portland*, 2: 45, 48; BL Add. MSS 23,242, fol. 18r; PRO SP 29/403/92; *CSPD 1678*, p. 201; *Blackader Mem.*, p. 223.

5. PRO SP 29/403/192, 243; 29/405/36; BL Add. MSS 23,242, fol. 66r; *CSPD 1678*, pp. 161–62, 185, 312; *RPCS*, 5: 460–61; *Blackader Mem.*, pp. 214–22.

6. *Copies*, p. 173; PRO SP 63/338/131, 132, 134.

7. PRO SP 29/403/15, 243; BL Add. MSS 23,242, fol. 18v; *Blackader Mem.*, pp. 210–13.

8. PRO SP 29/400/36.1; 29/405/227, 250; 29/406/19, 31; *Blackader Mem.*, p. 223. The religious aspect of these outdoor meetings is examined in Leigh

Eric Schmidt, *Holy Fairs: Scottish Communions and American Revivals in the Early Modern Period* (Princeton, N.J.: Princeton University Press, 1989).

9. BL Add. MSS 23,242, fol. 96r; PRO SP 29/406/127, 161, 180, 251; 29/407/105; Cowan, p. 92. Cf. *RPCS*, 6: 133, 138–40.

10. PRO SP 29/407/105; 29/411/34; NLS MSS 2512, fols. 215r–v, 229r; EUL MSS La.III.684.

11. Bodl. Carte MSS 45, fol. 504r; Sprat, pp. 34–35. See Greaves, *EUHF*, pp. 186–87.

12. NLS MSS 500, fols. 25r, 30r.

13. Long, *Compendious History*, p. 129; MacWard, *Poor Man's Cup of Cold Water*, sig. A3v. Radical literature was also available in Edinburgh and Aberdeen despite efforts to repress it. Among the publications the government found objectionable were Stewart's *Jus Populi Vindicatum*, another defense of the Galloway rebellion, and George Buchanan's *De Jure Regni apud Scotos*. *RPCS*, 6: 571–72 (cf. 5: 479). From England, but probably not for circulation at conventicles, came *The Common Council's Right in Electing of Sheriffs for London and Middlesex* (which does not appear in the *Short-Title Catalogue*) and Johnson's *Julian the Apostate*. Sir William Paterson strenuously objected to Johnson's book, "the maister-peice of villanie," because it argued that James should be destroyed, not simply excluded. *Letters to Aberdeen*, pp. 27–28. The bishop of Edinburgh was incensed in 1680 by James Gordon's *Reformed Bishop* because it attacked the bishops, doing more harm than the pamphlets of Brown and MacWard shipped from the Netherlands. BL Add. MSS 23,245, fols. 54r–v, 324r.

14. *MVB*, pp. 362–71; BL Egerton MSS 3325, fols. 53r, 54r. Wallace left the Netherlands temporarily, but died at Amsterdam in 1678. *MVB*, pp. 374, 376.

15. BL Add. MSS 23,242, fols. 20r, 99r; 35,125, fol. 303r; PRO SP 44/41, pp. 133–34, 158; London *Gazette*, 1341 (23–26 Sept. 1678); PRO SP 29/406/154; 44/143, pp. 218, 223.

16. PRO SP 29/366, p. 583; 29/406/183, 242, 233; 29/411/53, 68; 44/41, pp. 158, 160, 164–66; 44/42, pp. 46–47, 50–53, 59; 44/43, pp. 216–17, 219, 250, 268; *CSPD 1679–80*, pp. 105–6; *MVB*, pp. 99–102, 114. In September 1679 the Scottish minister John Erskine was jailed at Newcastle. BL Add. MSS 23,244, fol. 61r.

17. PRO SP 29/366, p. 595; 29/405/109, 109.1; 29/406/109; 44/43, p. 223; 63/338/132; Bodl. Carte MSS 45, fols. 482r, 486v; BL Add. MSS 23,246, fol. 48r; 35,125, fol. 302r; *RPCS*, 6: 457.

18. PRO SP 29/400/36.1; 29/406/109; *RPCS*, 5: 393–95. Cf. PRO SP 29/406/151.

19. BL Add. MSS 23,138, fol. 86r; 23,243, fol. 26r; *RPCS*, 6: 143–44, 155–57, 272, 300–301.

20. BL Add. MSS 23,243, fol. 34r–v, 40r; *CSPD 1679–80*, p. 122; *RPCS*, 6: 160–63, 166–68, 173–77. Cf. *Copies*, p. 173.

21. *RPCS*, 6: 177–78.

22. BL Add. MSS 23,243, fol. 20r; *ST*, 10: 811–23, 839–40; *RPCS*, 6: 180–82; *True Account of the Horrid Murther Committed upon the Late Archbishop*; *MVB*, pp. 103–5.

23. EUL MSS Dc.1.16, no. 24; Cowan, p. 94; *RPCS*, 6: 322–23. The others were George Balfour of Gilston; James Russell of Kingskettle; Robert Dingwell (or Dingwall) of Cadham; Alexander and Andrew Henderson, sons of John Henderson of Kilbrachmont; and George Fleeming, son of George Fleeming of Balboothy. *RPCS*, 6: 322–23.

24. *RPCS*, 6: 183–84, 511; EUL MSS Dc.1.16, nos. 23, 24, 25; *ST*, 10: 843–49; PRO SP 29/428/93; Erskine, pp. 9–10.

25. *CSPD 1680–81*, p. 69; *RPCS*, 6: 559; 11: 79; BL Add. MSS 41,812, fol. 36r. Among the persons arrested in connection with the assassination were William Falkener (or Falconar), who allegedly was in the assassination party but did not personally attack Sharp; Nathaniel Johnston, who was captured in Ireland; and Michael Cameron. EUL MSS Dc.1.16, no. 5; PRO SP 29/413/ 129, 145, 160; NLS MSS 597, fol. 275v; BL Add. MSS 23,246, fols. 48r, 62r; 32,095, fol. 190r; *RPCS*, 6: 534; Bodl. Carte MSS 45, fol. 555r–v. For others see, e.g., Add. MSS 28,747, fol. 23r; PRO SP 44/335, p. 215; *RPCS*, 6: 182, 392.

26. After Sharp's assassination, officials were concerned that the bishop of Argyll would be the next target; hence he was taken to Edinburgh by a protective guard. EUL MSS Dc.1.16, no. 3.

27. BL Add. MSS 23,245, fol. 79r; EUL MSS La.III.344, vol. 2, fols. 59v–60v; La.III.684 (which includes some of Cargill's sermons from this period).

28. EUL MSS La.III.344, vol. 2, fols. 61r–62r; La.III.684, pp. 352–53; Bodl. Carte MSS 45, fols. 484r–485r; *Blackader Mem.*, p. 238; PRO SP 29/ 411/150.1; *Copies*, pp. 173–74; *RPCS*, 6: 208, 210; Morrice, 1: 195–96.

29. *RPCS*, 6: 210. King and Douglass were soon rescued. Bodl. Carte MSS 45, fol. 496r–v.

30. EUL MSS La.III.344, vol. 2, fol. 62r; Bodl. Carte MSS 45, fols. 484r, 492r, 494r, 496r; BL Add. MSS 23,244, fols. 1r, 2r; PRO SP 29/411/150.1; *RPCS*, 6: 208, 211; NLS MSS 1004, fol. 2r.

31. PRO SP 29/411/150.1, 155; *RPCS*, 6: 208.

32. EUL MSS La.III.344, vol. 2, fol. 62v; *Copies*, p. 174; Bodl. Carte MSS 45, fol. 486r; *CSPD 1679–80*, p. 39; *Blackader Mem.*, pp. 229–30.

33. *Blackader Mem.*, p. 242; Ure, pp. 461–62, 466; *Copies*, p. 176.

34. Ure, pp. 463, 466–67; EUL MSS La.III.344, vol. 2, fols. 63r–64r; *Copies*, p. 176.

35. Cowan, p. 97; Ure, p. 462; NLS MSS 3473, pp. 46–47.

36. Ure, pp. 462, 464–65, 467–68.

37. *Blackader Mem.*, p. 242; EUL MSS La.II.89, fol. 136r–v; Bodl. Carte MSS 45, fols. 514r–515r.

38. Ure, pp. 470, 472.

39. BL Add. MSS 23,244, fols. 4v–5r; 25,124, fols. 200r, 201r; *CSPD 1679–80*, pp. 178, 324 (cf. 171); *RPCS*, 6: 239, PRO SP 44/29, p. 335; BL Althorp (Halifax) MSS H2, Coventry to Halifax, 16 June 1679.

40. London *Gazette*, 1417 (16–19 June 1679); 1418 (19–23 June 1679); 1419 (23–26 June 1679); BL Add. MSS 23,244, fols. 6r, 8r, 10r; PRO SP 29/411/156; *Blackader Mem.*, pp. 239–40; *RPCS*, 6: 216, 228, 231, 234, 236–37, 241.

41. PRO SP 29/411/150.1, 155; BL Add. MSS 23,244, fols. 2r, 12r; *RPCS*, 6: 218, 249; *Copies*, p. 177; London *Gazette*, 1419 (23–26 June 1679); *Blackader Mem.*, p. 241; Ure, p. 481 (Ure says there were 4,000 foot soldiers and 2,000 cavalry).

42. Orrery urged Essex not to send any troops from Ireland, since Ulster militants could have been inspired by the Scottish uprising to take up arms. BL Stowe MSS 212, fol. 357r–v.

43. PRO SP 29/411/155, 156; *RPCS*, 6: 219, 226, 249; London *Gazette*, 1417 (16–19 June 1679); 1419 (23–26 June 1679).

44. PRO SP 29/442/74; Ure, pp. 473–75; BL Add. MSS 23,244, fols. 14v–15r, 16r; *Copies*, p. 176; London *Gazette*, 1420 (26–30 June 1679).

45. EUL MSS La.III.344, vol. 2, fol. 67r–v; Dc.1.16, no. 7; BL Add. MSS 23,244, fol. 16r; NLS MSS 500, fols. 23r–24r; London *Gazette*, 1419 (23–26 June 1679); 1420 (26–30 June 1679); Ure, pp. 476–81, 483; *Blackader Mem.*, pp. 243–49; *Domestick Intelligence*, 2 (10 July 1679); *RPCS*, 6: 253–54, 256; *MVB*, p. 284. The prisoners were detained in an enclosure behind Greyfriars' Church in Edinburgh. *RPCS*, 6: 258, 277; London *Gazette*, 1420 (26–30 June 1679).

46. BL Add. MSS 23,244, fols. 45r, 47r, 49r; 35,125, fol. 310r; *RPCS*, 6: 264–65, 339–40; London *Gazette*, 1424 (10–14 July 1679); PRO SP 29/412/5.

47. *CSPD 1679–80*, pp. 208, 273; *RPCS*, 6: 265–66, 287–88, 296–97, 301–4, 327, 333, 340–41; PRO SP 29/339/30; EUL MSS Dc.1.16, no. 8; *Domestick Intelligence*, 9 (5 Aug. 1679); BL Add. MSS 23,244, fol. 53r.

48. *RPCS*, 6: 294–95, 306, 313–15, 338–39; *CSPD 1680–81*, p. 390; London *Gazette*, 1467 (8–11 Dec. 1679); 1475 (5–8 Jan. 1680).

49. London *Gazette*, 1566 (18–22 Nov. 1680); 1572 (9–13 Dec. 1680); *RPCS*, 6: 586; PRO SP 29/421/128. Alexander Hume of Hume Castle was also executed as a rebel in December 1682. *CSPD 1682*, pp. 596–97.

50. Crookshank, 2: 171–74; *Letters to Aberdeen*, pp. 118–20, 126; Erskine, pp. 3, 5, 23–24, 42–44, 55–56, 60, 77; *RPCS*, 10: 272–73; London *Gazette*, 1835 (18–21 June 1683); NUL MSS PwV 95, pp. 233, 322, 325, 327, 330; *True Protestant Mercury*, 134 (15–19 Apr. 1682); 135 (19–22 Apr. 1682).

51. PRO SP 29/418/159, 159.1; 29/428/43; 44/54, p. 45; *RPCS*, 6: 294–96; Bodl. Carte MSS 45, fol. 533r; *Domestick Intelligence*, 2 (10 July 1679); *Protestant (Domestick) Intelligence* 67 (24 Feb. 1680); *CSPD 1679–80*, pp. 397–98; *CSPD 1683–84*, p. 394; *Copies*, pp. 177–78. John Rae, one of those who fled, settled in London and married Mary Gladman, possibly the daughter of John Gladman. BL Add. MSS 41,804, fols. 74r–75r.

52. *CSPD 1679–80*, p. 238; *CSPD 1682*, pp. 141–42, 256; *RPCS*, 6: 283. John Cuningham of Bedlam and Thomas Cuningham of Montgreenan were both captured in 1679. *CSPD 1679–80*, p. 238.

53. *RPCS*, 7: 7, BL Add. MSS 32,095, fol. 194r; *CSPD 1680–81*, pp. 128, 345, 368; *CSPD 1682*, p. 256; *CSPD 1684–85*, p. 292; Cowan, p. 102; *Protestant (Domestick) Intelligence*, 67 (24 Feb. 1680); Erskine, pp. 6, 41.

54. *RPCS*, 8: 633–38.

55. Bodl. Carte MSS 45, fols. 433r, 500r–v; PRO SP 63/339/20, 24; James Seaton Reid, *History of the Presbyterian Church in Ireland*, new ed., 3 vols. (Belfast: William Mullan, 1867), 2: 337–38.

56. Bodl. Carte MSS 45, fol. 433r, 504r.

57. PRO SP 63/339/20, 23; Bodl. Carte MSS 45, fols. 530r, 531r–v. Eight Presbyterian ministers in Ulster, including John Hart, Robert Rule, and William Hampton, professed in September 1679 "to obey his [Charles'] lawfull commands, & wherein we cannot in conscience, actively obey his Majesties Lawes, yet peaceably to submit to his Majesties undoubted Authority over us, exhorting the people among whom we labour to beware of all seditious disturbances." PRO SP 63/339/39.1.

58. PRO SP 63/342/15, 15.1, 25, 29, 35, 44, 48, 48.1–2; *CSPD 1680–81*, p. 307; *True Protestant Mercury* 50 (25–29 June 1681). Reports of radical plotting in Ireland in 1680–81 were almost certainly spurious; cf. *CSPD 1679–80*, p. 609; PRO SP 29/415/8; 63/342/4.

59. *RPCS*, 6: 324; BL Add. MSS 23,243, fols. 11r, 22r; *CSPD 1679–80*, p. 198; *MVB*, pp. 117–20. The house in Edinburgh where Veitch once held a conventicle was destroyed in June 1680. NLS MSS 597, fol. 278r.

60. *Blackader Mem.*, pp. 256–58; BL Add. MSS 23,245, fol. 57r; 23,246, fols. 13r, 27r; *RPCS*, 6: 417, 426, 429–31, 447, 450, 501 (cf. 553); Bodl. Carte MSS 45, fol. 565r–v.

61. *ST*, 10: 869; *Copies*, pp. 178–79.

62. EUL MSS La.III.684, pp. 198–202, 204.

63. *Copies*, pp. 178–79.

64. *CSPD 1679–80*, p. 521; Erskine, p. 40; London *Gazette*, 1527 (5–8 July 1680); *RPCS*, 6: 481.

65. EUL MSS Dc.1.16, no. 22. A copy is printed in *ST*, 10: 795–805.

66. BL Add. MSS 23,246, fols. 45r, 48r; *CSPD 1679–80*, p. 510. Cf. PRO SP 29/413/159.1.

67. EUL MSS Dc.1.16, nos. 18, 21. Dalziel cited their original number as 50. Michael Cameron had been arrested in May 1679 on suspicion of complicity in the murder of Archbishop Sharp. EUL MSS Dc.1.16, no. 18; BL Add. MSS 32,095, fol. 190r.

68. EUL MSS Dc.1.16, no. 19. For other copies see EUL MSS La.III.350, fol. 8r; La.III. 684, pp. 354–56; BL Add. MSS 23,246, fol. 63r–v; *ST*, 10: 805–6. In Ireland four Presbyterian ministers—Patrick Adair, Alexander Hutcheson, Archibald Hamilton, and John Abernathy—denounced the Cameronians' manifesto as "absurd and rebellious" and their actions as "highlie sinnefull against God." PRO SP 63/339/113.

69. EUL MSS Dc.1.16, nos. 16, 18; La.II.20 (which dates the proclamation 1 July); La.III.684, pp. 146–60; London *Gazette*, 1527 (5–8 July 1680); *CSPD 1679–80*, p. 539; *RPCS*, 6: 481–85.

70. EUL MSS Dc.1.16, no. 24; London *Gazette*, 1534 (29 July–2 Aug. 1680); *ST*, 10: 843–50; *Collection of Letters to Sancroft*, p. 22.

71. Prinsterer, p. 444; EUL MSS La.II.27, vol. 1, fols. 22r–27r; La.III.350, fol. 12r; BL Add. MSS 23,247, fol. 22r–v.

72. BL Add. MSS 23,247, fols. 40r, 42r–44v; *ST*, 10: 856; *RPCS*, 6: 584; PRO SP 44/62, p. 87. Another copy of the excommunication statement is found in EUL MSS La.III.684, pp. 340–51.

73. *RPCS*, 6: 585–86; *CSPD 1680–81*, pp. 141–42; *ST*, 10: 859, 880, 883, 887; EUL MSS La.III.684, pp. 230–38.

74. EUL MSS La.III.684, pp. 272–82, 366–70; La.II.27, vol. 1, fols. 5r–12v.

75. Bodl. Carte MSS 45, fol. 565r–v; *RPCS*, 7: 704–5; Cowan, pp. 103–4; *ST*, 10: 853–55.

76. *CSPD 1680–81*, pp. 362, 385–86, 388, 516, 526; EUL MSS La.II.27, vol. 1, fols. 1r–4v; London *Gazette*, 1640 (4–8 Aug. 1681); *True Protestant Mercury*, 83 (19–22 Oct. 1681); *ST*, 10: 879. The three executed with Cargill and Smith were James Boig, an Edinburgh merchant; William Coothill, a Bo'ness seaman; and William Thompson, a servant from Stirling who had fought with the Bothwell rebels. *ST*, 10: 886–91.

77. *RPCS*, 6: 459–62. Cf. *CSPD 1679–80*, pp. 484–85.

78. Julia Buckroyd, *Church and State in Scotland 1660–1681* (Edinburgh: John Donald, 1980), pp. 134–35.

79. BL Add. MSS 23,246, fol. 51r; *RPCS*, 7: 35, 113–14, 133–34, 144–45, 147, 159, 163–66, 219, 390–91, 583–85; 8: 8–10, 29–30, 84–85.

80. *RPCS*, 6: 601; 7: 113, 137, 147, 301–3, 358, 362, 364, 398, 451–52, 456; 8: 9; *Letters to Aberdeen*, p. 5; *CSPD 1682*, p. 204; *Collection of Letters to Sancroft*, pp. 22–23; *Blackader Mem.*, pp. 260, 267–68. Blackader was arrested and imprisoned in April 1681 after holding a field conventicle in East Lothian near the Bass prison. He died in that jail nearly five years later. A story in the

Protestant Oxford Intelligence, 4 (17–21 Mar. 1681), wrongly suggested that many of the conventicle preachers were Jesuits or Catholic priests in disguise. Conventicles were reportedly meeting in the Highlands in the fall of 1682. *CSPD 1682*, p. 474.

81. *RPCS*, 7: 163–66, 583–84; 8: 41–42.

82. *Collection of Letters to Sancroft*, pp. 29, 34–36.

83. NLS MSS 3473, pp. 51–52. When Semple's wife became ill he returned to England and was incarcerated, but after his release he returned to Scotland. *RPCS*, 7: 172, 209–10, 240–41.

84. PRO SP 29/415/19, 125; 44/62, pp. 125, 145. Cf. *CSPD 1679–80*, p. 503.

85. *CSPD 1679–80*, pp. 624–25; *CSPD 1682*, p. 165; PRO SP 29/400/36.1; BL Add. MSS 23,247, fols. 29r, 38r. In January 1680 the duke of York informed the Scottish Council that those who troubled them were not as powerful as "the Republican Party" in England, with whom they corresponded. It is unclear which Scottish group James meant. London *Gazette*, 1485 (9–12 Feb. 1680).

86. NLS MSS 1038, passim (pp. 92 and 273 quoted).

87. BL Add. MSS 23,247, fols. 60r, 62r–64r. Hostility to Catholicism was manifest in January 1681 when students in Edinburgh burned an effigy of the pope, for which they were briefly detained by magistrates. The following day many people wore ribbons emblazoned "No Pope, no Papist." *True Protestant Mercury*, 6 (11–15 Jan. 1681). Cf. London *Gazette*, 1688 (19–23 Jan. 1682).

88. For examples of assaults on clergymen by a thief and extortionist see *RPCS*, 6: 455–56.

89. *RPCS*, 6: 440, 458; 7: 123, 155–56, 187–88; *CSPD 1682*, p. 143; Sprat, p. 37.

90. PRO SP 29/418/179; *RPCS*, 7: 364, 367, 398–400, 422–23, 431–32, 449–50, 456, 459–61; *CSPD 1682*, p. 256; *True Protestant Mercury*, 152 (17–21 June 1682).

91. Cowan, pp. 108–9; *RPCS*, 7: 296–97; *CSPD 1680–81*, p. 440. For the Test see *RPCS*, 7: 739.

92. BL Add. MSS 23,248, fols. 20r, 22r; 41,810, fol. 20r–v; *CSPD 1680–81*, p. 517; *RPCS*, 7: 261–62, 708–13.

93. *RPCS*, 7: 242–45, 290–93, 736; *Case of the Earl of Argyle*; BL Add. MSS 51,319, fol. 57r; *CSPD 1680–81*, pp. 599, 606; *CSPD 1682*, pp. 27, 170; London *Gazette*, 1678 (15–19 Dec. 1681); 1680 (22–26 Dec. 1681); 1682 (29 Dec. 1681–2 Jan. 1682); *Impartial Protestant Mercury*, 72 (27–30 Dec. 1681); *True Protestant Mercury*, 103 (28–31 Dec. 1681); 104 (31 Dec. 1681–4 Jan. 1682); Prinsterer, pp. 530, 533, 538.

94. Shields, pp. 9, 11–12; PRO SP 29/425/27; 29/427/101; *Copies*, pp. 150–51; *ST*, 9: 460–62.

95. EUL MSS La.II.89, fols. 137r–138r; for another copy see La.III.350, fols. 26r–27r.

96. *RPCS*, 7: 310–11, 329–30; *CSPD 1682*, p. 39; *True Protestant Mercury*, 115 (8–11 Feb. 1682).

97. *RPCS*, 7: 310–13, 326–27, 333–34.

98. *Letters to Aberdeen*, pp. 88, 107–11; Cowan, pp. 111–12; *Collection of Letters to Sancroft*, p. 54 (for an assault on the vicar of Kirknewton, Northumberland). Soldiers were attacked at Loudoun, Ayrshire, in July 1682. *RPCS*, 7: 487.

99. *RPCS*, 7: 358.

100. BL Add. MSS 15,892, fol. 136v; *Letters to Aberdeen*, pp. 23, 64, 117, 119, 128–29; *Collection of Letters to Sancroft*, pp. 48–49; *RPCS*, 7: 497–99. The duke of Hamilton was still searching for the authors of the Lesmahagow declaration in January 1683. In the same month, dissidents rescued a captured rebel at Dalserf, near Lesmahagow. *Letters to Aberdeen*, pp. 95–96. For examples of the rescue of other prisoners (or of rescue attempts) see *RPCS*, 6: 163, 454–55, 463 (Cargill), 557 (Cargill).

101. *RPCS*, 7: 451, 566–67, 624–25; *True Protestant Mercury*, 158 (8–12 July 1682); 168 (12–16 Aug. 1682); 182 (30 Sept.–4 Oct. 1682); *CSPD 1682*, p. 485; PRO SP 44/68, p. 184 (but cf. PRO SP 29/422/3).

102. *RPCS*, 7: 361, 373, 394, 396–97, 427.

103. *True Protestant Mercury*, 124 (11–15 Mar. 1682); *RPCS*, 7: 431; *ST*, 11: 909–16. There was a recurring need to punish lax or uncooperative magistrates. See *RPCS*, 5: 62–63, 83–84, 181–82, 406–7, 492–93, 495; 6: 164–65, 202, 493–94; 7: 113–14, 133–34, 144–45, 163–66.

104. BL Add. MSS 15,892, fol. 148r–v. James was probably also referring in a narrower sense to the leaders of the political nation.

105. Shields, pp. 16, 18–19, 21, 25, 28–30, 32–36, 41–45; EUL MSS La.III.350, fol. 38r; *Copies*, p. 151; *ST*, 11: 48; Sprat, p. 99; PRO SP 29/428/93; 29/432/103. According to Sprat (p. 100) Nisbet was Argyll's agent; I have found no evidence to support this. This Nisbet is not to be confused with John Nisbet of Loudoun, who was executed in April 1683 for his participation in the Bothwell Bridge rebellion. Crookshank, 2: 167. For the latter Nisbet's trial and conviction see *ST*, 11: 45–64; cf. EUL MSS Dc.1.16, no. 15. Nisbet of Loudoun had introduced Earlston to the Cameronians in 1681. *Copies*, p. 150.

106. EUL MSS La.III.350, fol. 94r–v.

107. Shields, pp. 49–51; EUL MSS La.III.350, fol. 54r.

108. Shields, pp. 58, 63–64.

109. Ibid., p. 64; PRO SP 29/427/101; 29/432/103; 29/433/62; *Copies*, pp. 142, 144–46, 152; *ST*, 9: 456–58, 462, 464–65; Mackenzie, pp. 9–10. John Cochrane, Sir John's son, had reportedly been with a group of rebels

at Cumnock, Ayrshire, a few days before the battle of Bothwell Bridge. However, both of the Cochranes and Sir Hugh Campbell of Cessnock were among a group of more than 50 men who formally denounced the Bothwell rebellion on 28 April 1679. Although Cessnock was indicted on charges of treason in 1684 for supporting the rebellion, the jury found him innocent. Erskine, pp. 38, 49, 52, 54–55; EUL MSS La.II.89, fol. 195r. For Murray see Haley, pp. 413, 424–26, 553n., 706n.

110. *ST*, 9: 462–63, 465; PRO SP 29/432/103. Johnston's letter of 2 May mentioned Andrew Young of Newcastle. Mackenzie, p. 10.

111. Shields, pp. 64, 66–67; PRO SP 29/427/101; 29/432/103.

112. Shields, pp. 67–71; PRO SP 29/424/46.

113. PRO SP 29/424/45; Shields, pp. 52–58, 74–78.

114. Shields, pp. 65–66, 74–78; *ST*, 9: 453–54; *RPCS*, 8: 173, 183–84; PRO SP 29/424/184; 29/425/115; 29/427/101; 44/56, pp. 72–73; 44/68, pp. 280, 282; 44/335, p. 4; *Copies*, pp. 130–31; Erskine, p. 9. On 10 June a company of grenadiers took Earlston to Edinburgh, where he subsequently confessed. NUL MSS PwV 95, pp. 231, 239; PRO SP 29/428/58; 29/435/41; 44/68, p. 335. Earlston was subsequently sentenced to death but given a reprieve and confined to the Bass prison after he confessed. In September 1684, he made an unsuccessful attempt to escape with the aid of an unidentified person. *RPCS*, 9: 232, 252–53, 264, 267; 10: 99, 141–42.

Chapter 3

1. London *Gazette*, 1609 (18–21 Apr. 1681); 1616 (12–16 May 1681); 1659 (10–13 Oct. 1681); 1660 (13–17 Oct. 1681); 1663 (24–27 Oct. 1681); 1664 (27–31 Oct. 1681); 1671 (21–24 Nov. 1681); 1672 (24–28 Nov. 1681); 1687 (16–19 Jan. 1682); 1770 (2–6 Nov. 1682); PRO SP 29/417/189; 29/421/74.

2. PRO SP 29/413/61; 29/414/109; 29/415/142; 29/416/49; 29/417/38, 140; 44/62, p. 103; CCRO MSS QSF/82, fol. 270r.

3. *Protestant (Domestick) Intelligence*, 97 (15 Feb. 1681); 107 (22 Mar. 1681); *True Protestant Mercury*, 70 (3–7 Sept. 1681); 76 (24–28 Sept. 1681); 86 (29 Oct.–2 Nov. 1681); 101 (21–24 Dec. 1681); 102 (24–28 Dec. 1681); 105 (4–7 Jan. 1682); 107 (11–14 Jan. 1682); PRO SP 29/416/117, 134; 29/417/25; 44/62, p. 282; *CSPD 1680–81*, p. 572. Cf. PRO SP 44/62, p. 358 (Marlborough, Wiltshire); *CSPD 1680–81*, p. 564 (hundred of Ossulston).

4. *True Protestant Mercury*, 110 (21–25 Jan. 1682); 119 (22–25 Feb. 1682); 124 (11–15 Mar. 1682); 126 (18–22 Mar. 1682); 141 (10–13 May 1682); *Impartial Protestant Mercury*, 88 (21–24 Feb. 1682); 99 (31 Mar.–4 Apr. 1682); PRO SP 29/418/26, 26.1, 27, 27.1, 197.

5. PRO SP 29/417/118, 130, 140, 151, 171, 182; 44/62, pp. 354–55, 365–66; 44/68, pp. 6–7.

6. For Dover, where the mayor was Nicholas Cullen, see PRO SP 29/416/

126, 173, 173.1, 174; *CSPD 1680–81*, p. 428. For Sandwich, where Bartholomew Coombes was mayor, see PRO SP 29/417/67, 68. For Reading see *Impartial Protestant Mercury*, 67 (9–13 Dec. 1681); PRO SP 44/62, pp. 370–71. Cf. PRO SP 29/419/98 for the mayor of Coventry's reluctance. A grand jury at Westminster refused to receive presentments of conventiclers. *True Protestant Mercury*, 113 (1–4 Feb. 1682).

7. PRO SP 29/417/274. Cf. *True Protestant Mercury*, 162 (22–26 July 1682).

8. PRO SP 29/416/134; 29/417/96, 156, 171; 29/418/43, 52, 89, 96, 167; 29/419/19; 29/421/127, 175; *CSPD 1682*, p. 272; *True Protestant Mercury*, 158 (8–12 July 1682).

9. PRO SP 29/417/144, 144.1, 156; *True Protestant Mercury*, 100 (17–21 Dec. 1681); *CSPD 1680–81*, p. 640. The jury that tried Vincent in January 1682 for holding conventicles returned a verdict of *ignoramus*. *Impartial Protestant Mercury*, 75 (6–10 Jan. 1682).

10. PRO SP 29/417/132. Nimrod was a name that had repeatedly been invoked against Charles I in the 1640s.

11. *CSPD 1682*, p. 128; *True Protestant Mercury*, 114 (4–8 Feb. 1682); 125 (15–18 Mar. 1682); 175 (6–9 Sept. 1682); 179 (20–23 Sept. 1682); *Impartial Protestant Mercury*, 108 (2–5 May 1682); PRO SP 29/418/120; 29/419/67. Cf. PRO SP 29/419/88.

12. PRO SP 29/418/30, 114; *CSPD 1682*, p. 255.

13. PRO SP 29/417/122.

14. *True Protestant Mercury*, 107 (11–14 Jan. 1682); PRO SP 29/418/106, 127. The others were the Presbyterians Samuel Annesley, Thomas Jacomb, Thomas Watson, Edmund Calamy, Thomas Doolittle, and Samuel Slater; the Congregationalist John Collins (or possibly the Presbyterian John Collinges); and Nicholas Blackley. PRO SP 29/417/122; cf. 29/417/144.1.

15. Owen, *Humble Testimony unto the Goodness and Severity of God*, sig. A3r–v.

16. Owen, *Brief and Impartial Account of the Nature of the Protestant Religion*, p. 12.

17. Haley, pp. 688–89; PRO SP 29/417/145, 155; Morrice, 1: 325, 326.

18. PRO SP 29/418/127; Haley, pp. 689, 695–96; Morrice, 1: 320.

19. *CSPD 1682*, pp. 147, 149–50; Luttrell, 1: 172, 176. Shaftesbury dined with Anglesey on 21 March. BL Add. MSS 18,730, fol. 95r.

20. Haley, pp. 694–95; Prinsterer, p. 549 (cf. p. 551).

21. Haley, pp. 697–704; Gary S. De Krey, "The London Whigs and the Exclusion Crisis Reconsidered," in *The First Modern Society*, ed. Lee Beier, David Cannadine, and James Rosenheim (Cambridge, Eng.: Cambridge University Press, 1989), pp. 470–72, 475, 477–78.

22. PRO SP 63/343/46; *CSPD 1682*, p. 390; Haley, p. 706 n.

23. David Allen, "Political Clubs in Restoration London," *Historical Jour-*

nal, 19 (Sept. 1976): 561–80; Tim Harris, *London Crowds in the Reign of Charles II: Propaganda and Politics from the Restoration Until the Exclusion Crisis* (Cambridge, Eng.: Cambridge University Press, 1987), pp. 92–94, 100–101, 119–20.

24. J. R. Jones, "The Green Ribbon Club," *Durham University Journal*, 49 (1956): 17–20; J. H. Plumb, *The Growth of Political Stability in England 1675–1725* (Harmondsworth, Eng.: Penguin, 1969), p. 53; Haley, p. 520; Gary S. De Krey, "London Radicals and Revolutionary Politics, 1675–1683," in *The Politics of Religion in Restoration England*, ed. Tim Harris, Paul Seaward, and Mark Goldie (Oxford: Basil Blackwell, 1990), p. 142; NUL MSS PwV 95, p. 237; Cambridge University, Pepys Library, Misc. MSS 7, pp. 465–91; BL Harleian MSS 6845, fol. 282r; PRO SP 29/429/184.

25. PRO SP 29/419/86, 87; 29/420/35; 29/429/61, 184; Allen, "Political Clubs," p. 573; Harris, *London Crowds*, p. 100.

26. PRO SP 29/420/18; 29/428/60, pp. 75–76, 89; 29/429/61, 194; 29/430/36, 76, 94; 29/430/111, p. 7; 29/437/100; 44/54, p. 276; 44/68, p. 113; John Latimer, *The Annals of Bristol in the Seventeenth Century* (Bristol, Eng.: William George's Sons, 1900), p. 418; Jonathan Barry, "The Politics of Religion in Restoration Bristol," in *Politics of Religion in Restoration England*, ed. Harris, Seaward, and Goldie, pp. 176–77.

27. Haley, pp. 605, 710; Milne, pp. 19–20; Grey, *SH*, p. 3; EUL MSS La.I.332, p. 6; Reresby, p. 195; Sidney, *Diary of the Times of Charles the Second*, 1: 298. Robert Ferguson, who was well acquainted with Shaftesbury, later denied he had known of such a conspiracy in 1680. Ferguson, "Rye House," pp. 412, 414–15. Royalists made spurious allegations in the summer of 1683 that Shaftesbury had first planned the conspiracy following his dismissal as lord chancellor in November 1673. NUL MSS PwV 95, p. 310.

28. *Copies*, pp. 199–200.

29. NUL MSS PwV 95, p. 256; Haley, pp. 643–44, 653, 672; PRO SP 29/420/79.1.

30. *Copies*, p. 196; *Last Speech*, p. 6.

31. BL Harleian MSS 6845, fol. 266r; PRO SP 29/425/56.

32. *MVB*, pp. 126–41; Andrew Lang, *Sir George Mackenzie, King's Advocate, of Rosehaugh: His Life and Times 1636(?)–1691* (London: Longmans, Green, 1909), p. 236; Mackenzie, p. 8; BL Add. MSS 37,981, fols. 35r–v, 57v; PRO SP 29/420/9; *CSPD 1682*, p. 327. The Hawick minister John Scot and George Pringle of Torwoodlee put Argyll into contact with Veitch. *MVB*, p. 133n.

33. Greaves, *EUHF*, pp. 107, 117, 236, 242.

34. *MVB*, pp. 142–43.

35. BL Add. MSS 38,847, fol. 88r–v; PRO SP 29/428/4; *HMC* 1, *Second Report*, Appendix, p. 214.

36. Grey, *SH*, pp. 3–5; Prinsterer, p. 553.

37. Morrice, 1: 362, 377, 417; *Letters of Eminent Men to Thoresby*, 1: 23–25.

38. Ferguson, "Rye House," pp. 415–16; Grey, *SH*, pp. 14–15.

39. Burnet, 2: 354–55; PRO SP 29/420/8, 9; *MVB*, pp. 140n., 152; cf. Haley, pp. 690, 710–11.

40. *MVB*, pp. 136–37, 145–46; PRO SP 29/421/122; *CSPD 1682*, pp. 567–68.

41. PRO SP 29/421/122; *CSPD 1682*, pp. 568–71.

42. Grey, *SH*, pp. 15–16. Shaftesbury's servant, Anthony Shepherd, acknowledged in July 1683 that Monmouth, Grey, and (unnamed) others had met with the earl in his home. PRO SP 29/428/116. John Rouse had heard something about the earlier plans for an insurrection in mid-1682 in connection with the shrieval election, but his sources were fragmentary and his account at this point highly unreliable. His claim to have participated in these early meetings is spurious. *Copies*, pp. 196–97.

43. BL Add. MSS 8127, fol. 67v; PRO SP 29/429/89; *Copies*, p. 194.

44. Walcott, whom Shaftesbury recruited, thought the plot began in August or September after Papillon and Dubois were rejected. PRO SP 29/428/60, pp. 36–42.

45. Grey, *SH*, p. 17; EUL MSS La.I.332, p. 6; Lacey, p. 350; Haley, p. 563; PRO SP 29/433/56.

46. In July 1683 Courtenay denied having known of the conspiracy. PRO SP 29/428/60, pp. 31–32. Another source asserted that Colonel (Edward?) Scott had been sent to the southwest to "make partys" for Monmouth. PRO SP 29/433/15.

47. Lacey, p. 450; Grey, *SH*, pp. 17–18; Elizabeth D'Oyley, *James Duke of Monmouth* (London: Geoffrey Bles, 1938), p. 210. Upon reading Grey's confession in August 1685, an unnamed government official, presumably a member of the Privy Council, made notes on specific points of interest, including the allegations against Macclesfield, Brandon, and Rotherham (after whom inquiries were to be made). BL Lansdowne MSS 1152, fol. 306r–v. By the time Grey wrote, Freke and Trenchard were in the Netherlands and Yonge had been arrested. Reportedly, around Michaelmas 1681 Trenchard had attempted to enlist men for an uprising, but this is highly unlikely. PRO SP 29/429/82; 29/430/44, 95, 100, 154.2, 162, 170; 29/431/17; 29/433/93.

48. BL Add. MSS 62,453, fol. 3r; Holloway, pp. 2, 14–15. Holloway erred in supposing that Howard of Escrick, with whom he had had no dealings, was involved in the conspiracy in mid-1682. Howard first became embroiled in October of that year.

49. BL Add. MSS 41,819, fol. 159r–160r.

50. PRO SP 29/414/54. On 14 August 1682 the bishop of Bristol told Jenkins he had information about a club of nearly 140 people who had taken an

oath of secrecy, corresponded with a club in London, and were engaged in a conspiracy. One of them, he claimed, was a government informer. PRO SP 29/420/18.

51. BL Add. MSS 38,847, fol. 71v; 62,453, fol. 3r–v; PRO SP 29/437/105.1, 139.

52. Ferguson averred, "The first resolution taken about flying to Arms, was imediately [*sic*] before the Duke of Monmouth's going to Cheshire." Since plans for the trip commenced in July, Ferguson's account also corroborates that of Grey. Ferguson, "Rye House," p. 417.

53. PRO SP 29/419/171 (cf. 29/420/22); Ferguson, "Rye House," p. 417; Grey, *SH*, pp. 16, 18; cf. Haley, p. 711.

54. PRO SP 29/420/38, 55, 58.1, 59, 60, 61, 66, 71, 72.1, 81, 82, 121, 126; 29/427/98; *CSPD 1682*, p. 401; ChRO MSS DDX7/1; DDX 383/2 (entry for 9 Sept. 1682); JRL Legh of Lyme MSS (depositions of Edward Sherman and Samuel Proudlove, 20 Sept. 1682). Cf. JRL Legh of Lyme MSS (report of Viscount Molyneux, 27 Aug. 1682). Macclesfield and his sons, Lord Brandon and Fitton Gerard, were part of a close-knit circle that included Delamere and his son Henry, Roger Whitley, Sir Thomas Mainwaring, and Sir Robert Cotton. This group also had ties to the earl of Derby, Lord Colchester, and Sir Thomas Armstrong. ChRO MSS DDX 383/2 (entries for 11 Nov. 1678–18 Aug. 1683, passim).

55. Cf. Ferguson, "Rye House," p. 417.

56. *CSPD*, 23: 370; D'Oyley, *James Duke of Monmouth*, p. 196; *Correspondence of the Family of Hatton*, 2: 18; Sir John Dalrymple, *Memoirs of Great Britain and Ireland*, 2nd ed., 2 vols. (London: W. Strahan and T. Cadell, 1771–73), vol. 1, pt. 1, bk. 1, pp. 13–14; JRL Legh of Lyme MSS (L. Jenkins to deputy-lieutenants of Cheshire, 15 Sept. 1682).

57. Grey, *SH*, pp. 18–25; EUL MSS La.I.332, pp. 6–7; Ferguson, "Rye House," p. 418; JRL Legh of Lyme MSS (L. Jenkins to deputy-lieutenants of Cheshire, 7 Oct. 1682). Cf. Haley, p. 712. Monmouth's bail was discharged in November. Morrice, 1: 346.

58. PRO SP 29/429/40.

59. Grey, *SH*, pp. 25–27; EUL MSS La.I.332, p. 7; Sprat, p. 30.

60. Greaves, *EUHF*, pp. 104–5, 108–9; BL Add. MSS 38,847, fol. 88v; *Copies*, p. 129; *Last Speech*, p. 9; PRO SP 29/425/71, 141; 29/428/4; 29/429/32; Sprat, pp. 29–30.

61. PRO SP 29/428/31, 60, p. 6; 29/428/79; 29/433/8, pp. 3–4; *Copies*, pp. 99–101; *Tryal of Delamere*, pp. 23–24. According to Howard's testimony at Delamere's trial, Walcott had previously given Howard a cipher and the two men had corresponded in a canting language using the terms of merchants. *Tryal of Delamere*, p. 22. Shepherd arranged for Shaftesbury to hide at Watson's house; Ferguson also visited the earl there. PRO SP 29/428/31.

62. Howard was imprecise in his dating; this meeting, he said, was on Thursday, 3 or 4 October; Thursday was the 5th.

63. *Copies*, pp. 102–3; NUL MSS PwV 95, p. 237; PRO SP 29/425/181; 29/427/88; 44/68, p. 296; *Tryal of Delamere*, p. 24; London *Gazette*, 1837 (25–28 June 1683); Sprat, pp. 36–37.

64. *Copies*, p. 103; PRO SP 29/428/116; Haley, p. 713; *Tryal of Delamere*, p. 26. A Captain Tracy had commanded a ship transporting foodstuffs in 1672. *CSPD 1672*, p. 572.

65. Ferguson, "Rye House," pp. 418–19, 422.

66. Ibid., p. 420.

67. Ibid., pp. 422–23. Charlton was Richard Baxter's brother-in-law.

68. Ibid., pp. 423–25; BL Add. MSS 38,847, fols. 89v–90r; London *Gazette*, 1845 (2–6 Aug. 1683). "I could never perceive," wrote Ferguson, "that my Lᵈ Russel had any intelligence" of the plan to use agents provocateur. "Rye House," p. 425.

69. *ST*, 11: 879; Ferguson, "Rye House," pp. 426–27; PRO SP 29/438/3.

70. BL Add. MSS 38,847, fols. 89v–90r; *Copies*, p. 69; West, *An Answer*, p. 1; PRO SP 29/425/49, 69; 29/428/5; Burnet, 2: 357. The duke of Buckingham had taken refuge with West when he was a wanted man in 1667. West was Aaron Smith's successor as Shaftesbury's solicitor, and Edmund Warcup accused him of suborning Lawrence Mowbray and other Popish Plot witnesses. West claimed Francis Shute had told him about the conspiracy in October. PRO SP 29/428/16. Rumsey averred that he had learned of the October scheme from John Row, whose source was West. *Copies*, p. 17. West's clerk, Benjamin Wetton, who had been an agent for Shaftesbury and had helped Stephen College "manage" Popish Plot witnesses, remained close to College's sister in the ensuing years. Wetton was arrested in June 1683, in the early stages of the discovery of the Rye House Plot, but apparently only after destroying West's papers, as he had been instructed. PRO SP 29/425/37, 42, 48, 58, 59. Richard Goodenough later confessed that he had first learned of a "design" about October 1682. BL Lansdowne MSS 1152, fol. 243r.

71. *Copies*, pp. 103, 108; PRO SP 29/428/31, 79. Prior to October, Howard insisted that he had heard plans for an insurrection referred to "only mistically." During October and November, he claimed to have had hints from Walcott, (Richard?) Goodenough, West, and Ferguson "of Striking at the Head" or shortening the work by removing two persons, which he assumed meant "some Attempt" on Charles and James; he received, he said, no details. According to Rumsey the conspirators distrusted Howard because of his loose tongue. PRO SP 29/428/31; *Copies*, pp. 25, 104.

72. BL Add. MSS 41,818, fol. 214r–v; 41,819, fol. 17r. Row was dismissed as swordbearer on 31 May 1683 for having spoken opprobrious words against

the government and prominent persons in Bristol. Latimer, *Annals*, p. 404.

73. Ferguson, "Rye House," p. 427; Grey, *SH*, pp. 27–28; *Copies*, pp. 103–4; Haley, p. 715.

74. Grey, *SH*, p. 28; *Copies*, p. 24; PRO SP 29/431/11. Thomas Shepherd may have been related to Anthony Shepherd, Shaftesbury's servant. Haley, p. 717. Anthony Shepherd later admitted the earl had gone to Thomas Shepherd's house, but provided no details. PRO SP 29/428/116.

75. Grey, *SH*, pp. 29–30.

76. PRO SP 29/429/89; *Copies*, pp. 193–94; Ferguson, "Rye House," pp. 427–28.

77. Grey, *SH*, pp. 30–32.

78. Ibid., pp. 32–33; PRO SP 29/434/98; Sprat, p. 470.

79. PRO SP 29/421/30; 29/424/114; 29/428/31; 29/430/34; EUL MSS La.II.89, fol. 182r; Carstares, *Deposition*, p. 4. Francis Smith also knew of the proposed uprising. PRO SP 29/424/114.

80. Morrice, 1: 341, 343, 344; Sprat, p. 47.

81. Grey, *SH*, pp. 33–35; PRO SP 29/425/139. Spence admitted that on his arrival in the Netherlands he consulted with James Stewart and Lord Stair, but he refused to say whether or not he saw Argyll. PRO SP 29/425/139.

82. Ferguson attributed Trenchard's hesitance to cowardice or venereal disease. "Rye House," p. 428.

83. Grey, *SH*, pp. 35–37; *Copies*, pp. 17, 24.

84. BL Add. MSS 38,847, fol. 97r–v; *Copies*, p. 67. West thought he had heard the information about Chepstow Castle from John Row or Joseph Foley. PRO SP 29/426, pt. 3, p. 33.

85. PRO SP 29/425/138, p. 29; 29/433/8, p. 39; 29/438/2, 3; Grey, *SH*, p. 37; *Copies*, pp. 14, 109.

86. Morrice, 1: 340, 358.

87. Armstrong later acknowledged he was present at gatherings in Shepherd's home. PRO SP 29/433/8. Grey claimed that Henry Cornish had attended one of these meetings, but not while the proposed insurrection was being discussed; Ferguson made the same point. Grey had been told that Cornish was privy to the plotting and was prepared to assist, but the source of this information was not identified and is almost certainly erroneous. Grey, *SH*, p. 39; Ferguson, "Rye House," p. 427. Rumsey did not mention Cornish. PRO SP 29/438/3.

88. *Copies*, p. 194; Grey, *SH*, pp. 38–39.

89. PRO SP 29/428/60, pp. 36–42; BL Add. MSS 38,847, fol. 90r–v; West, *An Answer*, p. 1; *Copies*, p. 88. Ferguson, disguised in "a coloured suit & a shabby perewig," met with Nelthorpe and Robert Blaney of the Middle Temple near the Young Devil tavern on 14 or 15 November. After his arrest, however, Blaney claimed he had first learned of the conspiracy on 27 December. PRO SP 29/426, pt. 2, p. 29; *Copies*, p. 31.

90. BL Add. MSS 38,847, fols. 90v–91r.

91. *Copies*, p. 129; PRO SP 29/428/4, 5; EUL MSS La.I.332, p. 7. In July 1683, Brandon denied knowledge of the conspiracy. Such testimony is not always reliable; Walcott made a similar statement before he confessed. PRO SP 29/428/4, 31.

92. BL Add. MSS 38,849, fol. 91r; Grey, *SH*, pp. 39–40.

93. *Copies*, p. 24; PRO SP 29/428/4, 5; 29/433/7; Ferguson, "Rye House," p. 429; Sprat, p. 49; Burnet, 2: 351; Haley, p. 723. Essex's mother-in-law, Anne Cecil, was the daughter of the second earl of Salisbury. Cokayne, 5: 145–46.

94. Haley, pp. 728–29; Ferguson, "Rye House," p. 429; Sprat, p. 49; Morrice, 1: 345, 370. Culliford does not appear in Plomer, *DBP* or *DPB*.

95. Greaves, *EUHF*, pp. 199, 298; Haley, p. 729; BL Add. MSS 35,104, fols. 78r–v, 82v; 37,980, fol. 256r, 257v–258r.

96. In late December, Shaftesbury was staying with Abraham Kicke (or Keck), who had betrayed the regicides Miles Corbet, John Okey, and John Barkstead in 1662. BL Add. MSS 37,980, fol. 273r; Greaves, *DUFE*, pp. 92–93.

97. BL Add. MSS 35,104, fol. 83r–v; 37,980, fol. 263r–v, 298r; 41,809, fol. 13r; 46,960A, fol. 21r.

98. BL Add. MSS 38,849, fol. 91r–v; *Copies*, p. 91; Grey, *SH*, p. 40.

99. Ferguson, "Rye House," p. 429.

100. BL Add. MSS 38,847, fol. 92r–v.

101. BL Add. MSS 38,847, fols. 92v–93r.

102. BL Add. MSS 38,847, fol. 93r; *Copies*, p. 61.

103. BL Add. MSS 38,847, fols. 93r–94r; *Copies*, pp. 60, 88; Sprat, p. 68. Cf. Add. MSS 41,818, fol. 214v, where Row reportedly claimed to have met with West, Aaron Smith, and Ferguson, after which he sought Trenchard's advice. In Amsterdam, Ferguson stayed with Israel Hayes, who allegedly believed that "the King was chiefe Actor, & Deepest in the Papist Plott then any whatsoever, [and] therefore must downe[,] must downe." PRO SP 29/433/39.

104. *Copies*, p. 17.

105. BL Lansdowne MSS 1152, fols. 245r–v, 249r.

Chapter 4

1. Grey, *SH*, p. 41.

2. BL Add. MSS 38,847, fols. 94v–95r; *Copies*, pp. 48, 56; PRO SP 29/425/56; 29/428/16; Sprat, p. 68.

3. *Copies*, p. 17; BL Add. MSS 41,819, fol. 159r.

4. BL Add. MSS 32,520, fol. 197v; 38,847, fol. 95r; PRO SP 29/425/138, pp. 25–26; 29/430/111; *Copies*, pp. 31–32; Sprat, p. 54. For Battiscombe, who

came from a prominent family in Bridport, Dorset, see PRO SP 29/427/128; Dorset Record Office MSS D239/f16.

5. PRO SP 29/422/13; BL Add. MSS 38,847, fol. 95r–v; *Copies*, pp. 27, 61–62, 88.

6. BL Lansdowne MSS 1152, fols. 249v–250v.

7. *Copies*, pp. 104–5; *ST*, 9: 609–10; Sprat, pp. 52, 84–85. The previous December, James had accused Monmouth (in a letter to Viscount Hyde) of making himself "the head of the Phanatical and republican party." BL Add. MSS 15,892, fol. 146r–v.

8. PRO SP 29/428/31, 32, 33, 60, pp. 4, 14; 29/428/79. During the period of intensive plotting commencing in October 1682, the earl of Anglesey had periodic social contact with a number of the conspirators, including Monmouth, Essex, Howard, and Grey, but no hard evidence proves his involvement in the scheming. BL Add. MSS 18,730, fols. 100v–104v.

9. *ST*, 9: 610–11; *Copies*, pp. 105–6; PRO SP 29/427/99; 29/428/4, 31; 29/428/60, pp. 5–6; 29/436/108, 109; 44/64, p. 181; Sprat, pp. 35, 52, 86. Smith may have been accompanied by his brother-in-law, Thomas Weeks, an avid Whig who had previously concealed the duke of Buckingham and Ferguson, and had posted bail for Smith. PRO SP 29/429/195. Starkey claimed to have overheard Smith, Simon Mayne, and Samuel Mayne discuss the possibility of shooting Charles and James and then planting the weapon on the earl of Feversham, thereby casting blame on the Jesuits. The conversation allegedly occurred about May 1680, when the king was ill at Windsor. PRO SP 29/430/82. According to West, Shaftesbury had previously sent for Cochrane and Sir George Campbell; if so, they either did not receive the message or declined to come. *Copies*, p. 69. Smith lived in the London house of the Congregationalist minister Jeremiah White, where his visitors included Nelthorpe, West, and one of the Goodenoughs. PRO SP 29/428/60, pp. 36–41.

10. *ST*, 9: 612. For Monmouth's visit to Chichester see PRO SP 29/422/83, 86, 91; NUL MSS PwV 95, p. 274. Major John Breman was also present.

11. Grey, *SH*, pp. 42–43.

12. Grey, *SH*, pp. 43–46; PRO SP 29/427/30; 29/428/31; 29/429/40, 89; BL Add. MSS 8127, fol. 68r. From the time of the second and third exclusion parliaments to at least March 1683, Monmouth met at Sir Thomas Player's house with such City Whigs as Sir Patience Ward, Sir Robert Clayton, Sir Thomas Pilkington, Richard Shute, and Henry Cornish. PRO SP 29/425/101.

13. BL Lansdowne MSS 1152, fols. 251r–252r.

14. BL Add. MSS 38,847, fol. 95v; *Copies*, pp. 17–18. In February 1683, Richard Goodenough attempted to overturn the election of North and Box by arresting the lord mayor, a sheriff, and three or four aldermen and threatening to arrest the other aldermen. JRL Legh of Lyme MSS (newsletter to

Richard Legh, 3 Feb. 1683); ChRO MSS DCH/K/3/6 (Hugh Beheathland to William Adams, 26 Apr. 1683).

15. BL Add. MSS 38,847, fols. 95v–96r; *Copies*, pp. 48–49; PRO SP 29/428/60, pp. 40–41.

16. PRO SP 29/428/60, pp. 102–3; 29/431/11.

17. BL Add. MSS 38,847, fol. 96r; *Copies*, pp. 24–25, 58–60; PRO SP 29/426, pt. 3, p. 33; 29/436/100.

18. BL Add. MSS 38,847, fol. 96r–v.

19. BL Add. MSS 38,847, fol. 96v; *Copies*, pp. 19, 23–25; PRO SP 29/436/100; Elizabeth D'Oyley, *James Duke of Monmouth* (London: Geoffrey Bles, 1938), p. 220.

20. Ferguson, "Rye House," p. 431.

21. PRO SP 29/421/140, 140.1.

22. Ferguson, "Rye House," pp. 431–32; West, *An Answer*, p. 1; Sprat, p. 53.

23. Ferguson, "Rye House," pp. 432–33; *Copies*, p. 28.

24. BL Add. MSS 38,847, fol. 97v.

25. Ferguson, "Rye House," p. 433.

26. Ibid., pp. 433–34. Ferguson identifies the person in question ("the first proposer") only as the man whom he had previously mentioned as having spoken of "Killing outlying Staggs & Beasts of spoile." Ferguson claimed "an intire friendship" existed between this person, who I believe was Wildman, and the three agents provocateur. Ibid., p. 434.

27. Ibid., p. 434.

28. Ibid., p. 436.

29. BL Add. MSS 38,847, fol. 96v.

30. BL Add. MSS 38,847, fols. 98r–99v; PRO SP 29/426, pt. 3, p. 3; *Copies*, pp. 56, 197–98; Sprat, p. 67. The Rye House also had a high tower with a commanding view.

31. Rumbold also allegedly claimed that approximately seven years earlier (c. 1676) he had plotted to blow up a theater when Charles and James were present but desisted because too many innocent people would have perished. BL Add. MSS 38,847, fol. 105v.

32. BL Add. MSS 38,847, fol. 99v; BL Lansdowne MSS 1152, fol. 243r (though Goodenough recalled that Rumbold had dated the plot at about 1678); Sprat, p. 69.

33. BL Add. MSS 38,847, fols. 99v–100r; *Copies*, p. 83.

34. BL Add. MSS 38,847, fols. 101v–102r.

35. PRO SP 29/425/87.1; 29/427/49, 98; 29/433/45; BL Add. MSS 38,847, fols. 100r–v, 103r, 105r–v, 117v; *Copies*, pp. 85–86, 90, 92; Sprat, pp. 22, 32; NUL MSS PwV 95, pp. 245–46. According to West, for reasons of security the conspirators considered assassinating Sir Nicholas Butler to undermine

his network of informers, but they opted instead to trust their compatriots. BL Add. MSS 38,847, fol. 100v. West had once hired Hone to wainscot his chambers. PRO SP 29/425/180.

36. BL Add. MSS 38,847, fols. 100v–101r; *Copies*, p. 63.

37. BL Add. MSS 38,847, fol. 101r–v; *Copies*, pp. 63–64. Cf. London *Gazette*, 1848 (2–6 Aug. 1683).

38. BL Add. MSS 38,847, fols. 102v–103v; *Copies*, pp. 64, 85. Two London citizens later claimed they had seen West, Nelthorpe, and a third person examining the Tower's defenses in March 1683. PRO SP 29/428/19.

39. BL Add. MSS 38,847, fol. 102r; *Copies*, p. 83. The publication of a manifesto ruled out the possibility of blaming Catholics for the assassination, an idea that was briefly considered. BL Add. MSS 38,847, fol. 102r–v.

40. PRO SP 29/428/15.1; BL Add. MSS 38,847, fol. 104v; *Copies*, p. 83; NUL MSS PwV 95, p. 296.

41. BL Add. MSS 38,847, fols. 103v–104r; *Copies*, pp. 82, 85, 90; Sprat, pp. 81–82.

42. BL Add. MSS 38,847, fol. 104v; NUL MSS PwV 95, pp. 259–60; *Copies*, p. 85; PRO SP 29/426, pt. 5, p. 9.

43. BL Add. MSS 38,847, fols. 103v, 105r, 106v; *Copies*, pp. 62, 82–83; Sprat, p. 59.

44. BL Add. MSS 38,847, fol. 106r–107r; *Copies*, p. 60.

45. Cambridge University, Pepys Library, Misc. MSS 7, p. 489; BL Add. MSS 38,847, fol. 107r; 62,453, fol. 3v; Morrice, 1: 317; J. G. Muddiman, *The King's Journalist 1659–1689: Studies in the Reign of Charles II* (London: John Lane, 1923), pp. 215–16; Sprat, pp. 32–33.

46. *Copies*, pp. 18, 20. According to Rumsey, at the ensuing meeting Ferguson said the indemnity could not be raised with the duke. Ibid., pp. 20–21.

47. Ibid., p. 24; BL Lansdowne MSS 1152, fol. 243v.

48. Walcott, *True Copy of a Paper*, pp. 1–2; PRO SP 29/428/4, 5; 29/429/32; *Copies*, p. 129. For Rumbold see *ST*, 11: 879–80.

49. PRO SP 29/433/8, p. 39.

50. BL Add. MSS 32,520, fol. 194v; *Copies*, pp. 1–2, 28–29.

51. BL Add. MSS 38,847, fol. 107r; *Copies*, p. 45.

52. BL Add. MSS 38,847, fols. 107v–108r; *Copies*, p. 45.

53. *Copies*, p. 23.

54. London *Gazette*, 1810 (22–26 Mar. 1683); 1811 (26–29 Mar. 1683); BL Add. MSS 28,875, fol. 238r; ChRO MSS DCH/K/3/6 (Hugh Beheathland to William Adams, 24 Mar. 1683).

55. BL Add. MSS 28,875, fol. 234r; 38,847, fols. 108v–109r; *Copies*, pp. 21, 39, 51, 109; PRO SP 29/438/2. During the investigation of the plot, the government learned that West had allegedly received £500 in March 1683. PRO

SP 29/425/59. Hone admitted that about the time of the fire he had been recruited by Goodenough and promised £20 with which to purchase a horse and weapons. Goodenough, he confessed, took him to Sergeants' cook shop, where they were joined by Rumbold and Keeling; the ensuing discussion was about "Clothes," apparently referring to the need to find more men for the party of assassins. *Copies*, p. 94.

56. BL Add. MSS 62,453, fol. 3r–v.

57. BL Add. MSS 62,453, fol. 3v; BL Lansdowne MSS 1152, fols. 247r, 296r.

58. PRO SP 29/417/207.1, 208; 29/418/53, 81; 29/419/93.

59. PRO SP 29/420/35, 36, 79.1, 122, 137, 156; 29/421/7, 30, 31, 78; 29/432/72, 73; cf. 29/429/184; 29/437/85, 85.1

60. PRO SP 29/422/88; cf. 29/427/87.

61. PRO SP 29/422/93.1; 44/68, p. 210.

62. PRO SP 29/422/152; 29/430/III, pp. 39–42. There is no evidence that the strategy detailed in this plan was discussed by West's group. The rebels purportedly would have disguised themselves as a foot company of the king's guards and made their appearance shortly before a regular relief company was due. A Mr. Powell had reportedly been involved in the attempted theft of the crown jewels; in January 1682, one Nathaniel Powell was fined 13*s*. 4*d*. for calling James a pimp and the son of a whore; and a Captain Powell was accused of conspiracy with such radicals as Breman and Mansell by Sir Robert Viner in February 1683. PRO SP 29/418/19; 29/422/88.

63. *Letters to Thoresby*, I: 23–24; Morrice, I: 362; PRO SP 29/423/98.

64. PRO SP 29/424/116; Ashcraft, p. 333. The letter was printed in the *Observator*, 2, no. 109 (4 Aug. 1684). Cf. Andrew Lang, *Sir George Mackenzie, King's Advocate, of Rosehaugh: His Life and Times 1636(?)–1691* (London: Longmans, Green, 1909), p. 240 n. 1. Walcott had written a letter to Jenkins sometime after 12 June, when the plot was disclosed. BL Add. MSS 32,520, fol. 196r.

Chapter 5

1. EUL MSS La.II.89, fols. 181v–182r. Carstares had been part of William of Orange's intelligence network and continued to corerspond with Hans Bentinck and Gaspar Fagel, the Grand Pensionary. Robert Herbert Story, *William Carstares: A Character and Career of the Revolutionary Epoch (1649–1715)* (London: Macmillan, 1874), pp. 29–30, 91.

2. EUL MSS La.II.89, fol. 181r. During his interrogation more than a year prior to Carstares' confession, Shepherd apparently provided no details about this episode, although he admitted that Carstares had been "the messenger." PRO SP 29/430/III, p. 16.

3. EUL MSS La.II.89, fol. 181r–v; PRO SP 29/436/90.

4. Haley, p. 706; *ST*, 9: 1021–54; PRO SP 29/436/54; *Letters to Aberdeen*, pp. 58–60, 69; *HMC* 34, *Fourteenth Report*, Appendix 3, p. 113; *HMC* 44, *Drumlanrig*, vol. 1, Appendix 8, pp. 175, 242; 2: 106; *RPCS*, 7: 599–600; Sprat, p. 36.

5. *HMC* 34, *Fourteenth Report*, Appendix 3, pp. 114–15; PRO SP 29/428/58; 29/432/4; 29/436/42; Sprat, pp. 35, 134–35. In Scotland, Smith was directed to Cochrane's house by Thomas Steill (or Steil), the marquis of Douglas' chamberlain. Steill subsequently went to Carolina with Cardross in July 1684. PRO SP 29/436/42; *Copies*, pp. 103–4; Erskine, p. 68. I owe this point to Patrick Riordan.

6. *MVB*, p. 143; *Tryal and Process Against Baillie*, p. 12; PRO SP 29/425/106; 29/435/55; *Letters to Aberdeen*, p. 152; *Acts of the Parliaments of Scotland*, vol. 8, Appendix, p. 40; Sprat, p. 139. Another Covenanting minister, George Brysson, was also in London at this time and was a friend of some of the Scots later imprisoned on suspicion of plotting. *MVB*, pp. 291–94.

7. EUL MSS La.II.89, fol. 181v; *Copies*, p. 194.

8. EUL MSS La.II.89, fol. 181v; PRO SP 29/427/98, 103; 29/428/60, p. 89; 29/430/111, p. 7; *Copies*, p. 185; Sprat, p. 32. Among the others who visited Ferguson at Bourne's house were Armstrong, Baillie, Ayloffe, Meade, Sir George Campbell, John Freke, and Sir Robert Rich. PRO SP 29/427/98, 111. Rich admitted knowing Ferguson and having cared for his wife when she was ill. PRO SP 29/427/127.

9. EUL MSS La.II.89, fols. 181v–182r; Sprat, pp. 124–25.

10. EUL MSS La.II.89, fol. 181v; *ST*, 10: 662–65; *Tryall and Process Against Baillie*, pp. 5, 12–13.

11. *ST*, 10: 671–82; Sprat, pp. 36, 121–37; *Tryall and Process Against Baillie*, p. 13.

12. PRO SP 29/425/138, pp. 1–2, 5–7; EUL MSS La.II.89, fols. 181v–182r; BL Add. MSS 38,847, fol. 113r. Holmes was the communications link between Argyll and Carstares. PRO SP 29/428/60, pp. 85–86, 89; 29/430/111, p. 7.

13. BL Lansdowne MSS 1152, fols. 247r–248r, 249r–v, 251r; EUL MSS La.I.332, p. 3. Holmes confessed that Carstares had informed him the conspirators had agreed to raise £10,000 for Argyll. PRO SP 29/433/8, p. 14. Shepherd insisted he had never discussed the conspiracy with Carstares, contrary to the latter's allegations. PRO SP 29/438/38, 39.

14. PRO SP 29/425/138, p. 29; 29/428/60, pp. 21–22, 25–27, 72–79; 29/431/11; 29/433/8, pp. 6, 13; 29/435/76; 29/436/90 (cf. 101); *Copies*, pp. 14–15, 185.

15. Grey, *SH*, pp. 47–49. In the spring of 1683, Howard spent three weeks at his estate in Essex followed by five weeks in Bath. *ST*, 9: 611.

16. Grey, *SH*, p. 50; PRO SP 29/438/2.

17. Grey, *SH*, pp. 51–58.

18. Ibid., pp. 58–59; PRO SP 29/428/60, p. 89; 29/430/111, p. 7.

19. Grey, *SH*, pp. 59–60.

20. PRO SP 29/424/55, 59, 68; 44/54, pp. 165–66; Grey, *SH*, p. 60; BL Add. MSS 28,875, fol. 251r–v; *HMC* 35, *Fourteenth Report*, p. 160. One of the Iretons and a Mr. Overton were arrested with Grey. Morrice, 1: 367.

21. *ST*, 9: 187–298; Morrice, 1: 367–68; London *Gazette*, 1823 (7–10 May 1683); 1837 (25–28 June 1683).

22. Grey, *SH*, pp. 61–62.

23. BL Add. MSS 38,847, fol. 109r–v; *Copies*, pp. 2–3, 18, 39; *ST*, 9: 574, 575; Sprat, p. 53.

24. BL Add. MSS 38,847, fols. 109v–110r; *Copies*, pp. 40, 51.

25. *Copies*, pp. 18, 21; PRO SP 29/425/73; 29/433/7.

26. BL Add. MSS 38,847, fols. 110r–111r; NUL MSS PwV 95, pp. 237, 259, 286–87, 289; *Letters to Aberdeen*, p. 130; PRO SP 29/425/56; 29/427/98; 29/428/79; *Copies*, pp. 21–22, 39–40, 78–80; West, *An Answer*, p. 2; Morrice, 1: 402; Sprat, p. 77. Cf. PRO SP 29/426, pt. 5, p. 6.

27. BL Add. MSS 38,847, fol. 111r; *Copies*, pp. 51–52.

28. BL Lansdowne MSS 1152, fol. 242r.

29. BL Add. MSS 38,847, fol. 111v; *Copies*, p. 18; PRO SP 29/425/73.

30. PRO SP 29/425/138, pp. 5–7; 29/428/30; BL Add. MSS 38,847, fols. 111v–112r. Cf. *Copies*, pp. 25, 50.

31. BL Add. MSS 38,847, fol. 112r–v; *Copies*, pp. 26, 52; Sprat, p. 63. During this period West tried to recruit Carleton Whitlock and Edmund Waller, but both, according to their own testimony, declined. Whitlock later claimed West had told him about the failed Rye House scheme and plans to purchase weapons in the Netherlands and had mentioned the involvement of Wildman, Sidney, Russell, and Ferguson. PRO SP 29/427/98; *Copies*, pp. 70–71.

32. BL Add. MSS 38,847, fol. 112v.

33. BL Add. MSS 38,847, fols. 112v–113r; *Copies*, p. 50.

34. BL Add. MSS 38,847, fol. 113r–v; *Copies*, pp. 22, 52; PRO SP 29/425/138, pp. 5–7; 29/438/3.

35. BL Add. MSS 62, 453, fols. 3v–4r. According to Bourne, at whose house Ferguson lived, the Scottish preacher's visitors in the spring included Armstrong, Rumsey, Walcott, Wade, Norton, Richard Goodenough, West, Nelthorpe, Charlton, Shepherd, Ayloffe, Blaney, Freke, Bethel, Sir Robert Rich, Baillie, Carstares, other Scots, and unidentified persons from Wapping. Ferguson also lodged with three other men in London. *Copies*, pp. 79–81, 185; PRO SP 29/428/60, pp. 77–78.

36. BL Add. MSS 62,453, fol. 4r.

37. BL Add. MSS 38,847, fol. 113v–115r; 62,453, fol. 4r–v; PRO SP 29/428/4; 29/436/100; 29/437/105.1; *Copies*, pp. 18–19, 40, 53–54. According to West's

account, each district leader would recruit fourteen or fifteen men, each of them being responsible for ten others.

38. BL Add. MSS 38,847, fol. 115r; 62,453, fol. 4v; *Copies*, pp. 19, 36–37, 53; PRO SP 29/437/105.1, 133 (where Armstrong indicates that Wade was absent when the City was divided into districts); Sprat, p. 56.

39. BL Lansdowne MSS 1152, fols. 241r–v, 242v, 245r–248r, 249r, 296r, 298r. Rope (or Roop, Rooke) may have been the Devon emissary sent by "Renolds"—probably Thomas Reynell, who had sat for Ashburton, Devon, in the Exclusion Parliaments—and the "honest" gentlemen of that county to learn what the conspirators planned to do. Before coming to London, Rope had reportedly conferred with Sir Francis Rolle, as instructed by Reynell. BL Lansdowne MSS 1152, fol. 250v. Cf. PRO SP 29/428/60, pp. 48–49. For Reynell see Lacey, p. 438.

40. BL Add. MSS 38,847, fol. 115v–117r; *Copies*, pp. 19, 54, 75; PRO SP 29/425/73; Sprat, pp. 52–53. According to Bourne, Walcott convened the session at the Salutation tavern so the plotters could confer with Shepherd. *Copies*, p. 80. Keeling claimed he had attended a meeting at this tavern on 7 June, at which (Richard?) Goodenough, Wade, Nelthorpe, West, and "Colonel" (Rumsey) were also present. *Copies*, p. 4.

41. BL Add. MSS 38,847, fol. 115v–116r; *Copies*, pp. 76, 96–97; PRO SP 29/425/87.1; 29/425/138, pp. 37–40; 29/428/4; Sprat, p. 61. Samuel Starkey, Aaron Smith's clerk, claimed to have seen a list of approximately 1,200 names of persons who were "known sticklers for their party[,] noe King's men but Down right Commonwealths men." The roster, he said, was in the possession of Peter Essington. PRO SP 29/431/68.

42. *Copies*, pp. 74–75; BL Add. MSS 38,847, fol. 116r. West's account corroborates Bourne's version. Lobb had been convicted of preaching at conventicles four times in July and August 1682. *Middlesex County Records*, 4: 165–68.

43. Morrice, 1: 348–49, 351–55, 357, 360; PRO SP 29/421/109, 177; 29/422/ 22, 79; 29/423/24; 44/66, pp. 187–88; 44/68, p. 237; *CSPD 1683*, 1: 50, BL Add. MSS 46,960A, fol. 22r.

44. PRO SP 29/431/4, 76, 99, 103; 29/433/93. Like Carstares, John Anderson obtained permission to travel to Scotland in March 1689; the two men may have been associated. *CSPD 1689–90*, pp. 15–16.

45. PRO SP 29/428/60, p. 97; 29/430/111, p. 33; 29/430/169; 29/431/3, 30 (which refers to William Dyke), 34, 58; 44/66, p. 261; Sprat, p. 32. The other members of Gladman's group were Dr. John Heath and Jeremiah House (or Houze); the latter knew Rumbold and Thomas Lee.

46. *Copies*, pp. 75, 80, 92–93; BL Add. MSS 38,847, fol. 116r; PRO SP 29/ 427/114; 29/430/40.

47. *Copies*, pp. 3–4, 5–7 (which dates Keeling's meeting with Goodenough on the 14th), 13, 86; PRO SP 29/413/64, 73, 81; 29/425/55; 29/425/138,

pp. 37–40; 29/427/98; 44/62, p. 9; *ST*, 9: 372; BL Lansdowne MSS 1152, fol. 242r. Cf. PRO SP 29/429/86. Bourne also noted that Goodenough had recruited Grange, who reportedly was to have enlisted men to attack Whitehall. PRO SP 29/427/98.

48. PRO SP 29/425/87.1; 29/425/138, pp. 45–50, 57–58, 61–63, 67, 81; 29/426, pt. 2, pp. 42–43, 45; 29/426, pt. 5, pp. 5–7; 29/427/98; 29/428/60, pp. 12–13, 23, 31–39, 50–51; 29/428/78, 79, 81; 29/430/III, p. 31; 29/434/45; 29/435/1; 29/436/61; *Copies*, pp. 16, 34–36, 96; NUL MSS PwV 95, p. 266; *ST*, 11: 467–74; *Last Speech*, pp. 7–8. Among the more improbable elements of Lee's testimony are his accusations that Francis Jenks promised to provide weapons for ten men and that Bateman consulted personally with Monmouth, apparently about the conspiracy. Lee claimed West had informed him that Robert Perrott, a former associate of Thomas Blood's, was engaged in the plot. PRO SP 29/436/31.

49. BL Add. MSS 38,847, fol. 116r–v. West claimed that Bourne had agreed to seize the lord keeper, who lived nearby; Bourne insisted that he had refused West's request to do so. *Copies*, p. 77. A woolcomber named Jeffreys confessed he had agreed to help Hone arrest the lord mayor. PRO SP 29/433/7; *Copies*, p. 80.

50. BL Add. MSS 38,847, fols. 116v–117r; *Copies*, pp. 26, 64–65, 76; *CSPD 1683*, 1: 352; Sprat, pp. 63–65. Bourne's confession substantiates West's account. *Copies*, p. 77.

51. *Copies*, pp. 12, 76–77; PRO SP 29/427/98.

52. BL Add. MSS 62, 453, fol. 4v; Sprat, p. 66; PRO SP 29/430/III, p. 29; 29/436/66.

53. PRO SP 29/428/9, 23, 37; 29/430/114; 29/431/28.

54. BL Add. MSS 38,847, fol. 115v.

55. PRO SP 29/429/239, 240.

56. BL Add. MSS 41,803, fols. 55r–57v; PRO SP 44/54, p. 202; Sprat, pp. 24, 32; *Calendar of Treasury Papers 1681–85*, p. 968.

57. *Copies*, pp. 6–8; BL Add. MSS 41,803, fols. 57v–58r.

58. BL Add. MSS 32,520, fol. 194v; 38,847, fol. 118r–v; 41,803, fols. 57v–58r; *Copies*, pp. 55, 77; PRO SP 29/428/4.

59. BL Add. MSS 38,847, fols. 118v–119r; 41,803, fol. 58r; *Copies*, pp. 54, 77–79; PRO SP 29/426, pt. 5, p. 8; Sprat, p. 78. Cf. BL Add. MSS 32,520, fol. 257r.

60. NUL MSS PwV 95, p. 235; BL Add. MSS 38,847, fol. 119r–v; *Copies*, pp. 66, 91; Sprat, pp. 91–93.

61. PRO SP 29/425/43; 44/68, pp. 293–94.

62. PRO SP 29/425/65, 67, 80, 111, 113, 129, 131, 148, 149; 29/427/11, 11.1, 15, 17A, 20, 39, 40, 60, 63, 66, 68, 71, 72, 73, 90, 92, 94, 97; 29/428/3, 112, 113, 143, 169, 186; 29/429/9, 106; 29/430/67; 44/68, pp. 301, 306–8, 310, 322, 326–27, 341, 349, 353; 44/69, p. 39; 44/335, pp. 8–10, 14, 20–21; NUL MSS PwV 95,

p. 237; BL Add. MSS 18,730, fol. 105v; BL Egerton MSS 2543, fol. 251v; CumRO(K) MSS WD/Ry, Box 35 (warrant of 20 July 1683); London *Gazette*, 1836 (21–25 June 1683). Cf. *CSPD 1683*, 1: 340.

63. NUL MSS PwV 95, p. 248; PRO SP 29/425/68; 29/427/18, 19; 29/428/21; 44/54, p. 182; 44/68, p. 309; 44/335, pp. 7–8.

64. *RPCS*, 8: 183–84, 187–89; 9: 173–74; 10: 46; PRO SP 29/438/47; *CSPD 1684–85*, p. 158.

65. PRO SP 63/343/139, 141, 142; BL Lansdowne MSS 1152, fols. 182r, 183r; Bodl. Carte MSS 40, fols. 55r, 57r, 63r, 73r, 88r, 90r, 100r; *HMC* 36, *Ormonde*, n.s., 7: 59, 63, 76; NUL MSS PwV 95, p. 306; Pinney, *Letters*, p. 15.

66. PRO SP 29/417/105; *True Protestant Mercury*, 117 (15–18 Feb. 1682); *Impartial Protestant Mercury*, 92 (7–10 Mar. 1682). Cf. PRO SP 29/420/107. For Nichols see Greaves, *EUHF*, pp. 263, 302.

67. BL Lansdowne MSS 1152, fols. 122r, 153r, 154r, 156r, 171r, 172r–v, 174r, 227r; PRO SP 29/425/83, 103, 104, 132, 134, 156; 29/427/16, 34, 119; 29/437/65; 44/64, pp. 159–60; 44/68, p. 311; 44/335, p. 444; 63/340, pp. 37, 39–42; 63/341, pp. 154–55, 158; 63/343/149, 149.1, 164, 164.1; *CSPD 1685*, p. 296; *HMC* 36, *Ormonde*, n.s., 7: 63, 65; Ashcraft, p. 374 n. 154. Owen was transferred from a Cork prison to one in Bristol in October 1685. BL Lansdowne MSS 1152, fol. 374r; PRO SP 31/1/135; 44/56, p. 282. For Anglesey's ties to Monmouth see, e.g., BL Add. MSS 40,860, fols. 89v, 90v, 92v, 98r. Rumbold's son, a sugar-baker, reportedly lived in Dublin, and his daughter was thought to reside in Ireland as well. *HMC* 36, *Ormonde*, n.s., 7: 76.

68. PRO SP 29/427/60, 119; 29/428/4, 8, 8.1, 22–24; 29/428/60, p. 31; 29/428/94. For the robbery of the exchequer at Taunton see Greaves, *EUHF*, pp. 7, 258 n. 15.

69. PRO SP 29/428/178, 178.1, 178.2, 179; 29/429/77, 129; 44/68, p. 340; Jonathan Scott, "England's Troubles: Exhuming the Popish Plot," in *The Politics of Religion in Restoration England*, ed. Tim Harris, Paul Seaward, and Mark Goldie (Oxford: Basil Blackwell, 1990), p. 126. Cf. PRO SP 63/343/137, 138.

70. BL Add. MSS 38,847, fol. 120r–v.

71. PRO SP 29/430/16.

72. NUL MSS PwV 95, p. 237; BL Add. MSS 32,520, fol. 195r; London *Gazette*, 1836 (21–25 June 1683); Grey, *SH*, pp. 62–63. Cf. PRO SP 29/426, pt. 3, p. 44; 29/428/16. The date of Rumsey's surrender is erroneously given as 25 June in NUL MSS PwV 95, p. 240. Cf. PRO SP 29/425/64.

73. PRO SP 29/425/23, 64, 79; 63/341, p. 151; NUL MSS PwV 95, p. 243; Prinsterer, pp. 577–78; Sprat, p. 24; *HMC* 36, *Ormonde*, n.s., 7: 53–54.

74. BL Egerton MSS 2618, fol. 140r; BL Harleian MSS 6845, fol. 268v.

75. Lois G. Schwoerer, "The Trial of Lord William Russell (1683): Judicial Murder?" *Journal of Legal History*, 9 (Sept. 1988): 144–45.

76. Grey, *SH*, pp. 63–64; BL Add. MSS 32,520, fol. 195v; NUL MSS PwV 95, pp. 240, 243, 245–46, 257, 274; PRO SP 29/425/77, 79, 115; 29/429/87, 133, 143, 204.1; 29/430/27, 41; 29/433/129; 29/434/19, 58; 44/54, p. 177; 44/68, pp. 299, 310; Morrice, 1: 339, 369, 371, 375, 381; JRL Legh of Lyme MSS (newsletter to Richard Legh, 17 July 1683); *RPCS*, 9: 133; *Letters to Aberdeen*, p. 135; *Copies*, p. 40; *CSPD 1683*, 2: 25, 145–46; V. Sackville-West, *Knole and the Sackvilles* (London: William Heinemann, 1922), p. 134.

77. PRO SP 29/425/79, 105, 115, 123, 128, 140, 151, 161, 165, 216; 29/427/6, 12, 91; 29/428/36; 29/430/149; *CSPD 1683*, 1: 359–60; *HMC 29, Portland*, 2: 236; *HMC 43, Fifteenth Report*, Appendix 7, p. 110; BL Add. MSS 4107, fol. 38v; 62,453, fols. 102–3 (printed); London *Gazette*, 1838 (28 June–2 July 1683). One of Monmouth's retainers, a Mr. Dynant, was arrested at Ipswich in late July and reportedly confessed various things concerning the conspiracy. Another, John Gibbons, had been apprehended earlier the same month. NUL MSS PwV 95, pp. 257, 278.

78. Grey, *SH*, p. 68; PRO SP 29/425/150; 29/427/116; 29/428/1; 29/428/60, pp. 46–49; 29/429/28, 51, 91, 121, 186, 186.1; 29/436/54; NUL MSS PwV 95, pp. 256, 330. When Grey arrived in the Netherlands he stayed briefly in the Rotterdam home of James Washington, a prominent member of the radical community. PRO SP 29/436/54; cf. Greaves, *EUHF*, pp. 13, 42, 109, 298. According to the bishop of Chichester, Grey was accompanied by Edmund Everard. PRO SP 29/429/50.

79. BL Harleian MSS 6845, fols. 268v–269r; BL Add. MSS 41,819, fol. 160r; NUL MSS PwV 95, pp. 268, 277; PRO SP 29/425/147, 157; 29/427/70; 29/428/53, 114, 127, 148, 187, 188; 29/429/67–71; 29/430/42; 29/436/43, 54; 44/54, p. 172; 44/68, pp. 297, 298, 329–30, 331; 44/335, p. 18; *CSPD 1683–84*, p. 392. Sir Patience Ward, who had been convicted of perjury for his testimony in Sir Thomas Pilkington's behalf when the duke of York sued the latter for *scandalum magnatum* in May, also fled. BL Add. MSS 28,875, fol. 251r; NUL MSS PwV 95, p. 239.

80. NUL MSS PwV 95, pp. 249, 251; BL Add. MSS 4107, fol. 38v; PRO SP 44/68, p. 300; *Copy of a Letter, Sent from a Person Present at the Apprehension of Meade*. Others arrested included Bateman, Rouse, Battiscombe, and Sir Henry Ingoldsby. NUL MSS PwV 95, p. 252; PRO SP 29/428/147, 176; 29/434/118; 44/54, p. 217; 44/68, p. 315.

81. PRO SP 29/428/13, 29, 47; NUL MSS PwV 95, pp. 254–55; John Carswell, *The Porcupine: The Life of Algernon Sidney* (London: John Murray, 1989), p. 206; BL Add. MSS 29,577, fol. 539r; 32,520, fol. 196v; Prinsterer, p. 579; HLRO, Committee Minutes, 22 Nov. 1689; Milne, pp. 83–84.

82. NUL MSS PwV 95, pp. 254–55, 259; PRO SP 44/68, p. 331; *CSPD 1683*, 1: 385.

83. PRO SP 29/430/1, 3, 19, 33, 34; 29/431/39; 29/436/90; 44/54, pp. 177, 178,

189, 197; 44/68, pp. 350–52, 355; NUL MSS PwV 95, pp. 284, 286–87, 289, 298, 300, 307; *Letters to Aberdeen*, pp. 135, 151–52; BL Add. MSS 28,875, fols. 257r, 259r, 261r, 265r; 29,577, fol. 545r; Sprat, p. 104; *True Account of the Taking of Casteers*.

84. PRO SP 29/416/62, 67, 69, 78, 166; 29/417/95, 107; 29/418/183; 29/421/77; 44/68, pp. 44, 53, 186; *CSPD 1680–81*, pp. 369–70.

85. PRO SP 44/68, p. 323 (cf. p. 355); 44/69, pp. 48–49; CumRO(K) MSS WD/Ry, Box 29 (instructions to magistrates, 11 July 1683); Box 35 (Privy Council to Sir Daniel Fleming, 4 July 1683; warrant to magistrates, 20 July 1683).

86. PRO SP 29/429/25; 29/431/50; 44/69, p. 65; NUL MSS PwV 95, p. 237; *Letters to Aberdeen*, p. 130; Sprat, p. 78. The London blacksmith Jacob Pierson, a Fifth Monarchist, made a "strange weapon" and also owned a musket. PRO SP 29/428/122. According to his clerk, Aaron Smith owned pistols, a blunderbuss, and three or four tilting swords. PRO SP 29/427/99.

87. BL Add. MSS 29,577, fol. 542r; 32,520, fol. 201r; NUL MSS PwV 95, pp. 240, 248; PRO SP 29/425/153, 154; 29/428/148, 185; 29/429/57, 97; 29/430/88, 174; 29/430/111, p. 53; 44/64, pp. 67–68; JRL Legh of Lyme MSS (newsletter to Richard Legh, 12 July 1683); *CSPD 1683*, 2: 389; Prinsterer, p. 579. No suspicious weapons were found in the homes of Papillon or Jenks. NUL MSS PwV 95, p. 239; PRO SP 29/428/144. Colonel Whitley and his two sons, Thomas and Roger Jr., had to provide security in October. PRO SP 44/64, p. 117.

88. PRO SP 29/428/27, 38–41; 29/428/60, p. 29; 29/428/72, 72.1–4; 29/429/56, 63–66, 85, 108; 29/430/135, 135.1; 29/431/82; 29/433/90; BL Add. MSS 32,520, fol. 201r–v.

89. BL Add. MSS 32,520, fol. 201r; PRO SP 29/427/14, 37; 29/428/22, 26, 177; 29/429/135, 175, 202; 29/430/111, pp. 41–42; 29/430/155; 29/431/115; 29/432/55; 29/433/3, 9, 32, 74.

90. PRO SP 29/424/93, 95; 29/429/76, 210, 211; 44/54, p. 181; 44/68, pp. 346–47; 44/69, pp. 90–92; NUL MSS PwV 95, p. 277. For earlier indications of dissident meetings in Northamptonshire see PRO SP 29/417/71, 176.

91. Cf. BL Add. MSS 29,560, fol. 54r; 29,577, fol. 537r; PRO SP 29/425/112; 29/425/138, p. 21; 29/427/36, 118; 29/428/60, p. 64; 29/428/71, 89, 154–56; 29/429/27, 131; 29/430/39, 131, 134.1, 141; 29/431/80.1; 29/432/54, 56, 57; 29/433/53, 137 (Thomas Palmer's house); 44/68, pp. 328, 335–36, 353.

92. PRO SP 29/427/59, 121; 29/428/145; 29/429/109, 110; 29/430/5, 88, 146; 29/433/67. Cf. 29/428/146 (Isle of Wight). Some arms were found in Sussex; PRO SP 29/427/12.

93. PRO SP 29/429/78, 136, 137; 29/430/39; cf. 29/407/123. This was also true of Berwick; PRO SP 29/427/4. For similar reports see PRO SP 29/425/93; 29/427/21, 104, 110.

94. PRO SP 29/425/144; 29/427/117; 29/428/20, 144, 185; 29/429/96; 29/430/93; 44/68, p. 339. See also PRO SP 29/427/120; 29/429/48, 97; 29/432/62.

95. PRO SP 29/425/114, 145, 146. In the Coventry area several weapons and four suits of armor were confiscated from Sir Richard Wardcot, and fourteen pair of pistols and nine suits of armor from Sir Richard Newdegate. NUL MSS PwV 95, p. 274; *CSPD 1683*, 2: 200–201.

96. NUL MSS PwV 95, pp. 236–37; PRO SP 29/425/116; 29/428/65, 199; 29/429/31; 29/432/61; 44/64, p. 80; 44/68, p. 349; *CSPD 1683*, 2: 200–201.

97. PRO SP 29/424/149.1; 29/425/24, 62, 160, 162; 29/427/129; 29/428/28, 173, 199; 29/430/12, 12.1, 161.

98. PRO SP 29/427/35, 35.1, 75, 98, 130–32; 29/436/113; NUL MSS PwV 95, p. 251. Cf. *CSPD 1683*, 2: 416; PRO SP 29/423/57.

99. *Letters to Aberdeen*, pp. 133–34. For earlier instances of possible arms smuggling see, e.g., PRO SP 29/417/107; 44/68, p. 44.

100. PRO SP 44/56, pp. 99, 103.

101. PRO SP 29/425/133; 29/428/93; 29/429/34, 35, 84; 29/433/8, pp. 16, 18, 21. The printed addresses belonged to John Noyes.

102. NUL MSS PwV 95, pp. 251–52; PRO SP 29/427/43, 43.1; 29/428/111.

103. NUL MSS PwV 95, pp. 239, 246; PRO SP 29/425/88, 89; 29/433/86.3; *Copies*, p. 172; *Letters to Aberdeen*, p. 137.

104. PRO SP 29/428/60, p. 89; 29/430/111, p. 7; 29/436/90; *CSPD 1683*, 1: 325–27.

105. *CSPD 1683*, 1: 325–27; PRO SP 29/425/19, 20; *State-Papers and Letters to Carstares*, p. 107. Another intercepted but undated letter in cipher, possibly to Carstares, indicated the earl's "strong desire to communicate some thoughts" to the recipient or to M.L., or to someone sent by them to meet with Argyll in Amsterdam, Zeeland, or Rotterdam. PRO SP 29/425/40. The M.L. referred to here and elsewhere in Argyll's correspondence is Mr. Lockzier, a code name. When Argyll's chamberlain was arrested in late June, magistrates found several letters and pocket books. One of them contained information about a sea voyage taken the previous November by Lockzier and Butler (Spence). Another was a letter from a Robert Langlands in Rotterdam to Andrew Grey, Lord Wharton's servant. PRO SP 29/425/124 (cf. 125).

106. PRO SP 29/427/93; 29/428/86; 29/436/90; 44/68, p. 313; Sprat, pp. 111–12.

107. *ST*, 9: 472–74; PRO SP 29/425/39; *State-Papers and Letters to Carstares*, pp. 113–24; Sprat, pp. 110–13. On 5 July, magistrates intercepted a letter to Grey's chief steward instructing him to transmit a substantial amount of money to Ireton in London. Grey was presumably trying to smuggle some of his funds out of the country. PRO SP 29/427/110.

108. PRO SP 29/436/90.

109. *Copies*, pp. 125–26. The Black Box is discussed in Chapter 1, above.

110. PRO SP 29/430/45; Basil Duke Henning, *The History of Parliament: The House of Commons 1660–1690*, vol. 2 (London: Secker & Warburg, 1983), p. 577.

111. PRO SP 29/425/92.

112. PRO SP 29/435/55; 63/343/144. I have been unable to locate the confiscated papers.

113. *ST*, 9: 473.

Chapter 6

1. BL Add. MSS 32,520, fol. 193v; 46,960A, fol. 182r; Morrice, 1: 371; Prinsterer, p. 579.

2. Kiffin, *Remarkable Passages*, pp. 51–52; *Letters of Eminent Men to Thoresby*, 1: 35; *Observator*, 372 (9 July 1683); 376 (18 July 1683); 379 (23 July 1683); 386 (14 Aug. 1683); PRO SP 29/431/7; D[avid] Jones, *The Secret History of White-Hall*, Letter LXIX; BL Add. MSS 29,582, fol. 23r.

3. London *Gazette*, 1839 (2–5 July 1683); 1844 (19–23 July 1683); 1846 (26–30 July 1683); 1847 (30 July–2 Aug. 1683); 1853 (20–23 Aug. 1683); 1854 (23–27 Aug. 1683); 1857 (3–6 Sept. 1683); 1858 (6–10 Sept. 1683); 1859 (10–13 Sept. 1683); 1872 (25–29 Oct. 1683); 1886 (13–17 Dec. 1683); 1894 (10–14 Jan. 1684); 1908 (28 Feb.–3 Mar. 1684); 1912 (13–17 Mar. 1684); 1927 (5–8 May 1684); 1979 (3–6 Nov. 1684); BL Add. MSS 34,152, fol. 13r; *HMC* 36, *Ormonde*, n.s., 7: 81; BL Egerton MSS 2985, fol. 305r; PRO SP 29/428/92, 149; 29/430/115. William of Orange dispatched Bentinck to congratulate Charles on his "Delivery from the plot." BL Add. MSS 4107, fol. 39r.

4. BL Egerton MSS 2985, fol. 301r; *True Account of the Presentment of the Grand Jury*, pp. 1–2; London *Gazette*, 1855 (27–30 Aug. 1683); 1856 (30 Aug.–3 September 1683); Michael Mullett, "Popular Culture and Popular Politics: Some Regional Case Studies," in *Britain in the First Age of Party 1680–1750*, ed. Clyve Jones (London: Hambledon, 1987), pp. 141–42. The discovery of the plotting understandably cowed dissidents for a time; one observer noted, "The Wiggs in the Citty dare not seeme to bee dissatisfyed." ChRO MSS DCH/K/3/6 (Robert Eddowes to William Adams, 18 Oct. 1683).

5. *ST*, 9: 519–50; NUL MSS PwV 95, pp. 259–60. Cf. West, *An Answer*. The trained bands were on duty in London during the Rye House trials to prevent disturbances. JRL Legh of Lyme MSS (newsletter to Richard Legh, 12 July 1683).

6. *ST*, 9: 552–59. Cf. Walcott's earlier admissions to the king and Privy Council; PRO SP 29/428/4; 29/428/60, pp. 40–41.

7. *ST*, 9: 550–51; *Copies*, pp. 126–28.

8. Walcott, *True Copy of a Paper*, pp. 1–2; *Proceedings to Execution of the Sentence Awarded Against Walcot, Hone, and Rouse*, p. 3; *Last Speech*, p. 14;

Execution and Confession with the Behaviour & Speeches of Walcot, Hone, and Rouse, p. 3; ChRO MSS DCH/K/3/6 (Hugh Beheathland to William Adams, 21 July 1683); *HMC* 35, *Fourteenth Report*, p. 162; *CSPD 1689–90*, p. 97. The other corpses displayed until 1689 were those of Hone, Bateman, Rumbold, and Nelthorpe; the latter three men died in 1685.

9. *ST*, 9: 571–78; PRO SP 29/425/138, pp. 37–40; 29/426, pt. 2, p. 45; 29/427/49. Four of the six alleged Bow Church conspirators were Hone; Harris, the butcher with ties to Blood; (William?) Smith, a London tailor; and Jeffreys, a London woolcomber.

10. *Last Speech*, pt. 2, p. 5; PRO SP 29/429/71 (summarized in *CSPD* as 29/429/33); *Proceedings to Execution of the Sentence Awarded Against Walcot, Hone, and Rouse*, p. 4; *HMC* 35, *Fourteenth Report*, p. 162.

11. *ST*, 9: 594.

12. *HMC* 36, *Ormonde*, 7: 74. This thesis is cogently developed by Lois G. Schwoerer, "The Trial of Lord William Russell (1683): Judicial Murder?" *Journal of Legal History*, 9 (Sept. 1988): 142–68.

13. The barristers were Sir Henry Holt, Henry Pollexfen, Edward Ward, and Mr. Dodsworth; the solicitor was Mr. Shaw. Advice for Russell's defense was also provided, via correspondence, by Sir Robert Atkyns; see his *Defence of the Late Lord Russel's Innocency*, sig. B1r–v and pp. 3–8.

14. BL Add. MSS 8127, fols. 62r–63v.

15. BL Add. MSS 8127, fols. 63v–64v.

16. BL Add. MSS 8127, fol. 64v.

17. BL Add. MSS 8127, fol. 67v.

18. *ST*, 9: 596–613. Shepherd had gone to Gloucestershire in a futile attempt to avoid testifying against Russell, an act that underscores his guilt. BL Add. MSS 41,803, fol. 25r; PRO SP 29/428/182.

19. *ST*, 9: 599, 601, 612, 614–18; *Copies*, p. 193.

20. *ST*, 9: 595, 602, 633, 636; Lois G. Schwoerer, *Lady Rachel Russell: "One of the Best of Women"* (Baltimore, Md.: Johns Hopkins University Press, 1988), p. 116; [Ferguson], *Enquire into, and Detection*, pp. 10–11. Russell's former chaplain, Samuel Johnson, was also convicted of sedition in November 1683. Morrice, 1: 389.

21. PRO SP 29/428/202; 29/429/40; NUL MSS PwV 95, p. 264; *HMC* 58, *Bath*, 1: 47.

22. PRO SP 29/429/89. For the execution see PRO SP 44/54, pp. 193–94 (warrant); BL Add. MSS 4107, fol. 39r; 29,577, fol. 543r ("The Hangman gave him 3 blows besides sawing with the axe before he cut his head of[f]"); JRL Legh of Lyme MSS (newsletter to Richard Legh, 21 July 1683); CumRO(C) MSS D/LONS/L1/1/30. One of Russell's friends allegedly offered the king £100,000 to spare Russell's life. Charles later reportedly told Monmouth he had been inclined to do so, but allowed the execution to

proceed; "otherwise he must have broke with" James. Welwood, Appendix, pp. 375–76; JRL Legh of Lyme MSS (newsletter to Richard Legh, 17 July 1683).

23. NUL MSS PwV 95, p. 274; *CSPD 1683*, 2: 215; *Letters to Aberdeen*, p. 148. Daniel Fleming paid 5*d.* for a copy of Russell's speech. CumRO(K) MSS WD/Ry, Box 29 (entry for 8 Aug. 1683). The publication of Russell's death speech once again inspired the Whigs to take up their pens against the regime. Sir Francis North observed, "Not one seditious pamphlett came out for a good while [after the plot was disclosed], hardly till the Lord Russells Execution." BL Add. MSS 32,520, fol. 195r.

24. *HMC 36, Ormonde*, n.s., 7: 88; *HMC 58, Bath*, 1: 47; NUL MSS PwV 95, p. 274; *Night-Walker of Bloomsbury*, a satire, refers to a scheme "to put the Lord *Russels* Speech upon Dr. *Burnett.*"

25. See Lois G. Schwoerer, "William, Lord Russell: The Making of a Martyr, 1683–1983," *Journal of British Studies*, 24 (Jan. 1985): 41–71.

26. *ST*, 9: 639, 653; Morrice, 1: 389.

27. *Last Speech*, pp. 7–10; Rouse, *Rouse His Case*; *Proceedings to Execution of the Sentence Awarded Against Walcot, Hone, and Rouse*, p. 4; London *Gazette*, 1844 (19–23 July 1683); *HMC 35, Fourteenth Report*, p. 162.

28. *Last Speech*, p. 8; *ST*, 9: 653–66.

29. PRO SP 44/68, pp. 334–35; *Observator*, 375 (16 July 1683); NUL MSS PwV 95, p. 275.

30. PRO SP 29/428/193; 29/429/132, 234, 234.1, 235; *CSPD 1683*, 2: 215–16.

31. NUL MSS PwV 95, p. 255; V. Sackville-West, *Knole and the Sackvilles* (London: William Heinemann, 1922), p. 134; *ST*, 9: 1127; PRO SP 29/428/60, pp. 1–6; BL Harleian MSS 1221, fol. 290r; Add. MSS 29,577, fol. 541r; 32,520, fol. 196v.

32. [Ferguson], *Enquirie into, and Detection*, pp. 7–8, 11; Danvers, *Murther*, p. 2; *ST*, 9: 1198; BL Harleian MSS 1221, fol. 316r; Add. MSS 29,577, fol. 541r; HLRO, Committee Minutes (25 Jan. 1689).

33. *ST*, 9: 1200; Evelyn, 4: 326; [Ferguson], *Enquirie into, and Detection*, p. 5; Danvers, *Murther*, p. 2; *HMC 36, Ormonde*, n.s., 7: 77; BL Add. MSS 32,520, fol. 199r; PRO SP 63/343/141.

34. BL Add. MSS 29,577, fol. 541r; [Ferguson], *Enquirie into, and Detection*, pp. 37, 62–63; Braddon, *Essex's Innocency*, pp. 31–32; BL Harleian MSS 1221, fols. 302r, 303r; BL Lansdowne MSS 253, fols. 475v–476r. BL Lansdowne MSS 253 contains the report of a special committee to investigate Essex's death; it was appointed in February 1689. Relevant committee reports are in the House of Lords Record Office.

35. BL Lansdowne MSS 253, fol. 475v; BL Harleian MSS 1221, fol. 302r. Although this is hearsay, the statement attributed to Charles accords with his comment on hearing of Essex's death: "He was sorry his Lordship should so much distrust his clemency." NUL MSS PwV 95, p. 259. Charles

as well as James was still in the Tower at the time of Essex's death. *HMC* 36, *Ormonde*, n.s., 7: 73; *HMC* 35, *Fourteenth Report*, p. 162; JRL Legh of Lyme MSS (James Rothwell to Richard Legh, 14 July 1683).

36. Ferguson, *Enquirie into, and Detection*, pp. 62–63.

37. *ST*, 9: 1199–1200, 1202, 1203; BL Lansdowne MSS 253, fol. 469v; *Account of How Essex Killed Himself*, pp. 3–4. Cf. *HMC* 35, *Fourteenth Report*, Appendix 4, p. 162.

38. BL Lansdowne MSS 253, fol. 469v–470r; Harleian MSS 1221, fol. 290r, 292r; *Account of How Essex Killed Himself*, p. 5; *ST*, 9: 1200–1201, 1203; HLRO, Committee Minutes (25 Jan., 4 Feb. 1689).

39. Braddon, *Essex's Innocency*, pp. 47–48. In April 1686, a former page to Charles or James went to Amsterdam, where he blamed the Stuart court for Essex's murder. According to Edmund Everard either this page or someone else had been sent by James after the earl's death "to command that the body should not be toucht nor nothing removed about it till the Coroner had viewed it & given his verdict in the Case." BL Add. MSS 41,819, fol. 17v.

40. HLRO, Committee Minutes (25 Jan. 1689); Braddon, *Essex's Innocency*, pp. 32–33; [Ferguson], *Enquirie into, and Detection*, pp. 53–54, 61; Danvers, *Murther*, pp. 4–5; *Letters of Eminent Men to Thoresby*, 1: 35; *HMC* 35, *Fourteenth Report*, Appendix 4, p. 162. Samuel Peck, one of Essex's servants, saw the corpse before it was cleaned up; he reported seeing a bloody footprint on one of the earl's stockings. [Ferguson], *Enquirie into, and Detection*, pp. 54–55; Danvers, *Murther*, p. 4.

41. *ST*, 9: 1133; *Account of How Essex Killed Himself*, p. 6; BL Lansdowne MSS 253, fol. 470r; Morrice, 1: 452–53.

42. *Account of How Essex Killed Himself*, pp. 3–4; Braddon, *Essex's Innocency*, p. 45; [Ferguson], *Enquirie into, and Detection*, pp. 44–45, 55; Danvers, *Murther*, p. 3; BL Harleian MSS 1221, fol. 313r, 314r. I am grateful to Dr. Thomas Wood, medical examiner for Leon County, Florida, and to Mr. Michael J. A. Thompson, a Yorkshire physician, both of whom discussed relevant aspects of this case with me.

43. BL Harleian MSS 1221, fols. 312r, 313r; Sloan MSS 78, fol. 5r; Braddon, *Essex's Innocency*, p. 45.

44. Cf. *Letters of Eminent Men to Thoresby*, 1: 35; Braddon, *Essex's Innocency*, p. 45. A servant named Martha Bascombe later testified that she saw three or four heads in Essex's window and heard a voice cry out, "Murder, murder, murder." BL Lansdowne MSS 253, fols. 474v–475r; BL Harleian MSS 1221, fol. 301r; BL Sloan MSS 78, fol. 5r.

45. *ST*, 9: 1141–52, 1163–64, 1181–85; BL Sloan MSS 78, fols. 4r, 17r, 18r; BL Harleian MSS 1221, fol. 304r, 305r; BL Lansdowne MSS 253, fol. 475r–v; PRO SP 29/428/60, pp. 44, 101–2, 105; 29/430/111, pp. 43–45.

46. *ST*, 9: 1202; BL Harleian MSS 1221, fol. 303r; BL Sloan MSS 78, fol.

4r; BL Lansdowne MSS 253, fols. 473v–474r; Braddon, *Essex's Innocency*, p. 42; [Ferguson], *Enquirie into, and Detection*, pp. 71–72. For others who reputedly saw the razor thrown from the window, see BL Sloan MSS 78, fol. 18v. Braddon insisted he had not been employed by the countess of Essex or Capel, though he claimed the latter had indicated that the family would be greatly obliged if he investigated. Capel retorted that he had urged Braddon to go to a secretary of state. PRO SP 29/430/III, pp. 39, 43.

47. BL Lansdowne MSS 253, fols. 473v–474r; BL Harleian MSS 1221, fol. 303r; Braddon, *Essex's Innocency*, pp. 41–43.

48. BL Harleian MSS 1221, fol. 299r; BL Lansdowne MSS 253, fols. 473v–474r; BL Sloan MSS 78, fol. 4r; HLRO, Committee Minutes (25 Jan., 4 Feb. 1689); Braddon, *Essex's Innocency*, pp. 27–28.

49. BL Lansdowne MSS 253, fol. 475r–v; BL Harleian MSS 1221, fol. 301r, 302r; BL Sloan MSS 78, fols. 11v–12v, 18r; Braddon, *Essex's Innocency*, pp. 31–32; [Ferguson], *Enquirie into, and Detection*, pp. 26–27, 37–38.

50. BL Sloan MSS 78, fols. 13r, 20v–21r; BL Harleian MSS 1221, fol. 299r; HLRO, Committee Minutes (23 and 25 Jan. 1689); Morrice, 1: 505–6; *Account of the Taking of Holland*; Braddon, *Essex's Innocency*, pp. 52–54. Holland complained to Lord Feversham that Braddon had tried to suborn him. Braddon, *Essex's Innocency*, p. 54. According to Ashcraft, Holland "wrote a letter professing to have information concerning Essex's death, and strongly implying" that Sunderland had asked him to participate in the assassination. This interpretation is based on a misreading of Holland's letter, which actually protests against Braddon's allegations: "He [Braddon] had a warrant from the House of Lords to take the writer [Holland], alleging he [Braddon] had evidence to prove him [Holland] one of the persons that committed the fact [Essex's murder], and that the King, his Lordship [Feversham], and Lord Sunderland had hired him to do it." Ashcraft, p. 381 n. 190; *HMC* 17, *Twelfth Report*, Appendix, pt. 6, p. 28.

51. BL Lansdowne MSS 253, fols. 471r–472v; BL Harleian MSS 1221, fols. 295r–298r; BL Sloan MSS 78, fol. 14r; Braddon, *Essex's Innocency*, pp. 22–26. Ferguson blamed Feversham as well as James and Sunderland. [Ferguson], *Enquirie into, and Detection*, pp. 23–24. Whig partisans also cited rumors in circulation *before* Essex's death that he had cut his throat; the rumors pointed, they argued, to the existence of a plot to kill him and disguise the murder as suicide. If there were rumors, they embodied only speculation. BL Lansdowne MSS 253, fol. 473r; BL Harleian MSS 1221, fols. 298r, 299r; BL Sloan MSS 78, fol. 16r; Braddon, *Essex's Innocency*, pp. 26–27.

52. Braddon, *Essex's Innocency*, pp. 43–44, 49; BL Sloan MSS 78, fol. 13r; BL Harleian MSS 1221, fol. 320r; Akerman, *Moneys Received*, p. 84; PRO SP 29/430/III, p. 43; [Ferguson], *Enquirie into, and Detection*, pp. 39–40, 42–43. Bomeny heard rumors that Burnet and Sir Henry Capel had urged

his dismissal on the grounds that it was not fit to retain him. PRO SP 29/433/8, p. 18.

53. Evelyn, 4: 326–27; Bodl. Locke MSS b.4, fol. 67r. Danvers also called for a new inquiry, to be prefaced by a grant of indemnity to those who confessed. Danvers, *Murther*, p. 7. Gilbert Burnet conducted an investigation for the Capel family, but nothing seems to have come of this. Milne, p. 135. A letter dated 19 March 1689 from Lady Russell to Essex's widow asks the latter, "[Do not] aggravate [unspecified] circumstances to your own wrong." Russell, *Letters of Lady Russell*, 1: 277. The state did not seize Essex's estate, which passed to his only surviving son, Algernon (1670–1710). Essex was buried on the family estate. PRO SP 29/428/119; JRL Legh of Lyme MSS (newsletters to Richard Legh, 17 and 21 July 1683); Cokayne, 5: 146.

54. *ST*, 9: 1127–1224; PRO SP 29/436/47; Braddon, *Essex's Innocency*, pp. 16–17; [Speke], *Secret History*, pp. 10–12; London *Gazette*, 1902 (7–11 Feb. 1684); 1923 (21–24 Apr. 1684); Morrice, 1: 418, 432.

55. PRO SP 29/431/33. Elegies for and against Essex appeared after his death, and in early 1685 pamphlets alleging the earl's murder were smuggled from the Netherlands. *Elegy on the Earl of Essex*; *Elegy upon That Renowned Hero*; Morrice, 1: 453–54, 466.

56. BL Harleian MSS 1221, fol. 300r; BL Lansdowne MSS 253, fols. 473v–474r; BL Sloan MSS 78, fols. 4r, 12v, 13v; Braddon, *Essex's Innocency*, pp. 50–51; HLRO, Committee Minutes (23 Jan. 1689); PRO SP 29/428/60, pp. 101–2.

57. [Ferguson], *Enquirie into, and Detection*, pp. 8–10, 12–13, Danvers, *Murther*, p. 6; BL Add. MSS 32,520, fols. 200v–201r.

58. BL Egerton MSS 2543, fol. 251r; PRO SP 29/429/21. James Stiles, James Burton, and William Thompson were also indicted on 12 July.

59. BL Add. MSS 29,582, fol. 83r; HLRO, Committee Minutes (6 Dec. 1689); NUL MSS PwV 95, pp. 245, 250, 305; Sprat, pp. 204–5 (misprinted as 164–65); London *Gazette*, 1872 (25–29 Oct. 1683); Luttrell, 1: 285; Morrice, 1: 383.

60. Welwood, p. 373; Foxcroft, 1: 401; PRO SP 29/430/149; 29/433/102; Maurice Ashley, *James II* (Minneapolis: University of Minnesota Press, 1977), p. 147. Gibbons, one of Monmouth's servants, had been arrested in July and committed to Newgate prison, where he remained until his release on £1,000 bail in November 1683. JRL Legh of Lyme MSS (newsletters to Richard Legh, 12 July 1683, 19 Nov. 1683).

61. Foxcroft, 1: 402; *ST*, 9: 832–33, 920–21.

62. PRO SP 29/434/68; Foxcroft, 1: 403–4.

63. *ST*, 9: 825–35.

64. ESRO Glynde MSS 794, fol. 22v.

65. *ST*, 9: 829–30.

66. ESRO Glynde MSS 794, fols. 1r, 10r, 17r, 20r, 21r, 24r–v.

67. *ST*, 9: 817–19, 838–49. Cf. PRO SP 29/425/118, 122; 29/428/31; 29/429/230.

68. *ST*, 9: 849–52. At the time, Roger Morrice (1: 389) noted: "[Howard] seemed to give a larger testimony and different from that he gave at my Lord Russells Tryall."

69. *ST*, 9: 853–59.

70. *ST*, 9: 859–80.

71. *ST*, 9: 879–95. The trial is summarized in Luttrell, 1: 289–91. Cf. Evelyn's caustic comment on the trial: Sidney was convicted "upon the single Wittnesse of that monster of a man the L: *Howard* of Escrick, and some sheetes of paper taken in Mr. Sidnys study, pretended to be written by him, but not fully proov'd, nor the time when, but appearing to have ben written before his Majesties restauration, & then pardon'd by the Act of Oblivion" (4: 353).

72. Reresby, p. 320; *CSPD 1683–84*, pp. 107, 108; BL Add. MSS 28,875, fol. 298r; PRO SP 29/434/98 (notes taken by James); 44/54, p. 224; Morrice, 1: 392–93, 401; ChRO MSS DCH/K/3/6 (J. Colley to William Adams, 4 Dec. 1683); JRL Legh of Lyme MSS (newsletter to Richard Legh, 24 Nov. 1683). Cf. Sprat, pp. 204–5 (misprinted as 164–65). According to Luttrell (1: 293) the sum given to Monmouth was £6,000.

73. John Carswell, *The Porcupine: The Life of Algernon Sidney*, p. 225; *ST*, 9: 899.

74. *ST*, 9: 899–901; BL Add. MSS 28,875, fols. 299v–300r.

75. *Correspondence of the Family of Hatton*, 2: 40–42; Foxcroft, 1: 407; PRO SP 63/341, pp. 155–57; London *Gazette*, 1880 (22–26 Nov. 1683).

76. Foxcroft, 1: 407. The prisoners, including Colonel Mildmay, Bateman, and Andrew Barber, were bailed on 28 November. Luttrell, 1: 292; Morrice, 1: 394; London *Gazette*, 1881 (26–29 Nov. 1683); 1899 (28–31 Jan. 1684). After their release they were reportedly "dicrying the plott." BL Add. MSS 28,875, fol. 303r.

77. Foxcroft, 1: 410–11.

78. BL Add. MSS 28,875, fol. 321r–v. In 1689, Charles Godfrey testified that Monmouth had shown him the signed confession, which (said Godfrey) confirmed the reality of the plotting with which Russell and Sidney had been charged. HLRO, Committee Minutes (22 Nov. 1689).

79. HLRO, Committee Minutes (16 and 20 Nov. 1689); Foxcroft, 1: 411; Evelyn, 4: 353; PRO SP 29/435/21, 22, 53; BL Add. MSS 28,875, fol. 305v; 41,803, fol. 45r–v; 41,809, fol. 190r; Prinsterer, p. 587. Morrice (1: 612) records two slightly different accounts of the transactions involving the duke's confession.

80. Morrice, 1: 414.

81. Sidney also petitioned the king, without success, for a personal con-

ference, and again for the remission of the death sentence to exile abroad. *ST*, 9: 904–6; PRO SP 29/434/116.

82. *ST*, 9: 916–50.

83. ESRO Glynde MSS 794, fols. 26v, 27v.

84. *ST*, 9: 907–16; BL Add. MSS 28,875, fols. 309r–v, 311r; PRO SP 29/435/25, 50; Morrice, 1: 398; Luttrell, 1: 294; Evelyn, 4: 353; *Correspondence of the Family of Hatton*, 2: 41; Reresby, p. 322. Stated one royalist, Sidney's gallows statement "damyn[s] the [radical] party, to see it thus Lined through with Scandall, falshood & Treason & not a word of those proofes (which they Expected) that there's no plott." BL Add. MSS 28,875, fol. 322r.

85. *ST*, 9: 1053–56, 1063–65; PRO SP 29/437/44; Luttrell, 1: 294–95, 306; Foxcroft, 1: 412; Bodl. Carte MSS 220, fol. 7r.

86. *ST*, 9: 1065–1104.

87. *ST*, 9: 1102.

88. *ST*, 9: 1104–26; London *Gazette*, 1903 (11–14 Feb. 1684).

89. HLRO, Committee Minutes (16 Nov. 1689); *ST*, 11: 479–94; *HMC 29, Portland*, 3: 392; *HMC 75, Downshire*, 1: 83–85, 93; London *Gazette*, 2099 (28–31 Dec. 1685); Luttrell, 1: 368, 381; BL Add. MSS 41,804, fol. 78r.

90. Luttrell, 1: 300–301; Morrice, 1: 420; London *Gazette*, 1903 (11–14 Feb. 1684); *CSPD 1683*, 2: 308, 313, 315; Reresby, p. 330. Bateman and Friend (who had been arrested in September) were released on bail in November 1683. Morrice, 1: 376, 387.

91. *Copies*, pp. 26, 50; BL Add. MSS 38,847, fol. 97r; PRO SP 29/427/38, 38.1, 38.2, 42, 54, 55, 64, 65, 69, 70, 95, 96, 108, 109, 122; 29/428/76, 153, 196; 29/429/54, 54.1, 55, 209; 29/434/56, 77, 77.1, 78; 29/436/34, 37, 121, 121.1; 44/68, pp. 318–19, 321–22, 330; 63/343/143.

92. PRO SP 29/427/24, 115; 29/428/43, 54, 55; 29/428/60, pp. 24, 57, 86–87; 29/428/74, 77, 140, 200; 29/429/98, 128, 161; 29/433/62, 44/54, p. 171; 44/68, pp. 317–19, 321; *Letters to Aberdeen*, pp. 142–44.

93. For Scots with possible ties to the plotting see PRO SP 29/428/75; 29/433/62; 29/436/5, 6; NUL MSS PwV 95, p. 275 (for two Scots arrested in Dublin).

94. PRO SP 29/433/86.3; 44/68, p. 335; NUL MSS PwV 95, p. 243. Holmes was imprisoned for many weeks in the Gatehouse in a room containing only a bed, an empty space measuring one by three feet, a small hole for light, and no heat; he nearly starved. Morrice, 1: 400.

95. The others were John Crawford, William Fairly, and John Hepburn. *CSPD 1683–84*, p. 67; PRO SP 44/56, p. 85; 44/335, pp. 58–61; Erskine, pp. 21–22. They reached Edinburgh on 14 November.

96. PRO SP 29/429/189, 201, 206; 29/430/51; 44/68, pp. 345–46; BL Add. MSS 41,809, fols. 127r, 137r, 138r–146r, 153r, 158r; 61,651, fol. 6r.

97. *ST*, 10: 919–88; EUL MSS La.II.89, fols. 169r–195r; Sprat, p. 104.

98. *ST*, 10: 989–1046.

99. Erskine, pp. 81–82, 84; PRO SP 29/438/41; *ST*, 10: 655–57; *CSPD 1684–85*, pp. 144–45, 167; Morrice, 1: 441–42; *RPCS*, 9: 142–44, 154, 159–60.

100. PRO SP 29/438/41; *CSPD 1684–85*, p. 152; *RPCS*, 9: 68–69, 73, 94, 97–98, 103–4, 117–20; Erskine, pp. 78–79; *MVB*, p. 125n. Sir William Scott of Harden fled in late December. Erskine, p. 102.

101. EUL MSS La.II.89, fol. 183v; *CSPD 1684–85*, pp. 156–57. During the revolution of 1688, Ferguson and Charlton claimed Carstares had made unjust accusations against them in his confession. Morrice, 2: 369.

102. *ST*, 10: 647–701, 722–24; *Tryall and Process Against Baillie*; *Acts of the Parliament of Scotland*, 8: 33; *RPCS*, 9: 134–38 (the indictment).

103. *ST*, 10: 701–11, 719–21; Erskine, p. 101; London *Gazette*, 1996 (1–5 Jan. 1685).

104. Another aspect of this campaign was the publication in Edinburgh of Carstares' depositions. *CSPD 1684–85*, p. 274.

105. *ST*, 10: 1065–80; Erskine, p. 103; *CSPD 1684–85*, p. 303; *RPCS*, 10: 128.

106. Holloway, p. 7; PRO SP 29/436/66, 66.1; 29/437/92, 93, 103; cf. 29/436/66.11, 66.14; 29/437/91, 100; 44/64, pp. 221–22, 224.

107. *HMC* 29, *Portland*, 2: 156; BL Add. MSS 62,453, fols. 3r–4v; PRO SP 29/437/106, 110.

108. *ST*, 10: 1–6; London *Gazette*, 1923 (21–24 Apr. 1684); PRO SP 29/437/126, 127.

109. Holloway, pp. 12–13; *ST*, 10: 7–13. Cf. PRO SP 29/436/66.11, 66.14; *CSPD 1684–85*, pp. 5–6. Holloway made a last desperate appeal for his life by offering to found a settlement for hundreds of English dissidents on an island near "bad" Puerto Rico, perhaps St. Croix, PRO SP 29/437/106.

110. BL Add. MSS 41,809, fols. 113v–114r; 41,810, fol. 74v; 41,811, fol. 132r; 61,651, fols. 6r, 7r, 10r, 13r; PRO SP 29/433/96.

111. BL Add. MSS 41,810, fols. 92r–v, 97r. Cf. Brandon's condemnation of the act; 41,810, fol. 121r.

112. Prinsterer, p. 588.

113. Under the terms of this statute, a fugitive had the right to a trial if he surrendered within a year of the outlawry. Jeffreys ruled that Holloway had not turned himself in but was captured. *ST*, 10: 105–16, 122–24; PRO SP 29/433/8, p. 40; *CSPD 1684–85*, pp. 54–55, 80; London *Gazette*, 1938 (12–16 June 1684). Fleming paid 3*d.* for a copy of Armstrong's gallows speech. CumRO(K) MSS WD/Ry, Box 29 (entry for 18 July 1684).

114. Burnet, 2: 412–15.

115. *ST*, 11: 410–13, 421–28; BL Lansdowne MSS 1152, fol. 242r; JRL Legh of Lyme MSS (newsletter to Richard Legh, 20 Oct. 1685). The draft of a 1689 bill to reverse Cornish's attainder is inaccurate. *HMC* 17, *Twelfth Report*, Appendix, pt. 6, p. 129.

116. *ST*, 11: 428–50; Morrice, 1: 484–86; DWL MSS 90.5.(3); *HMC* 29,

Portland, 3: 389; Luttrell, 1: 361. Ferguson denied that Cornish had been present when he read the declaration. *HMC* 17, *Twelfth Report*, Appendix, pt. 6, p. 129. Cornish's head and quarters were displayed on the Guildhall and the gates of London until November 1687. PRO SP 44/337, p. 355.

117. *ST*, 11: 467–74; DWL MSS 90.5.(8); Morrice, 1: 503; *HMC* 75, *Downshire*, 1: 72–73, 77.

118. To Charles' credit, he refused the offer of Stephen Dugdale, one of the Popish Plot witnesses, to testify in some of the Rye House trials. JRL Legh of Lyme MSS (newsletter to Richard Legh, 19 Nov. 1683).

119. *HMC* 29, *Portland*, 2: 156; 3: 377–79; BL Add. MSS 28,875, fol. 313r; PRO SP 29/429/199; 44/64, pp. 148–49; *ST*, 9: 1333–72; London *Gazette*, 1904 (14–18 Feb. 1684); 1922 (17–21 Apr. 1684). Barnardiston was fined £10,000.

120. BL Add. MSS 32,520, fols. 196v, 258r; *HMC* 36, *Ormonde*, n.s., 7: 53 (cf. p. 73); Ashcraft, p. 341. This is also the verdict of Milne, p. 120; and Schwoerer, "Trial of Lord Russell," 146. Cf. David Ogg, *England in the Reign of Charles II*, 2nd ed. (Oxford: Oxford University Press, 1956), p. 647. Not surprisingly, the early Whig position struck hard at the government: John Oldmixon, who denounced Thomas Sprat's *True Account* as a "Romance," contended that writing the history of the plotting from the official records was taking "the Vindication of the . . . Murders from the Murtherers themselves." [Oldmixon], *The History of England, During the Reigns of the Royal House of Stuart* (London: John Pemberton et al., 1730), p. 679 (cf. p. 680).

Chapter 7

1. BL Add. MSS 41,809, fol. 94r.

2. BL Add. MSS 41,818, fols. 159r–v, 206r, 214v; PRO SP 29/433/106; 29/436/54. Dr. Carney, who interrogated Row in March 1686, believed his allegations were frivolous. Carney, who lived at The Hague, was Irish. BL Add. MSS 41,818, fol. 265r; PRO SP 29/423/102.

3. BL Add. MSS 37,980, fol. 195r, 201r–204v.

4. Greaves, *EUHF*, p. 229.

5. PRO SP 29/422/30, 82, 120; 29/423/22, 102, 108; 29/425/41; 29/427/57, 81; 29/428/59; 29/429/172; 44/54, p. 162; 44/68, pp. 329–30; BL Add. MSS 41,811, fol. 119r; Prinsterer, p. 574. Cf. PRO SP 29/427/81; 29/433/39. Blunt also sought a pardon, but Charles guaranteed him only the safety of Whitehall until he had heard his confession. PRO SP 29/422/30. Mr. M. (Blunt?) claimed he had incriminating information about the Fifth Monarchist William Medley (alias Freeman), who had welcomed Shaftesbury to Amsterdam. PRO SP 29/423/102. See also the case of Nathaniel Powell, who admitted he had been a member of the party that was to have killed Charles and James near the Rye House. BL Add. MSS 41,809, fol. 259r; 41,810, fol. 12r–v; 41,811, fols. 136r–v, 175r–176r.

6. BL Add. MSS 41,803, fol. 264r; 41,809, fols. 95v, 138r–146r; 41,810, fols. 42r, 47r; 41,811, fols. 211r, 213r, 262r; 41,812, fol. 68v; 41,817, fols. 65v–66r; 61,651, fol. 7r.

7. BL Add. MSS 41,809, fols. 94r, 99r, 104v; 41,810, fols. 59r–v, 74v; 61,651, fols. 6r, 10r.

8. BL Add. MSS 41,809, fols. 95v, 103r, 113v–114r, 131r, 138r–146r; 41,811, fol. 132v; 61,651, fols. 7r, 13r; BL Harleian MSS 6845, fols. 263r, 269r; PRO SP 29/433/96; 29/435/157; 29/436/54. Nicholas Locke, who attended Baptist and Congregationalist churches, had been a friend of Shepherd's. BL Add. MSS 41,810, fol. 64r. Argyll, other Scots, Smith and his wife, and Locke visited Sir John Cochrane at Cleves in late October or early November. PRO SP 29/436/54.

9. BL Add. MSS 41,809, fols. 106v, 110v, 112r–v.

10. BL Add. MSS 41,809, fols. 113v–114r, 131r. Because of the importance of the pulpit in the exile community, Chudleigh tried, albeit without much success, to influence the appointment of ministers acceptable to the English government. BL Add. MSS 41,809, fols. 173v–174r; 41,810, fol. 28v; 61,651, fol. 15v. In August 1684, at the Scottish church in Rotterdam, Thomas Hogg thundered: "O Lord how long wilt thou suffer thy servants to be persecewted by Covenant brekers & tirants?" He exhorted his audience to "use any me[a]ns" rather than continue suffering. BL Add. MSS 41,811, fol. 242r.

11. BL Add. MSS 41,803, fols. 73r, 75r; 41,809, fols. 138r–146r; JRL Legh of Lyme MSS (newsletter to Richard Legh, 12 Sept. 1683); CumRO(K) MSS WD/Ry, Box 29 (William Orfeur's information, 20 Nov. 1684); CCRO MSS QSF/83, fol. 130v; PRO SP 29/430/38; 29/431/89, 89.1; 29/433/85; 29/435/146, 147; 29/436/117, 132; 29/438/103, 103.1.

12. BL Harleian MSS 6845, fol. 269r–v; Erskine, p. 179 (who refers to Ayloffe as J. Eleves). In January or February 1683, Rawlins had been taken by Shepherd to dine with Russell and Cornish at the Salutation tavern. The conversation may have involved contacts with the southwest or an appeal for financial support. PRO SP 29/428/60, pp. 53–55.

13. BL Add. MSS 41,810, fols. 14r–15r, 47r, 59r–v, 74v; 41,811, fols. 119r–v, 193r; BL Harleian MSS 6845, fol. 269r; Greaves, *EUHF*, pp. 30–31; *RPCS*, 8: 451, 509–11.

14. BL Harleian MSS 6845, fol. 269v; BL Add. MSS 41,810, fols. 63v–64r, 67r, 69r; Erskine, pp. 179–80.

15. Grey, *SH*, pp. 70–71, 73–74; Prinsterer, p. 586.

16. Grey, *SH*, pp. 73–74.

17. BL Add. MSS 41,810, fols. 63v, 67v, 69v, 74r–v, 91r, 119r, 125r–v, 128r, 130v; 41,811, fols. 213r, 224v.

18. BL Add. MSS 41,810, fol. 69v; Baxter, p. 197.

19. BL Add. MSS 41,810, fol. 97r; Grey, *SH*, p. 74. The key figures in

Armstrong's capture were Don Lewis and James Hodgson. BL Add. MSS 41,811, fol. 262r. Chudleigh paid the bailiff of Leiden £500 for issuing the warrant, and Constable, one of his own agents, £300. Morrice, 1: 440. Papers in Armstrong's possession indicated he was in contact with Joseph Hayes. BL Add. MSS 41,823, fol. 1r; *CSPD 1684–85*, p. 177.

20. BL Harleian MSS 6845, fol. 269v; BL Add. MSS 41,818, fol. 214v; Erskine, p. 180.

21. BL Add. MSS 41,811, fol. 226r. Barclay was accompanied by William Cleland and (unnamed) others. In October 1683 the duke of York received information that Scottish fugitives in the Newcastle area were discussing plans under way in London to avenge Russell's death. PRO SP 29/433/62.

22. PRO SP 29/438/43.1; *CSPD 1683–84*, pp. 398–99; *CSPD 1684–85*, pp. 55–56, 104–5, 158, 251; Erskine, pp. 73, 83–84, 88–89, 93, 99.

23. BL Add. MSS 41,811, fol. 226r–v. Cf. D'Avaux, 3: 135.

24. Grey, *SH*, pp. 74–77.

25. BL Add. MSS 41,810, fol. 168r; PRO SP 29/435/157.

26. BL Harleian MSS 6845, fol. 269v–270r; Morrice, 1: 407, 444; Kiffin, *Remarkable Passages*, pp. 51–52. Kiffin's son-in-law, Joseph Hayes, was accused of remitting a bill of exchange to Armstrong in the Netherlands after the latter had fled; Hayes was found innocent. While he was helping Hayes, Kiffin received a treasonable letter from someone allegedly attempting to trepan him. Kiffin's grandsons, Benjamin and William Hewling, fought with Monmouth in 1685. Kiffin, *Remarkable Passages*, pp. 51–56; Morrice, 1: 440, 449.

27. BL Add. MSS 41,809, fols. 178r, 193r.

28. Ashcraft, p. 337 n. 207.

29. BL Add. MSS 41,810, fols. 187v–188v; Bodl. Locke MSS f.8, pp. 72–73, 77, 98; Prideaux, pp. 139, 142. John Locke also stayed with Vandervelde, apparently for approximately a month, commencing on 19 July 1684, and then traveled extensively throughout the Netherlands between 15 August and 18 November, when he returned to Amsterdam. His route took him to such places as Franeker, Leeuwarden, Groningen, Zwoll, Deventer, Arnhem, Nijmegen, Utrecht, and Leiden. He may have been secretly enlisting support for the forthcoming rebellion. Bodl. Locke MSS f.8, pp. 98, 107–227.

30. Bodl. Locke MSS b.4, fols. 61r–66r; Ashcraft, p. 337 n. 207; [Ferguson], *Impartial Enquiry*, pp. 3–4, 10–11, 18, 21–25, 28, 36, 46–47, 53, 55–56, 60–61, 64–65, 77; BL Add. MSS 41,810, fols. 187v–188r. The case for Ferguson's authorship of *An Impartial Enquiry* is virtually clinched by the author's extensive references to Scottish affairs. Moreover, on 26 August (n.s.) Thomas Axton reported to Sir Francis North that Ferguson and Mr. Foster (possibly the Scottish minister Thomas Forrester) had written books harshly critical of Charles. BL Add. MSS 41,811, fols. 242r–243r; cf. 41,817, fol. 85r

(information dated 1 June [n.s.] that Ferguson and Everard had been writing or translating treasonable books).

31. BL Add. MSS 41,810, fols. 194r–v, 204r, 235r–236r; 41,811, fols. 268v, 270r–v; 41,823, fol. 2r. Ferguson's tract on Essex's death was also translated into Dutch: *Ondersoek en Ontdekking van de grouwzame moord, begaan tegens den gewesen Grave van Essex* (1684).

32. BL Add. MSS 41,810, fol. 234r. In late 1683, Kicke played a key role in helping a dozen dissidents become burghers at Amsterdam. Among them were Wilmore, Waller, Benjamin Harris, and Edmund Everard. BL Add. MSS 41,809, fols. 185v, 206r; 41,811, fol. 121r. Kicke was apparently the son of Abraham Kicke, a Delft merchant. Keith L. Sprunger, *Dutch Puritanism: A History of English and Scottish Churches of the Netherlands in the Sixteenth and Seventeenth Centuries* (Leiden: Brill, 1982), p. 410; Greaves, *DUFE*, pp. 92–93.

33. BL Add. MSS 41,810, fols. 237r–v, 243r–v, 246r, 248r–v, 250r; 41,811, fol. 274r–v; Sprunger, *Dutch Puritanism*, pp. 314–15.

34. PRO SP 29/438/43.1, 45.2, 46, 61.2; 44/335, p. 215; BL Add. MSS 41,803, fol. 98r–v.

35. *RPCS*, 8: 335; 9: 18–19, 30, 218–22, 275–76, 281, 286, 312–13.

36. Shields, pp. 78–81, 98, 104, 112, 129, 138, 149, 155–57, 162–63; EUL MSS La.III.350, fol. 79r; London *Gazette*, 1986 (29 Nov.–1 Dec. 1684); Erskine, pp. 94–95; BL Add. MSS 12,068, fols. 100r, 101r; 28,875, fol. 411r; PRO SP 63/340, p. 38; 63/343/162.7; *CSPD 1684–85*, pp. 219–20, 284–85; *CSPD 1685*, p. 12.

37. Clarendon and Rochester, *Correspondence*, 1: 99; BL Lansdowne MSS 1152, fols. 176r, 177r, 330r–331r; BL Add. MSS 41,823, fol. 112r; PRO SP 63/340, pp. 36–37, 77; Bodl. Carte MSS 40, fol. 301r.

38. PRO SP 63/343/162, 162.1–6, 164.2, 165, 166.

39. Erskine, p. 180; BL Add. MSS 41,810, fols. 188v–189r; Baxter, pp. 175, 192; Grey, *SH*, pp. 80–81.

40. D'Avaux, 3: 97; *MVB*, pp. 155–59; Thomas Carte, *An History of the Life of James Duke of Ormonde*, 2 vols. (London: J. Bettenham, 1736), 2: 539; Foxcroft, 1: 422–26, 433; Charles James Fox, *A History of the Early Part of the Reign of James the Second* (London: William Miller, 1808), pp. viii–ix. Burnet and Grey denied that Monmouth had seen Charles. Burnet, 2: 454.

41. Burnet, 2: 462; [John Oldmixon], *The History of England, During the Reigns of the Royal House of Stuart* (London: John Pemberton et al., 1730), pp. 691–92; *MVB*, pp. 160ff.; [James Ralph], *The History of England*, 2 vols. (London: Daniel Browne, 1744–46), 1: 836–39.

42. PRO SP 31/1/52A. Of the first two he was innocent, of the third possibly guilty, and of the fourth almost certainly innocent.

43. BL Add. MSS 41,810, fols. 189r–190r, 224r–v, 226r–v; Grey, *SH*, pp. 81–84.

44. Welwood, p. 376.

45. Baxter, p. 201; BL Add. MSS 41,810, fol. 262r; Grey, *SH*, p. 84; [Ralph], *History*, 1: 853; BL Harleian MSS 6845, fol. 270r. Louis XIV mistakenly suspected Monmouth of colluding with William against James in the winter of 1685. C. J. Fox, *History*, pp. xxv–xxvii, xl.

46. BL Harleian MSS 6845, fol. 270r; Add. MSS 41,810, fols. 168r, 188v, 236r–v.

47. BL Add. MSS 41,803, fols. 106r, 181r, 193r–194r; 41,809, fol. 99v; 41,811, fols. 189r, 211r; *CSPD James II*, 1: 1, 6; Morrice, 1: 456. Spence was soon released and by April was again apparently serving as a courier. BL Add. MSS 41,803, fol. 226r. William Ayloffe (John's son?) may also have served as a messenger about this time, for he arrived at Calais on the packet boat on 9 January 1685 (n.s.). BL Add. MSS 41,803, fol. 106r. The sons of other dissidents may have been similarly employed: Samuel Meade (Matthew's son) and Arthur and Maurice Thompson (Sir John's sons) took the packet boat to the Netherlands in early April 1685. BL Add. MSS 41,803, fol. 224r.

48. Ashcraft, pp. 444–46.

49. BL Add. MSS 41,803, fols. 107r, 108r, 110r–111r.

50. Ashcraft, pp. 443, 447; BL Add. MSS 41,803, fols. 227r, 229r.

51. BL Add. MSS 41,803, fols. 181r, 185r; Geoffrey F. Nuttall, "English Dissenters in the Netherlands 1640–1689," *Nederlands Archief voor Kerkgeschiedenis*, 59 (1978): 51. A warrant for Butler's arrest was issued on 2 March. *CSPD 1685*, p. 62.

52. Erskine, p. 180. English radicals in Utrecht reportedly celebrated Charles' death with feasts and revelry. D'Avaux, 3: 160.

53. Grey, *SH*, pp. 84–88; C. J. Fox, *History*, p. xxiii.

54. *RPCS*, 10: 78; *HMC 34, Fourteenth Report*, Appendix 3, p. 115. According to Wade, the initiative was Monmouth's. The duke went to Rotterdam, and while there sent Matthews to ask Wade and other members of Argyll's inner circle whether they "were enclined to Correspond with him." The duke was concerned, Wade continued, "for we had made complaints of him, that he made not use of his interest with his father . . . in favour of us who had Suffered for him." BL Harleian MSS 6845, fol. 270r.

55. Hume, pp. 5, 9.

56. Hume, pp. 9–16; *Tryal of Henry Baron Delamere*, p. 31. In English circles some of the distrust of Monmouth was owing to his perceived lack of religious sincerity. D'Avaux, 3: 167.

57. Grey, *SH*, pp. 90–92; Hume, p. 16; *Tryal of Henry Baron Delamere*, p. 31.

58. Hume, pp. 17–25; Grey, *SH*, pp. 92–93; *Tryal of Henry Baron Delamere*, p. 29.

59. Grey, *SH*, pp. 94–97; BL Harleian MSS 6845, fol. 270v; BL Lans-

downe MSS 1152, fols. 268r, 306r. Cf. *Tryal of Henry Baron Delamere*, pp. 29, 31.

60. BL Lansdowne MSS 1152, fol. 266r; BL Harleian MSS 6845, fol. 270r–v; Grey, *SH*, pp. 93–94; *HMC* 17, *Twelfth Report*, Appendix, pt. 6, pp. 392–93.

61. BL Harleian MSS 6845, fol. 270v. Cf. *Tryal of Henry Baron Delamere*, p. 29. Grey, Wade, and Richard Goodenough insisted that Cragg professed to have been sent by Wildman. BL Lansdowne MSS 1152, fols. 266v, 268r. Clifton (*LPR*, p. 151) plausibly accuses Ferguson of the duplicity.

62. Grey, *SH*, pp. 98–99.

63. Ibid., pp. 100–103; *Tryal of Henry Baron Delamere*, pp. 29, 31; BL Add. MSS 41,812, fol. 17r; BL Lansdowne MSS 1152, fol. 301r. Before his departure, Matthews was also told to seek support among the officers in the king's guards who were his friends. Grey, *SH*, pp. 103–4. The diary of Colonel Roger Whitley records a series of meetings (but not their subjects) between May 1684 and early March 1685 variously involving such dissidents as Macclesfield, Brandon, Sir Gilbert Gerard, Cornish, Manley, Charlton, Sir Walter Yonge, Player, Wildman, Anglesey, and (George?) Griffith. The discussions must have included the proposed rebellions. Bodl. English History MSS c.711, fols. 6v, 8v, 22v–23r, 25r–27v.

64. BL Add. MSS 41,812, fol. 72r; BL Lansdowne MSS 1152, fol. 306r; Grey, *SH*, pp. 104–5. Wade's account varies slightly from this. According to him Battiscombe had instructions to speak with Macclesfield and the others only if, by taking the packet boat, he reached England before Matthews. Battiscombe later insisted he had received no message to carry to England and that only Wade knew of his trip; although he admitted having talked with Cochrane, he denied knowing anything about Argyll's expedition. BL Harleian MSS 6845, fol. 271r; BL Lansdowne MSS 1152, fol. 309r.

65. Battiscombe and Spence disembarked in England on 8 April (o.s.). BL Add. MSS 41,803, fol. 226r.

66. Grey, *SH*, pp. 106–7; *CSPD 1685*, p. 136; BL Add. MSS 41,803, fols. 239r, 241r, 243r, 268r, 271r; 41,804, fol. 70r; BL Lansdowne MSS 1152, fols. 279r–282r, 290r–v, 310v.

67. *HMC* 17, *Twelfth Report*, Appendix, pt. 6, pp. 393–94; *Tryal of Henry Baron Delamere*, pp. 29, 31. Cragg arrived in Amsterdam two or three days after Matthews left. *HMC* 17, *Twelfth Report*, Appendix, pt. 6, p. 395.

68. BL Harleian MSS 6845, fol. 271r.

69. BL Harleian MSS 6845, fol. 271v; BL Lansdowne MSS 1152, fol. 300r; *Tryal of Henry Baron Delamere*, p. 31; Grey, *SH*, p. 106; *HMC* 17, *Twelfth Report*, Appendix, pt. 6, p. 394.

70. *HMC* 17, *Twelfth Report*, Appendix, pt. 6, p. 395; Grey, *SH*, pp. 105–6.

71. Grey, *SH*, pp. 108–9.

72. BL Harleian MSS 6845, fol. 271r. On Wildman's "Hieroglyphices" compare Henry Ireton's comment: "[Wildman] was alwayes such a cautious Sir Politick to me, that if ever he told me any peice of common newes though of no greater Moment than what one might heare in the Streete; he would talke of a Gyant, a horse, a Cocke & a Bull, & such kind of Stuff, & then say he us'd that way of talking, & that they who had not Witt enough to understand him, he car'd not for conversing with." BL Lansdowne MSS 1152, fol. 280r.

73. Grey, *SH*, p. 110.

74. *HMC* 17, *Twelfth Report*, Appendix, pt. 6, pp. 396–97; BL Lansdowne MSS 1152, fol. 266r. In the months before the invasion Delamere was in contact with Sir Thomas Mainwaring, who in turn was in touch with Brandon and Fitton Gerard. The subject of these meetings is not recorded. ChRO MSS DDX 383/2 (entries for 9, 13, 28 Feb.; 15 Mar.; 2, 28 Apr.; 1, 4, 7, 9, 13 May 1685).

75. BL Harleian MSS 6845, fol. 270v; Grey, *SH*, pp. 110–11.

76. BL Add. MSS 41,812, fols. 9v, 15r; 41,817, fol. 3r; Hume, pp. 34–37; Crookshank, 2: 308. The other seven Scots at the meeting on 17 April were Cochrane's son, James Stewart, William Denholm of Westshiels, George Hume of Bassendean, George Wishart, Charles Campbell, and Gilbert Elliot. Crookshank, 2: 308; *MVB*, p. 311.

77. London *Gazette*, 2036 (21–25 May 1685).

78. BL Lansdowne MSS 1152, fols. 242v, 258r. For a draft see BL Harleian MSS 6845, fols. 256r–259v. Disney was primarily responsible for printing it; a Mrs. Lee of London (who had previously supported Oates and Braddon) subsidized its publication. Copies were to be sent to Delamere in Cheshire. Skelton had obtained a copy from someone in Amsterdam by 26 June (n.s.), and three days later he reported the public sale of English, Dutch, and French versions. William finally ordered its suppression on 13 July, sixteen days after its denunciation by the States General. According to Skelton, "Monmouth's declaration hath galed him [William] to the quick." BL Add. MSS 41,804, fol. 26r–v; 41,806, fols. 255v–256r; 41,812, fols. 125r, 127r, 130v; (cf. 41,817, fol. 181v); BL Lansdowne MSS 1152, fol. 301r; *Tryal of Henry Baron Delamere*, pp. 41–43, Morrice, 1: 468, 472; D'Avaux, 3: 249.

79. Hume, p. 36; *MVB*, pp. 148, 153; BL Add. MSS 41,812, fol. 27r; 41,823, fols. 112v–113r.

80. *MVB*, p. 148; EUL MSS La.III.350, fol. 154r. For Robert Ker see Greaves, *EUHF*, pp. 82, 275.

81. Grey, *SH*, p. 112; BL Harleian MSS 6845, fols. 270v–271r; BL Add. MSS 41,812, fol. 138v; 41,817, fol. 17r; 41,818, fol. 106v; BL Lansdowne MSS 1152, fol. 306r. Erskine (p. 180) says Mrs. Smith donated £8,000, but does not indicate to whom the money was given. An English agent in Utrecht

described her as "a great fomenter of the Plotts." BL Add. MSS 41,817, fol. 219r.

82. BL Add. MSS 41,812, fol. 74r; D'Avaux, 3: 220. Henry Bull, the English agent in Amsterdam, reported on 12 May (n.s.) that Argyll's armaments included 60 large guns and carriages, 15,000 muskets, and 8,000 grenades. BL Add. MSS 41,812, fol. 65r. The report of a naval lieutenant lists only 160 barrels of gunpowder and bullets. BL Add. MSS 41,812, fols. 63r–64r.

83. BL Add. MSS 41,812, fols. 41r, 47r; 41,817, fol. 1r; Hume, pp. 38, 40; Grey, *SH*, pp. 111–12; *MVB*, p. 314; JRL Legh of Lyme MSS (Sunderland to Richard Legh et al., 19 May 1685). Prior to sailing, Cochrane left invitations to Scottish officers serving as mercenaries in Brandenburg and other German states to meet in Amsterdam to obtain instructions as to how they could serve Argyll. BL Add. MSS 41,817, fol. 65v.

84. Baxter, p. 204; BL Add. MSS 41,812, fols. 47r–v, 48v, 57v, 100r; 41,817, fols. 77r–v, 92r. The provinces of Utrecht and Zeeland also approved resolutions banning the rebels. BL Add. MSS 41,806, fol. 253r–v; 41,817, fol. 60r–v.

85. BL Add. MSS 41,806, fol. 251r–v; 41,812, fols. 47r–v, 58v, 68v, 94r. The initiative to ban the fugitives was James'. BL Add. MSS 41,823, fols. 11v–12r. A surprising amount of the information sent by Skelton to Middleton was erroneous, including the date of the expedition's departure and the rumor that Monmouth would command an army in Scotland around 30 May. Skelton also wrongly reported that an additional ten to twelve ships would join Argyll from such cities as Emden and Hamburg, and that more arms and men would be forthcoming from Emden, Rotterdam, Zeeland, and especially Bremen. BL Add. MSS 41,812, fols. 36r, 47v–48r, 57v (cf. 109r).

86. BL Add. MSS 41,812, fols. 26v, 36r, 57v; 41,817, fol. 13v; Erskine, pp. 113–14.

87. BL Add. MSS 41,812, fols. 36r, 65r; 41,817, fol. 13r; Erskine, pp. 114–15, 119, 124; Shields, p. 167; *MVB*, pp. 314, 320; *Blackader Mem.*, p. 321; PRO SP 63/351, fol. 26r–v.

88. *CSPD 1685*, p. 157; PRO SP 31/2, p. 31; London *Gazette*, 2036 (21–25 May 1685); 2038 (28 May–1 June 1685); 2039 (1–4 June 1685); 2040 (4–8 June 1685); 2044 (18–22 June 1685); 2045 (22–25 June 1685); 2046 (25–29 June 1685); 2048 (2–6 July 1685); *MVB*, pp. 314–32; NLS MSS 1004, fol. 4r–v. Cf. *HMC* 44, *Drumlanrig*, vol. 2, pp. 110–11.

89. EUL MSS La.III.344, vol. 1, fol. 133r; La.III.350, fols. 152r–153v; Shields, pp. 165–68.

90. *Collection of Letters Addressed to Sancroft*, p. 83; Erskine, p. 134; BL Add. MSS 41,817, fols. 102r, 114r–v. The government had feared that Argyll would land in northern Ireland, from which, in any case, Scottish fugitives had been returning home in the spring. Security measures were intensified,

especially from March forward. PRO SP 63/340, pp. 63, 75, 79, 81, 83–88; 63/351, fols. 11r, 14r, 16r; BL Lansdowne MSS 1152, fols. 329r, 331r–v, 344r, 347r–v; C. J. Fox, *History*, p. lxxx.

91. Grey, *SH*, pp. 113–17; *Tryal of Henry Baron Delamere*, pp. 29, 31; BL Harleian MSS 6845, fol. 271v; BL Lansdowne MSS 1152, fol. 310r; *HMC* 17, *Twelfth Report*, Appendix, pt. 6, p. 397. Skelton knew of Monmouth's plans to go to England "suddenly." BL Add. MSS 41,812, fol. 34r.

92. BL Harleian MSS 6845, fols. 271r–272r; BL Lansdowne MSS 1152, fols. 237r, 243v; BL Add. MSS 41,812, fols. 93v, 111v, 115r, 122v (cf. 77r–v); 41,817, fol. 274r; 41,818, fols. 10r, 234v; Grey, *SH*, pp. 112–13, 117–19; *HMC* 49, *Sackville*, 1: 23. Nicholas Locke is cited as the donor of the £400 by Burton and Richard Goodenough; BL Lansdowne MSS 1152, fol. 227r–v. But cf. Ashcraft's rebuttal, pp. 459–62.

93. BL Harleian MSS 6845, fol. 271r; Welwood, pp. 377–78. This letter may have been a response to one from an unidentified party in Taunton. Grey, *SH*, p. 112.

94. BL Add. MSS 41,812, fol. 75v.

95. Grey, *SH*, p. 118–19; *Tryal of Henry Baron Delamere*, pp. 32–34; BL Harleian MSS 6845, fol. 272v; BL Lansdowne MSS 1152, fols. 303r, 306v. Wade thought Jones had claimed he had been sent by Wildman.

96. Grey, *SH*, pp. 119–20; BL Harleian MSS 6845, fol. 272r–v; BL Lansdowne MSS 1152, fol. 308r; *HMC* 17, *Twelfth Report*, Appendix, pt. 6, pp. 398–99.

97. *Tryal of Henry Baron Delamere*, pp. 18–19, 30, 32, 34–39, 72; BL Add. MSS 61,690, fol. 80r. For pro-Monmouth sentiment in Chester see CCRO MSS QSF/83, fols. 76r, 77r, 110Ar, 177r–v, 224r, 234r, 237r, 238r, 239r, 241r, 247r; the following cases probably involved Monmouth partisans as well: CCRO MSS QSF/83, fols. 30r, 107r, 108r, 110r, 177Av, 234v. Rumors about Argyll's forces caused a disturbance in Chester. CCRO MSS QSF/83, fols. 73r, 96r–v. Peyton had been arrested in 1684 for stabbing his prospective son-in-law after the latter had refused to toast Monmouth. BL Add. MSS 28,875, fols. 415v, 419v.

98. Monmouth also sent Norton and Elizabeth Gaunt—whose husband, a former tallow-chandler, would sail with the duke—to instruct Macclesfield to be ready to act in Cheshire. BL Add. MSS 41,818, fols. 77r–v, 112v.

99. Elizabeth Gaunt was dispatched to the Netherlands to learn why the duke had been delayed. BL Add. MSS 41,812, fol. 138v; 41,817, fol. 181r. Jane Hall, "another Nurseing Mother or Messenger," also served as a courier for the radicals. BL Add. MSS 41,818, fol. 77v; 41,812, fol. 223v.

100. *HMC* 17, *Twelfth Report*, Appendix, pt. 6, pp. 399–403; BL Lansdowne MSS 1152, fol. 266v; Grey, *SH*, pp. 122–23. Brand, master of the Red Lion tavern, was arrested at the end of May along with Robert Perrott

(Blood's former colleague) and three others as they traveled to Exeter. BL Harleian MSS 6845, fols. 284v–285r; PRO SP 44/56, p. 210. Dr. Fell, bishop of Oxford, had a better insight into Wildman's character than did Monmouth: "Tis not to be thought that he put himself into the duke of Monmouths business, out of conscience." BL Add. MSS 29,582, fol. 268r.

101. BL Lansdowne MSS 1152, fols. 204r, 237r, 238r, 240r, 243v, 304r; Add. MSS 41,810, fols. 251v–252v, 254r–v, 258r–v, 266r; 41,812, fols. 36r, 59v–60r; 41,813, fol. 129v; 41,817, fols. 151r, 153r, 237r–v; 41,818, fols. 46r, 66r, 112r; 41,819, fols. 1r–2r; BL Harleian MSS 6845, fols. 280r, 286r; BL Sloan MSS 1983B, fol. 12r; PRO SP 31/2, pp. 61–62; SRO MSS DD/SF 3109 (29 July 1685); W. Bowles Barrett, "The Rebels in the Duke of Monmouth's Rebellion," *Proceedings of the Dorset Natural History and Antiquarian Field Club*, 5 (n.d.): 111; Hume, p. 44. Foulkes recruited soldiers for Monmouth. BL Add. MSS 41,819, fols. 1r–12r.

102. HMC 17, *Twelfth Report*, Appendix, pt. 6, pp. 403–5; HMC 49, *Sackville*, 1: 24; BL Lansdowne MSS 1152, fols. 237r, 238r, 242v, 266v; BL Harleian MSS 6845, fol. 282r; Grey, *SH*, p. 124. Manley was a correspondent of the Fifth Monarchist preacher Walter Thimbleton. BL Lansdowne MSS 1152, fol. 227r; *BDBR*, s.v. "Thimbleton, Walter." Several days after Manley's trip to London, Monmouth's chaplain, Nathaniel Hooke, went to the City to urge the duke's partisans to revolt. A day or two later, Manley's son gave Monmouth a message from Wildman's wife, conveying the assurance of her husband ("Mr. Indenture") that Delamere had left for Cheshire to head an insurrection and that London awaited the duke's command to revolt. Grey, *SH*, pp. 123–24; BL Harleian MSS 6845, fol. 282r.

103. BL Add. MSS 41,812, fol. 248r–v; HMC 29, *Portland*, 2: 158, 3: 385–86; JRL Legh of Lyme MSS (newsletter to Richard Legh, 7 July 1685).

Chapter 8

1. *RPCS*, 11: 96, 323–27.

2. *ST*, 11: 873–88; PRO SP 44/54, pp. 321, 323; London *Gazette*, 2047 (29 June–2 July 1685); 2048 (2–6 July 1685); 2081 (26–29 Oct. 1685); 2082 (29 Oct.–2 Nov. 1685); *RPCS*, 11: 83; HMC 29, *Portland*, 3: 387, 389.

3. BL Add. MSS 41,818, fol. 136r–v; BL Lansdowne MSS 1152, fol. 300r. Venner and Parsons left the insurgent army after ostensibly failing to persuade Monmouth to flee overseas, but according to Captain John Tillier the two men returned to the Netherlands at the behest of Ferguson, Wade, Tiley, and others to purchase arms and ammunition with which to mount an uprising in Ireland. Aided by Lieutenant-Colonel William More and other former Cromwellian officers, they allegedly planned to seize the forts at Cork and Kinsale, a castle near Carrickfergus, and the city of Limerick. They also had plans to blow up the arsenal in Dublin. If James dispatched

troops from Scotland, Cheshire would rise; if they came from England, London would revolt. Tillier may have concocted this account to save his life. BL Harleian MSS 6845, fol. 280r; BL Lansdowne MSS 1152, fols. 273r, 277r.

4. Earle, *MR*, pp. 97, 195; BL Lansdowne MSS 1152, fol. 243v. For Sedgemoor see Earle, *MR*, chap. 6, and Clifton, *LPR*, chap. 7. Some of the radicals had been led to expect help from sympathetic Europeans: John Row claimed that at the time of the rebellion hundreds of Swiss officers and landed gentlemen had offered to enlist and arm 10,000 Swiss soldiers at their own expense if Ludlow would lead the army. Ferguson, Wade, and other exiles purportedly declined the offer as unnecessary. According to Tiley and (unnamed) others, Ferguson and Le Blon had obtained a commitment—"a League and Engagement"—from the principal magistrates of Amsterdam to assist Monmouth, but the Dutch were supposedly not informed in time to act. Both stories are at best grossly exaggerated. BL Add. MSS 41,813, fol. 177v; 41,818, fol. 159v.

5. BL Add. MSS 41,806, fol. 259r–v; *HMC 49, Sackville*, 1: 22; BL Lansdowne MSS 1236, fol. 229r; PRO SP 31/1/104; 44/336, pp. 159–60; London *Gazette*, 2051 (13–16 July 1685); Luttrell, 1: 352–54; Evelyn, 4: 455–56; Morrice, 1: 474.

6. BL Sloan MSS 609, fol. 62r. Cf. Greaves, *EUHF*, pp. 175–76.

7. BL Add. MSS 30,077; 31,957, fols. 4r–34r; *True and Exact List of the Names; Further Account of the Proceedings Against the Rebels*; PRO SP 31/1/126; Clifton, *LPR*, chap. 8; Earle, *MR*, chap. 8; Whiting, *Persecution Expos'd*, p. 153 (cf. p. 144). For the cruel treatment of prisoners at Wells see SRO MSS DD/SAS S.E.83.

8. *Further Account of the Proceedings Against the Rebels*; London *Gazette*, 2046 (25–29 June 1685); 2066 (3–7 Sept. 1685); 2081 (26–29 Oct. 1685); 2082 (29 Oct.–2 Nov. 1685); BL Lansdowne MSS 1152, fols. 238v, 240v; BL Harleian MSS 6845, fol. 277v; PRO SP 44/56, pp. 284–85; Dorset Record Office MSS D239/f16; Morrice, 1: 471, 476–77, 487, 489. Dare was killed in a quarrel with another Monmouth supporter. BL Harleian MSS 6845, fol. 275v. Larke had been in trouble at Lyme in early 1682 for his illegal preaching. Cragg was sent to Newgate prison in December 1685 on charges of high treason. PRO SP 29/418/80; 44/68, p. 18; 44/336, p. 302. Hundreds of suspected dissidents, former Cromwellian soldiers, and nonconformist ministers, including Matthews, Manley, Gladman, Cornish, Ireton, and Yonge, were arrested during and in the aftermath of the rebellions. PRO SP 31/2, pp. 18, 34–36, 38, 41; 44/56, p. 245; 63/351, fol. 139r–v; BL Add. MSS 41,803, fol. 337r–v; 42,849, fol. 2r; Morrice, 1: 460, 462, 464, 466, 468–74, 476–77, 480–82, 492, 501; SRO MSS DD/SF 285.

9. *CSPD 1685*, pp. 349, 369; *CSPD 1686–87*, p. 132; PRO SP 31/1/139, 159;

44/337, pp. 9, 35, 199, 324, 363; 44/338, pp. 36–37; *HMC* 75, *Downshire*, 1: 56, 64, 282; Morrice, 1: 488, 541, 651, 657; BL Add. MSS 41,823, fol. 39r. Goodenough remained imprisoned in Jersey Castle until May 1687. PRO SP 44/337, pp. 64–65, 280.

10. Earle, *MR*, p. 178; *HMC* 29, *Portland*, 2: 238; SRO MSS T/PH/wig 2/5, p. 5 (John Coad); BL Lansdowne MSS 1152, fol. 256r; PRO SP 44/336, p. 312.

11. Luttrell, 1: 354, 355, 357, 364–65; Morrice, 1: 477, 496–97, 500–501; *CSPD 1685*, p. 275; London *Gazette*, 2067 (7–10 Sept. 1685); EUL MSS La.I.332, pp. 2–15; DWL MSS 90.5.(6); *HMC* 75, *Downshire*, 1: 56, 59–61; BL Lansdowne MSS 1152, fols. 262r, 263r, 265r; PRO SP 44/337, pp. 176, 315; JRL Legh of Lyme MSS (newsletter to Richard Legh, 28 July 1685). The government also gave up its case against Sir Gilbert Gerard (February 1686), who had been accused of conspiring to launch an insurrection, because it had only one witness. Luttrell, 1: 366, 371; *HMC* 75, *Downshire*, 1: 64. Finished with Rumsey, the government sent him to St. Nicholas Island, near Plymouth, in April 1686. PRO SP 44/337, p. 1.

12. *Tryal of Henry Baron Delamere*; *ST*, 11: 510–99; DWL MSS 90.5.(14); BL Lansdowne MSS 1152, fol. 294r; Morrice, 1: 510–12, 524; *Account of the Proceedings Against Saxon*; *Account of the Proceeding to Judgment*; JRL Legh of Lyme MSS (newsletters to Richard Legh, 9 and 14 Jan. 1686); *HMC* 75, *Downshire*, 1: 64, 74, 100–101, 107, 117; Luttrell, 1: 369, 372.

13. Luttrell, 1: 355, 360, 363, 364, 372, 374; *CSPD 1685*, p. 372.

14. Clifton, *LPR*, p. 231; BL Add. MSS 41,812, fols. 155r, 164r, 225v; 41,817, fols. 237v–238r, 264v; 41,818, fol. 112r.

15. BL Add. MSS 41,812, fol. 171v; 41,817, fol. 274v; *HMC* 34, *Fourteenth Report*, Appendix 3, p. 115. Bethel maintained contact with friends in England through correspondence sent to Abraham Kicke. BL Add. MSS 41,812, fols. 224v–225r.

16. BL Add. MSS 41,812, fol. 138r; 41,817, fols. 219v, 237v, 274v; 41,818, fol. 10r.

17. BL Add. MSS 41,812, fol. 222v; 41,813, fol. 15v; 41,818, fol. 125v; 41,819, fol. 60r. When Ann Smith learned on 22 June (n.s.) that Monmouth had landed in England, she had Cross preach on Psalm 34: 1–2 in a private house in Utrecht where Hogg usually spoke. BL Add. MSS 41,812, fol. 222r; 41,817, fol. 219r. Wilmore and Samuel Harris lived together in Utrecht. BL Add. MSS 41,820, fol. 85r.

18. BL Add. MSS 41,812, fol. 235v; 41,813, fols. 15r, 199v; 41,818, fols. 159r, 248v–249r, 280v.

19. BL Add. MSS 41,813, fol. 157r; 41,818, fol. 207r. Cragg also had incriminating information against Le Blon, Archer, Rotherham, and others. According to Everard, Cragg extorted money in London "from those that

corresponded with the Rebells for not discovering them." BL Add. MSS 41,818, fol. 181r.

20. BL Add. MSS 41,818, fols. 230r, 234r–v, 268r; PRO SP 31/3, fol. 237r. Perry had been captured after the rebellion but escaped in August 1685. He obtained his pardon in June 1686. BL Add. MSS 41,804, fol. 71r; PRO SP 44/54, p. 343.

21. BL Add. MSS 41,819, fols. 19r–20r.

22. BL Add. MSS 41,812, fols. 152r, 155r, 160v–161r; 41,813, fols. 9v, 11v–12r, 45r. Cf. 41,814, fols. 7r–9r; 41,818, fols. 196r, 198r; 41,820, fols. 102v–103r.

23. BL Add. MSS 41,812, fols. 195r, 199r, 228r, 229v, 232v, 242r, 260v; 41,814, fol. 7r; 41,818, fols. 127r–132v. Wildman and Charlton were in Amsterdam "under a strange disguise." BL Add. MSS 41,812, fols. 257r, 260v; 41,818, fols. 152r, 185v.

24. BL Add. MSS 41,812, fols. 154v, 174r, 177r, 256r; 41,813, fol. 3r; 41,823, fol. 33r; Erskine, p. 171.

25. BL Add. MSS 41,812, fols. 160r–v, 209r, 218r–v, 224r; 41,818, fols. 65r, 238r. Although not a fugitive, Wharton had taken leave of the king on the pretense that he was going to Montpellier. BL Add. MSS 41,818, fol. 106v.

26. BL Add. MSS 41,812, fol. 187v; 41,813, fols. 46r–v, 57r–58r; 41,818, fols. 19r, 21r, 23r, 53r, 54r–v, 106v, 188r, 256r.

27. BL Add. MSS 41,812, fols. 150r, 155r, 157r, 193r, 195v, 197r–v; 41,817, fols. 237v, 264r–v, 265v, 274v; 41,818, fols. 1r, 17r, 27r, 39r, 49r, 50r, 61r, 77r, 78r, 92r, 93r, 96r, 112r, 116r.

28. BL Add. MSS 41,804, fol. 158r–v; 41,813, fols. 54v, 58r, 139r, 142v, 185r; 41,818, fols. 242r, 281r; 41,819, fols. 20v, 61r. Denham had been spotted at Rotterdam with various Argyll fugitives in early January 1686. BL Add. MSS 41,818, fol. 208r. See also *CSPD 1689–90*, pp. 30, 191.

29. BL Add. MSS 41,813, fol. 168v; 41,819, fol. 161r.

30. BL Add. MSS 41,818, fols. 97r–99r. Everard maintained contacts with the radicals by providing hospitality, loaning them money, and finding them employment. Among those who shared his table were Manley, Meade, and Hilliard. BL Add. MSS 41,812, fol. 226v; 41,818, fol. 125r.

31. BL Add. MSS 41,812, fols. 211v, 223r, 225r–v; 41,818, fols. 17v, 103r, 106v–107r, 175r, 178r, 208v, 223v, 273v.

32. BL Add. MSS 41,818, fols. 106v, 108v, 238r. A member of the princess of Orange's entourage provided information to Sir John's wife. BL Add. MSS 41,818, fol. 108r.

33. BL Add. MSS 41,812, fols. 218r, 222r, 260v; Erskine, p. 174.

34. BL Add. MSS 41,813, fol. 179r; 41,818, fols. 273r–v, 274v, 283v; 41,819, fols. 59v, 60v, 84r; 41,820, fol. 85r. Wilmore lived in Utrecht. BL Add. MSS 41,819, fols. 60v–61r; 41,820, fol. 85r.

35. BL Add. MSS 41,812, fols. 208r–209r, 218r; 41,813, fol. 179r; 41,818, fols.

107r, 108r, 257r. Bethel was soon concerned about the statements Cornish made concerning him in his trial. BL Add. MSS 41,812, fols. 218v, 220v. English efforts to persuade the States General to banish Kicke in early July 1685 (n.s.) were unsuccessful. BL Add. MSS 41,812, fols. 134v, 137r.

36. BL Add. MSS 41,812, fols. 223v, 261r; 41,813, fol. 46v; 41,818, fols. 77r–v, 83r, 84r, 112v, 187r, 207r, 248r, 260r; PRO SP 44/54, p. 319.

37. *ST*, 11: 465–68; London *Gazette*, 2046 (25–29 June 1685); BL Add. MSS 41,804, fol. 26r–v; 41,818, fol. 125r. Malthus shared his London shop with John Harris, Samuel's brother. John Harris went to the Netherlands in the spring of 1686 and was seen with his brother and Wildman. BL Add. MSS 41,819, fol. 60r–v. For Malthus see Plomer, *DBP*, p. 196.

38. BL Add. MSS 41,812, fols. 226r–v, 235r; 41,818, fols. 79v–80r.

39. BL Add. MSS 41,818, fols. 106r, 229v, 269v; 41,819, fols. 19r, 229v. Cragg had also delivered Braddon's "Memoires concerneing Essex's Murder" to Ferguson in Amsterdam.

40. BL Add. MSS 41,806, fols. 261v–262r; 41,812, fols. 231v–232r, 244v–245r, 247r–v; 41,813, fol. 6v.

41. BL Add. MSS 41,804, fols. 194r, 284r, 295r–298r, 307v, 310r; 41,812, fol. 261r; 41,813, fols. 17r, 19r, 47v, 61v; 41,817, fol. 263r; 41,818, fols. 79v, 137v, 156v, 159r, 200r, 206r, 280v; SRO MSS Q/SR, Roll 169, fols. 1r–12r; CCRO MSS QSF/83, fol. 177Av. See also the deluded assertions of Elias Bragg, a veteran of Monmouth's rebellion, concerning the duke's imminent return to lead a new, grander insurrection. PRO SP 31/4, fols. 21r, 22r–v, 25r–26r, 30r, 33r; 44/56, p. 416. Feelings for and against the duke were still sufficiently strong in June 1687 to spark a riot between the residents of Huntspill and Burnham, Somerset.

42. BL Add. MSS 41,809, fol. 239r–v.

43. BL Add. MSS 41,810, fol. 262r; 41,813, fols. 96v, 112r; 41,818, fols. 58v, 234v, 249r, 256v; 41,819, fols. 13v, 64r.

44. PRO SP 29/435/157; BL Add. MSS 41,809, fol. 239r–v; 41,812, fols. 15v, 138v; 41,813, fol. 93r; D'Avaux, 3: 130.

45. BL Add. MSS 41,812, fol. 261r; 41,818, fols. 201r–203v, 274r; 41,819, fols. 121r–123v. Tiley and others also considered a plan to organize fugitives into a mercenary company or regiment for employment by the Swiss or the duke of Brandenburg. Waller actively sought recruits. BL Add. MSS 41,812, fols. 227r, 235v (cf. 248r); 41,818, fol. 279r.

46. BL Add. MSS 41,812, fol. 227r; 41,813, fols. 112v–113r, 114r, 142v, 150r; 41,818, fols. 125r, 226r, 229r–v, 234v, 235v; D'Avaux, 3: 130. Peyton, Manley, Row, and a draper named Foster boasted that they had £12,000 to invest at Leeuwarden. BL Add. MSS 41,818, fol. 229r.

47. BL Add. MSS 41,818, fols. 234r–v, 261r, 269v, 274r–v; 41,819, fols. 121r–123v, 125r–126r.

48. BL Add. MSS 41,803, fol. 115r; 41,818, fols. 256v, 269v, 280v.

49. BL Add. MSS 41,823, fol. 122r; *CSPD 1686–87*, p. 60. The attorney general advised that a proclamation prohibiting trade with traitors and fugitives in the Netherlands was legal. BL Add. MSS 41,804, fol. 120r.

50. BL Add. MSS 41,804, fol. 158r–v; 41,813, fol. 174r; 41,818, fols. 226r, 234v. Vile had reportedly gone to England in December 1685 to seek pardons for most of the rebels. BL Add. MSS 41,818, fol. 174r. Macclesfield, Brandon, Charlton, Wildman, and Trenchard were also excluded from the pardon. Morrice, 1: 528.

51. BL Add. MSS 41,806, fols. 263v, 265r–v, 267r–v; 41,813, fols. 130r, 136r, 142r, 156r; *HMC 75, Downshire*, 1: 188.

52. BL Add. MSS 41,813, fol. 96r–v; 41,818, fol. 291r–v; 41,823, fol. 37r–v.

53. BL Add. MSS 41,813, fols. 104r, 110r, 112r–113r, 122r, 128r–v, 130r; 41,823, fol. 39r; 41,819, fols. 16r, 57r–v, 71r; PRO SP 44/54, pp. 340, 343–44; 44/337, p. 90. Nicholas Locke offered to serve as an informer. BL Add. MSS 41,813, fols. 128v, 174r.

54. BL Add. MSS 41,804, fols. 182r, 185r, 187r, 189r, 191r–v; 41,813, fols. 150r–v, 156v; 41,819, fols. 103r, 125r–126r, 162r, 187r, 212r; *CSPD 1686–87*, p. 89.

55. BL Add. MSS 41,804, fol. 182r; 41,813, fols. 177v, 201v, 203r–v, 229v, 233r, 235v; 41,819, fols. 113r, 235v (cf. 108r).

56. BL Add. MSS 41,813, fols. 96v, 113v, 134v–135r, 189v; 41,818, fols. 289r–v, 290r–v; 41,819, fols. 45r, 58r, 97r, 116r, 161v, 186v, 206r, 272v; *CSPD 1686–87*, pp. 296, 319; PRO SP 44/337, p. 42.

57. Norton was the brother-in-law of the M.P. William Trenchard, a distant relation of Sir John's. BL Add. MSS 41,819, fol. 58r.

58. PRO SP 31/3, fol. 59r–v (Peyton's report); 44/337, pp. 199, 363; BL Add. MSS 41,813, fols. 113v, 134v; 41,819, fols. 51r, 69r, 93r, 95r–96r, 183r, 200r, 219r; *HMC 75, Downshire*, 1: 283. Other notable pardons were those granted to Ann Smith (August 1686), Sir Patience Ward (April 1687), and Benjamin Alsop (May 1687). PRO SP 44/337, pp. 89, 281; *CSPD 1686–87*, p. 403; cf. BL Add. MSS 41,814, fol. 85r–v.

59. BL Add. MSS 41,813, fols. 113v–114r, 249v; 41,819, fols. 162v, 240r–v.

60. BL Add. MSS 41,813, fol. 233v; 41,814, fol. 36r–v; Erskine, p. 219; PRO SP 44/337, p. 245. Another minister, Stephen Lobb, was pardoned in December 1686. PRO SP 44/337, p. 165.

61. BL Add. MSS 41,813, fols. 139r, 142v, 150v, 162v; 41,814, fol. 36r; 41,820, fol. 8r; Erskine, p. 190. Aaron Smith received a pardon in March 1688. PRO SP 44/337, p. 417; *CSPD 1687–89*, p. 175; Morrice, 2: 249.

62. BL Add. MSS 41,806, fols. 269r–270r, 271r–v, 273v–274r, 275r–276r; 41,813, fols. 156r, 229r, 254v, 256r; 41,819, fols. 80r, 235v, 272r; 41,823, fol. 123v; *CSPD 1686–87*, pp. 60, 127, 133; *HMC 75, Downshire*, 1: 186, 188.

63. BL Add. MSS 41,813, fols. 247r–v, 249v; 41,814, fol. 32v; 41,817, fols.

241v–242r; 41,818, fol. 229v; 41,819, fols. 20v, 162v–163r. The agent may have been Edward Woodward. BL Add. MSS 41,814, fol. 146v.

64. BL Add. MSS 41,814, fols. 32v–33r, 44v; 41,819, fol. 181r.

65. BL Add. MSS 41,814, fols. 44v, 48r–v, 52r–v, 53r, 56v, 64r–v, 76r, 87r–v, 93r–v, 105r–106v, 109r, 115r–v, 197r, 205r–v; 41,820, fols. 26r–27v, 33r–34r, 46r; 34,508, fols. 137r–139v; JRL Legh of Lyme MSS (newsletter to Richard Legh, 17 Mar. 1687); *HMC* 75, *Downshire*, 1: 225–26; Morrice, 1: 648.

66. BL Add. MSS 29,582, fol. 274r; 41,819, fol. 188r. Howe subsequently denied having seen Ferguson in the preceding four years. BL Add. MSS 41,819, fol. 213r.

67. BL Add. MSS 41,813, fols. 199r–v, 204r; 41,817, fols. 239r–242r; 41,819, fol. 187r. While Ferguson was in Amsterdam in July, Vermuyden interceded with Locke in his behalf. BL Add. MSS 41,819, fol. 191v.

68. BL Add. MSS 41,813, fol. 204r; cf. 41,814, fol. 1v. Everard was already disappointed because Skelton, who depicted him as a diligent agent but "a great villaine at bottom still," had opposed his appointment as consul in Amsterdam in April. BL Add. MSS 41,813, fol. 100v.

69. BL Add. MSS 41,813, fols. 190v, 215v; 41,819, fols. 221r, 223r; Erskine, p. 207; Baxter, p. 218; J. R. Jones, *The Revolution of 1688 in England* (New York: Norton, 1972), p. 217. White, an Irish Catholic, received his title from the Holy Roman Emperor. After Skelton's departure the best intelligence came from William Petit. In the first three months of the post-Skelton period, Petit expended 160 guilders on espionage; only postage (376 guilders) claimed a larger share of his budget of 812 guilders. BL Add. MSS 41,814, fol. 121r–v.

70. BL Add. MSS 41,814, fol. 206v; 41,815, fols. 110r, 114r–v, 119r; JRL Legh of Lyme MSS (newsletter to Richard Legh, 12 Mar. 1687). One Englishman in Amsterdam claimed he saw Ferguson board a ship for London in January 1688. BL Add. MSS 41,820, fols. 286r–287v.

71. BL Add. MSS 41,817, fol. 238r. In early November 1685 there were rumors of an embryonic plot to kill James with a pistol or poison. BL Add. MSS 41,818, fol. 112v.

72. BL Add. MSS 41,818, fols. 156v, 200r.

73. For Scottish conventicles see: *RPCS*, 11: 18–19, 58, 114–15, 206–7, 209, 373, 492–96, 501–2, 507–9, 540, 555–56, 599; 12: 87, 110–14, 117–18, 354–56, 367–72, 375, 377–78, 403–8; 13: 21–23, 101, 127–31, 192, 276–77, 282–83, 285–91, 293, 308–10, 343–44, 346, 352; BL Add. MSS 41,804, fol. 273r; *HMC* 75, *Downshire*, 1: 237; *HMC* 29, *Portland*, 2: 44; London *Gazette*, 2221 (28 Feb.–3 Mar. 1687). For attacks on ministers and the rescue of prisoners in Scotland see: *RPCS*, 11: 50–52, 554–55; 12: 373; 13: 271, 316–17, 326–28. For Irish security see: PRO SP 31/2, p. 40; 63/340, pp. 88–91, 98, 102–3; 63/344,

p. 170; 63/351, fol. 42v; BL Lansdowne MSS 1152, fols. 350r–v, 378r–v; Clarendon and Rochester, *Correspondence*, 1: 269; Morrice, 2: 231. For alleged conspiracies in Ireland see: *Letters of Eminent Men to Thoresby*, 1: 70; PRO SP 63/340, p. 235; 63/351, fols. 63v–64r, 151r–154r, 274r–275r; *CSPD 1685*, p. 236; *CSPD 1686–87*, pp. 14–15, 31; BL Add. MSS 15,893, fols. 41r, 47r, 49r, 50r, 117v; 15,894, fol. 48r; Clarendon and Rochester, *Correspondence*, 1: 498, 563–64, 569; 2: 78–79, 146–48.

74. BL Add. MSS 41,813, fols. 106r–107r; 41,820, fols. 91r–92v. Skelton was suspicious of Segar's allegations. BL Add. MSS 41,820, fol. 102r.

75. BL Add. MSS 41,804, fols. 136r–137v, 146r–147r, 154r, 155v–156r, 157r, 158r, 168r–169r, 280r, 281r; 41,813, fols. 88r, 90r–v, 94v–95r, 96r; 41,819, fol. 33r–v; Morrice, 1: 632, 636–37. Monmouth himself was compared to Warbeck by some of his critics. BL Add. MSS 28,876, fol. 13v; Add. MSS 62,453, fol. 104 (*A Relation of the Defeat of the Rebels in the West*).

76. BL Add. MSS 41,804, fol. 182r; 41,813, fols. 170v, 179r–v; 41,814, fols. 22r–23v, 45r; 41,819, fol. 185r–v; Erskine, p. 170.

77. BL Add. MSS 41,814, fol. 45r; 41,819, fol. 178v.

78. Erskine, pp. 211–14.

79. Erskine, pp. 170–219 passim.

80. Gilbert Burnet, *Bishop Burnet's History of His Own Time*, 2nd ed., 6 vols. (Oxford: At the University Press, 1833), 3: 180–81, 274–75; Ashcraft, p. 523.

81. BL Add. MSS 41,814, fols. 186r, 213v, 223r–224r, 226r–v, 229v–230r, 271v; 41,820, fols. 217r–218r; *CSPD 1687–89*, pp. 42, 44–45; *RPCS*, 13: 156–58; London *Gazette*, 2267 (8–11 Aug. 1687); *HMC 75, Downshire*, 1: 255.

82. BL Add. MSS 41,820, fols. 275r–276r; Lacey, pp. 469–70; J. R. Jones, *Revolution*, p. 222.

83. John Carswell, *The Descent on England: A Study of the English Revolution of 1688 and Its European Background* (New York: John Day, 1969), p. 78; BL Add. MSS 41,814, fols. 208r, 215v, 218v, 230r–v, 239r, 241v, 245v; 41,820, fol. 86r; Ashcraft, p. 552.

84. BL Add. MSS 41,804, fols. 311r, 313r, 315r–v; 41,815, fols. 6r, 17r, 20v–21r, 24v; PRO SP 44/54, p. 382; 44/56, p. 407; *HMC 75, Downshire*, 1: 279. Lambert professed not to know the skipper but admitted having conducted business in the past with Thomas Bassett and Thomas Sawbridge.

85. Morrice, 2: 181, 227; Maurice Ashley, *John Wildman: Plotter and Postmaster* (New Haven, Conn.: Yale University Press, 1947), pp. 269–70. The exiles were divided in their reaction to the indulgence, a policy they had anticipated as early as January 1686. BL Add. MSS 41,816, fol. 22r; 41,818, fol. 205r.

86. Carswell, *Descent*, pp. 107–10; BL Add. MSS 41,815, fols. 206r–v, 219r; *Reflexions on Monsieur Fagel's Letter*. Cf. PRO SP 31/8/1, pt. 2, fol. 157r.

87. BL Add. MSS 41,815, fols. 123v–124r, 132r, 211v, 223r, 228r, 252r; NUL MSS PwA 2141, fol. 5r; 2143, fol. 5r. Some feared that William himself was a target of James' plotting. NUL MSS PwA 2143, fol. 5r; 2149, fols. 1r–2v; BL Add. MSS 41,816, fol. 45v.

88. BL Add. MSS 41,815, fols. 239r–240r.

89. A copy of the poem may be found in BL Add. MSS 41,816, fols. 49–50. It was printed in Amsterdam by an unidentified Englishman (fol. 47r).

90. Not until 17 September 1688 (n.s.) did the Amsterdam magistrates and the court of Holland take steps to ban the publication of radical material. BL Add. MSS 41,816, fols. 106v, 145r, 166r, 167v, 182r, 186v–187v.

91. Carswell, *Descent*, pp. 119–24; BL Add. MSS 41,815, fols. 159v, 193v, 253r (cf. 131r); John Childs, *The Army, James II, and the Glorious Revolution* (Manchester, Eng.: Manchester University Press, 1980), pp. 130–32; G. H. Jones, "The Recall of the British from the Dutch Service," *Historical Journal*, 25 (1982): 423–35.

92. BL Add. MSS 41,815, fols. 193v, 202r, 250r; 41,816, fols. 26v, 34v, 38r, 46r; 41,821, fols. 58r, 77v, 83r, 88r, 93r, 205r–v. Information on alleged recruiting for William's army in England, with money for recruiters funneled through the Dutch ambassador, was provided by Captain Humphrey Okeover. BL Add. MSS 41,805, fols. 42r–43r. On 27 August (n.s.) Petit was still uncertain whether the fleet would invade England or attack France. On 14 September (n.s.) d'Albeville noted a general belief that England was the target, but he was not sure until 1 October. BL Add. MSS 41,816, fols. 159v, 177r, 209r.

93. BL Add. MSS 41,816, fols. 47r–v, 103v, 212v, 228v.

94. Lois G. Schwoerer, *The Declaration of Rights, 1689* (Baltimore, Md.: Johns Hopkins University Press, 1981), pp. 105–13; *HMC* 45, *Buccleuch*, 2: 33–35. Cf. Ashley, *John Wildman*, pp. 270–74; Ashcraft, pp. 549–50.

95. *CJ*, 10: 1–5.

96. BL Add. MSS 41,805, fol. 211r; 41,815, fols. 139v, 190r; 41,816, fols, 34v–35r, 209v, 238r–v, 257v, 264r–v; Carswell, *Descent*, p. 158; Hume, p. lxxvi; *Blackader Mem.*, pp. 325–26; Robert Herbert Story, *William Carstares: A Character and Career of the Revolutionary Epoch (1649–1715)* (London: Macmillan, 1874), p. 163. Another man who accompanied William was John Wolters (or Woolters), who had served Monmouth as a gunner; he had been pardoned in May 1687. Lords Melville and Stair were among others traveling with the prince or following him shortly thereafter. BL Add. MSS 41,805, fol. 288r; *CSPD 1686–87*, p. 440.

97. BL Add. MSS 41,816, fols. 173r–v (cf. 218v), 264v (cf. 231v, 248v). Some of the Huguenot officers in William's army reportedly swore to "joyne with such English as resolve to have at the Kings person." BL Add. MSS 41,816, fol. 242r (cf. 250r).

98. PRO SP 31/4, fol. 226r.

99. BL Add. MSS 35,852, fols. 203r, 204v; 41,805, fols. 232r–233r, 234r, 275r; Egerton MSS 3335, fol. 59v; *HMC 35, Fourteenth Report*, p. 209; Morrice, 2: 372; Luttrell, 1: 477–79, 483. Others who took up arms for William included Mr. Rope, who had been involved in the Rye House plotting, and Captain Hickes, son of an executed Monmouth rebel. Morrice, 2: 379; J. R. Jones, *Revolution*, p. 294. Trenchard brought William £250 that had been donated by two clothiers. BL Add. MSS 35,852, fols. 203r, 204v; *HMC 45, Buccleuch*, 2: 35.

100. [Speke], *Secret History*, pp. 24–30, 32–39, 43.

101. Ibid., pp. 43–49; Luttrell, 1: 472; Evelyn, 4: 602; BL Add. MSS 41,804, fol. 160r; Morrice, 1: 525, 623; 2: 310; *RPCS*, 12: xxvii–xxix, 29, 34, 41–44, 91–92. Among those who attacked the Lime Street chapel in London was James Chalmers, a west country Scot who lived with John Chalmers in Little Warwick Street; John was thought to support the radicals. BL Add. MSS 41,805, fol. 56r. For the role of Tories in the crowds see Tim Harris, "London Crowds and the Revolution of 1688," in *By Force or By Default? The Revolution of 1688–1689*, ed. Eveline Cruickshanks (Edinburgh: John Donald, 1989), pp. 49–64.

102. BL Add. MSS 41,805, fol. 148r–v; Luttrell, 1: 474, 477; Morrice, 2: 317; Evelyn, 4: 607; PRO SP 31/4, fol. 135Ar–135Bv; 44/97, p. 15; *HMC 35, Fourteenth Report*, p. 207; William L. Sachse, "The Mob and the Revolution of 1688," *Journal of British Studies*, 4 (Nov. 1964): 28. The Norwich incident occurred on 15 October 1686.

103. For a different interpretation see J. R. Jones, *Revolution*, pp. 301–2.

104. Luttrell, 1: 482, 484, 486; Morrice, 2: 338, 345, 351–53, 361–62; JRL Legh of Lyme MSS (John Chicheley to Peter Legh, 11 Dec. 1688); Sachse, "The Mob," p. 28; [John Oldmixon], *The History of England, During the Reigns of the Royal House of Stuart* (London: John Pemberton et al., 1730), p. 761; Sir John Dalrymple, *Memoirs of Great Britain and Ireland*, 2nd ed., 2 vols. (London: W. Strahan and T. Cadell, 1771–73), vol. 1, pt. 1, bk. 6, pp. 176–77; Evelyn, 4: 610; London *Gazette*, 2409 (10–13 Dec. 1688); 2412 (20–24 Dec. 1688); Reresby, p. 537; *HMC 29, Portland*, 3: 420. According to Morrice the residence of the Venetian representative was spared.

105. Luttrell, 1: 490; Morrice, 2: 359, 362, 389; CumRO(C) MSS D/LONS/L1/1/34, letters 21, 22, 25; JRL Mainwaring MSS E/1; Sachse, "The Mob," p. 31; London *Gazette*, 2410 (13–17 Dec. 1688); *HMC 35, Fourteenth Report*, p. 206; Dalrymple, *Memoirs*, vol. 1, pt. 1, bk. 6, p. 172; [James Ralph], *The History of England*, 2 vols. (London: Daniel Browne, 1744–46), 1: 1054–55; G. H. Jones, "The Irish Fright of 1688," *Bulletin of the Institute of Historical Research*, 55 (1982): 148–57.

106. Luttrell, 1: 488, 496; [Speke], *Secret History*, pp. 44–49; *RPCS*, 13:

lv. Scotland was further disrupted as some fled to the border region to avoid impressment. CumRO(C) MSS D/LONS/L1/1/34, Letter 19.

107. See Greaves, *EUHF*, pp. 195–97; Tim Harris, "The Bawdy House Riots of 1668," *Historical Journal*, 29 (Sept. 1986): 537–56.

108. Sachse, "The Mob," pp. 23–40.

109. PRO SP 31/4, fol. 135Ar–v; BL Add. MSS 41,805, fols. 109v–110r. James' forces included two captains who had served with the Monmouth rebels—Tucker and John Jones—and a small number of sectaries. Morrice, 2: 322.

110. BL Add. MSS 41,805, fols. 63r, 129r, 156r–v, 242r; Evelyn, 4: 600. James' cause was also undermined by the confusion in England over William's intentions in the months preceding the invasion. As late as 29 September 1688, Sir John Lowther of Whitehaven, London, reported to Sir John Lowther of Lowther, his father-in-law, that the court was certain only that William was making great preparations, possibly to attack the French, possibly to invade England. CumRO(C) MSS D/LONS/L1/1/34, Letters 12, 13, 15–17. "The apprehensions of invasion continues still," wrote Sir Edward Jennings of Ripon on 5 November. CumRO(C) MSS D/LONS/L1/1/34, Letter 18.

111. London *Gazette*, 2399 (12–15 Nov. 1688); PRO SP 44/97, p. 22; BL Add. MSS 35,852, fols. 201r–v, 204r; 41,805, fols. 168r, 180v, 190r, 200r, 201r, 207v, 245r, 264r; Morrice, 2: 319–20; Evelyn, 4: 609; Story, *Carstares*, pp. 156–57. The caution with which William was initially greeted is discussed by Eveline Cruickshanks, "The Revolution and the Localities: Examples of Loyalty to James II," in *By Force or By Default?*, pp. 28–43, and by Ian B. Cowan, "The Reluctant Revolutionaries: Scotland in 1688," ibid., pp. 65–81.

112. SRO MSS T/PH/wig 2/5, p. 17 (John Coad); Meade, *Vision of the Wheels*, pp. 39–40, 77, 97–98. A copy of Meade's sermon in the BL (1218.b.30) was given by Meade to "JN," probably Meade's friend John Nisbet.

Epilogue

The title of my epilogue is from the conclusion to Monmouth's declaration; BL Lansdowne MSS 1152, p. 8.

1. Jonathan Scott, "England's Troubles: Exhuming the Popish Plot," in *The Politics of Religion in Restoration England*, ed. Tim Harris, Paul Seaward, and Mark Goldie (Oxford: Basil Blackwell, 1990), pp. 108–9.

2. Morrice, 1: 331; BL Add. MSS 41,812, fol. 227r; 41,817, fol. 200v; SRO MSS T/PH/wig 2/5, p. 1; W. A. Speck, *Reluctant Revolutionaries: Englishmen and the Revolution of 1688* (Oxford: Oxford University Press, 1989), pp. 233–35.

3. PRO SP 29/425/138, pp. 37, 49, 57; BL Add. MSS 29,577, fol. 535r; BL Harleian MSS 6845, fol. 262r; Holloway, p. 13; *CSPD 1683*, 2: 5; Dorset Record Office MSS D239/f16.

4. BL Add. MSS 41,805, fol. 211r.

5. BL Lansdowne MSS 1152, fol. 243v; Clifton, *LPR*, pp. 178–79, 192; Friends' Library, London, Dix MSS H2S; SRO MSS DD/SFR(w) 1, p. 95; SS/SFR 10/2, fol. 48r–v; Richard L. Greaves, "Shattered Expectations? George Fox, the Quakers, and the Restoration State," *Albion*, 24 (forthcoming).

6. Gary Stuart De Krey, *A Fractured Society: The Politics of London in the First Age of Party 1688–1715* (Oxford: Clarendon, 1985), pp. 11–14, 24–25; idem, "London Radicals and Revolutionary Politics, 1675–1683," in *Politics of Religion*, ed. Harris, Seaward, and Goldie, pp. 133–62.

7. Jonathan Barry, "The Politics of Religion in Restoration Bristol," in *Politics of Religion*, ed. Harris, Seaward, and Goldie, pp. 163–89.

8. Throughout the trilogy I have attempted to provide the reader with a clear sense of the extent to which the government faced an incessant stream of allegations, much of which subsequently proved to be false, but which nevertheless could not be categorically dismissed upon receipt by government officials. Any suggestion that my discussion of such reports automatically attributes validity to the charges they encompassed is, of course, absurd.

9. Peter Fraser, *The Intelligence of the Secretaries of State & Their Monopoly of Licensed News 1660–1688* (Cambridge: at the University Press, 1956), pp. 27–28, 137–39.

10. Greaves, *DUFE*, pp. 51–52.

11. PRO SP 29/178/155, 156; Brown, *Miscellanea Aulica*, p. 429; *HMC 25, Le Fleming*, p. 43; *CSPD 1660–85, Addenda*, p. 165.

12. London *Gazette*, 1417 (16–19 June 1679); 1419 (23–26 June 1679); PRO SP 29/411/155.

13. ChRO MSS DCH/K/3/6 (Cholmondeley to William Adams, 1 July 1685); John Childs, *The Army, James II, and the Glorious Revolution* (Manchester, Eng.: Manchester University Press, 1980), p. 2.

14. Essex's son became a gentleman of the bedchamber. A number of Whigs, including William Kiffin, were appointed deputies lieutenant of London in March 1690. *CSPD 1689–90*, pp. 487–88.

15. A copy of Monmouth's declaration is bound in BL Lansdowne MSS 1152; the Declaration of Rights is reprinted in Lois G. Schwoerer, *The Declaration of Rights, 1689* (Baltimore, Md.: Johns Hopkins University Press, 1981), Appendix 1. Cf. Schwoerer: "Both the Declaration of Rights and the Bill of Rights are properly regarded as radical reforming documents, in the sense that they resolved long-standing disputes in ways favorable to Parliament and the individual, and according to libertarian political principles that had been articulated earlier" (p. 283). See also Schwoerer's "The Bill of Rights: Epitome of the Revolution of 1688–89," in *Three British Revolutions:*

1641, 1688, 1776, ed. J. G. A. Pocock (Princeton, N.J.: Princeton University Press, 1980), pp. 224–43; Richard L. Greaves, "Radicals, Rights, and Revolution: British Nonconformity and Roots of the American Experience," *Church History*, 61 (forthcoming).

16. Christopher Hill, *A Nation of Change and Novelty: Radical Politics, Religion and Literature in Seventeenth-Century England* (London: Routledge, 1990), pp. 110, 240–42. See also Schwoerer, "Propaganda in the Revolution of 1688–89," *American Historical Review*, 82 (Oct. 1977): 843–74; De Krey, *Fractured Society*, pp. 213–22.

17. See, e.g., De Krey, *Fractured Society*; Gary S. De Krey, "Political Radicalism in London After the Glorious Revolution," *Journal of Modern History*, 55 (December 1983): 585–617; Mark Goldie, "The Roots of True Whiggism 1688–94," *History of Political Thought*, 1 (June 1980): 195–236; H. T. Dickinson, "The Precursors of Political Radicalism in Augustan Britain," in *Britain in the First Age of Party 1680–1750*, ed. Clyve Jones (London: Hambledon, 1987), pp. 63–84; Robert Zaller, "The Continuity of British Radicalism in the Seventeenth and Eighteenth Centuries," *Eighteenth-Century Life*, 6, n.s. (Jan.–May 1981): 17–38; Linda Colley, "Eighteenth-Century English Radicalism Before Wilkes," *Transactions of the Royal Historical Society*, 5th ser., 31 (1981): 1–19.

18. *HMC* 36, *Ormonde*, n.s., 8: 13.

Appendix A

1. Nisbet was in fact preparing to go to the Netherlands after relinquishing his responsibilities as a contact between English and Scottish dissidents to Murray. PRO SP 29/425/27.

2. *ST*, 9: 454–56, 466–67; *Copies*, pp. 140–42. Bodl. Tanner MSS 34, fols. 286r–287r, is a contemporary copy. The letter is also printed in Mackenzie, pp. 11–12. Cf. Sprat, pp. 101–3; *Letters to Aberdeen*, p. 134. Robert Wodrow denied that this letter pertained to a plot, but Sir Francis North, who had considerable legal experience as lord chief justice, correctly if exaggeratedly concluded that it "plainly declare[d] the Conspiracy." Robert Wodrow, *The History of the Sufferings of the Church of Scotland from the Restoration to the Revolution*, ed. Robert Burns, 4 vols. (Glasgow: Blackie, Fullarton, 1829), 3: 471; BL Add. MSS 32,520, fol. 201v.

Select Bibliography

This bibliography includes the principal primary sources used in the preparation of the trilogy of which this book constitutes the third volume. These sources are divided into seven groups: (1) manuscripts; (2) calendars of major collections; (3) parliamentary and government materials; (4) miscellaneous correspondence; (5) diaries, journals, and memoirs; (6) pamphlets, broadsides, narratives, and church documents; and (7) newspapers.

Manuscripts

Algemeen Rijksarchief (The Hague): Letters of Johan de Witt to Coenraad van Beuningen.

Bodleian Library: Carte MSS 34, 35, 36, 37, 39, 40, 45, 46, 47, 68, 69, 72, 77, 79, 80, 81, 220. Clarendon MSS 75. Eng. hist. MSS c.487 (Edmund Ludlow, "A Voyce from the Watch Tower"). Eng. hist. MSS c.711 (diary of Roger Whitley). Locke MSS b.4, f.8. Rawlinson Letters 104 (Wharton correspondence). Rawlinson MSS A175. Smith MSS 31. Tanner MSS 34 (correspondence of the archbishop of Canterbury).

British Library: Add. MSS 4107 (Weymouth's diary); 8127; 12,068 (letters to Sir James Turner); 15,892–94 (Hyde papers); 18,730 (earl of Anglesey's diary, 1667–75); 21,484; 22,920 (letters to Sir George Downing); 23,119 (Lauderdale correspondence); 23,125 (Lauderdale correspondence); 23, 128–138 (Lauderdale correspondence); 23,242 (royal letters on Scottish affairs); 23,243–44 (Lauderdale papers); 23,245 (papers of the Scottish Parliament and Council); 23,246 (Middleton papers); 23,247 (papers relating to episcopacy in Scotland); 23,248 (Lauderdale papers); 25,124–25; 25,463; 28,093–94; 28,747; 28,875 (Ellis papers, 1672–86); 29,560 (Hatton papers, 1683–89); 29,577; 29,582; 30,077 (alleged Monmouth rebels); 31,957; 32, 094–95; 32,520; 33,770; 34,508 (correspondence from the Dutch envoys in London); 35,104 (letter-book of the earl of Conway); 35,125 (Lauderdale papers); 35,852 (Hardwicke papers); 37,980–81; 38,847; 38,849; 38,856; 40,860 (earl of Anglesey's diary, 1675–84); 41,254 (letter-book of Viscount

Fauconberg); 41,656 (Townshend papers); 41,803–23 (Middleton papers); 42,849 (papers of Philip Henry); 46,960A (Egmont papers); 47,021 (Egmont papers); 51,319 (state papers of Stephen Fox, 1656–1716); 56,240 (Hague correspondence, 1669–81); 61,651; 61,689 (Blenheim MSS—Wildman papers); 61,903 (Peter Le Neve's diary); 62,453. Althorp (Halifax) MSS H2. Egerton MSS 1527 (Monmouth's pocket-book); 2134; 2538; 2539; 2543; 2618; 2985 (Heath and Verney papers); 3325; 3327; 3535 (Scottish correspondence); 3340; 3349. Harleian MSS 1221; 4631; 6845 (including Nathaniel Wade's "Narrative" and other documents concerning Monmouth's rebellion); 7010; 7377. Lansdowne MSS 253 (depositions on Essex's death); 254; 1152 (examinations of Monmouth rebels); 1236. Portland MSS (Loan 29). Sloan MSS 78; 609; 1008; 1983B. Stowe MSS 186; 199–205, 207–17 (Essex papers).

Cambridge University: Pepys Library, Misc. MSS 7 ("The Journall of the Green-Ribbon-Clubb at the King's Head Taverne over against the Temple in Fleet-Street from 1678 to 1681").

Cheshire Record Office: MSS DCH/K/3/6; DDX 383/2 (Sir Thomas Mainwaring's diary); DDX7/1.

Chester City Record Office: Mayors' Letters. Quarter Sessions Files.

Cumbria Record Office, Carlisle: Lonsdale MSS.

Cumbria Record Office, Kendal: Fleming MSS.

Dorset Record Office: MSS D239/f16.

Dr. Williams's Library: Baxter MSS 59.1–6. Harmer MSS 76.2. Roger Morrice, "Entr'ing Book, Being an Historical Register of Occurrences from April, Anno 1677 to April 1691," 3 vols. MSS 90.5 (letters of Matthew Henry, 1685–86). Turner MSS 89.32.

East Sussex Record Office: Glynde MSS 794 (letters of Algernon Sidney to John Hampden, 1683).

Edinburgh University Library: MSS Dc.1.16 (documents concerning the assassination of Archbishop Sharp); La.I.332; La.II.20; La.II.27; La.II.89; La.III.344 (documents concerning the Covenanters); La.III.350 (documents concerning the Covenanters); La.III.684 (conventicle sermons).

Friends' Library, London: Dix MSS H2S.

Henry E. Huntington Library: Ellesmere MSS 8544; 8545. MSS HA 1950, 3146, 6786, 8528, 8540, 8542, 8543, 9602, 9606, 9607, 9609, 9805, 10,657 (Hastings Manuscripts). MSS STT 524, 718, 719, 721, 895–97, 1081, 2174 (Stowe Manuscripts).

House of Lords Record Office: Minutes of Committees, 1689.

John Rylands Library: Legh of Lyme MSS; Mainwaring MSS.

National Library of Scotland: MSS 500 (miscellaneous letters and documents); 573 (miscellaneous letters and documents); 597 (Lauderdale papers); 1004; 1038 (conventicle sermons); 2123 (conventicle sermons of

James Wodrow); 2512 (Lauderdale papers); 2762 (conventicle sermons of John Campbell); 3473 (autobiography of Gabriel Semple); 7006; 7024; 7025; 7033; 7034.

Nottingham University Library: MSS PwA 2141, PwA 2143, PwA 2149, PwV 95 (Portland Manuscripts).

Public Record Office: SP29 (state papers, Charles II). SP31 (state papers, James II). SP44 (entry books). SP63 (state papers, Ireland).

Somerset Record Office: MSS DD/SAS S.E.83; DD/SF 285; DD/SF 3109; DD/SFR 10/2 (Somerset Quarterly Meeting Minutes, Society of Friends); DD/SFR(w)1 (Minute Book, Western Division of Somerset Monthly Meeting, Society of Friends); Q/SR, Roll 169 (quarter session records); T/PH/wig 2/5 (John Load's narrative).

Calendars of Major Collections

Calendar of State Papers, Domestic Series, 1603–1714.

Calendar of State Papers Relating to Ireland.

Calendar of State Papers . . . Venice.

Calendar of the Clarendon State Papers Preserved in the Bodleian Library. Vol. 5, *1660–1726.* Edited by F. J. Routledge. Oxford: Clarendon, 1970.

Calendar of the Orrery Papers. Edited by Edward MacLysaght. Dublin: Stationery Office, 1941.

Calendar of Treasury Papers, 1681–85.

Collections of the Massachusetts Historical Society.

Historical Manuscripts Commission, Reports: 1 *Second Report*; 4 *Fifth Report*; 5 *Sixth Report*; 6 *Seventh Report*; 7 *Eighth Report*; 13 *Tenth Report*; 15 *Tenth Report*; 17 *Twelfth Report (House of Lords)*; 19 *Townshend*; 20 *Eleventh Report (Dartmouth)*; 21 *Hamilton*; 22 *Eleventh Report*; 24 *Rutland*; 25 *Le Fleming*; 27 *Twelfth Report*; 29 *Portland*; 31 *Thirteenth Report*; 32 *Thirteenth Report*; 33 *Lonsdale*; 34 *Fourteenth Report*; 35 *Fourteenth Report*; 36 *Ormonde*; 38 *Fourteenth Report*; 39 *Fifteenth Report (Hodgkin)*; 43 *Fifteenth Report*; 44 *Drumlanrig*; 45 *Buccleuch*; 49 *Sackville*; 50 *Heathcote*; 51 *Popham*; 52 *Astley*; 53 *Montagu*; 55 *Various Collections*; 58 *Bath*; 63 *Egmont*; 71 *Finch*; 72 *Laing*; 75 *Downshire*; 78 *Hastings.*

Parliamentary and Government Materials

The Acts of the Parliaments of Scotland. Vols. 7 and 8. Edinburgh, 1820.

Akerman, John Yonge, ed. *Moneys Received and Paid for Secret Services of Charles II. and James II.* London: Camden Society, vol. 52, 1851.

"A Brief View of the Public Revenue, Both Certain and Casual," 7 April 1659. In *The Parliamentary or Constitutional History of England from the Earliest Times to the Restoration of Charles II,* 21: 326–37. London, 1751–63.

Carstares, William. *The Deposition of Mr. William Carstares*. Edinburgh and London, 1684.

Churchwardens' Presentments (17th Century) Part 1. Archdeaconry of Chichester. Edited by Hilda Johnstone. Lewes: Sussex Record Society, vol. 49, 1947–48.

Cobbett, W.; T. B. Howell; et al., eds. *Cobbett's Complete Collection of State Trials and Proceedings*. 34 vols. London: R. Bagshaw, 1809–28.

Copies of the Informations and Original Papers Relating to the Proof of the Horrid Conspiracy Against the Late King, His Present Majesty, and the Government. 3rd ed. London, 1685.

D'Avaux, Jean Mesmes, Count. *The Negotiations of Count D'Avaux, Ambassador from the Most Christian King, Lewis XIV, to the States General of the United Provinces*. Vol. 3. London: A. Millar, D. Wilson, and T. Durham, 1755.

Debates of the House of Commons from the Year 1667 to the Year 1694. Edited by Anchitel Grey. 10 vols. London, 1763.

Depositions from the Castle of York, Relating to Offences Committed in the Northern Counties in the Seventeenth Century. Edited by J. Raine. Durham: Surtees Society, vol. 40, 1861.

Episcopal Visitation Book for the Archdeaconry of Buckingham, 1662. Edited by E. R. C. Brinkworth. Bedford: Buckinghamshire Record Society, vol. 7, 1947.

Extracts from the Records of the Burgh of Edinburgh 1665 to 1680. Edited by Marguerite Wood. Edinburgh: Oliver and Boyd, 1950.

Extracts from the Records of the Burgh of Glasgow, A.D. *1630–1662*. Edited by J. D. Marwick. Glasgow: Scottish Burgh Records Society, 1881.

Extracts from the Records of the Burgh of Glasgow, A.D. *1663–1690*. Edited by J. D. Marwick. Glasgow: Scottish Burgh Records Society, 1905.

Journals of the House of Commons 1547–1714. 17 vols. 1742ff.

Journals of the House of Lords. 1767ff.

The Lauderdale Papers. Edited by Osmund Airy. 2 vols. London: Camden Society, n.s., nos. 34 and 36, 1884–85.

Leicester, Sir Peter. *Charges to the Grand Jury at Quarter Sessions 1660–1677*. Edited by Elizabeth M. Halcrow. Manchester: Chetham Society, 3rd ser., vol. 5, 1953.

Middlesex County Records. Edited by John Cordy Jeaffreson. 4 vols. London: Middlesex County Records Society, 1886–92.

Notes Which Passed at Meetings of the Privy Council Between Charles II and the Earl of Clarendon, 1660–1667. Edited by W. D. Macray. London: Nichols and Sons, 1896.

Nottinghamshire County Records. Edited by H. Hampton Copnall. Nottingham: Henry B. Saxton, 1915.

"The Old Tolbooth: With Extracts from the Original Records." Edited by John A. Fairley. In *The Book of the Old Edinburgh Club*, vols. 4–6. Edinburgh: T. and A. Constable, 1911–13.

Ormond, James Butler, Duke of. *A Collection of Original Letters and Papers . . . from the Duke of Ormonde's Papers*. Edited by Thomas Carte. 2 vols. London: Society for the Encouragement of Learning, 1739.

Quarter Sessions Records. Edited by J. C. Atkinson. North Riding Record Society, vol. 6. London: Printed for the Society, 1888.

Quarter Sessions Records for the County of Somerset. Vol. 4, *Charles II. 1666–1677*. Edited by E. H. Bates-Harbin and M. C. B. Dawes. London: Somerset Record Society, vol. 34, 1919.

The Records of the Proceedings of the Justiciary Court Edinburgh 1661–1678. Edited by W. G. Scott-Moncrieff. 2 vols. Publications of the Scottish History Society, vols. 48 and 49. Edinburgh: T. and A. Constable, 1905.

The Register of the Privy Council of Scotland. Edited by P. Hume Brown. 3rd ser., vols. 1–13. Edinburgh: H. M. General Register House, 1908–32.

State-Papers and Letters, Addressed to William Carstares. Edited by Joseph McCormick. Edinburgh: W. Strahan, 1774.

Statutes of the Realm. 11 vols. London, 1820–28.

Surrey Quarter Sessions Records: The Order Book and the Sessions Rolls. Easter, 1663–Epiphany, 1666. Edited by Dorothy L. Powell and Hilary Jenkinson. London and Woking, Surrey: Surrey Record Society, no. 39, vol. 16, 1938.

A True Account of the Presentment of the Grand Jury for the Last General Assizes Held for the County of Northampton. London, 1683.

The Twysden Lieutenancy Papers, 1583–1668. Edited by Gladys Scott Thomson. Kent Archaeological Society, Records Branch, vol. 10. Ashford, Eng.: Headley Brothers, 1926.

Warwick County Records: Orders Made at the Quarter Sessions: Easter, 1665, to Epiphany, 1674. Edited by S. C. Ratcliff and H. C. Johnson. Warwick: L. Edgar Stephens, 1939.

Warwick County Records: Quarter Sessions Order Book. Easter, 1657, to Epiphany, 1665. Edited by S. C. Ratcliff and H. C. Johnson. Warwick: L. Edgar Stephens, 1938.

Miscellaneous Correspondence

Argyll, Archibald Campbell, Earl of. *Letters from Archibald Campbell, Earl of Argyll, to John, Duke of Lauderdale*. Edinburgh: Bannatyne Club, 1829.

Arlington, Henry Bennet, Earl of. *The Right Honourable the Earl of Arlington's Letters to Sir W. Temple, Bar*. Edited by Thomas Bebington. 2 vols. London: Thomas Bennet, 1701.

Clarendon, Edward Hyde, Earl of, and Lawrence Hyde, Earl of Rochester.

The Correspondence of Henry Hyde, Earl of Clarendon and of His Brother Lawrence Hyde, Earl of Rochester. Edited by Samuel Weller Singer. 2 vols. London: Henry Colburn, 1828.

A Collection of Letters Addressed by Prelates and Individuals of High Rank in Scotland and by Two Bishops of Sodor and Man to Sancroft Archbishop of Canterbury. Edited by William Nelson Clarke. Edinburgh: R. Lendrum, 1848.

A Copy of a Letter, Sent from a Person That Was Present at the Apprehension of Mr Meade and Five More. London, 1683.

Correspondence of the Family of Hatton: Being Chiefly Letters Addressed to Christopher First Viscount Hatton A.D. *1601–1704*. Edited by Edward Maunde Thompson. 2 vols. London: Camden Society, n.s., vols. 22–23, 1875, 1878.

Cosin, John. *The Correspondence of John Cosin, D.D., Lord Bishop of Durham*. Durham: Surtees Society, vol. 55, 1872.

Letters Addressed to the Earl of Lauderdale. Edited by Osmund Airy. London: Camden Society, n.s., no. 31, 1883.

Letters, Illustrative of Public Affairs in Scotland, Addressed by Contemporary Statesmen to George, Earl of Aberdeen, Lord High Chancellor of Scotland. MDCLXXXI–MDCLXXXIV. Aberdeen: Spalding Club, 1851.

"Letters of Early Friends." In *The Friends' Library*, edited by William Evans and Thomas Evans, vol. II. Philadelphia: Joseph Rakestraw, 1847.

Letters of Eminent Men, Addressed to Ralph Thoresby, F.R.S. 2 vols. London: Henry Colburn and Richard Bentley, 1832.

Orrery, Roger Boyle, Earl of. *A Collection of the State Letters of... Roger Boyle, the First Earl of Orrery*. Edited by Thomas Morrice. 2 vols. Dublin: George Faulkner, 1743.

Pinney, John. *Letters of John Pinney 1679–1699*. Edited by Geoffrey F. Nuttall. London: Oxford University Press, 1939.

Prideaux, Humphrey. *Letters of Humphrey Prideaux Sometime Dean of Norwich to John Ellis Sometime Under-Secretary of State 1674–1722*. Edited by Edward Maunde Thompson. London: Camden Society, n.s., vol. 15, 1875.

Prinsterer, G. Groen Van, ed. *Archives ou Correspondance Inédite de la Maison D'Orange-Nassau*. 2nd ser., bk. 5, 1650–88. Utrecht: Kemink, 1861.

The Rawdon Papers. Edited by Edward Berwick. London: John Nichols and Son, 1819.

Russell, Lady Rachel. *Letters of Rachel Lady Russell*. Edited by Lord John Russell. 2 vols. London: Longman, Brown, Green and Longmans, 1853.

The Tanner Letters. Edited by Charles McNeill. Dublin: Stationery Office, 1943.

Temple, Sir William. *Memoirs of the Life, Works, and Correspondence of Sir William Temple, Bart*. Edited by Thomas Peregrine Courtenay. 2 vols. London: Longman, 1836.

"Thirty-four Letters Written to James Sharp, Archbishop of St. Andrews, by the Duke and Duchess of Lauderdale ... 1660–1677." Edited by John

Dowden. In *Miscellany of the Scottish Historical Society*, vol. 1. Edinburgh: Publications of the Scottish Historical Society, vol. 15, 1893.

Diaries, Journals, and Memoirs

Angier, John. "Diary," *ad cal.* Oliver Heywood, *Life of John Angier of Denton*, ed. Ernest Axon. Manchester: Chetham Society, n.s., vol. 97, 1937.

Barnes, Ambrose. *Memoirs of the Life of Mr. Ambrose Barnes, Late Merchant and Sometime Alderman of Newcastle upon Tyne*. Durham: Surtees Society, vol. 50, 1867.

Crichton, Andrew. *The Life and Diary of Lieut. Col. J. Blackader, of the Cameronian Regiment*. Edinburgh: H. S. Baynes, 1824.

———. *Memoirs of Rev. John Blackader*. Edinburgh: Archibald Constable & Company, 1823.

Dering, Sir Edward. *The Parliamentary Diary of Sir Edward Dering 1670–1673*. Edited by Basil Duke Henning. New Haven: Yale University Press, 1940.

Erskine, John. *Journal of the Hon. John Erskine of Carnock. 1683–1687*. Edited by Walter Macleod. Edinburgh: T. and A. Constable, 1893.

Evelyn, John. *The Diary of John Evelyn*. Edited by E. S. de Beer. 6 vols. Oxford: Clarendon, 1955.

Fox, George. *The Journal of George Fox*. Edited by John L. Nickalls. Cambridge: at the University Press, 1952.

Henry, Philip. *Diaries and Letters of Philip Henry*. Edited by Matthew Henry Lee. London: Kegan Paul, Trench & Co., 1882.

Hodgson, John. *Original Memoirs*. Edinburgh: Arch. Constable; London: John Murray, 1806.

Jolly, Thomas. *The Note Book of the Rev. Thomas Jolly* A.D. *1671–1693*. Edited by Henry Fishwick. Manchester: Chetham Society, n.s., vol. 33, 1894.

Lowe, Roger. *The Diary of Roger Lowe of Ashton-in-Makerfield, Lancashire 1663–74*. Edited by William L. Sachse. New Haven, Conn.: Yale University Press, 1938.

Ludlow, Edmund. *The Memoirs of Edmund Ludlow*. Edited by C. H. Firth. Oxford: Clarendon Press, 1894.

———. *A Voyce from the Watch Tower Part Five: 1660–1662*. Edited by A. B. Worden. London: Camden Society, 4th ser., vol. 21, 1978.

Luttrell, Narcissus. *A Brief Historical Relation of State Affairs from September 1678 to April 1714*. 6 vols. Oxford: Oxford University Press, 1857.

Mackenzie, Sir George. *Memoirs of the Affairs of Scotland from the Restoration of King Charles II*. A.D. *M.D.C.L.X.* Edinburgh: n.p., 1821.

Newcome, Henry. *The Diary of the Rev. Henry Newcome*. Edited by Thomas Heywood. Manchester: Chetham Society, o.s., vol. 18, 1849.

Nicoll, John. *A Diary of Public Transactions and Other Occurrences, Chiefly in Scotland*. Edinburgh: Bannatyne Club, vol. 52, 1836.

Pepys, Samuel. *The Diary of Samuel Pepys*. Edited by Robert Latham and William Matthews. 9 vols. Berkeley: University of California Press, 1970–75.

Reresby, Sir John. *Memoirs of Sir John Reresby*. Edited by Andrew Browning. Glasgow: Jackson, Son, & Co., 1936.

Sidney, Henry. *Diary of the Times of Charles the Second*. Edited by R. W. Blencowe. 2 vols. London: Henry Colburn, 1843.

Turner, Sir James. *Memoirs of His Own Life and Times*. Edited by Thomas Thomson. Edinburgh: Bannatyne Club, 1829.

Veitch, William, and George Brysson. *Memoirs of Mr. William Veitch, and George Brysson, Written by Themselves*. Edited by Thomas McCrie. Edinburgh: William Blackwood, 1825.

Pamphlets, Broadsides, Narratives, and Church Documents

An Account of How the Earl of Essex Killed Himself. London, 1683.

An Account of the Proceedings Against Thomas Saxon. London, 1686.

An Account of the Proceeding to Judgment, Against Thomas Saxton. London, 1686.

An Account of the Taking of Captain Holland. London, 1689.

Adair, Patrick. *A True Narrative of the Rise and Progress of the Presbyterian Church in Ireland (1623–1670)*. Edited by W. D. Killen. Belfast: C. Aitchison, 1866.

An Advertisement as Touching the Fanaticks Late Conspiracy. 1661.

Another Cry of the Innocent and Oppressed for Justice. 1665.

An Answer to His Majesties Declaration. 1681.

The Arraignment and Plea of Edward Fitz-Harris, Gent. [1681.]

Atkyns, Sir Robert. *A Defence of the Late Lord Russel's Innocency*. London, 1689.

B., A. *The Saints Freedom from Tyranny Vindicated*. London, 1667.

Bacon, Nathaniel. *The Continuation of an Historical Discourse*. London, 1651.

Bagshaw, Edward. *The Great Question Concerning Things Indifferent in Religious Worship*. London, 1660.

———. *Signes of the Times: or Prognosticks of Future Judgements*. London, 1662.

B[aker], D[aniel]. *Yet One Warning More, to Thee O England*. London, 1660.

Baxter, Richard. *Reliquiae Baxterianae: or, Mr. Richard Baxter's Narrative of the Most Memorable Passages of His Life and Times*. Edited by Matthew Sylvester. London, 1696.

Bayly, William. *Pure Encouragements from the Spirit of the Lord*. [1664.]

Bedloe, William. *A Narrative and Impartial Discovery of the Horrid Popish Plot*. London, 1679.

Bennett, William. *God Only Exalted in His Own Work*. London, 1664.

[Blount, Charles]. *An Appeal from the Country to the City*. London, 1679.

Braddon, Lawrence. *Essex's Innocency and Honour Vindicated*. London, 1690.

A Brief Discourse Concerning Printing and Printers. London, 1663.

[Brown, John.] *An Apologeticall Relation, of the Particular Sufferings of the Faithfull Ministers & Professours of the Church of Scotland, Since August. 1660.* 1665.

Brown, Thomas. *Miscellanea Aulica*. London: J. Hartley, Rob. Gibson, & Tho. Hodgson, 1702.

Burnet, Gilbert. *Burnet's History of My Own Time*. Edited by Osmond Airy. 2 vols. London: Clarendon, 1897, 1900.

Burrough, Edward. *Antichrist's Government Justly Detected*. London, 1661.

Calamy, Edmund. *The Great Danger of Convenant-Refusing*. 1661.

The Case of the Earl of Argyle. 1683.

Certain Quaeres Humbly Presented in Way of Petition. London, 1648.

Clarendon, Edward Hyde, Earl of. "The Continuation of the Life of Edward Hyde Earl of Clarendon," *ad cal. The History of the Rebellion and Civil Wars in England*. Oxford: at the University Press, 1843.

The Common Prayer-Book Unmasked. 1660.

[Cooper, Anthony Ashley, Earl of Shaftesbury?] *A Letter from a Person of Quality, to His Friend in the Country*. 1675.

[———]. *A Speech Lately Made by a Noble Peer of the Realm*. [1681.]

[———]. *Two Seasonable Discourses Concerning This Present Parliament*. Oxford, 1675.

[Coven, Stephen.] *The Militant Christian; or, the Good Soldier of Jesus Christ*. London, 1668.

[Croft, Herbert.] *The Naked Truth*. 1675.

Danvers, [Henry]. *Murther Will Out*. [London, 1689.]

Dewsbury, William. *The Word of the Lord to All the Inhabitants in England*. 1666.

A Door of Hope. London, 1661.

[Drake, William.] *The Long Parliament Revived*. London, 1661.

Dyer, William. *Christ's Famous Titles, and a Believer's Golden Chain*. Philadelphia: Stewart and Cochran, 1743.

E., H. *The Jury-Man Charged; or, a Letter to a Citizen of London*. London, 1664.

An Elegy on the Earl of Essex, Who Cut His Own Throat in the Tower. London, 1683.

An Elegy upon That Renowned Hero and Cavalier, the Lord Capel, Who (for His Loyalty) Was Barbarously Murther'd. London, 1683.

Ellis, Thomas. *The Traytors Unveiled in a Brief and True Account of That Horrid and Bloody Design*. 1661.

Ellwood, Thomas. *The History of the Life of Thomas Ellwood*. Edited by C. G. Crump. London: Methuen, 1900.

Englands Sad Estate & Condition Lamented. 1661.

Englands Warning: or, Englands Sorrow for Londons Misery. London, 1667.

The Englishman, or a Letter from a Universal Friend. 1670.

An Exact Narrative of the Tryal and Condemnation of John Twyn. London, 1664.

The Execution and Confession with the Behaviour & Speeches of Capt. Thomas Walcot, William Hone, and John Rouse. London, 1683.

F[arnworth], R[ichard]. *Christian Religious Meetings Allowed by the Liturgie.* 1664.

F[arnworth], R[ichard], and Thomas Salthouse. *A Loving Salutation with Several Seasonable Exhortations.* 1665.

Ferguson, Robert. "Concerning the Rye House Business." In *Robert Ferguson the Plotter or the Secret of the Rye-House Conspiracy and the Story of a Strange Career*, by James Ferguson. Edinburgh: David Douglas, 1887.

[———]. *An Enquirie into, and Detection of, the Barbarous Murther of the Late Earl of Essex.* 1684.

[———]. *An Impartial Enquiry into the Administration of Affair's in England.* N.p., 1683.

[———]. *A Just and Modest Vindication of the Proceedings of the Two Last Parliaments.* [London?, 1681.]

[———]. *No Protestant-Plot.* London, 1681.

[———]. *The Second Part of No Protestant Plot.* London, 1682.

[———]. *The Third Part of No Protestant Plot.* London, 1682.

A Few Sober Queries upon the Late Proclamation, for Enforcing Laws Against Conventicles. London, 1668.

Fitzharris, Edward. *The Confession of Edward Fitz-harys, Esquire.* London, 1681.

[Ford, Thomas.] *Felo de Se, or the Bishops Condemned out of Their Own Mouthes.* [London], 1668.

Fox, George. *A Collection of the Several Books and Writings.* London, 1665.

Fox, George. *Narrative Papers of George Fox.* Edited by Henry J. Cadbury. Richmond, Ind.: Friends United Press, 1972.

Fox, George, et al. *A Declaration from the Harmles & Innocent People of God, Called Quakers.* London, 1661.

A Further Account of the Proceedings Against the Rebels in the West of England. London, 1685.

Gillespie, George. *A Dispute Against the English-Popish Ceremonies, Obtruded upon the Church of Scotland.* [Edinburgh], 1660.

[Goodwin, John.] *Prelatique Preachers None of Christ's Teachers.* London, 1663.

Gordon, James. *The Reformed Bishop.* 1679.

The Grand Debate. 1661.

Grey, Ford Lord. *The Secret History of the Rye-House Plot: and of Monmouth's Rebellion*. London: Andrew Millar, 1754.

[Hall, John.] *An Humble Motion to the Parliament of England*. London, 1649.

[Heath, James.] *A Brief Chronicle of All the Chief Actions So Fatally Falling Out in These Three Kingdoms*. London, 1662.

[Hicks, John.] *A True and Faithful Narrative*. 1671.

[Hill, William.] *A Brief Narrative of That Stupendious Tragedie*. London, 1662.

[Holles, Denzil.] *Some Considerations upon the Question, Whether the Parliament Is Dissolved by Its Prorogation for 15 Months?* [London], 1676 [i.e., 1677].

Holloway, James. *The Free and Voluntary Confession and Narrative of James Holloway*. London, 1684.

Holme, Thomas. *A Brief Relation of Some Part of the Sufferings of the True Christians . . . in Ireland . . . from 1660. until 1671*. 1672.

The Horrid Conspiracie of Such Impenitent Traytors as Intended a New Rebellion in the Kingdom of Ireland. London, 1663.

Hume, Sir Patrick. "A Narrative of the Events Which Occurred in the Enterprize of the Earl of Argyle in 1685." In *Observations on the Historical Work of the Late Right Honorable Charles James Fox*, by George Rose. London: T. Cadell & W. Davies, 1809.

Hunt, Thomas. *An Argument for the Bishops Right in Judging in Capital Causes in Parliament*. London, 1682.

———. *A Defence of the Charter, and Municipal Rights of the City of London*. London, [1682].

Ignoramus-Justice. London, 1682.

The Innocency and Conscientiousness of the Quakers Asserted and Cleared. London, 1664.

James, John. *The Speech and Declaration of John James*. 1661.

Jenks, Francis. *Mr. Francis Jenk's Speech Spoken in a Common Hall, the 24th. of June 1679*. [London, 1679.]

J[essey], H[enry]. *The Lords Loud Call to England*. London, 1660.

[Johnson, Samuel.] *Julian the Apostate: Being a Short Account of His Life*. London, 1682.

Johnston, Archibald, Sir. *Causes of the Lords Wrath Against Scotland*. 1653.

Jones, D[avid]. *The Secret History of White-Hall*. London, 1697.

[Jones, Roger.] *Mene Tekel; or, the Downfal of Tyranny*. 1663.

The Judgement of Foraign Divines as Well from Geneva as Other Parts, Touching the Discipline, Liturgie, and Ceremonies of the Church of England. London, 1660.

Kiffin, William. *Remarkable Passages in the Life of William Kiffin*. Edited by William Orme. London: Burton and Smith, 1823.

The Last Speech & Behaviour of William Late Lord Russel. . . . Also the Last Speeches, Behaviour, and Prayers of Capt. Thomas Walcot, John Rouse Gent. & William Hone Joyner. London, 1683.

Law, Robert. *Memorialls: or, the Memorable Things That Fell out Within This Island of Brittain from 1638 to 1684.* Edited by Charles Kirkpatrick Sharpe. Edinburgh: A. Constable, 1818.

[L'Estrange, Roger.] *A Brief History of the Times.* London, 1687.

———. *Considerations and Proposals in Order to the Regulation of the Press.* London, 1663.

[———]. *Treason Arraigned, in Answer to Plain English.* London, 1660.

Lilburne, John. *Englands Birth-Right Justified.* [1645.]

Lilly, William. *Mr. William Lilly's History of His Life and Times.* London, 1715.

Lloyd, Owen. *The Panther-prophecy, or, a Premonition to All People, of Sad Calamities and Miseries Like to Befall These Islands.* [London], 1662.

[Lockyer, Nicholas.] *Some Seasonable and Serious Queries upon the Late Act Against Conventicles.* [London, 1670.]

Londons Flames Discovered by Informations Taken Before the Committee. [London], 1667.

Long, Thomas. *A Compendious History of All the Popish & Fanatical Plots and Conspiracies.* London, 1684.

[Mackenzie, George.] *A True and Plain Account of the Discoveries Made in Scotland, of the Late Conspiracies Against His Majesty and the Government.* Edinburgh, 1685.

[MacWard, Robert.] *The Poor Man's Cup of Cold Water.* 1678.

Martindale, Adam. *The Life of Adam Martindale, Written by Himself.* Edited by Richard Parkinson. Manchester: Chetham Society, vol. 4, 1845.

Marvell, Andrew. *An Account of the Growth of Popery.* Amsterdam, [1677].

———. *The Rehearsal Transpros'd and the Rehearsal Transpros'd, the Second Part.* Edited by D. I. B. Smith. Oxford: Clarendon, 1971.

Meade, Matthew. *The Vision of the Wheels Seen by the Prophet Ezekiel.* London, 1689.

The Minutes of the First Independent Church (Now Bunyan Meeting) at Bedford 1656–1766. Edited by H. G. Tibbutt. [Bedford]: Publications of the Bedfordshire Historical Record Society, vol. 55, 1976.

Mirabilis Annus, or the Year of Prodigies and Wonders. London, 1661.

Mirabilis Annus Secundus. [London], 1662.

Mirabilis Annus Secundus: or the Second Part of the Second Years Prodigies. 1662.

Multum in parvo, aut vox veritatis. 1681.

Munster Paralleld in the Late Massacres Committed by the Fifth Monarchists. London, 1661.

A Narrative of the Apprehending, Commitment, Arraignment, Condemnation, and Execution of John James. London, 1662.

[Nedham, Marchamont.] *News from Brussels*. London, 1660.

The Night-Walker of Bloomsbury. 1683.

Omnia Comesta a Bello. 1667.

Original Records of Early Nonconformity. Edited by G. Lyon Turner. 3 vols. London: T. Fisher Unwin, 1911–14.

Owen, John. *A Brief and Impartial Account of the Nature of the Protestant Religion*. London, 1682.

———. *An Humble Testimony unto the Goodness and Severity of God in His Dealing with Sinful Churches and Nations*. London, 1681.

———. *The Works of John Owen*. Edited by William H. Goold. 16 vols. London: Johnstone and Hunter, 1850–53.

The Panther-prophecy, or, a Premonition to All People, of Sad Calamities and Miseries Like to Befall These Islands. 1662.

Parker, Samuel. *History of His Own Time*. Translated by Thomas Newlin. London: Charles Rivington, 1727.

[Patrick, Simon.] *A Friendly Debate Between a Conformist and a Non-Conformist*. 2nd ed. London, 1669.

[———]. *A Further Continuation and Defence, or, a Third Part of the Friendly Debate*. London, 1670.

[Penn, William.] *Commentary upon the Present Condition of the Kingdom and Its Melioration*. 1677.

A Phoenix: or, the Solemn League and Covenant. 1661.

Plain English to His Excellencie the Lord General Monck, and the Officers of the Army. London, 1660.

The Presbyterian Pater Noster, Creed, and Ten Commandments. [1681.]

Price, Evan. *Eye-Salve for England*. London, 1667.

The Proceedings to Execution of the Sentence Awarded Against Captain Thomas Walcot, William Hone, and John Rouse, for High-Treason. [London], 1683.

A Project for a Successor to the Crown. 1681.

Raree Show: or the True Protestant Procession. 1681.

The Records of a Church of Christ in Bristol, 1640–1687. Edited by Roger Hayden. [Bristol]: Bristol Record Society, vol. 27, 1974.

Reflexions on Monsieur Fagel's Letter. 1689.

A Relation of the Defeat of the Rebels in the West. 1685 (in BL Add. MSS 62, 453).

A Renuntiation and Declaration of the Ministers of Congregational Churches and Publick Preachers. London, 1661.

Rolle, Samuel. *A Sober Answer to the Friendly Debate*. London, 1669.

Rouse, John. *Rouse His Case, Truly Stated and Written with His Own Hand*. London, 1683.

S., T. *The Perplex'd Prince*. London, [1682].

[Sadler, John.] *Rights of the Kingdom*. London, 1682.

The Saints Freedom from Tyranny Vindicated. 1667.

Scott, W., ed. *Collection of Scarce and Valuable Tracts . . . of the Late Lord Somers.* 13 vols. London, 1809–15.

Sedgwick, William. *Animadversions upon a Book Entituled Inquisition for the Blood of Our Late Soveraign.* London, 1661.

Several Reasons Rendred by the People of God, (Called Quakers) Why No Outward Force, or Imposition, on the Conscience Ought to Be Used in Matters of Faith and Religion. 1668.

Shields, Michael. *Faithful Contendings Displayed.* Glasgow: John Bryce, 1780.

A Short Surveigh of the Grand Case of the Present Ministry. London, 1663.

[Smith, Francis?] *Trap ad Crucem; or, the Papists Watch-word.* 1670.

Smith, Nathaniel. *The Quakers Spirituall Cort Proclaim'd.* London, 1669.

The Speeches and Prayers of Major General Harrison . . . . [London], 1660.

[Speke, Hugh.] *The Secret History of the Happy Revolution, in 1688.* London: S. Keimer, 1715.

Sprat, Thomas. *A True Account and Declaration of the Horrid Conspiracy.* 3rd ed. London, 1686.

[Stewart, James.] *Jus Populi Vindicatum.* 1669.

[Stewart, James, and James Stirling.] *Naphtali, or the Wrestlings of the Church of Scotland for the Kingdom of Christ.* 1667.

Streater, John. *The Character of a True and False Shepherd.* 1670.

The Sufferers-Catechism, Wherein Are Many Necessary and Seasonable Questions and Cases of Conscience Resolved. 1664.

Tillinghast, John. *Mr. Tillinghasts Eight Last Sermons.* London, 1655.

A Treatise of the Execution of Justice. 1663.

A True Account of the Horrid Murther Committed upon His Grace, the Late Archbishop of Saint Andrews. London, 1679.

A True Account of the Taking of Mr. Casteers, at Tenderton in Kent, and Mr. Lobb, in Essex. London, 1683.

A True and Exact List of the Names of All the Men That Were Arraign'd and Condemn'd at Taunton in Somersetshire, in the Year 1685. London, 1689.

A True and Exact Relation of the Araignment, Tryal, and Condemnation. London, 1662.

A True and Faithful Account of the Several Informations. 1667.

The Tryal and Condemnation of Edw. Fitz-Harris. London, 1681.

The Tryall and Process of High-Treason and Doom of Forfaulture Against Mr. Robert Baillie of Jerviswood Traitor. Edinburgh, 1685.

The Tryal of Henry Baron Delamere for High-Treason. London, 1686.

Two Speeches. I. The Earl of Shaftsbury's Speech in the House of Lords the 20th. of October, 1675. II. The D. of Buckinghams Speech in the House of Lords the 16th. of November 1675. Amsterdam, 1675.

[Vernon, George.] *A Letter to a Friend Concerning Some of Dr. Owens Principles and Practices.* London, 1670.

Vox Populi, Fax Populi. London, 1681.

Vox Populi, Vox Dei: or, Englands General Lamentation for the Dissolution of the Parliament. 1681.

Walcott, Thomas. *A True Copy of a Paper Written by Capt. Tho. Walcott.* London, 1683.

[Wallis, Ralph.] *More News from Rome or Magna Charta, Discoursed of Between a Poor Man and His Wife.* London, 1666.

[———]. *Room for the Cobler of Gloucester and His Wife: With Several Cartloads of Abominable Irregular, Pitiful Stinking Priests.* [London], 1668.

Waterhouse, Edward. *An Humble Apologie for Learning and Learned Men.* London, 1653.

W[atkins], M[organ]. *A Lamentation over England.* 1664.

Watson, Thomas. *A Word of Comfort for the Church of God.* London, 1662.

The Weekly Pacquet of Advice from Rome. 4 vols. London, 1679–82.

Welwood, James. *Memoirs of the Most Material Transactions in England.* 3rd ed. London: Timothy Goodwin, 1700.

West, Robert. *An Answer to a Late Paper.* London, 1683.

The Whiggs Lamentation, for the Death of Their Dear Brother Colledge. London, 1681.

[Whitaker, Edward.] *The Ignoramus Justices.* London, 1681.

[———]. *The Second Part of the Ignoramus Justices.* London, 1682.

W[hitehead], G[eorge]. *The Conscientious Cause of the Sufferers, Called Quakers.* London, 1664.

———. *This Is an Epistle for the Remnant of Friends, and Chosen of God.* 1665.

Whiting, John. *Persecution Expos'd.* London, 1715.

The Whores Petition to the London Prentices. London, 1668.

Wigfield, W. M. *Recusancy and Nonconformity in Bedfordshire Illustrated by Select Documents Between 1622 and 1842.* [Bedford]: Publications of the Bedfordshire Historical Record Society, vol. 20, 1938.

[Wilson, John.] *Nehushtan: or, a Sober and Peaceable Discourse, Concerning the Abolishing of Things Abused to Superstition and Idolatry.* London, 1668.

[Wither, George.] *Sigh for the Pitchers: Breathed out in a Personal Contribution to the National Humiliation.* 1666.

[———]. *Vox & Lacrimae Anglorum: or, the True English-mens Complaints.* [London, 1668.]

Yarranton (or Yarrington), Andrew. *A Full Discovery of the First Presbyterian Sham-Plot.* London, 1681.

Newspapers

Democritus Ridens (1681).

Domestick Intelligence (1679–80).

Impartial London Intelligence (1681).

Impartial Protestant Mercury (1681–82).

Intelligencer (1663–65).
Kingdomes Intelligencer (1660–63).
London *Gazette* (1666–88).
Mercurius Publicus (1660–63).
Newes (1663–66).
Observator (1683–84).
Oxford Gazette (1665).
Parliamentary Intelligencer (1660).
Protestant (Domestick) Intelligence (1680–81).
Protestant Oxford Intelligence (1681).
True Protestant Mercury (1681–82).

Index

In this index an "f" after a number indicates a separate reference on the next page, and an "ff" indicates separate references on the next two pages. A continuous discussion over two or more pages is indicated by a span of page numbers, e.g. "pp. 57–58." *Passim* is used for a cluster of references in close but not consecutive sequence.

Library of Congress Cataloging-in-Publication Data

Greaves, Richard L.
    Secrets of the kingdom: British radicals from the Popish Plot to
the Revolution of 1688–1689 / Richard L. Greaves.
      p.   cm.
    Includes bibliographical references and index.
    ISBN 0-8047-2052-5 (alk. paper):
     1. Great Britain—Politics and government—1660–1688.
    2. Radicalism—Great Britain—History—17th Century. 3. Great
Britain—History—Revolution of 1688. 4. Popish Plot, 1678.
I. Title.
DA448.G7 1992
941.06'7—dc20
                                             91-44781
                                            CIP